THE PAPERS OF ALEXANDER HAMILTON

Alexander Hamilton, date unknown, probably between 1782 and 1792.
Artist unknown, but attributed to John Trumbull.
Collection of Richard N. Tetlie

THE PAPERS OF

Alexander Hamilton

VOLUME IX

AUGUST 1791–DECEMBER 1791

HAROLD C. SYRETT, EDITOR

JACOB E. COOKE, ASSOCIATE EDITOR

Assistant Editors

JEAN G. COOKE	CARA-LOUISE MILLER
DOROTHY TWOHIG	PATRICIA SYRETT

 COLUMBIA UNIVERSITY PRESS

NEW YORK AND LONDON, 1965

FROM THE PUBLISHER

The preparation of this edition of the papers of Alexander Hamilton has been made possible by the support received for the work of the editorial and research staff from the generous grants of the Rockefeller Foundation, Time Inc., and the Ford Foundation, and by the far-sighted cooperation of the National Historical Publications Commission. To these organizations, the publisher expresses gratitude on behalf of all who are concerned about making available the record of the founding of the United States.

PREFACE

THIS EDITION of Alexander Hamilton's papers contains letters and other documents written by Hamilton, letters to Hamilton, and some documents (commissions, certificates, etc.) that directly concern Hamilton but were written neither by him nor to him. All letters and other documents have been printed in chronological order. Hamilton's legal papers are being published under the editorial direction of Julius Goebel, Jr., George Welwood Murray Professor Emeritus of Legal History of the School of Law, Columbia University. The first volume of this distinguished work, which is entitled *The Law Practice of Alexander Hamilton*, was published by the Columbia University Press in 1964.

Many letters and documents have been calendared. Such calendared items include routine letters and documents by Hamilton, routine letters to Hamilton, some of the letters or documents written by Hamilton for someone else, letters or documents which have not been found but which are known to have existed, letters or documents which have been erroneously attributed to Hamilton, and letters to or by Hamilton that deal exclusively with his legal practice.

Certain routine documents which Hamilton wrote and received as Secretary of the Treasury have not been printed. The documents that fall within this category are warrants or interest certificates; letters written by Hamilton acknowledging receipts from banks, endorsing margins of certificate of registry, and enclosing sea letters; letters to Hamilton transmitting weekly, monthly, and quarterly accounts, or enclosing certificates of registry and other routine Treasury forms; and drafts by Hamilton on the treasurer. Statements of facts from the judges of the District Courts on cases concerning violations of the customs laws and warrants of remission of forfeiture issued by Hamilton have generally been omitted unless they pertain to cases discussed in Hamilton's correspondence.

The notes in these volumes are designed to provide information concerning the nature and location of each document, to identify Hamilton's correspondents and the individuals mentioned in the text, to explain events or ideas referred to in the text, and to point out textual variations or mistakes. Occasional departures from these standards can be attributed to a variety of reasons. In many cases the desired information has been supplied in an earlier note and can be found through the use of the index. Notes were not added when in the opinion of the editors the material in the text was either self-explanatory or common knowledge. The editors, moreover, did not think it desirable or necessary to provide full annotation for Hamilton's legal correspondence. Finally, the editors on some occasions were unable to find the desired information, and on other occasions the editors were remiss.

GUIDE TO EDITORIAL APPARATUS

I. SYMBOLS USED TO DESCRIBE MANUSCRIPTS

AD	Autograph Document
ADS	Autograph Document Signed
ADf	Autograph Draft
ADfS	Autograph Draft Signed
AL	Autograph Letter
ALS	Autograph Letter Signed
D	Document
DS	Document Signed
Df	Draft
DfS	Draft Signed
LS	Letter Signed
LC	Letter Book Copy
[S]	[S] is used with other symbols (AD[S], ADf[S], AL[S], D[S], Df[S], L[S]) to indicate that the signature on the document has been cropped or clipped.

II. MONETARY SYMBOLS AND ABBREVIATIONS

bf	Banco florin
V	Ecu
f	Florin
₶	Livre Tournois
medes	Maravedis (also md and mde)
d.	Penny or denier
ps	Piece of eight

£	Pound sterling or livre
Ry	Real
rs vn	Reals de vellon
rdr	Rix daller
s	Shilling, sou or sol (also expressed as /)
sti	Stiver

III. SHORT TITLES AND ABBREVIATIONS

Annals of Congress, I, II, III	*The Debates and Proceedings in the Congress of the United States; with an Appendix, Containing Important State Papers and Public Documents, and All the Laws of a Public Nature* (Washington, 1834–1849).
Arch. des Aff. Etr., Corr. Pol., Etats-Unis	Transcripts or photostats from the French Foreign Office deposited in the Library of Congress.
Archives Parlementaires	*Archives Parlementaires de 1787 à 1860* (Paris, 1868–).
ASP	*American State Papers, Documents, Legislative and Executive, of the Congress of the United States* (Washington, 1832–1861).
Bagnall, *Textile Industries*	William R. Bagnall, *The Textile Industries of the United States* (Cambridge, 1893).
Bayley, *National Loans*	Rafael A. Bayley, *The National Loans of the United States from July 4, 1776, to June 30, 1880* (Washington, 1882).
Bemis, *Jay's Treaty*	Samuel Flagg Bemis, *Jay's Treaty, a Study in Commerce and Diplomacy* (New York, 1923).
Boyd, *Papers of Thomas Jefferson*	Julian P. Boyd, ed., *The Papers of Thomas Jefferson* (Princeton, 1950–).
Brymner, *Canadian Archives*, 1890	Douglas Brymner, ed., *Report on Canadian Archives, 1890* (Ottawa, 1891).

Carter, *Territorial Papers*	Clarence E. Carter, ed., *The Territorial Papers of the United States* (Washington, 1934–).
Clark, *State Records of North Carolina*	Walter Clark, ed., *The State Records of North Carolina* (Goldsboro, North Carolina, 1886–1907).
Cole, *Industrial and Commercial Correspondence*	Arthur H. Cole, ed., *Industrial and Commercial Correspondence of Alexander Hamilton, Anticipating His Report on Manufactures* (Chicago, 1928).
Connecticut State Records	*The Public Records of the State of Connecticut* (Hartford, 1894–).
Davis, *Essays*	Joseph Stancliffe Davis, *Essays in the Earlier History of American Corporations* ("Harvard Economic Studies," XVI [Cambridge, 1917]).
Executive Journal, I	*Journal of the Executive Proceedings of the Senate* (Washington, 1828).
Freeman, *Washington*	Douglas Southall Freeman, *George Washington* (New York, 1948–1957). Volume VII of this series was written by John Alexander Carroll and Mary Wells Ashworth.
GW	John C. Fitzpatrick, ed., *The Writings of George Washington* (Washington, 1931–1944).
Hamilton, *History*	John C. Hamilton, *Life of Alexander Hamilton, a History of the Republic of the United States of America* (Boston, 1879).
Hamilton, *Intimate Life*	Allan McLane Hamilton, *The Intimate Life of Alexander Hamilton* (New York, 1910).
Hamilton, *Life*	John C. Hamilton, *The Life of Alexander Hamilton* (New York, 1840).

Hazard, *Pennsylvania Archives* — Samuel Hazard, ed., *Pennsylvania Archives* (Philadelphia, 1852–1856).

HCLW — Henry Cabot Lodge, ed., *The Works of Alexander Hamilton* (New York, 1904).

Hunt, *Calendar of Applications* — Gaillard Hunt, *Calendar of Applications and Recommendations for Office During the Presidency of George Washington* (Washington, 1901).

JCC — *Journals of the Continental Congress, 1774–1789* (Washington, 1904–1937).

JCH Transcripts — John C. Hamilton Transcripts. These transcripts are owned by Mr. William H. Swan, Hampton Bays, New York, and have been placed on loan in the Columbia University Libraries.

JCHW — John C. Hamilton, ed., *The Works of Alexander Hamilton* (New York, 1851–1856).

Journal of the House, I — *Journal of the House of Representatives of the United States* (Washington, 1826).

Laws of Massachusetts — *Acts and Laws of the Commonwealth of Massachusetts* (Boston, 1890–1898).

Miller, *Treaties* — Hunter Miller, ed., *Treaties and Other International Acts of the United States* (Washington, 1931–1948).

"Minutes of the S.U.M." — MS minutes of the Society for Establishing Useful Manufactures. City of Paterson, New Jersey, Plant Management Commission, Successors to the Society for Establishing Useful Manufactures.

Mitchell, *Hamilton* — Broadus Mitchell, *Alexander Hamilton* (1957–1962).

Pennsylvania Archives, 9th ser. — *Pennsylvania Archives*, 9th ser. (n.p., 1931–1935).

Pennsylvania Statutes — James T. Mitchell and Henry Flan-

	ders, eds., *The Statutes at Large of Pennsylvania from 1682 to 1801* (Harrisburg, 1896–1908).
PRO: F.O., or PRO: C.O.	Transcripts or photostats from the Public Records Office of Great Britain deposited in the Library of Congress.
Quincy, *Journals of Samuel Shaw*	Josiah Quincy, ed., *The Journals of Major Samuel Shaw* (Boston, 1847).
Records of Rhode Island	John Russell Bartlett, ed., *Records of the State of Rhode Island and Providence Plantations in New England* (Providence, 1856–1865).
Smith, *St. Clair Papers*	William Henry Smith, ed., *The St. Clair Papers: The Life and Public Services of Arthur St. Clair* (Cincinnati, 1882).
1 *Stat.*	*The Public Statutes at Large of the United States of America* (Boston, 1845).
6 *Stat.*	*The Public Statutes at Large of the United States of America* [Private Statutes] (Boston, 1856).
White, *Samuel Slater*	George S. White, *Memoir of Samuel Slater, the Father of American Manufactures. Connected with a History of the Rise and Progress of the Cotton Manufacture in England and America* (Philadelphia, 1836).

IV. INDECIPHERABLE WORDS

Words or parts of words which could not be deciphered because of the illegibility of the writing or the mutilation of the manuscript have been indicated as follows:

1. ⟨ – – – – – ⟩ indicates illegible words with the number of dashes indicating the estimated number of illegible words.
2. Words or letters in broken brackets indicate a guess as to what the words or letters in question may be. If the source of

the words or letters within the broken brackets is known, it has been given in a note.

V. CROSSED-OUT MATERIAL IN MANUSCRIPTS

Words or sentences crossed out by a writer in a manuscript have been handled in one of the three following ways:

1. They have been ignored, and the document or letter has been printed in its final version.
2. Crossed-out words and insertions for the crossed-out words have been described in the notes.
3. When the significance of a manuscript seems to warrant it, the crossed-out words have been retained, and the document has been printed as it was written.

VI. TEXTUAL CHANGES AND INSERTIONS

The following changes or insertions have been made in the letters and documents printed in these volumes:

1. Words or letters written above the line of print (for example, 9th) have been made even with the line of print (9th).
2. Punctuation and capitalization have been changed in those instances where it seemed necessary to make clear the sense of the writer. A special effort has been made to eliminate the dash, which was such a popular eighteenth-century device.
3. When the place or date, or both, of a letter or document does not appear at the head of that letter or document, it has been inserted in the text in brackets. If either the place or date at the head of a letter or document is incomplete, the necessary additional material has been added in the text in brackets. For all but the best known localities or places, the name of the colony, state, or territory has been added in brackets at the head of a document or letter.
4. In calendared documents, place and date have been uniformly written out in full without the use of brackets. Thus "N. York, Octr. 8, '99" becomes "New York, October 8, 1799." If, how-

ever, substantive material is added to the place or date in a calendared document, such material is placed in brackets. Thus "Oxford, Jan. 6" becomes "Oxford [Massachusetts] January 6 [1788]."

5. When a writer made an unintentional slip comparable to a typographical error, one of the four following devices has been used:

    a. It has been allowed to stand as written.

    b. It has been corrected by inserting either one or more letters in brackets.

    c. It has been corrected without indicating the change.

    d. It has been explained in a note.

6. Because the symbol for the thorn was archaic even in Hamilton's day, the editors have used the letter "y" to represent it. In doing this they are conforming to eighteenth-century manuscript usage.

THE PAPERS OF ALEXANDER HAMILTON

1791

To William Short [1]

(Duplicate)

Treasury Department
August 1st. [–2] 1791.

Sir,

Since my last letter to you,[2] yours of the 4th. of May has come to hand.

Pursuant to instructions recently received from the President of the United States,[3] I am at liberty to authorise you "to open at your discretion loans at such times and places and for such sums as you may find advisable within the limitations of the respective laws [4] authorising the loans" and which have been transmitted to you. This accordingly I now do; subject only to the following qualification: That with regard to such parts of principal of our foreign debt as will not fall due till after the year 1792, no loan is to be opened which will cost the United States in interest and charges more than four and a half per Cent on the sum actually received by them.

This restriction is founded on an expectation of being able ere that period arrives to borrow money within that limit.

You will now find yourself in condition to embrace any favorable opportunities which may present in either of the Countries which have been mentioned by you or in any other whatsoever. I hinted to you on a former occasion that the market of London would not be an undesirable one.[5] And I have some reason of late to suppose that it might not be found an impracticable one.

LS, William Short Papers, Library of Congress.
  1. Short had accompanied Thomas Jefferson to Paris in 1784 as his secretary and later served as secretary of legation. In 1789 he was appointed United States chargé d'affaires at Paris.
  2. H to Short, June 30, 1791.
  3. See George Washington to H, July 29, 1791.
  4. "An Act making provision for the (payment of the) Debt of the United States" (1 *Stat.* 138–44 [August 4, 1790]) and "An Act making Provision for the Reduction of the Public Debt" (1 *Stat.* 186–87 [August 12, 1790]).
  5. See H to Short, May 9, 1791.

I observe what you say in your letter of the 9th of April concerning the probable terms on which loans might be procured at Genoa. I should question exceedingly the expediency of opening a loan there or any where else on terms less advantageous than they can be made in Holland. Nevertheless it is not my intention to conclude you by this observation, if you judge that the future effect of the measure upon our loans in Holland may justify a temporary sacrifice. As to Genoa particularly it does not appear advisable to *go far*, unless on terms more advantageous than in Holland; because, for want of direct intercourse, remittances to pay the interest must be circuitous, and probably both inconvenient and comparatively disadvantageous.

In respect to France the case is very different. Equal terms there would appear eligible, if not preferable. But there is room to expect, from the progress of things in that scene, even better terms. To guard the lenders against the consequences of depreciation, the stipulations to pay in specie may be as precise as possible. There can be no objection to making the bonds, which should be given for the sums lent, receivable in payment for lands at the price or prices which *shall* be fixed by law, in other cases.

I send you herewith an official statement by the proper Officer certified under the seal of the Treasury of the product of the old duties for a period of one year, ending the 30th. of September last.[6] This I presume will be deemed sufficiently authentic. The productiveness of the new duties is as yet only partially ascertained. But there is every appearance that they will fully answer expectation. The product at the Port of Philadelphia, for a single quarter, including the months of April, May and June, exceeds three hundred and thirty thousand dollars; which, if you compare with the product of an entire year of the former duties, as exhibited in the statement above mentioned, will give you an idea of the very considerable increase which has taken place. All this, too, is independent of an interior duty on ardent spirits, which, in its progress, must afford an important accession of revenue.

You intimate the propriety of a plurality of persons to execute a trust such as that now reposed in you.[7] This however does not appear

---

6. See enclosure.   7. See Short to H, April 9, 1791.

necessary. And it is confided that you will chearfully execute it alone. Of your prudence and judgment all are satisfied.

With very great consideration and esteem   I remain,   Sir,   Your obedt Servant   Alexander Hamilton,
Secretary of the Treasury

Postscript Aug 2, 1791 When I speak of equal terms in France it ought to be understood in this sense—provided they are such as to realize the existing benefit of exchange between Holland & France.[8]

Willm. Short Esqr.

[E N C L O S U R E]

Nett amount of Duties on Goods Wares and Merchandize imported into the United-States from the 1st. October 1789 to the 30th. of September 1790.[9]

States	Nett Amot of Duties
New Hampshire	14,550.19½
Massachusetts	320,430.98¼
Rhode-Island	17,675.29½
Connecticut	64,336.20½
New-York	446,646.38
New-Jersey	4,291.85½
Pennsylvania	472,756.35
Delaware	9,914.21½
Maryland	206,750.27
Virginia	214,341.31¾
North-Carolina	14,340.15¼
South-Carolina	102,438.62
Georgia	15,237.64¾
Total Dollars	1,903,709.48½

The above Summary agrees with the General Accot. of Impost as rendered to Congress. It will receive an addition of about 30,000 Dollars upon the receipt of the quarterly Return commencing the 1st. July and ending 30th. Septr. 1790 for the district of Charleston So.

8. The postscript is in H's handwriting.
9. DS, William Short Papers, Library of Congress.

Carolina and of two or three of the smallest quarterly Returns from the State of Massachusetts.

Joseph Nourse Regr.[10]

Treasury Department
Registers Office 16th. Feby 1791.

10. On the reverse side of this document H wrote:
"I certify that the within is a true and authentic statement according to the purport thereof by the proper Officer of the Treasy of the United States and that full faith & credit are due to the same.
"Given under my hand and the seal of the said Treasury the first day of August in the year one thousand seven hundred and ninety One.
Alexander Hamilton
Secy of the Treasury"

From John B. Church [1]

[Down Place,[2] August 2, 1791]

My dear Sir

The enclos'd is the Answer sent me by Mr. Alchorne,[3] the Assay Master of the Mint, to the Enquiries respecting the Standard and Weight of Spanish Dollars which will I hope prove satisfactory. It is not in my Power at present to satisfy you respecting the Prices of Labor & Manufacturers, but I have taken Measures to inform myself of them and as it will take some Time, I shall hardly be able to send you the Account before the September Packet. I have been here about a Month and shall not return to London untill November, so that I know nothing of News or Politics but what I read in the public Prints. I fear there is no Disposition at present in our Ministers to treat properly with America. Lord Hawkesbury [4] is lately admitted into the Cabinet, and his Prejudices are strong against you, and the Enthusiasm for maintaining the Navigation Act is such that there is not a Shadow of probability they will in any Shape relax. I have heard nothing since my last [5] of Mr. Hammonds Appointment as Envoy to America [6] but I believe he is certainly to be sent out.

Angelica is well and joins me in best and most cordial Wishes to Mrs. Hamilton and yourself.

I am   My Dear Sir   ever sincerely   Yours &c &c   J B Church

Down Place
Augt. 2d: 1791

Alexr Hamilton Esqr.

ALS, Hamilton Papers, Library of Congress.
 1. Church, who had married Angelica Schuyler, H's sister-in-law, had become engaged in extensive business enterprises in the United States during the American Revolution. In 1782 he returned to England and in 1790 was elected to Parliament. During the seventeen-eighties H had managed his legal affairs in the United States.
 2. "Down Place," Church's country estate purchased in 1787, was located in Berkshire, about four miles northwest of Windsor and about twenty miles from London. This information was supplied by Mr. T. R. Hay, Locust Valley, New York.
 3. Stanesby Alchorne was assay master of the British Mint from 1764 to 1798.
 4. Baron Hawkesbury was president of the Board of Trade and Chancellor of the Duchy of Lancaster.
 5. Letter not found.
 6. George Hammond's instructions as Minister Plenipotentiary to the United States were dated September 2, 1791 (Bernard Mayo, ed., *Instructions to the British Ministers to the United States, 1791–1812* [Washington, 1941], 1–2).

From William Ellery

Collector's Office
Newport [Rhode Island] Augt. 2nd. 1791

Sir,
 This will be attended by a weekly return of monies received and paid, a monthly schedule of bonds; a List of a Post-note of the North American Bank for One hundred and ninety five Dollars, No. 8080, dated Philadelphia 9th. July 1791, one moiety whereof was transmitted by the last post, and the other moiety is now transmitted by this.
 The District Court which met here this day adjourned to the 15th of this month, the Atty. of the District [1] and the other Lawyers being obliged to attend a Court of the State, which this day sits at Providence; so that nothing has been done respecting the case of the Brig: Seven Brothers, and her late master, a Statement of which was trans-

mitted to you on the eleventh of the last month. Since that time we
have had an account of the Death of Capt. Browning.

Last Saturday I seized the Sloop Betsy of which Thomas Cotterell
was formerly sole Owner, and James Bissell Master on a complaint
made to the Surveyor of the Port of North Kingstown,[2] which excited a strong suspicion that on her arrival from Cape Francois a
twelve month ago the 10th. of this month, She had unladed, without
a permit, goods of the value of four hundred Dollars. I received a
letter from him dated July 27th, from which it appears that we shall
be able to prove beyond a doubt, that goods were landed out of that
vessel without a permit, and I think we shall be able to prove also that
they were of four hundred Dollars value and more. The Surveyor had
committed to writing the accounts which had been given to him of
this transaction; but they were too long, to be copied and it would
have been imprudent to have transmitted them. It is impossible for
me to give a regular Statement of this case untill I shall have seen him.

If these vessels or either of them, or any other should be seized,
condemned and exposed to sale I have reason to apprehend that the
principal merchants in this District would not bid at the vendue, and
that others might combine to favour the late owner or owners; in this
case unless the Offrs. of the Customs should interfere in the sale forfeited vessels would be struck off, at a price which instead of discouraging would tend to encourage transgressions of the Revenue
Laws. I wish for your instructn in this respect and am Sir [3]

Yr. most obt servt.   W Ellery

A Hamilton Esqr

LC, Newport Historical Society, Newport, Rhode Island.
    1. William Channing.
    2. Daniel Eldridge Updike.
    3. Ellery endorsed the letter book copy of this letter "Answered Sepr. 16
1791." H's reply has not been found.

To Elizabeth Hamilton

[Philadelphia] Aug. 2, 1791

I thank you my beloved Betsey for your letter [1] announcing your
safe arrival; but my satisfaction at learning this has been greatly al-

loyed by the intelligence you give me of the indisposition of my darling James.[2] Heaven protect and preserve him! I am sure you will lose no time in advising me of any alteration which may happen. I trust he will not be in danger.

Remember the flannel next his skin, and If he should not be better when this reaches, try the bark-waiscoat. Remember also the benefit he received from Barley water with a dash of brandy. Be very attentive to his diet. Indulge him with nothing that will injure him. Not much fruit of any kind. Be sure that he drinks no water which has not been first boiled in some iron vessel. I hope he will have had some rhubarb or antimonial wine. Paregoric at night in moderation will do him good & a little bark will not do him harm.

Take good care of my Lamb; but I need not recommend. It is among my consolations that he has Doctor Stringer[3] with him.

I am myself in good health & will wait with all the patience I can the time for your return. But you must not precipitate it. I am so anxious for a perfect restoration of your health that I am willing to make a great sacrifice for it. Remember me affectionately to your Father, mother & all the family & love me always as I do you.

Yr. ever tender

A Hamilton

E Hamilton

ALS, Hamilton Papers, Library of Congress.
1. Letter not found.
2. James Hamilton, H's third son and fourth child, was three years old.
3. Dr. Samuel Stringer of Albany.

To William Skinner [1]

[*Philadelphia, August 2, 1791.* On August 12, 1791, Hamilton wrote to Skinner and referred to "my letter to you of the 2nd instant." *Letter not found.*]

1. Skinner was commissioner of loans for North Carolina.

To William Cooper [1]

Philadelphia
Aug. 3, 1791

Dear Sir

Mr. Lincklaen, the bearer of this, is a Young Gentleman of Holland, nephew of Mr Cazenove, of whom you have heard.[2]

He is about to travel through the part of the Country in which you reside and has among other objects that of Examining what can be done with regard to the manufacture of the Maple Sugar. I have told him that you could give him more light on the subject than any other person and have assured him that you will do it with pleasure. The Connexion can bring with activity any Capital that may be necessary for the purpose.

With great regard   I remain Yr Obed Sr   A Hamilton

Judge Cooper

ALS, from a typescript supplied by an anonymous donor.

1. Cooper was a judge and an extensive landowner in Otsego County, New York. Between 1776 and 1786 Cooper, in partnership with Andrew Craig, acquired the greater part of the Otsego Patent, a vast tract of land in northern New York which had originally been granted to George Croghan. In the late seventeen-eighties Cooper founded the village of Cooperstown and undertook the settlement and development of his tract.

2. Jan Lincklaen was a representative of a group of Dutch firms which later became part of the Holland Land Company. In 1790 and early 1791 these firms joined the company of Van Beeftingh and Boon of Rotterdam in a plan to invest in the production of maple sugar in the United States. Théophile Cazenove also represented these firms in the United States. Lincklaen and Gerrit Boon were appointed to purchase suitable lands and begin business operations. The two men began their journey through the backcountry in August, 1791. For an account of their travels, see Paul Demund Evans, *The Holland Land Company* (Buffalo, 1924), 14–18.

From Elizabeth Hamilton

[*Albany, August 3, 1791.* On August 10, 1791, Hamilton wrote to Elizabeth Hamilton: "I received your precious letters of the 31 of July & 3d. of August." *Letter of August 3 not found.*]

To Charles Cotesworth Pinckney [1]

Philadelphia August 3d 1791

Dear sir

It is a cause of no small regret that there appears in a considerable part of the citizens of South Carolina a strong disinclination to the law laying a duty on distilled spirits; [2] and that in consequence of it, difficulties occur in obtaining proper characters to carry it into execution.

This was the more unexpected as the duty in question has been rendered necessary by a measure peculiarly interesting to South-Carolina (I mean the assumption of the state Debts) and its operation, as far as concerns the *part objected to*, falls with very trifling weight upon the state. While I console myself that in almost every other part of the united States, the law has thus far gone into operation with much greater facility than could have been expected, I rely that the citizens of South Carolina will not be long in discovering that their honor and their interest conspire with their duty to demand a ready acquiescence in the measure; and by affording it, will supersede the necessity of coercive expedients.

In the mean time impediments exist, and it has become necessary, on account of distance, to empower the Supervisor of the Revenue for the District comprehending your state [3] to nominate definitively the Inspectors of Surveys. This has accordingly been done, with only this restriction that he shall previously consult Mr Edward Rutledge, the Attorney of the District, and yourself, or such of you as may happen to be at any time accessible. In giving him this instruction, the President as well as myself has relied upon your zeal for the Support of the national laws, that it will not be disagreeable to you to afford your advice upon the occasion.

The Supervisor from the difficulty of procuring proper characters within the Surveys, has suggested the idea of deputing persons from Charleston. This appears a very questionable expedient, and I incline to think that rather than have recourse to it, it will be well to submit to a little delay. Nevertheless he has been left at liberty to pursue the idea, if upon a full consideration of circumstances it shall be thought eligible, as well by the Gentlemen to whom he is referred as by himself.

I am with very great consideration and esteem, Dear Sir   Your obedient Servt   Alexander Hamilton

General Pinckney
Charleston, South Carolina

LS, University of South Carolina Library, Columbia.
    1. Pinckney, who had served as a colonel during the American Revolution, practiced law in Charleston, South Carolina, after the war. In 1782 he was elected to the state legislature and later served as a delegate to the Constitutional Convention and the South Carolina Ratifying Convention.
    2. "An Act repealing, after the last day of June next, the duties heretofore laid upon Distilled Spirits imported from abroad, and laying others in their stead; and also upon Spirits distilled within the United States, and for appropriating the same" (1 *Stat.* 199–214 [March 3, 1791]).
    3. Daniel Stevens.

To Nathaniel Appleton

Treasury Department August 4th 1791

Sir,

The Treasurer has received directions to remit you a draft for six thousand, two hundred and ninety four Dollars to enable you to pay a half years pensions to the Invalids of your State, which according to a notification from the Department of war is to be paid on the fourth day of September ensuing. You are to pay under such regulations as shall have been communicated to you from that department as heretofore. The draft sent you is not to be presented for payment 'till a day or two before the period above mentioned.

I am sir   Your obedient servant   Alexander Hamilton

Nathl Appleton Esqr
Commr of Loans
Massachusetts

LS, The Bostonian Society, Boston.

From Nathaniel Appleton

Boston, August 4, 1791. "Agreeably to your directions I now improve the first oppo. to transmit an Account Current of 6 ₱ Ct. &

3 ℔ Ct. Stock funded in this Office to the 1st April 1791. They should have been sent forward sooner but a few errors occasion great delay in examining so many Accounts. The Acct. of the defered Stock shall be forwarded as soon as possible. About 1,300,000 Dollrs. have been subscribed by 450 persons to the Loan payable in Certificates of this State Debt. This branch of the business occasions much labor & attention as the endorsment of Interest on State Certificates are very various. . . ."

LC, RG 53, Massachusetts State Loan Office, Letter Book, 1785–1791, Vol. "259-M," National Archives.

To James Duane

Treasury Department, August 4th, 1791

Sir,

I find myself obliged to remit the proceedings on the Petition of John Osborn [1] in order that a further inquiry be had. Having had occasion heretofore to consult the British Acts of Parliament respecting the admeasurement of vessels,[2] I am satisfied that there must be some incorrectness in the evidence from which it has been stated that the Tonnage, according to the rule prescribed by the British laws, is so much greater than it appears to be by that which is prescribed by the Laws of the United States.[3] It would therefore be satisfactory to me to have the dimensions stated as they are found pursuant to each of those rules and to have a reference to the Act of Parliament from which the British rule is derived. I consider the reality of that rule as a material circumstance in the case.

I should unwillingly give the trouble of this revision had I not reason to suspect that there are examples of collusive registers in the quarter from which the vessel in question comes to evade the provisions of our Act.

I have the honor to be with great respect & consideration Sir
Your obedt Servant   Alexander Hamilton

The Honorable James Duane Esqr
Judge of the District Court of New York.[4]

LS, New-York Historical Society, New York City.

1. On August 13, 1791, under the terms of "An Act to provide for mitigating or remitting the forfeitures and penalties accruing under the revenue laws, in certain cases therein mentioned" (1 *Stat.* 122–23 [May 26, 1790]), H issued a warrant of remission for Osborn (copy, RG 21, Records of the United States District Court for the Southern District of New York, Warrants of Remission, 1790–1876, National Archives).

2. 13 Geo. III, C. 74 (1773). Section 1 of this law provided that in cases "where the tonage and burthen of any ship or vessel shall be necessary to be ascertained and known by any act or acts of parliament made, or hereafter to be made, concerning the revenues of customs, excise, or salt duty, the rule for admeasuring such ships or vessels shall be as follows; that is to say, the length shall be taken on a streight line along the rabbet of the keel of the ship, from the back of the main stern post to a perpendicular line from the forepart of the main stem under the bowsprit, from which subtracting three-fifths of the breadth, the remainder shall be esteemed the just length of the keel to find the tonage; and the breadth shall be taken from the outside of the outside plank, in the broadest place of the ship, be it either above or below the main whales, exclusive of all manner of doubling planks that may be wrought upon the sides of the ship, then multiplying the length of the keel by the breadth so taken, and that product by half the breadth, and dividing the whole by ninety-four, the quotient shall be deemed the true contents of the tonage; according to which rule the tonage of all such ships and vessels shall be measured and ascertained. . . ."

3. H is referring to Section 3 of "An Act for Registering and Clearing Vessels, Regulating the Coasting Trade, and for other purposes," which reads: *"And be it further enacted,* That to ascertain the tonnage of all ships or vessels, the surveyor or other person appointed by the collector to measure the same, shall take the length of every vessel, if double decked, from the fore part of the main stem to the after part of the stern post above the upper deck, the breadth at the broadest part above the main wales, and half such breadth shall be accounted the depth of every double decked vessel; he shall then deduct from the length three fifths of the breadth, multiply the remainder by the breadth and the product by the depth, dividing the product of the whole by ninety-five, the quotient shall be deemed the true contents or tonnage of such ship or vessel. To ascertain the tonnage of every single decked vessel, he shall take the length and breadth, as is directed to be taken for double decked vessels, and deduct three fifths in like manner, and the depth from the under side of the deck plank to the ceiling in the hold, and shall multiply and divide as aforesaid, and the quotient shall be deemed the true contents or tonnage of such single decked vessel" (1 *Stat.* 55–56 [September 1, 1789]).

4. This letter is endorsed "Answered 10th." Letter not found.

From Theodore Foster [1]

[*August 4, 1791.* On September 1, 1791, Hamilton wrote to Foster: "I have had the pleasure of receiving your two letters of the 23rd July & 4th of August." *Letter of August 4 not found.*]

1. Foster, a Providence, Rhode Island, lawyer, had served in the Rhode Island House of Representatives from 1776 to 1782, as town clerk of Providence from 1775 to 1787, and was appointed judge of the Court of Admiralty in 1785. In 1790 he was elected United States Senator from Rhode Island.

To Benjamin Lincoln [1]

Treasury Department August 4th 1791

Sir,

As the tea mentioned in your letter of the 13th of July is confessedly not simply Bohea but a different kind of black tea and was entered under a different denomination, I see not how it can be exempted from the duty laid on the second class of teas namely "Souchong and other black teas." [2] I cannot find that Bohea Congo is a species of tea known in the China Market, tho the Bohea of the District called Congo is said to be of superior quality. The price of the goods in question in the original Canton Invoice appears to be of consequence. The Bohea I understand is worth there about fourteen Tales [3] per pecul, [4] and the lowest Congo is worth twenty tales per pecul. *Campu* tea is not known as far as I can learn. I should suppose it intended for Confeu, but that I find a species of green. On the whole I am inclined to suppose that you will find this to have Cost ⟨20 tales or upwards⟩ [5] and that it will therefore be to be ⟨deemed a species of⟩ black tea other than Bohea and charged accordingly. The Bohea whole Chests weigh about 350 pounds. The fine teas (Congo, Souchong, Green) are imported in small chests from 70 to 90 pounds. If the teas in question should be in these small packages, it will afford a strong presumption that they are not really a species of Bohea.

With regard to the Spirits, which you mention to have been imported in Casks under fifty Gallons, it presents one of those cases in which, to further the general intent of the legislature and avoid the vexation of the Citizen, it is necessary for executive Officers at their peril to relax from the literal execution of the law. A reasonable time must be allowed for a knowledge of it to be communicated to distant parts; and in the interval pains must be taken to make foreigners acquainted with the provision.

I am Sir   Your obedt. Servant

Benj Lincoln Esqr

L[S], RG 36, Collector of Customs at Boston, Letters from the Treasury, 1789–1807, Vol. 4, National Archives; copy, RG 56, Letters to the Collector at Boston,

National Archives; copy, RG 56, Letters to Collectors at Small Ports, "Set G,"
National Archives.
   1. Lincoln was collector of customs at Boston.
   2. See Section 1 of "An Act making further provision for the payment of the
debts of the United States" (1 *Stat.* 180–81 [August 10, 1790]).
   3. Approximately twenty-one dollars.
   4. A pecul or picul is the equivalent of approximately 133 pounds.
   5. Words within broken brackets have been taken from the copy in RG 56,
Letters to the Collector at Boston, National Archives.

To William Seton [1]

[*Philadelphia, August 4, 1791.* On August 15, 1791, Seton wrote
to Hamilton: "I am honored with your Letter of the 4th." *Letter
not found.*]

   1. Seton was cashier of the Bank of New York.

Treasury Department Circular to the Commissioners of Loans

Treasury Department
Augt. 4th. 1791

Sir,
   It is deemed conducive to the general order of the department
that the respective Commissioners of loans should henceforth transmit to the Comptroller of the Treasury all such official statements
returns and documents respecting the public debt as they have been
or shall be directed to furnish, except the summary of the amount
of each kind of stock standing upon their books which has been required to be forwarded upon the closing of them in each quarter
preparatory to the payment of Interest, and which they will continue to address immediately to the Secretary of the Treasury. And
it is also deemed advisable that they should correspond generally with
the said Comptroller concerning whatever relates to the execution
of their several offices. They will therefore govern themselves accordingly, and will conform to the instructions which they shall
from time to time receive from that officer.
   This general direction is of course subject to the exception of all
such matters as shall hereafter be objects of special and direct communication from the Secretary of the Treasury.

In the course of past transactions respecting public business, considerable frauds and losses have resulted from the practice of signing papers with blanks to be afterwards filled up. It is confided that this practice will in no case obtain in any of the loan offices. No certificate or any other document which may bind the public is to be signed till after it shall have been filled up with whatever it is to contain.

I am, with consideration   Sir   Your most obedt Servant
                                      Alexander Hamilton

LS, to Nathaniel Appleton, The Turner Manuscript Collection at the Torrington Library, Torrington, Connecticut; LS, to William Gardner, Historical and Philosophical Society of Ohio, Cincinnati.

Treasury Department Circular
to the Collectors of the Customs

Treasury Department,
August 5th, 1791.

Sir,

Information has been given to me, that the Sloop Lurana, of Washington in North-Carolina, lately commanded by Thomas Eastwood, has been sold in Hispaniola to a person unknown, and there is some reason to apprehend that her certificate of registry has been disposed of with her, or retained for illicit purposes by the Captain. This certificate is numbered 28, and bears date at the port of Washington on the 9th day of December 1790. It states the vessel to be fifty three feet and one inch keel, eighteen feet two inches in breadth, five feet nine and a half inches in depth, and of the burden of forty six and two-thirds tons; that she has a round house, a billet head, and but one deck. Her late owner's name is James Eastwood. Should this vessel arrive in your district, you are to detain the certificate of registry till you receive my instructions, and to withhold from the Sloop and cargo the allowances and benefits granted to Vessels of the United States. If Captain Thomas Eastwood should be on board, you will proceed against him, after the expiration of eight days, for the nondelivery of the register on the occasion of the change of property, agreeably to the 9th section of the registering act.[1] It is said, however, that he has gone to France, and it is not therefore probable that he will appear in your district.

I have also received information, that the certificate of registry of the Schooner Fortitude, of New-York has been lost. The vessel having been stranded, and there being a possibility that the certificate of registry may have fallen into improper hands, it is necessary for me to put the Collectors on their guard, and to desire, that, if any vessel should enter with the certificate, it may be detained. It is No. 30, purports that the Schooner is of the length of fifty three feet, the breadth of seventeen feet four inches, the depth of six feet nine inches, and the burden of fifty two tons and one quarter, square sterned, round tucked, without badges, galleries or head, the property of George Scriba [2] of New-York, commanded first by Roderick Latesta, afterwards by Christian Geerman, and registered in New-York on the 24th of October 1789.

The papers which the legislature have directed to be prepared against their meeting, relative to the commerce of the United States, render it particularly necessary, that the returns of inward and outward tonnage, of decked vessels built in the several districts, of exports, and imports, should be made with as much expedition as may be found practicable, and that they be transmitted from time to time as soon as made up. No time ought to be lost in forwarding such as may be in arrear.

Having received information that the instruction communicated in my circular of the 30th November 1789, transmitting the opinions of Messrs. Jones and Harison,[3] has not been universally complied with, it becomes necessary to ascertain in what instances there have been deviations. If any such therefore have taken place within your district, it is my wish to be made acquainted with them, and with the considerations upon which they have been founded.

It has also been stated to me, that in some districts a practice has obtained of measuring *vessels of the United States previously registered,* and of charging for such admeasurement. This, though perhaps within the letter of the law,[4] does not appear to be within what may reasonably be supposed to be its true intent, and is of a complexion to excite dissatisfaction. It is with difficulty presumable, that the legislature could have intended to withhold credit from the acts and certificates of its own officers, so as to render an admeasurement in each district into which a vessel might happen to come necessary, and to subject the merchant to a repetition of the expence incident to that idea. The case of foreign vessels is different, because the documents they can produce are the acts of officers of another government. This practice therefore wherever it may have obtained is to be forborne; though if any reasons shall be offered in support of it they will be duly considered.

It will be satisfactory to receive a copy of the table of fees at each Custom-House, which is directed to be set up by the 54th section of the Collection Law.[5] Uniformity in practice as to the article of fees is particularly desirable. The want of it has already been a source of complaint, and is of a nature to produce both discontent and censure. I am, Sir   Your most obedient servant,   Alex Hamilton

Enclosed is a return of the Consuls and Vice-Consuls of the United States for the use of your Office.[6]

LS, to Jedediah Huntington, MS Division, New York Public Library; LS, to Jeremiah Olney, Rhode Island Historical Society, Providence; LS, The Andre deCoppet Collection, Princeton University Library; L[S], RG 36, Collector of Customs at Boston, Letters from the Treasury, 1789–1807, Vol. 4, National Archives; L[S], Office of the Secretary, United States Treasury Department; copy, United States Finance Miscellany, Treasury Circulars, Library of Congress; copy, RG 56, Circulars of the Office of the Secretary, "Set T," National Archives.

1. An Act for Registering and Clearing Vessels, Regulating the Coasting Trade, and for other purposes" (1 *Stat.* 55–65 [September 1, 1789]). Section 9 of the law stipulated that, when a vessel was transferred to foreigners, its certificate of registry had to be delivered up to a collector of the customs (1 *Stat.* 57).

2. Scriba was a New York City merchant.

3. See Richard Harison and Samuel Jones to H, November 18, 1789.

4. See Section 3 of "An Act for Registering and Clearing Vessels, Regulating the Coasting Trade, and for other purposes" (1 *Stat.* 55–56), which prescribed the rules for ascertaining the tonnage of ships or vessels.

5. H is actually referring to Section 55 of "An Act to provide more effectually for the collection of the duties imposed by law on goods, wares and merchandise imported into the United States, and on the tonnage of ships or vessels" (1 *Stat.* 173 [August 4, 1790]). For an explanation of the confusion over the numbering of the sections of this act, see H to Richard Harison, April 26, 1791, note 2.

6. William Ellery requested this information. See Ellery to H, June 26, 1791.

To Otho H. Williams

Treasury Department,
Augt. 6th, 1791.

Sir,
    It has been represented to me by Messrs. Sherman & Procter of

New Bedford, that some things which they deem improper have taken place. The Substance of the information is that their Brig Hawk, Hathaway Master, was remeasured in Baltimore altho she had been measured in New Bedford prior to her sailing [and was possessed of a Register of the U States] [1] that she was registered anew in Baltimore, that they paid charges, which were beyond those authorized by law, particularly the Surveyors fees and the fee of entry.[2] The enclosed papers are copies of the accounts of fees which they allege to have been paid at the Collectors and Surveyors offices.

Upon this Case I request to be informed what were the length and other demensions of the Brig Hawk, the circumstances that led to the remeasurement, whether she had a coasting licence, and whether any and what duties accrued upon the goods imported by her.

I also request to be furnished with the act or acts of the legislature of Maryland to which operation is given by the act of Congress of the 11th day of August 1790,[3] under which I presume the port duty of 2 Cents ℔ ton is charged.

I am with due consideration   Sir   Your obedt Servant
A. Hamilton

Otho H. Williams Esqr
Collr. of Baltimore

LS, Columbia University Libraries.
    1. The bracketed words are in H's handwriting.
    2. Section 53 of "An Act to provide more effectually for the collection of the duties imposed by law on goods, wares and merchandise imported into the United States, and on the tonnage of ships or vessels" prescribed the fees which might be charged by surveyors for the admeasurement of vessels (1 *Stat.* 171–72 [August 4, 1790]).
    3. "An Act declaring the assent of Congress to certain acts of the states of Maryland, Georgia, and Rhode Island and Providence Plantations" (1 *Stat.* 184–85) gave congressional consent to an act passed by "the General Assembly of the state of Maryland, at their session in April, one thousand seven hundred and eighty-three, intituled 'An act appointing wardens for the port of Baltimore-town in Baltimore county;' as also, another act of the General Assembly of the same state, passed at their session in November, one thousand seven hundred and eighty-eight, intituled 'A supplement to the act intituled, An act apppointing wardens for the port of Baltimore-town in Baltimore county.'"

From William Ellery

Newport [Rhode Island] August 8, 1791. ". . . On the 4th. of this month arrived here the Sloop Dove Pardon T. Slocum master from

Surinam and imported among other articles one hogshead and one barrel of Pumpings. Pumpings is a compound of the drainings from casks of sugar in the holds of vessels, and bilge water; which being pumped up is preserved in casks for sale. By distillation it yields some Spirit; but it is much inferior both in quantity and price to Molasses, and therefore it is thought should not pay the same duty. The Molasses imported in the Dove cost by the Masters account 15 cents per gallon and the hogshead and barrel of Pumpings one Dollar only. I am informed by Distillers that an hundred Galls of Pumpings will average from 10 to 20 galls. of Spirit. As the Law is silent with regard to this article I wish to know with what duty it is to be charged." [1]

LC, Newport Historical Society, Newport, Rhode Island.
    1. Ellery endorsed the letter book copy of this letter "Answered Augt. 24th 1791." Letter not found.

From Thomas Newton, Junior [1]

Norfolk [*Virginia*] *August 8, 1791.* "On monday last the foundation of the Light house was laid on Cape Henry; it was found necessary to go twenty feet deep below the water table, at the depth of thirteen there was nothing but loose sand, at twenty it appeared solid & firm. . . .I cou'd come to no others terms with Mr. McCoomb [2] than what is enclosed. . . .[3] He is perserving & merits much for his industry, the drifting of the sand is truly vexatious, for in an instant there came down fifty cart loads at least, in the foundation after it was cleansed for laying the Stone, which he bore with great patience & immediately set to work & removed it without a murmer. As to the time of payment for the additional work, it must be left to your determination. He has now above fifty hands at work & proceeds as fast as can be expected, but from a Conversation with him he does not think he will finish until October next, twelve months. . . ."

ALS, RG 26, Lighthouse Letters Received, Vol. "A," Pennsylvania and Southern States, National Archives.
    1. Newton was appointed inspector of Survey No. 4 in Virginia on November 1, 1791.
    2. John McComb, Jr., had contracted to build the lighthouse at Cape Henry.
    3. The enclosure was an undated contract between McComb and Newton for H (copy, RG 26, Lighthouse Letters Received, Vol. "A," Pennsylvania and Southern States, National Archives).

From William Short

Paris Aug. 8. 1791.

Sir

The letters which I have lately had the honor of writing to you are
of the dates of July 8.—19—24—26—27. In them I informed you of
what had been done with respect to the intended loan. Since then I
have recieved your letter of the 24th. of May, which increases my
powers both as to the repetition of the loans & the disposition of the
sums arising from them. At the time of its receipt a sudden & unexpected fall had taken place in the bonds of the U.S. at Amsterdam,
& previously to that, as already mentioned to you, the house at Antwerp had declined undertaking a loan at 4½. p. cent interest.[1] Our
bankers have since informed me that the fall was owing to local circumstances,[2] which they do not explain, & not to any discredit of
the bonds which are again on the rise.

Thus situated I had to chuse between the certainty of a loan at
Amsterdam & the experiment of one at Antwerp.[3] I should have preferred the latter, for the reasons formerly mentioned to you,[4] if it
had not been that I were advised to put off opening a loan there until
that for Russia should be completed, so as not to enter into competition with a power which gives such high premiums,[5] & also informed
that I must begin with small sums at first so as to insure success. The
sums on the market of Antwerp being inconsiderable when compared
with those at Amsterdam seemed to render such precautions proper.
When I considered therefore the amount of those which the U.S.
stood in need of & the advantageous mode of their present employment either at home or abroad I thought it most for their interest
at this moment to secure them at Amsterdam where they were offered
with certainty & without delay, on the terms of the last loan.[6] As the

AL, letterpress copy, William Short Papers, Library of Congress.

1. Short did not write about Charles John Michael de Wolf and Company's
refusal to make a loan until July 27, 1791.

2. See Willink, Van Staphorst, and Hubbard to Short, July 21, 1791, enclosed
in Short to H, July 26, 1791.

3. See Short to H, July 19, 1791.   4. Short to H, July 24–25, 1791.
5. See Short to H, July 27, 1791.
6. For a description of this loan, see Short to H, February 17, 1791.

bonds were above par it seemed to me just & reasonable that the charges should be somewhat reduced, but the bankers refuse it absolutely & say that the bonds will immediately fall to par as soon as a new loan is brought on the market. I am exceedingly sorry not to have been able as I expected, to reduce these charges; but the bankers, undertakers &c. are all so well acquainted with our position & the advantages we derive from the loans made there, & know so well that they depend on them in a great measure that I apprehend they would hold out against any attempt to reduce them lower.

I have thought it therefore, after an examination of the business in all its parts, most for the interest of the United States to subscribe to those terms for the present, & have accordingly authorized the bankers at Amsterdam to open a new loan [7] in the beginning of the next month for three millions of florins on the conditions of the last loan.

In their last letter they state that time as the proper one [8] & add a desire that I should leave them at liberty to extend it as far as six millions in case the moment should be favorable.[9] I have not done this as yet because I thought it best to make it the condition of their abating ½ p. cent on their charges in which case I have told them that I should have no objection to extending the loan, & added at the same time that it was to be understood that I allowed the 4. p. cent charges only on the condition that the undertakers still exacted 2. p. cent. I did not know but that they might have reduced them to 1½ p. cent as in the loan they formerly made, without allowing the U.S. the benefit of this reduction. If however I find that they persist in the 4. p. cent charges I shall probably authorize them under your last letter to go as far as the six millions & this as well because it will be easier, if the moment is favorable, to push it then to that amount than to make a new loan soon after, as because it will leave a greater space

7. Short did not send final orders for a new loan until August 11, 1791. On July 29, 1791, he discussed the terms but did not specifically order a new loan (Short to Willink, Van Staphorst, and Hubbard, July 29, August 11, 1791, ALS, letterpress copies, William Short Papers, Library of Congress).
8. See Willink, Van Staphorst, and Hubbard to Short, July 21, 1791, printed as an enclosure to Short to H, July 26, 1791.
9. On July 8, 1791, Willink, Van Staphorst, and Hubbard wrote to Short: "We have good hope We should succeed to carry it [the loan] even to the extent of Six Millions of Florins" (LS, Short Family Papers, Library of Congress).

of time between this & the next loan at Amsterdam which I should hope might be made, with a sufficient interval, at 4½. p cent interest. The balance which will remain due to France after the payment arising from this loan, may perhaps be provided for elsewhere either at Antwerp or Genoa. I leave Paris out of the question at present because I find from enquiry that although loans might be made here, they would afford less advantage to the U.S. in the payment to their debt to France than is derived from the rate of foreign exchange. Besides the foreign officers being not paid their interest here would of course prejudice the business of loans. I think it a misfortune the bill did not pass for re-imbursing them as it might have been done with much advantage on account of the exchange,[10] & the application which M. de Ternant [11] is to make in the names of the officers have been thus avoided.

I will take care Sir to keep you regularly informed of what is done with respect to the loan & shall desire the bankers also to announce it to you immediately on its being brought on the market, that no time may be lost with respect to the part which you intend to draw for. I suppose you find it most advantageous to receive these sums by drawing, otherwise there would have been less time lost perhaps in having the specie sent out.

I do not go to Amsterdam previous to the loan being made because it is not impossible that my presence there which would be known to the whole class of brokers & undertakers, by proving the want of a loan, might make them rise in their terms or render delay necessary in order to beat them down—or at least might furnish a pretext to the bankers for playing a game of that sort. Besides I do not see that any inconvenience can possibly arise from not being there at present. I shall go there to sign the bonds & at the same time stop at Antwerp in order to examine with more accuracy into the real situation of affairs at that place.

An offer has been lately made me indirectly, through Mr. Swan [12] of Boston & of course I suppose it comes from Schweizer & Jean-

10. See Short to H, July 19, 1791. For a description of the debt due foreign officers, see Short to H. August 3, 1790, note 5.

11. Jean Baptiste de Ternant presented his credentials as French Minister Plenipotentiary to the United States on August 2, 1791.

12. James Swan was a Boston merchant and speculator residing in France. See Short to H, January 15, 1791.

neret,[13] of furnishing the U.S. with all the money they want for paying off the French debt due & to become due & of taking their
obligations in Amsterdam. The source & chanel of this offer rendered
it impossible for me to have any confidence in it & as the terms they
offered were less advantageous than those found in borrowing at
Amsterdam to pay off this debt, I did not think it worth while to go
into a particular enquiry. They proposed to allow the U.S. 10. p. cent
for the exchange & 4. p. cent for the commission & asked charges on
the re-imbursement of their bonds. The exchange at present procuring
an advantage of 20. p. cent, this offer was of course inadmissible,
besides that they insisted on the debt to become due being included,
which was beyond my powers. I mentioned among other things that
I would not give the bonds payable at Amsterdam where our credit
was already established & where it might be injured by such an operation. Mr. Swan said the persons in question would consider whether
they would take the bonds payable at Genoa & London. I mention
this to you merely that nothing may be omitted, & have no idea that
any thing can be done in that way with the persons in question as I
suppose it merely an enterprize of some adventurers who have nothing to lose may risk any thing—who would be supported by people
of capital if this bargain was advantageous & abandoned if it should
turn out the contrary. It is possible however as I have formerly mentioned that in the crisis of the affairs of this country, the moment may
arrive when many may be disposed to withdraw their fortune from
the funds here by means of the American debt & thus put it in the
power of the U. S. to derive advantage from anticipating the payment
of their debt not yet due; as could be the case if such a change should
take place as should threaten bankruptcy, & render the circulation to
specie alone. In this situation the stockholders would be glad to get
out of the funds with the present rate of exchange, which would be
much more advantageous probably for the U.S. than that which
would prevail after the abolition of the assignats. Such a crisis & such
a turn in affairs is by no means impossible though I cannot undertake
to assert its probability, as it depends on foreign as well as domestic
operations.

The Honble. Alexander Hamilton Secretary of the Treasury—Philadelphia

13. The Paris banking firm of Jean Gaspar Schweizer and François Jeanneret.

To Elizabeth Hamilton

Brunswick [New Jersey] August 9. 1791

I came to this place my beloved Betsy a day or two since to meet some Gentlemen from New York on business.[1] Since you left me I have received but one letter from you,[2] which informed me of the indisposition of My Dear James [3] and left me in no small anxiety on his account. I hope on my return to Philadelphia I shall find a letter from you & Heaven Grant that it may assure me of your being all well!

I am myself in good health but I cannot be happy without you. Yet I must not advise you to urge your return. The confirmation of your health is so essential to our happiness that I am willing to make as long a sacrifice as the season and your patience will permit. Adieu my precious. My best love to all the family.

Yrs   ever & entirely   A Hamilton

Mrs. Hamilton

ALS, Hamilton Papers, Library of Congress.
1. The "business" was the organization of the Society for Establishing Useful Manufactures, which eventually obtained a charter from New Jersey and established a plant at what is now Paterson, New Jersey.
2. Letter not found.
3. See H to Elizabeth Hamilton, August 2, 1791.

Power of Attorney from the Society for Establishing Useful Manufactures

Brunswick in the State of
Jersey, August 9th. 1791.

Sir:

On behalf of a Society for the Establishment of Manufactures, of which we are Members, we request you to procure and Engage for the Service of the Society such Artists and Workmen, as you shall deem necessary, and upon such Terms, as shall appear to you reasonable, for the Purpose of Carrying on a Manufactory of Cotton in its various Branches, and printing the same. And we Engage to Indemnify you for all Expences which shall attend the Execution of this Request; and that the Society shall Ratify the Agreements, which shall be Enter'd into by you Concerning the same.

We are Sir, with Sentiments of Respect and Esteem   Your Obedt Hble Servts   Nichs. Low
                                                     Wm. Duer
                                                     Wm. Constable
                                                     Herman LeRoy
                                                     Richd. Platt
                                                     Mat. McConnell [1]

To Alexr: Hamilton Esqr.

DS, Hamilton Papers, Library of Congress.
    1. These men were among the original subscribers to the stock of the Society for Establishing Useful Manufactures. They were all New York residents except Matthew McConnell, who was a prominent Philadelphia securities broker.

From James Duane

[*New York, August 10, 1791.* On the back of Hamilton's letter to Duane of August 4, 1791, is the endorsement: "Answered 10th." *Letter not found.*]

To William Ellery

[*Philadelphia, August 10, 1791.* On August 23, 1791, Ellery referred to Hamilton's "letter of the 10th of this month, requesting the particular circumstances that led to a remeasurement of the Brig Sally." *Letter not found.*]

To Elizabeth Hamilton

[Philadelphia, August 10, 1791]

This day, my beloved, on my return from Brunswick I received your precious letters of the 31 of July & 3d. of August.[1] I was surprised to find you had received none from me; as without recollecting dates, I think one, which I wrote you, before my departure from New York,[2] ought to have got to hand previous to your last.

You will easily imagine how much pleasure it gives me to learn that my Dear James was better: [3] but then My Betsey, your health had suffered by your anxiety and you were not so well as when you left me! Think how afflicting an alloy this is. For Heaven's sake, do not yield too much to the little adverse circumstances that must attend us in this pilgrimage. Exert your fortitude. Keep up your spirits. Never forget for a moment the delight you will give me by returning to my bosom in good health. Dear Betsey—beloved Betsey—Take care of yourself—Be attentive to yourself—Use every mean that promises you benefit.

You say you have not forgotten your bark & Vitriol. But have you *constantly* remembered it? Have you used the other remedy also?

I have a wish that you would try the Cold bath, beginning by degrees. Take the air too as much as possible and *gentle* exercise.

I am myself in good health & only want you with me, & in health also, to be as happy as it is reasonable to wish to be. But I charge you (unless you are so anxious as to injure you, or unless you find your health declining more) not to precipitate your return. I cannot help hoping that your native air if taken long enough will be of service to you.

Adieu My angel. Assure yourself always of my tenderest affection & unceasing prayers.

Aug 10, 1791

AL[S], Mr. George T. Bowdoin, New York City.
  1. Neither of these letters has been found.
  2. Letter not found.
  3. See H to Elizabeth Hamilton, August 2, 9, 1791.

From Jeremiah Olney [1]

Providence, August 11, 1791. "A Sailor belonging to the Ship Providence, Entered here on the 5th Instant from Cape Francois, started out of a Barrel (which was included in the Manifest of her Cargo) about Eighty pounds of brown Sugar, and while she was unloading, attempted to carry it off in a Box before it was weighed; but the Surveyor [2] meeting him some distance from the Wharf, seized and deposited it in the Custom-House Store. This Sugar being forfeited by its removal without permission, with an evident design to defraud the Revenue, I purpose to proceed against it in the same manner as if it was an Article of greater value; and I hope it will prevent similar Practices in future. . . ."

ADfS, Rhode Island Historical Society, Providence; copy, RG 56, Letters from the Collector at Providence, National Archives.
  1. Olney was collector of customs at Providence.
  2. William Barton.

From William Skinner

United States Loan Office [Hillsboro] North Carolina
August 11th. 1791.

Sir.

In about eight or ten days after my inclosing you the Extract from the Council Books,[1] the Comptroller of the State[2] agreable to his instructions came forward with a small part of the Certificates collected from his office, with an intent to begin the business of subscribing in my office in behalf of the State for the Certificates in his and the Treasy. offices; this Subscription I considered it my duty to refuse admiting until I should receive your particular directions respecting that business, In consequence of my refusal another attempt was made two days past by the Comptroller to subscribe for the Certificates in his own name, this Subscription I also considered it my duty not to admit of, as it was going expressly contrary to the advice of the Council, and in a manner might be deemed sporting with the public property, for an individual to fund the Pub Securities in his own name; I am apprehensive the Governor of the State[3] (who has the business much at heart) will perhaps throw the Certificates into several hands that I may not suspect, and by that means obtain his wishes, however I shall be as much on my guard as possible to prevent the Subscription taking place until I receive your particular orders, but it is possible it may be accomplished by hands which I may not mistrust. The Checks to the small indents issued Mr. Jas Green[4] for the May & April Money, I am told is in the possession of the Admr. of Mr. Green but will not be delivered up without your orders and that cannot be accomplished so as to answer any good purpose before the first of October.[5]

I am most respectfully   Your most obedient Servant   W Skinner.

The Honble. Alexander Hamilton Esqr.

Copy, North Carolina Department of Archives and History, Raleigh. This letter was enclosed in H's "Report to the Governor of North Carolina," July 31, 1794.
    1. See the second letter that Skinner wrote to H on July 22, 1791.
    2. Francis Child.
    3. Alexander Martin.
    4. James Green, Jr., was appointed commissioner of the Continental loan office on December 24, 1777.
    5. The "May and April Money" to which Skinner is referring consisted of Continental bills of credit issued on May 20, 1777, and April 11, 1778. Under a resolution of January 2, 1779, these issues were called in because counterfeits had been detected. Those which were not used in payment of taxes might be received on loan or registered in the Continental loan offices and there exchanged for indented certificates (*JCC*, XIII, 22).

From Oliver Wolcott, Junior

Treasury Department
Comptroller's Office
11th: August 1791.

Sir,

On examining the Accounts of Daniel Benezet, Collector of the Customs, for the district of Great-Egg-harbour,[1] from the 1st: of January to the 31st. of March last; it appears, that he has collected duties on American Coasting Vessells, under 20 Tons burthen, at the rate of Six Cents per Ton, per annum, to the amount of one dollar & Eighty six Cents.

As the Collection of those duties, seems to have been made, contrary to the intent of your circular Letter to the Collectors, of 20th. November 1789,[2] I take the liberty of submitting the circumstance to your consideration.

I am &ca: O: W: Jr:

LC, RG 217, First Comptroller's Office, Revenue Letters Sent (Customs), National Archives.
    1. Great Egg Harbor is in New Jersey.
    2. No circular of this date on this subject has been found. Wolcott may be referring to "Treasury Department Circular to the Collectors of the Customs," December 23, 1789.

To Thomas Arnold and Others [1]

Treasury Department
August 12 1791

Gentlemen

In the month of July last Mr Thomas Arnold left at the Treasury a note relative to the tonnage and impost on the Sloops Betsy & Peace, stating that those duties had been paid at the foreign rates by their Captains on entries at Wiscassett and Bath *subsequent* to the adoption of the federal Constitution by the Convention of Rhode Island.[2] On examination it appears that the entries were made in the month of April, which, it will be perceived, puts it out of my power to direct a refund. Should there by any mistake in regard to dates, in either case, further attention will be paid to the matter, on your transmitting an accurate statement, with such original papers in proof as may be in your possession.

I am, Gentlemen,   Your Most Obedt. Servant

Alexander Hamilton

Messrs Thomas Arnold & Others,
Owners of the Sloops, Peace
& Betsy, Providence

LS, Rhode Island Historical Society, Providence.
  1. Thomas Arnold was the brother of Jonathan Arnold and uncle of Welcome Arnold. All three were Providence merchants.
  2. Rhode Island ratified the Constitution on May 29, 1790, and on June 14, 1790, Congress passed "An Act for giving effect to the several Acts therein mentioned, in respect to the State of Rhode Island and Providence Plantations" (1 *Stat.* 126–28).

Conversation with George Beckwith [1]

Philadelphia
August 12th [1791]

An Officer at the Head of an Executive Department

Mr. _____ Since I saw you, we have got Mr. Ternant, the minister plenipotentiary from France; I have seen him for a few minutes only. You will find him a man of easy, pleasing manners, and very fit for the objects of his appointment. There has been a sort of alarm in France, and a degree of jealousy of *your* having lately turned your attention more towards this Country than formerly.[2]

From the nature of our government foreign affairs are totally in the department of the Secretary of State; we have no Cabinet, and the heads of Departments meet on very particular occasions only, therefore I am a stranger to any special views, that may be in the contemplation of the French government from the appointment of this Minister, but I think it probable, that a revision of their whole commercial condition with *us* may be in agitation, in the Hope of acquiring thereby some share in the trade and consumption of this country; he is a fit man in many respects for such purposes.

Monsieur de la Fayette has written several letters by Mr. Ternant;[3] they contain his opinions of the state of France, and declare his expectation of a completion of the Revolution without a civil war.

Geo. Beckwith

D, PRO: F.O., Series 4, Vol. 12, Part II.

1. This document was enclosed in a letter Beckwith wrote to Lord Grenville, August 26, 1791.

Beckwith was the informal representative of the British government in the United States.

As Beckwith identified his informant as "An Officer at the Head of an Executive Department," and as H held frequent conversations with Beckwith, it has been assumed that the remarks recorded by Beckwith were made by H.

2. By England directing its "attention more towards this Country than formerly," H is probably referring to the recent appointment of George Hammond as Minister Plenipotentiary to the United States.

3. Among the letters sent by Lafayette was one to George Washington (*GW*, XXXI, 362). No letter from Lafayette to H has been found.

From William Duer [1]

[*New York, August 12, 1791.* On August 17, 1791, Hamilton wrote to Duer: "I have received your two letters of the 12th and 16th." *Letter of August 12 not found.*]

1. Duer, a prominent New York financier and speculator, had served as Assistant Secretary of the Treasury from September, 1789, until early in 1790.

From Henry Lee [1]

Alexa. [Virginia] 12th August 1791.

My dear sir

Our parting conversation has deeply employed my mind & I continue to lament exceedingly the existence of any event which puts us even politically opposite.

No man is more warmly attached to his friends than I am; among the first of whom my heart places you. I thoroughly confide in the unstained purity of your principles, altho I feel enmity to the measures flowing from them. I am solicitous for your encreasing fame & yet cannot applaud your system. The superiority of your understanding I am not a stranger to & therefore very often am led to doubt the accuracy of my own conclusions; my consequent apprehensions introduce re-deliberation which always terminates in confirmation of my opinions.

In one thing I am nearly decided, to advocate a patient trial for a few years of the fiscal plan, because by this the harmony of the community will be undisturbed & such alterations may be effected as will go to banish from among us bickerings & discord. Amendments of this nature yourself would surely patronise, because the undivided confidence of a nation is not only highly gratifying to a public minister but is the best foundation for complete success to just & wise measures. I wish I could know your mind on this subject & whether you cannot project a mode which will in our day gradually extinguish a debt which so many abhor & dread. This would cure the hurts of thousands, allay the fury of faction & re-laurel your brow.

I have partly contracted for your riding horse & as soon as I can will forward him to you.

Since my return, in consequence of a conversation with Mr. Cazinove [2] I have received a large sum in funded paper & shall send the same as soon as I get the transfer to Mr. Leroy & Bayard [3] recommended to me by Mr C to turn into cash.

The money being soon wanted & the price allowed by me very high, disappointment in the agency will be injurious & distressing. Therefore do I take the liberty to request you the moment you read this ltr. to walk to Mr Leroys,[4] see my letr. to him & urge him to do the business in the best manner for me, as I am a stranger to him.

By return of the post I expect to receive your reply; if you will then enclose Graysons [5] bond, I shall be able to put it on a probable road to paymt.

most affy. yours always   Henry Lee

Col. Hamilton

ALS, Hamilton Papers, Library of Congress.
    1. Lee, who was at this time a member of the Virginia Assembly, was elected governor of his state in 1791. Although, as this letter indicates, he objected to some features of H's economic policies, he remained an enthusiastic Federalist throughout his life.
    2. Théophile Cazenove, the representative in the United States of a group of Dutch banking houses.
    3. William Bayard and Herman Le Roy were prominent New York City merchants.
    4. Le Roy and Bayard had a branch office in Philadelphia at 323 High Street.
    5. Probably William Grayson of Virginia, who had been an aide to George Washington in the early years of the American Revolution and a delegate to the Continental Congress in the seventeen-eighties. Grayson was a member of the United States Senate from 1789 until his death in March, 1790.

To William Skinner

Treasury Department
August 12th. 1791.

Sir,
    In the hurry of writing my letter to you of the 2nd instant [1] an idea is expressed which does not conform to my real intention, namely that the Certificates of State Debt of which there are no Registers nor other checks, should be sent to the Treasury for examination previous to their admission by you as valid.

The reasons which dictated this regulation in regard to Certificates of Federal debt,[2] not being applicable to State Debt, it was never intended that it should extend to the latter.

You will therefore forbear to send onto the Treasury for previous examination the certificates of State Debt, ascertaining their authenticity in the best manner which circumstance will permit you will receive on loan all such as shall appear to you genuine. The enclosed extract of a letter of Hugh Williamson [3] Esquire points out guides which appear to me capable of being useful to you. I have received information that the State of North Carolina has passed a law for subscribing its own certificates which had been redeemed or called in.[4] On this point I refer you to my circular of the 1st. November. Nevertheless if the thing should be pressed upon you, you may receive the Certificates offered by the State and give a receipt expressing that they are to be submitted to the Secretary of the Treasury for his decision. And you will then inform me of the matter and receive my final determination, in order to which I shall perhaps take the advice of the Attorney General.

I am yours &c   A. H.

William Skinner Esquire
Commissioner of Loans.

Copy, North Carolina Department of Archives and History, Raleigh. This letter was enclosed in H's "Report to the Governor of North Carolina," July 31, 1794.
    1. Letter not found.
    2. See "Treasury Department Circular to the Commissioners of Loans," March 17, 1791.
    3. Williamson was a member of the House of Representatives from North Carolina. Letter not found.
    4. A "bill for subscribing on loan, in the office of the Commissioners of the United States, such continental monies and continental and state securities as are or may be in the hands of the Treasurer or Comptroller of this state belonging to the public, or which shall be in the hands of either of them on the last day of September next. . ." had been considered in the North Carolina legislature during November and December, 1790. Final action, however, was postponed until the following fall (*Journal of the House of Commons. North Carolina. At a General Assembly begun and held at Fayetteville, on the first day of November, in the year of our Lord one thousand seven hundred and ninety, and in the fifteenth year of the independence of the United States of America: Being the first session of this Assembly* [Edenton: Printed by Hodge & Wills, n.d.], 43, 44, 60, 62, 78).

Conversation with Thomas Jefferson [1]

[Philadelphia, August 13, 1791]

Aug. 13. 1791. Notes of a conversn between A. Hamilton & Th: J.

Th. J. mentioned to him a lre recd. from J. A. disavowing Publicola, & denying that he ever entertd. a wish to bring this country under a hereditary executive, or introduce an hereditary branch of legislature &c. See his lre. A. H. condemning mr A's writings & most particularly Davila, as having a tendency to weaken the present govmt declared in substance as follows. "I own it is my own opn, tho' I do not publish it in Dan & Bersheba, that the present govmt is not that which will answer the ends of society by giving stability & protection to it's rights, and that it will probably be found expedient to go into the British form. However, since we have undertaken the experiment, I am for giving it a fair course, whatever my expectns may be. The success indeed so far is greater than I had expected, & therefore at present success seems more possible than it had done heretofore, & there are still other & other stages of improvemt which, if the present does not succeed, may be tried & ought to be tried before we give up the republican form altogether for that mind must be really depraved which would not prefer the equality of political rights which is the foundn of pure republicanism, if it can be obtained consistently with order. Therefore whoever by his writings disturbs the present order of things, is really blameable, however pure his intentns may be, & he was sure mr Adams's were pure." This is the substance of a declaration made in much more lengthy terms, & which seemed to be more formal than usual for a private conversn. between two, & as if intended to qualify some less guarded expressions which had been dropped on former occasions. Th: J. has committed it to writing in the moment of A.H.'s leaving the room.

D, in writing of Thomas Jefferson, Thomas Jefferson Papers, Library of Congress.
    1. The background to this document is as follows: Early in 1791 the first part of Thomas Paine's The Rights of Man was published in England. In May, 1791, Jefferson read the book and at the request of John Beckley, clerk of the House of Representatives, forwarded it for reprinting to Jonathan B. Smith, brother of the printer Samuel Harrison Smith. Jefferson sent a note to Jonathan B. Smith approving of Paine's work, and this note was used by the printer in the preface of the work. Jefferson was quoted as writing: "I am extremely pleased to find it will be reprinted here, and that something is at length to be publickly said against the political heresies which have sprung up among us." Jefferson later made clear that he had in mind the "political heresies" in John Adams's Discourses on Davila, which had been serialized in Philadelphia papers. Then, beginning in June there appeared a series of letters to a Boston newspaper that were signed "Publicola" and that attacked Paine's views and supported those of Adams. Although Jefferson, like most other contemporaries, thought that "Publicola" was John Adams, the author of these letters actually was John Quincy Adams.

From Tobias Lear

[Philadelphia] August 13, 1791. Encloses the following commissions:

"A Commission for Thomas Marshal Inspector of Survey No. 7. in the District of Virga.

Do. for Sylvanus Walker, Inspector of survey No 3. in the Distt. of South Carolina.

Do. for William Ham second Mate of a revenue Cutter.

Do. for Bathurst Dangerfield, third mate of Do.

Likewise a commission for Josiah Murdaugh Inspector of the revenue at the port of Hartford in No. Carolina."

LC, George Washington Papers, Library of Congress.

From Jeremiah Olney

Providence, August 13, 1791. Asks that Jeremiah Greenman be appointed "Second Mate of the Cutter fitting in Connecticut." [1]

LS, George Washington Papers, Library of Congress; ADfS, Rhode Island Historical Society, Providence.

1. See Olney to H, February 17, 1791.

Promissory Note from William Adams

Augst. 13th, 1791

One Month after Date I Promise to pay to Alexr. Hamilton Esq Or Order fifteen pounds for Value Red.

Wm. Adams

£ 15..0..0

ADS, Hamilton Papers, Library of Congress.

Treasury Department Circular [1]

Philadelphia Augt. 13. 1791.

Dear Sir

Some investigations in which I am engaged induce a wish to be able to form as accurate an idea as can be obtained of the usual product in proportion to the value of cultivated lands in different parts of the United States.

As I am persuaded no person can better assist me in this object than yourself, I take the liberty to ask the favor of your assistance.

It has occurred to me that if the *actual* product on cultivated farms of *middling* quality could be ascertained with tolerable precision, it might afford as good a rule, by which to judge as the nature of the thing admits of.

With this view I have prepared a form with a number of Columns under heads specifying the different kinds of produce usual in your quarter in order that they may be filled in each case according to the fact and as the nature of each head shall require.[2]

There are besides some additional Columns which respect the Total value of the farm and the different kinds of Land of which it consists.

The value of the farm must be determined not by what it would fetch in Cash on a forced or sudden sale, but by what it would sell for at a reasonable and usual credit or perhaps by what the opinion of the neighbourhood would compute to be its true value.

The quantity of each kind of land must conform to the actual quantity in cultivation at the time for which the product is taken.

It is submitted to your judgment according to circumstances whether to determine the product by the average of a series of years, three or more, or by what has been considered as a year of middling fertility.

The price ought to express the value of each Article on the farm. Perhaps to determine this there is no better rule than to deduct the expence of transportation from the price at the nearest usual market. The high price of an extraordinary year would not be a proper criterion; but that which is deemed by intelligent and reasonable farmers a good saving price.

If not inconvenient to you to execute my present request, you will add to the favour by explaining in each case the rule by which you have proceeded; and if it would not be attended with too much trouble the extension of the inquiry to two or three different farms would be satisfactory.

In a matter with which I am not very familiar, it is possible I may have omitted circumstances of importance to the object of my inquiry. The supplying of such omissions will be particularly acceptable.

As whatever comes from the Treasury is apt to be suspected of having referrence to some scheme of taxation, it is my wish that the knowlege of this request may be confined to yourself. And I think it not amiss to add that *in truth* it has not the most remote referrence to any such purpose.

With great consideration & esteem   I remain   Sir   Your Obedt. servant   Alexander Hamilton

LS, Massachusetts Historical Society, Boston; LS, Historical Society of Pennsylvania, Philadelphia; LS, Mr. John E. Meals, Seattle.

1. H sent this letter to at least five individuals. See Richard Peters to H, August 27, 1791; Henry Wynkoop to H, August 29, 1791; Timothy Pickering to H, October 3, 1791; John Neville to H, October 27, 1791; John Beale Bordley to H, November 11, 1791.

H presumably sent this letter to obtain information for use in his "Report on the Subject of Manufactures," December 5, 1791. Copies of some of the answers received by H to this letter are in the George Washington Papers, Library of Congress. On June 18–21, 1792, Washington wrote to Arthur Young, the English agricultural reformer: "On applying to Colo. Hamilton for the statement mentioned in Mr. [Richard] Peters' letter he put into my hands, together with the statement, several communications which were made to him last year by some of the most respectable farmers in this part of the Country, in consequence of an application from him for information on certain points respecting farms, And as they appeared to contain some matters worth attention I had them copied, and they are also enclosed" (*GW*, XXXII, 71). For Peters's statement, see Peters to H, August 27, 1791.

2. D, Massachusetts Historical Society, Boston.

From Otho H. Williams [1]

Baltimore 13 August 1791

Sir

The Brigantine Hawke, Robert Hathaway, Master, arrived at this Port the 28th February last from Havre de Grace, having on board sundry articles of Merchandize, the duties on which amounted to sixty one dollars and eighty four Cents agreeable to the enclosed abstract.

The Brigantine Hawke was registered ninety eight tons, but some circumstance induced the Surveyor of this Port to remeasure her, and she was found to be of one hundred and ten Tons burthen as will appear by the enclosed certificate of admeasurement; she was not registered anew, but the tonnage duty and fees were charged agreeable to her *actual* tonnage, which I conceive to have been the intention of Congress, and which has invariably been the practice at this port.

I have enclosed an authenticated copy of the Act of the Legislature of Maryland that was ratified by Congress the eleventh day of August last,[2] and which authorizes the collection of two Cents ⅌ Ton, for the benefit of this port.

I am, Sir

ADf, RG 53, "Old Correspondence," Baltimore Collector, National Archives.
1. For background to this letter, see H to Otho H. Williams, August 6, 1791.
2. "An Act declaring the assent of Congress to certain acts of the states of Maryland, Georgia, and Rhode Island and Providence Plantations" (1 *Stat.* 184–85).

From Thomas Randall [1]

New York August 14th 1791

Sir.

Agreeably to your request,[2] I shall endeavor to communicate, in as clear a manner as my abilities will admit, the ideas which result to me, from my experience in the trade from this country to Canton.

It is needless to a gentleman of your historical information to make any remarks on the representation given by writers, on the government of China, as they must be merely speculative, and would not

ALS, Hamilton Papers, Library of Congress.
1. Little concerning Randall's early career is known beyond the fact that he was a resident of Massachusetts and that during the American Revolution he served first as a lieutenant in a Massachusetts regiment and then as a captain in a Continental artillery regiment. Samuel Shaw was a member of the same artillery regiment, and it was presumably during the Revolution that the two men became friends. In any event, when Shaw in 1784 became supercargo on the *Empress of China*, he secured the same position for Randall. Shaw writes:

"Soon after the close of the war between Great Britain and America, several merchants in New York and Philadelphia being desirous of opening a commerce with Canton, in China, a ship was purchased and loaded principally with ginseng, in order to exchange it for teas and manufactures of that country. My friend, Daniel Parker, Esq. agent for those concerned, having offered me the appointment of supercargo, I followed the advice of my friends in accepting it; and finding that Thomas Randall, Esq., my intimate friend, had an inclination to go the voyage, we agreed to try our fortunes together, and sailed from New York on Sunday 22d February, 1784, in the ship Empress of China, commanded by John Green, Esq." (Quincy, *Journals of Samuel Shaw*, 133.)

Arthur H. Cole confuses this Thomas Randall with another man of the same name. Cole writes: "Thomas Randall was a prominent New York merchant. He had been chosen a member of the committee of 100 to control the affairs of the city in 1775, and was the principal founder of the Marine Society of New York" (Cole, *Industrial and Commercial Correspondence*, 129).
2. Letter not found.

in the least elucidate those points of information, which you wish to consider from the noble motive that actuates you, of endeavoring to promote and secure a happy and prosperous trade to your country; but, it may be necessary to detail to you, how the merchants from this country trading to Canton, actually feel and suffer under the operations of the Chinese government, and which injuries, perhaps, may be remedied by regulating the mode of conducting the trade from hence to that port. I shall therefore begin with a recital of events & facts.

In the year 1784, on the 22d of February, the ship Empress of China, being the first ship that ever sailed from the United States for China, was sent to Canton by a company of American Merchants; her cargo consisted of Spanish dollars, about four hundred peculs of genseng, a pecul being 133 ⅓ lb English Avoirdu poids, some cordage, wine, lead, iron a few furs, with other trifling articles not worth enumerating. In this ship I went as a joint supercargo with Samuel Shaw Esq, the present Consul at Canton. Our reception from all the European nations who had factories there, viz the English, Dutch, French, Danes, Swedes, and imperialists,[3] was friendly and polite. From them we endeavoured to obtain all the information we could respecting the Chinese, and the mode of transacting business with them. We were informed that our ship must be measured in order to Ascertain the port duties she would have to pay, that the trade was put by the Chinese government in the hands of a body of Merchants, then eight in number, called Hong Merchants, that we must obtain one of these merchants as a security merchant whom the Mandarines* considered as responsible in his own person and fortune for all the improper conduct or trade that might be committed by the ship, that this was expensive, and no one would accept it, unless we dealt with him, and the appearance of our trade promised him a handsome profit. But, in this instance, on our application to the first Hong merchant named Pankikoa, he consented to become Trader, or Security merchant for the ship. However, it may be here necessary to remark, that when the funds of a ship are small, and that every

---

* Mandarine a term for every Officer of government whether civil or military.

3. The Imperial East India Company, which had been chartered by the Holy Roman Emperor and which had its headquarters in Ostend in the Belgian Netherlands.

Hong merchant declines the Office, the whole body of them under the name of the cohong are considered as security for said ship, and they name the first merchant of their number to act in that capacity, each paying their portion to him of the loss he sustains, in consequence of the trade of the ship not being sufficient, to enable him to pay the extra fees extorted by the mandarines. This merchant grants all your permits for either discharging or taking in your cargo. Our business of a Security merchant being settled, and our ship measured, we conceived ourselves at liberty to trade with any individual of the Cohong, or whom else we pleased, but in this pursuit we soon found ourselves exposed to intrigues of which we were not apprized. We experienced that this body of Hong merchants possessed more power than we were aware of; that they had an influence over all the other merchants in Canton, who are obliged to trade under the Chop, or permission of one of these Hong merchants, who each of them had their class of friends; and that private merchants could not ship any goods they might vend, or bring up any they might purchase, or even go to look at goods, without the Chop, or particular permission of one of the Hong merchants; that Pankikoa our security merchant was a mandarine, as well as a merchant of great opulence, and had an influence over all the rest of the Hong Merchants; and that not one of them would make us an offer equal to Pankikoa, who himself offered us but one hundred & fifty dollars the pecul, a price we thought far inferior to what we could get, if we could obtain a freedom in our trade. Perhaps Pankikoa in conjunction with the other Hong Merchants, had monopolized the business of purchasing our genseng, the only article of much consequence in our cargo, and over awed the other merchants not of the cohong from making us any offers, for future experience has led me to conclude, and the fact been verified, that this body of Hong merchants sometimes have agreed together to affix a price at which they would purchase merchandise, and that each individual of them has broke his engagement to the other, by giving a higher price, perfectly relying on the integrity of the European, that he would not betray him in the price given, but the fact being discovered, they have come to open rupture, broke their compact, and by court or mandarine influence, if I may be allowed the term, in gratification of their revenge ruined the weak hong merchant of their body, who has been so unfortunate as to be detected, although every one of them had been guilty of similar conduct.

In further confirmation of what I have writ, I must add that we were applied to by private merchants, who did go down to the ship to examine the genseng, came up, and offered us conditional prices according to the quantity we might sell, and that they would leave us earnest money to secure the purchase of our genseng at the price agreed on, which merchants have had the assurance and baseness to return next day, breaking their agreement & telling us they would give but one half of the price they had actually agreed to purchase for the preceding day, and others told us, they would, but could not purchase for fear of drawing on them the resentment of the Hong merchants. Thus situated, new adventurers in this commerce, anxious for the interests of our employers, and our minds agitated with doubts, we advised with an European friend, who told us, he knew of no remedy, but to wait and exhaust the Chinese patience, a difficult thing to do, if we had not resources independant of that article for our return cargo, especially as we had a larger quantity of genseng than ever had been brought to the Chinese market. Thus circumstanced we delayed selling our genseng from the time of our arrival which was the 27th August, 'till the 22d of September, when we sold to Shykinkoa, a hong merchant, for one hundred & fifty five dollars the pecul, but were afterwards obliged to abate five dollars on the pecul in consequence of it not all proving equal to the sample given.

I shall now make a few remarks on the article of genseng, and the quantity at Market that season, and observe upon the sales of the remainder of the Cargo.

Quantity of Genseng at market in the year 1784	
brought by ship Empress of China	445
Portuguese ships	300
English ships	135
about ten peculs of old genseng remaining at market	10
	890 Peculs.

The whole of this genseng was sold according to quality, and at various prices, from one hundred & fifty, to three hundred & fifty dollars the pecul, but in the year 1783 it had been sold for three thousand dollars the pecul.

I have further to observe that after the sale of our genseng to Shykinkoa, he offered to release us from our engagement from which we judged that he had no idea himself of its being a very lucrative bargain to him, and he did return us a small quantity of six or seven peculs belonging to the officers of the ship of better quality, and which we afterwards sold for them, at one hundred & eighty, and two hundred dollars the pecul. The remainder of our cargo sold for about the cost, the cordage and wine being bought by Europeans, the lead, iron, furs &c by the Chinese. Lead, is an article though it seldom yields any profit, will always sell for Cash; ours sold at four taels* per pecul. There was but three or four tons of iron belonging to the officers & I imagine it would have been very difficult to have got rid of a larger quantity.

I shall now proceed to relate a second and third voyage.

My second voyage commenced in February 1786 and we returned 2d August 1787.[4] There is scarcely anything new worthy remarking in the course of this voyage, than that there were four American ships at Canton of about three hundred tons burthen each, that the quantity of genseng brought that season to market was upwards of two thousand peculs, which sold from one hundred & fifty, to two hundred dollars the pecul, according to the quality, and the extortion of the mandarines for fees of every kind had rather increased. Our funds were small, and quite inadequate to the voyage. We were therefore obliged to obtain credit, and was defrauded in the quality

---

* 10 Cash makes a candareen ⎫
  10 Candareen a mace   ⎬ 72 cand. = Spanish dollar
  10 Mace a tael   ⎭

4. Of the origins of this voyage Shaw writes: "Towards the close of November, proposals were made to me by Isaac Sears, Esq., and other gentlemen in New York, to take a concern with them in a voyage to Canton, and, with Mr. Sears, superintend the business. To these proposals I agreed, on condition that my friend Randall should be admitted, and the business at Canton transacted by us jointly, or, in case of a difference of opinion, by a majority. A good ship, called the Hope, was accordingly provided, nearly of the dimensions of the Empress of China, and the command given to Captain James Magee. Immediately on engaging in this business, I resigned my appointment [as first secretary] in the war-office, and was shortly after honored by Congress with their commission of Consul at Canton, when Mr. Randall also received that of Vice-consul. A suitable cargo having been provided, we sailed from New York on the 4th of February, 1786, bound to Batavia and Canton" (Quincy, *Journals of Samuel Shaw*, 219).

of the teas, they not proving equal to the samples tried, and for which we in our next voyage obtained an abatement. I shall therefore without delaying your time proceed to relate my third and last voyage,[5] which commenced in December 1787 and was intended for India & China in one season, but some unexpected delays taking place at Madeira and finding on my arrival at Madrass the markets glutted with wine, the article of which my cargo was chiefly composed, but however having sold a part of the wines, I proceed to Batavia, where they granted me permission to sell the remainder of my wine, which I could not effect the market being glutted, and leave to purchase sugars, which I did, and carried to Bombay, where I sold the remainder of my wine, and obtained a handsome profit on the sale of my sugars. From Bombay I took a freight of cotton for Canton where I arrived the 16th of October 1789 and from thence took in a Cargo for this port where I arrived the 29th July 1790.

From Batavia by an English East India company's ship, I shipped my genseng to China, which arrived there in the beginning of the year 1789, which was sold by my agent there for 65 dollars the pecul, and to take bohea tea in payment. Large quantities of genseng also arrived in the year 1789, say upwards of two thousand peculs, and the price fell to fifty five dollars, to receive teas in payment, and I believe genseng of a tollerable good quality, would not have sold for Cash, for more than forty dollars the pecul. However, to conclude my remarks on the article of genseng, it appears to me from what I have observed respecting it, that there might be shipped to Canton annually from this country five or six hundred peculs, & perhaps a larger quantity, even to nine hundred peculs, provided none was exported from this country to Europe, although the Hong merchants say two hundred peculs annually, would be sufficient for the supply, and for that quantity they could contract to give a high price, that

---

5. Little has been found concerning this voyage. Shaw's journal, however, comtains the following entry: "Saturday morning, the 14th [of February, 1789], we anchored at North Island, where we found the Jenny, Captain Thompson, arrived the day before. The first mate of a Dutch ship from Batavia, stationed at this place . . . came on board and gave me the welcome information that Captain Randall and my brother in the Jay, were safe; that they arrived here the 3d instant, after five weeks' passage from Batavia. . . . Leaving this place, the 17th, we sailed for Krokatoa island, where we arrived the next morning, and, to my inexpressible joy, found the Jay there at anchor. Randall and my brother were soon on board of the Washington" (Quincy, *Journals of Samuel Shaw*, 318–19).

is four hundred dollars the pecul. This genseng however should be of the best quality, and well garbled,[6] in this situation, and the quantity not exceeding five hundred peculs: I believe it would bring readily four hundred dollars the pecul, especially as teas would be received in payment.

In Canton it is customary, unless a contrary agreement is made, for the Chinese to pay all duties either of import, or export, owing to the difficulty the Europeans have of determining what the duty realy is, or perhaps there is none, but what depends upon the caprice of the Mandarines, and varies very often the same year. They say genseng pays a duty to the Emperor of sixty dollars the pecul. They therefore start into bags all the genseng they purchase from the Europeans, and Americans, previous to their bringing it up from the ship to Canton,[7] as the Mandarines in weighing it, would make little or no abatement for tare if brought up in Casks. It is also to be observed that bad genseng pays a duty the same as good, and the bad being mixed with the good, it is a work of time to seperate it. Therefore every pecul of bad genseng adds to the cost of the good. For this last season although they bought the whole, good & bad together, yet after its being weighed to ascertain the quantity, and having allowed the price agreed for, yet they desired the worst to be thrown away, as not being worth the amount of the duty paid on it.

I am led from an examination of the Tartary genseng, which still sells for nearly its weight in gold, to conclude that this country produces two species of genseng, one of them nearly of equal quality to the Tartary genseng, provided proper pains was taken to gather it in due season, and care taken in properly drying it. But this I think cannot take place at present, as the trade is on the decline, and probably may be totally lost in the hands of individuals, it requiring too much capital for a single merchant to risque, and when a company is formed, it is made up in such a hasty manner, that they are obliged to purchase such genseng as is at market, and have never carefully attended to have it well garbled. Genseng shipped from England, though originally from this country, is in higher repute on this account, for they more carefully cull it.

6. As used here, "garbled" means "selected."
7. The ships anchored at Whampoa, about twelve miles downstream from Canton.

This year immense quantities of cotton was shipped by the English, on board their own & foreign bottoms from Bombay and a small quantity from Madrass to Canton, estimated to be near one half more than the annual demand, which, however, had increased, it was said owing to the failure of the Chinese crops, and the increased demand for tea, making them attend more to the culture of that article. Near fifty thousand bales of cotton arrived, averaging about four hundred pounds English weight per bale. This reduced the price from fourteen and fifteen taels the pecul, down to eleven and twelve taels cash. The cotton being at a high price, and freight at Bombay, the shippers suffered considerable loss, and were obliged also to credit the Chinese merchants a season over for large balances due them, on account of the sales of their cotton to them. These cotton ships, as well as other ships from Bengall, and other parts of India, (commonly called Country ships) [8] do not frequently get all money for their cargoes, and as they take but little merchandize in return, they therefore sell to the Chinese, and transfer the debt to the English East India company, and receive bills from them on London, at twelve months sight, at 5/3, to 5/6, Stg for the dollar. However this exchange varies, and the rate is declared by the English company's supercargoes at Canton every season. The English company therefore guard as carefully as they can, against English subjects trading to China, purchasing bills of any other person, as it saves them from making a considerable remittance in specie, but, it is what they cannot intirely prevent.

I shall now relate a few things respecting the sale of the sea Otter skin, that has been lately sold in China, both by the English and American vessels.

The ship Columbia, Robert Grey, Commander, a vessel fitted out from Boston,[9] arrived in Canton November 18th 1789. with about fifteen hundred sea Otter skins of various sizes and quality, the Commander of which ship, valued upon me for the transaction of his business, and I expected to have made a very advantageous sale of

8. These were ships owned by British merchants in India. The East India Company permitted them to trade from India as far west as the Cape of Good Hope.
9. The investors in this venture were Joseph Barrell, Samuel Brown, Crowell Hatch, and Charles Bulfinch of Boston, John Derby of Salem, and John M. Pintard of New York. They sent the *Columbia* and a sloop to the northwest coast of America to secure sea otter skins for sale in Canton.

those skins, from there being much wanted by the Mandarines. Pinqua, a Hong merchant, and others informed me, that probably, I should eventually obtain my price, if I waited with patience, as the Cohong, or body of Hong Merchants would be obliged to purchase them & present the best to the Viceroy of Canton, and the other Mandarines of rank, that the hong merchants would have to divide the cost of this involuntary present with each other, and that the remaining number of small skins would sell but for a trifling sum, also that no private merchant would dare to purchase them, as they were known to be wanted by the mandarines for their own use. I therefore, in order to make the best of the market, as Captain Gray had no other funds, advanced the necessary money to refit his ship to take in a cargo for America, and upon an estimate of the highest price I might probably obtain for the skins, found the sum would be insufficient, after defraying the expences of the ship, to load her fully with bohea teas. I then determined to fill her up on my own account with that article on freight, in order to render the voyage as lucrative as possible to the owners. With this idea, I contracted for the amount of bohea teas I intended to load on board the ship, and no part of my business as yet suffered any delay. After some difficulties in obtaining a security merchant for the ship, owing to the nature of her cargo, and the smallness of her funds, I was at last informed by the linguist, that she was secured in the name of the Cohong, and that Monqua, the then head hong merchant, would grant a chop for landing my skins at the factory. This was accordingly obtained, but produced an Altercation between Pinqua and myself, who said it would be a great injury to him, as he rented me the factory, the other part being occupied by himself; that on the skins being landed there, the Mandarines would come to look at them, and whatever they took he must pay for, and from policy must give them as a present, or it would draw upon him their resentment if he did otherwise, that I might land them at an European factory, where no Chinese merchant resided, and in that case he would be on a footing with the other Hong merchants, who would have to divide the amount of whatever skins the mandarines might take, and each pay his part of it. Being unwilling to injure Pinqua, with whom I was on friendly terms, I obtained a factory for the purpose. The skins were brought up, and accordingly stored there.

My patience was now exhausted by the various and continued applications to examine the skins, offers made to purchase, accepted by me, and then broke upon the part of the Chinese, who informed me they could not buy for fear of the mandarines. Matters continued thus through the months of December and January, when a private Chinese merchant offered to buy them, provided the Hong merchants would grant me in writing permission to sell them, which I applied for but could not obtain. He then made another proposition, that he would buy them, provided I would secure him from there being taken away afterwards by the Mandarines, or the hong merchants. There appeared to me something insidious in this proposition, and I answered I could not undertake to protect him against his own government. Pinqua soon after informed me, the Viceroy had given orders to Monqua the head hong merchant to purchase them, in order that he might make choice of the best, and there came out from the city a Mandarine of rank, who I was informed was an Officer in the Viceroy's family. He had them sorted, and made choice of about one hundred of them, and desired me by the interpretation of the linguist to fix my price for them. I told him I meant to sell them altogether, as parting with the best would injure the sale of the remainder. He then desired me to set my price for the whole, and if reasonable he would take them all. I accordingly did, and after some abatement he concluded to buy them, and desired permission to take those he had chose with him into the city. I replied that I could not suffer one of them to go from under my care 'till I was paid for the whole. He appeared incensed, and desired me to name the hong merchant who should pay me for them, which I declined, upon which he mentioned Pankikoa, the son of the Pankikoa named in the commencement of this letter, who was dead, and was succeeded by this son. Knowing him to be an opulent hong merchant, I made no objection. The Mandarine then asked me whether I would consent to have the bundle of skins carried to Pankikoa's house, and he would see me paid for the whole. I consented and accompanied them there. Pankikoa was at home, and as the Mandarine and he conversed in the Chinese language, I can only conjecture their conversation and trust to the inquiries I made for an interpretation of it. Pankikoa expostulated upon his being obliged to purchase the skins, not having sold me any goods; a reason that did not appear to satisfy the Mandarine,

who left him, and went in his Palanquin into the City, after making
some remarks which indicated that an incompliance with his request,
would be attended with serious consequences. After his departure,
the Chinese porters by the direction of Pankikoa took up the bundle
of skins, with an intention of carrying them into the city, but I opposed it, and they laid the bundle down again, upon which Pankikoa
appeared much agitated, told me I knew not the Chinese government
nor what I did, that this was a great disgrace to him, and to use his
own broken English expression, said it was, "a kill business"—in fact,
what I understood by the tenor of his language was, that the insult
offered the Viceroy, was as much as his life was worth, and that it
would ruin me, as well as himself, if the skins were not in the city
that night, before the gates of it were shut. He asked what I would
take for that bundle of skins now in his factory. I told him they were
the most valuable part, and I must have half the price I demanded for
the whole, which would amount to upwards of ten thousand dollars.
And I thought he meant to comply with my demand and pay me
the money, for he called for the key of his treasury, but recollecting
himself he sent for Monqua, Pinqua, and some other Hong merchants,
and the result of a long and passionate conversation, mixed at times
with a good deal of adulation towards Pinqua, was, as they interpreted it to me, that they had agreed to settle the matter amicably
among themselves, and that Pinqua with whom I had contracted for
the bohea tea shipped on board the Columbia, would pay me the
price I demanded for the whole of the skins, which Pinqua assented
to. As these were Hong merchants whose faces I was familiar with,
who dealt for large sums, who trusted, and were trusted by every
European, I thought it would be impudent to hesitate longer. I accordingly consented, and they took the skins into the city. The next
morning I applied to Pinqua for settlement, who referred me to
Pankikoa, and they trifled with me by referring me back to each
other for payment. At last Pinqua offered to settle with me for the
whole of the skins provided I took four thousand dollars less than
the price agreed on before, observing that he would not furnish me
with the passport for the ship Columbia to depart, and that I might
remain at Canton 'till the next season for ought he cared, that he had
been deceived by Pankikoa, and the other Hong merchants who had
promised to pay him their respective proportions of the price of the

skins taken by the mandarines, that they had broke their promise, saying as he had sold me tea, he must buy the skins and take the profit & loss together, and that he should lose fifteen thousand dollars by the business in consequence of the Mandarines taking away all the best skins, and that I must also suffer some loss. I waited a few days longer in hopes of Obtaining a more favorable conclusion to this business, when chance favored me with an opportunity of seeing the same Mandarine from the City, who had promised to see me paid for the skins. He was at a Mr Beales factory,[10] looking at some other skins of the same kind. I made application to him for redress, but could obtain none. I therefore from necessity was constrained to accept Pinqua proposition, upon which he obtained for me my grand Chop, or permit for sailing, and I left Canton the 15th of February 1790 for America being among the last ships that sailed. Had I refused Pinqua last offer, the ship would probably have lost her passage for that season round the Cape of Good Hope, for on the 17th February their holy days commenced, during which time their Public offices are shut, and no business transacted for near three weeks.

The demand in China, for sea otter skins, and other furs of the best quality is very great, and if you do not depend upon that article for your return Cargo, and can wait the season over you may obtain a good price, but transient merchants are subject to many more frauds and impositions in Canton, than those who have an established residence there. However, the English company are not exempt from them, for in the year 1784 they united with the other supercargoes in Canton in complaint to the Hoppo* against the increased extortions & delays in trade, and were promised redress, but an unfortunate accident prevented. An English Country ship in saluting Killed one Chinese and wounded two others. This brought on an event of a serious nature, for the Chinese seized the supercargo of the ship, Mr Smith,[11] and carried him into the City, declaring their laws re-

---

* The mandarine who superintends the trade at Canton.

10. Daniel Beale. "This gentleman was not long since a purser of an English company ship, but is now *Prussian consul*, and partner of Mr. Cox. The latter, in consequence of the recent regulations, could no longer, as an English subject, stay in Canton, but was obliged, at the close of the last season, to embark for England; while Mr. Beale, now become a *Prussian*, as such, in defiance of his late country, remains unmolested" (Quincy, *Journals of Samuel Shaw*, 296).

11. George Smith. For a longer and somewhat different version of this affair, see Quincy, *Journals of Samuel Shaw*, 186–95.

quired blood for blood, and that unless the person who fired the gun
was delivered up, they would detain Mr Smith. In this instance also
all the foreigners united, and I must say attempted to frighten the
Chinese, and had they possessed firmness adequate to the undertaking, I believe they would have succeeded, for in point of real force
or consequence, the Chinese are considered by most persons who
have seen them, as very contemptible, however importantly they
think of themselves. But to proceed. The Europeans brought up to
the factories between four & five hundred seamen armed, we also
had an armed boat up from our ship. On their passage up from
Wampoa to Canton, a distance of twelve miles, they were opposed
by so trifling a resistance on the part of the Chinese, as only slightly
to wound but one man, the boats passing in the night without returning their fire. On the arrival of the boats from the ships the Chinese
Citizens deserted the suburbs, and the Mandarines of war next morning, drew up an Armed force in the Common boats of the river,
opposite the factories, their arms consisting of Bows & arrows,
swords, spears, and Match lock fusees, with two or three Cannon
of about one pound caliber, mounted on a kind of three leg stools,
and the boats which contained their soldiers were sculled by the
women, who ply on the river for maintenance; the Chinese soldiers
preserved the most perfect silence, and paid a ready obedience to
orders. Negotiations for settleing the matter amicably now took
place, and the Chinese had the address to detach the other foreigners
from the English, who at last thought it most prudent to compromise
the matter by delivering up the gunner, whom they now said should
only be tried by their laws, and as it was well understood to be an
accident he would be returned unhurt. In the interim they restored
Mr Smith, and trade took place again, but they basely broke their
promise with respect to the gunner, for soon after the sailing of
great part of the European ships, they hanged him, nor did they
afterwards remove any of the impositions on the trade complained
of but rather increased them.

I shall now mention an instance to point out the necessity of a
nation showing an active protection to their subjects trading to
China. The Mandarines for some illicit act of a hong merchant, con-
fiscated all the property in his possession, to whomever belonging,
and sent him into banishment in an interior part of the country, nor

could the English Country supercargoes get any restitution of their property 'till the British nation sent a frigate, the Sea horse, Capt Panton,[12] with orders officially to demand and insist upon redress, and take such steps as he should think likely to obtain it. Captain Panton by a spirited conduct produced the desired effect, for the Mandarines after giving Captain Panton a hearing, directed the Hong Merchants to compromise the matter with the English company's supercargoes, which they did, and settled the debt by installments.[13]

Their mode of increasing their impositions upon all strangers is by stopping your trade, and even your supply of fresh provisions, knowing that the delay in your business as the season wears away, would eventually be more expensive to you, than to comply with their demand.

It is supposed that the Emperor is a stranger to this mode of conduct. An Ambassador was lately sent out from England, with an intention to obtain an audience with the Emperor and have some general laws established for the regulation of the English trade at Canton, but the death of the Ambassador during the passage, occasioned the ship to return, there being no successor appointed to carry the commission into execution, but it is expected they will again send one.

The English of late have shipped from England to Canton a quantity of tin, which they say the Chinese prefer to the Calin [14] that the Europeans procure from the different Malay settlements. However, it is my opinion, that the Americans might also make a profit on procuring Calin, and other Articles from the Malays if they were sufficiently united in pursuing the Commerce to China to enable them to extend their views to the different objects of commerce that would present themselves.

I shall enclose to you extracts from the English companies directions to their supercargoes,[15] also a list of the articles of import &

12. John (or Jonathan) A. Panton.
13. For the details of this affair, see Quincy, *Journals of Samuel Shaw*, 305–15.
14. Calin was an alloy whose composition is not known. Some eighteenth-century writers thought it consisted of pewter and lead, while others concluded it was tin and lead. The Chinese used it for manufacturing such utensils as coffee- and teapots.
15. These MS notes, which are located in the Hamilton Papers, Library of Congress, cover the East India Company's shipments to and from Canton. The most detailed information relates to quantities and varieties of teas sent to

export of the port of Canton,[16] with a list of all the ships at China in the year 1789.[17] I must remark that the two ships at Canton in the enclosed list, viz the Washington, and the Moise, were totally foreign property—the Washington & the Moise were I believed owned by Merchants at the Mauritius. The Moise, I had purchased of the Commander, Capt Oriolle, but finding it inconvenient to send her to America, I afterwards resold her to him. The other ship, the Washington, was commanded by an American, but from every inquiry I believe the property belonged to the French, and the American flag used to guard against the French Agent at Canton. The American Schooner Grace, was sold to an English subject, who sailed with her for the Northwest coast of America under American Colours. The unauthorized use of American Colours, may require some particular directions to the Consul at Canton, for his conduct on such an occasion, in the present instance, I thought it most prudent to pass it unnoticed, as a want of instructions upon the subject, might have rendered an interference productive of more evil than good.

On considering the disadvantages, the Americans trade under to Canton, owing to their seperate interests, and their not having an established factory there, it appears to me they require greater encouragement for the prosecution of it, by laying heavier duties on teas imported from Europe, for we still receive a considerable quantity of bohea tea from Amsterdam, although the Dutch are now prohibiting any teas being received in their ports from America. Bohea tea is an article of great consumption here, and being bulky would enable us to employ larger ships in the Canton trade, by which we should save considerably in port expences at Canton, as each ship however small, is obliged to pay besides her other expences, the present to the Hoppo, which is about two thousand eight hundred spanish dollars.

With respect to Spanish dollars, the only kind of specie which answers to export to China, and the command of which will always

Britain. The notes are printed in Cole, *Industrial and Commercial Correspondence*, 147–56.

16. This is a printed document which is entitled "November Price Current of Goods at Canton" and which is located in the Hamilton Papers, Library of Congress. The prices of the goods are inserted. The list is headed "Imports." If there was another such list for exports, it has not been found.

17. This MS list is located in the Hamilton Papers, Library of Congress, and is printed in Cole, *Industrial and Commercial Correspondence*, 157–59.

give you the preference of the Market, I feel myself unable to judge
of the amount that it would be necessary to annually ship, for want
of information of the Consumption of teas yearly in this country,
and the quantity of Silks, Nankeens Porcelain & other Chinese merchandize that would be requisite for a full supply for the United
states. Great quantities of raw silk are bought by the English dutch
& french, and would also be an article of import to us, if we established any silk manufactories in this country. You will, with the information you possess of the trade of this country, and observing in
the extracts from the English companies directions, the quantity of
specie shipped by them, be enable to judge how much it may require
to carry on the trade from this country. The danes & Swedes trade
principally with money, and I think it probable we should save in
the export of specie, considerably by a direct trade to China as we
otherwise should be obliged to pay higher by purchasing the Merchandize of China from any other nation.

I shall now close this letter with remarking that frauds and impositions are practised by the Chinese on every nation trading there, but
on these being detected in Europe they redress the established companies there who have been cheated, the hong merchants declaring
the fraud has been committed on them by the Country merchants,
but individuals are much more exposed to them than those com-
panys, from the idea that if they make a losing voyage they will not
be able to return and of course will be obliged to bear the loss, nor
can individuals obtain redress always, from want of property, and an
idea that the Chinese have, that being transient merchants they cannot redress themselves. And of course they can oblige them to suffer
the loss.

I know a respectable and opulent mercantile house in this city,
who have been greatly defrauded in the quality of their teas and
nankeens, and as they owe the Chinese money are determined to
retain sufficient in their hands to redress themselves. This leads me
to remark the failure of the Imperial company at Canton, who owe
the Chinese nearly two hundred thousand dollars, and they attempted
to detain the cargo of an English country ship, which came consigned to Mr Reid,[18] the imperial consul, and Chief-supercargo of
their company; but on the interference of the English supercargoes

18. John Reid.

it was paid for. How far, one American individual, may be made to pay the debts contracted by another, and thus annihilate the trade, future events may determine. It has been a maxim with the Chinese that when they could find redress at home, never to seek it abroad, and I have heard remarks made by them, that in case of a long & great delay in payment, that it was probable they would seize the property of one American to answer for the debt of another. They therefore to avoid this evil, express their wishes to see the trade carried on by a steady body of Merchants from this country. But supposing no accident of this kind should happen, the act of one American individual may expose the trade of all the rest to be injured. I shall mention an instance respecting the English. A country ship from Bengall, being unable to make an advantageous sale of her cargo, attempted to go away without paying her port duties, upon which the Hong Merchants told the English company's supercargoes that they would stop the trade of their nation 'till the duties were paid, upon which they interfered & obliged the Country Captain to settle his account. How far these may be guarded against by instructions to a Consul resident at Canton, your good judgement can determine.

I have prolonged the subject of this letter beyond my intention, led by an ardent desire to communicate every thing, I thought might be worthy your perusal. I must confess it is my opinion, that the trade to Canton will never flourish, but in the hands of a well regulated company, which will not be easily formed without the protection of government—for individuals have neither influence, nor consequence enough with the Chinese to withstand the rivalship of established companies. My own experience and situation in the trade enables me perhaps to pursue it with equal advantages to any private merchant, from which I might be excluded by an established company, but the desire of seeing the trade of my country prosper, supersedes every private interest. If what I have communicated should prove any way serviceable, it will afford great pleasure to

Sir Your most respectful, very obedient And most humble servant   Tho: Randall
late Vice Consul at
Canton in China

P.S. I last Saturday night received a letter from Mr. William Whitesides,[19] informing me that he had discovered one chest of Hyson Skin out of some sold him by me, contained a black leaf—something resembling tea, but of no possible use, a fresh instance of fraud in the Chinese, and an additional distress to the individual, who pays a duty here on an Article of no value, and whose poverty might prevent his return to obtain satisfaction in Canton. I applied once for Doctor Hunt of the Ship Hope, who was cheated in Nankeens, but could get no satisfaction in Canton from the Chinese who sold it to him. However if I detect no further fraud in the sale of the remainder of my teas it will be lucky. We never examine every chest we purchase, only a few, as opening or boring the Chests, injures the tea.

Honorable Alexander Hamilton Esquire
Secretary of the Treasury
Philadelphia

19. William Whiteside was a Philadelphia tea merchant.

From Fisher Ames

Boston August 15th 1791

Dear Sir

I have heard that the Bank of N York propose to reserve a number of their shares for the acceptance of the U. S. Bank, so as to create a kind of partnership.[1] Tho' little seems to be known of the particulars, yet it is insinuated that the idea is suggested under your

ALS, Connecticut Historical Society, Hartford.
1. Ames was a Federalist and a member of the House of Representatives from Massachusetts.
Following the incorporation of the Bank of New York under a charter granted by the state legislature on March 21, 1791, there was a rapid expansion of the bank's stock.
On August 7, 1791, Christopher Gore wrote to Rufus King: "The post of last evening bro't news that the Bank of New York had completed their number of Shares & that the Directors had reserved three hundred Shares, intending to offer them to the Governor & directors of the National bank—that, by this measure, they hoped to prevent the establishment of a branch from the National Bank in your city" (Charles R. King, *The Life and Correspondence of Rufus King* [New York, 1894], I, 400–01).

patronage.[2] When I wrote you last,[3] I was ignorant of all this. Tho'
the Bank is to govern itself, yet your opinion of the proper arrangements will, & ought to, have weight.

It is proper you should know how pliant our Massa. Bank wd.
probably be found, & what is thought here of blending the general
and local Banks. This is all the use that I suppose can be made of
my letters—for you are so much and I so little an actor in this Affair
that I do not ask your correspondence.

I think that any connection between the Banks wd. be generally
disagreeable in this quarter.

I think also that this (Massa) Bank is in the best disposition in the
world, ready to give up the ghost, and take a chance for a resurrec-
tion as a branch, which will be a joyful one, because the stockholders have a sure & certain hope of getting more Money in their future
than their present state. Tho' a few receive the idea of abolishing the
Mass. Bank with great repugnance, yet so many more own shares in
the U. S. Bank to a greater Amot., they hope so much from the one
and despond so totally of the other, that the present sanguine moment seems to be the critical one. Tho' this Bank never had much
popularity, yet it may hereafter be courted by a certain faction to
give weight & activity to their party, by their reputation & property. Other passions & persons may displace the present & change
the aspect of things. I draw my information from persons who well
know the temper of the stockholders & who have great merit in having prepared them for dissolution. Indeed, with their connections,
they are able to carry a major vote.[4]

I know that you are as much an Unitarian in politics as I am, and
therefore the reflections which this representation has produced in
my mind will rise in your's without my suggesting them.

2. It cannot be stated definitely whether or not this plan originated with H,
but it is clear that he favored some form of association with the state banks. See
H to William Seton, November 25, 1791; January 18, 24, 1792. In addition, on
August 20, 1791, Seth Johnson, a New York City merchant, wrote to Andrew
Craigie: "Mr. Seton informed me that in a Conversation he had with Mr H.
the latter observed it was difficult to say what plan the National directors would
pursue—he seemed to approve of this Bank offering the 300 shares—this in
Confidence" (Davis, *Essays*, II, 56).
   3. Ames to H, July 31, 1791.
   4. On June 23, 1791, the stockholders of the Massachusetts Bank voted that
the directors be authorized to purchase two hundred and fifty shares of the
Bank of the United States.

No proper means of strengthening the Govt. shd. be neglected. The Bank has been justly considered as one of the best. But it's efficacy will essentially depend on events posterior to it's legal establishment. It's uses to trade and to the Govt. can exist in the highest degree only in case of it's engrossing the whole business. The state Banks by dividing, not only take away part, but by opposing they will impair the value of the remainder. They are at liberty to issue Bills at pleasure. Their power, used ever so discreetly, will be an evil, and overcharge the channels of circulation, inasmuch as the issues of the U. S. Bank will be sufficient to fill them. If the latter should forbear, it's capital will lie idle, and it's rivals will fill the space it may have chosen to leave vacant. But suppose these rivals should want discretion, and, eager for profit, should multiply their bills unduly. This, it is true wd. be at their own risk, perhaps loss, and perhaps ruin. They wd. do a great deal of mischief, however, in the mean time. They wd. pour forth a torrent of paper money as baleful as a pestilence. Industry wd. sicken.

But without proceeding to extremes so hazardous to themselves, they might increase their paper to a point that wd. be injurious to the national Bank. The Massa. Bank under less favorable circumstances has acted this part. With a capital, buildings &c included, of 100,000 Dols., it has pushed it's operations as far as possible.[5] The dividend of 16 or 18 per Cent proves that they have done much with little. The seeds of public confidence in banks have been lately sown and the state institutions will not fail to gather part of the crop. They may issue bills very freely without much risk. So cheap an augmentation of capital wd. enable them to give longer credit and better terms than heretofore—and, if the national paper should be exchangeable only at Philada, in some measure to exclude it's currency. In that proportion, the U. S. Bank wd. lose part of it's profits, trade of it's facility & Govt. of it's resource. For the capacity of the Bank to aid Govt. must be measured by the prosperity of the former.

It is true that the increased paper of the state Banks might be rap-

---

5. There was a sharp rise in the circulation of the bank's notes in 1790–1791. The average amount of notes in circulation per week rose from $264,707 in 1790 to $487,000 in 1791. In the first half of 1791, circulation increased markedly, and by August 15–20 the average amount of notes in circulation per week was $637,159. See N. S. B. Gras, *The Massachusetts First National Bank of Boston, 1784–1934* (Cambridge, Massachusetts, 1937), 597–601.

idly returned upon them because of it's limited currency. But that may also be equally true of the national Bank paper. The latter, if managed with prudence & skill, wd. probably gain the ascendant at last. The political good effects wd. be delayed however, and some of them might never take place. The scramble of rival Banks wd. sharpen the acrimony of party humours, which at this moment are dulcified by the cream of speculation.

My corollary, or to proceed like a divine, my impr⟨ove⟩ment from all this preaching is, that the present is the most fa⟨vo⟩rable time for making progress with the Bank—that Sub⟨-Banks,⟩ if a safe plan for establishing them could be devised, and ⟨this⟩ I am told some knowing ones have no doubt, wd. be adequate to the object in view—and that any union connection of the general and local Banks wd. be inauspicious. It wd. give life, too long life, to those who are ready & willing to die. Like parasite plants having no root of their own they wd. subsist by sucking the sap from their supporter. They are rivals and I think cannot be partners. To apply a remark of your's on another occasion not dissimilar, it is establishing a qualified Anarchy—and that too in a system whose perfection is simplicity.

I make no doubt that you wll discern in my remarks that I have not the best means of judging of my subject, and that I have not made the best use of what I possess. For in truth I do not know the principles on whh the supposed ⟨union⟩ of Banks is to be contemplated. I am sure however that you will hold my leading principle as important as I do.

As I impose upon you the task of only reading my letter, you see I do not scruple to make it a long one.

The late rise of paper and bank stock, tho now declining,[6] has excited no small share of envy among those who might have made money by it, yet did not. But the fact redounds to the honor of the public counsels; and in that view, it seems to have it's full effect.

The price of paper being above par evinces the solidity of the principle on whh you founded your system of finance—as it shews

6. On July 4, 1791, the authorized stock of the Bank of the United States was oversubscribed. In the following weeks the price of public securities rose in a spectacular fashion. On August 11 there was a break in the security market in New York City, and on the following day its effects were felt in the Philadelphia security market. The sharp decline in security prices was halted on August 17.

the reduction of the rate of interest to be in fact as well as theory a fair ground of bargain with the creditors. I congratulate you on the vindication of the basis of your plan which some, even of your friends, treated as untenable. But a triumph of a nobler kind is found in the situation of our country. The body politic is certainly in high health. It's enemies, it's friends, chance & design seem to have conspired in it's favor. The very poison of the amendments has been food to it. Weak men feel their fears subside, sanguine men their hopes realized. The federal tree was in blossom almost as soon as it was planted. It is very lately that they have seen it bear fruit—and such fruit as makes their mouths water. They see too that tho every Antifederal puff has shaken it, the motion has given new vigor to the roots.

By seeing the effects of your public duties, you get rewarded for having performed them. With sentiments of respect and attachment, I am, dear Sir, Yr very hble. Srvt   Fisher Ames

Mr. Hamilton

P.S. The subscription for Mrs W's poetry [7] is closed and the Books are on sale for the Booksellers benefit. Tho I had told her husband that you had desired me to subscribe to the work on your behalf, yet I think it wd. be a departure from your intention to do anything in the matter, under these circumstances.

We have you exhibited here in Wax. You see that they are resolved to get money by you in every form.

Your's &c   F A

7. Mercy Warren. See Ames to H, July 31, 1791.

From Rufus King

[New York] Monday Evening. [August 15, 1791] [1]

The fall of Bank certificates [2] may have some good effects, it will operate to deter our industrious citizens from meddling in future with the funds, & teach them contentment in their proper vocations. So far as I am informed, the loss will be divided among a great number of individuals, and where it is heaviest, the sufferers will generally be characters who will neither excite nor deserve commiseration. The Fall having been hitherto gradual, the most timid have had an opportunity to retire with something less money, & much more wisdom, than they brought into the market. I see no reason to apprehend an alarming depression of the Stocks; they have risen within the last two months faster, & higher, than any prudent calculation would justify, but notwithstanding the pressing demands for cash, to discharge the contracts for Bank Certificates, as well as to support their credit under the present Check, & in opposition to the united exertions of some of the Dealers to tumble them lower, the other Stocks have not been greatly depressed. The 6 pr Cts. sold this evening for cash at 21/. the three per Cts. & deferred at upwards of 12/. and the Bank certificates at 160 Dollars.[3] If they do not fall below these prices, perhaps we may think ourselves fortunately extricated. The Business was going on in a most alarming manner, mechanicks deserting their shops, Shop keepers sending their goods to auction, and not a few of our merchants neglecting the regular & profitable commerce of the City. A check was necessary, the explosion will restore order, and we shall return to our regular pursuits. Several of the Speculators sold their Bank Certificates from 50 to 100 Dollars. The subsequent rise mortified them, and they don't fail among other means employed to depress the Stocks, to quote your opinion, that the Stocks are all too high.[4] They go further and mention prices, below the present market, as the value sanctioned by your authority. It can scarcely be believed that these gentlemen have any foundation for their assertions, but the fact will suggest to you the utmost caution on this subject. I know you must have regretted the late extravagance, but at the present juncture, the most unfair advantage may be made of your remarks, and consequences ruinous to individuals, and quite foreign from your wishes, may proceed from them.

In regard to our Bank,[5] although some specie has been drawn from us, and sent to the other States to purchase Stock, and the discounts are large; yet you are sensible of the prudence of the direction, and that they must be extremely well acquainted with the Circumstances of all the Dealers with the Bank. I understand that it has been reported, that the late check has been produced by the bank's having refused their usual discounts. This has by no means been the case. The Bank has continued, & will continue, to discount as far as their safety will authorize. The present agitation will render them cautious, but they will not under the influence of that temper withold those accomodations, which may be made with safety to the Bank, and which may likewise be essential in preventing a violent depression of the funds.

Yrs affectionately R King

I think Duer has been injured in being supposed to have been particularly engaged in raising the Bk Certificates.[6] So far as I can learn his conduct has been as correct as any Buyer's & seller's could be.

ALS, Hamilton Papers, Library of Congress.
 1. King was a Federalist Senator from New York.
 Although this letter is undated, H in his reply on August 17, 1791, refers to "Your Letter of Monday Evening." Since the decline of the bank script which King discusses did not occur until August 11, the letter must have been written on Monday, August 15.
 2. See Fisher Ames to H, August 15, 1791, note 6.
 3. By August 12, in Philadelphia, the six percents had reached 22s.7d., the three percents 13s.1d., the deferred 13s.6d. On August 11, Bank of the United States stock certificates in New York went as high as 280.
 4. Joseph Stancliffe Davis states that H "allowed himself to be quoted regarding the proper price of the speculative securities" (Davis, *Essays,* I, 204), but he gives no source for his statement.
 5. The Bank of New York, of which King was a director.
 6. See H to William Duer, August 17, 1791.

From Tobias Lear

United States
August 15. 1791.

By the Presidents command T. Lear has the honor to transmit to the Secretary of the Treasury a letter from Mr. Governr. Morris to the president [1] respecting the Debt of the United States in France; which the President requests the Secretary to take into consideration, and to draft such an answer [2] as will be proper for the President to give to Mr. Morris on this subject.

Tobias Lear
S.P.U.S.

LC, George Washington Papers, Library of Congress.
 1. See enclosure.
 2. H's draft has not been found, but Washington's reply to Morris, dated September 12, 1791, reads as follows:
 "Your letter of the 27 of may with its enclosures came duly to hand.

"During my absence on my late southern tour the proposals of Messrs. Schweizer and Jeannerett, made their appearance here, as well through Mr. [Louis G.] Otto, Chargé des Affaires of France, to the Secretary of State, as through Mr. Short, to the Secretary of the Treasury.

"In pursuance of certain arrangements, made previous to my departure, an answer was given—which answer was in substance that it did not appear to be for the interest of the United States to accept those proposals.

"The reasons which have been assigned to me as having dictated this answer are as follow.

"First, That the rate of interest to be stipulated in the new contract, as well upon the part of the debt which had not fallen due, as upon that which had fallen due was 5 ℔ cent. It was a question whether a contract stipulating such a rate of interest with regard to the first mentioned part of the debt was fairly within the meaning of that clause of the law which requires that the payment of it should be made upon 'terms *advantageous* to the United States,' and while there was no reason to apprehend that it would be necessary to allow a higher interest than 5 ℔ cent on any loans, which might be made to discharge the *arrears* of principal and interest, it did not appear expedient to forego the chance of a *lower rate*.

"2nd. The commission or premium of 5 ℔ ct. demanded in the proposals is one ℔ ct. more than is given upon the loans going on in Holland. This would amount to a loss of one ℔ct. on the part, which the United States were bound immediately to pay; and in respect to that, which had not become due, would be an unnecessary sacrifice of 5 ℔ cent.

"3rd. The immediate proposers are understood to be a House not of primary consequence themselves, and though they alledged, they did not prove, that they were supported by others who could be deemed Capitalists equal to the undertaking. From the difference of exchange between Holland and Paris they could afford sacrifices in the sale of the bonds of the United States; and if there was not great force of capital among those engaged in the undertaking, such sacrifices were to be expected. A great quantity of bonds, thrown suddenly into the market, by persons, who were pressed to raise money from them could not but have effects the most injurious to the credit of the U. S.

"4th. Paris being the stipulated place of payment, if, from the state of exchange payments could be made *there* in *gold* and *silver* with a saving to the United States, there could be no good objection to profiting by the circumstance—but this advantage, and more, even to the full extent of the depreciation of the Assignats, would be transferred by the proposed bargain to the undertakers.

"5th. The single advantage which the proposals held out, of a prolonged period of reimbursement would be obtained of course by loans in the ordinary way, and as to the effect of the measure upon loans for the redemption of the domestic debt, this would be good or bad according as the undertakers might or not have occasion to bring the bonds of the United States to market.

"The foregoing reasons appeared to me to have so much weight that I saw no ground for directing any alteration in what was done.

"It appears in their letter to you that the Gentlemen in question are willing to wave the claim of premium or commission on the part of the debt not yet due; but this obviates only one of the objections which have been stated.

"You observe also that they had given you proofs that persons of the first fortune were connected with them in the business. They were deficient in not having given the like proof to Mr. Short, whose enquiries had been directed to this object.

"The observations you make concerning the views, which ought to govern the United States in their reimbursements to France are founded in propriety.

[ENCLOSURE]

Gouverneur Morris To George Washington[3]

Paris 27 May 1791

public

Dear Sir

I have the Honor to enclose a Letter and sundry Papers relating to it from Messieurs Schweizer Jeanneret & Co.[4] I have referred these Gentlemen to Mr. Short telling them that it is most fitting in many Respects that they should apply to him.

As it is possible however that this Business may come before you, I think it a Duty to convey some Observations which occur to me, and which may not perhaps strike you because Matters of that Sort have not I believe much occupied your Attention. Previous thereto I beg Leave however to give you a History of my Acquaintance with it. In a Letter to Colo. Hamilton of the 31 of January 1790 I mentioned what had passed between Mr. Necker[5] and me respecting the Debt due by the United States to France and I hinted at the means of turning to useful Account a very precipitate step of the public Agents in Holland.[6] About this Time I received your orders to communicate with the british Ministers[7] and altho I did by no Means consider that in the Light of an Appointment to office yet from Motives of Delicacy I determined to extricate myself from the

_____

You may conclude that no unequitable advantage will be taken; and it is hoped that the measures now in execution will be more conducive to the real interests of that country than would have been an acceptance of the proposals of Messrs. S & J., who, it is presumable, founded their speculation chiefly upon the idea of availing themselves of the full benefit resulting from the depreciation of the Assignats.

"Thanking you for the communication you have made me on the subject, I assure you that I do justice to the motives which dictated it. . . ." (LC, George Washington Papers, Library of Congress.)

3. LC, Gouverneur Morris Papers, Library of Congress.

4. For the background of the attempt of Schweizer, Jeanneret, and Company to speculate in the American debt due to France, see William Short to H, December 18, 1790; February 7 and March 11, 1791.

5. In 1790 Jacques Necker was Director General of Finances.

6. The Dutch bankers, Willink, Van Staphorst, and Hubbard.

7. In two letters dated October 3, 1789, Washington instructed Morris to open informal discussions with the British ministry on various problems existing between the two countries (*GW*, XXX, 439–42).

Affair of the Debt as speedily as I could with Propriety. Various applications were made to me from different Quarters to which I replied evasively but on my Arrival in this City last November I informed the Parties that I had Reasons of a private Nature which deterred me from holding any share in their Speculation. I conversed with Mr. Short on the same Subject and communicated to him confidentially my Reason for declining an Interest as well as my Opinion respecting the use which might be derived from such Negotiation. A few Days after the President of the Committee of Finance [8] happening to meet me at the Count de Montmorin's [9] mentioned some Proposals then before them which to the best of my Remembrance were extravagant. I declined giving an Opinion without previously seeing and considering the terms upon which he and Mr. de Montmorin agreed together that before any thing was concluded the various Propositions which might be made should be submitted to my Examination. Here the thing dropt and the enclosed Papers shew the Reason why, for it appears from them that a Bargain was made shortly after by the Controleur general [10] with a different Company. Mr. Short mentioned this to me on his Return hither in the End of March telling me that the Parties concerned were as he was informed in Amsterdam Men of no Credit nor Capital.[11] I of Course agreed with him in Opinion that if so it was not worth while to listen to them. A few Days after one of them called on me, and after giving a History of the Affair begged me to make Use of my good Offices. I told him at once that it was ridiculous to ask a Commission of 5 ℔ % on changing the Nature of our Debt. That it was quite as convenient to owe France as to owe the Subjects of France and further that before any treaty was offered Persons of Credit and Capital should appear. As soon as I made this last Observation he drew out the Letter of the Comptroller general and shewing me the second Clause of it replied that after what was there contained no man had a Right to question the Solidity of the Society. He then added that for my private Satisfaction he would prove that People of the first Fortune were con-

8. Theodore Vernier, Comte de Montorient.

9. Montmorin was French Minister for Foreign Affairs.

10. Presumably Morris is referring to Charles Guillaume Lambert, who was Controller General of the Finances of France at the time of the Schweizer, Jeanneret, and Company proposals.

11. See Short to H, March 11, 1791.

nected therein, and indeed he gave me such Proof. I told him upon
this that they must apply to Mr. Short or to their own Ministry
whose support would be much more efficacious than the Sentiments
of any private Individual. I mentioned nevertheless to Mr. Short the
Substance of this Conversation. While he was in the country the
enclosed Letter was received. He returned to Town Yesterday and
called on me in the Evening when I communicated to him the Purport of it.

I have ever been of Opinion that as we are not in Condition to
pay our Debt to France a Bargain by which the Period can be prolonged without Loss to either Party is desirable. I say without Loss
because the Conduct of this Nation has been so generous to us that
it would be very ungrateful indeed to take Advantage of those
Necessities which the Succor afforded to America has occasioned.
Such Bargain must be either with the Government or with Individuals. But after the repeated Delay on our Part, to ask longer Time
now would not look well. Indeed no such Treaty could be made
without the Consent of the Assembly, and their Observations would
not be pleasant. A Bargain with Individuals has the Advantage of
bringing in the Aid of private Interest to the Support of our Credit,
and what is of very great Consequence it would leave us at Liberty
to make Use of that Credit for the Arrangement of our domestic
Affairs. And on this Head I must mention to you my dear Sir that
it has been my good fortune to prevent some publications which
would have been particularly injurious to us. Their Object was to
complain of the United States for speculating in their own Effects
with the Funds of France; Urging that while we owed heavy Installments already due here, all the Loans we obtain in Holland ought
to be applied to the Discharge of them and therefore that the Speculations in our domestic Debt were a double Violation of good faith,
&ca. &ca. &ca. The present State of things here has occasioned so
great a fall in the Exchange that Money borrowed in Holland is remitted with great gain consequently Loans made there just now answer well, & it is evident that the Parties who are endeavoring to
contract count on a considerable Profit from that Circumstance.
Much however is to be said on this Part of the Subject. First it is
questionable whether our Reputation may not be a little affected for
you will recollect that about one third of our Debt to France arose
from a Loan made on our Account in Holland of five Millions of

florins for which the King paid us here ten Million of Livres without any Deduction for Charges of any Sort.[12] The Nation is now
obliged to pay these five Millions in Holland and for us to borrow
that Amount there and then squeeze them in an Exchange which
distresses both their Commerce and Finances looks hard. There was
a good Deal of murmuring about it when the last operation of
F1.500,000. Guilders [12] took Place and I should not be at all surprized if some *Patriot* by way of shewing his zeal should make a
violent Attack in the Assembly when the next Payment is made.
There are many of these patriots who if they can inculpate Ministers
and distress those of different Sentiments don't Care a Jot for Consequences. But supposing this not to happen it is not possible for a
Nation to make the Advantage which Individuals do in such Things
because they must employ Individuals each of whom will be too apt
to look a little to his own Advantage. There is a Difference also between the Gain made upon Parts and that which would arise on the
whole for even if we could borrow all at once so large a Sum there
can be no Doubt that the Remittance of it hither would greatly
alter the Exchange. But it is not possible to borrow it speedily and
the present unnatural State of Things will in all Probability be
changed. In fact the leading Characters are very seriously alarmed
at it. If their Paper-Currency should be either redeemed or an-
nihilated or abolished To Morrow the Exchange would immediately
turn in favor of France and then we should loose on Remittances.
So much for this Affair in it's little Details, but there is a great View
of it which forcibly strikes my Mind. If we were at Liberty to turn
all our Efforts towards our domestic Debt we should by raising it's
Value prevent Speculations which are very injurious to the Country
if not to the Government. Millions have already been bought at low
Price and afterwards negotiated in Europe. Neither is that all, for
if we can borrow at five per Cent and buy up our six per Cent Debt
at Par we gain at once by that operation one fifth of the Interest or
twenty per Cent which besides all the other good Consequences is

12. For a description of the 1782 French loan of ten million livres, see Willink,
Van Staphorst, and Hubbard to H, January 25, 1790, note 3.
13. One and one-half million florins of the Holland loan of March, 1791, had
been used for payment on the American debt to France. See H to Short, April
13, 1791.

much more than ever we shall get by any Management of our Debts on this Side of the Water.

I have given you my dear Sir these Hints in Abridgement because my Time will not permit of dilating them. Attribute them I pray you to the true Cause and believe me always very sincerely yours

From Tobias Lear

United States August 15th. 1791

By the President's command T Lear has the honor to transmit to the Secretary of the treasury the proposals which have this day been submitted to the President, for rebuilding the lanthorn story & wooden work of the Light House in South Carolina which has lately been consumed by fire, and likewise proposals for plastering the same [1]—All of which have been approved by the President of the United States.

Tobias Lear
Secretary to the President
of the United States.

LS, RG 26, Lighthouse Letters Received, "Segregated" Lighthouse Records, Lear, National Archives; LC, George Washington Papers, Library of Congress.
1. See H to George Washington, August 15, 1791.

Meeting of the Commissioners of the Sinking Fund

[Philadelphia, August 15, 1791]

At a meeting of the Commissioners of the Sinking Fund of the United States, on the 15th day of August, 1791:
Present: The Secretary of State, the Secretary of the Treasury, and the Attorney General.

The Secretary of the Treasury having informed the Board, that a further sum, amounting, probably to between three and four hundred thousand dollars, may be applied, in pursuance of the act [1] constituting the Board: [2]

Whereupon it is Resolved

1. That the aforesaid Sum to purchase at the following rates—

To the purchase of Funded stock, bearing a present Interest of six per Centum, at twenty shillings in the Pound. Funded Debt bearing an Interest of three per Centum at twelve shillings in the Pound, and Deferred Debt at twelve shillings and six pence in the Pound.

2. That if any of the aforesaid Species of Debt be lower, than the rates here fixed, preference be given to it.

3. That any Surplus of the said Purchase Money or the whole as the case under the preceeding circumstances may be, be applied in the first instance to the purchase of the three pCents and the deferrd Debt as far as they can be obtained, and afterwards to the purchase of funded Stock of six per Cent.

4. That the Cities of Philadelphia and New York be the Places of Purchases. In behalf of the Board   Th. Jefferson

ASP, Finance, I, 235–36; copy, in the handwriting of William Seton, Hamilton Papers, Library of Congress.

1. Section 2 of "An Act making Provision for the Reduction of the Public Debt" provided in part "That the purchases to be made of the said debt, shall be made under the direction of the President of the Senate, the Chief Justice, the Secretary of State, the Secretary of the Treasury, and the Attorney General for the time being; and who, or any three, of whom, with the approbation of the President of the United States, shall cause the said purchases to be made in such manner, and under such regulations as shall appear to them best calculated to fulfill the intent of this act" (1 *Stat.* 186 [August 12, 1790]).

2. The preceding material is taken from the printed version in *ASP, Finance*, I, 235. The remainder of the document is taken from the copy in the Hamilton Papers.

To William Seton

Treasury Department
August 15. 1791

Sir

Inclosed is a resolution of the Trustees of the Sinking Fund appropriating a certain sum for the purchase of public Debt within certain limits therein specified.[1]

In consequence of that resolution I have concluded to apply One hundred and fifty thousand dollars towards purchases in the city of

New York and to ask you to undertake the execution of the business.[2] In thus forbearing to employ some officer of the United States and having recourse to your aid, I am governed by the consideration that your situation would lead to such an execution of the business as might at the same time best consist with the accommodation of the Bank of New York.

Inclosed is a letter to the Directors of the Bank [3] requesting them to pay to you the abovementioned sum. You will of course however only avail yourself of this authority in proportion to the actual purchases you shall make, and you will please to advise me weekly of such as you may be able to effect.

The Trustees have never yet determined on any allowance to the persons who have been employed in similar purchases, nor is it clear how much is in their power on this point. I can therefore only say that the same rule will govern in your case, as in that of others.

With great consideration   I am Sir   Your obed servant
Alexander Hamilton

William Seton Esquire
Cashier of the Bank of New York

ALS, Montague Collection, MS Division, New York Public Library; copy, in the handwriting of William Seton, Hamilton Papers, Library of Congress.
1. For this enclosure, see "Meeting of the Commissioners of the Sinking Fund," August 15, 1791.
2. Seton spent $116,542 from August 19 to August 27 and the balance from August 31 to September 5. See H to the President and Directors of the Bank of New York, September 7, 1791.
3. See H to the President and Directors of the Bank of New York, August 16, 1791.

From William Seton

[New York] 15 Aug. 1791

Sir

I am honored with your Letter of the 4th.[1] From the very sudden turn that Speculation has taken [2] We have only now remaining in Bank of the Treasurers Bills on Collectors undisposed of

No. 1648 for 200 Dollars on I. Gregory, Cambden [3]

1339   50   on G. Biscoe, Nottingham [4]

It is certainly of considerable importance & a great accomodation to the mercantile Interest of this City that the Bank be furnished with a proportion of the Treasurers Drafts on the Collectors in the different States. I therefore hope we shall continue to receive that favour from you. The Bills on the Eastern States we can more readily dispose of, but it is also very convenient to have a proportion of those upon the Southern.

I have the honor to enclose a Return of the Disposal of the Bills on Amsterdam for 300,000 Current Guilders amounting to Dollars 121984 71/100.

Mr Brasher the Goldsmith [5] begs that I will hand to you the Letter he has wrote to me upon the subject of the Dublon. I wish it may exonerate him in your opinion, for I am convinced he is a thorough honest Man. I return the piece of Metal enclosed agreeable to your desire and have the honor to be with the greatest respect   Sir   Your Obedt Hum Serv

LC, Bank of New York, New York City.
  1. Letter not found.
  2. See Fisher Ames to H, August 15, 1791, note 6.
  3. Isaac Gregory was collector of customs at Plankbridge in the District of Camden, North Carolina.
  4. George Biscoe, collector of customs at Nottingham, Maryland.
  5. Ephraim Brasher. See H to Seton, June 17, 1791.

To George Washington

Treasury Department, August 15, 1791. Recommends that the President accept the bid of Conrad Hook and John Naverson for rebuilding the "Lantern Story and all the wooden work of the Light house" in South Carolina.[1]

LC, George Washington Papers, Library of Congress.
  1. See Tobias Lear to H, August 15, 1791.

To George Washington

Treasury Department, August 15, 1791. Recommends that the President accept the bid of Robert McMahin "for plaistering, or rough casting the outside" of the lighthouse in South Carolina.[1]

LC, George Washington Papers, Library of Congress.
  1. See Tobias Lear to H, August 15, 1791.

From William Duer

[*New York, August 16, 1791.* On August 17, 1791, Hamilton wrote to Duer: "I have received your two letters of the 12th and 16th." *Letter of August 16 not found.*]

To the President and Directors of the Bank of New York [1]

Ty Dept. 16 Aug. 1791

Genn.

You will please to cause to be paid to Willm. Seton Esqr such sums not exceeding in the whole One Hundred & fifty Thousand Dollars as he may require to be applied by him towards purchases of the Public Debt at the request of the Trustees of the Sinking Fund.[2] The advances you shall make, when known, will be covered in the requisite forms.

Yours &c   A Hamilton

Copy, in the handwriting of William Seton, Hamilton Papers, Library of Congress.

1. Gulian Verplanck was elected president of the Bank of New York on May 11, 1791.

2. See H to Seton, August 15, 1791, and "Meeting of the Commissioners of the Sinking Fund," August 15, 1791.

To William Seton

Private

Philadelphia Aug 16. 1791

My Dear Sir

I send you herewith an official letter.[1] This private one I write as explanatory of it.

I hardly expect that you will be able to procure the debt within the limits prescribed—And yet I do not know what effect the imprudent speculations in Bank Script may produce. A principal object with me is to keep the Stock from falling too low in case the embarrassments of the dealers should lead to sacrifices; whence you will infer that it is not my wish that the purchases should be below the prescribed limits. Yet if such should unfortunately be the state of the market it must of course govern.

The limits assigned for the purchases of Three per Cents and deferred debt are founded on a calculation of the Government rate of interest being 5 ₩ Ct.[2] The same rule has not been extended to the Stock bearing an immediate interest of 6 ₩ Ct because the Government have a right to redeem it at par in certain proportions;[3] and though to individual purchasers it is worth more than par, because a part only can be redeemed, yet it is not at present the interest of the government to give more than par for it, because of the right to redeem a part. Indeed the law limits the Commissioners in this particular.[4]

You recollect that the act requires that the purchases should be made openly.[5] This has been construed to mean by a known agent for the public. When you make a purchase therefore it will be proper that it should be understood that it is on account of the United States but this need not precede the purchase, and it will be best that there should be no unnecessary demonstration lest it should raise hopes beyond what will be realised.

Yrs.   with great regard   A Hamilton

Wm Seton Esqr.

P S If the prices of Stocks should exceed the prescribed limits, you may retain the letter to the Directors.[6]

If there are any Gentlemen who support the *funds* and others who *depress* them, I shall be pleased that your purchases may aid the *former*. This in great confidence.

ALS, Mr. Pierce Gaines, Fairfield, Connecticut; copy, in the handwriting of William Seton, Hamilton Papers, Library of Congress.

1. H to Seton, August 15, 1791.
2. See "Meeting of the Commissioners of the Sinking Fund," August 15, 1791.
3. The relevant part of "An Act making provision for the (payment of the) Debt of the United States" (1 *Stat.* 138–44 [August 4, 1790]) reads as follows:
"Sec. 4. *And be it further enacted,* That for the whole or any part of any sum subscribed to the said loan, by any person or persons, or body politic, which shall be paid in the principal of the said domestic debt, the subscriber or subscribers shall be entitled to a certificate, purporting that the United States owe to the holder or holders thereof, his, her, or their assigns, a sum to be expressed therein, equal to two thirds of the sum so paid, bearing an interest of six per centum per annum, payable quarter yearly, and subject to redemption by pay-

ments not exceeding in one year, on account both of principal and interest, the proportion of eight dollars upon a hundred of the sum mentioned in such certificate; and to another certificate purporting that the United States owe to the holder or holders thereof, his, her or their assigns, a sum to be expressed therein, equal to the proportion of thirty-three dollars and one third of a dollar upon a hundred of the sum so paid, which after the year one thousand eight hundred shall bear an interest of six per centum per annum, payable quarter yearly, and subject to redemption by payments not exceeding in one year, on account both of principal and interest, the proportion of eight dollars upon a hundred of the sum mentioned in such certificate: *Provided*, That it shall not be understood that the United States shall be bound or obliged to redeem in the proportion aforesaid; but it shall be understood only that they have a right so to do." (1 *Stat.* 140.)

4. This provision is in Section 1 of "An Act making Provision for the Reduction of the Public Debt" (1 *Stat.* 186 [August 12, 1790]).

5. This provision is in Section 2 of "An Act making Provision for the Reduction of the Public Debt" (1 *Stat.* 186).

6. See H to the President and Directors of the Bank of New York, August 16, 1791.

From Thomas Smith [1]

[Philadelphia] Pennsa August 16. 1791

Sr

I now inclose accts of stock remaining on the Books of this office the 30th June 1791. I have paid the whole of the Indents last received & people are now waiting for Interest in Indents on their Certificates.[2]

I have the honor to be &c.

Honble Alexr Hamilton
Secety Treasy U states

Copy, RG 53, Pennsylvania State Loan Office, Letter Book, 1790–1794, Vol. "615-P," National Archives.

1. Smith was commissioner of loans for the state of Pennsylvania.

2. For background concerning the special requirements for indents in the Pennsylvania loan office, see Smith to H, February 14, 1791, note 1.

Contract with Thomas Marshall [1]

[*Philadelphia, August 17, 1791.* The minutes of the proceedings of the directors of the Society for Establishing Useful Manufactures for December 9, 1791, read: "The Governor laid before the Board a Letter from Collo Alexander Hamilton,[2] enclosing an Agreement entered into by the said Colo Hamilton in behalf of the Society. . . and Thomas Marshal dated 17th. August 1791." *Contract not found.*]

"Minutes of the S.U.M.," 3.
1. Marshall was appointed superintendent of the proposed cotton mill to be erected by the Society for Establishing Useful Manufactures.
2. H to the Directors of the Society for Establishing Useful Manufactures, December 7, 1791.

To William Duer

Philadelphia Aug 17 1791

My Dear Friend

I have received your two letters of the 12th and 16th.[1]

The Subscription Book for the manufacturing Society [2] did not remain with me nor with either of the two Gentlemen who came on with me. Is it with neither of those who accompanied you? If it is not, it must have been left at Brunswick & you will do well to write to some trusty person there to look it up & send it to you. I am impatient for the alterations which were agreed upon & a list of the Subscribers.[3]

La Roche may go to Scioto [4] if he can be back in the time you mention.

I fear that in the hurry of writing my letter [5] on the subject of Bank Script I must have expressed myself more strongly than was intended.

The conversation here was—"Bank Script is getting so high as to become a bubble" in one breath—in another, " 'tis a South Sea dream," in a third, "There is a combination of knowing ones at New York to raise it as high as possible by fictitious purchases in order to take in the credulous and ignorant"—In another "Duer Constable [6] and some others are mounting the balloon as fast as possible—If it dont soon burst, thousands will rue it" &c &c.[7]

As to myself, my friend, I think I know you too well to suppose you capable of such views as were implied in those innuendoes, or to harbour the most distant thought that you could wander from the path either of public good or private integrity. But I will honestly own I had serious fears for you—for your *purse* and for your *reputation*, and with an anxiety for both I wrote to you in earnest terms. You are sanguine, my friend. You ought to be aware of it yourself, & to be on your guard against the propensity. I feared least it might carry you further than was consistent either with your own safety or the public good. My friendship for you & my concern for the public cause were both alarmed. If the infatuation had continued progressive & any extensive mischiefs had ensued you would certainly have had a large portion of the blame. Conscious of this I wrote to you in all the earnestness of apprehensive friendship.

I do not widely differ from you about the real value of Bank Script. I should rather call it about 190 to be within bounds with hopes of better things, & I sincerely wish you may be able to support it at what you mention. The acquisition of too much of it by foreigners will certainly be an evil.

Yrs. Sincerely & Affect.   A Hamilton

Wm. Duer Esqr.

JCH Transcripts.
   1. Neither of these letters has been found.
   2. The Society for Establishing Useful Manufactures.
   3. The meeting of the subscribers to the Society for Establishing Useful Manufactures apparently began on August 7 and ended on August 9. See H to Elizabeth Hamilton, August 9, 10, 1791.
   4. Jean Baptiste de La Roche was one of a group of twenty-four Frenchmen, the Société de Vingt-Quatres, who contracted to purchase one thousand acres each of Scioto lands from Duer. Members of the group came to America in 1790 to take possession of their lands, but the purchase was never completed.
   5. Letter not found.
   6. William Constable, a New York merchant, was engaged with Duer in extensive stock speculation in 1790 and 1791.
   7. See Fisher Ames to H, August 15, 1791, note 6.

To Rufus King

[Philadelphia, August 17, 1791] [1]

Your letter of Monday Evening [2] has a good deal tranquillized me. I am glad to learn that the mischiefs from the over rise of scripts [3] are not likely to be very extensive.

I observe what you say respecting the quotation of my opinion. I was not unaware of the delicacy of giving any & was sufficiently reserved 'till I perceived the extreme to which Bank Script and with it other stock was tending. But when I saw this I thought it advise-able to speak out, for a bubble connected with my operations is of all the enemies I have to fear, in my judgment, the most formid-able—and not only not to promote, but as far as depends on me, to counteract delusions, appears to me to be the only secure founda-tion on which to stand. I thought it therefore expedient to risk something in contributing to dissolve the charm.

But I find that I have been misquoted. Speaking of sales on time at twenty four shillings for 6 ₱ Ct. &c. I think it probable, I may have intimated an opinion that they went faster than could be sup-ported. But it is untrue that I have given as a standard prices below those of the market as mentioned by you. On the contrary my standard on pretty mature reflection has been and is nearly as follows—

for Bank Script	195
6 ₱ Cents	22/
3 ₱ Cents	12/
Deferred *now*	12/8

I proceed on the idea of 5 ₱ Ct. interest—taking at the same time into calculation the *partial redeemability* of the 6 ₱ Ct.

I give you my standard that you may be able if necessary to con-tradict insinuations of an estimation on my part short of that stand-ard for the purpose of depressing the funds.

Yrs. sincerely & Affect   A Hamilton

Aug. 17
R King Esqr

ALS, New-York Historical Society, New York City.
  1. This letter is misdated August 7, 1791, in *JCHW*, V, 476, and *HCLW*, IX, 486.
  2. King to H, August 15, 1791.
  3. See Fisher Ames to H, August 15, 1791, note 6.

From William Seton

[New York] 18 Aug: 1791

Sir

I am desired by the President & Directors to acknowledge the receipt of your Letter of the 16th. They have ordered the Sum of 150,000 Dollars to be paid to me as it may [be] required for the purchases of public Debt for the Trustees of the Sinking fund agreeable to your request.

The Return of the Sale of the Bills on Holland was furnished last Monday.[1]

I have the Honor to be &c

LC, Bank of New York, New York City.
  1. See Seton to H, August 15, 1791.

From William Seton

New York 18 Augt. 1791

Sir

I am honored with your Letter of the 15th. enclosing a resolution of the Trustees of the Sinking fund, in consequence of which you direct me to purchase public Debt to the amount of 150,000 Dollars at the limits therein prescribed. I am very much flattered and very thankfull for this confidence reposed in me, the more so, as the execution of the business thro' me will be a great accomodation to this Bank.

The President & Directors have ordered the Sum of 150,000 Dols to be held at my disposal and I shall only avail myself of it in proportion to the actual purchases I may make, of which a weekly return shall be made to you.

I have this day purchased 52,500 Dollars of the deferred debt at 12/6 & 5000 Dolls. 3 ₱ Cents @ 12/—declaring the same to be on account of the United States. The Transfers will be made tomorrow & taken in my Name, till I receive your further orders on that point.

I have the honor to be with the greatest respect

LC, Bank of New York, New York City.

Treasury Department Circular
to the Commissioners of Loans

Treasury Department
August the 18th. 1791

Sir

I have directed the Treasurer to remit you drafts for Sixty five thousand Dollars towards payment of the quarters interest ending the last of September next. These Drafts are with blanks for the direction as heretofore, and may be filled with the name either of the Cashier of the Bank of Massachusetts or of New York or of North America or with the name of the Collector of Boston.

One half of these drafts may at once be disposed of, if a demand occurs, upon either of the Banks of North America or New York. The Residue it is presumed will find sufficient sums to answer them in the hands of the Bank of Massachusetts and of the Collector of Boston. You will do well however to consult with the latter in order to ascertain what sum you may rely upon from him in time and you will inform me without delay of the result.

You will also inform me as soon as possible how the probability stands of the sum remitted being adequate to the object, and you will report to me weekly the amount of the sales you may make.

I am, with consideration,　Sir,　your obedient servant

A Hamilton

LS, to Nathaniel Appleton, Historical and Philosophical Society of Ohio, Cincinnati; LS, to Jabez Bowen, Lloyd W. Smith Collection, Morristown National Historical Park, Morristown, New Jersey. The wording of these two circulars differs although the contents are similar.

To Jeremiah Olney

Treasury Department Aug 19th 1791

Sir

Your Letter of the 11th instant has come to hand.

Your intended proceedings with regard to the seizure of Sugar

You mention, appear to be proper, and conformable to the 13th Section of the Collection Law.[1]

I am, sir   Your obedt Servt   Alex Hamilton

Jere Olney Esqr
Collector
Providence

LS, Rhode Island Historical Society, Providence; copy, RG 56, Letters to the Collector at Providence, National Archives; copy, RG 56, Letters to Collectors at Small Ports, "Set G," National Archives.
    1. Section 13 of "An Act to provide more effectually for the collection of the duties imposed by law on goods, wares and merchandise imported into the United States, and on the tonnage of ships or vessels" provided that the penalty for unloading goods without authority was forfeiture (1 *Stat.* 157-58 [August 4, 1790]).

To Otho H. Williams [1]

Treasury Department August 19th. 1791

Sir,

In the documents which you transmitted to me concerning the goods of MacRae and Morrison which have been seized, I observe—

That one of the cases of Hats both in the Bill of Sale and deposition of Mr Frazer is numbered 12 and that no such number appears in the statement of the packages imported and of which the Goods seized are alleged to have been a part.

The numbers of all the cases stated to have been imported are 11. 10. 9. 11. 13.   1. 3. 4. The numbers of the cases seized are 1. 3. 4. 11. 12. 13.

I presume that this has arisen from some mistake not difficult to be explained, but a due regard to accuracy requires that an explanation should be called for.

I am Sir: Your obedt Servant   Alex Hamilton

Otho H. Williams Esqr
Collector
Baltimore

LS, Columbia University Libraries.
    1. For background to this letter, see H to Cyrus Griffin, February 15, 1791; H to Williams, June 4, 1791; Williams to H, June 10, 1791.

To Jabez Bowen [1]

[*Philadelphia, August 20, 1791*. ". . . It is a rule necessary to be strictly adhered to that the certificates of any state which have once been surrendered to such State shall be deemed to be extinguished and shall cease to be considered as a part of its debt, assumable on the principle of the Funding Act." [2] *Letter not found.*]

ALS, sold at Samuel Freeman Company, November 18, 1924, Item 167.
1. Bowen was commissioner of loans for Rhode Island.
2. "An Act making provision for the (payment of the) Debt of the United States" (1 *Stat.* 138–44 [August 4, 1790]). Text taken from extract in the dealer's catalogue.

Contract with William Hall [1]

[Philadelphia, August 20, 1791]

Agreement between AH on behalf of a certain Society or Comp for establis Manufactures in the state of N Jersey &   [2] Hall.

The said   Hall shall superintend and carry on for the said Society or Company the business of printing staining and bleaching of Cottons and Linnens, in all its parts, upon the like principles and in the like method, as the same is now carried on in the Kingdom of Great Britain, and to construct or direct the construction of all such machines as are in use in the said Kingdom in and about the said business; with all which, the said   Hall doth hereby declare himself to be well acquainted.

The said Society shall confide to the said   Hall the superintendence of the said business at such Factory as they shall establish and shall allow & pay to him for his services so long as they shall think fit to continue him in their employment, and he shall so continue, the yearly salary of 600 £ Sterling money of G B per annum together with a share in the nett profits of the said business at the rate of five per Centum of the said profits. In determining such nett profits no deduction shall be made for the interest of the Capital employed except such part of it as may be actually invested in the funds of the United States or in the stock of some public bank or as may be actually borrowed for the carrying on of the said business. The salary aforesaid shall commence from the time of the Incorporation of the said Society.[3]

The said Society shall make a reasonable compensation to the said   Hall for such machines as he shall introduce and furnish to their use, towards the prosecution of the said business—which compensation shall be agreed upon between the said Alexander Hamilton & the said   Hall, or if not so agreed upon, shall be ascertained by indifferent persons to be appointed by the parties.

For the performance of all which agreements severally & respectively the said parties do mutually and respectively bind themselves each to the other in the penal sum of Ten thousand Dollars.

In Witness whereof the said Alexander H   & the said Hall have hereunto respectively subscribed & set their hands & seals the   day of August 1791.

ADf, Hamilton Papers, Library of Congress.

1. Little is known concerning William Hall beyond the fact that he was an English or Irish artisan who had migrated to the United States. It seems likely that he was induced to migrate by Thomas Digges of Maryland. See Digges to H, April 6, 1792.

2. This and subsequent spaces were left blank in the MS.

3. The New Jersey legislature's bill incorporating the Society for Establishing Useful Manufactures became law on November 22, 1791.

From Charles Lee

Alexandria [Virginia] 20th. August 1791

Sir!

I have received your Circular of the 5th. of August and due attention shall be observed respecting the Certificates of Registry therein mentioned.

I have returned an account of Decked Vessels up to the 1st. of March last and of Imports and Exports to the 1st of July last; also of the Inward Tonnage to the last mentioned period; and the best account of the outward Tonnage in my power to make shall be soon transmitted. In keeping the Book of Clearances, the Tonnage of the Vessels has not been set down but from the documents in the Offices, some account may be rendered thereof.

I inclose a copy of the Table of fees as it has been and now is set up in the Office, which pursues the language of the Law verbatim.

If there has been any deviation from the opinions of Jones and Harrison [1] in my office it has been in the following instance, for example, —a licensed vessel above 20 Tons having on board foreign goods arriving in this District from Philadelphia and departing from hence to Philadelphia, has paid in full for all fees for coming and going one hundred and five cents, viz: a permit to land   20 Cents
For entering and receiving of and qualifying to her manifest 60 cents
For departing permit . . . . 25 cents
                                                           —————
                                                            105

This practice is legal, in the strictest construction of the 31st. Section of the Act of Congress,[2] as will appear from the Consideration that every service is rendered for which a fee is charged. The doubt or difference from the Opinion of Jones and Harrison if there be any is confined to the charge of sixty cents. How does this matter stand as to the facts? When the vessel arrives she is entered, and when she departs the manifest is received and qualified unto, and these services being performed, they are to be paid for. The clause of the 31st. section applying to this subject, it uses the most general language "for every entry of Inward Cargo directed to be made in conformity with this act, and for receiving of and qualifying to every manifest of Vessels licensed to Trade as aforesaid sixty cents." [3] The Case then meets the words of the Law which I have stated, and it can only be taken out of the words by very ingenious argument, and contrary to equity, as it is just that for every service, there should be a compensation. I own the opinions of Jones and Harrison are to me not sufficiently explicit to decide whether they coincide with the above construction or not. I have heard that in some there has been a custom of charging 60 cents for entry of a vessel as above described and the like fee of 60 cents for the receiving the Manifest and qualifying unto it, but this not being within the letter of the Law I have never done so, though the learned Counsel in Virginia who have been consulted have said it is warranted by the Law. I will not observe upon the trouble occasioned to the Collector in this part of his duty nor enlarge further on the subject now offered for your consideration, trusting that enough has been said to satisfy you of the legality of my practice. A Vessel of the United States being once registered as the Law directs has not been required to be again admeasured, except in the case of the register granted in another district, being delivered up to be cancelled in this District, and another Register demanded. An admeasurement has in this case been made by the Surveyor, here, who would not certify unless he actually measured the vessel and without his Certificate a new Register could not be issued by me. This is made necessary by the form of the Register itself one word or letter of which I could not presume to alter, the language being "The Surveyor of this District &c." In future I shall require the Surveyor to grant his Certificate upon the faith of the old register in like manner as if he had actually measured her in all cases whatever for so I understand your letter; but permit me to observe that the measurement here generally exceeds that expressed in the Eastern Registers. As to foreign Vessels they are measured when ever they come into this district and land goods, or come in Ballast from a foreign Port, unless they have been once measured by the Surveyor. Please to instruct me whether a foreign vessel having been once measured by the Officer here is liable to be measured every time she comes into this district.

I am Sir! respectfully   Your Obedient Servant

Charles Lee, Collector
at Alexandria

P.S. We have no Thermometer here, the one sent having been broken on its way.   Charles Lee.

Copy, RG 56, Letters to and from the Collector at Alexandria, National Archives.
  1. See Richard Harison and Samuel Jones to H, November 18, 1789. This opinion was transmitted to the collectors by H in "Treasury Department Circular to the Collectors of the Customs," November 30, 1789.
  2. "An Act for Registering and Clearing Vessels, Regulating the Coasting Trade, and for other purposes" (1 *Stat.* 55-65 [September 1, 1789]).
  3. 1 *Stat.* 64.

To Benjamin Lincoln

Treasury Department
August the 20th. 1791.

Sir

I have to acknowledge the receipt of your Letter of the 29th. Inst.[1]

In addition to the measures you have taken in the case you mention, I do not doubt you will also advert to the circumstance that the party who received the cotton is by the 26th. Section of the collection law liable to a penalty of four hundred dollars.² A rigorous prosecution of the receivers of run goods may produce a desireable effect, and is perhaps even more necessary than that of the principals.

I am

L[S], RG 36, Collector of Customs at Boston, Letters from the Treasury, 1789–1818, Vol. 5, National Archives; copy, RG 56, Letters to Collectors at Small Ports, "Set G," National Archives; copy, RG 56, Letters to the Collector at Boston, National Archives.

 1. See Lincoln to H, July 29, 1791.

 2. Actually H is referring to Section 27 (rather than Section 26) of "An Act to provide more effectually for the collection of the duties imposed by law on goods, wares and merchandise imported into the United States, and on the tonnage of ships or vessels" (1 *Stat.* 163 [August 4, 1790]). For an explanation of the confusion over the numbering of the sections of this act, see H to Richard Harison, April 26, 1791, note 2.

Section 27 prescribed the penalty for unloading goods without a permit and provided that "the master or person having the command or charge of such ship or vessel, and every other person who shall knowingly be concerned or aiding therein, or in removing, storing, or otherwise securing the said goods, wares or merchandise, shall forfeit and pay the sum of four hundred dollars for each offence."

From William Polk ¹

Wilmington [North Carolina] August 20th. 1791

Sir

When I wrote you last from Hillsborough ² I suggested to you that I was doubtfull of the Instrument for stamping the Certificates for the Inspectors would not be received before it would be incumbent on me to deliver them to the different Officers. In this I have not been deceived. No such instrument has yet been received & I have delivered to the Inspectors the Certificates without Stamping. No inconvenience will I hope insue, untill such time as the instrument may arive, more especially if the Officers in the different Districts are advertised of the same.

The Collectors ³ in more than half the Counties are appointed & am now on my rout to finish the same. The prospect is but gloomy. The lower Country have but few Stills & distill nothing but fruit, which there is none of this year and [in] the Western Counties many of the people have pulled down their Stills. Some threats have been thrown out; however, disregardless of them I have & will execute the Law with all my power. This will be handed you by Colo. Read,⁴

Inspector of Survey No. 1. To him I have committed some communications to be submitted to you, of the necessity of having Inspectors or Collectors with the powers of Inspectors at the Towns of Fayetteville Tarborough & Halifax for the greater security of the revenue & to prevent frauds.

There has [been] some charges for printing & paper already accrued & no means has been provided for the payment. Untill the first is made, which will not be before the last of January, could an order be given for draughts on the Collectors or any of them for such sums as may be wanting to satisfy these claims?

If it is admissable I would be glad to draw my Sallary from the Collector of the Customs at this place. It is contiguous or at least more so than any other in the District. If it could, I wish a form; if not I would wish to know where it is to be paid & the manner of application.

The forms of accounts & Books I have not yet recd. Indeed I have not had any information or instructions from you since Mr. Coxe's [5] letter of the 14th. of May.

I can never learn whether Inspectors for the Surveys No. 4 & 5 have been made by the President when passing thro' this State or at any other time.[6]

I have the Honor to be with   consideration your most   Obedient and very   Hbe. Servt.   Will: Polk

ALS, RG 58, General Records, 1791–1803, National Archives.
  1. Polk was supervisor of the revenue for the District of North Carolina.
  2. Letter not found.
  3. Although inspectors of the surveys or of the revenue were appointed by the President under the terms of "An Act repealing, after the last day of June next, the duties heretofore laid upon Distilled Spirits imported from abroad, and laying others in their stead; and also upon Spirits distilled within the United States, and for appropriating the same" (1 *Stat.* 199–214 [March 3, 1791]), minor officials called collectors could be appointed by the supervisor of the revenue to aid in the collection of the excise. See "Treasury Department Circular to the Collectors of the Customs," May 26, 1791.
  4. James Read.
  5. Tench Coxe, Assistant Secretary of the Treasury.
  6. See George Washington to H, March 15, 1791.

Receipt from William Pearce [1]

[*Philadelphia, August 20, 1791.* "Received Philadelphia Aug. 20, 1791 of Alexander Hamilton, one hundred dollars towards providing the use of Society for the establishment of Manufactures in the State of New Jersey certain machines & models of Machines to be delivered to the said Alexander Hamilton." [2] *Receipt not found.*]

AD, sold by Stan V. Henkels, Jr., May 15, 1931, Lot 23.

1. On December 7, 1791, H wrote to the directors of the Society for Establishing Useful Manufactures: "There is a William Pearce who has been employed by me in preparing Machines for the use of the Society. . . . He pretends to a knowlege of the fabrication of the most valuable Machines now in use in the Cotton Manufactory." In describing Pearce, Joseph Stancliffe Davis wrote: "William Pearce came over [from Belfast] also in July at the instance of Thomas Digges, who looked upon him as 'somewhat like a second Archimedes,' and gave him letters to the President, the Secretary of State, 'Governor' Dickinson of Pennsylvania, William Seton, cashier of the Bank of New York, and others. On Jefferson's promise that 'all charges would be faithfully repaid,' Seton paid Pearce's passage money, supplied him with funds to go to Philadelphia, and sent his precious models to Tench Coxe. Thus he came in touch with Hamilton, who at once set him to work and personally advanced him ample funds for constructing his machines" (Davis, *Essays*, I, 401).

Pearce had been engaged in cotton manufactures in Belfast, Ireland, when Digges encouraged him to emigrate to the United States. In a letter to Jefferson, dated April 28, 1791, Digges described Pearce's background as follows: "Pearce came last from Dorcaster in Yorkshire, & is the artist who erected the famous Mills of Messr. Cartwright of that place, which dress the wool, spin, and weaves it into Broad Cloth by force of water, Steam, or Horse. . ." (ALS, Thomas Jefferson Papers, Library of Congress). This letter also contains an account of the textile machines Pearce had developed in Belfast.

2. This quotation has been taken from an extract of this document in the dealer's catalogue.

An undated manuscript in the Hamilton Papers, Library of Congress, reads as follows:

"A list of Mr Willm Pearce's Machines

"1st A machine for spinning combed wool into yarns of various sizes by a combination of rollers (with a large cylinder) which take their movement from a wheel turned by hand, and capable with some variations of being moved by water or any other power, and that this machine is also capable of spinning yarns of flax & hemp.

"2nd A machine composed of rollers for the perpetual spinning of cottonwool into yarns of various sizes capable of being moved by hand, water or any other power with a Jack for winding by water or hand, that the said rollers, applied to the perpetual or water spinning machines, are capable of being so combined with the ordinary spinning Jenny as to form a highly useful hand machine denominated a Mule.

"3rd A machine denominated a Billy for roving or preparing cotton for the common spinning Jenny and other purposes, likewise for roving tow suitable for candle wick by means of a feeding Cloth, a roller and spindles.

"4th A machine or loom for weaving cloths of any material such as cotton, linen, wool silk or hair, capable of being moved by water or any other power.

"5th A loom for weaving cloths of various kinds which he denomiates *a multiplier,* capable of weaving two, three and perhaps more pieces of goods at one time. Connected with this Machine is a set of Temples in two, three or more pairs or parts for stretching the Cloth while in the loom—also a sett of unknotted hiddles or hells (sometimes called harness or geers) in two, three or more parts according to the number of pieces of Cloth in the multiplier."

To William Seton

[*Philadelphia, August 20, 1791*. On August 25, 1791, Seton wrote to Hamilton: "I have the honor to acknowledge the receipt of your Letters of the 20 & 22d." *Letter of August 20 not found.*]

To Elizabeth Hamilton

[Philadelphia, August 21, 1791]

I was made very happy, my beloved Betsey by the receipt of your letter,[1] informing me that one of mine had at length got to hand and that your spirits were recovered. I had suffered not a little at the idea that I must have appeared to you negligent. Nor am I able to imagine what can have become of my other letters. There is certainly some very foul and abominable practice, which it will not be my fault, if I do not detect.

You said that you would not stay longer at Albany than twenty days which would bring it to the first of September. How delighted shall I be to receive you again to my bosom & to embrace with you my precious children. And yet much as I long for this happy moment, my extreme anxiety for the restoration of your health will reconcile me to your staying longer where you are upon condition that you really receive benefit from it, and that your own mind is at ease. But I do not believe that I shall permit you to be so long absent from me another time.

Be chearful be happy my beloved, and if possible return to your husband with that sweet bloom in your looks which can never fail to delight him.

You must inform me before hand when you set out. My intention is to meet you at Elizabeth Town. For I am unwilling to go through the bustle of another visit to New York so soon after my last.[2]

Think of me—dream of me—and love me My Betsey as I do you.
Yrs. for ever   A Hamilton

Aug 21
Mrs. Hamilton

ALS, Hamilton Papers, Library of Congress.
1. Letter not found.
2. H had visited New York City in July.

From Edmund Randolph [1]

Philadelphia August 21st. 1791

Sir

In the opinion, given by Mr. Bradford [2] and Mr. Ingersoll,[3] I find the case of Mr. Robert Buchanan [4] to be accurately stated; but after paying a respectful attention to the sentiments of those gentlemen, I am compelled to say, that I differ in the conclusion drawn from that statement: for I cannot agree, that any interest is to be received upon ⟨the⟩ certificate for the year 1791.

I acknowledge that the certificate was issued in conformity with the Act of Congress, passed on the 4th. of August 1790; [5] and that it's silence as to interest is no objection to such a claim, if that Act warrants it.

A subscription to a loan is therein proposed, payable in certificates issued for the domestic debt. Among these are some bearing an interest of six per cent; and others, called indents of interest, bearing no interest at all. Mr. Buchanan's certificate is founded upon indents of interest; and had they been subscribed, he would have been entitled to a certificate, purporting that the United States owe to him, as the holder, or his assigns, the sum of 7500 dollars, bearing an interest of three per centum per annum.

He has not, however, subscribed those indents; but obtained the certificate from the Register of the Treasury before the first day of June 1791; to wit, on the sixteenth of February 1791; in pursuance of

LS, RG 60, Copies of Opinions, National Archives.
1. Randolph's letter is obviously in reply to a letter (which has not been found) by H requesting Randolph's opinion as Attorney General on Robert Buchanan's demand that he be paid interest on his certificate for 1791.
2. William Bradford had been attorney general of Pennsylvania in the seventeen-eighties. On the day after this letter was written, he was appointed to the Supreme Court of Pennsylvania, and in 1794 he succeeded Randolph as Attorney General of the United States.
3. In 1790 Jared Ingersoll succeeded Bradford as attorney general of Pennsylvania.
4. Buchanan was a resident of Philadelphia.
5. "An Act making provision for the ⟨payment of the⟩ Debt of the United States" (1 Stat. 138–44 [August 4, 1790]).

the tenth section of the abovementioned Act. Upon the construction of that section the decision depends.[6]

The opinion asserts the first part of that Section to be a substantive clause; and yet in the next sentence it connects that clause with the following parts of the section. The truth is, that the section itself forms one integer. The term, *creditors,* comprehends all holders of the domestic debt, which might be subscribed to the loan, and was not. It is immediately afterwards directed, that such of them as possess the original certificates, should exchange them for others, to be issued by the Register of the Treasury. Consequently all the non-⟨sub⟩scribing creditors are under the necessity of making this exchange; and being so, must submit to the conditions prescribed for it.

One of these conditions is, that the new certificate shall not only specify the specie amount of those which are cancelled; but shall be *otherwise* of the like tenor with those heretofore issued by the Register of the Treasury for the registered debt. These import that the debt bears an interest of six per centum; and it is not denied, that a new certificate given in lieu of cancelled indents, cannot carry an interest of six per centum. The question then is, whether a new certificate, which is not upon the most sanguine construction, capable of a higher interest than three per centum, is of the same tenor with one granting an interest of six per centum?

It does not seem to be correct, to resort to the popular & common acceptation of the words "*like tenor,*" when they are known to be peculiarly technical. Nor can I admit that this acceptation would establish, in this instance, a likeness of tenor between two papers, so substantially different as in three per cent: per annum. The gentlemen by confining their exposition to popular acceptation, virtually concede the interpretation of *law* to be against them. And without entering into prolix authorities, I take the liberty of saying, that in every law-proceeding which I can call to mind, it would be decided, that there is a *material variance* between two such documents; and therefore that they could not be of the same tenor.

But let us not content ourselves with resting on the criticism of single words; let us rather examine the context.

It is not for me here to estimate the merit of any scheme of finance.

6. For the provision for nonsubscribers made by Section 10, see Andrew Porter to H, April 23, 1791, note 2.

My office is to ascertain the sense of Congress. It strikes me then immediately, that the principal was far more respected than the interest; and that the higher interest allowed to the former, was intended to correspond with that stipulated by the old certificates; whereas no interest was originally stipulated on the latter. It appears probable, that being anxious that all the indents of interest should be subscribed, they might have satisfied themselves of the propriety of distinguishing between subscribed and unsubscribed indents; because interest not being *demandable* on the face of them, might in some measure be considered as a gratuity, which the Legislature might apportion at pleasure.

That such was the meaning of Congress, is confirmed by the first clause in the tenth section itself, which gives to non-subscribing creditors, interest during the year 1791, *including interest* to the last day of December 1790; thus shewing, that creditors whose demands would carry interest to that time, by force of the contract, were the persons contemplated. Of this kind were indents for interest. And this idea receives confirmation from the care, used in the third section, to be explicit as to certificates carrying no interest, when they are really designed.

Upon the whole, I cannot persuade myself, that with these strong features, indicating the purpose of Congress, the Courts of the United States would embarrass a system of finance, by a determination in favor of interest to Mr. Buchanan for the year 1791.

I have the honor, sir, to be   with great esteem & respect   yr. mo. ob. serv   Edm: Randolph

Secretary of the Treasury.

Contract with Joseph Mort [1]

[*Philadelphia, August 22, 1791*. The minutes of the proceedings of the directors of the Society for Establishing Useful Manufactures for December 9, 1791, read: "The Governor laid before the Board a Letter from Collo Alexander Hamilton,[2] enclosing an Agreement . . . with Joseph Mort dated 22d. August." *Contract not found.*]

"Minutes of the S.U.M.," 3.

1. On December 7, 1791, H wrote to the directors of the Society for Estab-

lishing Useful Manufactures that he had made "Joseph Mort . . . an Assistant in the Manufactory." Apparently Mort was an immigrant who was skilled in the manufacture of textiles. A short time after his appointment he married a daughter of Thomas Lowrey, one of the directors of the society.

2. H to the Directors of the Society for Establishing Useful Manufactures, December 7, 1791.

From Samuel Huntington [1]

Norwich [Connecticut] August 22, 1791. "I am favourd, with your letter of the 27th of June [2] which reached me the 8th: Instant. By the Certificate of the Comptroller of the public accounts in this State, which is herewith inclosed, you will be informed that this State hath not Issued any Certificates in exchange for those of the United States; which it is presumed, gives the needfull information requested."

ALS, University of Virginia.
1. Huntington was governor of Connecticut.
2. "Treasury Department Circular to the Governors of the States," June 27, 1791.

To Stephen Keyes [1]

Treasury Department, August 22, 1791. "I now request that you will endeavour to procure a Map which delineates the North Western parts of your State from actual Survey . . . and that you will send me a sketch protracted upon a larger scale . . . of so much of those parts including Alburgh and its vicinity as will serve to give an accurate idea not only of the situation of that Township but of any other place or places where in your opinion the office may be established with the greatest degree of propriety and utility free from the inconveniences of the situation which has been fixed upon. . . ." [2]

Extract, RG 217, Miscellaneous Treasury Accounts, 1790–1894, Account No. 2508, National Archives.
1. Keyes, a Burlington, Vermont, merchant, had been appointed collector of customs at Alburg in March, 1791.
2. Presumably this is a reference to the fact that Alburg lay within territory claimed by Great Britain. See "Conversation with George Beckwith," June 15, 1791, note 9.

From Henry Lee

[Alexandria, Virginia, August 22, 1791]

My dear friend.

Mr Cox [1] was about taking to you my riding horse, but my apprehension of yr. necessary hurry & my wish to compare him with a horse I have sent for, concluded a procrastination of my execution of your request & my ardent desire.[2] No other consideration could have induced me to postpone a measure you reckon essential to your health.

Nor shall time be lost in presenting you with this trivial testimony of the zeal with which I engage in any matter which goes to your comfort.

May success & happiness attend you.

Yours affy

Henry Lee
August 22d. 1791
Alexra

I wrote to you some time ago on the business of some of my friends.[3]

ALS, Hamilton Papers, Library of Congress.
　1. This was presumably Peter Cox, Lee's neighbor in Westmoreland County, Virginia.
　2. See Lee to H, August 12, 1791.
　3. See Lee to H, August 12, 1791.

To Thomas Mifflin [1]

Treasury Department, Aug. 22d, 1791.

The Secretary of the Treasury presents his respects to the Governor of Pennsylvania, and has the honor to inform him that the vacancy in the office of Auditor,[2] is no impediment to the adjustment of the affair of the lands with the Commonwealth of Pennsylvania. The only source of delay is a difference of opinion, concerning the Certificates in which payment is to be made; the Comptroller of the Treasury insisting that it ought to be in such certificates as bore interest at the time of the contract, and the Comptroller General of Pennsylvania offering the funded three per Cents in payment.

Samuel Hazard, ed., *Pennsylvania Archives* (Philadelphia, 1856), XII, 94.
  1. For background to this letter, see Mifflin to H, May 5, 1791, and the second letter H wrote to Mifflin, June 3, 1791.
  2. Nicholas Eveleigh, comptroller of the Treasury, had died on April 17, 1791. During the summer of 1791 Oliver Wolcott, Jr., the auditor of the Treasury, was appointed to succeed him (see H to George Washington, April 17, 1791; Washington to H, June 13, 1791). The appointment was confirmed by the Senate on November 7, 1791.

To William Seton

Treasury Department Aug 22d 1791

sir

I have to acknowledge the receipt of Yours of the 18th instant.

The Transfers of the stock, which You have purchased on account of the united states, must be made to the *vice President, the Chief Justice, the Secretary of the Treasury, the Secretary of State, and the Attorney General for the time being.*[1] In all future purchases, it will be most convenient to have the stock in the first instance transferred as here directed.

I am, sir   Your obedt Servt   Alex Hamilton

William Seton Esqr
Cashier of the Bank of New York

LS, Bank of New York, New York City; copy, in the handwriting of William Seton, Hamilton Papers, Library of Congress.
  1. These officials were the commissioners of the sinking fund. For background to this letter, see H to Seton, August 15, 16, 1791; Seton to H, August 18, 1791.

From William Ellery

Collrs Off. [Newport, Rhode Island] 23d. Aug: 1791

Sir,

This will be accompanied by a weekly return of monies recd. and paid, and the copy of an endorsment on Certife No. 22 granted Apl. 23d. 1791 at this Port.

To your letter of the 10th of this month,[1] requesting the particular

LC, Newport Historical Society, Newport, Rhode Island.
  1. Letter not found.

circumstances that led to a remeasurement of the Brig Sally &c I would answer; that the property of said Brig having been transferred to Messrs Lyon and Lawrance citizens of this District, and by them, before a new Register was granted, to Peleg Clark, a citizen of this Town, as appeared by regular bills of sale, it became necessary that she should be remeasured by the Surveyor of this Port [2] where she then lay. The tonnage at which she was registered in the Port of New Bedford Decr. 18 1789, as will appear by the Certife. of Registry No. 40 which was transmitted to you on the 18th. of July 1791 was sixty six tons; and this also appeared by a Certife. given by the Collector of New Bedford [3] to one of the former Owners of the Brig Sally of the tonnage paid by him, which Certife. was handed to me by Mr. Lyon. The length, breadth and depth of said Brig as taken by the Surveyor of the Port of New Bedford appears in the Certife. of Registry transmitted as before mentioned. Her length as taken by the Surveyor for this Port is Sixty eight feet nine inches, her breadth twenty feet, her depth eight feet, and she measured Ninety five tons and a half, which was twenty nine and one half tons more than the tonnage at which she was registered in New Bedford. This great difference led me to write to Col. Pope on the subject, to which he returned the following answer "On examining the papers in my office find that in making out the Regr. I took the [papers] of another vessel, which was consented to, signed and sworn to by one of the owners of said Brig prior to making out the Register. Whether he did it designedly or ignorantly I know not. William Gordon measured all the vessels within my District as soon as conveniently could be after the Act for Registering Vessels &c [4] took place: And the Certifs. of admeasurement he put on file in the Office, that whenever application was made for a Regr. I might resort thereto. In registering the above Brig I took a wrong Certife. I have sent you inclosed copies of the two Certifs that you may see how nearly Mr. Lymans measurement and Gordons agree. The Registry in your office must rectify the mistake." Inclosed are the copies referred to by Col. Pope. Upon the receipt of this answer I advised him to inform you of the mistake and how it arose; but have not received an answer to my letter. Thus, Sir, I have

2. Daniel Lyman.   3. Edward Pope.
4. "An Act for Registering and Clearing Vessels, Regulating the Coasting Trade, and for other purposes" (1 *Stat.* 55–65 [September 1, 1789]).

given you all the information I am possessed of respecting this matter, and more perhaps than your letter implied. I would only beg leave to observe that admeasurements of vessels anew conduce to an accurate ascertainment of their tonnage, and to correct errors. I have heard that in the reported amendment to the Act for Registering and Clearing vessels, Regulating the Coasting Trade &c it is proposed [5] that on the transfer of the property of a vessel to a person or persons residing in a district different from that in which her former owner or owners resided, she is not to be admeasured anew; but the first admeasurement is to be inserted into every subsequent Certife. of Registry. If this should take place the present form of Certifs. must I conceive be altered, and there will be no check in any case.

On the 11th. of July I transmitted a Statement of the case of the Seven Brothers, and of Joseph Finch her late master, on the 2nd. of this month I advised you of the death of Capt. Browning of whose testimony I hoped to avail myself on the trial of that Brig: of the adjournment of the District Court, of my having seized the Sloop Betsy, and of my apprehensions that vessels condemned would sell for a meer trifle unless the Offrs. of the Customs interfered in the sale.

A Special Court was ordered for the trial of the Betsy on the day after that to which the District Court had adjourned. The Courts have met. Every method was taken to serve summons on persons whose evidences were material in the case of the Seven Brothers; but methods more successful were taken as I suppose by the claimant and others concerned, to elude the service of them. Unfortunately the absence of the Marshall from the State,[6] and the sickness of the Deputy Marshall prevented the summons going out as early as was wished. The Witnesses having secreted themselves, or gone out of the State, the District Atty.[7] moved for a continuance, which was not allowed, and on the Sixth day of the term the claim of Topham was withdrawn and the Libel United States vs Brigantine Seven Brothers John Topham Claimant was discontinued. The cause United States vs Joseph Finch was tried, and the Jury gave a Verdict in favour of the Plaintiffs for Four Hundred Dollars and Cost.

The Libel of the Betsy has been tried, and I believe She will be condemned; if not, and the Atty. of the District should judge it

5. See H to Ellery, April 11, 1791, note 3.   6. William Peck.
7. William Channing.

proper, an appeal will be made to the Circuit Courts, there being some Persons absent whose evidences would I think ascertain the quantity of goods delivered from her without a permit, to be of four hundred Dollars value and more. That she did run goods the Witnesses at the trial placed beyond a doubt. These trials in my opinion, and in the opinion of others, will have a beneficial effect. The masters of vessels, and their owners will I think learn from them to pay a strict regard to the Revenue Laws, if they should not no pains will be spared to detect the violations of them. A Writ was issued against the Capt. of the Betsy, but he had departed from the State before the Depy. Marshall was well enough to serve it. It will be served upon him when he returns.[8]

I am, Sir,   Yr. most obedt. servant   W Ellery Collr

A Hamilton Esqr
Secry of Treasy

8. Ellery endorsed the letter book copy of this letter as follows: "That part of this Letter respectg the Seven brothers was answd. Sept. 16 1791." H's letter of September 16 has not been found.

To Jeremiah Olney

Treasury Department, August 23, 1791. Sends commission for Jeremiah Greenman as second mate for the revenue cutter "for the Connecticut & Rhode Island station."

LS, Rhode Island Historical Society, Providence; copy, RG 56, Letters to the Collector at Providence, National Archives; copy, RG 56, Letters to Collectors at Small Ports, "Set G," National Archives; copy, RG 26, Lighthouse Letters Received, Revenue Cutter Service, Letters Sent, Vol. "O," National Archives.

To Timothy Pickering [1]

[*Philadelphia, August 23, 1791.* On August 26, 1791, Pickering wrote to Hamilton: "I have received . . . your letter of the 23d instant." *Letter not found.*]

1. Pickering had been appointed Postmaster General on August 12, 1791.

From William Short

Paris August 23. 1791.

Sir

I acknowleged the reciept of your letter of the 24th. of May in my last of the 8th. of August. I have now the honor of acknowleging that of the 30th. of June inclosing one of the 25th. of the same month (both duplicates) which came to my hands yesterday by the way of the French packet.

My former letters will have informed you of the progress & issue of the affair of the reduction of interest.[1] Although abandoned for the present I have hopes that this flattering idea may be realized ere long either at Amsterdam or elsewhere. Every preparation should be made for effecting it at latest in June next, when the first re-imbursement is to take place on the loans made at Amsterdam. The proper previous steps seem to me to be for the U. S. to get as soon as possible all the money which they are in absolute want of, so as to leave a considerable term without making loans before the month of June. This being done gives time to their bonds to appreciate which will of course happen on the probability of no more loans being made at so high a rate of interest, & particularly if the U. S. shall have been able in the mean time to have established a credit in some other place.

The sums which may be considered as indispensable to the U.S. are those due to France—the interest of the debt to foreign officers [2] —the interest due on the loans in Amsterdam next february—& as the 2 ½ million of florins to be sent to America are to be taken out of the loans made, they may be considered of the same description. Supposing these sums to be provided for in the early part of the next winter so that the U. S. may be presented to the view of money jobbers as free of the necessity of making loans for some time, the practicability of reducing their rate of interest for June next at latest seems to me assured. Its being possible sooner will depend on the resources the U. S. may in the mean time find out of Holland. Their aspect is

ALS, letterpress copy, William Short Papers, Library of Congress.
    1. See Short to H, June 3, July 19, 26, 27, 1791.
    2. See Short to H, August 3, 1790; July 19, August 8, 1791.

promising at present, but it would be wrong to rely too much on them until the experiment shall be fully made.

I informed you in my last on what footing the intended loan at Amsterdam stood. Since then I have heard nothing from the bankers [3] on the subject although I expected it long before this. The only mode I had of attempting to reduce their charges was by leaving them the alternative of doubling the loan in the case of their fixing them at 3½ instead of 4. pc. I expected then to have recieved their answer early enough to have authorized them (as the loan was not to be opened before the beginning of the next month) to extend it even without the reduction of the charges. They know that you were satisfied with the late reduction of them to 4 pr c. They know also the advantages the U. S. derive from the payments they make at present to France, on the purchase of their own funds, by means of these loans: of course I fear much they will refuse the reduction. Still I thought it my duty to try it by every means in my power as well for the interest of the U. S. as my own personal satisfaction. I gave them to understand the possibility which the U. S. had of liquidating their debt to France by arrangements independent of loans at Amsterdam so as to make them suppose that we were not absolutely in their power at present. I did not chuse to say any thing to them about an idea of loans elsewhere. This would be dangerous so long as the U.S. are in the indispensable necessity of procuring so large sums as those at present in arrears. In such a case I should fear the malevolence of a combination of those concerned either directly or indirectly in our loans at Amsterdam, & know not what effect they might produce on our credit in other places. I do not precisely see what they would or could do, but still I should have apprehensions of them if they knew our wants of money to be great & so our credit not firmly established. The more we shall have obtained from them & the less we shall be in arrears with our debt to France, when they come to know our desire of making loans elsewhere the less we shall have to fear from their attempts or their power to injure us.

With respect to the practicability of our making loans in other places I have every reason at present to believe they may be ere long obtained either at Antwerp London or Genoa. It must be observed

3. Willink, Van Staphorst, and Hubbard, the bankers of the United States in Amsterdam.

however that my information on these subjects coming only from persons who are employed in making loans & who of course have hopes of being preferred if the U.S. should determine to make them, must be recieved with much caution & cannot be absolutely & unconditionally relied [upon]. It is however the only source of information that can be opened previous to actual experiment.

I have already put you in possession of this subject as far as it regards Antwerp. I wrote some time ago to a person in London, Mr. Alexander Donald, partner of a rich house [4] established there, informing him that it had been hinted to me that it was not improbable that moneyed men of that country would be disposed to place their cash in loans if such were opened there for the U.S. & desiring him to give me his opinion on the subject. Mr. Donald though not personally known to me, seemed the most proper person to be applied to in such a case as well on account of his commercial connexions with the U.S. as the high opinion which I know to be entertained of him by the Secretary of State to whom he has been long known & who will be able to tell you how far his information is to be relied on. I therefore send you in his own words the answer which I have this day recieved from him—it is dated London Aug. 19.

"I have had several conversations with the money brokers upon the subject of a loan to the U.S. From all of which I am inclined to think that the thing is practicable, but this cannot be ascertained unless I was empowered to make some specifick proposal. I said that I had no authority for doing so, nor did I even know if application would be made for a loan, that I was only desired by a friend to enquire if such application should be made whether it could be accomplished & upon what terms. All the brokers I have spoken to are of opinion that the regular payment of the interest must be guaranteed to be paid here —one more shrewd than the rest observed that men who had money to spare would rather purchase into the American funds, which he observed allowed an interest of 6. p. cent p. ann. & could now be purchased for 17. to 18/. in the pound. I could only say in reply to this observation, that if the moneyed men of this country were to turn their attention that way, that the 6. p. cents would soon rise to 120 or perhaps 130. I do think that the credit of Congress stands so

4. Donald had served as Robert Morris's agent for the purchase of tobacco in Virginia in the seventeen-eighties. Donald and Robert Burton were partners in a banking firm in London.

well & money is so very abundant in this country that a loan for half a million could be done provided the terms are made agreeable. If any further steps are taken in this business, the first to be adopted here will be inserting an advertisement in the publick newspapers intimating the business & calling a meeting of those who are disposed to lend the money at which time proposals will be laid before them for their consideration. I believe sir that the guarantee of Donald & Burton would be accepted for the payment of the interest which they have no objection to do upon being allowed a reasonable commission for their trouble." [5]

I shall write to Mr. Donald & inform him that the U.S. being able to make loans at Amsterdam at the present rate of 5. p. cent interest, the great inducement to make them elsewhere would be a reduction of that rate, & desire him to ascertain whether that can be done at 4½ p. cent p. ann. on a loan inferior to the one he proposes—& also to see if the advertisement he speaks of cannot be dispensed with, as it would be disagreeable in the extreme to take such a measure until the success was insured & then it would be useless. I have no idea of the commission which he would consider reasonable, but it will be necessarily higher than at Amsterdam where there is no guarantee. In England the loans cannot be opened in the name of a foreign power & of course the houses who undertake it must render themselves responsible to the lenders. I shall propose therefore to Mr. Donald in the case of this business being begun to join some other rich banking house with his, as presenting an additional security. If it were not for this security one house alone would be to be preferred for the reasons I have formerly mentioned to you.[6]

Mr. Grand [7] has written also to his correspondent at Genoa to sound him about the practicability of the U.S. making a loan there. He has just recieved an answer which gives hopes that one might be made for about a million of dollars at 5. p. cent interest, the whole of the revenues of the U.S. being pledged in general as well as some sufficient part in particular. This difficulty however I have no doubt might be got over. Should it be possible to effect a reduction of the

5. Donald to Short, August 19, 1791 (ALS, letterpress copy, William Short Papers, Library of Congress).
6. See Short to H, December 2, 1790.
7. Ferdinand Le Grand, French banker and member of the Paris banking house of Grand and Company.

interest in England or at Antwerp one of course would not be undertaken at 5. p. cent at Genoa. I have wished such inquiries to be made however as well to make us acquainted with the ground, without committing the U.S., as to excite the attention of those concerned in loans who being thus pushed on to be acquainted with the resources of America will necessarily consider them in a more favorable manner. I have formerly mentioned to you the inquiries that would be made by a relation of the Minister of Genoa at this court.[8] These circumstances will of course facilitate the business should the U.S. find it for their advantage to open them in that country. I shall take care to keep you progressively informed of these several matters.

It seems difficult to obtain particular information respecting the mint of Holland. It is kept at Dordrecht & carried on by contract. I have as yet been able to get only the inclosed account of the alloy, sent me from Amsterdam with a promise of further lights, which will be forwarded to you when recieved.[9]

You will have learned from the secretary of State that Drost [10] agrees to go to America to establish the mint agreeably to your wishes. You will find him useful I think in other parts of the subject as well as those which are merely mechanical. He seems to have considered it with a good deal of attention both in its theory & practice. I communicated to him the result of your enquiries & reflexions. He approves much the decimal division you propose [11] & the values annexed to the several pieces—except the small piece of gold. I mentioned to him your object in adopting it & the small number you purposed having struck. He thought it would be injurious, on account of its extreme diminutiveness, to the beauty & regularity of proportions which might otherwise be observed & that it would be wrong to have dyes made on purpose & as the U.S. have an entirely new ground to begin on he thinks they may with ease by avoiding the errors & abuses of the mints of all other countries, have the most

8. Christoforo Vincenzo de Spinola. See Short to H, April 9, May 4, June 3, July 8, 24-25, 1791.
9. H had asked Short to send information concerning the Dutch Mint. See H to Short, April 13, 1791.
10. Jean Pierre Droz. See H to Jefferson, April 14, 1791. Short had written to Jefferson on July 20 and again on July 27, 1791, to inform him that Droz was coming to the United States (RG 59, Despatches from United States Ministers to France, 1789-1869, January 16, 1791-August 6, 1792, National Archives).
11. See "Report on the Establishment of a Mint," January 28, 1791.

perfect coin that has ever existed. He seems to be well acquainted with these errors & abuses & will be able to point them out.

One which he considers as among the most considerable is the introducing alloy into money. He has fully examined all the arguments on both sides of the question & is well convinced of the propriety of money being struck only of pure metal. I have spoken on the subject with others supposed to be skilled in it. There is variance in their opinion but the soundest among them are in favor of pure metal & say that nothing introduced or has so long supported the doctrine of alloy, but the facility which it gives to those employed in the mints to fraud government. The principal argument which I observe in favor of alloy, is that it hardens the metal & also that the part which is lost by rubbing & usage being mixed the loss is less. You mention doubts on the subject & Drost insists that the loss is less when the metal is pure. In this he is supported as well by his own experience as the opinions of the learned here. The other advantages which he attributes to pure metal are the security against counterfeits (as the eyes of every one, in a simple experiment of putting them in a common fire will immediately discover impurity without affecting the substance) & the superior value of the metal since the same weight when pure is intrinsically worth more than when joined to others. He agrees that an observation which I made to him has weight & that is that our coin, being to be taken from the monies of other countries which are alloyed, the purifying them will be an object of trouble & expence. On the whole I am much too ignorant of this subject to appreciate the various ideas of Mr. Drost, but should your determination be suspended until his arrival you will perhaps find some of them useful.

You seem to be fully convinced of the propriety of attending to beauty in coinage. Mr. Drost observes that it is important before the diameters be fixed that it should be known what are the subjects that are to be represented that they may be proportioned thereto—as well as thickness of the piece. He is much in favor of the idea of representing an eagle on the coins & particularly the large gold piece. This bird all the artists consider as the most proper for presenting a fine form. For that purpose however it would be necessary to remove those heraldic parts which cover the body in the arms of the U.S. It is probable I think you will find it proper to employ Mr. Drost to engrave the dyes of the several pieces of money. He has much merit in this act & has applied himself to study it in its relations to coinage much more than engravers in general. What has happened here lately shews the necessity of the engravers having this kind of knowlege. The artist they have employed as the engraver for their new coinage is considered as the most eminent engraver of medals. By an error which he has committed for want of this practical knowlege the dyes have failed & been obliged to be renewed already several times & it is not yet certain whether the new figures represented on that money by his advice, though handsome & well adapted to a medal, can be executed in coinage, on account of the multiplication of the pieces. On one side is the effigy of the King with his constitutional title—on the other the genius of France in the figure of an Angel writing down the constitution on a table placed perpendicularly before it. The pieces which have been hitherto struck are somewhat better executed than their former coinage (they are of silver only & are of six louis & of fifteen sols) but are infinitely inferior to copper pieces struck by Drost's machine in England for Bolton & Co.[12]

I have the honor to be with perfect respect & attachment   Sir Your most obedient humble servant   W. Short

Alexander Hamilton secretary of the Treasury, Philadelphia

12. On April 23, 1790, Jefferson wrote to Ferdinand Le Grand: "You may remember that we were together at the Hotel de la Monnoye, to see M. Drost strike coins in his new manner, and that you were so kind as to speak with him afterwards on the subject of his coming to America. We are now in a condition to establish a mint, and should be desirous of engaging him in it. I suppose him to be at present in the service of Watts and Bolton, the latter of whom you may remember to have been present with us at the Monnoye. I know of no means of communicating our dispositions to Drost so effectually as through your friendly agency; and therefore take the liberty of asking you to write to him to know what emoluments he receives from Watts and Bolton, and whether he would be willing to come to us for the same? If he will, you may give him an expectation, but without an absolute engagement, that we will call for him immediately, and that with himself we may probably take and pay him for all the implements of coinage he may have, suited to our purposes. If he asks higher terms, he will naturally tell you so, and what they are; and we must reserve a right to consider of them. In either case, I will ask your answer as soon as possible. I need not observe to you that this negociation should be known to nobody but yourself, Drost and Mr. Short" (Boyd, *Papers of Thomas Jefferson*, XVI, 368–69).

Jefferson submitted the draft of this letter to H. See H to Jefferson, April 22, 1790.

Conversation with George Beckwith [1]

Philadelphia
August 24th [1791]

An Officer at the Head of an Executive Department.
Extract

Mr. _____ The National Assembly of France passed a decree a short time before Mr. Ternants [2] embarkation, authorizing the formation of a new treaty of commerce with this country; if the influence of La Fayette and his friends, shall finally prevail in The French Councils, their general dispositions towards us, will tend greatly to forward this object. George Beckwith

D, PRO: F.O., Series 4, Vol. 12, Part II.
　1. This document was enclosed in a letter Beckwith wrote to Lord Grenville, August 26, 1791.
　For the reasons for attributing these remarks to H, see "Conversation with George Beckwith," August 12, 1791.
　2. Jean Baptiste de Ternant, French Minister Plenipotentiary to the United States.

Election to the American Academy of Arts and Sciences

[Cambridge, Massachusetts, August 24, 1791]

To all Persons to whom these Presents shall come,
Greeting.

The American Academy of Arts and Sciences, established by a Law of the Commonwealth of Massachusetts, at a Meeting held the twenty fourth Day of August One Thousand Seven Hundred and Ninety one for the purpose of promoting the design of their institution, elected Alexander Hamilton Secretary of the Treasury of the United States of America a Fellow of their Society, and have granted unto him all the rights and privileges of a Member.

　　　　　　　　And In Testimony thereof, have affixed their
　　　　　　Seal to this certificate and caused the same to
　　　　be duly attested.

John Adams　President
Joseph Willard　Vice Presidt.

Attest }
Eliphalet Pearson } Secretaries
John Clarke }

DS, Hamilton Papers, Library of Congress.

To William Ellery

[*Philadelphia, August 24, 1791*. Ellery endorsed the letter book copy of his letter to Hamilton of August 8, 1791, "Answered Augt. 24th 1791." *Letter not found.*]

To Joshua Wentworth [1]

[*Philadelphia, August 24, 1791*. On September 7, 1791, Wentworth wrote to Hamilton: "I was honored by your's of 24th Ulto." *Letter not found.*]

1. Wentworth was supervisor of the revenue for the District of New Hampshire.

From Joseph Whipple [1]

Portsmouth, New Hampshire, August 24, 1791. "The Revenue Cutter being ready for Sea will proceed on a Cruize immediately; no arms or Military Stores having yet come to hand, I will borrow for the first Cruize Such as may be necessary. The person named for 3rd mate Should have been Samuel *Hobart* instead of Saml Hubert as copied in your letter of the 12th. Ulto. Herewith is inclosed a description of the Cutter received from the Surveyor. She will be accompanied with a Certificate from the Custom House by the Name of the ² till the instrument intended in lieu of a Register with Such Name as you will be pleased to give her Shall be received. I find that notwithstanding my Utmost endeavors to compleat this Vessel within your limitations the cost will exceed them. . . ."

LC, RG 36, Collector of Customs at Portsmouth, Letters Sent, 1791–1792, Vol. 3, National Archives; copy, RG 56, Letters from the Collector at Portsmouth, National Archives.
1. Whipple was collector of customs at Portsmouth.
2. Space left blank in MS. The name *Ferret* was proposed for the vessel. See Whipple to H, September 9, 1791.

To George Biscoe [1]

[*Philadelphia, August 25, 1791.* Letter listed in dealer's catalogue. *Letter not found.*]

LS, sold by Samuel Freeman, May, 1947, Item 502.
1. Biscoe was collector of customs at Nottingham, Maryland.

To George Cabot [1]

[*Philadelphia, August 25, 1791.* On September 6, 1791, Cabot wrote to Hamilton: "Being absent from home when your letter of the 25th ultimo arrived, it has been out of my power to answer the enqueries it contains until this day's post." *Letter not found.*]

1. Cabot, a wealthy merchant from Beverly, Massachusetts, had been elected United States Senator in June, 1791.

To Jedediah Huntington

Treasury Department August 25th 1791

Sir,

I have considered the case you State in your letter of the 22nd July [1] respecting the repairs of a french vessel.

I am of opinion that she will not be entitled to an American register if rebuilt in any manner whereby the identity of the Vessel is preserved. But if she be wholly taken to pieces, I perceive there can be no impropriety in making use of her Timber in the building of a new Vessel.

I am Sir   Your obedt Servant   A Hamilton

Jedh Huntington Esqr
Collr New London

LS, MS Division, New York Public Library.
1. Letter not found.

From Benjamin Lincoln

Boston August 25th: 1791

Sir

Your circular letter [1] came to hand by the last post.

Very particular attention will be paid to the certificates of Registers you mention.

In a few day will be forwarded all the papers due from this office.

Inclosed is a copy of the table of fees set up in this office, an exact copy from the law, which is literally followed here as explained by Messrs: Jones and Harison [2] excepting for the entery of an inward cargo, Coasters, we receive twenty five cents only. This fee we reduced as the coasters, who made many trips in a year, thought it a burden which the profits of their business would not support, and were therefore brought to enter with reluctance. That they should enter was a matter of great importance and be brought to it, if possible without a murmur was a circumstance to be desired. To effect these purposes we were induced to make the reduction.

In no instance has a vessel sailing under an american register arriving in this district been measured & a fee charged. Vessels measured in an other District and afterwards purchased into this have in all cases been measured before a new register has been granted from this district, and the fee taken because it appears by the form of the register that a certificate from the surveyor of the district from which the Register issues should be inserted in the body of it and therefore it has been thought necessary that he should be Satisfied as to the measure before he certifies it to the Collector. He only is answerable for the truth of it And because in many instances he has found, to what cause it is owing he knows not, that a vessel may as well be identified by the cut of her sails as by her papers. Foreign vessels are measured and the fee taken every time they arrive in this district. The surveyor [3] wishes to know whether he is right in these practices or not.

Captain Williams [4] is now I suppose some where in the province of Maine. I found his cruise would be too long for me unless the public good should be made to bend to my convenience. I therefore quitted my intentions of going with him into that country. He received your instructions [5] as he was ready to sail thought it best to take a run into that country as the cutter from New Hampshire is not out.

I am &c

Secretary of the Treasury

LC, Massachusetts Historical Society, Boston; LC, RG 36, Collector of Customs at Boston, Letter Book, 1790–1797, National Archives; copy, RG 36, Collector of Customs at Boston, Letters from the Treasury and Others, 1789–1818, National Archives; two copies, RG 56, Letters from the Collector at Boston, National Archives.

1. "Treasury Department Circular to the Collectors of the Customs," August 5, 1791.
2. See Richard Harison and Samuel Jones to H, November 18, 1789.
3. Thomas Melville (or Melvill).
4. John Foster Williams, captain of the Massachusetts revenue cutter.
5. See "Treasury Department Circular to the Captains of the Revenue Cutters," June 1, 4, 1791.

From Jeremiah Olney

Custom-House,
Providence 25th August 1791.

Sir.

I shall pay particular attention to the directions in your circular Letter of the 5th. instant, relative to the Certificates of registry, &c. of the Sloop Lurana and Schooner Fortitude. From your not noticing the loss of the Certificate of registry No. 56, granted by me the 13th. of December 1790, for the Schooner Nicholas, Wm. Cory first Master, I am led to suppose, that the Note at the bottom of the subsequent Register, Numbered 16, granted in the present year, copy of which was transmitted on the 26th of July last,[1] was not observed: On the 10th of Feby. the name of Thomas Potter, as the then Master, was endorsed on the first Register; he left the Vessel at Newport, where she was detained a considerable Time by the ice; during which Potter went to Sea, and has but very lately returned. She was navigated to this Port by John Holly, who taking the Oath required in such cases, a new Registry was made as the law directs. I think it probable, that on enquiry, which the Owners have promised to make of Capt. Potter, who is now at Newport, that the missing Certificate will be found among his Papers. I will acquaint you with the result of the enquiry.

My Return of outward Tonnage was transmitted on the 28th of July last; [2] but I have had no acknowledgement of its receipt. The other Returns shall be forwarded at the usual period.

In only One particular has there been, in my Office, any deviation from the Instructions in your circular Letter of the 30th of November 1789: In Two or three instances, Fees have been taken for Licences granted for Vessels under Twenty Tons, without adverting to those Instructions, from which a proper attention had been diverted by a more constant recourse to the Law allowing Fifty Cents for *every* Licence. However Sir, tho' the Coasting Fees are extremely inadequate to the Services, I shall not demand that Fee in future. I beg leave here to observe, that the exemption from Entering and Clearing, granted to these small Vessels, properly constitutes them *Licenced Smuglers;* and if it should not be withheld on a revision of the Coasting Act,[3] I am clearly of Opinion that the Revenue will, ere long, suffer more from that quarter than any other whatever.

No Vessels of the United States, registered or enrolled, have ever been remeasured here, except where a change of Property, if from another District, or an alteration in size, if belonging to this, made it essential to grant new Papers; in the former case, the Blanks contemplate a remeasurement, and in the latter, it is certainly necessary; a change of Property *within* the District, without an alteration in size, has never induced a second admeasurement.

I enclose a copy of the Table of Fees set up in my Office.

I have the Honor to be &c.   Jereh. Olney Collr.

To Alexr. Hamilton Esqr.
Secretary of the Treasury.

ADfS, Rhode Island Historical Society, Providence; copy, RG 56, Letters from the Collector at Providence, National Archives.

1. This letter deals with routine Treasury Department matters and has not been printed. Copies may be found in the Rhode Island Historical Society, Providence, and in RG 56, Letters from the Collector at Providence, National Archives.

2. This letter deals with routine Treasury Department matters and has not been printed. Copies may be found in the Rhode Island Historical Society, Providence, and in RG 56, Letters from the Collector at Providence, National Archives.

3. "An Act for Registering and Clearing Vessels, Regulating the Coasting Trade, and for other purposes" (1 *Stat.* 55–65 [September 1, 1789]).

From William Seton

[New York] 25 Augt. 1791

Sir

I have the honor to acknowledge the receipt of your Letters of the 20 [1] & 22d. Agreeable to your desire Mr. William Hill has been paid 4000 Dollars on account of his Clothing Contract & enclosed you have his receipt for the same.

The Transfers of the Stock purchased on account of the United States shall be made in the names you point out. Since my last [2] I have only purchased 6810 $^{30}/_{100}$ Dollars of the deferred debt @ 12/6. The transfers are not all made but will be between this and Monday when I shall transmit a proper return.

I have the honor to be with the greatest respect

LC, Bank of New York, New York City.
  1. Letter not found.
  2. Seton to H, August 18, 1791.

From Wilhem and Jan Willink, Nicholaas and Jacob Van Staphorst, and Nicholas Hubbard

[*Amsterdam, August 25, 1791.* On August 29, 1791, Willink, Van Staphorst, and Hubbard wrote to William Short: [1] "Begging leave to confirm our Respects to you of 25 Instant, We have now the honor to inclose you Triplicate of our Letter of same date to the Secretary of the Treasury of the United-States." *Letter not found.*]

  1. The letter from Willink, Van Staphorst, and Hubbard to Short is quoted in its entirety in Short to H, September 3, 1791, note 1.

From William Ellery

Collector's Office [Newport, Rhode Island]
Augt. 26th 1791

Sir,

Agreeably to my expectation the Sloop Betsy [1] is condemned, and is to be sold on the 14th. day of the next month. I should be happy

to receive your direction with respect to the conduct of the Officers
of the Customs as to the sale of said Sloop, prior to the day of sale;
and it would add to my happiness if at the same time you would give
me your opinion how the monies arising from the sale should be
distributed among the Offrs. of the Customs. The forfeiture of the
Betsy was for a breach of the old Collection Law [2] made at a time
when the Surveyor for North Kingstown [3] had not received his Commission; nor I believe any other Surveyor for this District excepting
the Surveyor for this Port; [4] and there is a difference between the
old and new Collection Law [5] with regard to the manner of distribution. By the old Law the United States are to receive one moiety,
and the other moiety is to be divided into *three* equal parts, and paid
to the Collector Naval Offr. and Surveyor of the *District* wherein
the same shall have been incurred &c.[6] By the new Law the moiety
which falls to the Offrs. is to be divided into equal parts, and paid
to the Collector and Naval Offe. of the District, and Surveyor of the
Port, wherein the same shall have been incurred, or to such of the
sd. Offrs. as there may be in the said District.[7] Has any Offr. a right
to a share of the moiety to be distributed in the present case, beside
the Collr. & Naval Offr., and if any what Surveyor?

    I am Sir   Yr. most obedt. servant   W Ellery Collr

A: Hamilton Secry of Treasy

LC, Newport Historical Society, Newport, Rhode Island.
    1. See Ellery to H, August 2, 23, 1791.
    2. "An Act to regulate the Collection of the Duties imposed by law on the
tonnage of ships or vessels, and on goods, wares and merchandises imported into
the United States" (1 *Stat.* 29–49 [July 31, 1789]).
    3. Daniel Eldridge Updike.
    4. Daniel Lyman.
    5. "An Act to provide more effectually for the collection of the duties imposed
by law on goods, wares and merchandise imported into the United States, and
on the tonnage of ships or vessels" (1 *Stat.* 145–78 [August 4, 1790]).
    6. See Section 38 of this act (1 *Stat.* 48).
    7. See Section 69 of this act (1 *Stat.* 177).

To Thomas Jefferson

Philadelphia
Aug 26. 91

The Secretary of the Treasury presents his respects to the Secretary of State. He returns the draft of Ratification [1] with some alterations to conform more accurately to the fact which are submitted. The Secretary of State will recollect that there is another loan (the contract for which was also forwarded to him) concluded by Messrs. Willinks & Van Staphorsts & of which likewise a Ratification is desired.[2] To possess the Secretary of State fully of the nature of the powers & course of the transactions in both cases, the drafts of the powers as well to the Commissioners as to Mr. Short are sent herewith.[3] When the Secretary of State has done with them he will please to return them.

AL, Thomas Jefferson Papers, Library of Congress.
    1. This was the ratification of the contract for a loan which had been negotiated by Willink, Van Staphorst, and Hubbard in January, 1790, and approved by H in August, 1790. It is dated September 1, 1791 (LC, George Washington Papers, Library of Congress; this document is printed in GW, XXXI, 353–54).
    2. This was the Holland loan of March, 1791, which was negotiated by William Short with Willink, Van Staphorst, and Hubbard. The ratification of it was also issued by the President on September 1, 1791 (LC, George Washington Papers, Library of Congress).
    3. See H to Willink, Van Staphorst, and Hubbard, August 28, 1790, and H to Short, August 29, September 1, 1790.

To Le Roy and Bayard [1]

[Philadelphia, August 26, 1791]

Gentlemen
    Being informed that you are drawing bills, if it is convenient to you to let me have 1000 pounds Sterling at 4 ⅌ Ct above par payable in London on my note at thirty days, including the discount, you may remit that sum by the Packet to John Barker Church Esquire & on notice of its being done my note shall be given accordingly.
    I remain with much consideration & esteem   Gentlemen   Your Obed ser   A Hamilton

Aug 26. 1791
Messrs. Le Roy & Bayard

ALS, Chicago Historical Society.
    1. The New York mercantile firm of Herman Le Roy and William Bayard. At this time the firm, acting for European clients, was engaged in heavy speculation in United States securities.

From Timothy Pickering

Genl. Post Office
Phila. Augt. 26th. 1791.

Sir

I have received and considered your letter of the 23rd instant,[1] proposing that a credit should be given to the Supervisors of the Revenue for the postage of Letters, until their collections should render it convenient to make payment. I shall as you request instruct the Deputy Postmasters, at the places by you enumerated, to open accounts with the respective Supervisors, and to accommodate the time of payments, to their reasonable convenience. To avoid the necessity of multiplying accounts beyond the number mentioned (which is one in each of the fourteen States) I would propose that each Supervisor should write his name on every letter sent to his Deputies (in the manner of franking) with the postage of which he should be charged: the postage of the letters addressed to the supervisors will be charged to them of course. If this arrangement will conform to your wishes, instructions will be given accordingly.

I am Sir &c   T. P.

LC, RG 28, Letter Books, 1789–1794, National Archives.
1. Letter not found.

To James Brown, John Graham, and George Pickett [1]

Treasury Department
Augt 27 1791

Sir

I learn, with real regret, the disappointment you experienced in your intended subscriptions to the Bank of the United States.[2] It was very much my wish that the property in the Stock of that Bank should be generally diffused throughout the States.

But its not having been foreseen, any where, that so rapid a subscription would take place, has been the cause that adequate provisions were not made in the law: [3] which might have been favorable to greater distribution.

I am sorry to be obliged to add that I do not at present perceive any mode by which the object of your letter [4] may be attained.

With great consideration, I am, Gentlemen, Your obed Servant

A Hamilton

Messrs Geo Picket, John Graham & James Brown, Richmond

LS, Hamilton Papers, Library of Congress.
1. Brown, Graham, and Pickett were Richmond businessmen.
2. The bank's stock was oversubscribed on July 4, 1791, the day on which it went on sale.
3. "An Act to incorporate the subscribers to the Bank of the United States" (1 *Stat.* 191–96 [February 25, 1791]).
4. Letter not found.

From Richard Peters [1]

Belmont [2] [Pennsylvania] 27 August 1791

Dear Sir

I send you the best Answer to your Enquiries on the Agricultural Subject I can at present think of.[3]

I thought it best to draw it up in the form of an Account tho' I have filled up the columns you sent me. The manner I have pursued will furnish you with every thing you require, tho' much of it may be useless to you & inapplicable perhaps to your immediate Object. If any thing is deficient inform me & it shall be supplied. You will perceive the miserable state of Agriculture in the part of the Country I live in.

Copy, George Washington Papers, Library of Congress; LC, George Washington Papers, Library of Congress.
1. Both H and Peters sent the President copies of this letter (see *GW*, XXXII, 71–72).
A member of the Board of War during the American Revolution, Peters served in the Continental Congress from 1782 to 1783, the Pennsylvania Assembly from 1787 to 1790, and the Pennsylvania Senate from 1791 to 1792. He was a practical farmer who also conducted many agricultural experiments, wrote papers on farming, and was the first president of the Philadelphia Society for the Promotion of Agriculture. Washington considered Peters "one of the best farmers in the state of Pennsylvania" (*GW*, XXXII, 71).
2. This was the Peters estate. It was located on the west bank of the Schuylkill River about six miles from Philadelphia.
3. Peters's letter was written in reply to "Treasury Department Circular," August 13, 1791.

It is bad enough every where, but the fertility of Soil in Lands recently cleared, or naturally better & readier Access to manure, give Advantages to Farmers more happily seated. The Account will explain the principles I went on & lest my calculations shd. be too conjectural I took four similar Farms I well know, which are situated not too far from each other, but far enough to give a general View of the State of the Country. I consulted the most intelligent of their owners, Men who happen to be the best informed on the Subject of any of my Neighbours. I averaged the actual produce in a year, the best of four years Cultivation in all of them. So that this added to my own experience convinces me that I am not far wrong in any particular. I omitted my own Farm because it far exceeds the produce of others, & tho' my expences are greater they are amply compensated by the difference of product. In all instances double, in many treble & in some quadruple. Yet with all this I find Farming but a bad Trade when Capital is calculated upon. There are few Men of any Talents who cannot employ themselves in any other Business to greater advantage. When I consider the actual profit of a Farm, I am the more astonished at the injustice & folly of those who have burthened the Land with such heavy Impositions. It is true Farmers are never on Velvet, for they pay their share of imperceptible Taxes. Yet these Taxes are also borne by those whose property is latent & cannot therefore be directly touched & the Owners of this kind of property are frequently the greatest Consumers. But it is useless to trouble you with such observations. Nor will it be of service to enter into Speculations, many of which are confirmed by successful Experience, to shew how the Agriculture of this Country may be improved. These Improvements depend not *directly* on Government. *Ultimately* they have no inconsiderable relation to it, but Farmers can only come in for their share of the beneficial Effects flowing from good general Systems. I can truly say that they ought to hope every thing in this View of the Subject & I am happy to be convinced that the Spirit of Improvement is rising rapidly among them. It has been a point of Patriotism with me for many Years past to promote this Spirit, & having set out with moderate Expectations I have not been without some Gratifications.

I am truly   Your Obedt servant   Richard Peters

A Hamilton Esquire

[ENCLOSURE][4]

The farms I have selected keep on an average 16 head horned Cattle, 4 horses, 12 Sheep & 12 Swine.

Dr. Farm

To annual Int: on capital 200 a[cre]s
£ 8 ⅌ acre £ 1600 @ £ 6 ⅌ cent £96. 0. 0

	4 horses at	
	£ 15 each £60. 0. 0	
	8 Cows at	
Stock	£6. do. 48. 0. 0	
and	cart, waggon,	
implements.	ploughs Har- 60. 0. 0	
	rows, geers	
	&c. . . .	
	12 Swine 12. 0. 0	

£180. 0. 0

on the above £180. I only charge
£6 ⅌ ct. 10.16.   £106.16. 0
tho' the annual loss in some articles is
£20 ⅌ Ct. & in none less than £10.
decrease in value by age in Horses &
cattle, accidents, wear & tear, are the
causes. I have made no accot. of annual
Losses by wear of buildings, or accidents to stock.

Annual expenditures besides the personal labour of the farmer & family,
and the produce & cash used for their
support.
one hired man & his maintenance £37.10. 0
Extra wages at hay & harvest, & expences   10. 0. 0
Days hire for occasional business 5. 0. 0
Smith's bill 3. 0. 0

4. LC, George Washington Papers, Library of Congress.

all the hay consumed by the Stock 90. 0. 0
Rye 30 bls. at 4/6 ....   6.15. 0
corn 100 bls. @ 3/. 15. 0. 0
Buckwheat 100 @ 2/6 ....   12.10. 0.
Potatoes 80 bls. @ 1/6 ....   6. 0. 0
Fire wood 20 cords @ 5/. ....   5. 0. 0.
Wheat 15 bls. @ 7/6 rye 5. @ 4/6 ......   6.15. 0.
Potatoes 12 bls. @ 1/6 ....   0.18. 0
Corn & Buckwheat ....   1.10. 0   199.16.

Direct Taxes of various descriptions
have in some years been £20. now
perhaps—but these are lessening   15.

                                                        £321.12. 0.

Contra

By 130 bls. wheat a 7/6. ....   £ 48.15. 0
   50 rye   @ 4/6 ....   11. 5. 0.
   180 corn   @ 3/. ....   27. 0. 0.
   30 Oats   @ 2/6 ....   3.15. 0
   175 buckwheat @ 2/6 ....   21.17. 6
   100 potatoes   @ 1/6 ....   7.10. 0.
   Roots & other vegetables in the garden .....   6. 0. 0.
   2 Cattle raised annually ....   4. 0. 0.
   Wool of 12. Sheep 36 lbs @ 2/. ....   3.12. 0.
   Pork 1400 @ 3 d. 17.10. 0
   Poultry in value 3. 0. 0
   Hay 30 tons @ £3 ....   90. 0. 0

Dairy 8 Cows
   6 Calves sold @ 20/. each ....   £ 6. 0. 0.
   (memo.—I allow 2 Calves raised).
   Butter 832 @ 1/3 ....   52. 0. 0.
   Cheese 100 @ 6d. ....   2.10. 0.   60.10. 0.
As to offal, milk &c. except a small part
for the family, it is consumed by the

calves & pigs, & accounted for in their
value.

Flax 150 lbs @ 7d.	£ 4. 7. 6.		
deduct ½ for breaking &c.	2. 3. 9.		
	£ 2. 3. 9.		
4 Bls. of seed @ 5/. ⎱ to be added ⎰	1. 0. 0.		3. 3. 9.
			£316.18. 3.
			4.13. 9.
Balce. agt. farmer			£321.12. 0.

N B. about 8 bushls. wheat pr. acre is a full allowance for the better
kind of Farms in these parts. Some do not yield 6., and 8 out of 10
do not come up to 8 bushls. per acre. The farms I have selected sow
from 15 to 20 a[cre]s. winter Grain. The average of actual crops is
however less than 8 bushls. to the acre.

From William Ellery

Collectors Office [Newport, Rhode Island]
Augt. 29th 1791

Sir,

I wrote a letter to you by the Post, last Friday,[1] because I wished
to receive as early an information on the subjects mentioned in it as
might be convenient.

I am informed that the situation and circumstances of Thomas
Cotterell late owner of the Sloop Betsy [2] are such that if the prosecutions to which he is liable should be commenced against him, and be
successful he and his family would be utterly ruined. Not long after
he had transgressed the Law, he sold said Sloop for six hundred Dollars, and the purchaser has since laid out upon her between two and
three hundred Dollars, which Cotterell must repay. He must also pay
for the detention of the vessel, and a bill of a cost arising from the
trial of the Libell against her amounting to about one hundred and
fifty dollars. The intention of the Law, in inflicting fines, penalties
and forfeitures in the violation of Law will, I think, by the seizure
and condemnation of the Sloop Betsy be fully answered with regard

to Cotterell, and it will restrain others, if there should be others, disposed to perpetrate like offences. I would therefore submit it to your better judgment whether prosecutions against him may not be suspended for the present.

I forgot to mention in my letter of the 23d: of this month, that the Ushers [3] submitted judgment, and their Council said that their causes would be carried up to the Circuit Court by writ of Error, to gain time that an application might again be made to you to mitigate the penalties they have incurred.

I have received your circular Letter of the 5th. of this month, and shall carefully attend to the several matters contained in it.

I have not deviated in any instance from the instruction communicated in your circular Letter of the 30th. of Nov. 1789, unless the taking of ninety cents for the Licenses of vessels under twenty tons should be considered as such, and this was done for the reasons which I assigned in my letter of the 12th of July 1790,[4] and because I found that such fees were taken in the District of Boston and Charlestown.

In this District a practice has obtained of measuring vessels of the United States previously registered, and of charging for such admeasurement; but only where there has been a transfer of property of the vessel from citizens of another District to Citizens of this, and the Vessel has been in this District at the time of Registry; and the remeasurement in such cases has been thought proper for the reasons suggested in my letter of the 23d. of this month, and has not excited any dissatisfaction here. Permit me to be more explicit by adding to the reasons suggested in that letter that Sec. 8 of the Act for Registering and clearing vessels &c expressly requires the Surveyor previous to the registering or granting of *any* Certife. of Registry &c. to deliver a true account in writing of the built &c of every vessel *to the person authorized to make such Registry and grant such Certificate thereof:* [5] and the form of the Certife. of Regy. expresses that _____ *Surveyor of this District* having certified *to Us* &c. Where no Certificate under the hand of a Surveyor of a port or District has been delivered to the Collector of a District in which a subsequent Register made, would it not be improper to issue a Certife. of Regy. expressing that the Surveyor of another District had certified *to Us* what he had not certified. Must not defacements by erasements and interlineations take place in subseqt. Certifs. of Regy. if new admeasurements should not be made, and would there be any check upon tonnaging? Perhaps the paragraph referred to doth not extend to admeasurements in the cases mentioned. There may have been admeasurements in Districts where vessels may have happened to come.

Inclosed is a copy of the table of fees set up in my office, No Offr. of the Customs is more desirous than I am, that Uniformity may take place with regard to fees, and all proceedings in the Custom Houses of the United States.

This letter is accompanied by a weekly return of monies received and paid, By a List of eight bank notes of the bank of N. York amg. to eight hundred dollars, one moiety of which is now transmitted to the Treasr.[6]

I am, Sir, yr. most obedt. servant   Wm Ellery Collr

A Hamilton Esqr
Secry of Treasy

LC, Newport Historical Society, Newport, Rhode Island.
    1. See Ellery to H, August 26, 1791.
    2. See Ellery to H, August 2, 23, 26, 1791.
    3. See also Ellery to H, February 15, 1791.
    4. This letter had not been found when Volume VII of *The Papers of Alexander Hamilton* was published. It has since been located and reads in part as follows: "I have read over the circular letter which contains the opinion of the eminent lawyers, and altho' I submit to their opinion, yet I do not think that part of it altogether unobjectionable which respects the exemption of Vessels under twenty tons from paying fees for their licences. The reason they assign is because the fee provided for *Licences to trade* appears to be appropriated to the particular description of licences, specified in the 23d. sect. &c. By the 31st. Sect. of the Coasting Act, it is enacted that for every licence to trade between the different districts of the United States, or to carry on the bank or Whale Fishery, for one year fifty cents are to be paid. Now if Licensed Vessels under Twenty tons may trade between the difft. districts of the United States, or carry on the bank or whale fisheries, as I conceive they may, it would seem to me that a fee for their licences is demandable. Perhaps I may view this matter through the medium of interest; but the fee for licences doth not appear to me to be appropriated fairly to Vessels whose licenses are attended with enrollments or registers, and I cannot conceive that it was the intention of the Legislature of the United States that its servants should do something for nothing. I could have wished that the fees for every service had been precisely ascertained; for nothing ought to be left to discretion where interest is concerned" (LC, Newport Historical Society).
    5. "An Act for Registering and Clearing Vessels, Regulating the Coasting Trade, and for other purposes" (1 *Stat.* 57 [September 1, 1789]).
    6. Ellery endorsed the letter book copy of this letter "Answered." H's reply has not been found.

From William Hall

New York 29th Augt. 1791

Sir

Mr. Mort [1] & myself have examin'd the Delaware as high as Pequest [2] about 94 miles above Philadelphia & have found several good situations. On the Raritan there are none. Our Money running short oblig'd us to come to New York for a supply. We propose going up the Pasaic in a few Days, after which you shall receive a report of our observations.

I call'd on Mr. Marshall and deliver'd your Letter.[3] He answered very freely every question I put to him. He seems to understand the theory of the Business but I am very doubtful if He is much acquainted with the practice. The Modells He is making will not work & I much fear some money will be expended and delays ensue on that acct. Mr. Mort I expect will be in Philadelphia in 6 or 8 days. To him I beg leave to refer you for particulars. He was present during the conversation but did not see the Modells. Mr. Marshall might have made the Modells to have worket much easier than larger Machines.

I have the honor to be   Sir   Your most obed. Servt.

William Hall

No. 57 Maiden Lane

ALS, Hamilton Papers, Library of Congress.
  1. Hall and Joseph Mort had been sent by H to look for sites for the factory of the Society for Establishing Useful Manufactures.
  2. The Pequest was a river in New Jersey which emptied into the Delaware River.
  3. Letter not found, but see Thomas Marshall to H, July 19, 1791, and July 24–31, 1791.

From Nathan Keais [1]

Washington [North Carolina] August 29, 1791. "Inclosed is a Copy of John Braggs & Stephen Tinkers Bond, taken in Consequence of a Contract for Staking out the Channel of news River [2] leading to New Bern. I have also Contracted with John Payne for Staking out the Channel leading to Edenton for Fifty dollars. . . ."

ALS, RG 26, Lighthouse Letters Received, Vol. "A," Pennsylvania and Southern States, National Archives.

1. Keais was collector of customs at Washington, North Carolina.
2. Neuse River.

From William Seton [1]

[New York] 29th Augt. 1791

Sir

I have the honor to enclose a Return of the Stock I have purchased on account of the United States to this day inclusive,[2] being 13291 8/100 of 3 ℔ Cents & 173708 88/100 Deferred, amounting to Dollars 116542 69/100 which Sum has been ⟨received⟩ from this Bank. I expect in a day or two to compleat the whole investiture of 150,000 Dollars.

I have the honor to be with the greatest respect   Sir &c

LC, Bank of New York, New York City.
1. For background to this letter, see H to Seton, August 15, 1791; H to the President and Directors of the Bank of New York, August 16, 1791; Seton to H, August 18, 1791.
2. This return is printed in *ASP, Finance*, I, 117.

From William Skinner

United States Loan Office, [Hillsboro] North Carolina August 29th. 1791.

Sir

I have heretofore at different times [1] taken the liberty of communicating to you the desire this State had of subscribing to the Loan for the Certificates in the Treasury and Comptroller's offices, and that attempts had been made for that purpose, in behalf of the State, That not answering their wish, That another attempt had been made to subscribe for them in the name of the Comptroller,[2] this much I believe I have heretofore communicated to you;

Wishing your particular directions respecting that business; None such having as yet come to hand,[3] I take the Liberty of observing further that I have sufficient reasons to believe, a third attempt is intended, and indeed in part has been accomplished. A young man, a stranger whom I did not suspect,[4] on the 20th. Curt. became a Subscriber on my Books for 22,415. dolls. 10 Cents, for which he obtained a rect. in the name of a Merchant at Fayetteville; [5] Since that the same young man came forward a second time with Certificates to a larger amount; Previous to his coming in I had reasons to believe a Deception had been made use of. I observed to the young man my suspicions, and wished to be satisfyd. whether the Certificates by him handed in were not the Pubs: he evaded giving me any satisfactory answer, the Business rests here, the young man has no rect. for the last Deposit nor have I suffered him to Subscribe. I shall keep him off until the close of the Subscription in expectations of your directions. I wish I might be ordered to administer an Oath, to suspected persons, which if it should not come to hand before the close of the Subscription, it might be complyd. with before issuing the Certificates on Interest. I expect the young man to come forward a third time (hourly). At present there dont appear to be a probability of the Loans being filld, in this State, as the whole Sum subscribed at this day amounts to only 991.600 Dollars & 90 Cents.

The Governor of this State [6] since taking the advice of Council has observed to me, that he had [been] misinformed; that New York has not Subscribed to the Loan but to the Bank.[7]

I am most respectfully   Your most obedient Servant   W Skinner

The Honble Alexander Hamilton Esqr

Copy, North Carolina Department of Archives and History, Raleigh. This letter was enclosed in H's "Report to the Governor of North Carolina," July 31, 1794.
  1. See the two letters Skinner wrote to H on July 22, 1791, and Skinner to H, August 11, 1791.
  2. Francis Child.
  3. See H to Skinner, August 12, 1791.
  4. Duncan McRae.
  5. Duncan MacAuslan.
  6. Alexander Martin.
  7. See enclosure to the second letter that Skinner wrote to H on July 22, 1791.

From Henry Wynkoop [1]

Bucks Coty Pennsylva. 29. Augt. 91.

Dear Sir,
Your Letter of the 13 instant,[2] I received this day week ago. I have

LC, George Washington Papers, Library of Congress.
  1. Wynkoop had served in the Continental Congress from 1783 to 1789 and was a member of the House of Representatives from Pennsylvania from 1789 to March 3, 1791.
  2. See "Treasury Department Circular," August 13, 1791.

endeavoured to comply with your request in the best manner I was capable, yet not altogether in the way you mentioned. The novelty of the subject—and never having kept any regular account of the annual produce of my lands—nor knowing any person to whom I could apply for such minute information, made it necessary for me to consider the different objects—and taking to my assistance an itelligent neighbouring farmer without letting him into the object of my pursuit, we together have formed an Estimate of what may be supposed the average annual product of the different articles raised on the Lands here, as you will perceive by the paper herewith transmitted, have added some articles not mentioned by you, and omitted what may be consumed by the family who occupy the farm, not doubting but in that particular you must be much more competent to judge than I am, have therefore only mentioned what I suppose the average number of persons on a two hundred acre farm. Altho' I have not filled the columns in the form you sent me, yet am in hopes you will be able to extract the necessary information & reduce it into such form as will be most convenient for your purpose. Happy in an opportunity afforded me, at least to endeavour to serve you, & anxious for the success of every measure which may tend to promote the general interests of our Country.

I am &c. &c.   Henry Wynkoop.

[ENCLOSURE] [3]

Bucks County Pennsylvania.

Quantity.	Two hundred acres being nearly the average quantity
200 acres.	of the Farms in this quarter, have taken that as the most
value	convenient portion from which to form the required
3.200 Ds.	Estimates.
Arable land	The arable Land divided into five fields of twenty
125 acres.	five acres each, makes in the whole 125 Acres.
Pasture	The course of cropping pursued here requiring three
50 acres	fields to be under tillage—two of course will be left for
	pasture, which make 50 acres.

3. LC, George Washington Papers, Library of Congress.

Orchard &c.   Orchard, Garden, House & barn yards, lanes &c. sup-
10 ac.   posed to occupy *ten* acres.

Meadow   The natural meadows in this part of the country being
15 acres.   few—yet as every farmer finds means for alloting some
portion of his land for that use, suppose the nearest
average 15 acres.

Woodland   Timber being an article indispensably necessary for
50 acres.   fuel, fencing, building &c. have allowed fifty acres for
that use.

Wheat   One of the aforesaid fields is alloted in rotation for
200 bushls.   wheat & rye, suppose twenty thereof to be sown with
90 Cents   wheat, will yield, communibus annis, ten bushels per
180 dolls.   acre—for altho' in seasons, on well improved grounds
twenty, thirty and even thirty five bushels may be produced from the acre—yet from the many casualties to
which land tillage is exposed, so that in some seasons the
best improved grounds may not produce even five
bushels, have from my own observation, and that of an
intelligent neighbouring farmer, taken the above as the
nearest supposed medium—making two hundred bushels, which at 90 cents pr. bushl. is 180 Dollars.

Rye   Rye likewise ten bushels to the acre, the remainder
50 bushels   of the field being five acres will yield fifty bushels,
@ 60 cents.   which at 60 cts. pr. bush: makes 30 dollars. N.B. the
30 dolls.   field on which the wheat & rye is sowed, is generally also put in with grass, and lays for pasture two
years.

Corn   One field is generally alloted to Indian corn & Buck-
300 bushs.   wheat in the same proportion with wheat & Rye. The
40 cents   twenty acres of Corn will average fifteen bushels pr.
120 dols.   acre making in the whole 300 bushels at 40 cts. ℔ bush:
is 120 dolls.

Buckwheat   This Grain is so precarious in it's growth that it is ex-
75 bushs.   tremely difficult to form an estimate of its general prod-
30 cents   uce; but suppose 15 bushs. pr. acre, which from five
22½ dols.   acres, being the remainder of that field occupied by the
Corn, will be seventy five bushels, valued at thirty cents
pr bushl. is 22 dollars 50 cents.

Barley.

So little of this Grain is raised here, that I did not think it worth notice.

Oats
100 bushs.
@ 20 cents
is 20 dolls.

By the course of cropping commonly used here, this Grain is sowed, for the sake of ease & convenience to the Farmer, upon some part of the fallow intended for wheat, to which it generally proves injurious—therefore is not largely propagated—have only allotted five acres which will average twenty bushels ℔ acre—making in the whole one hundred bushls. at 20 cents pr. bushl. is 20 dollars.

Flax &
Seed.
30 dolls.

This is also generally raised on part of the fallow—suppose two—which on an average may yield two hundred and fifty pounds of swingled Flax, & twelve bushels of Seed, which both together may be worth 30 dolls.

apples &
cyder
30 dolls.

Every Farm has more or less of orcharding. Eight acres allowed for that use—the product whereof in apples & cyder cannot be worth less than thirty Dollars.

Hay
20 tons
@ 6. dols.
each.
120 Ds.

Altho' fifteen acres only are allotted for meadow, which probably on an average will not yield more than that number of tons, yet as the farmers by sowing grass seed on their arable land, improved with dung, plaister of Paris &c., annually mow more or less of those, I have allowed 20 tons, worth 6 dollars each—120 Dollars.

Cattle
annual
product
70 Dolls.

I suppose a Farm of two hundred acres will on an average support twelve head of cattle. Of those I suppose five milch cows, which will each yield per annum one Calf; two of them to be raised and three fatted, the latter worth 6 dollars. Five milch cows will produce fifteen pounds butter pr. month each, for seven months which makes in the whole 525 lb. at nine cents pr. pound—is 47. Dollars & 25 cents. Five months allowed for their being farrow, or fatting the Calves. Two calves annually raised, affords opportunity for disposing of that number of Cattle annually, either in Beef or milch Cows, which being worth 16 dollars each, makes 32 dollars: making in the whole 79 dollars 25 cents. Deduct for accidents &c. 9 Dollars 25 Cents—leaves an annual product of 70 Dollars.

Horses.

☞

Whatever these may produce must be considered as included in the general product of the Farm, for the cultivation of which they are made—by the propagation of this animal—unless it be in the more interior parts of the country where no market can be procured for Grain &ca.

Sheep
annual
product
28. dolls.

Twenty store-sheep may be conveniently kept on a 200 acre farm. Their wool will average forty pounds per year, worth 23 Cents per pound, which makes 10 Dollars. Their increase in Lambs twelve—this number being to be disposed of annually either in Lamb, or fatted Mutton—they may be worth 1⅓ dollars each—makes 18 Dollars. Thus the whole annual product on Sheep will be 28 Dollars.

Hogs
annual
product
80 Dollars

Ten Hogs may be considered as the average number raised annually on a two hundred acre farm—weighing 200 lb. nett each; making 2000 lb., @ 4 cents per pound. The value of the annual product will be 80 Dollars.

Poultry
ann. prot.
10. Ds.

Suppose on an average ten dozen may be raised, worth one Dollar per Doz: their product will be Ten Dollars.

Wood
consumd.
in fuel
25 Cords.

Allowing one Kitchen fire which burns, more or less, the whole year; and one other fire during the winter, for the convenience of the Family, I suppose the two fires will consume twenty five cords.

Consumed by Cattle, Horses, Sheep, Hogs and Poultry—Indian Corn 200 bushels. Rye 25 do—Buckwheat 40 do.—Potatoes 75. do.—Hay 20 Tons.

The family consumption may be estimated by what will support nine persons vizt. the man, his Wife & three Children, one man hired by the year, one bound boy & Girl, the extra hiring of hands in harvest, & Hay making, spinsters, Visitors &ca equal to the maintenance of one person more during the year.

Tax paid annually for defraying the expences of the Country, supporting the poor & repairing the Roads, will average about 8 Dollars.

From William Short

Paris Aug. 30. 1791.

Sir

I make use of this conveyance by the English packet merely to announce to you that the bankers at Amsterdam have in consequence of my letters to them [1] had a loan contracted for in behalf of the U.S. for six millions of guilders.[2] The celerity with which it was taken up, as they inform me, shews the continuance of the high ground on which the credit of the U.S. stands at that place.

The bankers inform me that, agreeably to my desire, they announced this loan to you [3] immediately on its being contracted for. It will be considered as a double loan & appropriated as directed in your letter of the 24th. of May.

Having an opportunity by the way of Havre to-morrow I defer till then the details respecting the commission on this loan as contained in a letter of the bankers to me of the 25th. inst.[4]

I have the honor to be, Sir, your most obedient servant   W: Short

The Honble.
Alexander Hamilton Secretary of the Treasury—Philadelphia.

ALS, letterpress copy, William Short Papers, Library of Congress.

1. Short to Willink, Van Staphorst, and Hubbard, July 29, August 11, 12, 14, 1791 (ALS, letterpress copies, William Short Papers, Library of Congress). See also Short to H, August 8, 23, 1791.

2. On August 22, 1791, Willink, Van Staphorst, and Hubbard wrote to Short: "We have adopted the necessary Measures, to secure Success to a Loan of Six Million of Guilders for the United States at Five per Cent Interest per Annum, to be dated the first of the ensuing Month; the Completion Whereof We hope to announce to you next Post, on communicating you the further Particulars" (LS, Short Family Papers, Library of Congress).

3. Letter not found.

4. See Willink, Van Staphorst, and Hubbard to Short, August 25, 1791, enclosed in Short to H, August 31, 1791.

From Thomas Jefferson

[Philadelphia, August 31, 1791]

Th: Jefferson presents his respectful compliments to the Secretary of the Treasury and incloses him the proposed letter to the Minister of France,[1] in which however he shall be glad to make any modifications of expression to accomodate it more perfectly to the ideas of the Secretary of the Treasury. It will be necessary to shew it in it's ultimate form to the President before it be sent.

Aug. 31. 1791.

AL, letterpress copy, Thomas Jefferson Papers, Library of Congress; copy, Thomas Jefferson Papers, Library of Congress.

1. Jean Baptiste de Ternant. The draft of this letter reads as follows: "I have communicated to the President what passed between us the other day on the subject of the payments made to France by the United States in the assignats of that country since they have lost the par with gold and silver; and after conferences by his instruction with the Secretary of the Treasury, I am authorized to inform you that the government have no idea of paying their debt in a depreciated medium, and that they will take measures for making these payments in their just value, avoiding all benefit from depreciation, and desiring on their part to be guarded against any unjust loss from the circumstance of mere exchange" (*JCHW*, IV, 240).

To Thomas Jefferson

[Philadelphia, August 31, 1791]

Mr. Hamilton presents his compliments to the Secretary of State. He would think the turn of expression on the whole safer, if instead of what follows the words "depreciated medium"[1] the following was substituted—"and that in the final liquidation of the payments, which shall have been made, due regard will be had for an equitable allowance for the circumstance of depreciation."[2]

JCHW, IV, 240.

1. For the draft of the letter discussed by H, see Jefferson to H, August 31, 1791, note 1.

2. Jefferson accepted H's recommendation in the letter which was sent to Jean Baptiste de Ternant, dated September 1, 1791 (ALS, letterpress copy, Thomas Jefferson Papers, Library of Congress.)

To Tobias Lear

[Philadelphia, August 31, 1791]

Dr. Sir

The only person definitively concluded upon by the President, is Philip Thomas, as Inspector of the revenue for Survey No. 2, in the District of Maryland, comprehending the counties of Alleghany, Washington, Frederick, & Montgomery.

It is his intention also to appoint Mr. Morris,[1] the now 3d. mate of the Cutter at N.Y., to the Office of first mate, Mr. Boudenot[2] having written me a letter of resignation;[3] but, as he has not yet sent in his commission, the execution is suspended.

Mr. Carrington[4] wishes that a duplicate commission for Colo. Marshall[5] of Kentuckey may be forwarded through him, for fear of accident. I did not mention this to the President, but I believe it will be right to do it. Will you take the President's directon?

Yours wth great regard   A. Hamilton

August 31st. 91.

Be so good as to deliver the papers herewith to the President.

LC, George Washington Papers, Library of Congress.
  1. Richard Valentine Morris.
  2. Elias Boudinot.
  3. Letter not found.
  4. Edward Carrington, supervisor of the revenue for Virginia.
  5. Thomas Marshall, inspector of Survey No. 7, Kentucky.

From Benjamin Lincoln

Boston Aust 31 1791

Sir

When I reported to you[1] that I had contracted for the Cutter to be built in this State I mentioned that she was to be compleated fit for the sea that is with riging sails boats &c for 1440 dollars. After Captain Williams[2] was appointed master he suggested to me his wishes that there might be some deviation from the plan I had given and on which the agreement was founded. On this I wrote to the builders that they might gratify the wishes of Captain Williams but that they must always bear it on their minds that they must not as they regarded their own interest do any thing to augment the expence for no additional allowance could be made them. Notwithstanding this caution they attended so far to the request of Captain Williams as to increase the size of the vessel about seven tons besides she is orniminted with a handsom head, quarter badges and a considerable carved work about her stern. By building a larger vessel it not only increased the expence of the hull but also of the riging. After the vessel was finished the builders wished me to see their accounts. I told them as I could not make any allowance it would not be of any importance and therefore declined examining them. I understood however that the vessel cost them about two thousand & fifty dollars (six hundred more than the contract). As I could not make them any allowance for their extra expences, they wished to build an other vessel smaller and receive this back when the second should be finished & delivered. I did not feel my Self authorized to close with them on their proposition. I think notwithstanding that It will be for the interest of the United States to do it. This vessel is really too heavy for the number of hands assigned her. A vessel of the size I first mentioned of about 58 tons would in my opinion be much better than the one we now have all circumstances considered. She would be big enough to answer every purpose and the expences of repairs much smaller. If the builders should build a smaller one they will, I think, build her at the rate of 1440 dollars for 63 tons & $^{63}\!/_{95}$. This will reduce the expences and bring them nearer to your wishes.

On receiving directions to compleat the light house at Portland I employed for this purpose the same Gentlemen who had been appointed by this state to inspect the building of it in the first instance. The business being compleated I called for a settlement of their accounts. They have given them in & have charged to the United States the whole expence of the whole Light house and given credit for the sum they received in pay from this common wealth from which there is a large ballance due to them. I do not feel my self authorized to settle this account as stated. I do not consider the U. S. chargable with any expences prior to the Cession of the light house. The trustees are not satisfied with this decision. If I am wrong your suggestion of it will lead at once to close their accounts as stated. If right, your confirmation will end the dispute.

You mention in yours of the 20 inst the importance of prosecuting the receiver of run goods. How will this do after we have been obliged to use them as witnesses in a cause?

Here with you will receive my accounts for the last quarter, the exportation return is making out, and also my weekly return.

Secretary of the Treasury

LC, Massachusetts Historical Society, Boston; LC, RG 36, Collector of Customs at Boston, Letter Book, 1790–1797, National Archives; two copies, RG 56, Letters from the Collector at Boston, National Archives.
1. See Lincoln to H, July 23, 1791.
2. John Foster Williams, captain of the Massachusetts revenue cutter.

From William Short

Paris August. 31. 1791

Sir

I had the honor of announcing to you yesterday by the way of the English packet the loan contracted for at Amsterdam for six millions of florins.[1] I thought it best to give you the details of what has happened with respect to the charges & commission by this conveyance which is a person going to embark at Havre.

My several letters will have informed you of the several attempts I made to bring the bankers to undertake the loan at a rate of commission lower than the last.[2] As I was unable to persuade them by arguments drawn from the interests of the U.S. I endeavoured to prevail on them by considerations of their own advantage & therefore making use of the authority given me in your late letters [3] of repeating the loans, I agreed they should extend it to six millions, as they had asked to do; provided they would reduce the commission ½. p. cent—adding that if they refused this they must confine the loan to three millions only. It was possible that apprehending the U.S. might

AL, letterpress copy, William Short Papers, Library of Congress.
1. A copy of the contract for this loan may be found in RG 59, Records Relating to Foreign Accounts, 1782–1797, Letters, Accounts, and Contracts, National Archives.
2. See Short to H, July 19, 26, August 8, 23, 1791.
3. See H to Short, April 13, May 9, 24, 1791.

find other means of liquidating their debt to France through those who they knew wished to speculate in it, they might consider it more advantageous to make a loan of six millions at 3½. p. cent commission, than one of three at four p. cent. This was the only means left me of attempting to reduce them & I intended as I mentioned to you, that if they continued to refuse the reduction, then to authorize the extension of the loan to six millions, as I was persuaded at that time that it was the most advantageous measure that could be adopted for the U.S.

The bankers however, making use of their knowlege of the present situation of the U.S. & the advantages they derive from monies borrowed at Amsterdam, counting from past experience on the approbation of government, & supporting the measure by reasons of a local & momentary nature which they observe were necessarily unknown to me, have made this loan for six millions of florins & insist absolutely on the commission of four p. cent for the whole, notwithstanding the express condition of the contrary in the authority I gave them.

They have written me a voluminous letter [4] to prove their right to this commission in consequence of their agreement as mentioned in their letter to you of Dec. 23. 90.[5] approved & forwarded by me & also to shew that their present conduct cannot fail to be applauded. I do not send you a copy of this letter on account of its immense length & because I am persuaded they will have forwarded it to you as it contains all the reasons they could collect for their approbation.[6]

It is dated the 25th. of August & came to my hands by the last post so that I have not yet answered it. They assert that they acquired a right to insist on 4. p. cent commission on all future 5. p. cent loans & produce the clause of their letter of Dec. 23 to you, & my forwarding it as evidence of this right. My letter to you of Jan. 15. will explain that circumstance & shew that I did not suppose myself authorized to make any contract for any other loan than the one immediately undertaken. I even had the clause of their letter changed & forwarded it in the form you received it (as mentioned in my letter to you of Jan.

4. Willink, Van Staphorst, and Hubbard to Short, August 25, 1791. See enclosure.

5. Letter not found, but see extract quoted in the enclosure.

6. If the letter of August 25, 1791, from Willink, Van Staphorst, and Hubbard to Short was sent to H, no copy has been found among his papers. Since the contents of this letter are of importance in understanding the remaining portion of Short's letter, it has been printed below as an enclosure.

18.) [7] because what they told me was their reason for inserting it was to shew that they had not engaged to accept 4. p. cent commission on loans at a lower rate of interest. I made the less difficulty in forwarding their letter in the corrected form because as was understood necessarily between us every future loan was to be an object of future discussion & the more so as I could not know whether I should be employed to negotiate them. I own however I had no idea at that time of the commission's being reduced as it appeared to me certain that the profits of those employed were reduced as low as the usage of that place could admit of. Still I thought it useful to leave the subject open, that the U.S. might take such advantages as experience or their improved situation might give them & proper, that if any other person should succeed me in this business he might have the free exercise of his exertions for serving the U.S. in attempting to reduce the charges. Besides, a permanent engagement for the rate of commission wd. have been impolitic as it would have been binding on government & not on the commissioners, & of course never would have been consented to by me under any circumstance & particularly when I did not know how long I should continue to negotiate these loans for the U.S.

All the right which they claim therefore under their letter of the 23d. of Dec. I consider as groundless & their conduct in thus extending the loan contrary to the authorization contained in my letters, as by no means justifiable.

The reasons which they give for thus precipitating the loan as derived from local circumstances unknown to me, & which they say would have removed all their doubts of being approved if those mentioned above had left any, are 1. that the Province of Holland is to bring a loan immediately on the market for eight or ten millions of guilders for the service of the East India company & that it was therefore necessary to contract previously with the undertakers. 2. that it is now certain a tax is to be laid of 1. p. cent on all loans negotiated in Holland by foreign powers & that it will probably commence about the beginning of the next year, & of course it was to be desired to commence this loan immediately so as to make another before the new tax takes place. 3. that experience has shewn that a loan for six millions can be filled in nearly the same time as one of half of that sum.

7. Short evidently meant to refer to his letter of January 15, 1791.

These considerations add to my former persuasion that it is much for the advantage of the U.S. to push their loans at present, on the terms of the last [8] as to charges, if they cannot be reduced (the probability of success in London not being yet so established as to authorize the abandoning the resources of Amsterdam) [9] yet they will not prevent me from still endeavouring to bring the bankers as to the present loan to the conditions proposed in my letters.[10] I fear much however they are too fully masters of our situation to consent to the reduction, being fully persuaded the wants of government would prevent their disapproving a loan otherwise agreeable, on account of ½ p. cent commission. They will certainly have taken their precautions with the undertakers in the case of my accepting the loan only for three millions, or if they have recieved or should recieve the money they would pay it to the French government probably counting on your approbation, which they would see you in the impossibility of refusing under those circumstances.

Thus it would be imprudent for me to reject altogether the latter three millions of this loan; besides that would prevent me from announcing to you at present the sums at your disposal, since if the loan were three millions only, 1½. would be the part you destine for your service at home & if the whole six millions are accepted it will be 2½. And farther as matters stand at present, the question whether it is for the interest of the U.S. to accept the whole of this loan on the terms proposed, if they cannot be reduced, leaving no doubt I have thought it best to announce to you that you may consider 2½. millions of florins at your disposal as soon as you shall recieve this information, & without informing the bankers of this endeavour, by all the means in my power to bring them to the conditions of my letters, finally assenting to those they insist on, if they persevere. In the mean time the cash as recieved by them will be immediately paid to this government that there may be no double interest. I will inform you regularly of the progress of this business.

The bonds for this loan will be the same as those for the last, the conditions of re-imbursement &c. being the same. I shall go to Am-

8. For a description of the terms of this loan, see Short to H, February 17, 1791.
9. See Short to H, August 23, 1791.
10. Short to Willink, Van Staphorst, and Hubbard, July 29, August 11, 12, 14, 1791 (ALS, letterpress copies, William Short Papers, Library of Congress).

sterdam to sign them. The bankers recommend it to me to go there
towards the end of this year for that purpose as they observe that by
then signing the bonds for a new Loan, the tax may be avoided. I
shall defer my journey until I know fully what may be hoped for in
London or Genoa [11] as our proceedings in Amsterdam will of course
be directed by the prospects elsewhere. The undertakers have until
the end of January to complete their engagements, being obliged
however to pay an equal proportion of the sums they have contracted
for, in each month. The bankers are persuaded that they will for their
own advantage anticipate the epochs agreed on.

I omitted mentioning to you in my letter of the 23d. inst. that the
f 350,000 balance in the hands of the bankers had been paid to this
government under your order for extending the payments out of the
last loan, to 1½. million of florins [12]—this payment in addition to the
f 1,000,000 already paid out of the same loan making f 1,350,000. I
formerly mentioned to you the amount in livres of that million of
florins.[13] The f 350,000 produced agreeably to the exchange agreed
on with the commissaries of the treasury 941,175 ℔. 9s.

I have the honor to be with sentiments of the most perfect ⟨respect⟩

The Honble.
Alexander Hamilton Secretary of the Treasury, Philadelphia

[E N C L O S U R E]

Wilhem and Jan Willink, Nicholaas and Jacob Van Staphorst, and
Nicholas Hubbard to William Short [14]

Amsterdam 25 August 1791

Sir

We had the pleasure to address you the 22nd. Inst.[15] and now come
to reply particularly to your respected favors of 12 & 14 [16] ditto.

We must confess to you Sir, that your sticking to reduce the
Charges We fixed with you for the Five per Cent Loans of the United-
States, after We had placed them upon the very lowest footing, is

11. See Short to H, August 23, 1791.   12. See H to Short, April 13, 1791.
13. See Short to H, July 19, 1791.
14. LS, Short Family Papers, Library of Congress.
15. LS, Short Family Papers, Library of Congress.
16. ALS, letterpress copies, William Short Papers, Library of Congress.

truly surprizing to us, more especially as It is striving to recede from a Bargain already agreed between us, and approved by the Secretary of the Treasury of the United-States, as well as militating against the Mode ever practised here, in agreeing for the Charges in this Line of Business by the Lump; From which We informed you personally and You knew thro' the Communication of our Letters to the Treasury, It ought not to be expected We should depart.

To demonstrate the Truth of these Assertions, and thereby to convince you, that our Charges of Four per Cent for all Expences on the Five per Cent Loans, are already fixed, and independant of any Change in the Premium We may pay to the Undertakers, We beg leave to refer you to this Part of our Letter of 23 Decbr last to the Secretary of the Treasury,[17]

"Mr. Short informed us It was expected also, He should be able to fix more advantageous Conditions for the Charges of the future Loans, and notwithstanding We assured him the last Loan [18] at Four and an half per Cent for Commission, Premiums, Brokerage and all other Expences was as reasonable as It ought to be, as well as much cheaper than Russia and the other Powers of Europe paid, He stuck to this Point, with a Perseverance We must confess not to have a little surprized us: But considering the Relation We already have with the United-States, and the Injury any Application to others, would certainly have caused to their Credit and Interests, We consented to negotiate the future Five per Cent Loans, at Four per Cent, for Commission, Premiums, Brokerage & all other Charges, thereby offering a most unequivocal Testimony of the Value We set upon our Connexion with the United-States, and our Desire to satisfy and accommodate their Government all in our Power. Mr. Short having assented to the Offer authorised us &c."

The aforesaid Letter We delivered open to you—Sir, inclosed in One directed to yourself, with this Request, "We take the liberty to inclose you open, our Letter of this Date to the Secretary of the Treasury of the United-States, entreating you to peruse same, and approving the Contents to forward it." [19] The bare Inspection of this our Letter of 23 Decbr to the Secretary of the Treasury, wherein We tell him, You had consented to allow us Four per Cent, for Charges

17. Letter not found.
18. For a description of this loan, see H to Willink, Van Staphorst, and Hubbard, November 29, 1790, note 1.
19. LS, Short Family Papers, Library of Congress.

of Negotiation on the Five per Cent Loans, and your full Approbation in forwarding it without any remark, much less reclamation,
establishing most incontrovertibly, that the Charges of Four per Cent
were fixed for all the future Loans at Five Per Cent Interest; We shall
now proceed a Step further, and wave for a Moment only, our Right
to decline entering into any disenssion upon (the premium) an abstract Part of a general & compound Arrangement, moulded by our
Agreement with you into a single Result, by evidencing in an equally
strong Light, that this Agreement was however as well by you as ourselves, concluded upon the Basis, that the premium upon the American Loans would be more than 1½ per Cent; Which We do by a
Reference to our Letter of the 1 March last [20] to the secretary of the
Treasury, that was approved of by you here in all its Parts; We
therein merely satisfy the Secretary of the Treasury (as He confesses)
of the Mode of conducting and closing the Business of Loans here,
dissected the Charges upon the last Loan of March as follows

"You'll thereby see, that after deducting

  2 pr. Cent Premium
  ½ ⅌ Ct. Brokerage
  ½ ⅌ Ct. for Seals, Notary's Signatures, Charges &c. Adver-
       tisements, Papers for the Bonds and other incidental
       Expences, there remains but
  1 " " for our commission
  _____
  4 Per Cent that We fixed with Mr. Short to do the Business for:
  _____

We at that time calculated to give but 1½ per Cent Premium to the
Undertakers, But when It was question of only a Sacrifice of our Interest, to accelerate Mr. Short's Wish to open the Loan immediately,
We did not balance a Moment to make it, by allowing Two per Cent
premium, the least We could obtain the Money for."

In the aforegoing Instance, We to hasten the Accomplishment of
your Wishes, by giving up One half per Cent in the Premium, reduced
the Compensation for each of our Houses, below the Basis upon which
was calculated the Agreement between You and Us, and even to
what is paid for Brokerage only; An Allowance too disproportionate
in every respect, the Brokers having but very little Trouble and none

20. Letter not found.

of our great risques & responsibility, to be just in any degree, and much less to be rendered permanent, thro' your endeavors to establish our Resignation and Surrender of our Rights in one Instance, to be a Precedent for our being stripped of them in future Transactions, notwithstanding they are guaranteed to us by express Agreement.

Being most fully persuaded, that the aforegoing Eclaircissements, are more than abundantly sufficient, to convey irresistible Conviction to your Mind, of our being incontestably entitled to four per Cent Charged on the future Five per Cent Loans for the United States, and thus removing all Objections to extending the Loan You order us to open; We have presented it for Six Millions of Guilders at Five per Cent per Annum Interest, to be dated the First Day of September next, and reimbursable in Five Instalments of f 1,200,000—.— each, commencing the First Day of September 1802 and ending the First Day of September 1806. Which Loans by means of our preparatory Measures, has been immediately undertaken with all the Eclat You can wish, and has exhibited a new Proof of the Degree which the Credit of the United-States has attained here, to the great Satisfaction of their Friends, and Astonishment of some Persons, To whom the Prosperity and rising Power of the United-States, are by no means pleasing prospects.

Had We entertained any the least Particle of Doubt, of this our Conduct, meeting your hearty Approbation and securing us your Thanks, It would have been removed by the following Reflexion, The most important of which You could not know, and the others perhaps You were not perfectly acquainted with.

Before the Fifth Day of next Month, a Loan will be determined upon, to be raised by the Province of Holland for the Service of our East-India Company, to the large Amount of Eight or Ten Million of Guilders; To precede which was essentially necessary for the Success of the Loan for the United-States, and there every Moment was precious, to conclude the Bargain with the Undertakers.

It is now reduced to a Certainty, that One of the new Taxes to be laid upon this Country, and that will it is presumed take place about the Commencement of the ensuing Year, is a Duty of One per Cent upon the principal of all Loans that will be raised here for Foreign Powers, A very heavy Incumbrance; to spare which as much as possible for the United-States, demanded every exertion, to bring as soon as could eligibly be effected, the greatest Amount of Loans for the United-States upon our Market that might be practicable, especially as exclusive of the Honor and Advantage, of reimbursing at once all the Arrears of Interest and Reimbursment of the Instalments due upon the principal of their Debt to France; The United-States are subject to no useless Interest, as the Payments can be made to the National-Treasury of that Country as fast as We receive the Monies.

Experience has demonstrated by the last Loan of March, that It will be possible to launch a new Loan upon the Market for the United-States, as soon or very nearly so after the present Loan for Six Millions, as if We had confined it to half that Sum; Wherefore as the Credit of the United-States justifies our entertaining the hope, to have it in our Power to raise another Loan for them, towards the end of the present or Commencement of the New Year, We may flatter ourselves, that by arranging your Journey, so as to remain here about that Period, You may at same time as You sign the Bonds for the Loan of next Month, pass those for another Loan, so as to save the new Duty upon that also; An Economy much more essential and important than a triffling Difference upon our Charges.

Besides Sir, We have taken into consideration, What probably has not yet attracted your Attention, that the Time is now fast drawing near, when the United-States will have to reimburse the Instalments of the first Loan [21] they borrowed here, and that those will gradually become consequential.

Thus, the United-States having to provide here for

The Reimbursment of the Arrears of Interest & Instalments due on the principal of the French Debt.

The Payment by anticipation of the Instalments of ditto not yet due, to avail the United-States of the actual unprecedented favorable Exchange.

The large Sums annually to be paid here, for Interest upon the Loans raised in Holland, and which the Secretary of the Treasury, has given us a standing Order to discharge from the Monies in our hands.[22]

The Reimbursments of the Instalments upon the Dutch Loans as they fall due.

21. For a description of the Holland loan of 1782, see Willink, Van Staphorst, and Hubbard to H, January 25, 1790, note 3.
22. H to Willink, Van Staphorst, and Hubbard, June 30, 1791.

And It being highly probable, the Secretary will wish to provide for all these Objects by Loans here, until the full Organisation & complete Operation of the Bank of the United-States, and until the produce of the Taxes already laid or that yet are to be laid, to face the Civil List, Interest upon the Domestic-Debt, Interest upon the State-Debts assumed & other Objects of Expenditure of the United-States, shall yield a Surplus, to be remitted here to the Discharge of their Foreign Engagements; We cannot but judge, You will be deeply impressed as We are, with the propriety nay the absolute Necessity, of letting slip no Opportunity, to raise Monies for the United-States, to secure the punctual Fulfilment of all these Objects, since the Reimbursments to France, can be made to such immense Advantage to the United-States, without subjecting them to any useless Interest; And consequently fully approve our Zeal & Exertions to promote their Interests, and to facilitate the Plans of the Secretary of the Treasury; Who has in the most flattering Terms, sanctioned the whole of our Conduct in the Management of the Affairs of the United-States, and done Justice to our Moderation, in fixing the Conditions with you, for negotiating the future Five per Cent Loans.

The Bonds of the Six Millions Loan will be dated the First of next Month; But It would not have been possible to deviate from the constant practice here, of leaving to the Underwriters the faculty to receive them immediately after their signing a Contract or whenever they please, with the Enjoyment of the running Month's Interest as customary, that is, They benefit of the Interest upon the Months they take their Bonds in, and thus pay no more for them the last Day of the Month than they would have done the first Day; The reason, Why by far the major Part nay almost the whole Receipts of Monies, are on the very last Days of Months; Thus, by allowing Interest only from the First Day of September, We should have postponed the Opening of the Loan and Receipts of Money as for whole Month, without any good purpose whatever; But on the contrary, We should thereby have subjected the United-States, to a longer risque for profiting of the favorable French Exchange, and protracted for a Month, the Opening of a fresh Loan for the United-States, Which might have precluded the possibility to effect it, timely to save the Duty upon Foreign Loans. The Undertakers are allowed until the last Day of next January to receive their Bonds in, an equal Portion however in each Month. But You may depend Most of the Capital ones, will avail themselves of their priviledge to furnish their Monies as soon as they choose, to call for large Parcels of them early, and thus that our Receipts of Money will be important in the first Months: We even do not doubt, We shall have a good Sum the Commencement of next Month at your Disposal, About which We shall therefore expect your immediate Orders. At present the Exchange at Paris is more favorable for the United-States than at this place: Perhaps You may be able to fix with the Commissioners of the Treasury, the Course as at Paris, at which the United-States shall have credit, for our Payments to Messrs. Hogguer Grand & Cy.[23] Or, if You prefer leaving the Settlement of this Point to us, or that We should make Remittances for the Monies, You may depend upon our utmost Attention, to fulfill your directions, to the greatest advantage of the United-States.

By a Vessel on the point of sailing for New-York and likewise by way of England, We communicate to the Secretary of the Treasury as You desire, the Success and particulars of this Loan, at our Charges fixed with you and approved of by him, for the future Five per Cent Loans.[24]

Your draft on us advised in your Letter of 18 August for f 220—.— order Grand & Co: [25] for your Salary, will meet usual punctual Honor.

We are respectfully   Sir   Your most obedient and very humble Servants   Wilhem & Jan Willink
                                   N & J. Van Staphorst & Hubbard
Willm. Short Esqr.

23. Hogguer, Grand, and Company was acting as agent for the French government in Holland.
24. Letter not found.
25. Ferdinand Le Grand and Company, French bankers.

To George Washington

[Philadelphia, August 31, 1791]

The Secretary of the Treasury has the honor to transmit herewith to the President of the United States the result of the enquiry on the subject of Mr. Drayton.[1]

August 31.

LC, George Washington Papers, Library of Congress.
1. H may have misdated this letter to Washington or it was misdated by the

copyist, for "the result of the enquiry on the subject of Mr. Drayton" may be found in Oliver Wolcott, Jr., to H, September 1, 1791.

Stephen Drayton, who had served as deputy quartermaster general of the Southern Department during the American Revolution, wished to be appointed naval officer of Charleston, South Carolina.

From Tench Coxe

[Philadelphia, August, 1791]

The account of the Chinese trade [1] is in many respects similar to information and conformable to experience I have had. I do not observe any thing contrary to what I have heard from authority. The accot. of the East India trade is minute so far as it goes, and gives some useful information. The increase of the consumption of the finer kinds of Teas deserves notice. The quantity of Specie (at 2 to 3 Millions of Dollars) sent from England is very small considering their Trade.[2] 17,000 Tons, even as we load our Vessels, would require 7½ Millions of dollars, and the English take little Bohea Tea, & much raw silk and wrought silks, musk, drugs, &c which are valuable. The first cost of their China imports must be 9 or 10, Millions of Dollars. Their exports in European goods to China are not great. Bills must form a great part of their remittances, which bills arise out of the proceeds of the cotton and other articles taken thither by the Country Ships. The cotton Voyage deserves the Attention of our Merchants.

The subject of Ginseng, as usual is not satisfactorily explained. None of our Gentn. appear to understand the various uses to which it is applied, nor the extent of the consumption. I am satisfied an inspection of this article to take place early would be very useful. It ought not to be by a state law as it would only deprive of the trade that port which should be within the enacting State.

The Idea of a representation, concerning the frauds and impositions of the Chinese, to the emperor would deserve attention, were there not danger of its making things worse. Could it be general, it would be best, as no one Nation would be able to avail itself of the offence which might be given by the Measure.

The respectable proportion of the American Tonnage compared with any foreign nation, but the British is striking. It was equally so the following year as will appear by a paper in my hands.

If the papers [3] are to be retd. some of them should be copied first—particularly the English instructions.

AL, Hamilton Papers, Library of Congress.
1. See Thomas Randall to H, August 14, 1791.
2. One of the extracts which Randall enclosed in his letter to H stated that the East India Company sent £544,000 to Canton to pay its bills in 1788 or 1789.
3. This is a reference to the enclosures in Randall to H, August 14, 1791.

From Henry Guest [1]

[New] Brunswick [New] Jersey, August, 1791. Urges Hamilton to establish at New Brunswick "the public Manufactory" of the Society for Establishing Useful Manufactures.

ALS, Hamilton Papers, Library of Congress.
1. Guest, who had originally been a tanner by trade, was one of New Brunswick's leading businessmen.

Prospectus of the Society for Establishing Useful Manufactures [1]

[Philadelphia, August, 1791]

The establishment of Manufactures in the United States when maturely considered will be fo⟨und⟩ [2] to be of the highest importance to their prosperity. It ⟨is⟩ an almost self evident proposition that that com⟨muni⟩ty which can most completely supply its own w⟨ants⟩ is in a state of the highest political perfection. ⟨And⟩ both theory and experience conspire to prove that a nation (unless from a very peculiar

D, with insertions in writing of H, The Passaic County Historical Society, Lambert Castle, Paterson, New Jersey; copy, Hamilton Papers, Library of Congress; [Philadelphia] *Gazette of the United States,* September 10, 1791. The prospectus was also printed in a number of newspapers; for example, see the *Federal Gazette and Philadelphia Daily Advertiser,* September 5, 1791; [Philadelphia] *Dunlap's American Daily Advertiser,* September 7, 1791; *The* [Philadelphia] *General Advertiser,* September 7, 1791; *The* [Boston] *Argus,* September 23, 27, 1791.
1. Although no MS of this document in H's handwriting has been found, this prospectus has generally been attributed to him (Davis, *Essays,* I, 356; Cole, *Industrial and Commercial Correspondence,* 191). For an estimate of the view that Tench Coxe wrote all or part of this prospectus, see Davis, *Essays,* I, 349–57.
2. All the material within broken brackets in this document has been taken from the copy in the Hamilton Papers, Library of Congress.

coincidence of circumstances) cannot possess much *active* wealth but as the result of extensive manufactures.

While also it is manifest that the interest of the community is deeply concerned in the progress of this species of Industry, there is ⟨as⟩ little room to doubt that the interest of individuals may equally be promoted by the pursuit of it. What ⟨is⟩ there to hinder the profitable prosecution of manufact⟨ures⟩ in this Country, when it is notorious, that, independent of impositions for the benefit of the revenue and for the encouragement of domestic enterprise—the natural commercial charges of the greater part of th⟨ose⟩ which are brought from Europe amount to from fiftee⟨n to⟩ thirty per Cent—and when it is equally notorious that provisions and various kinds of raw materials are ev⟨en⟩ cheaper here than in the Country from which our principal supplies come?

The dearness of labour and the want of Capital are the two great objections to the success of manufactures in the United States.

The first objection ceases to be formidable when it is recollected how prodigiously the proportion of manual labour in a variety of manufactures has been decreased by the late improvements in the construction and application of Machines—and when it is also considered to what an extent women and even children in the populous parts of the Country may be rendered auxiliary to undertakings of this nature. It is also to be taken into calculation that emigrants may be engaged on reasonable terms in countries where labour is cheap, and brought over to the United States.

The last objection disappears in the eye of those who are aware how much may be done by a proper application of the public Debt. Here is the resource which has been hitherto wanted. And while a direction of it to this object may be made a mean of public prosperity and an instrument of profit to adventurers in the enterprise, it, at the same time, affords a prospect of an enhancement of the value of the debt; by giving it a new and additional employment and utility.

It is evident that various fabrics, under every supposed disadvantage, are in a very promising train. And that the success has not been still more considerable may be traced to very obvious causes.

Scarcely any has been undertaken upon a scale sufficiently extensive or with a due degree of system. To insure success it is desireable

to be able to enter into competition with foreign fabrics in three particulars—quality, price, term of credit. To the first, workmen of
equal skill is an essential ingredient. The means employed have not
generally been adequate to the purpose of procuring them from
abroad and those who have been procureable at home have for the
most part been of an inferior class. To cheapness of price, a capital
equal to the purpose of making all necessary advances, and procuring
materials on the best te⟨rms⟩ is an indispensible requisite—and to the
giving of ⟨Credit⟩ a Capital capable of affording a surplus beyond
wh⟨at⟩ is required for carrying on the business is not less indispensible. But most undertakings hitherto have been bottomed on very
slender resources.

To remedy this defect an association of the Capitals of a number
of Individuals is an obvious expedient—and the species of Capital
which cons⟨ists of⟩ the public Stock is susceptible of dispositions
which will render it adequate to the end. There is good reason to expect that as far as shall be found necessary money on reasonable terms
may be procured abroad upon an hypothecation of the Stock. It is
presumeable that public Banks would not refuse their aid in the same
way to a solid institution of so great public utility. The pecuniary
aid even of Government though not to be counted upon, ought not
wholly to be despaired of. And when the Stock shall have attained its
due value so that no loss will attend the sale all such aids may be dispensed with. The Stock may then be turned into specie without disadvantage whenever specie is called for.

But it is easy to see that upon a good Capital in Stock an effective
Credit may be raised in various ways which will answer every purpose
in specie, independent of the direct expedient of borrowing.

To effect the desired association an incorporation of the adventurers must be contemplated as a mean necessary to their security.
This can doubtless be obtained. There is scarcely a state which could
be insensible to the advantage of being the scene of such an undertaking. But there are reasons which strongly recommend the state of
New Jersey for the purpose. It is thickly populated—provisions are
there abundant and cheap. The state having scarcely any external
commerce and no waste lands to be peopled can feel the impulse of no
supposed interest hostile to the advancement of manufactures. Its situation seems to insure a constant friendly disposition.

The great and preliminary desideratum then is to form a sufficient capital. This it is conceived, ought not to be less than Five hundred thousand Dollars. Towards forming this capital subscriptions ought immediately to be set on foot; upon this condition that no subscriber shall be bound to pay until an Act of Incorporation shall have been obtained—for which application may be made as soon as the sums subscribed shall amount to One hundred thousand Dollars.

As soon as it is evident that a proper Capital can be formed means ought to be taken to procure from Europe skilful workmen and such machines and implements as cannot be had here in sufficient perfection. To this the existing crisis of the affairs of certain parts of Europe appears to be particularly favourable. It will not be necessary that all the requisite workmen should be brought from thence. One in the nature of a *foreman* for each branch may in some branches suffice. In others it may be requisite to go further and have one for each subdivision. But numbers of workmen of secondary merit may be found in the United States; and others may be quickly formed.

It is conceived that there would be a moral certainty of success in manufactories of the following articles—

   1st   Paper and Pasteboard

   2nd   Paper hangings

   3rd   Sail cloth and other coarse linen cloths, such as sheetings, shirtings, diaper, oznaburgs &ca.

   4th   The printing of Cottons and linens; and as incident to this but on a smaller scale the manufacturing of the article to be printed.

   5th   Womens shoes of all kinds.

   6th   Thread, Cotton and Worsted Stockings.

   7th   Pottery and Earthen Ware.

   8th   Chip Hats

   9th   Ribbands & Tapes

  10th   Carpets

  11th   Blankets

  12th   Brass and Iron wire.

  13th   Thread and Fringes.

It will be unnecessary to enter into the det⟨ails⟩ of the execution further than to observe that the employment of the labor-saving mills and machines is particularly contemplated.

In addition to the foregoing a brewery for the supply of the manufacturers, as a primary object, may be thought of.

When application shall be made for an act of Incorporation it ought to include a request that provision may be made for incorporating the Inhabitants of the district within a certain defined limit which shall be chosen by the Company as the principal seat of their factories and a further request that the Company may have permission to institute a lottery or lotteries in each year for the term of five years for a sum or sums not exceeding in one year One hundred thousand dollars. The State of Jersey if duly sensible of its interest in the measure will not refuse encouragements of this nature.

An incorporation of this sort will be of great importance to the police of the establishment. It may also be found eligible to vest a part of the funds of the Company in the purchase of ground on which to erect necessary buildings &c. A part of this ground divided into town lots may be afterwards a source of profit to the Company.

The lottery will answer two purposes. It will give a temporary command of Money and the profit arising from it will go towards indemnifying for first unproductive efforts.

The following scheme for the organisation of the Company will probably be an eligible one—

1. The Capital of the Company as before remarked to consist of Five hundred thousand dollars, to be divided into Five thousand Shares, each share being One hundred Dollars, [The Company nevertheless to be at liberty to extend their capital to one Million of Dollars.] [3]

2. Any person Copartnership or body politic may subscribe for as many shares as he she or they may think fit. The sums subscribed to be payable—One half in the *funded* six per Cent Stock, or in three per Cent Stock at two dollars for one, and the other half in deferred Stock. The payments to be in four equal parts. The first at the time of subscription,[4] the second in six months after, the third in six months after the second, and the fourth in six months after the third. Those who prefer paying in Specie to be permitted to do so, computing the funded six per Centum at par, and the deferred according to its pres-

---

3. The bracketed words in this sentence are in H's handwriting.
4. In the Library of Congress copy and in the *Gazette of the United States* "subscription" has been changed to "incorporation."

ent value at the time of payment discounting the interest thereupon during the suspension of payment at the rate of Six per Centum per annum.

3rd.   The affairs of the Company to be under the management of thirteen Directors to be chosen annually on the first Monday of October in each year by plurality of suffrages of the Stockholders. The Directors by plurality of voices to choose from among themselves a Governor and Deputy Governor.

4th.   The number of votes to which each Stockholder shall be intitled, shall be in proportion to the number of shares he shall hold that is to say one vote for each share. But neither the United States nor any State which may beco⟨me⟩ a Subscriber shall be entitled to more than One hundred votes. The United States or any State nevertheless, which may subscribe for not less than One hundred Shares may appoint a Commissioner who shall have a right at all times to inspect the proceedings of the Company and the state of its affairs but without any authority to controul. Every Subscriber may vote by Attorney duly constituted.

5th.   There shall be a stated meeting of the Directors on every first monday of January, April, July and October at the place which is the principal seat of the Manufactory. But the Governor for the time being or any three Directors may by writing under his or their hands, directed to the other Directors and left at their respective places of abode at least fourteen days prior to the day for Meeting, or by advertisement in one public Gazette printed in the State where the Corporation shall be established and in another public Gazette printed in the City of Philadelphia, and in another public Gazette printed in the City of New York for the space of thirty days prior to the time of Meeting convene a special meeting of Directors, for the purpose of transacting business of the company.

6th   No Director shall receive any emolument unless the same shall have been allowed by the Stockholders at a General meeting. But the Directors may appoint such Officers and with such compensations as they shall think fit.

7th   Not less than seven Directors, if the Governor or Deputy Governor be not one shall constitute a Board for the transaction of business. But if the Governor or Deputy Governor be one four shall suffice. In case it should at any time happen that there are two separate meetings of five or more Directors each, but both less than a majority of the whole, one having the Governor, and the other the Deputy Governor, that at which the Governor shall be present shall be the legal one.

8th.   The Directors to have power to make all Bye-laws, rules and regulations requisite for conducting the affairs of the Company.

9th   At every annual Meeting of the Stockholders for the purpose of choosing Directors the Directors shall lay before them a general state of the affairs of the Company exhibiting the amount of its Stock, Debts and Credits, the different kinds of Manufactures carried on, the number of persons employed in each and their respective compensations together with an account of profit and loss.

10th.   [The persons not exceeding five in number who at any general meeting shall have next after the Directors chosen the highest number of votes for Directors shall by force thereof be a committee of Inspection and shall have a right of access to all the books of the Company and of examination into all its affairs, and shall at each succeeding meeting report all such authentic facts as shall come to their knowlege to the Stockholders for their information.] The Stockholders may [also] [5] if they think fit at any general meeting appoint by plurality of suffrages any five of their number for the purpose of making such inquiries and investigations as they may think necessary.

11th.   The Stockholders at a General meeting may annul or alter any of the Regulations established by the Directors and make such others as they may think necessary.

12th.   Any Board of Directors or either of the Committees abovementioned may at any time call a general meeting of Stockholders; giving thirty days previous notice thereof in three Gazettes, one published in the state in which the Factory shall be established another in the City of Philadelphia and another in the City of New York.

13th.   Every Cashier or Treasurer of the Corporation shall before he enters upon the duties of his Office give Bond with one or more sureties to the satisfaction of the Directors for the faithful execution of his duty in a sum not less than Twenty thousand Dollars.

14th.   So much of the Capital Stock of the Company as may consist of public Debts shall be placed on the Books of the Treasury of the

5. The brackets around "also" and the preceding sentence were inserted by H. In the margin opposite this section H wrote "omitted."

United States in the name of the Corporation; and every Stockholder shall be entitled to a license under the Seal of the Corporation to inspect the account of the said Stock at his pleasure as far as may comport with the rules of the Treasury. This however shall not prevent the investment of the said Debt in Stock of the Bank of the United States, reserving to each Stockholder the like right of Inspection in relation to the Stock of the Company so invested.

15th   There shall be a yearly dividend of [so much of] [6] the profits of the Company [as the Directors shall think proper] for the first five years, and after that period a half yearly dividend.

16th   The Stock of the Corporation shall be assignable and transferable according to such rules as shall be instituted in that behalf by its laws & Ordinances.

17th.   The Corporation shall be at liberty to make and vend all such Articles as shall not be prohibited by law: Provided that it shall only trade in such articles as itself shall manufacture in whole or part or in such as shall be received in payment or exchange therefor. Provided nevertheless that this shall not prevent the investment of any sums paid in specie in Stock of the United States or in Bank Stock.[7]

18.   It shall be understood that a Majority of the Stockholders may at any time dissolve the Corporation; but this shall only be done at a general meeting which shall have been specially summoned for the purpose with public notice of the intent. And upon such dissolution the Directors for the time being shall be ipso facto trustees for settling all the affairs of the Corporation disposing of its effects paying its debts and dividing the surplus among the Stockholders in proportion to their respective interests in the Stock; [unless the Stockholders at a General Meeting previous to such dissolution shall have nominated other persons as trustees; in which case those persons shall be trustees for the purposes aforesaid.] [8]

19.   The Stock and other property of the Corporation to be exempt from Taxes.

6. The bracketed words in this sentence are in H's handwriting and are not included in the Library of Congress copy or in the *Gazette of the United States*.

7. This sentence is in H's handwriting. It is not included in the Library of Congress copy or in the *Gazette of the United States*.

8. The bracketed words in this sentence are in H's handwriting and are not included in the Library of Congress copy. The wording varies in the *Gazette of the United States*.

The management of the Affairs of this Company will require that an Agent should be appointe⟨d⟩ to Superintend all the different works and the disposition of the Articles manufactured in conformity to the general regulations of the Directors. This Agent ought to have such a compensation as will command the services of a man every way competent and trustworthy. Such a man may doubtless be found. It is not necessary that he should be a technical man in any of the branches of manufacture; but a man of information, thoroughly a man of business, of probity, and diligence and energy.

We [9] the Subscribers for ourselves respectively and not one for the other and for our respective heirs, executors and administrators do severally covenant promise and agree to and with each other and with the heirs Executors and Administrators of each other that we will respectively contribute and pay in the manner and at the times specified in the plan hereunto annexed the respective sums against our respective names hereunder set for the purpose of establishing a company for carrying on the business of manufactures in one of the States of New York New Jersey and Pennsylvania (giving a preference to New Jersey if an incorporation can be obtained from the said State on advantageous terms) according to the general principles of the plan aforesaid, but subject to such alterations as shall be agreed upon at any time previous to the obtaining an Act of Incorporation either in the principles or details thereof by the major part of us whose names are hereunto subscribed, or in the details thereof only, as shall be thought fit by the major part of the persons hereinafter named. And we do hereby jointly and severally constitute and appoint   [10] one and each of our Attorneys who or the major part of them or the major part of the survivors of them are hereby empowered as soon as the sum of One hundred thousand Dollars shall be subscribed hereto to make application on our behalf to either of the States aforesaid (giving such preference as aforesaid to the State of New Jersey) for an Act or Acts of Incorporation according to the principles of the plan aforesaid with such alterations in the details

9. The remainder of this document has been taken from the copy in the Hamilton Papers, Library of Congress.

10. Space left blank in MS. In the *Gazette of the United States* the following names have been inserted at this point: Elias Boudinot, Nicholas Low, William Constable, William Duer, Philip Livingston, Blair McClenachan, Matthew McConnell, and Herman Le Roy.

thereof as shall appear to them eligible, or with such alterations whatsoever, as shall be previously agreed upon by us; And further to take
such measures at our joint expense as shall appear to them necessary
and proper for engaging workmen in the several branches of manufacture mentioned in the said plan.

In testimony whereof We have hereunto subscribed and set our
hands and seals, the   day of   [11] in the year of our Lord One
thousand seven hundred and ninety One.

11. These two spaces were left blank in MS.

From Nathaniel Appleton

[*Boston, September 1, 1791.* On September 27, 1791, Hamilton
wrote to Appleton: "You observe in your letter of the first instant."
Letter not found.]

To Theodore Foster

Philadelphia, 1 Sept., 1791.

Dear Sir:

I have had the pleasure of receiving your two letters of the 23rd
July & 4th of August.[1] You concluded rightly that it could require
no apology for entering into the detail with which you have favored
me. On a subject so interesting to your State, your desire to communicate information was indulged with peculiar propriety, & on any subject I shall always esteem myself obliged by your sentiments. Thoroughly impressed with the hardship of a decision against the certificates which had been surrendered to the State by their Proprietors, I
did not come to it without a serious struggle between my Judgment &
my Wishes; but after mature deliberation I saw no way of allowing
those Certificates to be received on the proposed loan which would
not involve inextricable embarrassment. All the States have called in
large portions of their respective Debts.

There is good reason to believe, that on a close investigation Rhode
Island might not be found to be the only State in which they had
been so called in for a very inadequate consideration. And tho' it
might be urged to distinguish the case, that Rhode Island alone com-

pelled the surrender, on pain of forfeiture, it might be answered that in sound equity, there is no very material distinction between obliging Persons to surrender their property for less than its value, under the penalty of confiscation and laying them under a necessity of doing the same thing, from the total and deliberate neglect of a better provision. Be this as it may, I saw no safe rule, that would be admitted to be such by even the candid part of those, whose interest it might be to dispute it, by which I could pronounce that Certificates surrendered and cancelled *by the Mutual Acts* of the Creditor and Debtor should be permitted to receive and acquire validity in respect to one State and not in respect to another. And without such rule, all the extinguished portions of the Debts of all the States might, if they should think proper to make it so, acquire a capacity of being subscribed towards the assumption. Where this would lead it is not necessary to say. The two Carolinas have actually passed laws for subscribing the portions of their respective Debts which have been extinguished by them [2]—the only answer I can give is that a Bond surrendered as discharged constitutes *no Debt* and that in every such case, there is no Debt to be assumed.

I cannot allow an after act of a State [3] to create a Debt within the meaning of the funding Act,[4] which it cannot be admitted to have contemplated as then in existence. It may be asked, How then shall the Certificates which remained in the hands of Individuals, but which were forfeited by the law of the State, be admitted upon the Loan, any more than those which were surrendered? This is a question not wholly free from difficulty; but if I had found no distinction satisfactory to my own mind, I should have been obliged to reject the whole. Such a distinction, however, was in my opinion to be found. Upon principle, it is a general rule, that the dissolution of a contract by one party without the concurrence of the other, is void.

The Creditors who did not concur may claim the benefit of that rule and it is to be supposed that it was the intention of Congress, they should have it. It may be said to be a legal presumption that Congress, at the time of passing the funding Act, was acquainted with the laws of Rhode Island respecting the Certificates. And in point of fact the generality of them were so at least in substance. They must, therefore, have been apprised, that if the forfeiture annexed in those laws to the not bringing in the certificates for payment was to prevail, there was no debt of the State of Rhode Island to be assumed. By assuming a Sum of 200,000 Dollars, a sum by the way nearly corresponding with the amount of the outstanding Certificates, the clear inference is that they meant to consider those Certificates as in force, and the forfeiture as far as regarded the assumption, as inoperative. But it is not a reasonable presumption, that they could have intended to comprise the surrendered Certificates, which could not even be repossessed by the individual proprietors without a subsequent act of the State.

I have made some suggestions in this letter, which I should perhaps have omitted if I had considered it as strictly official, and therefore request that it may be received as a private and in some sort a confidential communication.

I cannot lose the opportunity of expressing to you that I feel myself truly and very much indebted to the Senators of Rhode Island for the very flattering manner in which they have made mention of the Secretary of the Treasury in their late communication to the State.[5]

The measure of their approbation certainly exceeds that of his services or pretentions.

With respectful consideration and real regard, I have the honor to be   Dear Sir   Your obedient Servant.

HCLW, X, 220–23.

1. Letters not found.

2. On February 19, 1791, the South Carolina legislature had passed "An Act for loaning to the United States, a sum of the Indents of this State under certain Limitations therein mentioned" (*State of South Carolina. At a General Assembly, begun and holden at Columbia, on Monday the third day of January, in the year of our Lord one thousand seven hundred and ninety-one, and from thence continued by divers adjournments, to the fourteenth day of February, in the same year, and in the fifteenth year of the Independence of the United States* [n.p., n.d.], 72–74). See also William Skinner to H, July 22, 1791. For an account of the actions of the North Carolina legislature in this matter, see H to Skinner, August 12, 1791.

3. In June, 1791, the Rhode Island legislature passed "An Act relative to certain securities heretofore granted by this state, and for repealing certain acts of the legislature of this state hereinafter mentioned." It reads in part as follows:

"Whereas, during the war between the United States of America and the kingdom of Great Britain, this state (from its eminently exposed situation, and its great exertions in support of the war,) for the common defence, in raising and keeping up its quota of troops, in the federal army, and from the long continued depredations of the enemy . . . was subjected to the unavoidable necessity of incurring great and heavy charges, whereby the debt of the state was greatly accumulated, insomuch that after the close of the war it became impracticable for the state, in the then scarcity of specie, to discharge the same in the usual mode by taxes in specie.

"And whereas, to facilitate the payment and discharge of the said securities, paper-bills of credit were issued pursuant to an act of the legislature of said state, passed at their session in May, A.D. 1786, which the holders and proprietors of the said securities were required to receive from time to time, in payment and discharge thereof, on the penalty of forfeiting the same, and many of the said holders and owners of the said securities in compliance with the said several acts of the legislature before mentioned, received the said paper bills of credit for their said securities, or part thereof, when the same had greatly depreciated. . . . And whereas, at the second session of the Congress of the United States . . . by . . . 'An Act making provision for the debts of the United States,' it was provided that certain descriptions of the debts of the several states therein mentioned, within the purview and meaning whereof are the greatest part of the beforementioned securities, required to be discharged by the said paper bills of credit of this state as aforesaid, and the sum of two hundred thousand specie dollars was by the said act of Congress assumed, to be paid by the United States, as part of the debt of this state, required by the acts of the legislature of this state to be paid by the said paper money bills as aforesaid, which said bills having gradually depreciated to the discount of fifteen for one, compared with gold and silver coin, at which rate they are finally to be discharged, agreeable to an act passed by the legislature of this state in October, in the year of our Lord 1789, so that without the interposition of this General Assembly very great and manifest injustice will be done to those who received the said paper money bills in a state greatly depreciated, for their said securities. Therefore, that equal justice may be done, as well to those who received the said paper money bills for their securities respectively, as beforementioned, agreeable to the requisitions of the laws of this state, as to those who did not comply with the said requisitions.

"Be it enacted by this General Assembly, and by the authority thereof it is hereby enacted, that all the acts, laws, and resolutions of the legislature of this state, passed at different times between the first day of September, A. D. 1786, and the first day of January, A. D. 1790, requiring the holders and owners of the said securities to bring them into the general treasury, and to receive the said bills of credit in payment and discharge of the said securities, so far as the said several acts, laws and resolutions, declare and enact, that the said securities should become null and void and of no effect, in case the same should not be brought into the general treasury, and the said bills received in discharge thereof, within certain limited periods, be, and the same are, hereby repealed. . . .

"And be it further enacted by the authority aforesaid, that each and every person who delivered into the general treasury any of the securities of this state, dated prior to the first day of July, A. D. 1788, and which were lodged there, and the said bills of credit received thereon at any time between the first day of December, A. D. 1786, and the first day of July, A. D. 1789, be, and they are, hereby authorized, by themselves, or their lawful representatives, agents, or attorneys, after the beforementioned endorsement shall have been made thereon, to receive from the said general treasurer, any, or all of such securities of him, her or them respectively belonging. . . .

"That thereupon, it shall and may be lawful for such owner or proprietor of any such security or securities, to receive the same, and to apply to the commissioner of the loan office to this state, and to have such part loaned and funded as shall remain undischarged of such securities, as would have been receivable in the National Loan Office open in this state, if no acts of the legislature of this state had been made for calling in and discharging the said securities by the paper money as aforesaid, on the same terms and conditions as any other of the securities of the said state, whereof no part hath been paid by the said paper money bills as aforesaid." (*Records of Rhode Island*, X, 447-49.)

4. 1 *Stat.* 138-44 (August 4, 1790).

5. On February 17, 1791, Joseph Stanton, Jr., and Foster, Senators from Rhode Island, had written an account of Government activities to Arthur Fenner, governor of Rhode Island. The section of the letter concerning H reads as follows:

"The confidence of the nation at large in the secretary of the treasury is deservedly great. Possessed of a contemplative, comprehensive, energetic, independent mind, he unites the strictest integrity to the most indefatigable industry, which on all occasions he incessantly applies to the service of the public. Prudent, active yet deliberate, studious, firm and candid, he may be said to invigorate the whole fiscal system of our country. Ability, foresight, decision, and a comprehensive view of the remotest consequences, are so conspicuous in all his reports respecting the finances and national arrangements, which he recommends that they seem generally to carry conviction as they go. With a fertile invention, added to real science and patriotic views, he has the talent of bringing his information into action, with that perspicuity, method and forcibleness of reasoning, that his country generally acquiesces in the propriety of the measures he recommends." (*Records of Rhode Island*, X, 424.)

From Le Roy and Bayard

New york 1 Septber 1791

Dr Sir!

Your Esteemed Favor of the 26 Ulto. only reached us this day, and that after the Sailing of the Packet. We were done drawing, or Should have been happy in Supplying you with a bill for £1000. Stg. We desired Mr. Mc.Evers [1] to Spare you whatever he had left of those, we sent him for Sale. The Exchange we sold at was from 4½ to 4 p ct Cash. Probably we may again Shortly be drawing, when we will cheerfully furnish you with the Sum required if Still wanted. Constable [2] is drawing now at 4½ p ct. We have this day received a Letter from a Committee chosen by the Subscribers [to the] National Bank, requesting that a meeting of the Stockholders may be called here, in order to devise some plan of coopperation as to voting for Directors. An opinion here we think Seems prevalent, as to the choice of Electors, wch. if we recollect, was what you wished to take place. We presume that a meeting Shortly will be called here. We Subscribe ourselves respectfully & with much Esteem   Dr Sir.   Your humble Servants   LeRoy & Bayard

Alexander Hamilton Esqr

LS, Hamilton Papers, Library of Congress.
1. Charles McÈvers, Jr., was a business associate of Herman Le Roy and Wil-

liam Bayard. In the seventeen-eighties the name of the firm had been Le Roy, Bayard, and McEvers.

2. William Constable was one of a large group of New York merchants, which included the firm of Le Roy and Bayard, who were engaged in heavy speculation in securities, usually as the agents of foreign purchasers.

From Oliver Wolcott, Junior [1]

[Philadelphia, September 1, 1791] [2]

Mr. Wolcott respectfully informs the Secretary of the Treasury, that Stephen Drayton Esq: of south Carolina, is charged on the Books of the Quarter Master Department, with between, three & four Millions of Dollars in old emissions recd. by him, principally during the years 1779. & 1780. Also that certificates of Specie value, to a large amount, were issued by said Drayton & his assistants, which have been settled by the State of So. Carolina, & for which the said Drayton will be held accountable.

On enquiry I have full reason to believe that no accounts or documents have been transmitted to the late commissioner for the Quarter Master Department,[3] or to the Treasury, respecting the expenditure of moneys, or the applications of supplies for which certificates were issued; & therefore no opinion can be given of the manner in which Mr. Drayton will account.

Thursday Sept. 1. 1791.

LC, George Washington Papers, Library of Congress.
1. Wolcott was comptroller of the Treasury.
2. This letter may have been misdated by Wolcott or by the copyist, for it was enclosed in H to George Washington, August 31, 1791.
3. Jonathan Burrall had served as commissioner for settling the accounts of the quartermaster general and commissary general departments from 1786 to 1789.

To William Short

(Duplicate)   Treasury Department
                                               September 2. 1791

Sir

Since my last to you of the first of August I have received your several letters of the 3d. 5. 10 & 19th of June.

Most of the points mentioned in those letters will find sufficient answers in my several communications of the 9th & 24th of May, June 25 & 30th & the 1st of August, all of which having gone, by duplicates at least, and some by triplicates, I take it for granted have gotten or will get safe to hand.

Previous to saying any thing further, by way of answer, it is proper to inform you of a circumstance which has recently taken place here. Mr. Ternant, shortly after his arrival,[1] made a representation against the payment of the monies due to France in its depreciated paper or assignats. You will readily conclude that the answer to such a representation could only be, *that was not the intention of the United States to take advantage of the circumstance of depreciation,* and that an equitable allowance would be made for that circumstance in the final adjustment of the payments which shall have been made.[2]

It therefore becomes important to distinguish *mere depreciation* from *rate of exchange.* To illustrate my meaning, I observe, that you state in your letter of the 3d of June the exchange between Amsterdam and Paris as upwards of twenty ℔ Ct (say 20) in favor of the former. You also state the rate of the depreciation of Assignats at Paris, or in other words, the difference between equal sums in *specie* & *Assignats,* at 10 ℔ Ct. Here then the rate of exchange, exclusive of depreciation, was 10 ℔ Ct above par, in favour of Amsterdam.

Two modes of adjusting this matter occur—one, to note at each period of payment the rate of exchange and the rate of depreciation and to pay the money, if desired, in Holland at a rate of exchange corresponding with the difference; the other, to sell bills on Amsterdam for *specie,* and pay the proceeds into the French Treasury.

As it may hereafter be questioned whether the rate of depreciation can be distinguished from the rate of exchange, it will be well to endeavour to put this point out of doubt. If circumstances permit the sale of bills at Paris, in *specie,* at a rate of exchange, which is *nearly a mean* between the nominal or declared rate of exchange and the actual rate of depreciation, (which on the data noticed above ought to be 10 ℔ Ct) this would afford an incontestible criterion. For Paris

LS, William Short Papers, Library of Congress.

1. Jean Baptiste de Ternant, newly appointed French Minister Plenipotentiary to the United States, had arrived in Philadelphia on August 10, 1791.

2. For Thomas Jefferson's stand on this question, see Jefferson to H, August 31, 1791, note 1. For H's view, see H to Jefferson, August 31, 1791.

being the stipulated place of payment there could be no colorable claim upon us to make payments at Amsterdam, when we could make them in gold or silver at Paris, at 10 or any other rate per Cent (which might correspond with the above mentioned mean) less.

The management of this point will require delicacy. It is probable that the French Ministry will not choose to *mark formally* a rate of depreciation. And it is not wished to create any embarrassment on the point. It is hoped that you will be able so to conduct the thing as to conciliate a due regard to equity with the interest of the United States, and the scruples which the conjuncture may impose on the French Ministry.

If the sale of bills for specie will afford the equitable line of demarkation, it would seem the simplest operation for the French Administration to purchase your bills on our Bankers at Amsterdam [3] at the market *specie rate* of exchange; in case, as I understand to be the fact, they wish to remit to Holland.

I observe the expectation of our bankers of a reduction of the rate of interest on the loans of this Country, and your reasons for doubting that their expectation will be realized. Those reasons have great weight. Yet the accounts from this Quarter, of the progressive rise of our Stock, and the rapid filling of the national bank must, ere this, have given a strong impulse to whatever causes might exist favorable to a reduction of interest. And without expecting sanguinely, I do not despair of the event having happened, or speedily happening.

An increased premium, though not desirable, ought not, as you intimate, to be an obstacle; if within limits that, on calculation, shew that more is gained in the reduction of interest than lost in the increase of premium. And it is probable enough that an augmentation of benefit to the Undertakers may induce them to exert efficaciously their influence to persuade the money lenders to be content with a rate of interest which will considerably overbalance to the United States the additional compensation given to them. The observations in my first instructions, which have relation to this point, had an eye chiefly to the sacrifices which in the loan of two millions of florins at 4 ⅌ Ct were made to a mere appearance of low interest; and which, if I remember right, in fact gave to the lenders about 7 ⅌ Ct.[4] A small

3. Willink, Van Staphorst, and Hubbard.
4. For a description of this loan, see H to Short, September 1, 1790, note 22.

additional premium, which would be an object to Agents or Under-takers, would be easily overbalanced by a slight diminution of the rate of interest.

The course marked out in my letter of the 24th of May will obviate, in future, any injurious delay in the employment of the sums bor-rowed—if, as I have no doubt will be the case, I am accurately advised of the time of commencing each loan and the prospects concerning it; in order that I may regulate the drafts for the parts, which are intended to be applied here.

The probability of an extension of loans abroad for the purchase of public debt beyond the limit of 2 000 000 of Dollars depends on that of a fall of interest. When I inform you that I expect in future to be able to borrow in the United States at 5 ⅌ Ct, you will perceive, that it cannot long be their interest to give 5 in Europe.

As you have now a latitude of discretion coextensive with the whole amount of our foreign debt, and indications of my opinions on various points, I forbear to multiply details which perhaps would only serve to perplex. I shall therefore content myself with barely adding, that, in regard to places of payment for monies borrowed my speculations on the probable course of exchange, resulting from the future rela-tions of commerce, would lead me to prefer, on equal terms, first Paris & next Amsterdam. Neither any of the Italian States, nor the Austrian Netherlands, nor London appears to me equally eligible. But too much stress ought not be laid on such a preference, the grounds of it being far from certain.

The affair of Shweizer Jeanneret & Co [5] is more & more out of the Question. Mr Ternant discountenances instead of promoting it. And the President has sanctioned the dasapprobation of the meas-ure.

The Postcript to my letter of the 2d of August [6] is to be construed with a reference to what is said in this letter concerning the adjust-ment of the payments to France.

I thank you for the different documents you have forwarded me,

5. Short had written H frequently concerning Schweizer, Jeanneret, and Com-pany's proposals to buy the French debt. The last letter Short had written to H on this subject which H had at this time received was Short's letter of June 3, 1791.
6. H's letter to Short is dated August 1, 1791; the postscript to the letter is dated August 2.

and assure you of the increasing consideration & esteem with which I have the honor to be,   Sir,   Your Obed Servant.   A Hamilton

A ratification of the contract for the loan by the President has been sent to Messrs Willinks & Van Staphorsts [7] by a direct opportunity which has been deemed safer than a circuitous one through you.

7. The ratification referred to was either for the Holland loan of August, 1790, for three million florins or for the loan of March, 1791, for two and one-half million florins. Both ratifications, dated September 1, 1791, may be found in the George Washington Papers, Library of Congress. For an account of the 1790 loan, see H to Willink, Van Staphorst, and Hubbard, November 29, 1790, note 1. The loan of March, 1791, is described in Short to H, February 17, 1791.

From Samuel Breck [1]

Boston Sept. 3d. 1791

Dear Sir

In conformity with your wishes [2] it wou'd afford me great pleasure to make you acquainted with the exact State of the Duck & Glass manufactories in this Town, but an Account of the former having already been communicated, by our Agent, to Mr Gorham to be forwarded to you [3] will render any observations on that branch unnecessary except that the demand for our Sail Cloth far exceeds the quantity made, which indeed might be augmented if the Country produced plenty of Flax. The high price however which is now given cannot fail of encouraging the Farmer to raise enough for that & every other object. If the representation above refered to has not reached you I will procure a Copy & forward it. We wait only for Workmen, which are engaged & probably on their passage, to commence making Sheet and other Glass. The *director*, who appears competent to the business, has prepared every thing. The Ovens, Furnaces & implements of every Kind are in perfect order. Their Cost including the building materials &ca, about Eleven thousand Dollars. It is supposed the quantity capable of being manufactured at these Works will more than supply this Commonwealth, indeed as the materials are abundent in this Country, it may be so extended as to furnish many other States with that necessary article. The bounty given by this State for raising Hemp is ample [4] & will, I presume, render our dependence on Rushia much less, & probably in a few years anihilate that Commerce. If the bounty on Duck [5] should be continued after January next, it must produce the same effect, but as the *Act for that purpose* expires in December we fear it will not be revived; however there is much consolation in the reflection that it is always within the power of the united States to *secure these great objects*.[6] I know how precious your time is & therefore will not occupy more of it, except to request you will present Mrs & the Miss Brecks best regards to Mrs. Hamilton & beleive me to be with sentiments the most sincere [7]

Dear Sir   Your Obedient Servant   Saml Breck

Honble. Alexander Hamilton Esqr

ALS, Hamilton Papers, Library of Congress.
  1. Breck was a Boston merchant who was associated with the Boston Duck or Sail Cloth Manufactory and with a glass factory known as the Boston Glass House, to which in 1789 the legislature had granted a fifteen-year monopoly of glass manufacturing.
  2. H's letter to Breck requesting this information has not been found.
  3. See Nathaniel Gorham to H, October 13, 1791.
  4. In 1791 the bounty on hemp grown by citizens of Massachusetts for manufacture within the commonwealth was twelve shillings per "Hundred for every gross Hundred Weight of good merchantable Hemp" (*Laws of Massachusetts, 1786–1787*, 382, 880; *1788–1789*, 668).
  5. The bounty on duck manufactured in Massachusetts was eight shillings for each piece thirty-eight yards by twenty-eight inches (*Laws of Massachusetts, 1786–1787*, 880; *1788–1789*, 668).
  6. In the "Report on the Subject of Manufactures," December 5, 1791, H recommended a bounty of two cents a yard on sailcloth.
  7. Davis writes: "In 1791 the works [of the Boston Duck or Sail Cloth Manufactory] were enlarged, and in September of that year Hamilton was informed that two hundred women and girls and fifty men were employed and that the capital invested amounted to $4000 in buildings and $2200 in tools, etc." (Davis, *Essays*, II, 261). Davis gives as his source for this statement: "Breck to Hamilton, Sept. 3, 1791, in *Hamilton Papers* [Library of Congress]." This information is not in the letter printed above, but may be found in the enclosures to Gorham to H, October 13, 1791.

From Daniel Delozier [1]

Baltimore
Collector's Office, Septr. 3d. 1791

Sir

It appears by the books and Invoices of this Office, that Mr Thomas Fraser imported in the Ship Hope, Andrew English, Master, from

Liverpool the 23 June 1790 five Cases hats marked $\underset{\times}{\overset{N}{T}\!\!\!/\!\!\!F}$ and numbered from 9 to 13 inclusive.

Cases, number 9, 10, 11 & 12 were assorted alike and cost £26..9..3 sterling each, and number 13 cost £54. 13..9 Sterling.

Mr. Fraser avers that in his acco. of packages imported, he inserted No. 9 instead of number 12 which was one of the Cases he sold to McRea and Morrison, and was actually shipped on board the Sloop Polly, for Petersburg.

I am, Sir   Your very Hble Servant   D. Delozier, Dep. Collr.

Alexander Hamilton Esqr.
Secretary of the Treasury

ALS, RG 56, Original Letters to the Collector at Baltimore, National Archives.
    1. For background to this letter, see H to Cyrus Griffin, February 15, 1791; H to Otho H. Williams, June 4, August 19, 1791; Williams to H, June 10, 1791.

To George Gale [1]

[*Philadelphia, September 3, 1791*. Letter listed in dealer's catalogue. *Letter not found.*]

LS, sold by Charles F. Heartman, April 6, 1929, Lot 96.
    1. Gale was supervisor of the revenue for the District of Maryland.

From Tobias Lear

[*Philadelphia*] *September 3, 1791*. "The enclosed letter, which I have the honor of transmitting to you by the President's order, will shew the necessity of making a change in the commissions for the Port of Charleston. . . ."

LC, George Washington Papers, Library of Congress.

From William Short

Paris Septr 3. 1791.

Sir

I received last night the inclosed copy of a letter from the bankers at Amsterdam which they desire me after perusal to forward to you.[1] In my two last of the 30th & 31st ulto I announced to you the loan therein mentioned & informed you it would be appropriated agreeably to your directions—so that from the time of your recieving this information you may consider the 2½ million of florins at your disposal. I take it for granted it will be from three to four months from this time before bills which you may draw could be presented. I know not at what usance you generally draw, but imagine it will always leave time for allowing the receipts to answer them & particularly as you will not probably be able to dispose of bills for the whole sum at once. I shall continue to have the sums recieved, paid to this country until I hear from you that there may be as little double interest as possible.

In my last I informed you of the circumstances of the charges on this loan. I did not then send you a copy of the letter of the commissioners to me on this subject, on account of its length & because I supposed you would have recieved it from them. From this letter however herein inclosed I infer that they did not send you a copy of theirs to me. I therefore transcribe that part of it which relates particularly to their commission—the rest, relative to the propriety of pushing the loans at Amsterdam & of taking up six millions at present instead of three, is contained literally in their letter to you. I therefore save myself the trouble of copying it here.

"Amsterdam 25. August 1791.

"Sir

We had the pleasure to address you the 22d.[2] inst. & now come to reply particularly to your respected favors of 12 & 14 ditto.[3] We must confess to you, Sir, that your sticking to reduce the charges we fixed

---

ALS, letterpress copy, William Short Papers, Library of Congress.

1. The letter to H from Willink, Van Staphorst, and Hubbard, dated August 25, 1791, has not been found, but the letter to Short enclosing it reads as follows: "Begging leave to confirm our Respects to you of 25 Instant, We have now the honor to inclose you Triplicate of our Letter of same date to the Secretary of the Treasury of the United-States; Which We request you after Perusal, to forward by a Conveyance from some Port in France, the Original having been dispatched direct from this Place, and the Duplicate via England" (Willink, Van Staphorst, and Hubbard to Short, August 29, 1791, LS, Short Family Papers, Library of Congress).

2. Willink, Van Staphorst, and Hubbard to Short, August 22, 1791 (LS, Short Family Papers, Library of Congress).

3. ALS, letterpress copies, William Short Papers, Library of Congress.

with you for the five p.cent loans of the U.S. after we had placed
them upon the very lowest footing, is truly surprizing to us, more
especially as it is striving to recede from a bargain already agreed
between us & approved by the Secretary of the Treasury of the U.S.,
as well as militating against the mode ever practised here, in agreeing
for the charges in this line of business by the lump; from which we
informed you personally, & you knew through the communication
of our letters to the treasury, it ought not to be expected we should
depart.

To demonstrate the truth of these assertions & thereby to convince
you *that* . . .[4] others perhaps you were not perfectly acquainted
with." (here follows the several objects mentioned in their letter
to you).

I enclose you a copy of my answer thereto written by the post
of to day.[5] It is an effort I make in order to bring them to the reduction of ½ p.cent on the charges which I think the U.S. have in strict
justice a right to insist on, although I think at the same time that it
is much for their advantage to push the loans even without this reduction if it cannot be effected. When I shall have done whatever
depends on me to reduce it, if I should not succeed, I flatter myself
you will approve its being granted. Perhaps the bankers may desire
that this contestation should be referred to you. If so I shall not refuse
it, as I should be better satisfied that they should recieve this ½. p.cent
from governmental munificence (if judged proper) than from my
compliance with what they insist on.

Nothing new has been recieved from London since I had the honor
of writing to you on the 23d. of August respecting our prospects
there.

I am with perfect respect   Sir,   Your most obedient humble Servant   W: Short

The Honble
Alexander Hamilton Secretary of the Treasury Philadelphia

4. These are Short's ellipses. Short noted on the letterpress copy "the pages
copied are omitted. The next page begins *others*." The letter of August 25, 1791,
from Willink, Van Staphorst, and Hubbard to Short is printed in its entirety
as an enclosure to Short to H, August 31, 1791.

5. See enclosure.

[ENCLOSURE]

William Short to Wilhem and Jan Willink,
Nicholaas and Jacob Van Staphorst, and
Nicholas Hubbard [6]

Paris Sep 3 1791

Gentlemen

Your letter of the 22d of August [7] informed me that you had opened a loan for six millions of ⟨florins⟩ & it gave me real pleasure as it never could have entered into my mind that any other conditions than those presented & repeated in my several letters authorizing the loan could have been adopted. Your letter of the 25th [8] informs me that you have ⟨presented⟩ other conditions for this loan not only different from but in ⟨opposition⟩ to those prescribed in the authority I gave for the opening the loan. Upon examining the subject ⟨ — ⟩ the result of my judgment was that I should subscribe to the conditions of the last loan if they could not be ameliorated ⟨limiting⟩ its amount in that case to three millions of florins determining however to take on myself to extend it to six millions if the charges could be reduced ½ ℔ cent—this was what my view of the situation of the U. S. dictated to me as proper. You have had a different view of the subject it seems & have of your own accord opened a loan of six millions—but it was absolutely of your own acct. & I suppose you will readily agree since I not only did not authorize it but stipulated precisely against it in the ⟨directions⟩ I gave. Your letter informs me that you consider yourselves entitled to ⟨charges⟩ to this measure ⟨ — ⟩ because you had a right to 4 p. cent commission ⟨in the case of⟩ future 5 p. cent loans as appears by your letter to the sec of the Treasury [9] approved of and forwarded by me— ⟨ — ⟩ because it is advantageous for the U. S. at present to make a loan of six millions at 5 p. cent.

6. ALS, letterpress copy, William Short Papers, Library of Congress.
7. LS, Short Family Papers, Library of Congress.
8. Willink, Van Staphorst, and Hubbard to Short, August 25, 1791, enclosed in Short to H, August 31, 1791.
9. The letter from Willink, Van Staphorst, and Hubbard to H, December 23, 1790, has not been found. For a description of it, see Willink, Van Staphorst, and Hubbard to Short, August 25, 1791, enclosed in Short to H, August 31, 1791.

As to the first part, I think you will easily see how far it is from being grounded if you will recollect what past at the time of that letter being written. You shewed me the rough draught of it desiring my observations as stated in your letter. I approved all except the clause relating to the commission, which indicated that the commission was to be raised ⟨ – – – ⟩ I objected absolutely to this clause & insisted on its being struck out on the principle of my having no right to take such an engagement ⟨ – ⟩ not knowing whether I should be ⟨ – ⟩ employed at that time I could not have taken ⟨it⟩ on me to prescribe terms to those who might succeed me. I mention particularly that ⟨any⟩ loan must fix its own terms & certainly it would be ⟨observed⟩ in any government to fix terms in this manner, where from the nature of the case they would be binding only on the government not on the commissioners. You promised therefore to strike out the clause. You will here recollect that you shewed me the rough draught of the letter because you were so excessively pressed at that time that the writing the letter twice would have been troublesome. You kept the rough draught a considerable time after my observations & then sent me the letter corrected & drawn up in the form you quote. I still observed that I did not see the use of the clause & observed that I expected it would have been left out altogether instead of its being changed to its present form. Your observation then was that it was intended to shew that if in future the rate of interest could be lowered by augmenting the profits of the undertakers; that ⟨ – ⟩ taken was not to affect you; that you were not to be expected to make loans at ⟨ – – – – ⟩ at the same rate of commission. I still mentioned to you that the clause was obscure, but on your giving this explanation of it &c, its being fully understood that I could not undertake to bind the U.S. as to the conditions of the future loans & as I know also the ⟨United States⟩ have no right to expect that you should make loans at a lower rate of interest for the commission of 4 ℔ cent (which you assured me to be what the clause was intended to provide against), I saw no inconvenience in forwarding the letter to the Sec. of the treasury ⟨therefore not⟩ obliging you, in the press of business which you then told me you were, to write it over again so as to express this ⟨ – – – ⟩ more clearly. I therefore forwarded it & gave the secretary of the treasury at the same time the explanation which I since have repeated to you. I certainly did not expect at that time that this clause was to have been thus interpreted to suppose that I had been guilty of the absurdity of binding the United States as to the terms of all their future 5 ₱ cent loans when I could not know whether I should be employed even to make a second—& also when no one good consequence could be derived from being so bound.

So much is the right supposed to be derived from your letter to the Secretary of the treasury forwarded by me. As to your ⟨views on⟩ the advantages of the U.S. resulting from making the loan of six millions your observations & view of that subject may be just & might be proper for those who have sufficient powers to act in consequence of them—you will recollect however that I do not consider myself in that class since when I was at Amsterdam at the time of the last loan, the same arguments were used ⟨ – – – – ⟩ 2½ millions further in ⟨ – – – ⟩ in case of my refusal ⟨ – – – – ⟩ all humours of the undertakers. You will remember I allowed ⟨ – – – – ⟩ & yet judged it proper not to take it on me to extend it on that account—what I then ⟨ – – ⟩ your view of the subject taken at Amsterdam may have induced you to have supposed yourselves authorized to adopt this measure—from the same view I thought differently at the time of the last loan—from my view ⟨ – ⟩ at this time I thought ⟨ – – – ⟩ & in consequence prescribed a different amount ⟨ – – – – ⟩ debt to France must have been known to me which could not be to you. If I had thought it proper to extend this loan to six millions at 4 ₱ cent commission I should probably have told you so—my silence therefore must have been proof of the contrary—but I went farther to express my disapprobation of it. This ⟨sight⟩ of the arguments which determined what it appeared proper to me to be done, ⟨ – ⟩ and charged I can only refer you to the authority then given & which stipulated expressly that the loan should be limited to three millions unless the commission was reduced. I must therefore insist on a compliance with the conditions then presented not only for the interest & credit of the U.S. but for my own justification in this case.

I have gone into this full discussion of the subject to shew that the U.S. have an unquestionable right to insist on the charges of 2½ ₱ cent of the loan if extended to six million & that you may see that it is not my wish that you should have less profits on this than the last loan. I will ask your attention to a single consideration which will shew that there will be no undersirable conditions agreeable to the state of your letter. . . .[10]

10. The remainder of this letter is indecipherable.

From Daniel Stevens [1]

Charleston [South Carolina] 3rd. September 1791

Sir

Agreeable to your request,[2] have wrote a circular Letter to the most leading Characters, throughout the State, relative to the Manufactures that may be carried on in the several Counties. As yet, have only two Letters [3] on the subject, one contains some small Samples of the Cotton and Linen manufacture carried on in families for their own wear. As any others come to hand, I will transmit them to you, and shall shortly give you some account of what Manufactures are carried on in Charleston.

I am With regard　Sir　Your Most Obt. Servt.　Danl. Stevens

[ENCLOSURE]

Silvanus Walker to Daniel Stevens [4]

Septr 1st 1791

Sir.

Agreeable to your request I am to inform you that there is no manufactories carried on in the interior parts of this State only in private families; and they in general manufactor as much as they commonly wear a few samples of which I have enclosed you but am convinced from the small knowledge I acquir'd of that business and situation of that part of the country if the people could meet with proper encouragement even from having a tolerable market that manufactor might be carried on to great advantage and perfection as there is the most convenient Mill seats I have ever seen in that part of America which have been acquainted with and flax cotton & Hemp grow exceedingly well and very good sheep is raised here and might be much improved also silk is very easy raised in this country I am Sir with due Reverance your Obliged Servt   Silvs: Walker

ALS, Hamilton Papers, Library of Congress.
1. Stevens was supervisor of the revenue for the District of South Carolina.
2. "Treasury Department Circular to the Supervisors of the Revenue," June 22, 1791.
3. Only the enclosure printed with this letter has been found. Arthur H. Cole also includes as an enclosure to this letter a letter from Bazile Lanneau and William Rouse to Stevens (Cole, *Industrial and Commercial Correspondence*, 90). Cole, however, is mistaken, for the letter from Lanneau and Rouse is dated "October 1791" and therefore could not possibly have been enclosed in Stevens's letter of September 3. The original letter from Lanneau and Rouse is in the Hamilton Papers, Library of Congress.
4. ALS, Hamilton Papers, Library of Congress.
Walker's appointment as inspector of Survey No. 3 for South Carolina was confirmed by the Senate on November 7, 1791.

From William Hall[1]

New York 4th. Sepr. 1791

Sir

Last night Mr. Mort & myself return'd from the Pasaic Falls.[2] One of the finest situations in the world (we believe) can be made there. The quality of the water is good & in sufficient quantity to supply works of almost any extent. Every thing nescessary as to situation is here to be found. The Lands ly well are shelter'd from the winds & are not subject to inundations. This situation so far exceeds our expectations that we are very desirous you shou'd see it. If convenient shou'd wish to meet you there with any other person you think a judge & explain to you our reasons for prefering this situation, after which we flatter ourselves you will agree with us in opinion. We have seen Coll. Duer.[3] He says He will write you on the subject by this Post & will accompany us to the Falls. We think it unnesscessary to trouble you with our report of the Delaware till we have the pleasure of seeing you.

Shall be happy to hear from you as soon as convenient.

I have the honor to remain   Sir Your most obedt. Hble Servt.

William Hall

No. 57 Maiden Lane

ALS, Hamilton Papers, Library of Congress.
1. For background to this letter, see Hall to H, August 29, 1791.

2. These falls are located in what is now Paterson, New Jersey, and they were to become the site of the Society for Establishing Useful Manufactures.

3. William Duer had been active in drafting plans for the Society for Establishing Useful Manufactures in the spring and summer of 1791. For a description of his activities for the society, see Davis, *Essays*, I, 270-72.

To Elizabeth Hamilton

[Philadelphia, September 4, 1791]

My beloved Betsey

I hoped with the strongest assurance to have met you at Eliz Town; but this change of weather has brought upon me an attack of the complaint in my kindneys, to which you know I have been sometimes subject in the fall. So that I could not with safety commit myself to so rude a vehicle as the stage for so long a journey. I have therefo⟨re⟩ prevailed upon Mr. Meyer [1] to go to Elizabet⟨h⟩ Town to meet you in my place. He will b⟨e⟩ there on Tuesday Evening; when, or the day f⟨ollowing⟩ I hope it will be convenient to you to ⟨be⟩ there. For as the moment of seeing you ap⟨proaches⟩ my impatience increases. I am pained beyon⟨d⟩ measure, that I cannot execute my intention of meeting you.

But dont alarm yourself nor hurry so as to injure either yourself or the children. I am not *ill* though I might make myself so by the jolting of the carriag⟨e⟩ were I to undertake the journey. I am indeed better than I was, this Evening, and if I can get a proper machine I shall make use of a warm bath to which I am advised and from which I am persuaded I shal⟨l⟩ receive benefit.

Inclosed my angel yo⟨u⟩ will find 200 Dollars in bank Notes. You will have to put your name upon them before you pass them. If you find any difficulty in passing them you can send to Mr. Seton [2] who I dare say will find means to accommod⟨ate⟩ you.

Give my Love to Peggy.[3] I hope she will come on with you—as I shall be very glad to see her.

God bless you my beloved   A Hamilton

⟨Sun⟩day Evening 4 Sep

If wind & weather serve, you had better come by water. Otherwise engage a carriage or carriages to carry you to E Town where you will find one to bring you on, under the care of Mr. Meyer. Mr. Meyer is desired to inquire for you at Mr. Boudinots.[4]

Mrs. Hamilton

ALS, Hamilton Papers, Library of Congress.
  1. John Meyer was a clerk in the Treasury Department.
  2. William Seton, cashier of the Bank of New York.
  3. Margaret (or Margarita) Schuyler Van Rensselaer, Elizabeth Hamilton's sister and the wife of Stephen Van Rensselaer.
  4. Elias Boudinot, one of H's oldest friends, was at this time a Federalist member of the House of Representatives from New Jersey.

From William Campbell, Benjamin Smith, Henry Toomer, George Hooper, M. R. Willkings, Auly Macnaughten, and Thomas Withers [1]

Wilmington [North Carolina] September 5, 1791. "We take the present favourable opportunity of replying to yours of the 11th. June by inclosing all the answers We conceived necessary to your queries. . . ."

[ENCLOSURE] [2]

Quere 1st.	When was the building commenced?
Answer.	About the 1st. June 1788.
Qr. 2d.	Is there any the least appearance of its suffering from the winter or winters it has sustained since it was built and in what parts?
A.	Not materially. Indeed the brick work not at all but the frames of the windows a little, the Lumber on the beach which was provided for the light house and not yet made use of is how ever suffering very much.
Q. 3d	What parts of the building are of stone and particularly as to the foundation, water tables Cills of the doors and windows, and the Curbs?
A.	None of stone, The Cills of the doors and windows are of yellow pine. There are no Curbs.
Q. 4.	Is the lime used Stone lime or Oyster shell lime?
A.	Oyster shell lime.

Q. 5   Are the frame and sashes of the Lanthern to be of Iron or wood?

A.   Of wood.

Q. 6   What is the thickness of the base in feet and inches the plan calls it 7 bricks thick, but it is not known wether it is seven times the length, the breadth or the thickness of a brick?

A.   The plan already sent is wrong in this instance. The foundation walls in parallell lines is ten feet through at the extremity of the foundation but being octagonal inside, at the angles is eighteen feet six inches through.

Quere 7.   Was there a solid bottom in the Earth on digging down for the foundation?

Answr.   There was a bank of drifted sand about 20 feet in height which was cut down thus far to bring it on a level with the adjacent land, after which 5 feet more was dug down for a foundation, it was apprehended that going deeper would have brought the workmen to a quick sand.

Q 8.   Is the spot an eminence or is it a level with the land for 100 or 200 yards around it?

Answ   Exclusive of the sand bank before mentioned it is a level for several hundred yards around.

Q. 9.   Is it in any degree a drifted sand hill and if it is did the workmen take care to go down thro it to the solid Earth?

Ansr.   See answer to query 7th.

Q. 10.   Is there any frame work laid under the foundation as proposed and what is its construction and the kind of timber used?

Ansr.   There is no frame work for this purpose.

Q 11   What are the several thicknesses of the walls of the pyramid in feet and inches in those parts above the foundation which are represented to be six bricks, five bricks and four and half bricks?

Answr.   The part of the pyramid represented as six bricks thick is four feet 8 inches through, five bricks three feet 11 inches, and four and a half bricks, three feet 6 inches. In short the bricks are 9 inches long.

Query 12.   Is the diameter the same at the top of the Story in which the doors are as at the bottom of that Story and what is that diameter from outside to outside?

Ansr.   The diameter of the story in which the doors are is the same at the top as bottom, which is 32 feet from out to out.

Query 13.   What is the diameter of the top of the masonry immediately under the Lanthern proposed to be?

Ansr.   The building immediately under the lanthern is twelve feet diameter.

Query 14.   What is the diameter and height of the lanthern exclusive of the dome roof and what is the height of the dome or roof?

Ansr.   The diameter of the lanthern is 12 feet, the height 16 feet, the height of the dome exclusive of the ball 8 feet.

Query 15   What is the height of the building from the Earth to the ball on the top of the Lanthern?

Ansr.   The Building from the Earth to the ball is 125 feet.

Query 16.   Will the thickness of two bricks which I suppose to be 17 inches be sufficiently strong at the height of 75 to 90 feet from the Earth and will the thickness of six bricks (or 4½ to 5 feet) be thick enough for the lower part of a building of so great height?

Answer.   It appears to us that the dimensions of every part of this building be sufficient for the height.

LS, RG 26, Lighthouse Letters Received, Early Lighthouse Letters, National Archives.
  1. These men were North Carolina commissioners to regulate shipping on the Cape Fear River.
  2. D, RG 26, Lighthouse Letters Received, Early Lighthouse Letters, National Archives.

To Tobias Lear

[Philadelphia, September 5, 1791]

The Secretary of the Treasury presents his compliments to Mr. Lear and sends the two commissions for south Carolina.[1] He would wait on the president to day but is prevented by a slight attack of a disorder common to him at the change of weather usual at this season.

Septem: 5. 1791.
LC, George Washington Papers, Library of Congress.
    1. See Lear to H, September 3, 1791.

From William Seton [1]

[New York] 5th Sep 1791

Sir

Having compleated the full investiture of the 150,000 Dollars directed by you to be laid out in the purchase of Stock for acct. of the United States, I have the honor to enclose a Return of the same,[2] & your account in Bank is debited with the amount.

I am with great respect

LC, Bank of New York, New York City.
    1. For background to this letter, see H to Seton, August 15, 1791; H to the President and Directors of the Bank of New York, August 16, 1791.
    2. This return is printed in *ASP, Finance,* I, 117.

From William Seton

[New York] 5 Sept 1791

Dear sir

By my Public Letter you will see I have compleated the investiture of the 150,000 Dollars in the purchase of Stock—in fact it was finished the middle of last week but I could not get some of the Transfers passed till this day. The whole stands now in the Name of the Vice President &ca. I wish to know if I am to take out the Certificates & forward them & to whom. Great as this relief has been to the holders, it is far short of preventing that universal panic & want of money which now prevails. Deffered debt was actually sold under 12/ to day & Scrip at 150—merely to save credit. Was it possible to extend your purchase here to 150 M Dollars more—even 2d or 3d under the Acct limitts (if that is to be wished) it would be of immense consequence to this Community, & I believe would readily fill.

We have a great demand for the Treasurers Bills on the Southard

particularly Virginia & Maryland of which we have not had any for
some time.

I hope you will excuse the liberty I take in mentioning these things
to you, & believe that I am with the highest respect & esteem

Dear sir &c

LC, Bank of New York, New York City.

From George Cabot [1]

Beverly [Massachusetts] Sept. 6th. 1791

Dear Sir

Being absent from home when your letter of the 25th ultimo [2] arrived, it has been out of my power to answer the enquiries it contains
until this day's post.

Almost 4 years have expired since a number of Gentlemen in this
place associated for the purpose of establishing a manufactory of cotton goods of the kinds usually imported from Manchester for men's
wear.[3] The various parts of this complex manufacture are performed
by machines, some of which are very intricate & others delicate. A
want of skill in constructing the machinery & of dexterity in using it,
added to our want of a *general* knowledge of the business we had
undertaken, have proved the principal impediments to it's success.
Destitute of the necessary information ourselves we were subject to
be misled by every pretender to knowledge. A number of Europeans
chiefly Irish have been successively employed by us, but as no one of
them was master of any branch of the business, & most of them proved

ALS, Hamilton Papers, Library of Congress; copy, Hamilton Papers, Library of
Congress.
    1. Cabot, whose home was in Beverly, was one of the leading merchants and
Federalist politicians of Massachusetts. In June, 1791, he had been chosen United
States Senator from Massachusetts. H had asked him about manufacturing because he was a prominent stockholder and leading promoter of the Beverly
Cotton Manufactory. This company is mentioned in H's "Report on the Subject
of Manufactures," December 5, 1791.
    2. Letter not found.
    3. Cabot's two older brothers, John and Andrew, were also among the
founders of the Beverly Cotton Manufactory. John, moreover, was the company's largest stockholder and one of its two managers. Although the company
was organized in 1788, it did not obtain a charter of incorporation until 1789.
When President Washington paid a visit to this famous factory in 1789, its
principal product was corduroys.

deficient in some quality essential to usefulness, one only has remained in our service. Satisfied from experience that we must at last depend on the People of the country *alone* for a solid & permanent establishment, we have for a long time directed our efforts to their instruction, so that of the 40 Persons now employed in our workshop 39 are natives of the vicinity. Our machines are

- 1 carding engine which with the labor of 1 man cards 15 lb per day & with the labor of 2 men is capable of carding 30 lb per day
- 9 spinning jennies of 60 to 84 spindles each
- 1 doubling & twisting machine constructed on ye principle of ye jenny
- 1 slubbing machine or coarse jenny to prepare the Ropings for the finest jennies whereon they are fitted for doubling & twisting
- 1 warping mill sufficient to perform this part of the work for a very extensive manufactory
- 16 Looms with flying shuttles—10 of which are sufficient to weave all the yarn our present Spinners can furnish
- 2 cutting frames with knives guides &c
- 1 Burner & furnace with apparatus to singe the goods
- Apparatus for coloring drying &c.

A summary of our accounts lately exhibited by the managers shews our actual expenditures to have been about 14,000 Dollars against which may be placed

"Buildings &c worth as they cost	3,000
Machinery & apparatus now worth	2 000
Goods & unwrought materials	4 000
sunk in waste of materials extraordinary cost of first machines in maintaining Learners compensating Teachers &c	5,000
Dols.	14,000

It shou'd be noticed however that the legislature of Massachusetts having granted aids in land & lottery tickets that may amount to about 4,000 Dollars,[4] the neat loss to the Proprietors may be estimated at only 1000 Dollars actual money & the interest on their advances for about 2 years.

At present we manufacture at the rate of 8 to 10,000 yards per

4. In 1789 the Massachusetts legislature granted the company land in Maine worth five hundred pounds, and in 1791 the legislature granted it seven hundred state lottery tickets.

annum worth in the market on an average 3/6—these goods cost us
3/ without adding any thing for the use of that part of the capital
which is constituted by Buildings Machinery & apparatus; if the proper
allowance for rent & repair of these be added it wou'd raise the cost
of the goods 6d higher, which is indeed the true cost & is equal to what
they bring in the market. The enclosed specimens numbered 1 & 2
shew the proficiency we had made 2 years ago, & by comparing with
these the other specimens on the same paper which were executed
lately, may be readily seen the improvement we have made since that
period.

With respect to our future prospects, they are less discouraging
than they have been. We have subdued the greatest difficulties, & we
shall not be exposed again to many extravagant charges which heretofore have swallowed up our funds without any reproduction. Many
expences such as the rent of buildings, wages of the Dyer, compensation to managers & some others will remain nearly the same, tho' the
scale of business shou'd be greatly encreased, consequently the proportion chargeable on each yard of goods will be lessened as the whole
work extends. Beside we are not without expectation of placing many
parts of the work in private families where we can avail ourselves of
the cheapness of household labor.

Our machinery has been bad & dear; it is now perfectly well made
& cheap. Our artists have been learning their trades at our expence;
their work is now worth more than it costs, & as they improve in
skill & adroitness we expect that they will perform more & better
work for the same compensation.

On a comparison of the prices of labor in this country with those
of Great Britain, we perceived that altho' the wages of *common labor*
is much higher here yet *that* of *artificers* is not. Here the demand for
labor is chiefly for agriculture & the wages seem to be regulated by it.
There the mechanic arts afford so much employment that the demand
for every species of skill & ingenuity is constant & high. Hence it
happens that we can satisfy our artists with wages very little above the
common Labor of the country while those who come from Europe
will not work without a much greater price. It is on considerations of
this kind that our hopes principally rest, & with these ideas we shall
proceed to extend our business as fast as we can train the Laborers to
the proper execution of the work. This however must be very slowly

as the heavy losses on ill wrought goods discourage extension beyond a very limited ratio.

We have yet had no experience of the cotton of the southern states, but it appeared early to be essential to our interest to use cotton of the longest fibre & the best cleaned. That of Cayenne Surrinam & Demerary [5] has been preferred tho' at a price 2 or 3 pence higher than the cotton of the Islands. In proportion as our workers are awkward & unskillful is the necessity of furnishing the best materials— bad materials woud be wasted altogether. At present we wish to have the cotton that grows nearest to the Equator, but when our Spinners are more perfect an inferior kind may perhaps be wrought with advantage.

with the highest respect & esteem   I have the honor to be Sir your mo. obt. & mo. hble Servant   George Cabot

Honorable Mr. Hamilton

5. Demerara, British Guiana.

From William Ellery

Newport [*Rhode Island*] *September 6, 1791.* "I have recd. your letter respecting the article of Pumpings, and shall attend to your directions.[1] Please to favour me with an answer to my letter of the 6th. of June relative to the lawful portion of the compensations Surveyors are to receive for Regrs &c., to the question in my letter of the 4th. of July Should not every vessel receive her first Certife. of Registry from the Collector of the District where she is built? to my letter of the 18th. of July relative to repairing the Light-House, and to the question in my letter of the 25th. of July touching what is to be performed by a person usually residing in one District, who being in another there purchases a vessel, in order to entitle him to a Register of such vessel. Joseph Finch to gain time, as I suppose, has purchased a writ of Error to the next Circuit Court. . . .[2] An iron chest is very much wanted for the Custom House. If you approve of it, I will purchase one and charge it to the United States." [3]

LC, Newport Historical Society, Newport, Rhode Island.
    1. Letter not found, but see Ellery to H, August 8, 1791.
    2. See Ellery to H, July 11, August 23, 1791.

3. Ellery endorsed the letter book copy of this letter "Answered." H's reply has not been found.

From Tobias Lear

[*Philadelphia, September 6, 1791.*] Transmits Isaac Holmes's commission "appointing him collector of Charleston in South Carolina."

LC, George Washington Papers, Library of Congress.

To Le Roy and Bayard

[*Philadelphia, September 6, 1791*. On September 11, 1791, Le Roy and Bayard wrote to Hamilton: "Your esteemed favor of the 6 Instt has been complied with." *Letter not found.*]

From Jeremiah Olney

Providence, September 6, 1791. "The missing Certificate of Registry for Schooner Nicholas, mentioned in my Letter of the 25th Ulto. proves to have been all the Time in the Collector's Office at Newport: Capt. Potter,[1] who is now here, says he took it from thence to bring up with him, but left it at Home through forgetfulness. He promises to send it hither on his return, which will be in a few Days. I enclose the Certificate of registry No. 25, granted by me in 1790, for Brign. Trinanada; she having been lately sold at a foreign Port."

ADfS, Rhode Island Historical Society, Providence; copy, RG 56, Letters from the Collector at Providence, National Archives.
  1. Thomas Potter. See Olney to H, August 25, 1791.

From Tobias Lear

United States
Sept: 7, 1791

By the Presidents command T. Lear has the honor to transmit to the Secretary of the Treasury for his information a letter from Colo. Ballard,[1] Inspector of the port of Baltimore, stating the trouble & expence attending the execution of the duties of his Office, for which there is no compensation.[2]

At the same time the President directs the enclosed letter from Genl. Lincoln [3] to T. L. (which has been submitted to the president's inspection) to be laid before the Secretary, as it points to the same subject relative to the Inspector of the port of Boston.[4]

Tobias Lear.

S. P. U. S.

LC, George Washington Papers, Library of Congress.
1. Robert Ballard was surveyor of the port of Baltimore.
2. On September 7, 1791, Lear wrote to Ballard as follows: "It is impossible for the President to attend to the minutiae of business which may be communicated by Individuals, he wishes always to receive such information as may be proper to come before him, relating to the several Departments through the heads of the Departments to which the business properly belongs. Upon this view of the matter the President is persuaded, Sir, that you will not consider his declining to reply to the subject of your letter at this time, as a singular case; for he observes the same conduct on all occasions of this nature" (*GW*, XXXI, 360, note 84).
3. Benjamin Lincoln, collector of customs at Boston.
4. Thomas Melville (or Melvill).

To the President and Directors of the Bank of New York

Ty Dept. 7th Sepr. 1791

Gent.

I request you to furnish the Cashier of your Bank with the further Sum of Fifty thousand Dollars to be by him applied towards purchases of the Public Debt on acct. of the United States.[1]

P. S. A Warrant will issue tomorrow to cover the 150,000 Dollars already advanced for the same purpose.[2]

Copy, in the handwriting of William Seton, Hamilton Papers, Library of Congress.
1. See the second letter William Seton wrote to H on September 5, 1791, and H to Seton, September 7, 1791.
2. See H to Seton, August 15, 16, 1791.

To Jeremiah Olney

Treasury Department
September 7 1791

Sir

It has been represented to me that a Brig, called the Trinidada, lately belonging to Messrs. Brown & Francis [1] of your district, has arrived in the district of Wilmington on Delaware with a copy of a register issued from your Office which does not agree with the vessel in two material particulars. The register, which is No 25 & bears date on the 25th of Augt. 1790, appears, from the copy, to describe the vessel as having "*a head*" and as being "*pink* sterned," and the copy in this Office agrees with that, but the brig has not a head, and tho' said to be narrow abaft, is square sterned. This case naturally excites extraordinary attention, as the bill of sale of the Agents of Brown & Francis, which the present Owner possesses, is confirmed by other information, that the vessel was actually sold by the persons named as Agents, and to the person appearing to be the purchaser.

It is my request that you will immediately transmit to me a copy of the Surveyors certificate to you, on which you issued the Register, No 25, and, if you have it, the original register under the State of Rhode Island which was delivered up to you when the register in question under the United States was obtained by Mr Brown. I also wish to be informed whether the Trinidada ever had a head, and if she had, when and for what reason it was taken off—also whether any vessels are called pink sterned in the State of Rhode Island, the ends of whose after planks are not actually butted against the Stern post. Any circumstances which will throw light upon the fact relating to the place at which the Trinidada was built you will also communicate: [2] or if a mistake has happened any circumstances tending to ascertain and explain it will be acceptable.

I am, Sir, Your Obedt Servant.   A Hamilton

The Collector of the Customs,
Providence

LS, Rhode Island Historical Society, Providence; copy, RG 56, Letters to the Collector at Providence, National Archives; copy, RG 56, Letters to Collectors at Small Ports, "Set G," National Archives.
    1. See Olney to H, September 6, 1791. John Brown and John Francis were Providence merchants.
    2. The remainder of this sentence is in H's handwriting.

Receipt from William Pearce

[Philadelphia, September 7, 1791]

Received Philadelphia Sep 7. 1791 of Alexander Hamilton, Fifty Dollars towards providing Machines for a Cotton Manufactory.[1]

Wm. Pearce

D, in writing of H and signed by Pearce, Hamilton Papers, Library of Congress.
    1. For a list of these machines, see "Receipt from William Pearce," August 20, 1791, note 2.

To William Seton

Treasury Department
Sept. 7. 1791

Sir

I write herewith to the Directors of the Bank of New York to advance you a further sum of fifty thousand Dollars, towards purchases of the public Debt ⟨on⟩ account of the United States, on the ⟨sa⟩me principles with the sum heretofore advanced to you for the like purpose.[1]

With great consideration   I am Sir   Your Obed servt

A Hamilton

Wm. Seton Esquire
Cashier of the Bank of New York

ALS, Bank of New York, New York City; LS, Bank of New York; copy, in the handwriting of William Seton, Hamilton Papers, Library of Congress.
    1. See H to Seton, August 15, 1791.

To William Seton

Philadelphia Sepr. 7. 91

My Dear Sir

I regret though I am not surprised at what you disclose in your private letter of the 5th. I have for sometime foreseen the effects of a too sanguine disposition in the dealers of your City; particularly in relation to Bank Script; and have anticipated that it would lead to a necessity of sacrifices injurious to the funds. We got beyond the force of our own capital & beyond the point to which foreigners were *yet prepared* to go.

I trust however the evil is temporary. The Bank is as good a thing as it ever was. The United States are as solid as they were. The provision for the debt appears every day more and more ample. In short every thing promises well. And the timid will soon rally.

You will find by the letters herewith that you are furnished with a further sum of 50000 Dollars for purchases.[1] I wish I could have gone further but my hands are tied by the want of a majority of the Trustees[2] being present—Mr Jefferson being just gone to Virginia. The 50.000 now authorised & the sum appropriated here for the same purpose complete what has yet determined to be applied.

You may however make it known that the Treasurer is purchasing here.

You need never make an apology for any intimation you give me. The truth is however that for some time past *drafts* have been suspended to let money accumulate for the payment of the accruing Quarters interest. Considerable sums will be to be drawn for in the course of the next Month. I remain with great regard & truth

    Yr. friend & serv.   A Hamilton

William Seton Esqr.

ALS, Bank of New York, New York City; extract, in the handwriting of William Seton, Hamilton Papers, Library of Congress.

    1. H to the President and Directors of the Bank of New York, September 7, 1791, and H's other letter to Seton on September 7, 1791.

    2. This is a reference to the commissioners of the sinking fund. See H to Seton, August 15, 1791.

From Joshua Wentworth

Portsmo. New Hamps. Septr. 7th. 1791.

Sir

The 2d Instant I was honored by your's of 24th Ulto.[1] inclosing five forms of the System for the government of the Revenue, those Compleats my receipt of the whole. And inclosed is a return of form No. 1. This I shou'd have forwardd. some time past, but supposing others might be necessary to accompany it, delayed transmiting this return until the whole of the System had reached me, to which and your explination of the Act[2] I shall pay every attention.

The opperation of the Law meets with no Embarrassment nor have I reason to suppose any will ensue in the execution of it, in this District.

Agreeably to the power vested in me by the Law I have appointed Mr George Wentworth[3] Collector of Revenue, an Inhabitant of this Town, formerly a Ship Master in the Merchants Service, and their being but one Distillery in this District at present, Mr. Wentworth's is the only appointment taken place.

The necessary Oaths of Office were attended to, and are forwarded to the Comptroller of the Treasury as the Law prescribes. A Bond likewise is taken of the Collector of Revenue agreeably to your Directions.

Your letters of the 7th May & 22d June[4] were duly received & every attention are paid to their Contents. With all possible convenience I will transmit a reply to your enquiries of the latter. Remaining respectfully   Sir yr most obedient   & very hble servt.

Josh. Wentworth

Alexander Hamilton Esquire

ALS, RG 58, General Records, 1791–1803, National Archives.
   1. Letter not found.
   2. "An Act repealing, after the last day of June next, the duties heretofore laid upon Distilled Spirits imported from abroad, and laying others in their stead; and also upon Spirits distilled within the United States, and for appropriating the same" (1 *Stat.* 199–214 [March 3, 1791]).
   3. George Wentworth was Joshua's brother.
   4. Neither letter has been found. The letter of June 22, 1791, may have been the Treasury Department circular which H sent to the supervisors of the revenue on this date.

From Fisher Ames

Boston Sept 8, 1791

Dear Sir

The immoderately long letter which I took the liberty to write you some time ago,[1] will, probably, have surprised you. You will wonder why I should take pains to establish opinions which you have never held in dispute. I will confess to you that the rumour of the intended connection between the U.S and NY. Banks gave me some uneasiness. My friend Mr Gore [2] will leave this town next week, and you will learn from him that the good disposition of the Massa. Bank proprietors, at the time when that report was diffused, made it very unwelcome. Everything had gradually ripened their minds to an acquiescence in the Unity of the Bank and it's branches. I think you are acquainted with Mr Gore, and as he will not fail to converse with you, it is unnecessary for me to notice any further the causes and circumstances of my apprehension respecting the Bank of the U. S.

The arrangements of the Bank are expected with some impatience. Here the general wish is to have Branches. I hope they may be safely adopted, not so much with a view to the profits of the stock, (tho' that is a thing to be noticed) as for reasons which I have formerly given.[3] Mr. Gore is one of the few men whom I consider as sound and thorough patriots. Tho a great Stockholder,[4] you will find him *national*. The possession of an ample fortune has not contracted his heart, nor twisted his intellects. He will leave this place for Philada next week, and as he will, probably, represent a great many proprietors, with whom his opinion and reputation will weigh a great deal you will find him able to inform of the views of the eastern stockholders. I confess I have my fears that party schemes will be nursed in the City. Should any improper designs be formed, you will naturally reckon upon his steady opposition to them. In short as your acquaintance with him is slight, I think it will be useful & almost necessary that you should *know* him. Few Men are so worthy of esteem and confidence.

The distillers here are framing a petition to Congress for a reduction of the duty on home made Rum 3 Cents and an augmentation of

3 Cents on imported Rum &c. You may possibly think this immoderate, and a symptom of discontent. Tho' I wish they had thought fit to ask for less, I will venture to vouch for their good dispositions. Some change of the ratio of duties would be highly acceptable to them and favorable to their manufacture. But they will not make a clamor against the Excise Act as it is.[5]

You will doubtless remark that I am writing confidentially.

I very much approve the Letter you wrote to our Assessors.[6] But many country gentlemen have thought less favorably of it. They say why not tax property equally. The spirit of envy, an evil spirit! in times of prosperous adventure can bear the day light. That spirit would rejoice in the spoil of the possessors of public paper by assessment. Assessments are so arbitrary, so various in the different states, and even in different towns, and so much applause would be secured in many towns by acts of rapine in the shape of a tax, that the value of property in paper may be made eventually, very insecure. The inequality of it's operation on different proprietors, and the bad policy of holding such a terror over opulent citizens whom we may wish to fix as residents would, if dilated on, make some impression upon the public. At present, no uneasiness seems to subsist in this town on that head. But when the state valuation shall be settled, as it will be within a year, I apprehend the seeds will sprout again.

I am, dear Sir, with sentiments of esteem &c your most obedt. hble servant   Fisher Ames

Mr Hamilton

ALS, Connecticut Historical Society, Hartford.
    1. See Ames to H, August 15, 1791.
    2. Christopher Gore, United States attorney for the District of Massachusetts.
    3. See Ames to H, July 31, August 15, 1791.
    4. Gore was a stockholder in the Massachusetts Bank.
    5. "An Act repealing, after the last day of June next, the duties heretofore laid upon Distilled Spirits imported from abroad, and laying others in their stead; and also upon Spirits distilled within the United States, and for appropriating the same" (1 Stat. 199–214 [March 3, 1791]).
    6. H to the Board of Assessors of the Town of Boston, July 27, 1791.

To Sharp Delany

Treasury Department
(Private)   Septemr. 8th 1791

Sir

I am informed there is reason to believe, that a vessel belonging to Elizabeth Town in New Jersey has been employed by a merchant in Philadelphia to run a cargo of rum, by carrying the hogsheads in the hold and a quantity of shingles on the Deck.

The intelligence comes to me in such a way as to render it proper that you know it for the purpose of giving the necessary intimation to the officers of your District.

I am, Sir,   Your obedt. Servt.   Alexander Hamilton

Sharp Delany Esquire
Collector Philada.

LS, Bureau of Customs, Philadelphia; two copies, RG 56, Letters to the Collectors at Small Ports, "Set G," National Archives.

To Sharp Delany

Treasury Department
Sept. 8. 1791.

Sir

I have considered the case proposed to me in your letter of the 11th. July,[1] and do not find myself authorised to instruct you to set off the drawback against the bond of the importer Mr. Telles.[2] The legislature had not seen fit to make any provision of this nature in the first collection law,[3] and in the existing act [4] they have only extended it to the *importer*, and not to the purchasers from him which you state Messrs. Willing Morris & Swanwick [5] to be. [And the outward entry at the Custom House is the only admissible evidence of who is the Importer.] [6]

I am, Sir,   Your obedt. servant   A Hamilton

Sharp Delany Esq.

LS, Bureau of Customs, Philadelphia; two copies, RG 56, Letters to Collectors at Small Ports, "Set G," National Archives.

1. Letter not found.

2. John Telles was a Philadelphia merchant.

3. "An Act to regulate the Collection of the Duties imposed by law on the tonnage of ships or vessels, and on goods, wares and merchandises imported into the United States" (1 *Stat.* 29–49 [July 31, 1789]).

4. "An Act to provide more effectually for the collection of the duties imposed by law on goods, wares and merchandise imported into the United States, and on the tonnage of ships or vessels" (1 *Stat.* 145–78 [August 4, 1790]). Section 61 of this act reads as follows: "*And be it further enacted,* That if any goods, the duties upon which shall have been secured by bond, shall be re-exported by the importer or importers thereof, and if the said bond shall become due before the expiration of the time herein before limited for payment of the drawback upon such goods, it shall be lawful for the collector of the district from which the said goods shall have been exported, to give farther credit for so much of the sum due upon such bond, as shall be equal to the amount of the said drawback, until the expiration of the said time limited for payment thereof" (1 *Stat.* 174–75).

5. The partners in this firm were Thomas Willing, Robert Morris, and John Swanwick.

6. The bracketed sentence is in the handwriting of H.

To William Seton

[Philadelphia] Sep 8, 91

D Sr,

I wrote you a private letter last Evening which went by a private opportunity. Its principal object was to inform you—

That I could not exceed the sum now directed to be advanced for want of authority—the present 50000 completing the sum heretofore appropriated by the Trustees & there not being here a sufficient number for a board.

That purchases by the Treasurer were going on here.

That there had been for some time past a suspension of drafts on Collectors in order to the payment of the accruing Quarters interest.

But that in the course of the next month there would be considerable drafts of which N York would have its share.

Yrs. with great regd.   A Hamilton

Wm. Seton Esq

ALS, Bank of New York, New York City; extract, in the handwriting of William Seton, Hamilton Papers, Library of Congress.

To William Skinner [1]

September 8th. 1791.
Treasury Department

Sir

Your letter of the 29th. of August is just come to hand. My circular of the first of November which you had received required that you should not admit on loan the Certificates of the State of North Carolina upon its own account. The reason of this would operate in regard to the Comptroller [2] or any other Officer of the State, or any individual who might be the acknowledged or secret Agent of the State, or to whom the State might have disposed of such Certificates. For if they are not receivable from the State itself on loan, it is on the principle that a Bond once surrendered to the Debtor, as satisfied or discharged extinguishes the Debt; and consequently there is in such case, no *debt* in existence, to be assumed. A transfer of the Certificates therefore to any other person even if real can make no alteration in the thing. You were of course right in refusing to receive them, in the name of the Comptroller and you were not less right in your objection to the Gentleman whom you did not name who effected the first and offered the second subscription you speak of, if by his conduct or other circumstances there was good ground to believe that the certificates he tendered were of the kind above mentioned. Were it not for the suspicion you express it would never have entered into my imagination that the Government of your State could resolve by any secret or indirect method to effect the receipt by you of certificates which you were not at Liberty from your instructions to receive. And even after what you communicate, I am obliged to suppose, either that your suspicion is without foundation or that some subordinate officer, whose zeal for the interest of the State makes him forgetful of what is due to its dignity to propriety and to fair dealing, has without authority or instruction resorted to so improper an expedient. Confiding that the Governor [3] will be anxious to arrest a proceeding so exceptionable in every view, I desire that you will immediately make known to him your suspicion and the grounds of it, in order that being appraised of the thing he may take measures to prevent a repetition of the attempt. In my letter of the 12th. of August a copy of which accompanies this, you are authorised to receive the certificates in question from the State in order to their being submitted to me. This I did from a disposition to give the matter every possible chance which could result from the fullest consideration and with a view to taking finally the opinion of the Attorney General after hearing whatever might be offered on the part of the State. This you are still at liberty to do. But as you appear to think secret means were taking to pass the certificates upon you—you will do well to continue upon your guard. You will however receive the Certificates offered; giving a descriptive receipt for them as in other cases—but inserting in that receipt *expressly* that they are to be specially submitted to the decision of the Secretary of the Treasury whether receivable or not upon the loan. You will understand also that none of the *receipts* you have given in any case for certificates deposited are to be considered by you as conclusive upon the public. The Certificates are all liable to revision and may be rejected if they appear forged, or in any other respect not proper to be admitted on the loan. The only reason for a distinction between the forms of the receipts to be given for suspected certificates, and those to be given for such as are not suspected is to put purchasers on their guard.

The attempts you have announced are of such a nature as to oblidge me to desire; that before you issue any certificates of Stock in lieu of the State debt deposited, you advise me of the total amount of the sums subscribed, noting all such cases in which you have reason to believe the Certificates are of the kind not properly admissible on the loan. In making this communication you will use *all possible dispatch.*

I am yours &c

William Skinner Esquire
Commissioner of Loans
for North Carolina.

Copy, North Carolina Department of Archives and History, Raleigh. This letter was enclosed in H's "Report to the Governor of North Carolina," July 31, 1794.

1. For background to this letter, see the two letters that Skinner wrote to H on July 22, 1791, and Skinner to H, August 29, 1791.

2. For the attempt which Francis Child, comptroller of North Carolina, had made to subscribe redeemed certificates of state debt, see Skinner to H, August 11, 1791.

3. Alexander Martin.

From Aaron Dunham [1]

Supervisors Office
Trenton 9th. Septr. 1791

Sir,

On the 19th of June I wrote a Circular letter to such Gentlemen in the Different parts of this State, as I conceived would be likely to give me the best information respecting Manufactures of every kind carried on Within their knowledge. The letter inclosed is the only one as yet received in answer; as they come to hand shall forward.

I am Sir,   with all due respect   your Very Humb Sert.

Aaron Dunham

Alexander Hamilton Esquire

[E N C L O S U R E]

Silas Condict to Aaron Dunham [2]

Morris Town [New Jersey] 25 augt. 1791

Sir

I have to acknowledge the receipt of of your favour of the 19 ult. on the important Subject of our Manufactories. I Should be happy to have had it in my power to give you a more favourable account of the matter than I can do. However, in General I can Say that Industry and an attention to Mechanism is gaining Ground, tho' we have no established Companies, or Manufactories carried on here, the principal branch of business that we can call Such, is that of the Iron Manufactory; and that is carried on by individuals. We have in this County, two Furnaces, at which are made various Castings of hollow ware pig &c. two Slitting & Rooling mills; and a large number of Ironwork: Some refining but most of them are Bloomeries, and there are a number of Naileries, that are carried on, these Several branches of the Iron business employs a great Many People, which is one of the principle advantages attending it. And if some mode of Inspection, could be adopted to prevent the vending of Iron, Nails &c, not well made or unfit for Market it would I think be of great utility & tend much to perfecting the business.

Our part of the Country is well adapted for keeping Sheep, and their numbers are fast increasing among us and I doubt not but that a Woollen Manufactory might be carried on here to advantage, had we a Sufficient number of Men of Spirit and Capital to engage in it.

The Silk making Seems to ware the most favourable aspect altho it is yet only in Embrio. One Gentm. has procured Seed & has now from 60 to 100.000 plants in nursery and has got a Sufficient Quantity of the Eggs to produce a Considerable Stock of Worms next Spring, and our People Seem engaged as Soon as time maturates the Trees to apply themselves to this branch of business, and if the Legislature of the U.S. would encourage it, by Premium, or Laying a heavy Duty on imported Silk, I flatter myself that this part of the State in a Short time would benefit much by the Culture of Silk, my hopes of Success are raised more on this than any other branch, because the People in general Seem more engaged to try the Experiment, in this than any other. As I have not been engaged in the Iron business nor in the Merchantile line, it is not in my Power to give you an Estimate of the produce of the Iron, but probably you may have it from Some gentlemen that are better Qualifyed to do it than your

Huml Sert.   Silas Condict

Aaron Dunham Esqr.

ALS, Hamilton Papers, Library of Congress.
    1. Dunham was supervisor of the revenue for the District of New Jersey. H's letter to Dunham has not been found, but see "Treasury Department Circular to the Supervisors of the Revenue," June 22, 1791.
    2. ALS, Hamilton Papers, Library of Congress.
    Condict was a large landholder in Morristown, New Jersey, and served in the state General Assembly in the seventeen-nineties.

From Benjamin Lincoln

Boston Sept. 9th: 1791

Sir

The day before yesterday came on the trial at Salem of Capt Davis & yesterday his mate charged with landing good at tarpaulien cove as mentioned to you July 29. Although the fact was clearly established to the satisfaction of the Court, and so far as I can learn, to every by stander even the defendants Council gave up the matter Yet the Jury did not in either case find a verdict though sent out repeatedly by the Judge. They said they could not agree. It has been hinted that they were satisfied with regard to the fact but would not say so because the penalty they said was too high. The next term the cause will be given to a jury in this County.[1]

Secy of the Treasury

LC, Massachusetts Historical Society, Boston; LC, RG 36, Collector of Customs at Boston, Letter Book, 1790–1797, National Archives; two copies, RG 56, Letters from the Collector at Boston, National Archives.
  1. The case concerning Samuel Davis was referred to the Massachusetts Circuit Court during its November, 1791, term. Davis pleaded guilty to false swearing and was fined fifty dollars (Massachusetts Circuit Court Records, Federal Records Center, Boston).

From Joseph Whipple

Portsmo. [New Hampshire] Sep. 9th. 1791

Sir

With my letter to you of the 24 Ulto. I inclosd a description of the Cutter & gave a name for her which was handed to me at the Moment of closing the letter. Since which I have been informed there is a British public Vessel of the Name of the Ferret in Nova Scotia or Newfoundland. I conceive there woud be an impropriety in giving a Cutter of the United States the Same Name & therefore request that you will be pleased to direct the insertion of such other name in the instrument intended in lieu of a Register as will be more proper.

I directed Cap. Yeaton [1] to deal out the Provisions at the rate of 1 lb B[r]ead & 1 lb Beef or 3/4 lb Pork ℔. man ℔. day and to assure the people, whatever may be the established Rations, whether of liquers or other articles would be made up to them on Settlement, when Such Rations Shoud be known. At present they furnish their own Liquers, which is an article they expect will constitute a part of their Rations. On this point be pleased to give me instructions.

The Cutter Sailed the 26th Aug having on board a few borrowed Small arms & other Military Accoutrements.

ADf, RG 36, Portsmouth Collector, Letters Sent, 1771–1792, Vol. 3, National Archives; copy, RG 56, Letters from the Collector at Portsmouth, National Archives.
  1. Hopley Yeaton, commander of the New Hampshire revenue cutter. The cutter was eventually named the Scammell.

From John Jay

New York 10 Septr 1791

Dear Sir

I send you Copies of a Letter of 3 Augt. from Jacob Cuyler,[1] and of my answer of this Date.[2] It is natural for men circumstanced as he is, to be anxious; and as adversity too often begets neglect, marks of attention are doubly acceptable to men in his Situation. I fear you will find it difficult to do much for his Son. A little will to him be much. At any Rate write to him, and let him percieve that altho you cannot create opportunities of serving him, yet that you wish him well.

    adieu   Yours sincerely   John Jay

Col. Hamilton

ALS, Hamilton Papers, Library of Congress.
   1. Cuyler to Jay, August 3, 1791 (copy, in writing of Jay, Hamilton Papers, Library of Congress). In this letter, Cuyler, an Albany merchant, asked Jay to speak to H about the possibility of a position in the Treasury Department for Cuyler's son Richard. See also Richard Cuyler to H, May 10, 1791.
   2. Jay to Cuyler, September 10, 1791 (copy, in writing of Jay, Hamilton Papers, Library of Congress). Jay wrote that he had spoken to H about Cuyler's son, but that at present there were no vacancies in the Treasury Department.

From Eliphalet Pearson [1]

[Cambridge, Massachusetts, September 10, 1791]

Sir,

I feel myself happy in the honor of acquainting a gentleman of Mr. Hamilton's merited distinction that the American Academy of Arts & Sciences has elected him a Fellow; of which the instrument, herewith transmitted, is a Certificate executed in the usual form.[2]

   With sentiments of highest esteem, I have the honor to be,   Sir, Your most obedient &   very humble servant,

Eliphalet Pearson
Correspg. Secretary.

Cambridge 10 Septr. 1791.

ALS, Hamilton Papers, Library of Congress.
1. Pearson was Hancock Professor of Hebrew and Oriental Languages at Harvard College.
2. See "Election to the American Academy of Arts and Sciences," August 24, 1791.

From Joseph Whipple

Collectors Office Portsmo. New Hamp. Sep. 10. 1791

Sir

Your Circular letter dated the 5th. of August respecting two missing Certificates of Registry, Enjoining the Seasonable transmission of Returns, Noticing the failure of complying with the opinions of Messrs. Jones and Harrison,[1] The Information Stating a practice of Measuring Vessels of the United States previously Registered, And requesting a Copy of the Table of Fees, was received the 25th. Ulto.

Being Apprehensive that the possibility of a failure in the Conveyance of returns thro' the post offices or erroneous informations may have led to the forming unjust Ideas of the proceedings in Custom Houses which a conciousness of not falling under the imputations does not fully Satisfy, I think it necessary and judge it will be also more Satisfactory to you that answers be given to the Several paragraphs of that letter, except those respecting the Registers.

All Returns hitherto directed have been regularly transmitted from this District as soon as they could be made up. The quarterly & Monthly returns have in no instance exceeded the Month Suceeding the periord to which the Returns extended, and the Shorter delays have been Occasioned by unavoidable detentions in ascertaining duties & liquidating Bonds or in the nonpayment of Tonnage Duties which it was desirable Should be comprehended in the returns for the term in which they Occurd.

The Instructions on the Opinions of Mess. Jones & Harrison have been carefully attended to & complied with, excepting the Opinion respecting the receiving the fee of 60 cents on the 27th Section of the Coasting Act,[2] which has not in all instances been received. As no penalty is annexed to a failure of Coasters making entry as directed by that section, it is seldom complied with by Coasters, nor do I perceive in what manner they can be compelled unless by an action of debt for the fee, which if proper would be a disagreeable method when this trifling fee only is depending & it is not enjoined as an official duty.

The Measuring of Vessels of the United States previously registered and receiving a fee for such Admeasurement has never been considered in this district as a possible intention of the Legislature, or Construction of the law & the Charge for the like fee on Foreign Vessels, before measured in the port and known to have undergone no alteration of Tonnage has in some instances been given up, tho' the Same Idea is entertaind of its proprity as conveyed in your letter.

A Copy of the Table of Fees fixed up in the Custom House is enclosed.

I beg leave upon this Occasion [to] take notice that the exemption from entering & clearing of certain descriptions of Coasters exposes the Revenue to frauds—as also does the manner of entering Coasters as directed by the 28th. Section,[3] in which case a master is under no restraint by his oath, from receiving Smuggled goods on board after clearing & before his arrival at another port, as no oath is required at his entry at which time rather than at his clearing I conceive it would be proper.

I will also take the Occasion to observe that the term of 15 days allowed by law for the discharge of Vessels from foreign ports is subject to abuse, by increasing the expence of Inspectors attendance & affording opportunities for Smuggling.[4] Was the clause in the Act qualified by a proviso that the No. of hands of which the Vessel consisted Should be dayly employd till such discharge, these delays would be prevented without Subjecting the owner to any hardship. Instances have happened in which a Cargo consisting of 30 or 40 hhds Molases & 300 or 400 bushels of Salt only has been detained on board 12 or 15 days, the hands being discharged on the day of arrival & the Vessel employed as a Store.

The Hon. Alex Hamilton Esqr

ADf, RG 36, Collector of Customs at Portsmouth, Letters Sent, 1791–1792, Vol. 3, National Archives; copy, RG 56, Letters from the Collector at Portsmouth, National Archives.
    1. See Richard Harison and Samuel Jones to H, November 18, 1789.
    2. Section 27 of "An Act for Registering and Clearing Vessels, Regulating the Coasting Trade, and for other purposes" (September 1, 1789) reads as follows:

"*And be it further enacted,* That the master of every ship or vessel of the burthen of twenty tons or upwards, licensed to trade as aforesaid, not having on board rum or other ardent spirits, exceeding four hundred gallons, and arriving from one district to another in the same state, or from a district in one state to a district in the next adjoining state, with goods, wares or merchandise, of the growth or manufacture of the United States only, within twenty-four hours, Sundays excepted, next after his arrival at any place or port where a collector or surveyor resides, and before any part of the cargo on board such ship or vessel be landed or unloaded, deliver to such collector or surveyor a manifest thereof, and shall make oath or affirmation before such collector or surveyor, that such manifest contains a true account of all the goods, wares and merchandise on board such ship or vessel, and thereupon shall receive from such collector or surveyor a permit to land or unload the same." (1 *Stat.* 63.)

3. This section reads as follows: "*And be it further enacted,* That in all other cases the master of every vessel of the burthen of twenty tons or upwards, licensed to trade as aforesaid, shall within twenty-four hours, Sunday excepted, next after his arrival at any port or place within the United States, where a collector or surveyor resides, and before any part of the cargo on board any such ship or vessel be landed or unloaded, deliver to such collector or surveyor the manifest thereof, authenticated before and received from the collector or surveyor of the port or place where the said cargo was taken on board, together with his permit to depart from the place of lading, whereupon it shall be the duty of such collector or surveyor to grant a permit to land or unload such cargo" (1 *Stat.* 63).

4. Whipple is referring to Section 33 of "An Act to provide more effectually for the collection of the duties imposed by law on goods, wares and merchandise imported into the United States, and on the tonnage of ships or vessels" (1 *Stat.* 145–78 [August 4, 1790]). This section reads as follows:

"*And be it further enacted,* That if at the expiration of fifteen working days after the time within which the report of the master or person having the charge or command of any ship or vessel, is required to be made to the collector of a district as aforesaid, there shall be found on board any goods, wares or merchandise, other than shall have been reported for some other district or a foreign port or place, the said inspector or inspectors shall take possession thereof, and deliver the same to the order of the collector of the district, taking his receipt therefor, and giving a certificate thereof to the master or person having such charge or command of such ship or vessel, describing the packages and their marks and numbers. And the said goods shall be kept with due and reasonable care at the charge and risk of the owner or owners for a term of nine months; and if within that time no claim be made for the same, the said collector shall procure an appraisement thereof by two or more reputable merchants, to be certified under their hands, and to remain with him, and shall afterwards cause the said goods to be sold at public auction, and retaining the duties and charges thereon, shall pay the overplus, if any there be, into the treasury of the United States, there to remain for the use of the owner or owners, who shall upon due proof of his, her or their property, be entitled to receive the same; and the receipt or certificate of the collector shall exonerate the master or commander from all claim of the owner. *Provided,* That where any entry shall have been duly made of such goods, the same shall not be appraised; and that where such goods are of a perishable nature, they shall be sold forthwith. *Provided further,* That the said limitation of fifteen days shall not extend to ships or vessels laden with salt or coal; but if the said master or owner of any such ship or vessel requires longer time to discharge her cargo, the wages or compensation of the inspector for every day's attendance exceeding the said fifteen days, shall be paid by the said master or owner. And if by reason of the delivery of a cargo in different districts, more than the said term of fifteen working days shall in the whole be spent therein, the wages or compensation of the inspector or inspectors who may be employed on board of any ship or vessel, in respect to which the said term may be so exceeded, shall for every day of such excess be paid by the said master or owner." (1 *Stat.* 165–66.)

To Charles Lee

Treasury Department
September 11 1791

Sir

An application has been made to me for a boat for the use of the Customs at one of the ports on the Potomack below Alexandria. I am informed that the boat belonging to your district is found too large for harbour service, and that it would be more convenient to the Surveyor to have a small boat fit for the purpose to board vessels within a short distance of the Town. I wish to be informed if such an exchange appears to you expedient, and, if so, I wish to have a Seamans inventory of the boat you now have, specifying her dimensions and all her appurtenances.

The admeasurement of *foreign* vessels at every entry into your District is a practice that ought to be observed, as there can be, otherwise, no certainty of the identity of the vessel, nor of her remaining unaltered. The documents they produce are from Officers not amenable to our laws, and whose deviations from fact, therefore subject them to no penal consequences from the United States.[1] I am, with consideration, Sir,

Your Obed Servant   A Hamilton

⟨Ch⟩arles Lee Esqr.
Alexandria

LS, RG 56, Letters to and from the Collectors at Alexandria, National Archives; copy, RG 56, Letters to Collectors at Small Ports, "Set G," National Archives.
   1. Lee requested this information in his letter to H of August 20, 1791.

From Le Roy and Bayard

Newyork 11 Septber 1791

Dr Sir!

Mr. Mc.Evers [1] informed us that you would take £2000 Stg in bills on London at 4 pct; we accordingly a few days since sent him to that amount, wch. we make no doubt he will have delivered to you. Thus the Contents of your esteemed favor of the 6 Instt [2] has been complied with. We presume that you have already been informed that a Comittee from the Stockholders to the National Bank, in Boston, have addressed Several Gentlemen in this City, upon the Subject of a coopperation between the two Cities, as to Voting for Directors at the ensueing Election. A Meeting of the Stockholders, has in consequence of those Letters been convened, and they have Unanimously appointed 11 Electors who are to represent them at the Ensueing Election, and to form a junction with those of Boston. A Committee is appointed here to Correspond with that of Boston, who have in Strong terms recommended the adoption of Similar measures there, wch. may tend to prevent numerous parties wch. by holding up any particular list of Directors, would have created. Mr. Smith [3] of S. Carolina, who is appointed the Agent General from Charleston, a⟨tte⟩nded the private Committee, to whome he declared his readiness to join this and the Eastern States, in voting for Directors. The Eastern States are accordingly apprised of these measures and it is to be hoped they may have beneficial effects.[4] The choice of Electors will we presume, meet your approbation, as it was your opinion, similar measures ought to be adopted.[5]

We have the honor to remain respectfully and with Much Esteem Sir   Your humble Servants   LeRoy & Bayard
Alex. Hamilton Esq

LS, Hamilton Papers, Library of Congress.
    1. Charles McEvers, Jr. See Le Roy and Bayard to H, September 1, 1791.
    2. Letter not found.
    3. William Loughton Smith, a Federalist member of the House of Representatives from South Carolina.
    4. This and the preceding sentence refer to plans to prevent Philadelphia from controlling the Bank of the United States. In discussing the struggle for

control of the bank, James Wettereau has written: "From the outset there was marked determination on the part of New York and New England capitalists not to permit Philadelphia to dominate the Bank. The citizens of Charleston, South Carolina, were no less resolved to safeguard their interests. Under the leadership of their Hamiltonian Congressman, William Loughton Smith, they systematically organized a campaign which speedily resulted in pledges for between 650 and 1,000 shares with the avowed purpose of obtaining a branch for that city" (James O. Wettereau, "The Branches of the First Bank of the United States," *The Journal of Economic History*, II [December, 1942], Supplement, 72).

  5. See Le Roy and Bayard to H, September 1, 1791.

To Charles Lee

[*Philadelphia, September 12, 1791.* On September 21, 1791, Lee wrote to Hamilton: "Your letter of the 12th. shall be duly attended to." *Letter not found.*]

From William Seton

[New York] 12 Sep. 1791

Sir

  I am desired by the President & Directors to acknowledge the receipt of your Letter of the 7th. They have directed 50,000 Dollars to be paid to me agreeable to your desire, and the same is invested in the purchase of Stock, on account of the United States, as specified in the enclosed return.[1] I have the honor to be with great respect &ca.

LC, Bank of New York, New York City.
  1. This return is printed in *ASP, Finance,* I, 117.

From William Seton

New York 12th Sept. 1791

Dear sir

  I had the pleasure to receive your Letter of the 7th by Mr. Eddie [1] on fryday morning, but not early enough to answer you with propriety by that post. The bearer of the Letter I apprehend knew or conjectured at the Contents as it flew over the Town like Wildfire that I had orders to purchase, therefore before I got to the Coffee House at Noon, every one was prepared, and no one would offer to supply at less than the former prices.[2] I thought it prudent to accept at that, and to diffuse the benefit I divided the purchases into 5000 Dollar Lots, and held them at that, so long as to give every one a chance, and be assured it has been a very great relief. Scrip since I wrote you last [3] has been down to 110 and great sacrifices made, Saturday and today they have gone at 135 to 145 and rather bear the appearance of rising. They are now getting into the proper hands and I have no doubt will soon come up to their real value, if the price of the other funds can be now & then supported by your purchases. You have the blessings of thousands here, and I feel gratified more than I can express, at being the dispenser of your benevolence.

I am with the greatest respect   Dear sir   Your obliged Obedt Humble Sert   Wm Seton

Alexr. Hamilton Esqr.

ALS, Hamilton Papers, Library of Congress.
    1. Thomas Eddy was a New York City merchant.
    2. Three percents were purchased at 12*s*. and six percent deferreds at 12*s*. 6*d* (*ASP, Finance*, I, 117). See also Seton to H, August 18 and September 5, 1791.
    3. See Seton to H, September 5, 1791.

To Charles Lee

Treasury Department
Septr. 13. 1791

Sir,

As it is possible The President of the United States may have occasion for some Money in Alexandria,[1] you will retain for his own use one thousand Dollars. The receipt of any of the Gentlemen of his family for such part of the said sum as he may desire, when transmitted to this office will be duly covered with a warrant.

I am,   Sir,   Your obedt Servant   A Hamilton

Charles Lee Esquire
Collector
Alexandria

LS, RG 56, Letters to and from the Collectors at Alexandria, National Archives; copy, RG 56, Letters to Collectors at Small Ports, "Set G," National Archives.
    1. On September 15, 1791, Washington left Philadelphia for Mount Vernon.

From George Fox[1]

Philada. Septemr. 14th. 1791

Sir

I did myself the honor of waiting on you to mention some difficulties which have occurred in transacting business at the Treasury under a Power of Attorney received from some Gentlemen in London.

As I was not fortunate enough to meet with you I will beg permission briefly to state the circumstances of the case in hopes that some mode may be suggested to enable me to fulfill their intentions.

In consequence of a purchase made by Mr. W. T. Franklin[2] of Mr. Gouvr. Morris, Messrs. Baring Boehm & Henchman[3] transmit me (at the request of Mr. G. Morris) their Power of Atty. (accompanied by authenticated copies of several certificates) to receive the Interest due on 382,878 60/100 Drs. with instructions to transfer 66,666 2/3 Drs. to Mr. Franklin & the remainder thereof to Mr. G. Morris. At the same time Messrs. Willing Morris & Swanwick[4] receive A Power of Attorney from the same Gentlemen to loan to the United States 226,460 42/100 Dollars being I presume a part of the 382,878 60/100 Dollars mentioned before; in consequence of this power & the Instructions he had received, Mr. Swanwick transferred to my Credit 40,762 87/100 Drs in the 3 ⅌ Ct. Stock being the whole of that Stock to which those Gentlemen were intitled upon the Sum which Mr. Swanwick had subscribed to the Loan in their name—a deficiency of near 26,000 Drs. in the sum which they had directed me to transfer to Mr. Franklin appearing & Mr. Gouvr. Morris having engaged under a Penalty that the said sum of 66,666 2/3 Dolls. should be vested in the name of Mr. Franklin in the 3 ⅌ Cent Stock on or before the 15th day of Septemr. 1791 I am desirous of learning if any means could wth safety be adopted to prevent Mr. G. Morris from incurring that Penalty by securing Mr. Franklin in due time the sum directed to be transferred to him.

I have the honor to be &c

The Honble The Secretary of Treasury of the United States

1. Fox was a Philadelphia attorney. For background to this letter, see Gouverneur Morris to H, June 28, 1791.

2. William Temple Franklin, Benjamin Franklin's grandson, had been sent to Europe in 1790 by Robert Morris to sell New York wilderness land.

3. Sir Francis Baring, Edmund Boehm, and Thomas Henchman, London bankers.

4. The Philadelphia firm of Thomas Willing, Robert Morris, and John Swanwick.

From Henry Marchant

Rhode Island District
Newport Sept. 14. 1791

In pursuance of an Act of the Congress of the United States "to provide for mitigating or remitting Forfeitures and Penalties accruing under the Revenue Laws, in certain Cases therein mentioned" [1] I have recd. the Petition of Peleg Saunders [2] hereto annexed, and thereupon caused William Ellery Collector, Robert Crooke Naval Officer, and Daniel Lyman Surveyor of Newport District, the Persons claiming a moiety of the fifteen Hogshead of Rum and one Keg of Medecines upon forfeiture thereof upon their Libel filed before me, if such forfeiture should take Place, and also William Channing Esqr. Attorney of the United States for said Rhode Island District to be noticed to appear before me and shew Cause if any they had against the mitigation or remission thereof, and who declar'd they had no Cause to offer against the Remission prayed for by the said Petitioner, nor had They any Reason to disbelieve the Facts and Circumstances as stated and set forth in said Petition. Whereupon I proceeded to examine into the Truth of the Facts so set forth by the said Petitioner in a summary Manner And by the Report by him openly made signed and deliverd to the said Collector, of the said Goods, by the Declaration of the said Petitioner under solemn Oath to me made, As also by the Testimony of Oliver Burdick of Westerly within sd. District, who also under Oath declared that he was no way interested in said Vessell or Goods, but was a Hand on Board said Vessell in the Employ of the said Petitioner &c at the Time said Effects were taken on Board and hath so continued ever since. As also by the Certificates of the Inspector of New London mentioned in said Petition, and which the said Danl. Lyman Surveyor for the District of Newport acknowledgeth, strictly compares and agrees with the Marks &c

upon the said Hogsheads. It appears The Facts and Circumstances stated and set forth in said Petition are true. All which I do hereby certify to the Secretary of the Treasury of the United States.

Henry Marchant
Judge of Rhode Island District

ADfS, Rhode Island Historical Society, Providence; ALS, sold at Parke-Bernet Galleries, April 10, 1962, Lot 126.

1. Under the terms of this act "any person who now is, or hereafter shall be liable to a fine, penalty or forfeiture, or interested in any vessel, goods, wares or merchandise, or other thing which may be subject to seizure and for-feiture . . . shall prefer his petition to the judge of the district in which such fine, penalty or forfeiture may have accrued, truly and particularly setting forth the circumstances of his case, and shall pray that the same may be mitigated or remitted; the said judge shall inquire in a summary manner into the circumstances of the case, first causing reasonable notice to be given to the person or persons claiming such fine, penalty or forfeiture, and to the attorney of the United States for such district, that each may have an opportunity of showing cause against the mitigation or remission thereof; and shall cause the facts which shall appear upon such inquiry, to be stated and annexed to the petition, and direct their transmission to the Secretary of the Treasury. . ." (1 *Stat.* 122–23 [May 26, 1790]).

2. Saunders was a resident of Westerly, Rhode Island. In 1787 he had served as a justice of the peace for Westerly.

George Washington to George Clinton [1]

[*Philadelphia*] *September 14, 1791.* Discusses the possibility of the British establishing a post south of Lake Champlain.

Df, in the handwriting of H, RG 59, Miscellaneous Letters, 1790–1799, National Archives.

1. Clinton was governor of New York.

From Jeremiah Olney

Custom-House,
Providence 15th September 1791.

Sir.

On the Thirteenth instant Entered here, from Bordeaux, the Brigan-tine Betsey, John Arnold Master, the Property of Mr. Stephen Dexter of this Place: In her were imported Ten Kegs of Brandy, consigned to James Johnson of New-York; which, together with the Vessel, being forfeited by the 33 Section of the Excise Act,[1] I have requested the District Attorney to proceed against them as the law directs; tho in justice to the Master, I declare that I have no suspicion of his having the least Intention to defraud the Revenue, and that I believe the forfeiture had been incurred through ignorance of the Law in both him and the Shipper.[2]

I have the Honor to be &c.   Jereh. Olney Collr.

Alexr. Hamilton Esqr.
Secy of the Treasury.

ADfS, Rhode Island Historical Society, Providence; copy, RG 56, Letters from the Collector at Providence, National Archives.

1. Section 33 of "An Act repealing, after the last day of June next, the duties heretofore laid upon Distilled Spirits imported from abroad, and laying others in their stead; and also upon Spirits distilled within the United States, and for appropriating the same" reads in part as follows: "*And be it further enacted,* That after the last day of June next, no spirituous liquors excepting gin or cordials in cases, jugs or bottles, shall be brought from any foreign port or place, in casks of less capacity than fifty gallons at the least, on pain of forfeiting of the said spirits, and of the ship or vessel in which they shall be brought" (1 *Stat.* 199–214 [March 3, 1791]). As a keg held no more than ten gallons, it was a clear violation of the law to import brandy in kegs.

2. On October 15, 1791, under the terms of "An Act to provide for mitigating or remitting the forfeitures and penalties accruing under the revenue laws, in certain cases therein mentioned" (1 *Stat.* 122–23 [May 26, 1790]) H issued a warrant of remission to Dexter (DS, Columbia University Libraries).

To William Ellery

[*Philadelphia, September 16, 1791.* On October 4, 1791, Ellery wrote to Hamilton: "I have received your letter of the 16th of Septemr." *Letter not found.*]

From Tobias Lear

[*Philadelphia*] *September 16, 1791.* "T: Lear has the honor to transmit to the Secretary of the Treasury a Commission for Benjn. Cudworth, Inspector of Survey No. 2. in South Carolina."

LC, George Washington Papers, Library of Congress.

To Benjamin Lincoln [1]

Treasury Department.
Septr. 16th. 1791

Sir,

The practice of the Surveyor of Boston [2] in measuring American vessels (not new) only when they are transferred into your district, as also in measuring foreign vessels at every entry is perfectly regular.

It will be agreeable to me that the builders of the cutter receive her back on delivering a vessel equally good, and well fit, and not exceeding *the rate* of 63 $63\frac{6}{95}$ tons for 1440 dollars. The Cutter constructed at the district of Portsmouth New Hampshire is of 51 $51\frac{81}{95}$ Tons and she is deemed equal to the service on that coast and Massachusetts.

In thus expressing myself however I do not mean to preclude a different Judgment of yourself and others on the spot. For the sufficiency of the vessel is of primary consequence. But I shall be glad to find that, on full consideration, *one* short of the dimensions you propose may be found adequate to the object. The smaller the vessel, if of competent size, the more cheaply she may be kept in good condition, the more manageable she will be with the number of hands allowed and the more certain I shall be of not exceeding the pecuniary limits prescribed by the Legislature.

You are right in your ideas that only such expenditures as have been incurred in relation to the Portland light house since the time of your authorising the gentlemen you refer to, in your letter, to superintend the completion of the building under the authority and for the account of the United States are to be admitted. By exhibiting the act to the Gentlemen you will find no difficulty in convincing them it does not apply to any expenditures prior to its date.[3]

My ideas on the subject of prosecuting the receivers of run goods are not intended to preclude exemption in favor of those whose testimony has been previously made use of, with hopes of exemption.

You will find enclosed a copy of a return of the Surveyor of Portsmouth,[4] containing the Dimensions of the Cutter.

I am with great consideration   Sir   Your obedt Servant
Alex. Hamilton

Benjn. Lincoln Esqr
Collr.
Boston

LS, RG 36, Collector of Customs at Boston, Letters from the Treasury and Others, 1790–1817, Vol. 10, National Archives; copy, RG 26, Lighthouse Letters Received, Revenue Cutter Service Letters Sent, Vol. "O," National Archives; copy, RG 56, Letters to the Collector at Boston, National Archives; copy, RG 56, Letters to Collectors at Small Ports, "Set G," National Archives.

1. H wrote this letter in reply to Lincoln to H, August 25, 31, 1791.
2. Thomas Melville (Melvill).
3. The first section of "An Act for the establishment and support of Lighthouses, Beacons, Buoys, and Public Piers" reads in part as follows: "*Be it enacted* . . . That all expenses which shall accrue from and after the fifteenth day of August, one thousand seven hundred and eighty-nine, in the necessary support, maintenance and repairs of all lighthouses, beacons, buoys and public piers erected, placed, or sunk before the passing of this act . . . shall be defrayed out of the treasury of the United States" (1 *Stat.* 53–54 [August 7, 1789]).
4. Thomas Martin.

To George Washington

[Philadelphia, September 16, 1791]

Sir,

I have the honor to enclose the copy of a letter from Mr. Brown [1] of Kentucke, to Genl. Irvine,[2] giving an account of some interesting particulars in the Western Country. Part of the letter, I have understood, has been forwarded to you, but not the whole. Genl. Irvine is of opinion that the waters will be still so far practicable as to permit the progress of the Troops under Genl. Butler; by the expedient of dragging the Boats in the shallowest places.[3]

With perfect respect &c. &c.   A: Hamilton

Philada.
16th. Septr. 1791.

[ENCLOSURE]

John Brown to William Irvine [4]

[Danville, Virginia, August 22, 1791]

Sir,

An Express from Gen: Wilkinson [5] has this moment reached this place informing of his success. He has destroyed a large Indian Town situated at the banks of the Wabash; also a Kichapoo town containing about 30 houses, & has killed & taken 42 of the enemy. His loss two men killed & one wounded. I have not as yet heard where the Express left him, but expect he has repassed the Ohio before this time. Genl. St. Clair is now here endeavouring to procure aid from the Kentucke militia. His regular force, as yet, does not exceed 500 or 600 men & the river is too low to admit of Boats descending from Fort Pitt. I fear he will meet with great difficulty in obtaining assistance from this Country as the Militia are extremely averse to a co-operation with the regulars, & I am doubtful whether they can be compelled by the Laws of this State, especially as the Executive of Virginia [6] has given no orders upon the subject to the Lieutenants of this District. [7] The Bearer will only allow me time to assure you that,

I am   With very great respect   Sir,   Your Mo: Hble Servt.

J: Brown

Danville
22d. Augt. 1791

P. S. Have lately received two packets from you.

LC, George Washington Papers, Library of Congress.

1. John Brown had been a member of the Virginia Senate from the District of Kentucky from 1784 to 1788 and a member of the Continental Congress from the Kentucky District of Virginia in 1787 and 1788. When this letter was written, he was a member of the House of Representatives from Virginia. In May, 1791, he accompanied the expedition of Brigadier General Charles Scott against the Indians on the Scioto River.

2. William Irvine, who had risen to the rank of brigadier general during the American Revolution, had been a member of the Continental Congress from Pennsylvania from 1786 to 1788.

3. Arthur St. Clair began his ill-fated campaign against the western Indians in September, 1791. His second-in-command was Richard Butler, Indian Superintendent of the Northern District. During the summer of 1791 Butler was engaged in recruiting and provisioning in Pittsburgh, but his failure to move

his troops by the end of the summer from Fort Pitt to Fort Washington near Cincinnati caused serious concern to both Knox and St. Clair. Although he did reach Fort Washington on September 7, word of his arrival had still not reached Philadelphia by September 24 (Knox to Washington, September 24, 1791, Smith, *St. Clair Papers*, II, 241-42).

4. LC, George Washington Papers, Library of Congress.

5. During the American Revolution James Wilkinson had served as a brigadier general and after the war had settled in Kentucky where he engaged in various separatist intrigues. In August, 1791, he led an expedition against the Indians north of the Ohio. For an account of this expedition, see Wilkinson to St. Clair, August 24, 1791, Smith, *St. Clair Papers*, II, 233-39.

6. Beverley Randolph.

7. Concerning the difficulties St. Clair faced in obtaining militia from Kentucky for the western campaign, Knox wrote to Washington on September 24 as follows: "He called upon the county lieutenants to meet him the 3d of September, in order to obtain from them as many militia as he might require. He was induced to this measure from the advice of Judge Innes, and others, in order to persuade the lieutenants, to a measure, which it seems they would enter with an order from the Governor of Virginia, which they had not received. I wrote to the Governor of Virginia, by your authority, on the 15th of July, requesting him to instruct the county lieutenants of Kentucky that, in case General St. Clair should call for militia, that there should be no obstruction. He answered on the 4th of August, 'that he had embraced the first opportunity to instruct General Scott to use every exertion to insure them of ample compliance with the requisition of the general of the Federal troops for militia.' But I flatter myself that he will not think proper to require any militia, excepting, perhaps, two or three hundred mounted volunteers." (Smith, *St. Clair Papers*, II, 241-42).

From George Washington

[Head of Elk, Maryland, September 16, 1791]

Dr. Sir,

Whilst I was in Wilmington [1] waiting breakfast to day, I made the best enquiry time & circumstances would permit, for some fit character to fill the office lately held by Doctr. Latimer.[2] Several persons were mentioned, but the weight of information was in favor of one Andrew Barratt. He was spoken of by Mr. Vining[3] as a man of respectable character, of decision and temper. He now is, or lately has been high Sheriff of the county of Kent; & no man, it is said, could have discharged the duties of that Office better. Mr. Bedford,[4] though he had another person in view, (Majr. Jacquet),[5] accords in this opinion of Barratt. Doctor Latimer, whom I afterwards called upon, at New port, for the purpose of enquiry, also speaks well of Barratt. He did indeed, before I mentioned the name of Barratt to him, say that he thought Majr. Patten[6] of Dover the best person that readily occurred to him for this office, but yielded a ready assent to the qualifications of Barratt. None knows whether he would, or would not accept the appointment. Among other things, urged in his favor by Mr. Vining, are his living near the centre of the State—amidst the Stills, and where the most discontent is said to be. To Mr. Chew [7] of Philada. Mr. Vining particularly appeals for the character of Mr. Barratt.

If his testimony is in favor of this character, I think it will be an eligible appointment.[8] A blank commission, signed, has been left with Mr. Lear for the Supervisor of the Delaware District.

With much esteem & regard   I am Dear Sir,   Your Mo: Obt. Servant   G: Washington

Head of Elk
16th. Septr. 1791.

LC, George Washington Papers, Library of Congress.
1. Wilmington, Delaware. Washington was en route from Philadelphia to Mount Vernon.
2. Dr. Henry Latimer had resigned as supervisor of the revenue for the District of Delaware.
3. John Vining was a member of the House of Representatives from Delaware.
4. Gunning Bedford, Jr., a signer of the Constitution, was a Federal judge for the District of Delaware.
5. Peter Jaquett, who served in the Delaware Regiment throughout the American Revolution and was brevetted a major in 1783, had unsuccessfully sought appointments from Washington on two earlier occasions (April 18, 1789, and January 16, 1791). See Hunt, *Calendar of Applications*, 66.
6. John Patten rose to the rank of major in the Delaware Regiment during the Revolution. He was taken prisoner at Camden, South Carolina, on August 16, 1780, and was on parole until the close of the war.
7. Benjamin Chew, a lawyer, became president and judge of the Pennsylvania Court of Errors and Appeals in October, 1791.
8. Barratt's appointment was confirmed by the Senate on November 7, 1791.

From Joseph Whipple

Portsmouth [*New Hampshire*] *September 16, 1791.* "The Dicas's Hydrometer forwardd me to replace the One first Sent which proved defective came to hand but having found a workman who has effectually repaired the defective one, I have two on hand one of which I will direct as you will please to order. The Thermometer that was forwardd from the Treasury is by Accident broken. It was in the hands of one of the Inspectors, a very careful man, who was assisting the Surveyor. A Similar Accident befel a Neat Thermometer before in use which was borrowd of a Physician, (& wch. I have Sent to London to repair). I have endeaverd to procure one in Boston & Other places in this Vicinity without Success—be pleased to order one from Philadelphia for *the use* of this District. I have the pleasure to enclose you herewith the State of a Manufactory of Sail Cloth lately established in New Hampshire." [1]

LC, RG 36, Collector of Customs at Portsmouth, Letters Sent, 1791–1792, Vol. 3, National Archives; copy, RG 56, Letters from the Collector at Portsmouth, National Archives.

1. For a discussion of textile manufactures in Portsmouth at this time, see Bagnall, *Textile Industries*, I, 134.

From Jeremiah Olney

Custom-House,
Providence 17th Septemr. 1791.

Sir.

I have received your Letter of the 7th Instant, relative to the Brigantine Trinidada; and agreeable to your request I enclose a copy of the Surveyor's Certificate of her Measurement and Description, together with the Register granted under this State. By an additional Certificate upon the former, you will perceive that the disagreement between the Vessel, and the Register granted by me, in the two particulars you mention, was occasioned by an error in Judgement, and a mistake in the Surveyor. And in the latter, it is said she was built at Philadelphia in the Year 1786: this Register not being produced when she was registered in my Office (it having been found, since the receipt of your Letter, among the Papers of the late State Collector) Mr. Brown has doubtless forgot when and where she was built; but Capt. Joseph Cooke of this Place, who purchased her for Messrs. Brown & Francis at Trinidada, says, that in the Certificate of registry he had with her, which cannot now be found, it was declared that she was built at, either Chester in Pennsylvania, or Wilmington in Delaware, but which of them he does not recollect. Mr. Francis being absent, it is not in my power to account for the disagreement between the enclosed Register and the Information of Capt. Cooke, the truth of which I have no reason to doubt. The Certificate of Registry granted by me, I transmitted on the Sixth Instant.

Mr. Coxe's Letter, acknowledging the receipt of a Draft for 1490 Dollars, paid by me, I have received.

I have the Honor to be &c.   Jereh. Olney Collr.

Alex. Hamilton Esqr.
Secy. of the Treasury.

ADfS, Rhode Island Historical Society, Providence; copy, RG 56, Letters from the Collector at Providence, National Archives.

Receipt from William Pearce

Philadelphia Sepr. 17. 1791

Received of Alexander Hamilton, Fifty Dollars, towards procuring Machines [1] for a Cotton Manufactory.   Wm. Pearce

DS, in handwriting of H, Hamilton Papers, Library of Congress.
1. For a "list of Mr Willm Pearce's Machines," see "Receipt from William Pearce," August 20, 1791, note 2.

From William Ellery

Collrs. Office Sept. 19th: 1791
Port of Newport [Rhode Island]

Sir,

The Schooner Lydia Peleg Saunders master burthen 34 26/95 tons arrived here from the Port of Stonington in the District of New London on the 12th. of this month, with a cargo consisting of fifteen hhds. of West India Rum, One box and one kegg of medicine and eight cords of oak wood; without a manifest or permit. The Schooner was duely enrolled and licensed. The master produced to the office Certificates of the Rum subscribed by the Inspector of the Revenue for the Port of Stonington,[1] which, when comparison made by the Inspector of the Revenue of this Port,[2] agreed with the marks on the hogsheads. It appeared upon examining the master and the shipper of the Rum, that the Schooner was bound from Connecticut river with a Load of firewood for this port, that she stopped at Stonington, that the master was perswaded to land there the wood on his deck, and take thereon the Rum and medicine and proceed with them to this Port, that through ignorance he departed from the Port of Stonington for this Port without a manifest and permit and that he had no intention to defraud the Revenue. Indeed his coming to the office on his arrival, and producing certificates of the Rum showed that he had no fraudulent design. But by Sec. 29 of the Act for Regg. & Clearing Vessels, Regulating the Coasting Trade, and for other purposes, the said goods being subjected to seizure and forfeiture, and the master to forfeit & pay the sum of four hundred Dollars,[3] and the office not being invested with any discretionary powers in this regard, I seized the goods, and they are libelled, and a suit is instituted against the master. He has petitioned the District Judge,[4] and the Judge will transmit the facts stated and annexed to the attestor's petition by this Post.

The Sloop Betsy, Thomas Cottrell claimant,[5] was sold on the 14th. of this month at public auction for five hund. and sixty three Dollars, which was nearly her value. I should be very happy to have your sentiments as to the manner of distributing the moiety which doth not appertain to the United States.

This will be accompanied by a weekly return of monies received and paid, by a Certife. of Registry No. 3. granted at the Port of Washington dated Apl. 13th 1790, and delivered up on a transfer of property, and a Copy of endorsment of change of master on Regr. No. 34. granted at this Port 20th. Sepr. 1790.[6]

I am Sir   Yr. most obedt. Servant   Wm Ellery

A Hamilton Esqr
Secry of Treasy

LC, Newport Historical Society, Newport, Rhode Island.
1. John Chester.
2. John S. Dexter.
3. "An Act for Registering and Clearing Vessels, Regulating the Coasting Trade, and for other purposes" (1 *Stat.* 63 [September 1, 1789]).
4. See Henry Marchant to H, September 14, 1791.
5. See Ellery to H, August 2, 23, 26, 1791.
6. Ellery endorsed the letter book copy of this letter "Answered." H's reply has not been found.

To Joseph Whipple

[*Philadelphia, September 19, 1791*. In a letter to Hamilton dated October 7, 1791, Whipple referred to "your letter of the 19th. Ulto." *Letter not found.*]

From Terence O'Neill

[Philadelphia, September 20, 1791]

Sir

A plan having been suggested to establish a Cotton as well as other Manufactories in the United States, on principles devised by your wisdom, and in consequence of which a subscription is set on foot, Mechanics encouraged, and Machines imported to put this National work into execution.[1] Notwithstanding that artists well qualified in every branch necessary to promote the undertaking may be procured, yet it is as essential that persons qualified to superintend these several Manufactures and who may have a general knowledge of the Manufacturing business should also be engaged. Having been bred for many years to the Business of superintending & keeping the Books of a very extensive Cotton Manufactory in Ireland, together with my experience in the Manchester trade, acquired by carrying on business extensively in that line for some years on my own account; I am induced from these qualifications to offer myself as a person capable of Conducting the Cotton Branch in every particular whatever. I'll assert myself capable of planing the Books for this business, in a suitable and concise manner and in such order that the accounts shall correspond so as to shew the disposition of every ounce of the Raw Materials and the several operations at one view which will be a means of preventing fraud in any part of the business, if any shou'd be attempted. The prime cost of every article shall also be calculated, that the Commissioners who may be appointed to make the sales, cannot be imposed on in any respect. In short, I think I may without arrogance assert myself qualified to observe & correct any errors that may occur in any part of this branch of business, as well as to detect any fraud or defect that might appear either thro' neglect or design.

Should I on this occasion, Sir, meet with your approbation, as doubt-less yours will be necessary for every person who may be employed in this undertaking, I shall deem myself highly gratified, and in the mean time shou'd you wish to have any conversation with me on the subject, I shall do myself the honor to wait on you, whenever it may suit your Convenience. Such security for my good conduct shall be given as may be required. In case you would favor me with your sentiments in this occasion, I beg leave to inform you I lodge at the corner of Front and Race Streets, No. 137.

I have the honor to be Sir, your most obedt. very humble servant

Terence O Neill

Philadelphia 20th, September 1791

ALS, Hamilton Papers, Library of Congress.

1. See "Prospectus of the Society for Establishing Useful Manufactures," August, 1791.

Treasury Department Circular
to the Collectors of the Customs

Treasury Department
Sept 20th 1791

Sir,

It has been suggested to me that the Grocers in one of the Seaport Towns of the United States have received applications from Persons concerned in foreign trade for the purchase of their Casks marked "Old Stock." It will be quickly perceived that such a measure affords the strongest reason to suspect, that illicit practices, evasive of both the Revenue and impost are intended. To prevent the mischiefs which would arise from such purchases, I recommend that due notice be given to the Dealers in Rum, and others concerned, that on applica-tion to the Revenue offices, an officer will attend at their Rumstores for the purpose of seeing the marks of "Old Stock" &c. completely dubbed or taken off, and receiving the certificate, which had accom-panied the Cask into their hands. These certificates should be can-celled by cutting a hole thro the signers name and should be returned and filed in your office. The Casks may then be sold or used for any other purpose, which will prevent the necessity of selling them.[1]

I am with consideration   Sir   Your obedt Servant
                                                    Alex Hamilton

LS, The Andre deCoppet Collection, Princeton University Library.
    1. For the significance of casks marked "Old Stock," see Section 26 of "An Act repealing, after the last day of June next, the duties heretofore laid upon Distilled Spirits imported from abroad, and laying others in their stead; and also upon Spirits distilled within the United States, and for appropriating the same" (1 *Stat.* 205 [March 3, 1791]).

From Charles Lee

Alexandria [Virginia] 21st. Septr 1791

Sir!

    Your letter of the 12th.[1] shall be duly attended to. The Scale Beam and Chains, Scale plates and Triangle intended for the Collector of George Town [2] have arrived and will be forwarded to him by the first opportunity.

    The inclosed is a copy of a claim in favour of Charles Page [3] which is submitted to you for your direction as to the payment expected from me. Without further authority from the Treasury Department I do not conceive myself authorized to discharge it.

    I am Sir! with respect   Your most Obedt. Servant
                                                    Charles Lee
                                                    Collector at Alexandria

Copy, RG 56, Letters to and from the Collector at Alexandria, National Archives.
    1. Letter not found.
    2. John Cogdell was collector of customs at Georgetown, South Carolina.
    3. This claim concerned compensation for Page as a witness in a suit against William Simpson.

To Benjamin Lincoln

Treasury Department
Sepr. 21 1791

Sir

    You will pay into the Bank of Massachusettes whatever monies may be in your hands, on the last day of this month, over and above what it may be necessary for you to retain to satisfy any Treasury drafts which you may have accepted and to fulfil any services which have been committed to your superintendence. For the sum you may pay in, you will take duplicate receipts, one of which you will forward here as a voucher for covering the payment with the usual warrant.

Benj Lincoln Esqr &c

AL[S], RG 36, Collector of Customs at Boston, Letters from the Treasury, 1772–1818, Vol. 6, National Archives; copy, RG 56, Letters to the Collector at Boston, National Archives; copy, RG 56, Letters to Collectors at Small Ports, "Set G," National Archives.

To the President and Directors of the Bank of New York

[*Philadelphia, September 21, 1791*. On October 1, 1791, William Seton wrote to Hamilton: "I am desired by the President and Directors to acknowledge the receipt of your Letters of the 21 & 24 Sepr." *Letter of September 21 not found.*]

From Jean Baptiste de Ternant [1]

Philadelphie 21 Sepre. 1791

Mr.

Une revolte dans les atteliers de la partie francaise de st. Dominque [2] m'oblige d'y faire passer sans delay des secours de tous les genres dont le Gouvernemen annonce avoir le plus pressant besoin. Mes moyens ne pouvant Suffire aux achats indispensables dans cette occasion, je vous prie de vouloir m'accorder sur le Tresor federal un credit de 40 mille dollars à valoir en à compte de ce que les Etats unis doivent à la france.

Le cas est si urgent, et je suis tellement convaincu de votre sincere attachement aux interets de ma patrie que je ne doute nullement de votre empressement à accueillir ma sollicitation. Je ne manquerai pas de la mettre au plutot sous les yeux du President des Etats unis, et je suis persuadé qu'il ne desapprouvera pas le parti que vous aurez pris d'acquiescer à ma demande.[3]

J'ai l'honeur d'etre &c.

Copy, *Arch. des Aff. Etr., Corr. Pol., Etats-Unis*, Vol. 35; LC (English translation), George Washington Papers, Library of Congress.
    1. Ternant, the French Minister Plenipotentiary to the United States, arrived
in Philadelphia on August 10, 1791.
    2. The slave revolt on the plantations in Haiti began on August 23, 1791. It
resulted in widespread property damage in most of the northern plain around
Cap Français.
    3. Washington was at Mount Vernon.

To Jean Baptiste de Ternant

Treasury Department
Sept. 21st. 1791.

Sir

Regretting most sincerely the calamitous event announced in your
letter of this day, it is with real pleasure, I find myself in a condition
to inform you, that the sum you desire is at your command to operate
as a payment, on account of the debt due to France.

It will be most convenient to the Treasury if you can accommodate
the objects you have to fulfill to the following installments—of a
sum of Ten thousand dollars immediately—of a further sum of fifteen thousand dollars at the end of thirty days—and of the remaining
fifteen thousand at the end of sixty days, the whole advance to be
completed in sixty days.

I presume you will find this arrangement not less favorable to your
purposes than the immediate possession of the intire sum. But you
are, nevertheless, at liberty to draw for the whole or any part of it
as fast as you may find it necessary. I reserve to myself, only the
option of paying either here or at New York.

I have the honor to be   Sir,   Your most obed s   Alex Hamilton

His Excellency
The Minister Plenipotentiary of France.

LS, *Arch. des Aff. Etr., Corr. Pol., Etats-Unis*, Vol. 20; copy (French translation), *Arch. des Aff. Etr., Corr. Pol., Etats-Unis*, Vol. 35.

Treasury Department Circular
to the Collectors of the Customs

Treasury Department
September 21 1791

Sir

It being necessary to fix the rates at which the additional rations for the Officers of the Cutters are to be paid for, I have determined, on consideration, to instruct you to allow to the Captain & other Officers of the Cutter, under your Agency, the sum of nine Cents for every ration which they shall not draw, and for which they shall prefer to receive payment in money. It will also be agreeable to me that you should allow the Captain the like sum for all other rations, whether for himself, the Officers or the hands, provided he will engage to furnish for the same a sufficiency of the component parts of the Rations (not less than those underwritten) to the several persons belonging to the Cutter who shall be entitled to draw the same.

It will readily be understood that this arrangement has for object a due supply of the Seamen, (as far as it relates to them) and that it is expected that the whole sum to be allowed in lieu of the ration be expended in the Supply.

I am, Sir,   Your Most Obedt. Servant   Alex Hamilton

Component parts of a Ration—
One pound of beef or 3/4 lb of pork
One pound of bread or flour
Half a jill of Rum, brandy or whisky.
One quart of Salt
Two quarts of vinegar
Two pounds of Soap   } per 100 Rations
One pound of Candles

LS, to Jedediah Huntington, MS Division, New York Public Library; LS, Office of the Secretary, United States Treasury Department; copy, United States Finance Miscellany, Treasury Circulars, Library of Congress; copy, RG 56, Circulars of the Office of the Secretary, "Set T," National Archives.

Treasury Department Circular
to the Collectors of the Customs

Treasury Department,
September 21, 1791.

Sir,

It being necessary to ascertain correctly the state of the public monies in the several Custom-Houses, I enclose you a form of a return of bonds which may not be paid with punctuality, which it is my desire that you regularly transmit at foot of every monthly return of bonds, though there should be none unpaid, noting in the proper column that the fact is so.

Those parts which are printed in Italic characters, are proposed to be varied as the dates, parties, names, sums, &c. shall, in the future course of business, require. In order to shew the state of things at the time of commencing the transmission of these returns, it will be proper that the first monthly schedule of bonds, which you shall send forward after the receipt of this letter, shall be accompanied with a general return of bonds unpaid (if any such there be) from the opening of the Custom-House in your district to the time of making up the return.

It will be proper in future that all draughts of the Treasurer upon you have a hole cut or punched through his signature, about one half of an inch in diameter, prior to your transmitting them to this office.

The following regulation is proposed hereafter with respect to cancelled certificates of registry and enrolment. When a master or owner of a vessel, or any person in their behalf shall deliver a certificate of registry or enrolment to any Collector from whose district the same shall not have been issued, the said certificate or enrolment is before filing to be punched or cut through, in the place of the signature of the Secretary of the Treasury or Collector, with a hole of not less than half an inch diameter. After which the said certificate is to be transmitted by the first post to this office, where the margin containing the subscription and seal of the Custom-House officers will be cut off, and transmitted with the requisite memorandums for cancelling the bond, and may be filed in your office.

In regard to the admeasurement of vessels I think it necessary to give the following instructions. 1st. All foreign vessels are to be ad-measured whenever they shall arrive in your district under circumstances, which occasion the tonnage duty to *accrue* upon them, and 2d. all vessels of the United States are to be admeasured anew upon every change of property, or upon their introduction as vessels belonging to your district from some other district in which they were before owned; or in other words whenever it is necessary to grant a new register.

Alex Hamilton

I am, Sir,   Your obedient Servant,   Secretary of the Treasury.

P.S. It is much wished that the returns of duties on Tonnage and goods imported for the quarter ending the last of Septr. may be forwarded with all possible *dispatch;* in order to prepare for Congress early in the session a general return for the year preceding.

LS, to Jeremiah Olney, Rhode Island Historical Society, Providence; LS, Massachusetts Historical Society, Boston; LS, MS Division, New York Public Library; L[S], RG 36, Collector of Customs at Boston, Letters from the Treasury and Others, 1789–1809, Vol. 1, National Archives; L[S], RG 56, Circulars of the Office of the Secretary, "Set T," National Archives; copy, Circulars of the Treasury Department, 1789–1814, Library of Congress.

From William Ellery

Collrs Office
Port of Newport [Rhode Island] Sepr. 22 1791

Sir

I am informed by the Surveyor of the Port of No. Kingstown,[1] that it is common for fishing Vessels belonging to that Port to bring grindstones, and the masters of them declare that the rough Stones are taken from shores in the Brith. Dominions as ballast and manufactured by the hands on board on their passage home. On this information permit me to raise the following questions. Supposing on Inquiry it should turn out that Grind-stones said to be so obtained and manufactd. were purchased of the British? or that the raw materials were given by or purchased of them, and manufactured by fishermen on shore; or that the materials should in fact be taken from British shores without purchase, and be manufactured as before mentioned what penalty or forfeiture would be incurred in either of these cases?

The 23d. Sec: of the Coastg. Act requires that bond shall be given that such vessels shall not be employed in any illicit trade or commerce.[2] I am in doubt whether the expression *illicit* trade and commerce comprehends either of the cases mentioned. If it should, then the bond in that case would be forfeited, and the goods liable to forfeiture: if not I would then ask, is any penalty or forfeiture incurred and what? or are the goods subject only to the payment of duties? If the Sec: referred doth not touch the cases put, I have not been able to find any one that doth.

I conceive that articles manufactured of foreign materials by the cits. of the U. S. on foreign shores are to be considered as foreign, and on importan. in Licensed vessels are subject to the same penalties, forfeitures or duties, as if manufactured by and purchased of foreigners, but I am doubtful whether raw materials of foreign growth manuf. by cits. of these States in foreign ports or places on board Licensed vessels of the U States, and imported in them are in the same predicament. Cabinets made any more than vessels built by such citizens of foreign materials in foreign territories would not I imagin be deemed to be of the manufe. of the U. S.: but might not cabinets or grind stones made of such materials on board such vessels by such citizens in foreign ports or places be considered as of the manufacture of the U. S.?

I hope I shall not be thought too particular in my enquiries; and it gives me pain to divert an attention engaged in the most important objects; but a wish to know my duty and to be prepared to perform it must be my apology for desiring your sentiments as soon as may be convenient on the foregoing questions. I will only beg leave to add that the arrival of several fishing vessels in this District is daily expected, and they may be under one or the other of the circumstances I have stated.

I am   Sir   Yr. most obedt. servant   Wm Ellery Collr

A Hamilton Esqr
Secry Treasy

LC, Newport Historical Society, Newport, Rhode Island.
1. Daniel Eldridge Updike.
2. "An Act for Registering and Clearing Vessels, Regulating the Coasting Trade, and for other purposes" (1 *Stat.* 61 [September 1, 1789]).

To Benjamin Lincoln

Treasury Department Sept 22d 1791

Sir

A certificate of Registry No 16, granted by you, for the Ship Lucretia, has been delivered up, at the Port of Newbern in north Carolina, and returned to this officer by the Collector of that port.[1] Inclosed you will receive part of the certificate,[2] containing the official Seals and signatures of yourself and the naval Officer; [3] which is transmitted to you, in order that the Bond given agreeable to law, may be allowed to be cancelled.[4]

I am sir   Your obedt Servt   A Hamilton

Benj Lincoln Esqr
Collector
Boston

LS, RG 36, Collector of Customs at Boston, Letters from the Treasury, 1790–1807, Vol. 4, National Archives; copy, RG 56, Letters to the Collector at Boston, National Archives; copy, RG 56, Letters to Collectors at Small Ports, "Set G," National Archives.

1. John Daves.
2. This reads as follows: "Register No 16—January 14th 1790 Ship Lucretia, John Callahan master, succeeded by Erasmus Thomson, master and afterwards commanded again by sd Callahan, first & last owner the said John Callahan, built at Boston in Massachusetts" (D, RG 36, Collector of Customs at Boston, Letters from the Treasury, 1790-1807, Vol. 4, National Archives).
3. James Lovell.
4. This was in conformity with Sections 10 and 11 of "An Act for Registering and Clearing Vessels, Regulating the Coasting Trade, and for other purposes" (1 Stat. 57–58 [September 1, 1789]).

To George Washington

[Philadelphia, September 22, 1791]

Sir,

I have received a letter from the Minister of France, of which the inclosed is a copy.[1] Having full authority from you in relation to payments to France, & there being funds out of which that which will constitute the succour requested may with propriety be made; and being fully persuaded that in so urgent & calamitous a case, you will be pleased with a ready acquiescence in what is desired, I have not hesitated to answer the Minister that the sum he asks is at his command.[2]

With the most perfect respect and truest attachment, I have the honor to be Sir, Your Most Obedient & Most Hble Servant

A: Hamilton

Philadelphia
22d. Septr. 1791.

LC, George Washington Papers, Library of Congress.
1. Jean Baptiste de Ternant to H, September 21, 1791.
2. H to Ternant, September 21, 1791.

To William Ellery

[*Philadelphia, September 23, 1791.* On October 10, 1791, Ellery wrote to Hamilton: "I have received your Circular of the 21st. of last month . . . I have also received your letter of the 23d. of the same month." *Letter not found.*]

From William Short

Paris Sep. 23. 1791.

Sir

My letters lately addressed to you by different chanels were of Aug. 8, 23, 30, 31, & Sep. 3. They will have informed you of the loan lately opened at Amsterdam for six millions of florins [1]—the success with which it was attended & my attempts to reduce the charges on it. In my last [2] I inclosed you a copy of my letter to the bankers on this subject. I have since recieved from them a letter of the 8th. by which it appears that they adhere to their claim of the 4. p. cent charges. I save myself the trouble of copying it as they will forward it to you.[3] I inclose here a copy of my answer to them.[4] As it has not become

ALS, letterpress copy, William Short Papers, Library of Congress.
1. For a description of this loan, see Short to H, August 31, 1791.
2. See Short to H, September 3, 1791.
3. Since the copy of this letter which was sent to H has not been found, the letter received by Short has been printed here as an enclosure to clarify the contents of Short's answer.
4. See enclosure.

indispensable for me to accede to their demands I have not done it. Of course the rate of their charges is left a matter of discussion between the U.S. & them. As a matter of right they certainly cannot claim more than 3½. p. cent & since in my letters authorizing the loan I stipulate expressly & repeatedly that the loan shall not be extended beyond three millions unless the charges are reduced & in strict justice they ought not to claim it since their profits are greater at 3½. p cent, the loan being six millions, than they would have been at 4. p. cent (the terms they agreed to) if the loan had been only three millions. I have thought it proper that you should have our correspondence on this subject, because finally it may be to be settled by you, to whom they will probably appeal from my refusal—if so it will be when they come to state their accounts with the U.S. I thought it possible they might insist on my accepting their terms before they paid the monies arising on this loan & in that case I should have thought it for the advantage of the U.S. to have assented to them. As yet however I have discovered no symptom of this intention.

They have already made two remittances out of this loan amounting to 1,723,771. 2. 3 livres tournois.[5] They do not inform me at what rate of exchange these remittances are made. I have written [6] to ask this information of them, which may be necessary to me in the case of the commissaries of the treasury desiring any part of this loan to be paid at Amsterdam. As yet they say they prefer having remittances made here.

Mr. Donald left London soon after writing me the letter communicated to you [7] in mine of the 23d of August. His partner has since informed me [8] that it does not appear to him possible that a loan could

5. On September 15, 1791, Willink, Van Staphorst, and Hubbard wrote to Short:

"On the 8 Instant, We had the honor to advise you our Remittances to the Commissaries of the National Treasury   £ 642,896. 9.9

And now inform you, of our further Remittances to them this Date 1,080,874.12.6

For account of the United States   £ 1,723,771. 2.3

They will be followed by others, so fast as We can procure good Bills, to the Amount of your Order for One Million and an half of Florins. . . ." (LS, Short Family Papers, Library of Congress.)

6. See enclosure.

7. Alexander Donald, a London banker. Donald's letter to Short, dated August 19, 1791, is quoted in Short to H, August 23, 1791.

8. Robert Burton to Short, September 6, 1791 (LS, William Short Papers, Library of Congress).

be effected in London for the U.S. at less than 5. p. cent, although he thinks it might be done at that rate. He observes that it being necessary that the agents there should guarantee the loan & the payment of interest, no house of any solidity would do this, & particularly if the loan is to continue ten years, for 5 p. cent commission. They would expect also a commission on paying the interest, which he estimates ⅓ p. cent for recieving & ½ p. cent for paying. He observes also that the proper time to attempt a loan would be in the spring after Mr Pitt shall have brought forward his budget. This is a less favorable view of the subject than that presented by Mr Donald. I am the more sorry for it as it leaves me in a doubt of what is proper to be done, not knowing how far you would desire a sacrifice should be made in the charges of a loan in order to effect it in London where you contemplate other advantages from its being made. I still hope however that it will be found that if it is practicable for the U. S. to make a loan there at all that it may be done at a reduced rate of interest so as to compensate the increased commission which will be indispensable on account of the guarantee. I shall continue my correspondence on this subject & inform you of the result. I learn that the domestic funds of the U S have been sold in London & that the six p. cents went as high as 10s.

I have heard nothing for some time from Antwerp. The Russian loan brought on there will of course prevent the U.S. from attempting one at a reduced rate of interest until it shall have been completed.

You will recieve by the way of Havre in a box addressed to the Secretary of State several books & pamphlets on the subjects of mint & coinage. I was advised to procure them & send them to you which I have done on the authority of others, having not sufficient knowlege of the subject to judge of their merit myself. I am told by M. Drost [9] & the Abbé Rochon [10] one of the members of the monetary commission here, that they will be useful to you in the researches you are making.

Mr. Brantsen [11] late Ambassador from Holland here & employed

9. Jean Pierre Droz. See Short to H, August 23, 1791, note 10.

10. Alexis Marie de Rochon was a noted astronomer and navigator. In April, 1791, he was appointed by the King to the newly created Commission on Money in France.

11. Gerard Brantsen had served as Minister to France from the Netherlands from 1782 to 1787. H had requested information from Short on the Dutch Mint. See H to Short, April 13, 1791; Short to H, June 3, 1791.

in the mint of that country promises to give me an account of their manner of proceeding & the establishment of their mint. If he keeps his word I will forward you the information I may collect from him.

I have the honor to be with the most perfect respect Sir Your most obedient humble servant   W: Short

The Honble.
Alexander Hamilton Secretary of the treasury Philadelphia.

[E N C L O S U R E]

Wilhem and Jan Willink, Nicholaas and Jacob Van Staphorst, and Nicholas Hubbard to William Short [12]

Amsterdam 8 September 1791

Sir

We have before us your respected favors of 28 Ulto.[13] and 3d Instant,[14] the latter rendering that Justice to our Views, in the Conduct of the last Loan for Six Millions, which they merit, and that Circumstances are fast developing the extreme Propriety of, since the probable Acceptance of the French Constitution by the King, greatly augments the hopes and expectations of People here, in a rapid Rise of the Exchange as well as of the Public Funds of that Country: The Effects have begun to operate and will speedily extend their Influence, Wherefore We have this date bought all the good Bills upon Paris We could collect, to the Amount of £ 642.896. 9. 9 that We remit per this Post to the Commissaries of the National Treasury, to be placed to the Credit of the United-States; And We shall lose no opportunity of securing good Paper to the Amount of One and an half Million You desire use to remit; A Disposal We are able immediately to fulfill and even to exceed if you direct, solely owing to the Loan being for so large a Sum; Whereby the United-States will most probably, profit infinitely more by the favorable Exchange, than by any saving in the Charges, triffling to them, altho' essential to us in every Point of View.

12. LS, Short Family Papers, Library of Congress.
13. ALS, letterpress copy, William Short Papers, Library of Congress.
14. See enclosure to Short to H, September 3, 1791.

Our Disposition, to evince our Zeal and Attachment, to the Interests of the United-States, and our sincere Wish to oblige you Sir, would induce us to any Complaisance or sacrifice, that could be effected, without resigning what is essentially due to ourselves; On the other hand We trust in return to be treated with Justice. All We desire and that is requisite, to demonstrate that our Charges of Four per Cent are not susceptible of any deduction, having been founded upon the lowest Calculation for the Nature of the Business, and being precisely what You agreed to allow us for the Loan of 2½ Millions,[15] on calculating the Premium of the Undertakers at only 1½ per Cent.

Waving any particular Reply, to your Objections against the Expressions of our Letter to Mr. Secretary Hamilton, as they will be corroborated by the following series of Facts, We proceed to call to your Recollection, that,

On your Arrival here, We asked the same Charges for the future Loans, as We had received upon the One of Three Millions,[16] which were 4½ pr. Cent altho' the Premium to the Undertakers was but 1½ per Cent, the lowest We could flatter ourselves to obtain it for: We contended as is really the case, that no Power borrowed Money here upon such cheap Terms: Yet, to place beyond the possibility of a Doubt, our sincere Wish & Zeal to serve the United-States, We acceeded to your pressing Efforts, to obtain One half per Cent Reduction upon the Charges. At the Moment of our doing it, there was no question, nor could it exist in Your or Our Ideas, that the Loans to be raised by us at those Charges, would be at an higher premium than 1½ per Cent; A Truth established beyond equivocation, as We informed the Secretary of the Treasury of the Terms, thus, "4 per Cent that We fixed with Mr. Short to do the Business for; We at that time calculated to give but 1½ pr. Cent premium to the Undertakers, but when It was question of only a Sacrifice of our Interest, to accelerate Mr. Short's Wish to open the Loan immediately, We did not balance a Moment to make it, by allowing Two per Cent premium, the least, We could obtain the Money for." [17]

15. The Holland loan of March, 1791. For a description of this loan, see Short to H, February 17, 1791.

16. The Holland loan of 1790. For a description of this loan, see H to Willink, Van Staphorst, and Hubbard, November 29, 1790, note 1.

17. Letter not found. This letter is dated March 1, 1791, and is quoted in Willink, Van Staphorst, and Hubbard to Short, August 25, 1791, which is printed as an enclosure to Short to H, August 31, 1791.

From this clearly results, What our Memories likewise perfectly retain

That, the Reduction of one Half per Cent Charges, was on the supposition of the future Loans, being raised by us at 1½ per Cent promd. to the Undertakers.

Thus, It was calculated between You & us, that our Profits were to be upon the Basis of 4 per Cent Charges, when the premium was 1½ per Cent.

That, they were rendered less solely by our giving the Undertakers 2 per Cent premium, to accelerate and secure the Loan of 1 March, was a Sacrifice of One Half per Cent of our acquired and covenanted Profits with you, in order not to procrastinate longer the Completing of your Wishes.

The Difference then between us, is only, Whether, We are to be allowed the Charges You agreed We should enjoy on the Loan of 2½ Millions, Or, Whether You shall avail yourself, of our having sacrificed Part of our acquired Right in that Instance, purely & solely to oblige you and accomplish your Views, as a Motive and Ground for your depriving us of it in the present; No Sir, We cannot think You will strive to maintain it; for if We had not paid 2 p ct. Prem on the last Loan,[18] You would have had no pretext whatever, to expect a Reduction of Charges on the present One, especially when you will recollect that our giving One Half per Cent extra Premium was merely to evince our Desire to oblige you: We are therefore persuaded a further and more calm Investigation of the Subject, will convince you of the propriety and justice, of your desisting from your Endeavors, to convert our Deference and Complaisance towards you, into a Weapon to wound our own Interests and destroy our Rights; And consequently, that you will consider the Charges upon the Loan of 2½ Millions as agreed & fixed with you, to be the Standard for those of Six Millions; And not what our Profits on that Business were unexpectedly both to you and us reduced to, by our sacrifice to oblige in that Instance.

Having always viewed the Matter in this Light, We naturally & justly concluded, Your Limitation of the present Loan upon account of Charges, originated from a false Conception of the subject, by removing which We overcame the Objection; And growing more and

18. See note 15.

more convinced of the propriety & Justice of our Conduct, in proportion as We revolve it in our Minds, We must persevere in maintaining our Right.

We beg of you Sir, to dispense, our replying fully to the Calculations, by which you look upon our Commission as the Labor of Mechanics: In this Point of View, We should certainly be more than amply rewarded, Which We assure you We are not, considering what others receive for the Negotiation of Loans here, A Business that every One is not competent to, any more than It would be safe to trust every One with it. The Allowance upon these Transactions, is always a per Centum upon their Amount, And is no more proportioned or applicable to the payment for a Mechanical Labor, than is the Influence necessary to their success, or the Responsibility lodged in the Persons who execute them, without taking into account the great Risques attending the Manutention of such large sums.

We will chearfully forward the Secretary of the Treasury, Copy of our Letter to you of 22 Ulto,[19] But shall not dispatch it, until We have your Approbation to accompany it with a Copy of the present.

We are respectfully   Sir   Your most obedient and very humble servants   Wilhem & Jan Willink
                                   N & J. Van Staphorst & Hubbard
Willm. Short Esqr.

[ENCLOSURE]

William Short to Wilhem and Jan Willink, Nicholaas and Jacob Van Staphorst, and Nicholas Hubbard [20]

Paris Sep 16 1791

Gentlemen

I received after the departure of the last post your letter of the 8th inst.[21] ⟨I⟩ am really sorry to find that you persist in pretensions which I should have hoped must have been removed by the observations

19. Although Willink, Van Staphorst, and Hubbard refer to their letter of August 22, 1791, Short in answering this statement in his letter to them of September 16, 1791 (enclosed below), refers to their letter of August 25, 1791. The letter of August 25 is printed as an enclosure to Short to H, August 31, 1791. The letter of August 22, 1791, is quoted in Short to H, August 30, 1791, note 2.
20. ALS, letterpress copy, William Short Papers, Library of Congress.
21. See preceding enclosure.

contained in mine of the 3d. instant [22] & of which you acknowlege
the receipt. It becomes useless for us to discuss this subject longer.
For my part I examined it in all its parts not so much to establish the
right of the U. S. to the reduction of the charges (for that right is un-
contestable as will appear from reading over my letters on the authorizing this loan) as to shew that it was just in them to exercise that right.

Leaving the circumstance of the commission you give to the undertakers out of the question, as being a matter of indifference as to the
right of the U. S. to fix the conditions on which they will open loans,
I think you cannot deny that Congress were at liberty to open this
last loan or not to open it at Amsterdam—& also at liberty to employ
your house or not to employ them in making it. If then they had this
right they had also that of fixing with you the terms on which they
would open it. Where are those terms to be found if it is not an authority given for opening the loan? In perusing my letters containing
this authority the extension of the loan to six million is so expressly
stipulated to be authorized only on the condition of the charges being
reduced & others so often repeated that it is difficult to say how a
pretension of the contrary could ever be taken up. So far I think you
yourselves will not object to and must admit to the right of the U. S.
to insist on a reduction of the charges on the 2½ million loan. It only
remained therefore to put in question whether it would be just in
them so as to use this right. I know nothing wch. would render it unjust except its being burthensome to those they imploy. This can only
be understood by considering the terms on which you acknowlege
you were willing to make the ⟨ – ⟩ the profits which you yourselves
consider as competent in this business. According to your own statement your profits on the 2½ million loan were ⅛ p cent each. You
object however to the raised commission of the undertakers being
taken in to the acct. wch. was a sacrifice you made of yourselves—
leaving that out of the question then the profits to wch. you consider
yourselves as just would have been ¾ p cent each. If then the U. S.
had chosen to employ your houses separately each to make a loan of
three million & offered you 1 p cent clear commission you would certainly have accepted it or at least have considered these profits sufficient. As it is you have the appearance of acting jointly but not being

22. See Short to Willink, Van Staphorst, and Hubbard, September 3, 1791. This
letter is printed as an enclosure to Short to H, September 3, 1791.

bound for each other & may be considered as separately & your profits on the six million loan produce the same result. You object to this view of the subject as comparing your agency to mechanic labor. I cannot see the justice of this objection, but see on the contrary that you cannot have grounds to complain of the U. S. exercising an incontestible right where it is evident that instead of your being injured your profits are greater than those stated by you as being just on the 2½ million loan.

The right of the U. S. to insist on the charges of the loan of six million being reduced to 3¼ p cent being thus put beyond the possibility of a contradiction & the justice of exercising this right being also demonstrated, I cannot flatter myself that I shall be able to contribute to induce you to acknowlege them if these observations should not satisfy you. I hope therefore you will excuse me from a repetition of them. I have discussed them thus fully because I am desirous that you should be convinced that the U. S. in this instance not only claim a right, but one which it is highly just they should exercise. This consideration I should hope would induce you in your next to enable me to inform the Secretary of the Treasury that you retreat from the pretensions hitherto mentioned. Although this circumstance does not affect the right of the U. S. yet it is necessary for other reasons that there should be no further delay in this business.

You say you shall comply with my request to send to the Sec. of the treasury a copy of your letter to me of the 25th of August [23] on having my approbation to send likewise a copy of that of the 8th inst. I do not see the necessity of having waited for this approbation as you might have taken it for granted that I would not have had any objection to your sending a copy of that or of any other of your letters to me, but on the contrary must have wished him to be furnished with whatever could give him lights in this business. I hope therefore you will transmit the copy of the letter in question or any other that you may suppose may have that tendency.

You mention the advantages resulting from the present rate of charges render the probability of the rise as being much greater for the U. S. than any saving in the charges on the loan. I can only repeat

23. Willink, Van Staphorst, and Hubbard to Short, August 25, 1791, enclosed in Short to H, August 31, 1791.

in answer to this what I have formerly mentioned, that although it may be just I do not consider myself or my powers competent to judge of it in consequence of such considerations & that I gave you a strong proof of this at the time of making the 2 ½ million loan in refusing to extend it notwithstanding the same observations were then made use of. I cannot help however thinking it a little singular that you should at that time have been so urgent for extending the loan so far as it could be carried: whilst the high commission of the undertakers left you only ½ p cent each & that you should now make so much difficulty about receiving the same rate on the whole.

I am sorry that you did not mention to me at what rate you made the remittance mentioned in your last letter of 642,896 £ 9. 9. I will thank you to inform me of that circumstance & the rate of future remittances as well as the rate of exchange, The day of the departure of your letters & your ideas as to the rise or fall. These circumstances will be essential to me in treating with the commissioners of the treasury & settling with them agreeably to what I may suppose most for the advantage of the U. S. whether the payments shall be made at Amsterdam & on what terms—or by remittances here.

You informed me in your last that you were already able to remit the 1 ½ p ct. loan of florins desired. I now desire you to continue the remittance as far as 1 ½ millions more (3 millions on the whole) in the manner you may suppose most for the advantage of the U. S. but not to exceed that sum until you hear further from me. In the mean time I shall hope you will keep me regularly informed of the progress of this business that I may know how to meet the commissioners of the treasury in the case of their desiring to change the rate of payment. I am gentlemen very sincerely yours   W Short

To Charles Lee

Treasury Department
September 24. 1791

Sir

You were right in declining to pay the order which was made upon you by the District Court in relation to Charles Page.[1] It was altogether irregular, and of course I cannot authorise its being complied with.

I am with consideration   Sir   Your obedient ser   A Hamilton

Charles Lee Esqr
Collector Alexandria

ALS, RG 56, Letters to and from the Collector at Alexandria, National Archives; copy, RG 56, Letters to Collectors at Small Ports, "Set G," National Archives.
1. See Lee to H, September 21, 1791.

To the President and Directors of the Bank of New York

[*Philadelphia, September 24, 1791*. On October 1, 1791, William Seton wrote to Hamilton: "I am desired by the President and Directors to acknowledge the receipt of your Letters of the 21 & 24 Sepr." *Letter of September 24 not found.*]

To Jeremiah Olney

Treasury Department
Septr. 24. 1791

Sir,

Your letter of the 15th. instant, respecting ten Kegs of Brandy imported in the Brigantine Betsey from Bordeaux in violation of the thirty third Section of the act of the 3rd of march last,[1] has been received.

There appears to be reasonable ground for a presumption that the importation of the Brandy in kegs proceeded from ignorance of the law, and if no legal process is yet instituted with regard to the forfeiture, it is my wish that you will forbear to proceed further against it. The vessel and Brandy may of course be released. If a prosecution has been commenced the course of relief will be by petition through the district Judge.[2]

I am with consideration   Sir   Your obedt Servant   Alex Hamilton

Jeremh. Olney Esqr.
Collr Providence

LS, Rhode Island Historical Society, Providence; copy, RG 56, Letters to the Collector at Providence, National Archives; copy, RG 56, Letters to Collectors at Small Ports, "Set G," National Archives.

1. "An Act repealing, after the last day of June next, the duties heretofore laid upon Distilled Spirits imported from abroad, and laying others in their stead; and also upon Spirits distilled within the United States, and for appropriating the same" (1 Stat. 199–214).

2. This sentence is in H's handwriting.

To Eliphalet Pearson

Philadelphia
Sepr. 24, 1791

Sir

I have the honor of your letter of the 10th. instant transmitting me a testimonial of my election as a fellow of the Society of The American Academy of Arts of Sciences. I entertain too high and respectful opinion of that Society not to esteem myself particularly flattered by so honorable a mark of their distinction; for which I request you to make my most cordial acknowlegements to them; permitting me at the same time to thank you for the obliging manner in which you communicate their act.

I have the honor to be With great consideration Sir Your Obed ser   A Hamilton

Eliphalet Pearson Esqr
Corresp Secretary

ALS, American Academy of Arts and Sciences, Cambridge, Massachusetts.

To George Washington

[Treasury Department, September 24, 1791]

Sir,

I have the honor to transmit you a letter of the 8th. of August from Governor St. Clair, together with sundry papers which accompanied it; the whole relating to the subject of the Settlements which have been made under purchases from Judge Symmes.[1]

A: Hamilton

Treasy. Departmt.
24th. Sep. 1791.

LC, George Washington Papers, Library of Congress.
  1. For the controversy between John Cleves Symmes and Arthur St. Clair, see St. Clair to H, May 25, 1791.

From George Washington

[Mount Vernon, September 24, 1791]

Sir,

I have received your letter of the 22d. inst: enclosing a copy of one from the French Minister; [1] I have to inform you, that your proceedings with respect to the request of the Minister of France, meet my entire approbation.

I am Sir   Your hble Servt.   G: Washington

Mount Vernon
24th. Septr. 1791.

LC, George Washington Papers, Library of Congress.
  1. Jean Baptiste de Ternant to H, September 21, 1791.

To Otho H. Williams

Treasury Department
September 24 1791

Sir

An account has been transmitted by Mr. Porter, [1] One of the Officers of the Cutter, for the time prior to the date of his Commission. It will be proper that you transmit to the Treasury some information, carefully taken, of the time when each of the Officers commenced *effectual* and *continued* service in the preparations for & fitting of the Cutter.

I am, Sir,   Your most Obed servant   Alexander Hamilton

Otho H Williams Esqr.
Collector of the Customs,
Baltimore

LS, Columbia University Libraries.
  1. David Porter was first mate of the Maryland revenue cutter.

From Thomas Mifflin [1]

[Philadelphia, September 26, 1791]

Sir.

Upon receiving information, that a difference of sentiment had arisen between the Comptroller of the Treasury of the U.S.[2] and the Comptroller General of Pennsylvania,[3] as to the mode of paying for the tract of Land on Lake Erie, agreably to the terms of the Contract, I referred the subject to the Attorney General of this Commonwealth; and I have now the honor of transmitting to you a copy of his opinion.[4]

As the accomplishment of this purchase has been long suspended, and appears to be anxiously desired by the Legislature, permit me to hope, Sir, that you will either concur with me in making the settlement conformably to the principles of Mr. Ingersoll's opinion, or suggest some other mode by which the ground of dispute may be speedily removed.

I am, with great respect,   Sir, Your most obed Servt.

Phila. 26. Sept. 1791
To Alexr. Hamilton, Esqr.
Secretary of the Treasury of the United States.

[ENCLOSURE]

Jared Ingersoll to Thomas Mifflin [5]

[Philadelphia, September 25, 1791]

Dear Sir

I have carefully examined and considered the documents transmitted me on the twenty second instant respecting a doubt that has arisen between the Comptroller of the Treasury of the United States and the Comptroller General of Pennsylvania as to the manner of paying for the Tract of Land on Lake Erie agreably to the Contract between the Members of Congress from this State and the late Board of Treasury.

The Instructions to our Delegates in Congress their proposals to the Board of Treasury, and the Boards acceptance of the Terms—offered, I have not seen, I give my Sentiments upon the papers furnished, I presume the others are unimportant.

I am of Opinion that all the Securities of the United States bearing Interest at the time the Contract was executed, are payable agreeably to the Terms of the Contract.

I conceive that Indents of Interest funded at three prCent or to express myself in General terms the three per Cent stock is not payable agreeably to the Terms of the Contract.

It appears to me however that the arrears of Interest on the unfunded Certificates, as well previous as subsequent to January 1788 are admissible and ought to be computed in discharge of the said debt equally as the principal.

The distinction attempted by the Comptroller of the Treasury of the United States between the arrears of Interest before and after January 1788 does not appear to me to be well founded the seperation of Interest of Principal in the antecedent period was at the option of the holders and in the hands of many may be found united.

As I am exceedingly pressed for time preparing for the Circuit, I beg the the favor of you to presere a Copy of this Letter for me as I have not time to transcribe it myself.

I am Dear Sir   With much esteem   Your Most O[b]edient Humble Servant   Jared Ingersoll.

Philadelphia
September 25th 1791

Df, in the handwriting of Alexander Dallas, Division of Public Records, Pennsylvania Historical and Museum Commission, Harrisburg; LC, Division of Public Records, Pennsylvania Historical and Museum Commission; copy, Division of Public Records, Pennsylvania Historical and Museum Commission.
    1. For background to this letter, see Mifflin to H, May 5, 1791; H to Mifflin, June 3, August 22, 1791.
    2. Oliver Wolcott, Jr.
    3. John Nicholson.
    4. See enclosure.
    5. *Pennsylvania Archives*, 9th ser., I, 222–23.

To Nathaniel Appleton

Treasury Department
Sept. 27. 1791.

Sir

You observe in your letter of the first instant [1] which did not strike me on the first perusal, or it would have been sooner noticed, that "you think it probable the sum remitted will be sufficient for the payment of the next quarter's interest, *though it must be matter of conjecture only till the close of the loan.*"

The last clause leads me to conclude, that you have misapprehended a late instruction of the Comptroller, directing you to continue to *receive subscriptions* to the several loans *to the end of the month*. But this was not meant to alter the preceding instruction, to close your books as to transfers fourteen days previous to the termination of each quarter, and to make up your *dividends of interest* according to the *then* state of the stock on your books. Any deviation from this rule will necessarily interfere with the punctuality of payment, and with the order of the business, and will be particularly unfortunate.

With consideration, I am, Sir   Your obedient servant

Alexander Hamilton

Nathaniel Appleton Esq.
Commissioner of Loans
Massachusetts.

LS, New Hampshire Historical Society, Concord.
   1. Letter not found.

From Joseph Whipple

Portsmouth New Hamp Sep. 27, 1791

Sir

Inclosed herewith I transmit you my Account of payment for the Support of the Lighthouse Establishment in this district from the commencing of that expence on the 15th. of August 1789 to the 30th. of June last. This Return has been detained with a view of accompanying it with a plan of the Lighthouse and the Land Adjacent lately

Ceded by this State to the United States, but the Surveyor who took it, having mislaid the rough minutes has not yet furnished me with the draughts.

I also now inclose for the approbation of The President, a New Contract for the Support of the Lighthouse for Six Months commencing the 1st. day July 1791.

The usefulness & conveniency to trade and Navigation attending the hoisting the Flag at the Fort [1] as answered by Merchants whose opinions I requested are

1st. That when it appeard by such Signal a Vessel (the different Colours as Ensign, pendant &c designating the kind of Vessel whether Ship Snow or Brig) was approaching the harbour, an owner expecting such Vessel was enabld to Stop her coming up the River, if the Cargo was intended for any other port for a Market.

2nd. That it was an inducement to suspend orders for Insurance whereby they might Sometimes Save the premium.

3rd. That it gave Notice to the pilot whose Residence did not admit of his seeing the Vessel so soon as a person Stationd at the Fort.

4th. That it Shows a respect to Strangers which has been in practice Since the first Settlement of the Country. To which I would add as it respects the public, that notice of a vessels appearance in the offing would excite the attention of the Officers of the Customs, especially the Inspector residing at New Castle, to whom I have given directions to observe the Conduct of Vessels approaching the harbour, whose entrance in it, would probably be in the Night, & to attend to their proceedings after such entrance. To this I was induced from having heard that Vessels had dallied off the harbour, with intention of entering in the Night unseen, & after coming to Anchor in the harbour, have attempted and probably sometimes effected their fraudulent purposes.

The Expence of hoisting the Flag as demanded by the person who now attends the light woud be 25 Cents pr. day which I conceive to be more than its Value & am of opinion that a much less sum aded to the expence of the Lighthouses after the present Contract is expired would obtain the Service.

I would take this Occasion to observe that the former practice under the State Government of hailing Vessels on their passing the Fort & the Authority for bringing them too when necessary, & subjecting those to punishment who did not give true answers, was found to be a useful regulation, and would be so under the General Government as it respects the Revenue, if Authorized by Law. The entrance of the harbour is so narrow that no Vessel can escape the command of the Fort, or pass out of hearing. Many Vessels from foreign ports enter the harbour, bound to different ports of Massachusetts, & a greater Number of Coasting Vessels passing between the districts of Maine & Massachusetts, meeting a head wind put in for Shelter at all times of day & night, many of the latter description, having the appearance of foreigners are visited by the Inspector while entering the harbour, or when laying at Anchor within, which is attended with a considerable expence that in many instances might be preventd if enquiry was made of the destination &c of Vessels at their passing the Fort.

Under any new regulation respecting the Fort I conceive it would be a Saving of expence & a Security to the Revenue if the persons employed at the Fort Should be connected with the Custom House. They might be selected from the Military Invalids now entitled to a pension, from whom boatmen might be appointd & a person to attend the Lighthouse.

I am, Sir, very respectfully   Your Most Obedt. hume. servt.

Joseph Whipple

Honble. Alexander Hamilton Esq.

ALS, RG 26, Lighthouse Letters Received, Vol. "B," New Hampshire and Massachusetts, National Archives; ADf, RG 36, Collector of Customs at Portsmouth, Letters Sent, 1791–1792, Vol. 3, National Archives; copy, RG 56, Letters from the Collector at Portsmouth, National Archives.

1. Fort William and Mary on New Castle Island. See Whipple to H, June 28, 1791, and H to Whipple, July 12, 1791.

To Otho H. Williams

Treasury Department
Septr. 27. 1791

Sir

You will retain, in your hands, such monies as you shall receive after this letter reaches you 'till the whole sum shall amount to ten thousand Dollars; which is destined as an advance to Messrs. Elliot and Williams,[1] and for the payment of which you will receive directions as soon as their bond with the proper sureties shall be received by me.

I remain with great consideration   Sir   Your Obed ser

Alexander Hamilton

Otho H. Williams Esqr
Collector of Baltimore

ALS, Columbia University Libraries.
1. The firm of Elie Williams and Robert Elliot had contracted to supply the western posts.

From William Allibone [1]

Philadelphia, September 28, 1791. Encloses estimates for "the Present quarter" and for "one year comencing the 15th of August." Reports that the navigational aids in the Delaware River "are now in good order."

ALS, RG 26, Lighthouse Letters Received, Vol. "A," Pennsylvania and Southern States, National Archives.
1. Allibone was master warden of the port of Philadelphia.

To Benjamin Lincoln [1]

Treasury Department
Sepr 28. 1791

Sir

The law making provision for the reduction of the public debt requiring that an account of the purchases should be laid before Congress within the first fourteen days of each session,[2] and as I am informed that only a part of the purchases made by you, yet appears on the books of the Treasury, I am to request that you will without delay have this business completed and all such stock as may stand on the books of any Commissioner of loans transferred immediately to those of the Treasury in the names of the Trustees of the Sinking Fund as described in the Act.[3]

You will observe the particulars which by the 3d. Section of that act are to enter into the Report of the Trustees; as these particulars must necessarily come from you, I request an abstract or statement of your purchases in which they shall be specified.

With great consideration &   esteem   I am Sir   Your obedient
                                                         A Hamilton
Benjamin Lincoln Esqr

ALS, RG 36, Collector of Customs at Boston, Letters from the Treasury, 1789–
1808, National Archives; copy, RG 56, Letters to the Collector at Boston, National Archives; copy, RG 56, Letters to Collectors at Small Ports, "Set G,"
National Archives.
    1. For background to this letter, see H to Lincoln, February 1, 1791.
    2. Section 3 of "An Act making Provision for the Reduction of the Public
Debt" reads as follows: "*And be it further enacted*, That accounts of the application of the said monies shall be rendered for settlement as other public accounts, accompanied with returns of the amount of the said debt purchased
therewith, at the end of every quarter of a year, to be computed from the time
of commencing the purchases aforesaid: and that a full and exact report of the
proceedings of the said five persons, or any three of them, including a statement
of the disbursements and purchases made under their direction, specifying the
times thereof, the prices at which, and the parties from whom the same may be
made, shall be laid before Congress, within the first fourteen days of each session
which may ensue the present, during the execution of their said trust" (1 *Stat.*
186–87 [August 12, 1790]).
    3. Section 2 of "An Act making Provision for the Reduction of the Public
Debt" reads in part as follows: "*And be it further enacted*, That the purchases
to be made of the said debt, shall be made under the direction of the President
of the Senate, the Chief Justice, the Secretary of State, the Secretary of the
Treasury, and the Attorney General for the time being; and who, or any three
of whom, with the approbation of the President of the United States, shall cause
the said purchases to be made in such manner, and under such regulations as
shall appear to them best calculated to fulfill the intent of this act" (1 *Stat.* 186).

To Thomas Mifflin

Treasury Department
Sepr. 28. 1791

Sir
    I am very sorry that the absence of the Comptroller of the Treas-
ury, in consequence of ill health, renders it impossible to complete
at this time the adjustment of the purchase, which is the subject of
your Excellency's letter of the 26th instant.
    Immediately after his return, which will probably be in about ten
days, the most particular attention will be paid to the business.
    I observe with pleasure that the opinion of the Attorney General
of Pensylvania obviates a material part of the question which has
existed between the Comptroller of the Treasury of the United States
and the Comptroller General of Pensylvania; and I imagine that a

very simple inquiry on the return of the former to this place will remove any remaining difference of construction.

I have the honor to be with perfect respect Sir Your most Obedient & humble servant   Alexander Hamilton

His Excellency Thomas Mifflin Esqr. &c &c

ALS, Lloyd W. Smith Collection, Morristown National Historical Park, Morristown, New Jersey.

To ——————— [1]

[Philadelphia, September 30, 1791]

Dear Sir:

If you can conveniently let me have twenty dollars for a few days, be so good as to send it by the bearer. I have just put myself out of cash by payment of Major l'Enfants' bill.[2]

James A. Hamilton, *Reminiscences of James A. Hamilton* (New York, 1869), 7.
   1. James A. Hamilton does not identify the addressee beyond saying that he was a "friend" of H. According to James Hamilton, the letter was endorsed "Gave a check dated September 30, 1791, for fifty dollars."
   2. Pierre Charles L'Enfant, who had served in the Continental Army as a captain of the Corps of Engineers during the American Revolution. At this time he was engaged in drawing up plans for the new Federal city.

From Nathaniel Hazard [1]

[New York, September 30, 1791]

Dear Sir

Mr. Wolcott [2] going sooner than I expected, gives me little Time. The Council of Appointment [3] met Yesterday, & appointed Willett Sheriff again.[4] The Governor it is thought, gained Webster.[5] Miles Hughes,[6] tried for it. I negotiated for him, with I. Roosevelt; Tillotson we suppose was for Willett. Peter Schuyler was sick at Home. Miles's Practice I apprehend is not large. Mel. Smith [7] & N. Lawrence [8] countenance Hughes' Views; all three dislike Clinton. Burr keeps his State Attorney-ship, he wants to put it into Nat Lawrence's Hands. Clinton wants to give it to Ned Livingston,[9] this must not be; he will propagate wrong Policy thro' out the State. Lawrence looks up to

Burr with Veneration, has formed a favorable Opinion of you, but is shy. He is honest, but very wary & cold blooded for a young Man. He has suspected Harrison [10] wished the State Attorney-ship. Harrison however respectable, is no Statesman. I believe it would be good Policy to give it to Lawrence. It would be deemed so far as you could countenance it, an *indubitable* Proof of your sincere Good Will to Burr & himself. Allow me for Brevity Sake to conclude with a Word which means like all lengthier Subscriptions of Address, Nothing or everything just as this Heart feels—to say *cordially*

Vale   N. H

P.S. Clinton is staggered, he is afraid to turn Burr out, & Burr wont resign untill a new Council, if he can avoid it.[11] We want to make Dr. Minima [12] Sheriff of Queens County.

Septr. 30th. 1791

ALS, Hamilton Papers, Library of Congress.

1. Hazard was a New York City merchant and ironmonger.
2. Oliver Wolcott, Jr.
3. The Council of Appointment was a distinctive feature of the New York State Constitution of 1777. Consisting of the governor and one senator from each of the four senatorial districts, selected each year by the Assembly, it exercised complete control over the selection of personnel for the appointive jobs in the state government.
4. Marinus Willett was sheriff of New York County from 1784 to 1787 and from 1791 to 1795.
5. Alexander Webster of Washington County was a state senator from the eastern district from 1789 to 1791.
   In 1791 the members of the Council of Appointment in addition to Governor George Clinton were Webster, Isaac Roosevelt, Thomas Tillotson, and Peter Schuyler.
6. This is apparently James Miles Hughes, a New York City lawyer, a master of chancery, and a notary public.
7. Melancton Smith, a prominent New York City lawyer and merchant, had served in the Continental Congress from 1785 to 1788. A leading Antifederalist, he had opposed the ratification of the Constitution in the New York Ratifying Convention. He was elected to the New York legislature in 1791.
8. Nathaniel Lawrence of Hempstead represented Queens County in the New York Ratifying Convention. In 1790 he was appointed secretary to the state regents, and in 1791 he was elected an assemblyman from Queens.
9. Edward Livingston, a lawyer, was the youngest brother of Chancellor Robert R. Livingston. At this time he held no public office.
10. Richard Harison, United States attorney for the District of New York.
11. Aaron Burr had defeated Philip Schuyler in January, 1791, for the seat in the United States Senate, but his term did not commence until Congress met in October. Meanwhile he continued to exercise his authority as attorney general of New York State. The new Council of Appointment would not meet until January, 1792, to choose another attorney general.
12. Daniel Menema was appointed sheriff of Queens County in 1792.

To William Seton

[*Philadelphia, September 30, 1791.* Letter listed in dealer's catalogue. *Letter not found.*]

ALS, sold at Parke-Bernet Galleries, May 12, 1947, Lot 261.

Treasury Department Circular to the Supervisors of the Revenue

Treasury Department
Septr. 30. 1791

Sir

Increasing embarrassments concerning the seizure of spirits for want of being accompanied with Certificates render it necessary that the ideas communicated in particular cases should be made general. I therefore make them the subject of this Circular letter.

A disagreable dilemma presents itself. This is either to forbear seizures for want of marks and certificates, which will materially impair an important check designed by the law, or to give something like just ground of complaint for seizing the property of Citizens for the want of a *thing*, which in many cases is not made necessary by the law.

It is required by the law that all the old Stock on a certain day in the hands of importers and distillers from foreign materials generally and in Cities Towns and Villages, from domestic materials should be marked and certified; [1] but it omits to extend this requisition to old Stock in the hands of dealers who are not importers, and of distillers from Stills, rated according to the capacity of the Still, and indeed of all other descriptions of persons except the two which have been mentioned. It equally omits to provide for marking and certifying Spirits made after the commencement of the law, at Country distilleries of domestic materials, and altogether for the case of Spirits drawn off from one Cask and put into another, in the course of retail dealing.

Attempts have been made to supply these deficiences; by special regulations depending on the consent of parties; but these have not been capable of embracing all the differences of circumstances and on a full reflexion, it does not appear practicable to adopt any plan, which not being authorised by law can effectually provide for all the cases which require to be provided for, so as to render it proper to enforce vigorously by the provision which authorises the seizure of Spirits, not accompanied with marks and Certificates.

In a situation like this a great relaxation appears unavoidable; and it is deemed preferable to weaken the efficacy of the provision respecting certificates than to give just cause of complaint of the rigorous execution of the law in a particular in which it is improvident in its provisions.

It is therefore my wish that the want of Certificates may in general rather be considered as a ground for careful enquiry and examination than of *itself* a *sufficient* cause for seizures; and that the Officers of Inspection under you may have an instruction to this effect.

When the spirits, if of the imported class, are in Hhds. of upwards an hundred Gallons, or from any evident marks, in the original packages, in which they are imported; or when they can be traced to have been brought from any distillery of foreign materials, or of domestic materials in a city, town or Village, in every such case, the presumption of fraud from the want of certificates will be strong enough to justify a seizure. But it ought to be impressed upon all concerned, that great circumspection is to be used in every instance in making a seizure on the mere score of want of marks and Certificates.

With great consideration   I am Sir,   Your obedient servant

A Hamilton

Copy, to John Dexter, Rhode Island Historical Society, Providence.
    1. This is provided in Section 26 of "An Act repealing, after the last day of June next, the duties heretofore laid upon Distilled Spirits imported from abroad, and laying others in their stead; and also upon Spirits distilled within the United States, and for appropriating the same" (1 *Stat.* 205–06 [March 3, 1791]).

To George Washington

[Treasury Department, September 30, 1791]

The Secretary of the Treasury has the honor respectfully to submit to the President of the United States a contract entered into by the Deputy Collector of Wilmington in North Carolina with James Mc-

Stephens & Henry Toomer for the stakage of the shoals of Cape Fear River.

The sum stipulated to be paid, not being considerable, the fixing of new sets of stakes being a part of the business, as well as the preservation of them as usual, the Secretary does not perceive any reason to object against the terms agreed on. Should the contract receive the President's approbation, the Secretary humbly suggests that the public service would be promoted by an instruction to the Gentleman acting as the President's Secretary to signify the same to the Collector of Wilmington.[1] A: Hamilton

Treasy. Departmt.
30th. Sep: 1791.

LC, George Washington Papers, Library of Congress.
  1. James Read.

From ——————— [1]

[September–October, 1791]

Sir

I have had the honor to transmit to you a sketch, which you appeared to desire of the arrangements necessary for the execution of the plan chalked out in your prospectus.[2] I confined myself to class the objects with which you propose to begin the business on each of these heads. I might have entered into more particular details, and given, if not an exact estimation, at least an Idea of the expense of their Establishment, their support, their consumption and produce. I have occupied myself with this business, at least as much as one Could, who has only a general Knowledge, but not the exact information which a Workman only can possess.

Now that I see, Sir, the business ready to begin, I will take the liberty of communicating to you my private opinion on the subject; and my reason for not expressing it in the paper I transmitted to you was, that it differed in some degree from the ideas contained in the

Copy, Hamilton Papers, Library of Congress.
  1. Joseph Stancliffe Davis (*Essays*, I, 482) attributes this letter to Thomas Marshall.
  2. "Prospectus of the Society for Establishing Useful Manufactures," August, 1791.

prospectus. I had at first with you the idea That an Establishment comprehending a dozen different objects well chosen, conducted by an able direction, enlightened and honest managers and skillful Workmen might have the greatest success, and I think so still; but would not the union of so many qualities, on which the success entirely depends, be an absolute miracle? and would it be prudent to depend upon it? But if one of them is Wanting, you will find bad goods come out of the hands of unskillful workmen; dishonest managers make a fraudulent advantage at the expense of their employers, which in such a multitude of details will escape the eye of the directors; and directors who for want of particular knowledge of each of the different branches conduct well that with which they are best acquainted, and be continually exposed to be decived in all the others. The more I think on This affair, the more I am persuaded that there is a great risk in pursuing it in the manner in which it is proposed, and its advantageous execution must depend on fortune, more than on reason. I have seen in Europe individual manufacturers employ two or three hundred hands, but in the same branch, and the undertakers had occasion only to be acquainted with that branch; besides they were employed for their own profit, and not as hirelings, and after all were often cheated in the details. In the establishment proposed we must in the first place [have] as many faithful and enlightened directors as there are different branches; then a number of managers each capable of following the branch entrusted to him with the eye of a real and intelligent manufacturer, without which it will be necessary to depend absolutely on the head-Workmen, who, even if they should be all honest, can never be stimulated by that interest which animates those who work for themselves. The expense of such an establishment is immense in buildings, machines, looms, the purchase of raw-materials of so many kinds, the Wages of workmen, Salaries of managers, Directors &c. These articles alone, without counting the purchase of lands and unforeseen expenses, will demand an immense capital if they are calculated in a reasonable manner, and present in their details a multitude of means of loss to The Corporation. I repeat it, Sir, unless God should send us saints for Workmen and angels to conduct them, there is the greatest reason to fear for the success of the plan.

I am far from thinking, however, that there are not other means to accomplish the object in your view which, if I understand it right, is 1st. to encourage and protect the establishment of the manufactures necessary for This country. 2dly. To take advantage of The crisis in which affairs now are in several country of Europe, to Engage as many manufacturers in as many different Branches as possible to Emigrate to this country. It seems to me that these objects may be equally accomplished by the corporation undertaking three or four of the principal branches, and Which I Should Chuse connected together that The Details may be more easy to follow. 3dly. by becoming partners in the other branches with undertakers of known abilities and charac⟨ter⟩ [3] on the terms that may be thought proper.

A General spinning house, and the employment of its prod⟨ucts⟩ are in my opinion Worthy of préférence. The extent to Which th⟨ey⟩ may be carried is sufficiently great while their connection makes The Business easy to be followed. These two articles require ot⟨hers⟩ as accessary, viz. the dying of cotton, Wool &c. before they are manufactured. I am perfectly convinced that it would be much ⟨more⟩ easy to manage well 600 hands in such a manufacture, Th⟨an⟩ 200 divided among different branches which have no depen⟨dence⟩ on each other.

As to the proposal I make of engaging the corporation as pa⟨rtners⟩ with private manufacturers, it is not a new idea. I have seen in France the gouvernement concerned in many private undertakings in Which they appointed a commissary to take care of their interests. This was one of the means of encouraging and protecting manufactures. Here it has another advantage, that of procuring able Workmen from Europe. The corporation might engage in Such undertakings in several ways; either by advancing the necessary capital to individuals; by building and renting to them the necessary works; or by taking upon them selves the expenses of the first establishment, always in proportion to the solidity and talents of The undertakers.

Such are the observations which I take the liberty to lay before you. I know that to you I have no occasion to develope them more particularly, and I hope that you will consider the freedom With Which I venture to discuss your opinion, as a new Tribut of Esteem paid to your private Character, and patriotic Virtues.

I am with respect,

3. The material within broken brackets is taken from Cole, *Industrial and Commercial Correspondence*, 202.

From William Playfair [1]

[Paris, September–December, 1791]

Sir,

I must once more request your Pardon for the liberty which I again take of writing to you about the affairs of the Sioto but they are in So extraordinary a State and the Interests of Such a Number of Individuals are at Stake that I hope you will excuse me.

I have written to Mr Dewer [2] by this Same Packet and have Entered into the affair at great length but as it would be very improper to trowble you with these details and Reasonings I shall confine Myself to what is Realy Matter of Importance.

The Present Moment is become from the State of affairs in France exceedingly favourable for the Emigration Much More so than Ever. A Mr Gervais [3] Who is a very honest intelligent Man who lived 9 Months on the Sioto lands is Returned & has brought Such letters & Gives Such a favourable account of the Establishment that the Public opinion has Changed and is actually favourable to that enterprise. All Persons agree that if this Winter is let Slip it will Run hard to Ruin the Affair. Several other Sales of Land in America are opening or opened & this derives its great advantage from having been the First French Colony. Should Another get footing then that advantage is at an End. At the Same time that things are in so favourable a Situation for Selling there Are infinit difficulties occasioned by former Transactions the Procuration which the Company of Mr Dewer Sent here having Sold the Whole of the Land 2ce neither of which Sales indeed have been consummated but likewise Neither has been undone Regularly. There is however a possibility of going on with a Sale for Some Months in Spite of all & the Plan I propose is—One tenth of the Price of the Land to be paid here four Tenths at Philadelphia by the Purchaser when he arives either to the Public Treasury or to a Person whom Mr Dewer May appoint and the Remaining five tenths or half to be paid in 2 years & till paid to Remain a Mortgage upon the Land Sold. Thus No Single acre will be delivered without touching $\frac{4}{10}$th in Cash & $\frac{1}{2}$ in obligation on the land itself. Mr Dewer never Expected better than that & according to the arrangements his Procuration made he never could have had near so much therefore his Interest is Secured And it gives Confidence here to the Buyers.

As the Matter will in 10 days from this time be begun in that Manner which with Regard to the Persons who are interrested in America is *Unexceptionable* I have written to Mr Dewer to Send over New Powers *limited* & to the purpose of Selling on these terms. The *Unlimited* Powers which have hitherto been Sent Should be Annulled certainly & when the powers Go No farther than to Sell upon the Above Conditions Mr Dewers interests will be Secured let the Seller be well or ill inclined. With Regard to myself I have allways considdered My Interest as being included in the general one & therefore have not in any case bargained for Myself but as I have contracted obligations which it will be difficult for Me to pay if the affair does not go on And as the Courts of Justice have decided that I Personally Am bound to pay whatever is owing for that affair, If any Procuration Should come that will tend to Stop the operation I shall be obliged tho' with Reluctance to have the Effect of Such Procuration Suspended & to go on with the Sale if that Shall Still continue to be possible after a Law Suit shall have been begun. I beg of you Sir to have the Goodness Not for My Sake because I have not the honour to be known to you but in general for the Sake of all those who are embarked in that Enterprise to Use Your Endeavours with Mr Dewer & others concerned to the Purpose of Powers being Sent over in that limited Sence so that the Sale may go on without interruption.

You will probably have a letter from Monsieur Duval D'Ésprimenel the Famous Member of the Ancient Parliament who intends going to America with his Family & A Number of other Families Next Spring.[4] All the French Nobility Are in the Intention of Emigrating to One place or Another & Most of the Clergy add to that the Best Part of the Artists Are Ruined as trade And Manufactures are at a low Ebb. If things are well Managed America will gain More in Population and Imported Wealth in three years to come than She would otherwise in thirty for let things here take what turn they may one quarter of the Inhabitants must be discontented & a great portion of them will leave the Country.

Were I to permitt my self Another liberty after that which I take of writing the present letter it would be to Request your taking the trowble of throwing your Eyes over the letter which I have Sent to

Mr Dewer by this Same Packet which letter explains many things that it would be impertinent to trowble you with in this letter.

The Sooner that Mr Dewer takes a Party in this affair the better it will be for all concerned and thus for the Sale in general & certainly he has Nothing to dread from Sending the Procuration in the Way I mention.

I have the honour to be Sir, Your Most Obedient and Most humble Servant   William Playfair

To Hamilton Esqr a New yorke

ALS, Hamilton Papers, Library of Congress.
   1. For background to this letter, see Playfair to H, March 30, 1791.
   Playfair was an English adventurer who in 1789 was associated with Joel Barlow in the formation of a French company to sell the Scioto lands.
   2. William Duer.
   3. John Gervais, one of the original settlers on the Scioto lands at Gallipolis.
   4. Duval d'Epremesnil was a prominent member of the Parlement of Paris in 1787 and 1788 who achieved popularity by his opposition to the Crown. Elected by the nobility to the Estates General in 1789, he opposed the middle-class demands for the unification of the three Estates. The launching of the French Scioto Company in 1789 caught his imagination, and he bought 10,000 acres of land on the Ohio. He planned to colonize his purchase and eventually to live there. In September, 1791, he sent a new agent to America to manage his lands and began preparations to emigrate in the spring.

From Oliver Wolcott, Junior

[Philadelphia, September, 1791]

Observations on the question, whether it is expedient for the Bank of the United States to operate by Departments?

It is first necessary to determine, whether any limitations in the constitution of the Bank of the United States, render it improper for the Corporation to operate by departments. A fair construction of the law [1] must decide this point.

The only limitation in the act of incorporation which can affect this inquiry, is contained in the ninth section of the Law,[2] and is ex-

ADfS, Connecticut Historical Society, Hartford.
   1. "An Act to incorporate the subscribers to the Bank of the United States" (1 Stat. 193–95 [February 25, 1791]).
   2. Section 7 of the act enumerates the "rules, restrictions, limitations and provisions" to be incorporated into the constitution of the Bank of the United States. Wolcott's reference is to number IX of these provisions.

pressed in these words. "The total amount of the debts which the said corporation shall at any time owe, whether by bond bill note or other contract, shall not exceed the sum of ten millions of dollars over and above the monies then actually deposited in the bank for safe keeping, unless the contracting of a greater debt shall have been previously authorised by a Law of the United States."

It is presumed to be the effect of this provision, that the debts of the bank ought to be so limited that the *debts due for deposits* may at all times be for such amounts only as can be satisfied, *out of the deposits*, and the *debts contracted on account of the capital Stock*, such as the *capital Stock will satisfy*. There is no limitation with respect to the *debts which may be due for deposits*, which may rise to any amount that individuals, may intrust to the Bank. The profits of the Bank can in no sence be said to result immediately from debts due *from* the Bank. The profits will always result from operations which will occasion debts to be due *to the Bank*, and in this respect the bank of the United States is not limited by Law. From this view of the subject, it is evident, that nothing in the Law, forbids the bank of the United States to lend the whole of the Specie part of its capital and the whole of the deposits—though it is not contended that it will be consistent with the exercise of a good discretion to lend or discount to this extent.

The Bank being therefore at liberty to lend or discount to an indefinite amount taking care that the debts due by the bank, in no instance exceed its credits; it follows, that no restriction in the Law, forbids the establishment of departments.

The next enquiry is, can the right of establishing departments be excercised, so as to render it expedient?

To solve this question it is necessary to consider how banks operate & from what sources their profits result.

It is presumed that the capital Stock of a bank, is principally intended to serve as a pledge to its customers, that any losses which it may suffer, shall not impair its ability to satisfy the demands of those who may deposit money in its coffers. A bank may indeed trade on its capital Stock, but it is not for this purpose that banks are incorporated. If the capital Stock of a bank is considered seperately from the deposits, the former, instead of being rendered more profitable is rendered of less value, by being employed in a Bank of discount

& Deposit by the tendency which such banks ever have to reduce the rate of interest and by the increased expences of management which attend such institutions. If such a bank receives deposits without being permitted to lend them the capital is charged with the risque of safekeeping which is an additional expence. Hence it follows that the capital of a bank need not and ought not in most cases to exceed what is necessary to insure against all contingencies—and hence the importance of wisdom, prudence and integrity in the administrators, which being the chief causes of credit, by diminishing the chances of loss, render the less capital necessary.

In every community there is a sum reserved in the hands of individuals which is to them an unproductive or dead Stock. The amount of this Stock is continually varying with every change in society, and can only be calculated by observation. As this stock can never be profitably employed by the proprietors, it will be deposited in a bank, if sufficient assurance is given, that it will be refunded on demand. The inducement for making these deposits will in the first instance be, to avoid the risque of safe keeping. After the effect of a bank for discounts and deposits is perceived, such deposits will be continued from motives of private advantage, for by the aids received, every man in business, will find, that he can trade on the whole amount of his capital, by paying interest to the bank, on that part thereof, which would otherwise be unproductive.

The administrators of such a bank, will soon find, a sum of money continually remaining in their Coffers, which though demandable at a moment, will never be called for, while the bank retains its credit, and which they may safely lend on Interest. From lending this money, the chief profits of the bank will arise.

From these data the inference results, that an institution which should be able to produce satisfactory security of its ability to indemnify its customers from all losses & also to make payments on demand and also deservedly possess the confidence of the community, in respect to wisdom, prudence, & integrity, might excercise the business of banking with the fullest success, without employing one dollar of money as a capital. It is presumed that a capital of ten millions of Dollars is sufficient to ensure against all losses in any prudent negociations which may be made, in the United States and the sagacity of the individuals who are interested in the capital Stock, may be safely trusted to call into their service the most able and upright administrators.

It is also presumed that the plan for establishing departments, which is herewith submitted, is attended with no risque, which would not attend the operations of a single bank, which should operate to the extent of the principal bank & the departments.

If the plan now proposed is observed, the debts can never exceed the resources of the bank; compleat information will be attainable by the Directors of the Bank of the United States, of all the business done by the Departments & the operations of the Bank may be extended wherever the deposits will amou[n]t to such a sum, that the interest of that part which may be loaned out, will defray the expences of a proper establishment. The profits resulting from an extensive operation upon this plan, appear to be sufficiently alluring to the corporation of the Bank of the United States and the advantages which will result to the community from banks well conducted, render it important, that the benefits should be extended to as wide a scene as possible.

Respectfully submitted by   Oliv. Wolcott.

Phila. Sept. 1791.

[ENCLOSURE] [3]

[Philadelphia, September, 1791]

Plan for establishing departments of the Bank of the United States, submitted to the Secretary of the Treasy. by Oliver Wolcott.

1st.   The Directors of the Bank of the United States shall appoint   [4] directors for each Department.

2d.   The Directors for each department shall choose one of their number for President of the directors of each respective department.

3d.   The Directors of the Bank of the United States shall appoint the Cashiers of departments.

4th.   The Cashiers of departments shall appoint their respective

3. ADf, Connecticut Historical Society.
4. Space left blank in MS.

Tellers & Clerks & the surities of said Tellers & Clerks shall be approved by the Directors of the Bank of the United States.

5th. The Cashiers of departments shall be responsible for all deficiencies which shall finally appear either by the default of themselves, their Tellers, or Clerks.

6th. The compensations to the Presidents Cashiers Tellers & Clerks of departments shall be established by the directors of the Bank of the United States.

7th. The manner of keeping stating and rendering the accounts of departments, shall be prescribed by the Directors of the Bank of the United States, and the observance of the rules established, shall be enforced by the President of the Bank of the United States, to whom the accounts of departments shall be rendered.

8th. The Capital Stock of the Bank of the United States consisting of 6 ℀ Cent funded Stock, shall not be divided, but shall remain under the controul of the Directors; and the Departments shall trade and discount only on such part of the Specie Capital of the sd. Bank as the Directors shall apportion to them together with such part of the deposits which shall be lodged with them from time to time, as the directors of departments shall judge safe and expedient.

9th. All Notes to be issued at the Departments, shall be numbered, signed and registered by the President of the Bank of the United States and shall be delivered to the Cashiers of Departments, who shall sign duplicate Receipts for the same, for which they shall be accountable—one of which receipts shall be lodged with the President for the Department and the other with the President of the Bank of the United States.

10th. No Notes shall be issued at the Departments, except for money lodged with the Cashier of the Department or except for Notes which shall have become worn or unfit for circulation and which shall have been previously cancelled in the presence of the President and   [5] directors of the department and said Notes so cancelled shall be forthwith transmitted to the President of the Bank of the United States.

11th. All Notes to be issued at the Departments shall be counter-

5. Space left blank in MS.

signed by the Cashier for the department and shall contain each a promise to be payable at the Department from which they issued.

12th. No contract to charge the Bank of the United States or any department thereof shall be made, unless in pursuance of some rule established by the Directors of the Bank of the United States; and all such contracts shall be signed by the President of the Bank of the United States and shall be countersigned by the Cashier of the Department where such contract is to be fulfilled.

To John Davidson [1]

Treasury Department, October 1, 1791. "By a circular instruction of March 30 1790 you have been directed to transmit all paid draughts of the Treasurer to this office. A deviation from this rule has taken place in your remitting draughts to the Treasurer. You will in future adhere to the Instruction."

Copy, RG 56, Letters to and from the Collectors at Bridgetown and Annapolis, National Archives; copy, RG 56, Letters to Collectors at Small Ports, "Set G," National Archives.
    1. Davidson was the collector of customs at Annapolis.

From Meletiah Jordan

Collectors Office. Frenchman's Bay [District of Maine] October 1st. 1791

Sir

Your circular Letter of the 14th. of April I have but very recently received which will apologize for so late an answer. As you have been good enough to give me liberty to disclose my sentiments to you on the subject, You will I hope pardon the freedom of my answer to your Circular. I will answer as particularly respecting myself as possible. The salary of fifty dollars a year commences but the 1st. of October 1790 which is granted I presume by the eligibility of such a Salary appearing to the House of Representatives due to me & persons of my situation for services to the State. As one year has elapsed previous to the granting such salary and in which it must be supposed

I must be put to an extraordinary expense in hiring an Office, Books &c with the additional expense of jaunting round the District which by the by is very detached and difficult destitute of Roads or any convenience for travelling but by water exclusive of my services for that year I should imagine that consequently my salary ought to be paid as well as the year subsequent thereto. Agreeable to your request I have herewith inclosed a minute of the money paid by me on account of the United States for the year 1790. From the tenor of your letter I dont understand that you wish to have an account of what money I paid away on Official account they being already forwarded with the different Vouchers. But I conceive you mean any extraordinary expense that has accrued in the course of the business but of which no charge could be made by me with propriety to the United States. I have therefore taken the liberty to inclose you also such minutes. If upon an investigation of the matter an addition of salary should take place or extra expenses take place I for my part shall be very happy & grateful and I hope upon an impartial judgement it will appear that the present Salary will be thought inadequate to the purpose intended. But should it be determined otherways I also am content to render every service my poor abilities will admit to the United States.

I beg leave to subscribe myself   Your humble Servant

Meletiah Jordan.

Honble. Alexander Hamilton
Secretary of the Treasury.

Copy, RG 56, Letters to Collectors at Gloucester, Machias, and Frenchman's Bay, National Archives.

From Meletiah Jordan

Frenchman's Bay [*District of Maine*] *October 1, 1791.* ". . . I am sorry to observe that the last Quarter has been so unproductive of profit to the Revenue. The unusual demand of Lumber from the different parts of the State has drained the Country so much as to prevent Foreign Vessels loading. You will observe a manifest difference between the Account Current and Abstracts of Duties on tonnage which you will give me leave to elucidate. The Schooner Goodintent Benj. Pierce Master who entered the 12th. of July, some time after she drifted from her moorings in bad weather and bilged—the Master has since endeavoured to repair her but want of money to do it effectually has obliged him to go back to St. Johns to procure money for that purpose and to discharge his Duties at this Office. I have got the Register and the Vessel is in such a situation that she cannot float until she has a thorough repair and the Revenue secured. I have adopted this method in preference of entering a process at Law knowing the money to be secure, the Vessel in distress and conceiving that a lawsuit would by no means expedite the business. From Mr. Lamb [1] of New York I have to acknowledge the Receipt of a Thermometer and a Hydrometer which came to hand but two days ago, and the Thermometer in such a situation as to render it useless the Glass Globe at the Bottom being broken and the Mercury gone. . . ."

Incomplete copy, RG 56, Letters to Collectors at Gloucester, Machias, and Frenchman's Bay, National Archives.
1. John Lamb, collector of customs at New York City.

To Charles Lee

Treasury Department
October 1 1791

Sir

An enquiry was made at this Office, during your absence from Alexandria relative to the case of Teas arriving in your district not accompanied with certificates. In consequence of which I request that you would inform the Surveyor, that in all cases wherein the marking of the packages or other circumstances prove the Teas to have been imported since the first of April last, the production of a certificate is to be required, and, if not produced, that the package or packages are to be seized. But in cases wherein there is no ground to believe that the Teas were imported since the 1st April 1791, after a very careful examination into circumstances, the Teas must be permitted to pass.[1]

I am, Sir,   Your Most Obedt Servant   A Hamilton

Charles Lee Esqr.
Collr Alexandria

LS, RG 56, Letters to and from the Collectors at Alexandria, National Archives; copy, RG 56, Letters to Collectors at Small Ports, "Set G," National Archives.

1. Section 4 of "An Act making farther provision for the collection of the duties by law imposed on Teas, and to prolong the term for the payment of the Duties on Wines" reads as follows:

"*And be it further enacted,* That all teas which, after the first day of April next, shall be imported into the United States from any foreign port or place, shall be landed under the care of the inspectors of the revenue for the ports where the same shall be respectively landed; and for that purpose every permit which shall be granted by any collector, for landing the same, shall, prior to such landing, be produced to the said inspector, who by an endorsement thereupon under his hand, shall signify the production thereof to him, and the time when; after which, and not otherwise, it shall be lawful to land the teas mentioned in such permit. And the said inspector shall make an entry of all such permits, and of the contents thereof; and each chest, box or package containing any teas, shall be marked by the officer under whose immediate inspection the same shall be landed, in legible and durable characters, with progressive numbers, and with the name of the vessel in which the same shall have been imported. And the said officer shall grant a certificate for each such chest, box or package, specifying therein the name or names of the importer or importers, the ship or vessel in which the same shall have been imported, and the number thereof to accompany the same wheresoever it shall be sent.

"And whereas, for the payment of the duties accruing on Maderia wines, and which may be secured by bond, the term of twelve months is allowed; and it is proper to extend, in like manner, the payment of the duties accruing on other wines." (1 *Stat.* 220–21 [March 3, 1791].)

From Edmund Randolph

Philadelphia October 1. 1791.

Sir

I have done myself the honor of calling at your house and office, with a view to say a word to you, on the claim, which the holders of a certain description of certificates have set up.[1] But being disappointed in meeting you, I beg leave to give you the result of my reflections on that subject.

What degree of obligation lies upon the United States to gratify them, is at this time immaterial, Because I am opposed to their pretensions, in a principle, not connected with such an inquiry.

The secretary of the Treasury is to execute the funding law.[2] In that are contained his text and rule of conduct. From that therefore those creditors must derive the support of their pretensions. I shall not repeat, what I wrote to you on a former occasion;[3] altho' it would constitute a considerable part of what I should now write, were I minute. I shall also waive those reasons, which weigh with me in addition. For the creditors sent me your correspondence with them; [4] and in your construction of that law, as expressed therein, I wholly acquiesce. I make this reference; because my observations, being intended solely for your own satisfaction, are as explicit by such a reference, as they would be by a particular repetition. I certainly can add nothing to the sentiments in those letters.

As the time of subscription was running out so rapidly, one of the creditors desired to know, what opinion I should forward to you. I did not hesitate to inform him, that it would square with the foregoing; as I thereby gained more time to settle my judgment upon the questions, by rendering an immediate answer unnecessary.

You forgot to return the rough original of my last letter.[5]

I have the honor, sir, to be, with real esteem   yr. mo. ob. serv.

Edm: Randolph

The Secretary of the Treasury.

ALS, RG 46, Second Congress, Records of the Office of the Secretary of the Senate, National Archives.

1. H endorsed this letter "concerning loan Office Certificates bearing interest on Nominal sum." See H to Thomas Forrest, John Nicholson, and Others, Public Creditors, May 27, 1791.

2. See "An Act making provision for the (payment of the) Debt of the United States" (1 *Stat.* 138–44 [August 4, 1790]).

3. Randolph to H, August 21, 1791.

4. Only one of these letters has been found. See H to Thomas Forrest, John Nicholson, and Others, Public Creditors, May 27, 1791. See also Blair McClenachan *et al.* to H, March 16, 1791.

5. Letter not found.

From William Seton

[New York] 1 Oct 1791

sir

Immediately upon the receipt of your Letter of the 30th.[1] I informed the Commissioner of Loans [2] that the Sum of 20,000 Dollars should be passed to the credit of his Account in Bank agreeably to your desire.

I have the honor to be &c.

LC, Bank of New York, New York City.

1. Letter not found.

2. John Cochran.

From William Seton

[New York] 1 Oct. 1791

Sir

I am desired by the President and Directors to acknowledge the receipt of your Letters of the 21 & 24 Sepr [1]—the first requesting a payment to be made of Ten thousand Dollars to Mr. De la Forest Vice Consul of France,[2] which was immediately complied with & enclosed. I have the honor to transmit his receipt for the same.[3] Your directions respecting ballancing the weekly Returns of the Treasurers Account with this Bank shall be punctually attended to; we have closed the Account to the 30th Sepr. inclusive of which I now transmit a State which will precisely shew the Cash in hand belonging to the United States. I have the honor to be &c.

LC, Bank of New York, New York City.
1. Neither letter has been found.
2. Antoine René Charles Mathurin de La Forest, who served in the French legation in the United States during the American Revolution, was made French vice consul at Savannah in 1783. He assumed the duties of consul general in 1785, but was not officially appointed to the post until March 2, 1792.
3. See Jean Baptiste de Ternant to H, September 21, 1791, and H to Ternant, September 21, 1791.

From George Beckwith [1]

Philadelphia, October 2nd. 1791.

Sir.

Having received from Lord Dorchester, a copy of his Lordship's answer to a late address from deputies of the confederated western nations of indians,[2] I am induced to transmit to you herewith an authenticated copy of that paper for the information of the Executive Government, in the hope that it may have a tendency to dispel the remaining prejudices of individuals, and to promote the peace of the frontiers.

I have the honor to be   Sir,   Your most obedient,   and most humble servt
                                                    Geo: Beckwith

Alexander Hamilton Esqr:
&c &c &c

Copy, George Washington Papers, Library of Congress; copy, Connecticut Historical Society, Hartford.

1. This letter was enclosed in a letter which Henry Knox, Secretary of War, wrote to George Washington on October 4, 1791 (LS, George Washington Papers, Library of Congress). H, in a letter to Knox, dated October 3, 1791, had submitted Beckwith's letter to the Secretary of War.

2. According to Samuel F. Bemis, Dorchester's address to a deputation of the confederated Indian nations is in the British Public Records Office. Dorchester informed the Indians that Great Britain would not join them in hostilities but that he would mediate between them and the United States (Bemis, *Jay's Treaty*, 116). Dorchester sent a copy of his address in a letter to Lord Grenville on August 17, 1791 (see Brymner, *Canadian Archives*, 1890, 302). It presumably was prepared in answer to a message from the English traders of the Northwest, dated August 10, 1791, which had been forwarded to Dorchester by Sir John Johnson, Superintendent of Indian Affairs. The traders had asked Johnson to "represent to Dorchester the alarming situation of their trade to the Southward of Detroit." They expressed the hope that "His Excellency will use his influence to persuade the Indians to listen to terms of peace" (Brymner, *Canadian Archives*, 1890, 302).

To Angelica Church [1]

[Philadelphia, October 2, 1791]

Betsey according to your hint cries "Atlantic" [2] and defies any thing that either of us can say or do. She consents to every thing, except that I should love you *as well as herself* and this you are too reasonable to expect.

But I do not know how far I shall avail myself of her generosity if you do not mend your manners. You hurt my republican nerves by your intimacy with "*amiable*" Princes. I cannot endure that you should be giving such folks dinners, while I at the distance of 3000 miles can only console myself by *thinking* of you.

But I pray you dont let your Vanity make you forget that such folks are but men and that it is very possible that they may not be half as worthy of the good will of a fine woman as a parliament man or a Secretary of the Treasury.

You are not however to conclude from what I have said that I am in a violent fit of dudgeon with you. If it will give you pleasure, assure yourself that you are as much in my good graces as ever and that you must be a very naughty girl indeed before you can lose the place you have in my affection. I earnestly join Betsey in the favourite

wish that we may meet again—And heaven permitting, it shall be so.
Adieu very *dear sister in law*   A Hamilton

October 2d. 91

ALS, Judge Peter B. Olney, Deep River, Connecticut.
1. H wrote this letter as a postscript to a letter which Elizabeth Hamilton
wrote to her sister on this date.
2. At the conclusion of her letter to Angelica, Elizabeth wrote: "My Hamilton and I often talk about you with great pleasure and earnestly wish that you
could again be aded to our little circle but we dare scarcely hope for so great
a happiness. We will not how ever dispair of Meeting again on one or the other
side of the Atlantic."

From *Thomas Marshall* [1]

Octr. 2d: 1791. Newark [New Jersey]

Sir

At the particular desire of Coll. Duer I Yesterday visited the great
falls of the Pasaic, Accompanied by a Monsieur Allon [2] of this Town.
I was requested not to make enquiries on the Spot, for fear of my
design being discover'd, which being known Col: Duer thought
wou'd Affect the Price of Land. I am fearful that it will be found
Impossible to take the Necessary steps, however cautious the persons
may be, without their design being discover'd. Col: Duers recommendation of Monr: Allon for a Companion was attended with some
particular Circumstances. This Gentlemen is totally unacquainted
with English, and I Ignorant of French, and of course our Conversation for 32 Miles was very Interesting to the Society. On our arrival
at the Falls I concluded Monsr. A. wou'd have conducted me to the
place destin'd for the Canal, but after a Bewilder'd ramble in the
Woods, I found he had mistaken the Side of the River. Being Inhibited
from Enquiries I found myself in an awkward Situation. At length we
gain'd the Falls, still I was dissatisfied as *this* appear'd not to be the
place destin'd for the Cut. I Understood that Col. Duer had requested him to take me to the *Exact Spot*. I used every means in my
power to make him sensible of this and I thought he was proceeding
to the place, when after persuing the run of the Pasaic for about four
hundred yards above the falls thro' thick woods, at length we were

stopt as we found them Impenetrable any further. I must confess Sir, I found myself much at a loss how to Account for the Events of the Day. If there was a design or wish for *me* to fix upon a spot without being apprized of the Choice of *others,* I shou'd have been permitted to have follow'd my own Inclinations and not to have been *led* by Monsr: Allon, but I really think Sir, 'twas nothing more than the *Forgetfulness* of my Companion. I therefore took every means in my power to relieve the Anxiety his mind was evidently in, but was obliged to return with only a transient View of the Falls and Aspect of the Country. The Body of Water is beyond Compare, and that it may be drawn off in any Quantity appears extreemly probable from the Situation of the Adjacent Country. The Expence of the Canal I understand from Col. Duer, Mosr. Allon estimates at 2000 £. The Navigation he asserts may be brought within a small distance of the Works at a very trifling Expence, but I have some reasons to differ in Opinion on the latter Subject as far as concerns Expence but cannot speak positively. Stone is in abundance, and some of it I think doubtless good, tho' what I Saw had no very powerful recomendations. The Country about the Falls is cover'd with Wood, Consequently that Article cannot be very dear; Beef & Mutton at 3½ and 4d. pr Lb; by Land exactly 10 Miles from N York and 16 from Newark. This, Sir, is all I am enabled to say at present, but must confess that I am favourably imprest from the Transient view I had of things. The Expence attending the Canal and making the Pasaic Navigable for such a distance are Objects Sir that I respectfully recommend for your Consideration, and when the Pasaic is froze Land carriage for such a distance will fall heavy. If Sir, these Objections are nothing compared to its requisites, I am of Opinion it will be found to be the best Situation, that is Sir, it will have more Water, & the Land may be had cheaper here than at Second River. In point of Water Second River bears no Comparison with the Pasaic, but it has almost every thing else to recommend its preeminece over the latter. Thus Sir, I venture to differ in Opinion from others who have gone before me, and if I am wrong in my Statements it arises from Ignorance only, for I think myself as warmly attatch'd to the Prosperity and Interest of the Society as any individual directly or indirectly concern'd and have endeavour'd to guide my conduct by these Sentiments in the little concerns that have hitherto fallen to my lot. If

Sir, I receive no other Commands I shall proceed from Trenton to Pitts-Town [3] on Tuesday, and am Sir with the utmost respect

Yr. Most Obedient   Humble Servant   Thomas Marshall

The Honble: Alexr Hamilton

ALS, Hamilton Papers, Library of Congress.
1. For background to this letter, see William Hall to H, September 4, 1791.
2. Allon (or Allou) had supplied William Duer with an estimate of the cost of constructing a canal between Great Falls and Vreeland's Point on the Passaic River. Marshall seems to have acted under the instructions of Tench Coxe to whom he reported in detail (Marshall to Coxe, September 18, 21, 27, October 10, 1791, Hamilton Papers, Library of Congress). These letters are printed in Cole, *Industrial and Commercial Correspondence*, 208–14, 217–18.
3. Pittstown is in Hunterdon County, New Jersey, on a tributary of the south branch of the Raritan River about thirty miles north of Trenton.

From George Washington [1]

[Mount Vernon, October 2, 1791]

Sir,

Your letter of the 24th. ulto., (enclosing a letter from Govr. St. Clair, and sundry papers relating to the subject of the settlements which have been made under purchases from Judge Symmes) I have duly received. The Secretary of State, as well as I recollect, has already written both to Govr. St. Clair [2] & Judge Symmes [3] on this subject; but whether he has or has not, it can make no material difference to let the matter rest until my return to Philada. when I shall pay the necessary attention to it.

I am Sir,   Yr. most hble Servt.   G: Washington

Mount Vernon
2d. Octor. 1791.

LC, George Washington Papers, Library of Congress.
1. For background to this letter, see Arthur St. Clair to H, May 25, 1791.
2. Thomas Jefferson to St. Clair, August 6, 1791. This letter is printed in Carter, *Territorial Papers*, II, 349.
3. Jefferson to John Cleves Symmes, August 6, 1791. This letter is printed in Carter, *Territorial Papers*, II, 349–50.

To Henry Knox

Philadelphia, October 3rd. 1791.

Sir.

I transmit you, as relating to your department, a letter just received by me from Lieutenant Colonel Beckwith forwarding a copy of a paper purporting to be a speech of Lord Dorchester, in answer to an address of the deputies of certain indian tribes.[1]

You will observe that the object of this communication is stated to be "the information of the executive government." In conversation, a reliance on the candor of all comprehended in that description has been expressed, that no use will be made of it which might be disagreeable to Lord Dorchester; and it has been particularly intimated, that any promulgation of it in the papers, or the furnishing of any copy to any officer in the western country would be undesireable.[2]

I consider myself as having received the paper with these qualifications, and generally under the idea of a discreet and delicate use of it.

I have the honor to be very respectfully, Sir, Your obedt: servant.   A Hamilton

The Secretary for the
Department of War.

Copy, George Washington Papers, Library of Congress. This letter was enclosed in Knox to Washington, October 4, 1791, George Washington Papers, Library of Congress.
1. See George Beckwith to H, October 2, 1791.
2. No record has been found of the conversation in which Beckwith made these requests of H.

To Jeremiah Olney

Treasury Department, October 3, 1791. "As letters to and from the Treasurer now go free of postage, there is no longer a necessity for enclosing them to me. You will therefore in future transmit them directly to him. . . ."

LS, Rhode Island Historical Society, Providence; copy, RG 56, Letters to the Collector at Providence, National Archives; copy, RG 56, Letters to Collectors at Small Ports, "Set G," National Archives.

To William Seton

Treasury Department
October 3. 1791.

Sir,

I do not find among the papers of the office any return of the investment of the last fifty thousand dollars in purchases of the debt; though I have a confused recollection of having received it.[1] I therefore request that it may be forwarded, if not yet sent, or a duplicate, if a return has already been made.

I request also, that you will cause the requisite steps to be taken, for effecting a transfer of the whole amount of the debt purchased, to the Books of the Treasury; as the session of Congress approaches, and it is an express requisite of the Act that a report be made to that body of all preceding purchases, within fourteen days after the commencement of each session;[2] in order to which it is necessary that they be first placed on the books of the Treasury. I beg your immediate attention to the matter.

With great consideration, I remain Sir, Your obedt. servant

A Hamilton

William Seton Esq.

LS, Bank of New York, New York City; copy, in the handwriting of William Seton, Hamilton Papers, Library of Congress.

1. See Seton to H, September 12, 1791.
2. Section 3 of "An Act making Provision for the Reduction of the Public Debt" reads as follows: "*And be it further enacted,* That accounts of the application of the said monies shall be rendered for settlement as other public accounts, accompanied with returns of the amount of the said debt purchased therewith, at the end of every quarter of a year, to be computed from the time of commencing the purchases aforesaid: and that a full and exact report of the proceedings of the said five persons [the Vice President, the Chief Justice, the Secretary of State, the Secretary of the Treasury, and the Attorney General], or any three of them, including a statement of the disbursements and purchases made under their direction, specifying the times thereof, the prices at which, and the parties from whom the same may be made, shall be laid before Congress, within the first fourteen days of each session which may ensue the present, during the execution of their said trust" (1 *Stat.* 186–87 [August 12, 1790]).

To William Short

Treasury Department
October 3. 1791

Sir

I acknowlege the receipt of your letters of the 26th and 27 of July.

The fall which you announce in the price of the effects of the United States was certainly artificial. The cause ere this will have been better ascertained to you. 'Tis open to various conjectures.

I have thought it adviseable to drop a line to our Bankers in Holland [1] (of which a copy is inclosed) merely to *mark* my attention to the circumstance.

It will deserve to be further considered whether it be expedient to press any more the reduction of charges. Perhaps the principal effort ought hereafter to be towards a reduction of the rate of interest. But you, who best know the ground, can best judge.

I shall be anxious to know the issue of your experiment at Antwerp.

I have the honor to remain with great consideration and regard
Sir   Your most Obedient servt   A Hamilton

William Short Esquire &c

ALS, William Short Papers, Library of Congress.
    1. See H to Willink, Van Staphorst, and Hubbard, October 3, 1791.

To Joseph Whipple [1]

Treasury Department
October 3rd. 1791.

Sir,

Another Thermometer will be sent on to you, but I request that you will enjoin on the Inspectors great care in the handling of it.

The spare Hydrometer of which you are possessed may be delivered to the Supervisor of the Revenue for the District of New Hampshire [2] for the use of the officers in his Department. It will be proper that, his receipt for the instrument be transmitted to the Treasury.

I am   Sir   Your obedt Servant   A Hamilton

Joseph Whipple Esqr
Collector
Portsmouth

LS, RG 56, Letters to the Collector at Portsmouth, National Archives; copy, RG 56, Letters to Collectors at Small Ports, "Set G," National Archives.
1. This letter is in reply to Whipple to H, September 16, 1791.
2. Joshua Wentworth.

From Otho H. Williams

Baltimore 3d. October 1791.

Sir

There have lately been two importations of Horses from England into this port—two in each.

It was customary, under the laws of this state, which were silent on the subject, to consider live Stock as neither goods, wares nor merchandize; and they were consequently admitted duty free. The Laws of Congress are silent also, and the custom is continued. But I am not confident enough to rely upon custom only for my justification. The reasons which were urged in favor of this indulgence, to wit, that the importation of Live Stock improved the breed of our Cattle does not always apply. In one of the late instances a pair of Geldings for a Gentleman's carriage were imported. I request your opinion whether Horses, or any other live animals, may be legally imported without payment of duties.

Your most Humble Servant.

Alexander Hamilton Esqr.
Secretary of the Treasury

ADf, RG 53, "Old Correspondence," Baltimore Collector, National Archives.

To Wilhem and Jan Willink, Nicholaas and Jacob Van Staphorst, and Nicholas Hubbard

Treasury Department
October 3d. 1791.

Gentlemen

I have learnt with some surprise, through Mr. Short, that the price of the effects of the United States had undergone a sudden depression in the market of Amsterdam.[1]

This is so different from the tenor of the hopes I had built upon those expressed by you, and so contrary to all the calculations I can form on the *natural course* of the thing, that I cannot but be curious for a particular devellopment of its cause.

It will therefore be satisfactory to me to receive from you, as early as may be, a full explanation of the circumstances which shall appear to you to have occasioned so unexpected a turn of the thing.

With great consideration, I remain   Gentlemen   Your Obedt. servant

Messrs. Willinks, VanStaphorsts & Hubbard
Amsterdam.

Copy, William Short Papers, Library of Congress.
1. See Short to H, July 26, 27, 1791.

Account with Manasseh Salter [1]

[New York, October 4, 1791]

Mr. Hamilton   To Manasseh Salter Dr.

1791

Septr 28 To	73	Yds	Carpetting (pr Mrs Coloen)[2]	8/6	£31.	0 6
To	3	„	Towe Cloth	1/6		4.6
Oct 4 To	7	”	Carpetting	9/	3.	3.0
					£34.	8.0

D, Hamilton Papers, Library of Congress.
1. Salter operated a store at 34 and 35 Broadway, New York City.
2. According to the New York City directory for 1789, this is presumably the Widow Colon of Barclay Street.

From Edward Carrington

Richmond. October 4th. 1791

Sir

The enclosed papers [1] contain parts of the information which I expect to furnish upon the subject of Manufactures in Virginia, and are transmitted agreeably to your request.[2] These papers have come from the two lower Surveys of the District; the information they contain as to the particular Neighbourhoods from which they are drawn, may be applied, with propriety to the whole of those Surveys: indeed, so equally do the people of Virginia go into Manufactures within themselves, that the application might be made to the whole Country, with only a few allowances, from a consideration of their respective staples which I will in some degree enable you to make, upon the following principles. In regard to staples, Virginia is contemplated under three divisions, the Lower, the Middle, & the Upper: the first is comprehended between the Sea and the falls of our great rivers; the Second, between these falls and the blue ridge of Mountains; the latter takes all the Country beyond the Mountains.

The staples of the first are Indian corn principally, small crops of indifferent Tobacco, small crops of wheat, &, in some parts, lumber.

The Middle Country produces our great exports of Tobacco & wheat.

The Upper Country produces Hemp, Flax & wheat principally, and small and indifferent crops of Tobacco.

I have observed that the people of the whole Country, are in habits of Domestic Manufactures pretty equally, except that some allowances must be made on Account of field labour upon their respective staples. These are as follow; the staples of the lower country require moderate labour, and that at particular seasons of the year. The consequence is, that they have much leisure and can apply their hands to

LS, Hamilton Papers, Library of Congress.

1. Thomas Newton, Jr., to Edward Carrington, September 28, 1791; Robert Twiford to Thomas Newton, Jr., August 14, 1791; Anselm Bailey to Thomas Newton, Jr., August 23, 1791; Drury Ragsdale to Edward Carrington, September 29, 1791. These letters are printed below as enclosures.

2. "Treasury Department Circular to the Supervisors of the Revenue," June 22, 1791.

Manufacturing so far as to supply, not only the cloathing of the Whites, but of the Blacks also.

The great staple, Tobacco, in the Middle Country requires much labor when growing, and, what with fitting it for market, and preparing land for succeeding Crops, leaves but little time for the same hands to Manufacture. The consequence is, that the latter business is carried on only by the white females in poor families, and, in wealthly families, under the Eye of the Mistress, by female slaves drawn out of the Estates for that purpose, aided by the superfluous time of a superabundance of house-servants; the consequence is, that less is manufactured here than in the lower Country, yet the difference is, I beleive, no greater than as to the cloathing of the field slaves, for which purpose Kendal Cotton, oznabrigs,³ & hempen rolls ar[e] purchased, but the owner of every plantation tans the hides of the Cattle which are killed or casually die, and, by that means, supplies the slaves in shoes for winter.

The staples of the upper Country require somewhat more field labour than those of the lower, and much less than those of the Middle, & having however but few slaves, and being distant from foreign intercourse, the people depend principally upon home Manufactures, and, at least, equal the lower Country in them.

As to raw materials, no Country under the sun, is capable of producing more than Virginia. The lower Country, produces fine Cotton & Wool, and, both might be increased even to satisfy great foreign demands—in many parts good flax is also made. The Middle Country produces fine Cotton, but the more valuable staples of Wheat and Tobacco, confine the production to the demands of the private Manufactures of the Country itself. It is also well adapted to Hemp & Flax: of the first, some is produced for market; of the latter, every family makes for its own use: to the same extent Wool is also produced. The Upper Country supplies our Markets with great quantities of hemp, said to be equal to any in the World. Flax is also here produced in high perfection, and in great quantities, the people using it for purposes to which Cotton is applied below. For supplying the article of Wool this part of Virginia is so favorable that large droves of sheep go from it, to the lower Town Markets.

3. Osnaburgs.

The mountainous parts of Virginia, abound in Iron Ore, from which most of the Iron, and some of the steel, used in the state, are supplied, and the productions of both might be so increased as to make great exports. We have also a valuable lead mine, in the Southwestern part of the Upper Country, from which new Manufactures are daily coming into practice, such as sheet lead for roofing, shot &c.[4] There is a shot factory in Richmond, well established by the present worker of this Mine, and the same hand has furnished the lead for covering the roof of our *Capitol*, or State House. This mine was, during the War, worked under the public direction of this state, and supplied all the lead used in the Southern service; supplies of it, also went to the Main Army, but whether for the whole service, I will not undertake to say.

As to regular Trades we have but few. They are, however, increasing daily. In the upper Country, there are several fulling Mills, from which good Cloth is seen. I will endeavour to obtain samples.

I have now endeavoured to give you, in addition to the enclosed papers, such information as will furnish a general idea of the Manufactures throughout this Commonwealth, and having been tolerably attentive to these circumstances, for several years, as I have passed through the various parts of the Country, am persuaded you may rely upon it, as well founded. I have been led to do it, from a consideration, that the approach of the session, requires an early communication, and from the information expected from the upper Inspectors, having not yet arrived. When I receive their reports, they shall be forwarded immediately.

I beg you to be assured, that this business has been attended with no material trouble or inconvenience, and that it has given pleasure to both myself & the Inspectors that you requested our assistance in obtaining the desired information.

I have the Honor to be   with great respect   Sir   Your Most Obt. sr.   Ed Carrington
                          Supervisor D: Virga.

---

4. This lead mine was in southwestern Virginia along the Great Kanawha River about twenty-five miles from the state's southern boundary. After reduction in a nearby furnace, the lead went overland to the James River and down the river to Richmond. This lead mine is mentioned in H's "Report on the Subject of Manufactures," December 5, 1791.

N.B.   D. Ragsdales [5] return is made upon 20 Families in one neighbourhood, comprehending all classes in life from the richest to the
poorest. Upon my Census returns of the district of Virga. (exclusive
of Kentucky) 70,825 Families appear. This note is made upon a supposition that it may possibly be useful in calculations which the Secretary may wish to make.[6]

Alexr. Hamilton Esq.

[E N C L O S U R E]

Thomas Newton, Junior, to Edward Carrington [7]

Norfolk [Virginia] 28. Sept. 1791.

Dear Sir,

Having been much hurried by my private affairs since I left you
at So. Hampton Court, prevented my information of the State of
Manufacturies in this port of my Survey. The inhabitants of Princess
Anne County makes most of their Negroes Cloathing & their coarse
Cloaths, with Shoes & Stockings. The Counties of Norfolk & Nansemond the Same. In the Town of Norfolk there is a very extensive
Tannery, which supplies most of the lower Counties with Leather,
together with the little that is made by the Country people at their
Own Houses & but few but have a Vat or Trough to tann the hides
of the Cattle they kill themselves. There is also a Ropery carried on
here to a Considerable extent, but the owner thinks the Duty laid on
imported Cordage is not Sufficient to encourage him as most of the
Ships are British & give a preference to English Cordage at 10 ⅌ Ct.
higher than American made, *altho* the last is best being prejudiced in
favor of their Own Manufactury. We have plenty of Shoe-makers,
Taylors Blacksmiths, House & Ship Carpenters, Cabinet makers, Carriage makers & Wheel wrights, that with what they do & what comes

5. Drury Ragsdale was appointed inspector of Survey No. 1 in Virginia on
October 31, 1791.
6. The postscript is in Carrington's handwriting.
7. ALS, Hamilton Papers, Library of Congress.
    Newton, a Norfolk lawyer, was appointed inspector of Survey No. 4 in Vir-
ginia on October 31, 1791.

in from the Northern States, we cou'd do very well without any thing from Europe that they can make. In Portsmouth there is a small Tannery, but is not carried on with Spirits, Shoemakers &c Sufficient to make for their Consumption. I endeavored to Comply with your request in making a return According to the form sent me, but found the people averse to giving in. I Judged it improper to say more & have given you to the best of my knowledge a true State of our Situation as to Manufacturies here.

am with respect   Yr. Obt. Servt.   Tho Newton Jr

Colo. Carrington

[ENCLOSURE]

Robert Twiford to Thomas Newton, Junior [8]

Pungoteague [Virginia] August 14th. 1791

Dear Sir,

I Recd. yours dated the 25th July the 10th Instant together with sum Advertisements; I have fixed two Auxiliary officers in Northampton & two in Accomack above my house & one at My house, so that I beleve that the Destilaries are all within ten miles of an office except a few at Marenty Bay; I have informed my self Respecting the Manufactries as well as the length of time would allow. 45000 yds. all yarn 30000 do. Cotton 45000 do. wollen what we call Lintsewoose [9] Flax linnen coars & fine 315000 do. I suppose that ¾ of the people are clothed in their own Manufactury; Leather shoes we make cheafely within our selves & common Stocking; I Shall indeavour to Inform my self beter by the next Oppertunity and will write you more fully; When I am with

Respect Dr. sir Your Hubl   Servt.   Robert Twiford Collector [10]

---

8. ALS, Hamilton Papers, Library of Congress.
Twiford operated a stage wagon on the Eastern Shore of Virginia.
9. Before this word Carrington placed an asterisk, and then opposite an asterisk at the bottom of the page he wrote "Say linsey-Woolsey."
10. At the end of this letter, Carrington wrote: "Mr. Twiford includes in the above estimate the two Counties of Accomac & Northampton on the Eastern shore in Virginia, which contain, upon the Census return, 2,729 families. E. C."

[ENCLOSURE]

Anselm Bailey to Thomas Newton, Junior [11]

Surry [Virginia] Augt. 23d 1791

Dr Friend,

Thine of the 26th. of last Mo. I received & set about with much chearfulness to comply with thy request, but thou'l be perhaps surprised at hearing that most of the people in these parts have got into such a spirit of Jealousy that they suspect some design unfavorable to them in every thing that is attempted of a public nature. "What are they going to Tax our Cloath too" was the reply of several, and as nothing I cou'd say in respect to the real intention wou'd satisfy, was inclined to think it would be best to decline the attempt. I suppose however that several of the neighbours make from three to four hundred yards of Clo. each year, which is mostly Cotton, a small proportion of it is mixt Cotton & Wool and Cotton & Flax but there is very little made that is all Wool or Flax. I am inclined to think that for ten Miles round me the avarage quantity of Clo. would be nearly two hundred yards to each Family. That at least $\frac{5}{6}$ of all the cloth Shoes. & Stockings that are used in those Families are home made. The average price of which are nearly as follows. Cloth 2/- Shoes 5/6 or 6/- & Stockgs the same. . . .[12]

Thy Friend   Anselm Bailey

[ENCLOSURE]

Drury Ragsdale to Edward Carrington [13]

King William County [Virginia] Sept. 29. 1791

"Inclosed you will receive a return of Cloth &c. manufactured in my Neighbourhood.

11. ALS, Hamilton Papers, Library of Congress.
Bailey was a Surry County physician.
12. The remainder of this letter, which was of a personal nature, was crossed out by Carrington.
13. Extract, in Edward Carrington's handwriting, Hamilton Papers, Library of Congress.

It may not be amiss to inform you that it is my opinion that the manufactures in my Survey carried on in private families consist principally if not all together of Cotton and Wool, most of the fine cloth is of cotton alone, made into such Cloth as Table linnen sheeting, Jeans for Breeches and Waistcoats, in imitation of the Manchester manufactures, Bed ticking much superior to the cheap and common imported from Europe, Muslings in immitation of those from Scotland, striped cottons for Womens gowns; some patterns hansomer and more durable than the printed imported cottons. There being a scarsity of Wool it is generally mixed with Cotton, the warp being filled in with wool makes the cloathing of the Young and Domestic Negroes, and, though not yeilding equal warmth with the cheap Kendal Cotton, is generally, when wove double, more durable than those Cottons, as they are called. Fine Stockings are knit to every degree of perfection, principally of Cotton. Course Stockings are knit generally of Cotton & Wool & the Negroes prefer these to those imported.

As to the Article of leather there seems to be a scarsity owing to a distemper that has been very fatal for some years amoung the horned cattle, but what there is in the Country distant from Towns, are generally manufactured by the families themselves tho' it may be supposed from the manner of carrying on this business in the Country, that it cannot be in any great state of improvement.

The manufacturing of Iron seems to exceed all the manufactures carried on amoung us; most of the Blacksmiths in the Country are capable of making every Article Necessary for Domestic use of the planter, as hoes, axes, Plows, shovels, spades, tongs, wrought hand irons, nails, (this article can be imported cheaper than we can make them owing to the want of slitting mills) in short, almost every article in iron (except the more refined cutlery) can be made as cheap and I think of Better quality than what is imported to us from Europe, but it may be necessary to remark that Iron comes dear to us in the Middle [14] Counties, generally retail'd at 4d ⅌ lb. and considered as a cash article."

14. Before this word Carrington placed an asterisk, and at the bottom of the page opposite an asterisk he wrote: "Middle Counties here are not meant of the whole State but the interior parts of the lower Country, or those which are distant from the trading Cities or Towns. E. C."

Heads of Families	White Male Tithes	W. Female Tithes	White Children	Male Slave Tithes	F. M. Slave Tithes	Children	Total no. in Family	Fine such as Family Cloathing. Beding Table Linnins &c.	Course such as Negroes Cloathing Blanketing &c.	Total No. of Yards.	Value of fine Cloath ⅌ yd.	Value of Course.	Fine ⅌rs	Course.	Fine	Course.	Total Amount of Value of Cloath &c.
Thomas Avera	1	3	1	3	3	3	13	196.	67.	263.	3/6	2/6.	9.	6	5/-	2/6.	£ 45.13.6
James Ruffin	1	1	5.	7.	10	16.	43	296.	172.	468.	3/6	2/6.	17.	17.	5/	2/6.	80: 1.0
Steeling Ruffin	1	1	2	7.	13	14	35.	187.	100.	287.	3/6	2/6.	6.	20.	5/	2/6.	49. 7.0
David Pannell	1	2	5.	6.	3	10	31.	284.	116.	400.	3/6	2/6.	20.	13.	5/	2/6.	69.16.6
John King	2	2	1	—	—	1	8.	98.	29	127.	3/6	2/6.	8.	2	5/	2/6.	22: 5.6
Hickerson Bagwell	1	1	—	1	1	—	13	56.	13	69.	3/6	2/6.	5.	1.	5/	2/6.	13: 1.0
Nathaniel Fox Junr	1	—	3	3	3	3	20	120	80	200	3/6	2/6.	6.	8	5/.	2/6.	33.15.
Wm. Towler	1	1	2	1.	1	1.	4.	46.	22	68.	3/6	2/6.	7.	—	5.	2/6.	7. 4. 6
Bernard Lipscomb	1	—	2	—	1	1	8	70.	60	130	3/6	2/6.	6.	—	5/.	2/6.	8.15
Mathew Towler	1	—	8.	—	2	2.	31.	26.	30.	56	3/6	2/6.	8	—	5/.	2/6.	10.6
James Howard	1	1	2	1	1	1	18.	30	22.	52	3/6	2/6.	8	—	5.	2/6.	21.5
Samuel Howard	2	—	2	4	2	7.	5.	27.	12.	39	3/6	2/6.	4.	—	5/.	2/6.	12.6
Wm Starke	1	1	3	—	—	—	9.	—	—	—	—	—	3.	—	—	—	33.15.
John Hollins	1	—	1	1	2	3	4	27.	6.	33	3/6	2/6.	4.	3	5/.	2/6.	6. 9. 6
Mrs. Hawse	—	1	—	—	1	1	5.	22.	18.	40	3/6	2/6.	6.	—	5/.	2/6.	7.14. 6
Charles Lipscomb	1	2	3	1	2	—	5	27.	15.	50	3/6	2/6.	4.	5.	5/.	2/6	9.12. 6
Peter Richeson	1	2	1	3	1	3	16	35.	35.	147.	3/6	2/6.	16.	8.	5/.	2/6	28.12.
Edward P. Chamberlayne	1	1	—	4	2	6	17	112	35.	70	3/6	2/6	6.	9.	5/.	2/6	9.15
Wm Newman	1	—	3	7.	4	5	19.	75.	70.	145.	—	2/6	12.	15.	5/.	2/6.	26. 0
Drury Ragsdale	1	3	1	8.	4	3	19.	200.	70.	270	3/6	2/6	14	6	5/.	2/6	49. 2. 6
Total amt. of the whole	20	26	50	58	61	86	301	1907	1007.	2914	—	—	152	108			£ 501: 2: 0

This return contains the Quantity of Cloath &c Manufacturd in the Familys it contains from the 1st. day of Janry. 1790 to the 1st. day of January 1791.

King William Virginia.   Drury Ragsdale
Sept. 29th. 1791

General remarks.

From William Ellery

Collector's Office [Newport, Rhode Island]
October 4th 1791

Sir,

I have received your letter of the 16th of Septemr.[1] on the 27th of the same month, and am much obliged for your answers to my several questions, and for the consent you have given respecting the sales of vessels of which may be condemned. If measures had not been taken the Sloop Betsy would not have sold so high as she did.[2]

I told the Council for the Ushers,[3] that their case having been fairly stated to you, and received your determination, I thought they had no reason to expect that an application to you for a mitigation of the penalties they had incurred would prove successful.

As the District attorney [4] will without doubt write to you on that part of your reflexions which relates to the service of summonses, I will only observe here, that, if it had been conceived that summonses could be served by other than Officers I should have taken them out of the Clerk's office and delivered them to persons who, not being suspected of being charged with such processes, might have probaly served them. He will also doubtless inform you what he suggested in his motion for a continuance. I was occasionally absent when the motion was made, but was present when the District Judge [5] gave his opinion. He observed that there was no ⟨lack⟩ on the part of the Officers of the Customs, but as there was no evidence of collusion between the claimant and the Witnesses in his opinion the cause was continued. This as well as I can recollect was the substance of what he said.

On Saturday last I reseized the Brig Seven Brothers; [6] and immediately delivered a summons to the Depy. Marshall to be served on a person who had heretofore eluded the service, and who, I presume will be a material evidence in the case. After much difficulty the summons has been served, and this day at 10 o clock his deposition is to be taken before the Judge of the District Court. The substance of it I will communicate to you by the next post. A writ is ready to be served on Cotrell, I only wait to hear from the Marshall,[7] to whom I have written respecting a witness who I presume is at Providence,

This will be accompanied by a Certificate of Registry No. 41. granted at the Port of Dighton Novr. 6 1790 and delivered up on a transfer of property, a Certife. of Regy. No. 19th. granted at this port Apl. 6 1791 and delivered up on a transfer of property, and a copy of an endorsment of change of master on Regr. No. 38. granted at this Port Augt. 2nd 1791: a weekly return of monies received and paid.

I am, Sir, yr. obedt. servant   Wm Ellery Collr

A Hamilton Esqr
Secry Treasy

LC, Newport Historical Society, Newport, Rhode Island.
  1. Letter not found.
  2. See Ellery to H, August 2, 23, 26, 29, September 19, 1791.
  3. See Ellery to H, February 15, May 9, 1791.
  4. The attorney for the District of Rhode Island was William Channing.
  5. Henry Marchant.
  6. See Ellery to H, July 11, August 2, 23, 1791.
  7. William Peck.

From Benjamin Lincoln

Boston 4 Octr [1791]

Sir

I received your circular Letter of the 21st. Ulto and your letter respecting a cancelled register [1] by the last post.

Knowing sir how anxious you are to œconomise the public money and how just your expectations are that all officers of the revenue will aid you in a measure so important to the general interest I take the liberty to suggest, as the weather will soon be so inclement as to prevent our boat going out of the harbour, that we may without injury to the revenue dismiss three out of four of our boat men. One is quite sufficient to take care of the boat & at all times, when we want to put an officer on board a vessel in the harbour a man can be obtained for a small consideration compared with the constant pay of a man. These boat men cannot be wanted again untill the next April.

Inclosed is a receipt from the bank of Massachusetts for twenty five thousand dollars. This I had on hand On the first instant after retaining a like sum for Mr. Appleton [2] and a sum necessary for other demands.

By the next post I shall be able to state to you what the rations for the men on board the cutter have cost us. The rations as state will not keep one New Englander on board. I, at first, attempted to confine the men to the fixed ration. The consequence was that they instantly deserted.

I have seen Mr. Searl the builder of the present Cutter & he has informed me that he will build a smaller vessel and at the rate ℔ ton as he engage to build the present one.[3]

LC, Massachusetts Historical Society, Boston; LC, RG 36, Collector of Customs at Boston, Letter Book, 1790–1797, National Archives; copy, RG 56, Letters from the Collector at Boston, National Archives.
1. H to Lincoln, September 22, 1791.
2. Nathaniel Appleton, commissioner of loans for Massachusetts.
3. See Lincoln to H, August 31, 1791; H to Lincoln, September 16, 1791.

From Jeremiah Olney

Providence, October 4, 1791. "I have recd. your Letter of the 24th of September. A Libel had been previously filed agt. the Brigt. Betsey and the Ten Kegs of Brandy; and the Owners are pursuing the Steps of the Law for relief, which I hope will be attended with no great Expence. . . ."

ADfS, Rhode Island Historical Society, Providence; copy, RG 56, Letters from the Collector at Providence, National Archives.

To William Bingham [1]

[*Philadelphia, October 5, 1791.* On October 6, 1791, Bingham wrote to Hamilton: "I received your Letter of yesterday." *Letter not found.*]

1. Bingham was a founder and director of the Bank of North America, a land speculator, the founder of Binghamton, New York, and one of the richest men in the United States. He was a member of the Pennsylvania Assembly from 1790 to 1795.

From William Bingham

[Philadelphia, October 5, 1791]

Dr sir,

I herewith return you the Subscription Book of the Manufacturing society,[1] & must apologize (from hurry of Business) for having detained it So long.

I approve exceedingly of the Plan, both as indicative of public Spirit, & as affording a well grounded hope of private Emolument. I will therefore give it every support in my power, & influenced by these Considerations, do Subscribe 5000 Dollars.[2]

I am with regard & Consideration   Yours Sincerely
Wm Bingham

Philada.
Octr 5th 1791
Honble Col Hamilton

ALS, letterpress copy, Historical Society of Pennsylvania, Philadelphia.
   1. The Society for Establishing Useful Manufactures.
   2. This sum bought fifty shares of stock in the Society for Establishing Useful Manufactures.

From Sharp Delany

[*Philadelphia, October 5, 1791.* On October 10, 1791, Hamilton wrote to Delany: "Your letter of the 5th instant has been received." *Letter not found.*]

From Edward Stevens [1]

[St. Croix, October 5, 1791]

My dear Friend
   The Bearer of this Letter, Mr. Jasper Parsons intends visiting the united States with his Lady and Family to spend the Winter Months in an agreeable Manner, & restore his Health which has been slightly impaired. This Gentleman & his Lady are such respectable Characters, are so universally esteemed in this Island & have excited in my Mind so sincere a Regard for them, that I feel very much interested in every Thing that concerns them. I could not, therefore, let them depart without introducing them to an Acquaintance with you and your worthy Family. I have taken this Liberty from a Conviction that they will meet with every Civility & Attention from you that your Leisure will permit you to shew them, during their short Stay in

Philadelphia. I recommend them with Confidence as I am convinced you will find them every Way worthy your Politeness & friendly Patronage. I remain wh: best Wishes for your Happiness & Prosperity and an ardent Desire of hearing from you.

My dear Friend   Your's very sincerely & affecy:

Edward Stevens

St: Croix   Octobr: 5th. 1791.

ALS, Hamilton Papers, Library of Congress.
  1. Stevens and H had been boyhood friends in St. Croix, and H's first extant letter is addressed to Stevens. A graduate of King's College who studied medicine at the University of Edinburgh, Stevens practiced medicine in St. Croix from 1783 to 1793, when he moved to Philadelphia.

From William Bingham

Philadia Oct 6th 1791

Dear sir

I received your Letter of yesterday [1] with your Remarks on what I wrote to you.[2]

If any Person has offered the sum that you mention to be the price of the Lot, & will make the Same Payment, I certainly will not hesitate a Moment in giving it to you.

At any Rate, we will Settle the Matter whenever you come to Town.

I am   Dear sir   Yours Sincerely   Wm Bingham

A. ⟨Ham⟩ilton Esqr

ALS, letterpress copy, Historical Society of Pennsylvania, Philadelphia.
  1. Letter not found.
  2. Bingham to H, October 5, 1791.

To Elliot and Williams [1]

[*Philadelphia, October 6, 1791.* "The Collector of Baltimore is authorized to advance to you immediately Ten Thousand Dollars, and is informed that it is my intention to make you a like advance, on the first of January next." *Letter not found.*] [2]

ALS, sold at Anderson Galleries, April 14, 1913, Lot 365.

1. The firm consisted of Robert Elliot and Elie Williams. For background to this letter, see Elie Williams to H, October 10, 1789; H to Elie Williams, October 17, 1789; H to Otho H. Williams, September 27, October 6, 1791.

2. Text taken from extract of letter in dealer's catalogue.

From William Seton

[New York] 6th Oct. 1791

Sir

I am honored with your Letter of the 3d. On the 12th of September I transmitted to you a Return of the investment of the 50,000 Dollars in purchases of Stock for account of The United States. I have now the honor to enclose a Duplicate of the same. On the 5th. September I informed you that all the purchases of Debt made to that day had been transferred on the Books to the Names of the Vice President &ca.; all subsequent purchases were made in those Names so that on the 12th of September for the 200,000 Dollars you ordered me to invest, there stood on the Books of the office here, $67439^{96}/_{100}$ Dollars 3 ₱ Cents & $255,257^{71}/_{100}$ Deferred Debt in the Names of the Vice President &ca. I shall call at the office of the Commissioner of Loans [1] tomorrow and do every thing that may be further necessary to comply with your orders.

I have the honor to be with the greatest respect &ca

LC, Bank of New York, New York City.

1. John Cochran. See Seton to H, October 1, 1791.

To George Washington

[Philadelphia, October 6, 1791]

Sir,

Mr. Chew having confirmed the character received by you, of Mr. Barratt,[1] I have written to Mr. Vining [2] requesting him to ascertain whether the appointment will be acceptable to him.

Mr. Houston of Georgia [3] declines the offer made to him, on the score of want of a familiar acquaintance with figures, and its being inconsistant with the State of his affairs, to translate himself *wholly* to the seat of Government. I beg leave to remind you of Mr. Pleasants,[4] if an opportunity of enquiry concerning him should present itself. Mr. McComb,[5] the present auditor of the State of Delaware, has offered himself as a candidate & Mr. Stoddard [6] of Maryland has been mentioned as a proper person, if he would accept. I as yet know not enough of either of these characters to hazard an opinion.

The Packet has brought me a letter of the 2d. of August from Mr. Church which contains the following paragraph—"I fear there is no disposition at present in our Ministers to treat properly with America. Lord Hawkesbury is lately admitted into the cabinet, & his prejudices are strong against you, & the enthusiasm for maintaining the navigation Act is such, that there is not a shadow of probability they will in any shape relax. I have heard nothing since my last of Mr. Hammond's [7] appointment to America, but I believe he is certainly to be sent out."

With the most respectful attachment, I have the honor &c.

A: Hamilton

P.S. I have this day the honor of your letter of the 2d.

Philadelpha.
6th. Octor. 1791.

LC, George Washington Papers, Library of Congress.
    1. Benjamin Chew and Andrew Barratt. See Washington to H, September 16, 1791.
    2. John Vining, a member of the House of Representatives from Delaware. Letter not found.
    3. On March 7, 1791, Senator James Gunn of Georgia recommended John Houston (or Houstoun) for a judicial position (Hunt, *Calendar of Applications*, 62). In 1792 Houston was judge of the Superior Court of Georgia.
    4. John P. Pleasants, a Baltimore merchant.
    5. Eleazer McComb of Wilmington.
    6. This may be a reference to Benjamin Stoddert, a well-to-do merchant of Georgetown. In 1798 he became the first Secretary of the Navy.
    7. George Hammond was appointed Minister Plenipotentiary to the United States on September 2, 1791.

To Otho H. Williams

T D October 6th 1791

Sir,

In pursuance of the intimation in a former letter [1] I am to request that you will pay to Messrs Elliot & Williams as an advance upon the

Contract lately entered into with them, out of the amount of the duties accruing in your district, ten thousand Dollars.

It is my intention to make them a further advance, on the first day of January next of an equal sum.

With great consideration   I am Sir   Your obedt Servt   A H

Otho H Williams Esqr
Collector &ca.

Copy, American Antiquarian Society, Worcester, Massachusetts.
    1. See H to Williams, September 27, 1791, and H to Elliot and Williams, October 6, 1791.

Conversation with Jean Baptiste de Ternant

[*Philadelphia, October 7,*[1] *1791*] ". . . M. Hamilton m'ayant parlé fort longuement de l'importance que les Etats unis attachoient à l'extension de leur commerce avec nos colonies, je lui ai observé que la France avoit déjà beaucoup accordé à cet égard, qu'elle étoit la premiere puissance qui au prejudice de ses négocians, et par un pur motif de bienveillance de la part du Roi, eut ouvert ses ports des Antilles aux Americains, que de nouveaux avantages, ne pouvoient être raisonnablement sollicités de la part de ces derniers que dans le cas où ils auroient à offrir une compensation convenable, et qu'enfin si le Gouvernement fédéral avoit quelque chose de cette nature à me communiquer, je m'empresserois surement de mettre ses propositions sous vos yeux. Comment, des propositions! a-t-il dit moitié d'un ton serieux et moitié en riant, que veut donc dire le décrèt du 2 de Juin?[2] 'Ce decrèt,' ai-je repliqué, 'est l'expression des sentimens d'interêt et d'attachement dont la nation française est animée envers les Etats unis, et une assurance des dispositions de l'Assemblée Nationale à accueillir tous les arrangemens de commerce que le Gouvernement pourra juger à propos de conclure avec vous, pour l'avantage reciproque des deux peuples.' Vous savez que cette reciprocité d'avantages est la base du traité de 1778, et que le Roi ne s'en est écarté que pour vous accorder par l'édit de May 1784, de nouveaux avantages sans compensation,[3] tandis que le Gouvernement fédéral a agi dans un sens absolument contraire, soit en établissant entre les batimens americains et françois une difference d'impots à l'importation qui n'existe point en France, soit en faisant payé à nos batimens un droit de cabotage qui n'est point exigé des americains dans nos ports.[4] M. Hamilton a fort bien senti que je voulois lui rappeller les reclamations infructueuses faites par M. Otto [5] conformément à vos ordres, et il s'est efforcé de me prouver que des circonstances imperieuses et dont pouvoit dépendre le succès de la nouvelle constitution fédérale, avoit empeché le Congrès de faire dans ses loix fiscales les exceptions qu'il avoit eû d'abord intention d'etablir en faveur du commerce de France. Les raisons qu'il m'a données étant les mêmes que celles dont M. Otto a déjà eu l'honneur de vous rendre compte, je crois pouvoir me dispenser de les rapporter ici. J'observerai seulement que dans nos discussions sur le sens de l'article 5. du traité [6] il m'a fait esperer qu'en prouvant l'exemption du droit de grand cabotage pour les Americains en France, je parviendrois probablement à en faire exempter aussi les François dans les ports des Etats unis, et même à obtenir le remboursement des sommes reclamés par le commerce de France sur cet objet. . . . Je reviens à mon entretien avec M. Hamilton à la suite de ses dernieres observations, il m'a dit qu'il seroit possible de lever toutes les difficultés par un nouveau traité qu'il en desiroit vivement la conclusion, et que si elle avoit lieu, il n'hésiteroit pas à proposer lui même toutes les exceptions fiscales en faveur de la France qu'exigeroit la teneur de ce nouveau traité, ou que le seul principe de la reciprocité poirroit justifier. Après lui avoir temoigné là-dessus le zèle ardent avec lequel je m'occuperois dans toutes les circonstances d'améliorer et de consolider les liaisons de politique et de commerce qui subsistent entre la France et les Etats unis, j'ai cru devoir encore lui faire sentir qu'il importait avant tout que le gouvernement federal se montrat religieux observateur des premiers traités, et que de là dependroit probablement la conclusion du nouveau qu'il paroissoit désirer. M. Hamilton a beaucoup cherché à decouvrir ce que mes instructions pouvoient me prescrire à cet égard, mais il n'a pas été satisfait. Il m'a parlé ensuite de la nomination de M. Hammond à la place de Ministre d'Angleterre auprès des Etats unis, et il m'a assuré qu'il seroit rendu à Philadelphie dans les premiers jours de novembre. L'indifference que j'ai montrée sur l'arrivée prochaine, ainsi que sur les négociations de ce ministre, a paru surpendre M. Hamilton, ce qui l'a probablement engagé à entrer avec moi dans quelques détails sur les vuës de l'Angleterre. Il m'a paru persuadé que le gouvernement fédéral ne consentiroit à un traité de commerce avec cette puissance, qu'autant que les batimens americains seroient admis dans tous ses ports des Antilles indistinctement: Ce sera là assure-t-il, une condition sine quâ non. Quant à un traité d'alliance le Secrétaire de la Trésorerie pense que l'Angleterre voudra le conclure en même tems que celui de commerce, et en faire une négociation indivisible, mais que cette proposition sera rejetée ici, et que l'on y demandera même comme une autre condition sine quâ non, de négocier et de conclure izolément le seul traité de commerce. M. Hamilton m'a fait au reste les plus grandes protestations d'attachement à la France, et il a beaucoup cherché à me convaincre, de la persuasion où il étoit que le veritable interèt des Etats unis excluoit toute autre alliance politique que celle qu'ils avoient avec nous. J'ai cru m'apercevoir au-reste qu'il n'étoit pas entierement venu de lui même, et que le President avoit bien pu le charger d'avoir avec moi quelques entretiens. Nous nous sommes quittés grands amis, et avec promesse mutuelle de nous voir souvent et de mettre toujours loyauté et franchise dans nos entretiens. . . ."

Frederick J. Turner, ed., "Correspondence of the French Ministers to the United States, 1791–1797," *Annual Report of the American Historical Association for the Year 1903* (Washington, 1904), II, 57–59. This conversation is taken from a letter from Ternant to Comte de Montmorin, October 9, 1791.

1. Ternant dated his letter to Montmorin October 9, 1791, but in the opening sentences of the letter he indicates that the conversation had taken place on October 7.

2. On June 2, 1791, the National Assembly approved a decree that provided for opening negotiations with the United States for a new commercial treaty (*Archives Parlementaires*, XXVI, 710). Through Ternant the King proposed that the United States Minister in Paris be instructed to undertake the negotiations.

3. Ternant is presumably referring to the *arrêt* of August 30, 1784, which placed the number of free ports in the French West Indies at seven and added coal, salt beef, salt fish, rice, maize, and vegetables to the list of permitted imports.

4. Ternant is complaining about the Tonnage Law. See "An Act imposing duties on the tonnage of ships or vessels" (1 *Stat.* 135–36 [July 20, 1790]).

5. Louis Guillaume Otto was French chargé d'affaires in the United States. For Otto's complaints to Jefferson on American policy, see *ASP, Foreign Relations*, I, 111–12.

6. Article V of the 1778 Treaty of Amity and Commerce between France and the United States exempted the United States from "the Imposition of 100 Sols pr Ton, established in France on Foreign Ships; unless when the Ships of the United States shall load with the Merchandize of France for another Port of the same Dominion, in which Case the said Ships shall pay the Duty above-mentioned so long as other Nations the most favour'd shall be obliged to pay it. But it is understood that the said United States or any of them are at Liberty when they shall judge it proper, to establish a Duty equivalent in the same Case" (Miller, *Treaties*, II, 7).

To Benjamin Lincoln

Treasury Department
Octr. 7. 1791

Sir,

The account rendered by Capt. Williams [1] will be transmitted for Examination to the accounting officers of the Treasury, of which I request you to inform him.

The account you give of the Conduct of the Jury in the Cases of Capt. Davis and his mate is such as to create great uneasiness.[2] I approve your intention of having a jury for the next experiment from Suffolk. It is certainly proper that on occasions when there is an appearance of favor or partiality in the Jury of one County the cases be tried by a Jury of some other County.

Benjn. Lincoln Esqr
Collector Boston

L[S], RG 36, Collector of Customs at Boston, Letters from the Treasury, 1789–1818, Vol. 5, National Archives; copy, RG 56, Letters to Collectors at Small Ports, "Set G," National Archives; copy, RG 56, Letters to the Collector at Boston, National Archives.

1. John Foster Williams was captain of the revenue cutter for Massachusetts.
2. See Lincoln to H, September 9, 1791.

From Benjamin Lincoln

Boston Octr 7 [–8] 1791

Sir

I was very unhappy the last evening on the receipt of your letter [1] by the post to find that the papers I forwarded in April last [2] respecting my purchase of the public securtes had not answered your wishes. Before I forwarded them I examined the law [3] & your instructions [4] and intended fully to comply with both. I therefore was induced in the statement of my account of my transactions in the business to mention in each charge the time of purchase, the person of whom purchased, the different species of the public debt, the amount of each security, the sum I paid for each kind, and the full sum paid to each person of whom I purchased, with this statement I forwarded my vouchers.

At the time of transacting the business I supposed I had nothing more to do in order to bring it to a close than to forward to you the different kind of public securites received. This caused some delay, but on finding they were to be changed I immediately attempted it and sent as soon as they could be obtained transfers to the Commissioners of the sinking fund of the public stock amounting to fifty thousand & twenty odd dollars estimating the 6 ℔ Cents at 18/9 & the 3 ℔ Cents & the deffered debt at 9/9 the price I gave saving about nine dollars in the whole

The ballance is in my favour saving a little interest the amount of which with a transfer in the name of the Commissioners I now inclose with a new statemen of the whole business which I hope will meet your approbation.

In my letter to you, covering my accounts, in April last, I mentioned this matter of interest and requested your direction whether it should be forwarded in Cash or whether I should, with it, purchase public securities as with the sum I received from the treasury.

I have been this particular in this representation to remove if possible from your mind any impressions which may have been made that the delay in compleating this business has arisen from an unjustifiable inattention on my part.

Saturday Octr 8   I am just returned from Mr. Appletons [5] Loan office, I find there that the interest due on the public securities which have been transferred in his office to the Commissioners of the Sinking fund purchased by me stands part credited to me & part to the said Commissioners. A doubt arises in Mr. Appletons mind how the interest which stands Credited to them shall be discharged. He wishes your direction on the subject. As the whole interest stand precisely on the same bottom, the whole being public property, and as you may wish the same line of Conduct should be pursued, respecting that Cr. to me & that Credited to the Commissioners I think it best to postpone any farther proceedings respecting it until I shall have your directions so that you will not find the transfer inclosed which I yesterday intended should be.

Secy of the Treasury

LC, Massachusetts Historical Society, Boston; LC, incomplete copy, RG 36, Collector of Customs at Boston, 1790–1797, National Archives; two copies, RG 56, Letters from the Collector at Boston, National Archives.
1. See H to Lincoln, September 28, 1791.
2. See Lincoln to H, April 27, 1791.
3. "An Act making Provision for the Reduction of the Public Debt" (1 *Stat.* 186–87 [August 12, 1790]).
4. See H to Lincoln, February 1, 1791.
5. Nathaniel Appleton was commissioner of loans for Massachusetts.

To Jeremiah Olney

Treasury Department, October 7 1791

Sir

The remark made by you on the additional two columns in the return of Tonnage appears to be just. Some other mode of obtaining the end must be devised, of which you will be informed. In the mean time you will insert the destination of vessels which appear in your return, so far as your knowledge of the fact renders it practicable.

It would certainly have been preferable that you suffered the embarrassment on the Ship Warren,[1] incurred by the conduct of her Owners, to have lain upon her. You will find, on examination of the laws, that you are not authorized to issue permits or registers, or to certify manifests of Vessels not actually within your district.

You observe that you do not comprehend my meaning in that part of my letter of the 30th of May, wherein I say that "the nature of the Cargoes & the places from whence coasting Vessels come with expired licenses, are to determine the fees &ca. exactly as if they had never been licensed." [2] By this I mean that they will be exactly in the situation in which they would have been if they had never been licensed. Some of the consequences of this will be that such of them as may have neither registers nor enrollments in force, if they have goods on board, taken in at another district to be delivered in yours, will be liable to foreign Tonnage, if they have registers in force they will pay no Tonnage in such case; but they will pay six Cents per Ton if they bring goods from a district in any other than an adjoining State. If this explanation does not meet your point of Enquiry, it will be well to state some of the cases which you had in view.

I observe the request you make, in your letter, of final explanation in the case of Mr Arnold.[3] You may assure yourself that no representation concerning your department, as a public Officer, shall make any impression on my judgment until it shall be first made known to you, and time shall have been given for your explanation and justification.

Attention will be paid to your remarks, relative to Coasters, in your letter of the twenty fifth of August.

I am, Sir, with great consideration & esteem, Your Obed Servant.

A Hamilton

Jere. Olney Esqr.
Collr Providence

LS, Rhode Island Historical Society, Providence.
1. See H to Olney, May 30, 1791; Olney to H, June 14, 1791.
2. See Olney to H, June 14, 1791.
3. Welcome Arnold. See Olney to H, July 29, 1791.

From William Seton

[New York] 7 Oct 1791

Sir

I had the honor to write you by last nights post enclosing a Duplicate of the Return of the investment in Stock of the last 50,000 Dolls.

This morning I called upon the Commissioner of Loans [1] to know what was requisite to be done to comply with your orders respecting a transfer of the whole amount of the Debt purchased to the Books of the Treasury.[2] He informs me that as the whole stands now in the Name of the Vice President, the Chief Justice, the Secretary of the Treasury, the Secretary of State and the Attorney General for the time being, it will be necessary that I should have a Power of Attorney from them to enable me to transfer it to the Books of the Treasury.

I have the honor to be &c.

LC, Bank of New York, New York City.
1. John Cochran.
2. See H to Seton, October 3, 1791.

From George Washington

[*Mount Vernon, October 7, 1791.* On October 11, 1791, Hamilton wrote to Washington: "The Post of this day has brought me your letter of the 7th. instant." *Letter not found.*]

From Joseph Whipple

Portsmo New Hamp. Octo. 7 1791

Sir

Mr. Flag [1] who was appointed 1st mate of the Revenue Cutter having been absent ever since his appointment has lately returned home, & having enterd into engagements in the Service of a Merchant as Master of a Vessel declines the Acceptance of his Commission which I now return inclosed herewith.

I beg leave to name John Parrot the 2nd Mate to fill the Station of 1st. Mate, his Conduct since he has been in the Service intitles him to this recommendation.

I also beg leave to name John Adams as a suitable person to take the place of Mr. Parrott as 2nd Mate, he is a young man of a reputable Family, has been Several Voyages as Mate of a Vessel & is recommended by several respectable persons—as there was only one Mate on duty, at Capt. Yeatons [2] request I consented that Mr. Adams shoud go on board the 27th. Ulto. & if it shoud please the president to appoint him I hope there will be no impropriety in his Commissions bearing date on the day of his entering on duty.

Mr. Hobert [3] who was recommended for 3rd Mate is at Sea & is soon expected home.

Before the Cutter sailed on the first Cruize I proposed to Cap. Yeaton his supplying the People with Bread & meat at the rate Specified in the Army Rations—and desired him to inform them that the residue of articles or their Value, shoud be made up in Settlement & in the Mean time money shoud be advanced them for the purpose of supplying themselves, with which they were perfectly Satisfied. During the Cruize they fell in with the Cutter Massachusetts whose people they found were furnished with provisions of Bread & Meat & Peas without restriction & with Coffee So this had Such effect on Cap. Yeatons people that he was obliged to dismiss three of them on his return into port. I mention this circumstance to show the Necessity of a Uniformity in the Supplies to these Vessels, as they will have communication with each other. The Scammels Crew caught Fish & were therefore well off for provisions, but Cap. Yeaton is of opinion that without the Aid of Fish which is an uncertain Supply, the quantity of Meat is not Sufficient for people at Sea who cannot be Supplied constantly with Vegetable. I have therefore been under the Necessity of consenting that Cap. Yeaton should Supply his people for the present in the Same manner that Capt. Williams's [4] people are Supplied managing the Same with prudence. The result of this experiment shall be laid before you.

In consequence of the P.S. to your letter of the 19th. Ulto.[5] I have consulted, what rate pr. Ration in lieu of articles would be satisfactory to the Seamen & find it would greatly exceed the Value of a Sufficient Supply of Provisions, & I do not conceive that any engagements of the Seamen for Supplying themselves would be safe for the Service as no dependence can be had in their providing a sufficient quantity for the Cruize. A person on whom I can depend has proposed to supply the 4 Seamen at 12 Cents ⅌ Ration with a quantity of Provisions which Cap. Yeaton is of opinion would be Satisfactory to the People & which he conceives in necessary, but this quantity exceeds the rations fixed by Law [6] & are as follow.—for 4 Men a Week or 28 Rations

> 30 lb Beef
> 8 lb Pork
> 28 lb Bread
> 1½ lb Coffee
> 3 pints Molases
> 4 Qts. Peas
> 14 Jills Rum

This will give one & half pound Beef or one pound pork in lieu of the Army Ration & adds Coffee Molss. & Peas instead of Vinegar Salt & Soap. This Might be Contracted for, for a year or any less term.

In conformity with your Circular letter of the 21st. Sep. I have proposed to Cap Yeaton & he agrees to receive Nine Cents for the Ration which he is entitled to draw for himself & boys as well as his extra Rations, to which proposal his Mate Also Accedes, So that no rations will be drawn but for the 4 Seamen. Capt. Yeaton would furnish the Component parts of the fixed Ration for 9 Cents but insists on the impossibility of Satisfying the people therewith.

ADf, RG 36, Collector of Customs at Portsmouth, Letters Sent, 1791–1792, Vol. 3, National Archives; copy, RG 56, Letters from the Collector at Portsmouth, National Archives.

1. Presumably John Flagg of Portsmouth.
2. Hopley Yeaton, captain of the revenue cutter *Scammell,* which was based at Portsmouth.
3. Samuel Hobart.
4. John Foster Williams was captain of the revenue cutter for Massachusetts.
5. Letter not found.
6. See postscript to "Treasury Department Circular to the Collectors of the Customs," September 21, 1791.

From Edward Carrington

Richmond October 8th. 1791

Sir,

Since mine of the 4th. Instant, covering some information upon Manufactures, I have received an additional report from General Stevens,[1] Inspector of Survey No. 2, which, together with his letter, and a Copy of one he received from one of his Collectors I now do myself the pleasure to enclose.[2] It was my intention, at first, to have obtained the Reports of all the Inspectors, and then have made a general one, with certain allowances, and remarks, for you. This would have been attended with but little trouble, and although you was good enough to desire that it might be dispensed with, yet I should have done it. The detached manner in which my information comes, & the late period at which I should be enabled to communicate it to you, were I to delay for this purpose, dictates the greater propriety of complying with your dispensation, and giving you the information by parts, as it comes in. You find that Genl Stevens & Mr. Ragsdale, have, both, reported the domestic manufactures made in twenty families, comprehending the various classes of life, from the richest to the poorest.[3] This is done in consequence of a request I made of each Inspector, in order to form a principle of calculation upon the whole number of families in the State, expecting that, as these Gentlemen reside in different parts, such reports might enable

ALS, Hamilton Papers, Library of Congress.
1. Edward Stevens, a veteran of the American Revolution, was a member of the Virginia Senate from 1782 to 1790. He was formally appointed inspector of Survey No. 2 for Virginia on October 31, 1791.
2. See Stevens to Carrington, October 6, 1791; Charles Yancey to Stevens, October 1–5, 1791. These enclosures are printed below.
3. See Drury Ragsdale to Carrington, September 29, 1791, printed as an enclosure to Carrington to H, October 4, 1791.

us to judge how far a general principle of calculation might be relied upon, or what deviations might be proper to lead the nearest the truth. You will observe that each of these reports already received, take in the whole year 1790; the others will do the same, and as they come to my hands, they shall be forwarded to you.

The enquiries upon this subject gave rise, at first, to suggestions from the Enemies of the Government, that the object was, a Tax upon manufactures. This led to the necessity of the Inspectors effecting their inquiries in such manner as would not favor such an alarm; and this they have been so judicious in, that there is nothing said about it now. Indeed it is generally viewed in the true light, as leading to some project for the encouragement of home Manufactures.

I am with the greatest respect   Sir   Your Most Ob st.

                                              Ed Carrington
                                              Supervisor D V.[4]
Alexander Hamilton Esqr

[E N C L O S U R E]

Edward Stevens to Edward Carrington [5]

Culpeper Court House [Virginia] October 6th. 1791

Sir

Expecting this to be nearly about the time you would wish to be receiving the reports respecting the manufactures of this State, I have made Out and now Inclose you such a one as (I conceived) you required of me; at least as nearly so, as was in my power, And I hope it may be such as will answer. You will understand the information was taken entirely from persons of this County, indeed I found great reluctance in many of my Acquaintances and refusal from others, at least their conduct produced the same effect, as they never could find a proper time to detail to me or set down an Accot. themselves. I trust it will make no diference my geting this intelligence entirely from persons of this County, as I think the circumstances of all the Countys in my Survey is nearly similar, as to Cultivation Produce and Domestic manufactures; except perhaps one or Two of

4. District of Virginia.
5. ALS, Hamilton Papers, Library of Congress.

the little County's in the Lower parts of it. In averaging the Prices of
the diferent Articles, I governed myself from the information, as well
as by the following Principles. The Linnen Cloth made by the Rich
is generally for their negroes which is coarse, that made by the midling Kind, a great proportion is also used in the same way, and that
by the lower Sort for their own wear. Therefore a greater part of
theirs would be some what of a finer Quality. In the Woolen Cloth
both the Rich and the middling by what I could learn was nearly
the same Kind, for negroes, and Children some of it mixted colours
& others, in the Shape of a Stuff which is imported from Britain and
called Jersy's. The poorest people among us raise few or no Sheep,
and what wool they commanly have I fancey is mostly made into
Stockings. The Cotton Cloth made by the Rich, a great proportion
is for Coverlets, Bedtyckes, Mens wear Jeans &c which is valuable.
It is also nearly the case with the middling or at least what they may
be deficient in Coverlets Jeans &c they make up in Womens fine
Gowns. The Poorest is generally coarse. With respect to Stockings
and Shoes, The Rich commonly purchase the greater part of the fine
Kinds which they wear and the other Classes dont make such use
of them, therefore after taking into Accot. that the largest Quantity
are for negroes and the poorest people, think I may be pretty near
the value of these Two Articles.

I have received one report of the Stated Trades, or rather a List ⟨of⟩
the names of the diferent Tradesmen, distinguishing whether living
in Town or Country; from Mr. Adams of Loudon, he says it was
not in his Power to do more, he seems to be of a disposition to oblige
and has the Character of a very active attentive, Industrious good
man. I have also received from Mr. Yancey of Lousia by way of a
Paragraph of a Letter something on the Subject, but in order to
give you a better Knowledge of it, than a description, I have taken
the Liberty to inclose you a Coppy. In what manner do you wish
me to hand them to you? I mean as to waitg until they all come
forward to me, and make a General report. I am with very much
respect

Sir   Your most hum. Servt   Edward Stevens Inspector
                                      Revenue Survey No. 2

ACCOUNT of Manufactures made in Survey No. 2 by Twenty Families from the Richest to the Poorest in the Space of One Year from the 1st. January to 31st December 1790

Classes of Four Families in each Class	Linnen Cloth Yards	Yarn Cloth Yards	Cotton Cloth Yards	Stockinges dift. Kinds Pairs	Shoes dift. Kinds Pairs
First	187	225	700½	51	112
Second	225	95	440	46	57
Third	320	24	296	40	38
Fourth	254	"	177	28	17
Fifth	109	"	68	9	13
	1095	344	1681½	174	237
	* 1	† 2	3	4	5

[ENCLOSURE]

Charles Yancey to Edward Stevens [6]

[Louisa County, Virginia, October 1–5, 1791]

Inclosed you will receive a list of the Stills with their Contents in our County you will please to excuse any Inaccuracies in the want of form as I have greatly hurried in the Business oweing among other causes to the want of Health and being anxious to make my return by the time you directed having found it a very fatigueing troublesome Business. However I have been happy to find the People willing to submit to the duties though not without some disapprobation of the Law through Ignorance of the true meaning, but after explaining the same appear to be tolerably satisfied. And agreeably to your directions I have appointed persons to receive the returns of all the Stills within ten Miles of each of them, to wit Capt James Dabney in the lower part of the County, and Mr William Wash in the upper part of the said County, so that at present, there are Offices opened within ten Miles of every Still in the County and, in order to give the Business the greater Credit the persons I have appointed are of

6. Copy, Hamilton Papers, Library of Congress.

Average Price of Each Article wch. was obliged to be conjectural					
Lin. Cloth	Yarn do	Cotton do	Stockgs	Shoes	
					* 1. 82. 2. 6
					† 2. 43. 0. 0
					3. 294. 5. 0
					4. 39. 3. 0
					5. 79. 0. 0
					537.10. 6
1/6	2/6	3/6	4/6	6/8	

Note in some instances their was a little mixted Cloths. I should have made a Column for it but as it was not taken notice of in your request, was apprehensive it might derange your System, therfore I proportioned it according to the Stuff it was made of

Edward Stevens Inspector
Revenue Survey No. 2
October 5th: 1791

the best Credit & Character. With respect to the other requisitions of the Secretary I do not well know what to say as I have so little time and their being no publick manufactures In Our County except one gun Smith to wit Francis Giddins who Works part of the Year at that Business, And one Wheel rights Shop, to wit Butler Bradburn, though their Are several Persons that do some thing at the Business in the Winter Season, when their Crops are Secured &c. We have a Considerable Number of Carpente⟨rs⟩ Joiners and Blacksmiths. The latter is Cheifly done by Blacks but little more is done then Working and farming Tools &c. Manufactures of Common home Spun is very Considerable in private Families, but we have no fulling Mills in our County, a pretty deal of Cotton & Flax is raised; wool is on the Increase And the Culture of Tobo is on the decline; The farming Business is gaining the assendencey among our People, and upon the whole we are on riseing Ground & becomeing more wealthy and Independent. As to the defects of the Excise Law,[7] I have ha⟨d⟩ very

7. "An Act repealing, after the last day of June next, the duties heretofore laid

little leasure to peruse it or to spend much thought about ⟨it⟩ but think if the Collectors in the deferent Counties were Aided ⟨by⟩ Assistants it would be convenient. And that the profits at present are no ways equal to the expence and trouble & suppo⟨se⟩ few in the Country can find their Account in holding their Appointsments. You will please to signify to me any furthe⟨r⟩ Instructions that may be necessary as I shall be happy in rendering any service I am able while in my present Office I am &c.

P S   The Price of Mr Giddins Rifles is £4 and smooth Boars £3. The Price of Cart & Waggon Wheels are various from 30/ to 50/ According to their size. Tanner'es we have none but in private families since Mr Culp [8] has removed. The time I have marked against the Stills being employed is as near as we could guess at the usual time, Though few of them will be employed this Year as we have very little fruit. There are also some few Stills in the Country not noticed, as they are not intended to be used and are not in furnicies.

upon Distilled Spirits imported from abroad, and laying others in their stead; and also upon Spirits distilled within the United States, and for appropriating the same" (1 Stat. 199–214 [March 3, 1791]).
    8. Daniel Culp.

From Henry Marchant

Rhode Island District
Newport Octr 8th 1791

In pursuance of an Act of the Congress of the United States "to provide for mitigating or remitting forfeitures, and penalties, accruing under the Revenue Laws, in certain Cases therein mentioned" [1] I have received the Petition of Samuel Westgate of Providence in said District hereto annexed, and thereupon caused Jeremiah Olney Collector, Ebenezer Thompson Naval Officer and William Barton Surveyor of Providence District, the persons claiming a moiety of the said five Chests of Tea upon forfeiture thereof, if such forfeiture should take place, and also William Channing Esqr. Attorney of the United States for Said Rhode Island District to be noticed to appear before me, and shew cause if any they had against the mitigation or remission of the forfeiture thereof and penalty incurred thereon, and who declared they had no cause to offer against the remission prayed for by the said Petitioner, nor had they any reason to disbelieve the circumstances as stated & set forth in said Petition. Whereupon I proceeded to examine further into the Circumstances of the Case in a summary manner and it appears by a Certificate from the Collector for Newport District,[2] that the said Petitioner Samuel Westgate Master of the Sloop Clementina burthen twenty nine tons came to his Office late in the afternoon of the first day of this month to be cleared out for the port of Providence but being in a great hurry desired that two manifests might be made out for him, and to effect that, left five Certificates for five Chests of Tea in the Office, that two manifests were accordingly made out for him, and that he might not be delayed a permit to proceed for the Port of Providence was also made out for him & completed, except the insertion of the day of the month Certified Copies of which manifests and also of said five Certificates and of said permit were produced to me. And the said Petitioner under solemn Oath to me made, declared the matters & things set forth in his said petition were just and true and that immediately upon his arrival at Providence as soon as Office Hours, he waited upon the Collector & informed him of the Goods taken on board, & having forgot to call upon the Office at Newport for his permit &c. All which I do hereby certify to the Secretary of the Treasury of the United States.

Hy. Marchant Judge
of the District Court for
Rhode Island District

Copy, Rhode Island Historical Society, Providence.
1. 1 *Stat.* 122–23 (May 26, 1790).
2. William Ellery.

From Jeremiah Olney

Custom House
Providence 8th. Octr. 1791

Sir

There has lately been instituted in this Town a Bank [1] which will Commence discounting on Tuesday Next, the plan or Constitution of which I have the Honor to enclose you. The President and others, are very desirous that the public monies Received in my office should be Deposited therein, and that Bank notes should be received by me in discharge of Bonds taken for duties. Tho I am Fully sensible of the many advantages that a measure of this sort would afford to the Public and Merchantle Interest, yet as I am not authorized to enter into any Negotiations with the President and directors, I am induced Respectfully to request your particular advice and Instructions on this Subject.

I have the Honor to be with Esteem   Sir   Your most Obed. Hum Serv.   Jereh Olney Collr.

Alexr. Hamilton Esqr.
Secy. of the Treasury

ADfS, Rhode Island Historical Society, Providence; copy, RG 56, Letters from the Collector at Providence, National Archives.
    1. The Providence Bank was established in 1791 under the auspices of John and Moses Brown, the firm of Brown and Francis, and other leading Providence businessmen. The plan for the bank was drawn up by Moses Brown, and the bank was incorporated by the Rhode Island legislature in October, 1791.

To William Seton [1]

Treasury Department
Octr. 8th. 1791

Sir,
    It is necessary to inform you that the Treasurers check or order for thirty thousand dollars of the *first* instant in favor of John Cochran Esq the Commissioner of loans for New York was intended to include your payment of Twenty thousand Dollars on the 1st instant, and the further sum of ten thousand Dollars. I think it proper to apprize you of this lest you may suppose that the Thirty thousand Dollars were to be additional to the Twenty thousand.

    The duplicate receipt for Ten thousand Dollars of the 29th Ulto. by the Vice Consul General of France (and Mr. de la Forest) [2] is at hand.

    I am   Sir,   Your obedt Servant.   A Hamilton

Willm. Seton Esqr
Cashier of the Bank of
New York

LS, The Andre de Coppet Collection, Princeton University Library.
1. For background to this letter, see Seton to H, October 1, 1791.
2. The "Vice Consul General of France (and Mr. de la Forest)" were the same person. Antoine René Charles de La Forest became vice consul at Savannah in 1783 and in 1785 assumed the duties of consul general, although he was not formally appointed to the post until March, 1792.

From Vincent Gray [1]

[*Alexandria, Virginia, October 9, 1791*. On November 10, 1791, Hamilton wrote to Charles Lee: "Mr Gray's letter of the 9th Ultimo . . . has been received." *Letter not found.*]

1. Gray was the deputy collector of customs at Alexandria, Virginia.

To John Cochran

[*Philadelphia, October 10, 1791*. On October 10, 1791, Hamilton wrote to William Seton that he was sending a letter to the commissioner of loans for New York State. *Letter not found.*]

To Sharp Delany

Treasury Department, October 10, 1791. "Your letter of the 5th instant [1] has been received. The requisite instructions relative to the boat have been forwarded to the Collector of Wilmington. . . ." [2]

Copy, RG 56, Letters to the Collector at Philadelphia, National Archives; copy, RG 56, Letters to Collectors at Small Ports, "Set G," National Archives.
1. Letter not found.
2. The collector of customs at Wilmington, Delaware, was George Bush.

From William Ellery

Collector's Office [Newport, Rhode Island] Oct 10th: 1791

Sir,
    I have received your Circular of the 21st. of last month, and shall

observe your directions contained in it. I have also received your letter of the 23d. of the same month [1] with the marginal part of Certife. of Registry No. 60.

I wish to know whether cancelled bonds for Registers may be delivered up to the obligors, or destroyed. I don't know that they can be of any use after cancelment, and the keeping of them in the office, if useless, will only serve to accumulate papers, which collect very fast. I should be glad too to be informed whether upon Licenses being delivered up, the bonds which relate to them are to be cancelled, and whether such Licenses and bonds, if to be cancelled, or either of them are to be preserved in the office after being delivered up and cancelled. A licensed vessel may have been employed in some illicit trade, and it may not be known until after the License is delivered up, in this case if the bond is cancelled on the delivery of the License, the obligors are discharged from the penalty of the bond.

The substance of the Deposition which in my last [2] I promised to communicate in this, was that he was certain that twenty barrels of sugar, two barrels of Molasses, and between twenty and thirty bags of Coffee were landed from the Brig Seven brothers about 10 or 11 o'clock of the night he arrived in Newport, the value whereof is more than four hundred dollars.

At the same time that a summons issued for the Deponent, the Substance of whose Deposition I have just given, a Summons issued for another person who was also a seaman on board the Seven Brothers in the voyage at the close of which goods were landed from her without a permit; but he has avoided the service and gone to Sea. Indeed if the Deponent had not been hunted and harrassed by the Officer, and influenced by the strong perswasions of his father, who is Inspector of the Port of Bristol,[3] he would not have submitted to a service of the Summons.

A Writ is served on Thos. Cottrel, and a summons issued for a Seaman, who lives in Providence, to appear forthwith before the Judge of the District Court at his Dwelling house to give his deposition in that case. I suspect the Marshall will not be able to serve it, and if he should he cannot compel him to appear in the first instance; and before a compulsory process could issue he would probably be gone. A summons issued for the same man to give evidence at the trial of the Sloop Betsy, and he avoided the service, as the other Seaman referred to did the summons for him in the case of the Seven Brothers.

Permit me on this occasion to observe, that, considering Custom-House Officers, and Informers are, on account of their being interested, not admissible as Witnesses, and seamen are strongly attached to their employers, and under their influence, unless a law is passed by the United States, admitting a capias to issue in the first instance, and to be served by persons other than Officers, it will be extremely difficult to prosecute transgressors of the Revenue Law to Conviction. Marshalls and Depy. Marshalls are almost universally known and whenever a seizure is made, or a prosecution commenced and they appear in any place suspicions are excited, the alarm given, and they who could give testimony disappear.

I send by this post a weekly return of monies received and paid, a monthly schedule of bonds, an Abstract of distilled Spirits exported from 1st. of July to 30th Sept. 1791. Register of Ship Ascension No. 2 granted at Sagg Harbour Decr. 26 1789 Copy of an endorsmt. on Regr. No. 57. granted at this port Novr. 23 1790, a like endorsmt. on Regy. No. 41. granted at this Port Oct. 1 1790, and a like endorsement on Regr. No. 5 granted at this Port 1791, also my quarterly returns, and copies of Certifs. of Registry and Enrollments for the Quarter ending Sept. 30th 1791, and a list of a bank note amg. to One hundred Dollars, one moiety whereof is now transmitted to the Treasy.

I am Sir, Yr. most obedt. servt.   Wm Ellery Collr

A Hamilton Esqr
Secry of Treasy

LC, Newport Historical Society, Newport, Rhode Island.
1. Letter not found.
2. See Ellery to H, October 4, 1791.
3. William Munro.

From Jedediah Huntington

[*New London, Connecticut, October 10, 1791.* On November 22, 1791, Hamilton wrote to Huntington: "I do not think, it will be necessary to require a refund from the officers of the revenue cutter . . . as mentioned in your letter of the 10th. October." *Letter not found.*]

From Thomas Mifflin [1]

[Philadelphia, October 10, 1791]

Sir.

The Register General of Pennsylvania,[2] conceiving, that the possession of an accurate list of the State Debt subscribed to the Loan of the United States, would be a considerable improvement to the arrangement of the public accounts in his office has made a request upon the subject, which I beg leave to submit to your consideration; with a view that, if it will not be improper or inconvenient, your acquiescence may be obtained.

I am, with great esteem   Sir,   Your most obedient sevt.

Thomas Mifflin.

Phila: 10 Oct. 1791
To Alexander Hamilton Esqr
Secret. of the Ts of the U. S.

Df, in the writing of Alexander Dallas, Division of Public Records, Pennsylvania Historical and Museum Commission, Harrisburg; LC, Division of Public Records, Pennsylvania Historical and Museum Commission.
    1. For background to this letter, see Mifflin to H, June 2, 1791.
    2. John Donnaldson was authorized to implement the Pennsylvania law compensating creditors of the state who subscribed to the Federal loan.

From Thomas Newton, Junior

Norfolk [Virginia] October 10, 1791. Reports that John McComb, Jr., has completed the foundation of the Cape Henry lighthouse.

ALS, RG 26, Lighthouse Letters Received, Vol. "A," Pennsylvania and Southern States, National Archives.

To William Seton

Treasury Department
October 10. 1791

Sir

The duplicate return of your last purchases has come to hand.[1]
The Commissioner of loans [2] might have issued the requisite Cer-

tificate in order to a Transfer to the books of the Treasury, upon the strength of your original Agency; especially as the Transfer was to be in the same names.

But as a different idea has struck him I have written to him the enclosed [3] to obviate difficulty.

With very great consideration I remain Sir Your obedient servt   A Hamilton

William Seton Esqr.

ALS, Bank of New York, New York City; copy, in the handwriting of William Seton, Hamilton Papers, Library of Congress.
1. See Seton to H, October 6, 1791.
2. John Cochran. See Seton to H, October 7, 1791.
3. Letter not found.

From William Short

Paris Oct 10. 1791.

Sir

The last letter which I have had the honor of writing to you was of the 23d. of September. I have since then recieved yours of August 1st.

I inclose you at present a copy of my last letter to the bankers at Amsterdam [1] written in answer to theirs in which they propose of themselves, as I had formerly mentioned it was probable they would do, that the rate of commission on the last loan should be settled between you & them.[2] I have sent you regularly copies of my letters to

ALS, letterpress copy, William Short Papers, Library of Congress.
1. See enclosure.
2. On September 22, 1791, Willink, Van Staphorst, and Hubbard wrote to Short: "It is painful to us, to learn your perseverance, in rejecting our reasons for extending the last Loan to Six Millions; We now agree with you, that a further Discussion of the Matter between us is useless, especially after your continuing to judge of the Charges upon Loans as a simple Mechanical Compensation, and not on the true invariable Considerations they are granted for. The Charges of making Remittances alone are Half per Cent. Deducting this, would upon your Basis, reduce our Profits to One Half per Cent, which is totally inadmissible; Wherefore, We propose to you Sir, that We shall settle the Matter with the Secretary of the United-States, From whose official Knowledge of the Business, and the Justice He will render to our Motives, We are persuaded We shall experience full approbation. . ." (LS, Short Family Papers, Library of Congress).

them on this subject. They will also send you theirs to me which will save me the trouble of copying them. Thus Sir you will be furnished with all the materials on this subject. They will put out of doubt the right of the U.S. to insist on the 3½ p.cent commission. The expediency also it is now for you to judge of. Having thus put the question entirely within your decision is all that I could do. Should considerations for the former services of the bankers of the U.S. on which they seem to count a good deal induce you to make the sacrifice of this ½. p. cent in their favor I think it would be proper to make them see clearly that the concession was made on that account. As to my own part I cannot undertake to fix the weight you may think proper to give to such considerations, but as far as I can judge of them they do not appear to me to require that the U.S. should make a sacrifice of a right so clearly ascertained. It was my intention as I formerly mentioned to you to have submitted to the 4. p. cent commission if it had become indispensable—as that was not the case I did not do it & am happy to have been thus able to put the business entirely at your discretion.

When I announced to you this loan I mentioned that you might consider the 2½. millions of florins as at your disposal from the time of your recieving that letter.[3] Although the undertakers were not obliged to pay more than one million a month yet it was certain they would pay more. The bankers have not informed me precisely of the sums they have recieved, but from the remittances they have announced to me it appears that the reciepts have been much more considerable than the million a month. On the 22d. of Sept. they informed me they had remitted to the public treasury here 4,088,786.₶—the bills from about 43 ⅞ to 44. groats p. crown. This includes the remittance mentioned in my last. They have since informed me in their several letters of remittances to the amount of 1,643,313₶ 7 sols, the bills of the greater part at about 44½, the rate of the rest not mentioned.

Since the departure of Mr. Donald[4] from London his partner[5] has continued the correspondence with me on the subject of a loan there for the U.S. The final result of his researches is less favorable

3. See Short to H, August 31, 1791.
4. Alexander Donald. See Short to H, September 23, 1791.
5. Robert Burton, member of the London banking firm of Donald and Burton.

for the present moment than Mr Donald had given reason to hope. On more precise enquiry he found that no house of solidity would undertake to guarantee a loan for any commission and that no loan could be opened *publicly* for a foreign power. Still he was well convinced that the U.S. might *privately* obtain a loan in London provided the interest was at 5. p. cent, & that it was not brought on until the next spring. As I did not understand precisely what was meant by the term *privately* & of course could not judge whether the dignity of the U.S. would admit of their making use of that mode I have written to ask an explanation of it as an indispensable preliminary, & have not yet recieved an answer. I take it for granted however that no loan can be made there before the spring. Mr. Burton observes also that it will be absolutely necessary for me to go to London before any thing final can be determined on.[6] I have written also to know in what respects he considers my presence primarily requisite, that I may be the better able to judge how far such a journey may be proper. Unless it may appear essentially necessary at present I shall suppose it best to postpone it until next spring—or until the time which may appear proper for opening such a loan. Should it be found that the U.S. can make a loan in London I cannot help still hoping from a general view of circumstances that it may be done at a lower rate of interest than 5. p. cent notwithstanding what Mr. Burton has said on the subject. This however is a circumstance which as you will readily see, can only be reduced to certainty at the time of the loan being made, & on the spot. Should that be found impracticable & should it be possible to reduce the charges to the point at which they stand at Amsterdam, I shall have no doubt of the propriety of a loan being opened there, as it will necessarily assist in enabling the U.S. to reduce the rate of interest elsewhere.

  With respect to Antwerp I have hitherto informed you how the business stood there.[7] Since my last I have at Mr. Morris's request [8]

6. Burton to Short, September 13, 1791 (LS, William Short Papers, Library of Congress); Donald and Burton to Short, September 27, 1791 (LS, William Short Papers, Library of Congress).

7. See Short to H, July 27, August 8, September 23, 1791.

8. On October 5, 1791, Short wrote to Gouverneur Morris:

"After reflecting on the conversations which have passed between us in consequence of your opinion that loans might be made for the U. S. at Antwerp at a rate of interest inferior to those made at Amsterdam I think it for their advantage that an experiment should be made there provided it be done with the authorized the opening a loan there provided it can be effected at 4½ p. cent interest & 5. p. cent commission: As he observed it would be necessary in that case for the U.S. not to open loans in Holland at an higher rate of interest, I have agreed that that shall not be done before the 1st. of Jany. next provided three millions of florins can be procured at Antwerp at that rate & in that time. I had no difficulty in taking this engagement as it is consenting only to what the interest of the U. S. would dictate. No answer had been as yet recieved to this letter written only a few days ago. I must own however I am not very sanguine in the expectation of any thing being done there at present in consequence of it. I shall be more able to ascertain what may be expected from that source after having been there which will be in the course of the next month. I pass through that place on my way to Amsterdam whither I shall go in order to sign the bonds of the last loan.[9] Having signed those of the loan made last spring,[10] the bankers then informed me that it would be necessary for uniformity sake to sign the others. I have directed the bonds to be prepared in consequence thereof, as I thought it might not be improper to take a view of Antwerp & Amsterdam at present so as to be better able to judge of the real situation of affairs there as relative to the U.S. & as I inferred also from the tenor of your first letters that you expected I should go there.

What I have said above will make you acquainted as far as I am, with prospects at Amsterdam, London, & Antwerp. The progress of our credit at home will inevitably continue to increase them & leave the U. S. still more the arbiters of the use they may chuse to make of them. As to Genoa I have little doubt we should be able in the course

---

caution & prudence so indespensably requisite in a case of this kind. Agreeably to your request therefore I now express to you in writing that you may assure the house with which you have corresponded on this subject at Antwerp, that I will engage to open no loan in Holland for the U. S. in the course of the year 91 at an higher rate of interest than 4½ p. cent; provided three millions of florins can be procured for them in the same time at Antwerp, at that rate of interest with 5 p. cent for commission & all charges whatsoever.

"You know that I rely altogether on your Knowledge of the ability integrity & prudence of the house with which you have corresponded for the certain fulfillment of the engagements which may be entered into, & particularly for nothing being undertaken in this business without its success being certain." (ALS, Columbia University Libraries.)

9. The Holland loan of September, 1791. For a description of this loan, see Short to H, August 31, 1791.

10. The Holland loan of March, 1791. For a description of this loan, see Short to H, February 17, 1791.

of the Autumn to make a loan there for a million of dollars. From what you say however with respect to that place,[11] which is evidently founded in reason & policy, I shall think it adviseable not to do it unless the terms should be better than those wch. may be offered at Amsterdam or in London, or unless it may be found proper to suspend the loans for some time at Amsterdam in order to ameliorate the terms there.

With respect to Paris, the hopes which I had formerly concieved of the resources here have not been realized although it is possible they may be in some future crisis. Hitherto the obstacles have been 1. that the difference between the assignats & specie has been less than the difference of exchange. 2. that the French having more confidence in the assignats than foreigners would not have loaned them for any length of time even at the current difference. 3. that the French monied men are not accustomed to lend to foreigners & have little confidence in the U.S., knowing little of them or only what is least favourable to their credit & punctuality; as for instance their arrears to their debt to the French government—to the farmers general [12] & particularly to the foreign officers.[13] Under such circumstances I have thought it most adviseable not to attempt to push such business against stream. Should *assignats* continue in circulation however after we shall have cleared off these several arrears I have no doubt Paris will be found a favorable soil to derive means from of liquidating our French debt. It is for this reason among others that I shall accelerate as far as depends on me the wiping off these arrears—& I don't doubt what relates to the foreign officers strikes you too forcibly to need further mention.

I recieved in your last [14] a properly authenticated copy of the revenue to Octob. 90. Such papers will enable me to shew the real situation of the debt of the U.S. & will contribute eminently to enhance their credit on this side of the Atlantic. I will ask the favor of you to send similar information of the present year & such matters as you may publicly report thereon to the next session of Congress. I cannot too often repeat the propriety of exposing the U.S. (particularly in whatever relates to their finances) to the public eye in Europe. The

11. See H to Short, August 1–2, 1791.
12. For a description of the 1777 loan from the Farmers–General, see H to Short, September 1, 1790, note 26.
13. For a description of this debt, see Short to H, August 3, 1790, note 5.
14. See H to Short, August 1–2, 1791.

more they are known the more they will be independent of those few whose business it has been hitherto to make themselves acquainted with them.

I want words Sir to express the high sense I entertain of the satisfaction you are pleased to express of my conduct & the extensive confidence placed in me. I feel definitely the obligation this imposes on me not to use every effort in the prosecution of the business. I must report however with all the candor & sincerity of which I am master that I have not sufficient reliance on my skill & judgment to be exempt from apprehensions that the interests of the U.S. may suffer in my hands if alternatives should present themselves of such a nature as formerly mentioned to you. So long as the business is confined simply to the paying off the debt in one country by making loans in another less skill will be required, & I will endeavour by my zeal to merit a continuance of your confidence to which I feel I have that alone to entitle me; renewing however what I have already mentioned of being incompetent to acting alone in any negotiation for changing finally the nature of our foreign debt & begging that in that case some other person may be joined to me.

You may rest assured Sir that I shall keep you regularly advertised of all the symptoms which may take place with respect to these several matters, so as to recieve your earliest instructions thereon. I beg you to be persuaded of the sentiments of sincere attachment & profound respect with which I have the honor to be

Sir,   Your most obedient &   most humble servant   W: Short

The Honble.
Alexander Hamilton Secretary of the Treasury. Philadelphia.

[E N C L O S U R E]

William Short to Wilhem and Jan Willink, Nicholaas and Jacob Van Staphorst, and Nicholas Hubbard[15]

Paris Sep. 30, 1791

Gentlemen
    I have barely time to acknowledge by the extraordinary of to-

15. ALS, letterpress copy, William Short Papers, Library of Congress.

morrow the receipt of yours of the 22d. inst. in which you propose that the sec. of the Treasury should settle the rate of commission on the last loan.¹⁶ It would seem that the rate at which any business is to be transacted should be looked for in the powers authorizing the transaction of that business—still if you think this matter will be settled more to your satisfaction by the Sec. of the treasury I can have no objection to your addressing yourselves to him & I can assure you very sincerely that if he & you are well satisfied in whatever manner it may be terminated I shall be perfectly so. The correspondence which has passed between us on the subject will put him fully in possession of the circumstances attending it. I am persuaded that the decision which he will form thereon will be completely conformable to the rules of justice & of course free from objections of any kind. I have the honor to be very sincerely Gentlemen, your most obedient humble servant   W. Short

Messrs. W & J Willink N. & J Van Staphorst & Hubbard
—Amsterdam

16. See note 9.

From George Washington

[Mount Vernon, October 10, 1791]

Sir,

Your letter of the 30th. September enclosing a Contract entered into by the Collector of Wilmington in North Carolina ¹ with James McStephens & Henry Toomer for the stakage of the shoals of Cape Fear river, I have duly received. As I approve of the Contract, I have transmitted the same with my approbation to the Collector of Wilmington.

I wrote to you from the head of Elk,² informing you of my having made enquiries for a proper character to fill the Office of Supervisor of the District of Delaware, & that the weight of information which I collected, was in favor of one Andrew Barratt ³ &c. Whether a commission was ever filled up for him, or what was done in the matter, you have not informed me. I now however, transmit to you a letter from the Hone. Jno: Clayton ⁴ Esqr., by which it appears that no person has been appointed, & that he has recommended his son [5] to you as a fit character to fill that office. I wish you to look into this business, and to let me know what, or whether anything has finally been done therein.

I am Sir,   Your Most hble Servt.   G: Washington

Mount Vernon
10th. Octobr. 1791.

LC, George Washington Papers, Library of Congress.
   1. James Read.
   2. Washington to H, September 16, 1791.
   3. Barratt was appointed supervisor on November 7, 1791.
   4. Washington is referring to Joshua Clayton, president of Delaware.
   5. James Clayton.

From John Chester [1]

[Wethersfield] Connecticut, Office of Supervisor,
October 11th 1791.

Sir.

In compliance with the request in your Circular of 22d June last,[2] herewith are forwarded a number of letters,[3] which have been recieved, & relate to the subject of Manufactures carried on in this State; together with sundry samples.

After having revolved in my mind several plans for obtaining the necessary information, none was thought of which afforded so flattering prospects, as that which was adopted, of writing to each member in the upper branch of our legislature, as well as to many of the principal manufacturers. The most of my letters have been answered; and if the information is not so full, & complete, as could be wished, still it is the best which could be obtained, & may possibly be of some service.

Accounts of the silk manufactured at Wallingford, and of the linnen & cotton made at N Haven, also letters from several gentlemen

ALS, Hamilton Papers, Library of Congress.
   1. Chester was supervisor of the revenue for the District of Connecticut.
   2. See "Treasury Department Circular to the Supervisors of the Revenue," June 22, 1791.
   3. These enclosures are printed below.

on this subject are expected, and shall as soon as they are recieved be transmitted.

I am with the greatest consideration, Sir, Your most obedt servant.

John Chester.

[E N C L O S U R E]

Peter Colt to John Chester [4]

Hartford July 21. 1791

Dear Sir

The conversation which I had with you some days past on the subject of the Secretarys Letter respecting our manufactures, has given occasion the imperfect History of that Business which accompanies this. I shall leave it to your judgment to make such use of it in your correspondence with the Secretary as you may deem proper—or wholly to suppress it; I am not possessd of sufficient documents on which to ground any details or calculations as to the amount of the products of our different Manufactures or their annual value, a very superficial History of them is all I can pretend to, & this I trust you will find to be the Case with other Gentlemen to whom you may apply for information on this Subject. I have only to subjoin the Names of those persons most likely to give you information respecting this Business in the different parts of the State.

Mr. Josiah Burr of New Haven is the Manager of the Linen manufacture, & is a person of good information. Mr. Robert Walker of Stratford will probably be best able to inform you of the present Situation & Extent of the Duck Manufacture established in that Town. James Davenport Esq of that at Stamford, Mr. Saml Richards that at Farmington, Chaney Whitelsey Esq that at Middletown, Mr. W. Hubbard [5] that at Colchester, Mr. Job. Tabor that at N London, Mr. Daniel L. Coit that at Norwich, Coll. J. Trumbull [6] that at Lebanon

4. ALS, Hamilton Papers, Library of Congress.
Colt was a Hartford businessman who in the seventeen-eighties had been an associate of Jeremiah Wadsworth in the Hartford Woolen Manufactory. In 1793 he became superintendent of the factory founded by the Society for Establishing Useful Manufactures in Paterson, New Jersey. At the time this letter was written he was treasurer of Connecticut.
5. William Hubbard.
6. Jonathan Trumbull, Federalist member of the House of Representatives from Connecticut.

& Maj Daniel Putnam of Brooklyne that at Killingsly & its neighbour-hood. If it should be judged necessary, I believe I can procure you an accurate return of the Wool purchased & worked up into Cloth & the quantity of each kind manufactured at Hartford since the Commence-ment of the Business.

I am dear Sir with very sincere regard your most obedient hume servant   P. Colt

Colo Jno Chester.

July 1791

A succinct account of the Manufactures carried on in the State of Connecticutt.

The Manufactures of this State naturally present themselv to our view under the following Heads; Those carried on in Families merely for the consumption of those Families; Those carried on in like man-ner for the purpose of barter or sale; & those carried on by Tradesmen, Single persons, or Companies for supplying the wants of others; or for the general purposes of merchandise, or Commerce.

Those which come under the first description, & which are purely domestic, are the most extensive & important; there being Scarcely a Family in the State either so rich or so poor as not to be concerned therein. These domestic Manufactures are of Linen, of Cotton & of Wool, in their various modifications. Out of those raw materials are made an abundance of Linen, Cotton, Woolen & woosted Hose, worn by all ranks of people; so as greatly to lessen the Importation, particu-larly of the more ordinary kinds, notwithstanding our increased pop-ulation & wealth has greatly increased the consumption of those articles. Next to those Branches may be reckoned those of tow cloth, coarse Linens, Linen & Cotton for Shirting & Sheating, table Linen, checked & Striped Linens, and Bedticks; also coarse fustians & Jeenes for mens wear, & white Dimity for the Women. The manufactures of Wool are of various kinds of Cloth for Servants and the ordinary wear of the whole class of our Farmers & most of those who follow any of the usual Trades or labourous occupations. This branch of domestic manufactures is extending itself very fast, both as it respects the Quantity & Quality of the Goods. A great proportion of our most substantial Farmers and mechanicks appear dressed on *Sundays* and *holy days* in the manufactures of their Wives & daughters; & this is becoming every day more reputable. We may add to the foregoing list *thread*, both white & colourd, Lace & fringe for various purposes, and of late sewing Silk.

There is manufactured also large parcels of allmost all the denominations afore recited for the purpose of barter, or sale to the merchants, who export them out of the State—within these few years attempts have been made to extend our manufactures, & for improving the fabricks. This has been attempted either by single persons or by companies, with various success. Of this discription is the Linen manufacture established at *New-Haven*, from whence large parcels of coarse Linens have been Shiped to the Southern States & to the West Indies. The same kind of manufacture has more recently been established at Middletown and New-London; the Stock at all those places being raised by Subscription, & managed by an Ajent for the benefit of the adventurers. To these may be added the manufacture of Cottons set up by merchants at Glastenbury & Lebanon, on rather a small Scale; & that at Norwich on a more extensive plan, backed with a larger capital. At Farmington there is a small manufacture of checks, both Cotton & Linen, of Bedticks, and of Fustians & Jeenes. The Same person has made some attemps in the Woosted and Woolen Branches, but his Stock is too limited to make much progress. At Stamford is a similar manufacture. All these are carried on by Single persons or merchants trading in Company; and their Stock is generally small. To these may be added the manufacture of Duck in Stratford (which however is principally confined to Families) & that established at Colchester, on the plan of those at Boston. That is both warp & woof are spun, not on wheels, but drawn out in the same Manner as the Yarns for Riggin are in Rope walks.

At Killingly there is a small Manufacture of Woolens begun under the care of a Mr. Kundall, who has received Some encouragement from Goverment,[7] I believe he has only made coarse cloths & Coatings; & those only narrow. I believe neither his capital or knowledge of this Business will justify our expecting much from this attempt, untill he connects himself with persons of more information, & who

7. William Candal (Cundall), a manufacturer of woolens at Killingly. During the May, 1787, session of the Connecticut legislature Candal was granted a lottery to promote the manufacture of woolen goods (*Connecticut State Records*, VI, 323–24).

shall be possessed of the Means of carrying their projects into effect.

I have purposly omited mentioning the Woolen Manufacture which has been established, or rather attempted, at Hartford, as being on the most extensive plan, & which has the fairest Prospect of Succeeding. This Manufacture commenced about *three* years agone, with a Capital of £1200, raised by voluntary Subscription in shares of £10. each; some of the Subscribers taking more, Some less, as their patriotism or circumstances dictated. This Stock being found too small to effect the veiws of the Company (which were to determin the Question if *American Wool* would make Cloths equal to *British Cloths* out of *British Wool,* & at reasonable prices) was extended by new Subscriptions to £2800. which is the amount of their present Capital. This Stock has been employed in buying Wool, & working it up into Woosted Goods, Narrow & Broad Coatings & Cloths after having been Sorted & prepared in the Manner practised in Great Britain. This Company have received Some aid from Goverment— viz a trifling bounty the first year on Spining—then an exemtion, for two years, of their Workmen from a *Poll Tax;* & their work Shops from all taxes for the same term of Time.[8] These Same priviliges were extended to the manufactures established at Farmington, New Haven & Killingly.[9] But this indulgence is no longer continued to any of them.

The Company at Hartford had expended So much of their Small capital in Buildings, Impliments &c that they found themselves under the necessity of applying to Goverment for Some Aid. The Legislature being sensible of the Importance of encouraging this infant establishment, granted them a Lottery to raise £1000 to enable them to procure a more compleat Set of machinery, & for extending their Business.[10] This Lottery will probably Net them three Thousand Dollars & enable them to make a further tryal in this laudable attempt,

8. "An Act for the Encouragement of certain Manufactures within this State" (*Connecticut State Records,* VI, 406–07).

9. "An Act for the encouragement of the Woollen Manufacture within this State" (*Connecticut State Records,* VI, 501–02).

10. In October, 1790, the Connecticut legislature resolved that permission be granted "for the setting up a Lottery to raise the Sum of One Thousand Pounds lawfull Money exclusive of Expence . . . for the purchase of . . . Machines, Implements and Stock and the carrying on and establishing of said Woollen Manufactory, and that said Lottery be drawn within One Year from and after the first Day of January next" (*Connecticut State Records,* VII, 205).

to establish so valuable a manufacture. The Event is yet, hower, very problematical. Those persons concerned in seting up new Manufactures have every obsticle to Surmount which can arrise from clashing Interests, or ancient prejudices; as well as from the smallness of our capitals, the scarcity of Materials & workmen, & the consequent high prices of both. In this respect the obsticals which are opposed to the Woolen manufacture are the greatest. The reasons are too obviouse to need reciting. Some kind of aid therefore, from the General Goverment of the United States will be necessary in order fully to establish Manufactures, for the purpose of Barter or merchandize. Those for domestic purposes only, will be continued from mere necessity. How this is to be effected, those who administer the Goverment must determin. In addition to the foregoing List should be subjoined the manufactures in Wood, in Iron & in Leather, both for home consumption & for exportation. Household Furniture & wheel Carriages of all kinds are made in plenty & prety good Stile, & considerable is exported to the Southern States & to the west Indies. The manufactures of Iron are variouse & extensive & exceed our demands for home consumption, except Cutlery & some part of the Tools used by Tradesmen. Our manufactures of Leather are considerable; so as to make a full supply of Shoes & Boots; Saddles, Bridles, Horse Harness &c even for Exportation. We make also stuff & Silk Shoes nearly Sufficient for the consumption of the State.

As to the quantum of all these manufactures, either those used amongst ourselves, or those exported; or the value of them in Money, I dare not hazard an oppinion, not having the details on which to make the calculation, or ground such an oppinion. But considering the Number of our laborious & active Citizens, & our modes of Living, it cannot otherways than be considerable & it is yearly increasing. The manufactures carried on in our Families may be calculated to increase the value of the products, beyound that of the *raw materials* as three to one. Those established in factories, such as the woolen manufacture at Hartford, not less than four to one, or even five to one.

When the active Stock of the Citizens shall no longer be embarked in paper Speculations, then we may expect to see part of it turned to the promoting & extending our manufactures & then those which languish and dwindle for want of being supportd with proper Capitals may be expected to prosper & this Country freed from a disgracefull dependance on Europe for their ordinary Cloathing.

P.S. I might have mentioned Tin men, pewterers, Hatters &c & Silver Smith in a great plenty—Braizing Brass founders—& of late Button makers. This last Business is of a recent date, but promises to become extensive.

[ENCLOSURE]

Elisha Colt to John Chester [11]

Hartford August 20th. 1791

Sir

    In answer to you favour of 16th. Inst on the subject of the Woolen Manufacture established in this place, I am now to observe, that the Business commenced in June 1788 with a Capital of £1280. raised by Subscription in shares of Ten pounds each. The first season we purchased about Seven thousand pounds of Wool, and such Implements as were of prime necessity in carrying on the Business, which was managed by an Agent in behalf of the Company; This was meant as an essay only, to determin if this Branch of Manufactures could be made profitable in this Country. We were at that period not only totally unacquainted with the various parts or subdivisions of the Labour; but equally destitute of every kind of machinery and Labourers for executing such a project. But the news of this infant attempt to establish so usefull a manufacture soon collected a number of Workmen about us, who had been bred to different branches of the Woolen & Worsted Business in England. These were chiefly old Soldiers who had deserted the British Army, or having been taken prisoners during the late War, remained in the Country. From these men we have acquired some usefull Knowledge, tho at a dear rate; as every one had some project to his own to propose, or improvement to make in the various Implements &c. used in our Business, but none of them had a sufficient mechanical Knouledge to give proper directions, or make themselves understood by our mechanicks: of course

    11. ALS, Hamilton Papers, Library of Congress.
    Elisha Colt, a nephew of Peter Colt, was manager of the Hartford Woolen Manufactory.

we expended considerable Sums from which we received no manner of Benefit. We have had to struggle with every kind of embarrassment which can attend the setting up a new Business; either from the Ignorance, the Knavery or the fickleness of the workmen; the high price of materials; the smallness of our Capital, and the prejudices of the Community against *home made* Cloths, and the interested views and Jealousy of the British Factors and agents in this Country. So much of our small Capital was Consumed in building our works & procuring the necessary Implements for carrying on our Business (as there was not a single Loom in the Country in which a piece of Broad Cloth could be wove; nor a pair of Stocks in which it could be fulled, or a board on which it could be sheared &c.) that the proprietors found it absolutely necessary to enlarge their Stock. This was done, the *second season,* by new Subscriptions by which our Capital was raised to Two thousand eight hundred pounds. Notwithstanding our Stock was more than doubled, we found ourselves, *last fall,* so cramped in our Business, by losses and improvident bargains, and by having so large a part of our fabricks on hand, that the Business was in danger of totally failing, when the Goverment interposed and granted us a Lottery for raising One thousand pounds to enable us to procure a Stock of Wool for the present season, and such further Implements as may be necessary effectually to establish our Works.[12] This Lottery will probably nett the Factory Nine hundred pounds and has proved a most seasonable aid. We have now erecected a Building well calculated for carrying on this Business in the various parts, in which we have three Broad & five Narrow Looms at work, which will consume about 12,000 pounds of Wool ℗ annum. Our wool is collected about the Country from the Farmers who raise it, it costs from 1/2 to 1/6 the pound, taken at their Houses. When it comes into the Woolstore, the Fleeces are broken up and sorted exactly in the manner practised in England, by workmen regularly bred to that branch. We make *six* sorts besides the coarse hairy parts which is only used for *listing.* After this operation the wool is washed clean and dried, when it is passed thro' a Machine called a *Willow,* which operation serves to pull the Wool in pieces and seperates the dirt & dead hairs, after which it is oiled and then *Scribled,* by which operation it is prepared for the Spinners. This is a very labourous &

12. See note 10.

expensive part of the process in making Cloths (particularly mixtures, which require to be repeated three times) and is now performed in England by machines that are worked by Water. So far the work is performed under our Eye and immediate management. It is then put out in Families in the neighbouring districts to be spun into yarn, when it is returned to the Factory and there warped into proper peices and wove into Cloth in our own Looms, as the Country Looms will not make even the narrow Cloths of sufficient width for our purpose. From the Loom they go to the fulling Mill, to be scoured & partly fulled, when they go thro a process called *burling*, by which all knots, lumps &c. are taken out; and in mixtures, every thing that would disfigure the Cloths when finished. They are then returned to the Mill & the Fulling is compleated; when they are delivr'd over to the head Clothier or finisher, who raises the nap, shears, presses & stacks the Cloths for market. Every part or branch of the Business is managed in the same manner as practised in England. We dye both in the Wool and in the Cloth; tho we are perhaps more deficient in this Branch than any other part of the Business.

Since the commencment of this Business in the summer of 1788 (when we were destitute of Implements and Workmen) we have purchased and worked up (previous to the present season) about 20,000 pounds of Wool into Goods of different kinds & values, and which have been sold at al prices from 1/6 to 28/. ℔ yard vizt.

69 peices	Narrow Baizes	makg.	2308 yards	averaging @ 2/- in sales	
17	"	Shallons	465	"	do	2/6-
21	"	Lastings	510	"	do	4/6
45	"	Serge	1007	"	do	5/6
24	"	Elastick Cloth	524	"	do	7/-
84	"	broad & narrow Coatings	2252	"	do	4/9 & 7/6
97	"	narrow Cloths	2557	"	do	6/6
89	"	broad Cloths	1833	"	do	12/or 13/
39	"	Casimers	1072	"	do	8/

Besides a considerable quantity of Yarns and Cloths in different stages not yet finished. The making of Baizes, Shallons & Lastings, we have declined, as unprofitable.

Samples of some of our Fabricks that are *now on hand* will accompany this for the Inspection of the Secretary of Treasury.

At present we enjoy no exclusive priviledge, or indeed any emolument from Goverment.

The Embarrassments we labour under arrise from the Scarcity of Wool, and the consequent high price of that article; and the frauds and impositions we are subject to in purchasing Wool, from a total want of inspection or regulations in packing Wool for market; from the scarcity of Workmen; particularly dyers and finishers of Goods; from the want of machines for expediting Labour; such as Scribling or Carding Machines, that are worked by Water, and Jennies for spinning yarn.

The present use of Machines in England give their Manufacturers immence advantages over us. This we expect to remedy. But the price of Wool must be high with us, untill the people of the middle & southern States can be induced to turn their attention to raising Sheep. Should this take place, in a very few years we may raise wool enough for the consumption of this Country & make every kind of Woolen Goods suitable for every discription of People from the highest Class of Citizens to the Negro Slaves. Whilst Wool is so scarce we are obliged to purchase our years stock as soon as it is taken off the Sheep. As our Capital is so small this is an unfortunate circumstance and the impossibility of hiring Money on legal Interest adds to our embarrassments. This evil we endeavoured to remedy by contracting for spanish Wool; but we were so imposed upon by the Merchant in the quality of the Wool that we have been detered from recuring to this expedient again. We are daily making improvements in the manufacture of Cloths and are in hopes of procuring Machines for scribling Wool & Spinning it into yarns, so as to enable us to meet the British on equal terms in market: and that as soon as the rage for Speculation in the funds of the United States shall have ceased, part of the Money of the Country, which now circulates only in paper trafic, may be directed into this channel for the aid of our infant Manufactures.

What encouragement it will be proper for the General Goverment to afford us; either by exemptions, by Bounties, or by duties on Importation the Legislature of the United States must determin. They alone are Competent to this Business, the seperate States having neither authority or Funds for the purpose.

By giving you this *History* of our Manufactory, I have answered your various queries in best manner in my power

and am with great respect Sir Your most obedient & Most Humble Servant   Elisha Colt

John Chester Esquire

[ENCLOSURE]

Heman Swift to John Chester [13]

Cornwall [Connecticut] August 22d. 1791

Sir

I receiv'd your favour of the 10th. instant, yesterday, and should be very happy to comply with your request in making Out a statement respecting the Manufactures in this County, but am obliged to set out on a journey into the state of Vermont the day after tomorrow which will prevent my being able to get the Necssary information before you will be oblieged to make returns. I consider those matters you mention of very great importance to this State, and wish to pay every attention in my power to ascertain them; I am so well acquainted in the County that I am sure very Little attention is paid to manufactures therein except in the Domestic & Iron manufactures both of which are carried on to considerable advantage; and with suitable encouragement might be increased to considerable perfection, as this County is peculiarly calculated for carrying on the Iron manufacture as there is a great plenty of wood & Ore. There has lately been discovered two beds of ore which I think will prove good: There is in the County one Furnace and twenty six Forges that I recollect, All owned by Individuals, and two Slitting works. The Forges are too many of them Owned by Men that are not Able to stock them well, and of consequence are not carried on to advantage, yet there are others that are carried on to the best advantage: There are other new works Erecting and that branch of business is increaseing fast but in the smaller branches of the Iron Manufactures very Little attention has been paid except in One works where is carried the making of Ancors and Mill Irons: which are carried on to the best advantage. Common bloom Iron is sold at 20/ pr. hundred but the smaller branches are exceedingly Neglected and want encourageing; as to Domestic Manufactures they are carried on in almost every family so far as to make coarse woolen and Linnen cloth for the consumtion of their own family. But the Iron made in this County is principally of the Bloom-

13. ALS, Hamilton Papers, Library of Congress.
Swift was a member of the Connecticut Council.

ery kind yet of the best quality. An addition of a Furnice or two I think would be very profitable to increase the Quantity of refind Iron. You will please to excuse the inaccuracy of my information as I am oblig'd to write in haste.

I am sir with every sentiment   of Esteem your Obdt. servt

Heman Swift

The Honl. John Chester Esqr.

[E N C L O S U R E]

Benjamin Huntington to John Chester [14]

Norwich [Connecticut] August 24th 1791

Sir

Your Letter of the 10th Instant has been Recd but being Necessarily Abscent last week could not Attend to the Subject you mention untill Monday last and being on the same Business this Day I found Col Leffingwell [15] on the Same Employ through the Request of Mr. Learnand [16] & we have agreed on a Report as near as we can state one, not only for this Town but for the whole County N London (exceptd) which you will Receive in a Short Time from him. It is Impossible to State the amount of Articles Manufactured in the Several Branches with Accuracy but have done it as near as we can.

There are no Manufactures of Consequence in Stonington Groton Lyme Colchester Franklin Lisbon or Montville saving such as are mentioned in Mr. Leffingwells report. Ship Building and the Cod fishing are the Principal in Stonington but I Suppose these are what the Secretary has had a better account of than we can Collect. The Domestic Manufacture of Coarse Linins and Wollens is very considerable more than Sufficient for the Consuption of farmers Families. As to Inpediments and Encouragements I know of None but what you are Perfectly Acquainted with. The Impediments Complained of by the Mechanics are the assessments on the Trade of Facutised

14. ALS, Hamilton Papers, Library of Congress.
Huntington was a member of a prominent Norwich mercantile family and a member of the Connecticut Council.
15. Christopher Leffingwell, a prominent Norwich merchant and stocking manufacturer.
16. Amasa Learned had served in the Connecticut General Assembly and in 1791 was elected to the Federal House of Representatives.

Persons,[17] the Poll tax on apprentices,[18] Equipments & Loss of Time for Military Service and the want of an Increase of Duties on Goods Imported which might be manufactured here.

I will Remember the Design of Congress in Directing the Secretary to Report was the better to Enable the Next Session of Congress to judge what Manufactures to Encourage and to adopt measures for that Purpose (This will extend Principa⟨ll⟩y to Articles Imported which might as well be made here) and to Increase the Commerce between the Northern & Southern States & by that means at once to Increase our Internal Trade & Strengthen the Union as also to promote an Acquaintance and assimulation of Manners among the People in the several States. The good Effects of this Design when accomplished were very Obvious.

I am sir with Esteem & Regard   your Friend & Hume Servt
                                                    Benj Huntington
Col. Chester

[E N C L O S U R E]

Christopher Leffingwell to John Chester [19]

Norwich [Connecticut] 26th. Augt 1791

Dear Sir

In Consequence of your Application to Mr Learned and Mr Huntington to procure a Statement of the Manufactories in the County of New London they have both applied to me to give you the best information I could collect which I here inclose the principal part of which is in this Town which Imagine will at Some future day become a very Considerable manufactoring place. My reasons are these it is at the head of a Navagable River in a Very plentiful

17. The tax laws of Connecticut provided for "*assessments* proportioned to the estimated gains or profits arising from any, and all, lucrative professions, trades, and occupations, excepting compensations to public offices, the profits of husbandry, and common labor for hire." See *ASP, Finance,* I, 423. The term "faculty" was applied to this tax.
18. The poll tax in Connecticut applied to two groups, persons twenty-one to seventy years old and those eighteen to twenty-one years old (*ASP, Finance,* I, 454). Apprentices would fall into the latter group, and presumably their masters would be responsible for the payment of the taxes.
19. ALS, Hamilton Papers, Library of Congress.

Country for every kind of Provisions. There is a plenty of fuel which will always be Cheeper than in any other Considerable Town I know of.

The Stream which runs thro this Town has many Mill Seats more & better than in any Other in this State and a great Variety of Manufactoring will be done by Machinery turnd by Water. I do not know what Establishments the Secretary Colo Hamilton has in View respecting Manufactories, but I concieve if he has it in Contemplation to Establish Several on the large Scale he cannot find a better place in the United States than Norwich. Suppose a Cotton Manufactory for making every kind of Cotton Goods should be thought an Object. The Carding Spinning & considerable weaving may be done by Water Machines.

The Calandering the Stamping or printing & almost every part may be done in that way & Save ⅞ths. of the Manual Labour. Suppose the Crockery Business in the Variety of its branches Should be thought an object & I concieve it to be a Capital one. The Consumption of that Article is immense and the freight from Europe amounts to an Amazing sum. The Materials may be Ground & prepared by Water Machines and fuel is a Considerable Article.

Suppose the Cutlery Branch Should be thought worth attending to. Seven Eights of the forging & finishing may & Ought to be done by Water Works. Hammers Bellows & Grindstones ought all to Go by water. Having dipt considerably in the manufactoring line before the Warr & having procured Some information Since the Naval office in this Town has been absorb'd in the district of New London and Loosing the little Living I recieved from the Office has induced me to make enquirys into the Nature and process in Manufactoring Several kinds of Goods. Am fully Convinced the Articles I have mentioned and Sundry others may be made in this Country Cheaper & better than they can possibly be procured from any Other. You will if you think proper Suggest Some of these Ideas to the Secretary or Suppress them & beleive me very respectfully

Your Most Obedient Servt   Chrisr. Leffingwell

Colo Chester

[ENCLOSURE]

Christopher Leffingwell to John Chester [20]

Norwich [Connecticut] 30th Augt 1791

Dear Sir

Since forwarding Statement of Manufactories have discoverd an Omission of the Manufactoring of Carding Machines and Jennys for Carding & Spinning on the large Scale. Those in Mr Lathrops works [21] were wholly made here by an Inhabitant of this Town who is a Great Mechanical Genius. Machines for Cutting doubling & Crooking Card wire for making Common Cotton & Wool Cards are also made in this Town. Those at Philadelphia & Several in Boston were made by a Nathan Cobb of this place.

I am your most Obed sert   Chrisr Leffingwell

Colo Chester

[ENCLOSURE]

William Hillhouse to John Chester [22]

Montville [Connecticut] Sepr. 6th. 1791.

Sir

As Mr. Huntington and Mr. Learned reside in the two principle Manfacturing Towns, and have Easy access to all the other Towns in the County of New London, Shall depend on their giving the information you Desire in respect to the Manufactures in them.

This Town is altogether in the Farming way, & little or nothing is done with us in the way of Trade or Manufacture Except for use of the Inhabitants, we have Blacksmiths, that do the Common work needfull for the Farmers, Shoemakers, Carpenters, Cloathers ⟨when⟩ Necessary for the peoples wants. The Familys ⟨ma⟩ke plain Cloth,

20. ALS, Hamilton Papers, Library of Congress.
21. This is a reference to the cotton manufactory established at Norwich in 1790 by Dr. Joshua Lathrop and Cushing Eells.
22. ALS, Hamilton Papers, Library of Congress.
Hillhouse, a lawyer, was elected to the Connecticut legislature in 1792.

Bearskin, Thin Cloth, & Linnen for Family use. They also make Checkd. flanning & Tow Cloth, which the Women Barter with the Shopkeepers for Calicoes, Muslins, and other Female Clothing and ornaments. This Sir is near as I can recollect the State of the case with respect to us and has been nearly the same for Years past.

It is Easy to Supply the flax for the linning Clothing as about half an Acre of flax Ground upon an Average will Supply a Sufficient Quantity of flax for all the Inhabitants of this State.

The Woollen Manufacture, in this Cold Climate, is an Important Object, which is not Easy to get a long with for Want of Wool. I have not made Exact Calulations But will Suppose for Once, that to Cloathe the People of this State only, it will require a Number of Sheep to be Shorn Yearly not less than 1000,000. What the number in the State was, the Last Deduction from the List I have forgot, but very Short of the Number that is Wanted.

You have I believe, often heard it Mentioned that Two of the Most Material Objections to keeping Sheep are, In the first place Sheep are apt to be unruly and Troublesome, and in the Next place they will not pay the Expence of keeping Equall to other Stock, which is in a Measure True.

I know of no remedy for the last objec⟨tion⟩ but for the Good People in their Patroism to Eat and Make away with as Much Lamb and Mutton Sheep as posible instead of other Meat, which would make Such Demand for Sheep as would induce the raising them, for it is a Well None fact, that the Wool that is Shorn from the Sheep is no Compensation to the Farmer for Keeping them. I could perhaps give you a more perticular account (Why and Wherefore) but will Omit it not Doubting but you Well understand the Matter.

Something I believe might be done to better the Texture and Quality of the Wool, but that would Need Encouragment as Course Wool is More profitably raised than fine, but Enough as I am not Certain that Your Enquiries lead to This Subject, however I will Suggest a remedy to the first objection to keeping Sheep, their being unruly, it is Easy to remedy it. Keep Your Sheep Well, attend to Your fences to keep them in repair and dont let Your Sheep Choose for themselves but Govern Them, and there is no more Dificulty in Managing Sheep than any other Stock,

I am Sir with Great respect   and Consideration, your   most Obet.
Hume. Servt.   William Hillhouse

The Honrable John Chester

[ENCLOSURE]

Joseph P. Cooke to John Chester [23]

Danbury [Connecticut] Septr. 12th. 1791.

Sir

In pursuance of your request communicated in your letter the
10th. ult. I have endeavoured to obtain the best information in my
power respecting the several manufactures in the northern parts of
the County of Fairfield, expecting you will receive from Mr. Davenport [24] all necessary information from the towns upon the Sea-coasts.
The inland parts of this County, not yet overstocked with inhabitants,
afford the people the means of persuing Agriculture very generally
which is their favourite employment, consequently the spirit of
manufacturing has not much prevailed, except in the domestic way;
that however in the aggragate is very considerable, as their families
are principally cloathed in their own manufactures, but to what
amount cannot be ascertained with any degree of precision. Making
of Nails is also become part of the trade of almost every blacksmith,
whereby the importation of that article is entirely at an end. The
manufacturing of Hats of all kinds is prosecuted upon a large scale in
this town; from the factory of O. Burr and Co.[25] which is probably
the largest of the kind in this State, large quantities of hats are sent
abroad, as also from several others, although to a much less amount.
I took the liberty to communicate your letter to Mr. White one of
the partners of that company, and desired him to give such a State-

23. ALS, Hamilton Papers, Library of Congress.
Cooke, a Danbury merchant, had served as a member of the Continental
Congress from 1784 to 1788. At the time this letter was written he was a member
of the Connecticut Council.
24. James Davenport, a Stamford lawyer and a member of the Connecticut
Board of Assistants, had served in the Connecticut General Assembly from 1785
to 1790.
25. O. Burr and Company operated a hat factory in Danbury. The members of
the firm were Oliver Burr and Colonel Russell White.

ment of their business as would correspond with your ideas; he engaged to do it; and I doubt not he will give a satisfactory account of this business in a letter addressed to you, which I expect will accompany this.

A Cotton manufacture has also been carried on in this town for about two years past, but not to any considerable degree; a company however has been formed this summer past for that purpose; they have purchased a Jenny for spinning and a Carding Machine, have manufactured several pieces of cloth which meet with a ready sale; the prospect is somewhat promising; the greatest difficulty as present is in procuring good workmen that will be steady in business.

The manufacturing of Pot and Pearl Ashes is carried on in much the same manner as I suppose it is in other parts of the State; one or more works in almost every town: the owners complain of too great an interference in this business, perhaps some general regulations on that account might be proper.

The manufacturing of Bar Iron has made a rapid progress within a few years: four years ago there was not a single Forge for that purpose in this County, and I believe never was; within that time eight or nine Iron Works have been erected, in most of which there are two Forges producing upon a mean about twenty tons of bar iron annally, of which a large quantity, after supplying the home consumption which is very great, is exported to New-York, where it meets with a quick market at about 70 Dollars ⅌ ton. These works are supplied with Ore of a good quality from an inexhaustible Bed about seven miles from this town just within the limits of the State of New-York. This important branch of business, being liable to many disasters, requires the unremitted exertions of the Proprietors, and demands public encouragement. A Sliting Mill has for some time been in contemplation, but nothing as yet done, such works would be of great utility to this part of the Country, but they ought not to be too frequent.

With great respect and esteem I am Sir your most obedient Servant   Joseph P. Cooke

Honble. John Chester.

[ENCLOSURE]

O. Burr and Company to John Chester [26]

Honble. J. Chester Esqr   Danbury [Connecticut] Sept 12. 1791.

Sir,

Your circular Letter of the 10th. ult., desiring Information respecting the Rise & Progress of Manufactures, was handed to us by the Honble. Joseph P. Cooke Esqr & as you observe, that any Communications by Letter, will answer your Purpose, we have taken the Liberty of addressing this to you, stating the Rise & Progress of our Hat Manufactory, & that of the Saddle Cloth under the Care of Judson White.

And we have subjoined several Impediments under which we concieve, the Hat Manufactory labors.

Perhaps from local & contracted Views, we have not given the Subject that extensive Consideration, which it demands. If we have given any Hints which maybe serviceable to the manufacturing Interest, our Purpose will be answered. Such as they are, we submit to your Candour.

We began the Hatting Business in Janry 1787, with only one Journeyman & one Apprentice. You will see the Progress of it, by the Statement on the other Page. We now employ seven Journeymen & ten Apprentices.

The Price affixed to each Quality of Hats, is at what they now sell by the Dozen, in Lawful Money.

	Felt Hats	Girls Do.	plain Castors	Napt Rorums	Beavers.	Beaveretts
1787	305	....	73	146	10	....
1788	450	4	50	408	8	17
1789	609	60	65	1104	47	6
1790	443	9	19	1862	85	....
1791	98	....	21	1629	30	....
	1905 @ 5/	73 @ 7/6	228 @ 24/	5149 @ 15/	180 @ 39/	23 @ 30/

	Plain Rorums	Napt Castors	Ladies
1787	17	....	....
1788	10	....	....
1789	14	11	....
1790	....	99	....
1791	....	180	237
	41 @ 10/	290 @ 24/	237 @ 15/

26. LS, Hamilton Papers, Library of Congress.

The Article of Muskrats of which we use large Quantities in napping our Rorum Hats, have advanced in Price within 15 or 16 Months 30 ⅌ Cent at least, & Hats have fallen in Market full 20 ⅌ Cent in the same Time, owing in a great measure to Persons setting up the Business who never served for the Trade, & not being Judges, have bad Work done which goes to Market, & has injured the Credit of American Hats very much, & must in Time ruin it entirely, except Government adopts some method to prevent such injurious Practices, & make it necessary for Men to serve such a number of years as shall perfect them in the Business. Our Trade is not learned by Observation nor by mathematical Calculation, but by practical Experiments.

This Practice of setting up the Business without serving an Apprenticeship, has the hurtful Tendency to make Apprentices discontented in their Master's Service, as they see those who have not served at the Trade more than one or two years, employed as Journeymen at full Wages in these Shops: therefore as soon as they have learned to form a Hat, they will say; "if we can by any means get clear of our Masters, we may be Journeymen on Wages too, as we can work as well as those who are employed by these Men." Hence we see the great Propriety of the English Laws which no doubt have been the means of the Improvements which have brot their Manufactures to such Perfection. What Improvement can be expected in a Shop where the only Person interested is ignorant of the Business?

The Rise of Stock & Fall of Hats, makes it necessary for us to enlarge our Business & as Journeymen are scarce, we are obliged to take a Number of Apprentices; the Poll Tax on these will be a heavy Burden;[27] add to this, the Assessments on Mechanicks which the Listers think must be laid on,[28] in Proportion to the Business appearing to be done. Now as our Hats must be sold in New York by the Dozen, & the Price is from 30 to 50 ⅌ Cent. below what they are sold for by Retail at the Hatters Shops in the Country, this Assessment, you will readily see is very unequal on us.

The Principal Reason of the high Price of Furrs, is ⟨our⟩ not having the Command of the Furr Trade; & a great Part of ⟨the⟩ Furrs which come into this Part of the Country is purchased in Canada by a Person in New York & shipped to England, & from there to that City. And as

27. See note 18.
28. See note 17.

there is no other Person in that Business at present, he is able to engross the whole of the Furrs, & command the Price.

Some kinds of Furrs are lately imported from Germany & other Parts of Europe, which we hope may be a Relief to us; & together with our Improvements in extending the Stock, will enable us to continue the Business to the Advantage of ourselves & Country, should Government make such Regulations or to encourage Improvements by those who are capable of making them, & prevent Practices which are hurtful to the Credit of the manufactoring Interest.

We are with great Respect, Sr Your   obedt humble Servts

O. Burr & Co.

Judson White began the Saddle Cloth Manufactory in Septr 1790. Since that Time he has manufactured 1258 Yards which sells from 3/6 to 3/9 ℔ Yard by the Piece, Several Samples of which, we inclose. As it is not convenient to send a Sample of the Hats, we would just inform you, that they may be seen either in our shop in Danbury, or in New York Maiden Lane where we expect to open a Shop sometime this Month.

[ENCLOSURE]

Amasa Learned to John Chester [29]

New London [Connecticut] 14th Septr 1791

Dear sir,

Agreeably to your request, I have written to several Gentlemen in each Town, in this County, to collect and forward to you, before the 20th Septr, such information on the subject of Manufactures in their respective Towns as the Secretary required.

The domestic manufactures of this Town are the same kind that you find in every other Town; but rather inferior to most, in quantity & quality. The incidental trades, such as Boat-building, sailmaking, Ropemaking, Blockmaking &C &C. varies as the Tide of Business ebbs or flows. They need no laws directly in their favour, depending wholly on the State of Commerce. There are two Saddlers in this Town, who make about 500 Saddles each every year & as many bridles. The prices vary according to the quality from 8 dollars to 20.

29. ALS, Hamilton Papers, Library of Congress.

Most of them are exported to the West Indies some to the Southern States, where they meet the same wares from England. These manufacturers, suppose that the duty on imported Saddles is not sufficiently high. Some Complaint there has been that the duty on tanned leather is too low. In the Island of Hispaniola from whence they formerly brought many raw hides the tanning business has greatly increased & leather is imported instead of hides. I know of no other trades in this Town that labor under any impediment which it is in the power of Government to remove. To enter into a particular detail of all the incidental & domestic trades of this Town, of thier origin, annual produce & State of improvement would be an arduous task and as useless as difficult. Norwich will be able to furnish more necessary information than all the rest of the County. I wrote to Colo Leffingwell, Coit [30] & Lathrop, Gentlemen deeply interested in Manufactures.

With Sentiments of Esteem   Dear sir, your Obedt & hble Sert

Amasa Learned

[ENCLOSURE]

Jonathan Palmer, Junior, to John Chester [31]

Stonington [Connecticut] Sept. 15th. AD 1791

Sir

At Mr. Learneds request with respect to Manafactures have to state to you, That we have No regular Established. Factories in this Town, and therefore no pecuniary Incouragements. Our Domestick Are Considerable but to what amount is very doubtfull. The business of Hattmaking has been caryed on long in this Town, but for about One Year has been followed with peculiar Attention And perseverance. They Manafacture enough for the Use of the Town of different Qualities, and which Are I think preferable to ye English. These Hats are Caried, Many of them, to differant States in ye Union for Sale, but ye Hattars Complain that foreign Importations Yet, very Much Injure the business here. Cabinett making has been followed here

30. Daniel L. Coit, a nephew of Joshua Lathrop, was a partner in the Norwich drug firm of Coit and Lathrop.
31. ALS, Hamilton Papers, Library of Congress.
Palmer was a representative in the Connecticut General Assembly and surveyor of the port of Stonington.

time Immemorial, and for many years Sufficiently for ye use of this Town and Considerable Shipd. to ye southern States for sale. Our Wollen Manufactory is wholly of the family kind and Judge Sufficent to furnish the Inhabitants, of there Corse wairing aparel, those of a fine Quality are chiefly of Foreign Inportation. Of Coarse Lining in the family way we Manafacture Sufficent for Our Own Inhabitants but our fine, as in the case of wollen we Import from Forigners. The above is the best Statement can at present make as particular valuations would be Intirely matter of gess.

Am sir with Sentiments of Esteem & Friendship   Devotedly Yours

Jona. Palmer Junor

Colo. John Chester

[E N C L O S U R E]

James Davenport to John Chester [32]

Stamford [Connecticut] Sept. 16th Ad 1791

Sir

I am honored by the receipt of your Letter of the 10th Ult. in which you inform me of the request of the Secretary of the Treasury to have as accurate information as possible of the state of Manufactures of every kind in this State & desire me to collect & communicate to you information on the subject from this County. I should have answered you Letter sooner but absence from home prevented.

It is impossible to give you the Minute information you wish, but can generally inform you that domestic manufactures of Woolen Linnen & Cotton have since the conclusion of the war very greatly increased. I believe more than three fourths of that description of Goods used by the Inhabitants are manufactured in that way the fabricks are generally of the coarser kinds but are esteemed much better than those imported of the same degree of fineness & are made at less cost than the price of the imported goods.

A manufacture of Sail Cloth & Coarse Linnen was set up in this Town about two years since by Jno. Wm. Holly; he has not carried it on very Extensively but has manufactured in that period about Eighty peices of Duck of Thirty Eight yards each the price of which has been from Eleven to twelve Dollars per peice. He has also made about

32. ALS, Hamilton Papers, Library of Congress.

14,000 yards of Oznaburghs & other linnen Cloth the prices at which it sold were various from Forty to Twelve Cents. The manufacture of Nails is also carried on in this Town by Mr. Jarvis.[33] It was begun about five years ago & ten Tons of Nails have been made per year & the same article has been manufactured in the Town of Norwalk for about Three years in greater quantities than in this Town by Burral & Gruman.

I know of no other manufactures but of the domestic kind in this County excepting at Danbury where the manufacture of Linnen & Cotton & Hatts is carried on. Col. Cook I suppose will give you particular information from thence.

I ought to have mentioned that considerable quantities of linnen Cloth which sells for about 20 Cents per yard are made in the domestic way in the County & sold in the southern States.

I shall be glad if this information can be of any service to you & wish I could have been more particular. The subject is important & merits Legislative consideration & it will be peculiarly serviceable to this State if Manufactures are properly encouraged.

I have seen a plan (said to be the plan of the Secretary) for the incorporation of a Company with a Capital of 500.000 Dollars to be imployed in the business of Manufactures [34] & its operations are to be confined to one of the three States next south of this & New Jersey is to have the preference, why is New Jersey preferable to Connecticut for the carrying on such business?

I am with sentiments of esteem & regard Sir your   most Obdt servant
James Davenport

[ENCLOSURE]

Roger Newberry to John Chester [35]

Windsor [Connecticut] 16th Septr. 1791

Sr

Since I received yours of the 10th. of August My Son on whome

33. Samuel Jarvis.
34. See "Prospectus of the Society for Establishing Useful Manufactures," August, 1791.
35. ALS, Hamilton Papers, Library of Congress.
    Newberry, a Windsor lawyer and merchant, had served as a major general in the Connecticut militia during the American Revolution. At the time this letter was written he was a member of the Connecticut legislature.

my dependance has been has been sick and unable to assist me in my business, so that I have been unable to pay much attention to the Subject of your letter. I have wrote to several Gentlement and have recd. no answer except from Alexander King [36] Esq of Suffield whose letter I herewith send you.

The Manufactures of this Town are Mostly in the domestic way such as most of our coarse Woolens & Linnens, chec'd Linnens we import none they are all of home manufacture as are all Linnens under 2/ per yard, and notwithstanding the great increase of population there is not one quarter part of coarse imported Woollens used that there were four year ago. Our Axes Siythes, Hoes, and many other of the large & heavyer kind of edged tools are manufactured among our selves. The Prisons at New Gate will probably manufacture from 15 to 20 Tons of Nails in a year which are sold by large quantities at 6d per pound by retaile at 7d. There is usually in the country large quantities of Tow cloth from 1/ to 1/3 per yard made in the domestick way, brought to market and sent to the Southen States, but this year there has been but little more made than is necessary for home consumption, owing I suppose to moderate crop of Flax last year and the great demand for that article for Sail Cloth and Cordage. It is difficult to fix any time when the above mentioned Manufactures began. They have been gradually increasing ever since the first Settlement of this Country, but have been rapidly improveing ever since the commencement of the late War but more especially since the conclusion of it. And what farther incouragement is necessary I am unable to say. The two cloth is sold according to the labour and expence about it, very low, and I could wish some better incouragement might be given to that manufacture as it imploys a great many women in the country. I am very sorry I have not been able to pay greater attention to the subject, as it is a subject of importance and in which this State is deeply interested. If I shall receive any answers from the other Gentlemen to whome I have wrote I will forward them to you, and am

Your Obedient   Humle Serv   Roger Newberry

Honle John Chester Esq

36. King was a Suffield physician who served in the Connecticut General Assembly from 1778 to 1784.

[ENCLOSURE]

Alexander King to Roger Newberry [37]

Suffield [Connecticut] 12th. Septemr. 1791

Sir.

In Compliance with your Request of 29th August last, I have sent as Accurate an Estimate as at present can be obtained of the State and produce of the Manufactures of this Town.

The Wollen Manufacture is the Principal and the most Beneficial to the Inhabitants of any that is carried on in this Place. There are in Suffield about 400 Families and about 5 Thousand grown Sheep, which will produce about 25 lb wt. to a Family on an Average. This is all manufactured in the Domestic way except Fulling and Dressing which is done at the Cloathiers Works.

We have One Cloathier in Suffield who carries on a pretty large Branch of Bussiness. In the year 1788 he fulled and Dressed 1500 yd of Wollen Cloath; besides Dying and pressing half as much More; in the year past he has fulled & Dressed 3500 yds of wollen and dyed and presd. about 1800 more which was not fulled; the Cloath thus made is consumed by the Particular Families who manufacture it. The late Premium granted by the Legislature of this State, has in my Opinion contributed to the Increase of Sheep.[38] They have doubled in Number in this Town in less than Four Years; and by proper Attention may yet for a long Time become an increasing Source of Wealth to the Farmer and Manufacturer.

Of this Article no great Quantities are manufactured in this Place. Some particular Families do a little.

About 20 Thousand Wt. of Flax is Annually manufactured in this Town which is Another important Article of Manufactures, and is

37. ALS, Hamilton Papers, Library of Congress.
38. "An Act for the Encouragement of certain Manufactures within this State," passed in May, 1788, by the Connecticut legislature, had provided for a bounty of one penny on the pound of woolen yarn spun into cloth at the Hartford Woolen Manufactory before June, 1789 (*Connecticut State Records*, VI, 406).

done like the Wool in the Domestic Way. The whole of this however is not the Produce of this Town, perhaps One Quarter is purchased from other Places, the usual price of Flax is from 4d to 6d pr lb.

Hemp

The Culture of Hemp has been attempted this year by some of Our Farmers, how it will produce or how far Succeed is yet unknown. The growth of this year may be Estimated at Two Tuns.

Iron

There is a Forge for making Iron Shovels, the Plates are drawn under a Trip Hammer carried by Water. Two Workmen have made the year past One Hundred Dozen. They compute Two & ½ Tuns of Iron and 2500 Bushels of Coal to make 100 Doz. The Owners are now erecting Works upon a larger Plan, to carry Three Trip hammers. They calculate to make 300 Doz yearly for the future and intend to use better Iron than what was work'd last year which was but in-different. The Price from 7 to 9 Dollars per Doz.

Cotton &
Wool
Cards

Mr Thompson has lately set up making Cotton & Wool Cards in the year past he has made about 12 Hundred pair, he intends to enlarge his Works and expects to make Three Thousand pair a Year.

Nails

Very little of this Business is carried on here possibly a Tun of Nail Brads may be worked up in a Year.
Our Black Smiths furnish the Husbandry and Mechanic Tools for the Inhabitants.
Mr Taylor is noted for makeing the best narrow Axes many of which are carried out of the State to Vermont. He makes about 300 a Year Price 6/.
About Ten Tuns of Iron is annually workd up in Suffield & about 10 Thousand Bushels of Coal.

Hides &
Tallow

400 Head of Beef Cattle are commonly Bucherd. in Suffield Annually exclusive of those which are killed by perticular Families for their own Consumption. The Hides are manufactured chiefly in Town. Mr Phelps carries on a large Branch of Bussiness and has a very convenient Yard and proper Buildings for the Works, he Usually Tans about 600 grown Hides & 400 Calf Skins besides Sheep and Other Skins. The Other Tanners in Town about 200 grown Hides and one Hund Calf

Skins. The price of Hides 2 ½ d calf Skin 5d Seal Leather 1/3 pr lb wt. The Tallow is usually sold to the Tallow Chandler and Soap Boilers in Hartford, fetches about 4d Ruff.

There are made about [39] more than what the Inhabitants want for their own Use which are mostly sold out of the state. The Other Branches of Leather Manufactures are mostly made in Town & consumed by the Inhabitants.

Mr Swan [40] commonly manufactures 5 or 6 Hundred wt. of Wool into Hats Yearly. He has made very considerable improvments in making Wool Hats. I have not seen Handsomer or better made Felt Hats either imported or manufactured in America. The price of Hatters Wool is about 2/3 pr lb. wt. Hats from 5/ to 12/.

This Manufacture was early introduced into Suffield in the Year 1761. Mr Zuell and Others Coy of Merchants in Glascow Scotland, Erected Works in this Town to make Potash, which they managed pretty largely for some Years. The Potash then Sold for 60 £ Sterling pr Ton (whether the Bounty was included in that Sum I am not able to say). Since those works were thrown up the Bussiness has been carried on by some of the Inhabitants. To this Time it is computed about 600 Bushels of Ashes will make a Tun after the Old Manner & Process. The New has never yet been tried here. The average price of Ashes about 7d delv'd at the Works. They make about 5 Tons a year which sells in New York for 30 or 31 lawful Money.

Grangers & Elys Mill erected on the west Bank of Connecticutt River, saws about 300 Thousand feet of Boards Plank and Other Stuff a year. There are 5 or 6 Other Mills in Town which Alltogether probably saw half as much more. Most of the Timber is white Pine floated down connecticutt River in the Spring Freshets. The average price of Boards about 33/ Lawful Mony pr Thousand. 400 Thousand Shingles are made Annually from Timber which comes down the River likewise price about 12/ pr Tousand.

39. Space left blank in MS.
40. Timothy Swan, a hatter and merchant, had come to Suffield from Worcester, Massachusetts, in 1782.

Wheel Carriages — Mr. Dewey [41] is noted for making the Best Wheels for Carriages of all Sorts. He makes some Chairs and Chaises every year but generally this kind of Work is for the Use of the Inhabitants and Also ye Cabinet work which is made in Town.

Casks — There may be a Thousand Casks made in Town yearly besides what the Inhabitants use for Cyder.

Salt Petre — Has been manufactured in the Time of the War, but is now imported cheaper than we can make it.

Earthern Ware — A Small Quantity of this Article is made in Town about 9 Kilns a year valued at 12 £ pr Kiln. This Bussiness was first set up here in 1782.

Wooden Dishes — The Ancient Characteristic Manufacture of Suffield is Over. Our Materials are gone.

Perhaps I have enumerated Articles in the foregoing Account, which were not expected if so you will use them or not according as you think proper. I am Sir with Respect & Esteem
  Your Humble Sert   Alexr. King

Honble: Roger Newberry Esquire

[ENCLOSURE]

John Treadwell to John Chester [42]

Farmington [Connecticut] Septr. 21st AD 1791

Sir
  Pursuant to your request I wrote to a Gentleman in each of the towns of Southington Berlin and Bristol for the necessary information on the subject manufactures in those towns, but have received no answer except from Mr Andrews of Southington.[43] The account he has given and the estimates he has made I have reason to conclude are

41. Presumably John Dewy of Suffield.
42. ALS, Hamilton Papers, Library of Congress.
  Treadwell was a member of the Connecticut Council. From 1776 to 1785 he had served in the Connecticut General Assembly.
43. Elezur Andrews.

pretty correct, and with very little variation, as to common manufactures, will apply to the towns of Berlin and Bristol whose circumstances are very simular to those of Southington regard being had to the number of inhabitants in the respective towns, and indeed for substance will apply to this Town, though I believe a greater proportion of foreign Cloths are used here than in those towns, and from a general view of the Subject I should conjecture that something more than one third of the whole expense of clothing the inhabitants of this town is laid out in foreign Articles.

The manufacture of articles of clothing in this town has hitherto been carried on in the family way chiefly and these manufactures particularly the woollen have of late, in some families attained a good degree of perfection. The woollen manufactuory at Hartford has contributed much to the defusion of knowledge in this branch to the people particularly in the vicinity, and in that respect, at least, has been highly useful, but the woollen & cotten manufactures of various fabrics and various qualities are carried on with apparent success, by a Mr. Brownson [44] of this town as a regular trade. He has employed for a year or two past perhaps about fifty persons in his Business though not all or the most of them at his factory. He expects the present year to make about ten thousand yards of cloth of woollen & cotten. Some of his fabrics are very fine and good, and generally his cloths, are found for service to excell those of like fineness that are imported, but he has not as yet been able to give them that complete finish which foreign cloths have, and consequently, they do not command that ready market in cash that imported cloths do. He finds a market for them however in the way of barter, but it commonly takes two or three turns before he can convert them into money and this is an inconvenience he cannot remove for want of proper machinery to give a high finish to his cloths, which his property will not enable him at present to procure. His profits however notwithstanding this disadvantage are sufficient to enable him to pursue the business, and he seems to be in a state of gradual progression toward perfection.

Mr Martin Bull of this Town a Goldsmith ⟨for⟩ about two years past set up the manufacture of Coa⟨t⟩ buttons being I suppose the first who has set up the business in this State. This manufacture is in its infancy but is however by no means unworthy of Notice in its present

44. Stephen Brownson.

state. The buttons are made of hardned tin, very serviceable and of a good appearance, and in no respect inferiour to a great proportion of imported buttons. He has made several thousand dozen, and informs me that a boy of sixteen may make 200 Gross in a year, the profits would be considerable were it not for the exceeding ⟨low⟩ price of some of the Matthewman buttons import⟨ed from⟩ Europe. He can afford them for 10/ pr gross for co⟨at &⟩ for vest buttons but it seems the Merchant will not take large quantities at that price as imported ones are something cheaper, a sample of the buttons is inclosed.

The manufacture of Hats is about to be carried on here upon a pretty large Scale. About twenty persons are expected to be employed in the House erected for that purpose but what success the Undertakers will have is uncertain. The furr branch of that business be sure labours under great embarrassments at present which cannot be removed without the aid of Government, whatever may be done with it.

Since the receipt of your Letter I have been wholly occupied in business I was appointed to do by the General Assembly in October last, and on that account have found it impracticable to pay that attention to this Subject, which was necessary to afford you the expected information or to do it within the time requested, add to this the failure of two of the Gentlemen to whom I wrote for information, I presume it will not be thought strange that the Information I am able to give you on the Subject is so very imperfect.

I am   Sir   your most obedt humbe Servt   John Treadwell

[E N C L O S U R E]

Elezur Andrews to John Treadwell [45]

Southington [Connecticut] Septemr. 14th. 1791

sir

Agreeable to your Request I have endeavoured to obtain such Knowledge as to give you as Just a statement as I possibly could as to the Manufactories in this Town.

It is not in my power to give you accurate account as I could wish. The greatest part of Woolen & Linen Cloaths wore in this Town are Manufactured by different Families in this place. (A very Small pro-

45. ALS, Hamilton Papers, Library of Congress.

portion of Foreign cloaths are made use of.) Silk is made by a number of Families in this Town. Hatts Chiefly worn by the Inhabitants are made in Town. Boots and shoes are mostly made of Leather Tanned in Town and by Shoemakers who reside here. We have an Oil Mill nearly compleated owned by Mr. Asa Barns which I believe will make a very considerable of oil from Flaxseed.

I have made an estimate not fully found on my own Judgment but the opinion of some Others of the undermentioned articles Manufactured in this Town & their prices.

2000. yards fulld. Cloath	at 4/6
1800. Do. not fulld. Do.	2/–
6000. Do. Linin Do.	1/2
800 Hatts . Do.	@ 6/–
80. p. Boots	24/.
2000 pr Shoes great & small	@ 5/–
1000 runs Silk	@

I am sir with Respect your huml servt.   E Andrews

[ENCLOSURE]

Chauncey Whittelsey to John Chester [46]

Middleton [Connecticut] Septr. 27th. 1791

Col: Chester

Sr:

I have recd. but two Letters in answer to those I wrote, in Consequence of your Application upon the Subject of Manufactures, one from Chatham, the other from Killingworth; the one from Killingworth was accompanied by one from Mr. Elliot [47] to Mr. Lane,[48] which I forward you as it contains some Information, upon the Subject of manufacturing Steel, which may eventually prove of some Consequence.

46. ALS, Hamilton Papers, Library of Congress.
Whittelsey had been quartermaster general for Connecticut during the American Revolution. He was elected to the Connecticut General Assembly and was appointed collector of customs at Middletown, Connecticut, in 1797.
47. Aaron Elliott was an iron manufacturer in Killingworth, Connecticut.
48. Hezekiah Lane, who had served in the commissary department during the American Revolution, was a member of the Connecticut legislature.

In the Town of Chatham are the two distilleries one of Rum, the other of Geneva, the one lattle set up, the other about eighteen years since, but did but little, untill last year; when the former distilled about 30,000 Gals, the latter about 10,000. There is likewise a forge for Iron, sett up thirty years agone, or more, but is at such a distance from the place of Landing, & the owners so poor, it is not carried on to very great Advantage, it produces but about twenty Tuns of Iron annually; which is sold for 25/. pr. hundd. There are two Quarries of Freestone, the one worked for a great Number of years, the other lately opened; from thence are obtained Stones for every use, for which those kind are proper, & which are there worked, for the various purposes for which designed. Parhaps it is the best Quary in this part of America.

In this town is a Snuff Mill, first set to work last fall, which has done some Business; what it is annuall produce will be is not easey to determin; the Snuff is sold in Bottles of half a pound each, for 30 Dolrs pr. Gross; the works are carried on under the protection of a Patent, granted to a Company at East Hartford.[49]

The Business of making pot & pearl Ashes, is carried on in several parts of this State; but as I have recd. no particular Information, I can only observe, that in this Town one sett of works makes about five Tuns annually.

We have in this Town a Stock of about 250 £ — L Money employed in a Linnen Manufactory. It is a temporary Matter sett agoing about two years & an half ago, for the purpose of an Experiment, by a Number of Subscribers; and will probably fail, when the term of their Subscription expires. The articles principally made, are coarse Linnens under the name of oznaburgs, of which are made about 4000 Yds in a Year, which are sold on an Average @ 10d. pr. Yd by the Bolt.

Checks sold @ 1/6 and upwards by the piece
Striped Linnens @ 1/6
Sheetings from 1/6 to 1/9

49. The snuff mill at East Hartford had been established in 1784 by William Pitkin. Pitkin had been granted by an act of the General Assembly of Connecticut, in May, 1784, "the Sole and exclusive Right and privelege of manufacturing all and every kinds of Snuffs in this State . . . for the Term of fourteen Years . . . and that he . . . be exempt for that Term from any Taxes or Assesment for or on account of said Business, or any Proffits that may thence arise" (*Connecticut State Records*, V, 400).

Of the last Articles no large Quantities are made.

The difficulty of disposing of the Goods for Cash in hand; & of getting a price that will afford a small profit on the Stock, is an embarrisment upon any Business of this kind.

Thro' out the County we are furnished with Tanners who supply Leather for almost if not quite every Use, for which it is wanted. This is wrought up by different Tradesmen, into the various Articles which are wanted by their several Customers, such as, Shoes, Boots, Saddles, Harnesses &c &c. Most of our riding Carriages are likewise made by our own Mekanicks.

The Smith supply us with Scythes & Axes, in Abundance; one Shop in this Town, turn out about one hundred Dozen of those Articles in a Year, which he sells for ten Dollars pr. dozen. This is done beside the other Smith work, he carries on.

The Articles of Nails is principally made among ourselves, and sold by retail 9d. pr. lb. The Business is carried on by our common Smiths; I am not acquainted with any, that make it their capital Object.

As to the domestic Manufactures from Woollen, Flax, Cotton, I can add nothing to the observations, you read to me when last at your house; The Subject is such as not to admit of vary exact Calculations, without more labour and expence than can be expected under present Circumstances. I can only observe in general, That our farmers are mostly clothed by the produce of their farms, improved by the labour of their Families; and those Woollens which are made in this, are parhaps equal to any in the World, for the use of the day-Labourer. Considerable Quantities of Cloth are made for the purposes of barter; in that Way as well as for private Cloathing the Manufactures of this State, appear to be continually extending themselves.

I omitted in its proper place to mention an Iron works in Killingworth set up in 1763 which manufactures about eight Tuns pr. Annum, and sells @ 30/. pr. C. In the same Town are three Works for Pot and Pearl Ashes, which manufacture, one that was erected in 1766, 3½ Tuns pr. Annum, one 1786, 26 Tuns, one lately set up, has worked but one Tun.

I am Sr: with Respect   Your Obedient Humble Servant

Chauncey Whittelsey

[ENCLOSURE]

Hezekiah Lane to Chauncey Whittelsey [50]

Killingworth [Connecticut] Sept. 16th. 1791

Sir

Since writing the Letter respecting Manufactures I have received this which I send you for more particular Information about the Steel Works.   Hezh: Lane

Chauncey Whittelsey Esq.
Middletown

[ENCLOSURE]

Aaron Elliott to Hezekiah Lane [51]

Killingworth [Connecticut] Sept 14th Ad 1791

Sir

Agreeable to your request of information, respecting the Steel Furnace, from the Supervisor of Middlesex County; for the information of the Secretary, of Congress; I would Observe

The Furnace, was built by My Father Colo Aaron Elliot, about Fivety, Yeares past, for the purpose of Manufacturing Blistered Steel. It was at first but small, for the sake of Experiment: afterwards inlargd, so as to contain about 25 Ct: (And was the only one in the New England States at the time of the act of Parlement prohibiting aney others being built)[52] And remain in that cituation untill the commencement of the War, between Great Britain, & the Colonies; at which time the demant became so great, that my Father found himself under the necessity if Inlarging it; which was accordingly done, so as to contain about 2 Tun 10 Ct.

My Father, usd commonly to Manufacture, about 40. or 50. Tuns pr. Year: The price he commonly sold at; was £ 42 Y: Mony, pr Tun. It might now be afforded at £32: as I have made sundry improve-

50. ALS, Hamilton Papers, Library of Congress.
51. ALS, Hamilton Papers, Library of Congress.
52. 23 Geo. II, C. 24 (1750).

ments, & lately, at considerable expence, Inlargd the Works to contain 4 Tun, at a blast; & with but small additional expence is manufacring of it. And were there sufficient encouragemt might easily, inlarge it now so as to contain 10. or 12 Tun.

As to encouragement from this State; there is none; of a bublik nature.

My circumstances, are such, that I am not able, to carrey it on extensively; I have manufatured this Year 4 Tun only; but the Works, is capable of Turning out One Hundred Ton, with Ease, Yearly.

As to Quality; I make Blister, & Faggt, Steel, which answers well, for all kinds of Country use. And had I encouragement, coud make German, Steel, equal in quality to aney made in Germaney.

In hast, am Sir, your Friend. & Humb. Servt   Aaron Elliott

Hezekiah Lane Esqr

[ENCLOSURE]

William Williams to John Chester [53]

Lebanon [Connecticut] 29 Sepr 1791

Sir

In answer to your Letter of ye 10th Augt Ulto. thro the multiplicity of Business & avocations, I am able to give you a very imperfect account of Manufactures in this County, & I suppose quite inadequate to the Secretarys Wishes. There are manufactures of Linnen Cloths carried on in very many Families in this Town & County, & large quantities are made, many private Looms for weavg in Families beside what is wove by those whose stated business it is, the Cloths are of perhaps every quality below superfine; and are sold at about the prices which foreign Linnens of the same fineness are, but generally more durable. Also large quantities of wool is spun up in Families, & generally wove by professors of that are, & dressed & prepared by the Clothiers of which there are three or four in this Town, & ye same proportion I believe in other Towns of ye County of Windham. The Cloths are of good qualities & various, most of them of the midling

53. ALS, Hamilton Papers, Library of Congress.
Williams, a signer of the Declaration of Independence, had been a member of the Continental Congress and at this time was serving on the Connecticut Council.

kind, very durable; Colours fixed & hansome of almost every hue are given them by the Dyers. There is one Cargill [54] at Pomfret who carries on the Clothier Business to a very considerable degree, one Condall [55] at Killingley. They manufacture large quantities of Woollen Cloths, many of them in Colour & quality fit for Gentlemen of any Character, also at Windham & such other Towns, Workmen who have considerable skill in the business. These Cloths, considering their quality & durability, are sold lower than imported Cloths, the particular quantities it is impossible for me to assertain, without more time & expense than can be afforded by one, who has spent almost all his hitherto Life in public Service with little emolument to himself thereby. The high price of Labour, & plenty of Lands prevent greater progress & perfection in these & other ⟨–⟩ of Manufactures. What is done in this County is by Individuals at their own cost & risque. The Genl Assembly granted a small Lottery for the encouragement of Condalls Works,[56] which I believe is not yet drawn. The Silk manufacture in this County is principally at Mansfield the best Information I can give you respecting that & sample of ye work, is contained in a Letter from Consnt Southworth Esq.[57] which is inclosed. There is a Cotton Manufacture in this Town set up about a year since by Majr Tilden [58] & 2 or 3 Partners. They have made considerable quantities of Fustian, Jeans & various Cloths, equal in Color & quality to the wishes of ye Consumers, & they are not deficient in Pride & ambition, they are I trust more durable than imported of the same quality, & are sold rather under. They have no public encouragement, & I fear will not be able to prosecute the business, to advantage much longer, without some public aid, their Buildings & Machinery having been expensive, & they not yet sufficiently furnished.

There [are] also almost every kind of Handy Crafts men among us professing the several Trades. Edge Tools of every kind are made in great perfection & the prices of all kinds of Manufactures are very much governed by that of imported, as the makers (think they) can't afford their articles under & cant get more.

54. Presumably Benjamin Cargell.
55. William Candal. See note 7.
56. See note 7.
57. Southworth, a resident of Mansfield, Connecticut, had served in the Connecticut legislature from 1770 to 1779.
58. Presumably Daniel Tilden of Lebanon.

I had ye fullest assurance of Col. Grosvenor,[59] of a particular Information relative to Cargill & Condalls, Woolen Factories, & have delay'd writing you on ye Acco. in daily expectation of it, but have yet reciv'd nothing.

All the Information I am able to give at prese⟨nt⟩ will be of little advantage to the Secretar⟨y⟩ I trust, but I hope & doubt not, but ⟨what⟩ he will obtain, aided by his own Genius ⟨and⟩ penetration will enable him to make a Report as satisfactory useful, & acceptable as they have hitherto been.

I am Sir with esteem & regard, your   most obedt & very humble Servant   Wm. Williams

PS if I sho'd. not attend ye Supreme Court of Errors, it will be on acco. of my concern with my two Sons, who were lately innoculated for ye small Pox at N London.
Happen to be out of paper, fit to use.

Honble Jno. Chester Esqr

[ENCLOSURE]

Constant Southworth to William Williams [60]

Mansfield [Connecticut] Septr 1st 1791

Sir

The manufactures carried on in this Town, are in the domestic way, and differ very little from those of other Towns in the County, except in the Article of Silk; Woollens and Linens are made here in most Families for domestic Use, and are many of them nearly equal in beauty to European Cloths of the second rate, and far exceed them in strength and durability.

The culture of the Mulberry tree and raising of Silk has been attended to, by a considerable number of people in this Town for some years past. It was first set on foot by Messrs. Hanks [61] and Aspenwall,[62] natives of this place, who became inspired with a sort of

59. Lemuel Grosvenor, a woolen manufacturer of Pomfret, Connecticut.
60. ALS, Hamilton Papers, Library of Congress.
61. Presumably Uriah or Benjamin Hanks of Mansfield.
62. Presumably Prince Aspenwell.

Agricultural enthusiasm, on reading the late Doct Elliots Treatise on Field Husbandry,[63] with great pains and after many disappointments they at length introduced the White Mulberry, which is now cultivated with great facility in a high and free Soil; low and marshy ground being unfavourable to this tree, by its exposure to the late, and early frosts in Spring and Autumn, which prove fatal oftener than the severity of Winter: there is made in this town the present year about Two hundred pounds weight of raw silk after being properly wound from the cacoons and dried; on which there is a Bounty given by Government of two pence per Ounce, to continue to the year 1794.[64] The business of Winding, or as it is commonly called realing the silk, is now well understood, though at first it was very indifferently performed. Silk is made from twelve pounds weight in a family, down to the Smallest quantity, without much detriment to other Business; two or three weeks however of laborious exercise, and Strict attention is necessary, for those who raise the largest Quantities. The Silk is of a good Quality, and might be wrought into the most Useful and elegant fabrics in the Silkway, could persons Skilled in the business be Obtained—by the force of genius and application *Some* have been produced; particularly handkerchiefs of the Barcelona Wale, Buttons in imitation of the Imperial, and ribbands of the Padusoy kind, all of which are very durable. As you Sir desire this information for the benifit of the Secretary of the Treasury of the United States, I have inclosed a sample of the Sewing Silk and buttons, into the former of which the raw silk is chiefly manufactured, and sold at much the same price with that imported. A number of persons concerned in this business applied to the Legislature of this State and Obtained a Charter of Incorporation in 1789 with ample powers; and exemption from taxation of public works they might erect, for the term of twelve years under the Name and Firm of the

63. Jared Eliot, *Essays upon Field Husbandry in New England, as It is or May be Ordered* (Boston, 1760).

64. In May, 1784, the Connecticut legislature had passed "An Act in alteration of the Act entituled an Act to promote the making of Raw Silk within this State" providing that "whoever shall make any Raw Silk from Worms and Mulberry Trees of his own raising within this State by properly winding the same from Balls or Cocoons after the first Day of July next and for ten Years next thereafter, shall as a Bounty from the Treasury of this State have and receive two pence lawfull Money for each ounce of such Silk well dryed, which such Person or Persons shall make as aforesaid, which Bounty shall be paid out of the Duties arising on the Importation of foreign Articles into this State" (*Connecticut State Records*, V, 342–43).

"Director, Inspectors and Company, of the Connecticut Society of Silk Manufacturers." [65] No special advantage can be derived from this grant, however generous, until workmen can be obtained Skilled at least in some One branch of the silk manufacture, I imagine *that* of Stockings would be the most advantagious as the Silk is capable of being so wrought as to make them both elegant and serviceable, and I think there are few gentlemen who would not be fond of Wearing American silk in that way. I have not a sample of the ribband by me, but you may be assured sir that it is the most durable of any thing possible that can be wrought, which has flexibility enough in it, to tie up the hair, for which purpose they are worn by the Honorable Mr Wadsworth [66] Representative in Congress, and by the Honble Mr Chester and other gentlemen in this State.

The culture of the Mulberry tree is increasing, and I believe it would be very easy in a few years for most families in this State to produce annually each one pound weight of raw silk without injury to other domestic business, *this,* with the larger quantities that would naturally be raised by many, whose situation was favourable in a particular degree, would find employment for Some, and amusement for others, and supersede the necessity of importing an Article which has long drained this State of her money and richest commodities. But you will pardon me Sir for presuming to hazard any Opinion on a Subject so diffuse, and be pleased to accept the above Information from Sir your most Obedient and very humble servant

Constant Southworth

Honorable William Williams Esqr

[E N C L O S U R E]

John Mix, Junior, to John Chester [67]

New Haven [Connecticut] October 5th 1791

Respected Sir

I had the Honour of receiving a Letter From you Dated 15th of September 1791 In which you are pleas'd to inform me of the Desire

65. The Company of Connecticut Silk Manufacturers was composed of a group of thirty-two Mansfield residents interested in developing the culture and manufacture of silk in Connecticut.
66. Jeremiah Wadsworth.
67. ALS, Hamilton Papers, Library of Congress.

of the Secretary of the Treasury to be Inform'd Relative to the different Manufactories which are carried on in this State, and as Sir the object of your writing me is with regard to the Button Manufactory in which I am Engaged, I have therefore Sir herewith inclosed a short detail with regard to my first motives of Seting up the business of the Progress of the same and the Quantity and Quality made at different Periods, and the main Obstacles that appear to me to be a great Barr and almost unsurmountable difficulty of Bringing the Button Manufactory to great Perfection. I have also herewith Inclos'd a Sample of the Buttons that are made at our Factory and the Number and Prises. I have not sent a Sample of Each Number that we make, but such a number of them that any Person will have an Idea of the Sorts & Sizes there made.

If Sir I have hereby Communicated any thing that will be Serviceable to my Country and Accepable to you and the Secretary of the Treasury, I shall think myself amply compensated for the Trouble.

I am Sir with Esteam and Respect Your most   Obedient and very humble servant   John Mix Junr.

Honoule. John Chester Esqr.

[ENCLOSURE]

John Mix, Junior, to John Chester [68]

New Haven [Connecticut] September 30th 1791

Sir

I was not bread up to any Mechanical Business, but had part of an Education at Yale College. After I left College I entered into the Mercantile Line, but Just at that time the War Coming on I entered into the Service with a Commition in which I remained untill my Ill State of health oblidged me to Quit the Service. Being ever a Friend and Supporter of the Rights of my Country and finding agriculture and Manufatories must be the main Supporters of the Country, I applyed my attention to find out some kind of Manufactories that had not met with the perticular attention of the Publick.

68. ALS, Hamilton Papers, Library of Congress.

In September 1789 I accidentally Cast my Eye on a Perticular hard metal Button; after Examination of it I was fully Persuaded in my own mind that I could find out the Composition, and that they might be made to advantages. I soon after this Communicated my Ideas with regard to this kind of Buttons to a Mr. Bradley of this Town. Not haveing the Button at that time I attempted to give him a Description of the kind, but he Endeavoured to discourage me with regard to the attempt, telling me that Mettal Buttons was Imported from Europe so Low that I could not find my Account in it. But this so far from discourageing me that it servd to Stimulate me to Attempt it. Some time in October following I Procured a Sample of those kind of Buttons which I shewed to Mr. Bradley (he being Skilld. in Metals) and after close Examination on the Subject he came fully into my Opinion and Said he did not doubt but they Could be made to good advantage and that he would assist me, and that he would make Experiments with me which we accordingly did. We pursueed different Experiments and methods with regard to the Composition from October 1789 to the December following, when after the Numberless & unwearied Prossesses we at length hitt on the right Composition. The Next matter was to form a method to make them, and to Construct machienery for the finishing, which we accomplished in a very Imperfect manner, and the first Buttons that we were able to make for Sale was on the 23rd of February 1790. I then undertook the Business by myself and I proseaded and made from time to time as Follows.

	Gross	Doz.
From the 23rd of February 1790 to the 8th of March was made 12 Gross of Vest Buttons & 3 Gross of Coat do.	15.	
From the 8th March to 21st of April was made 33 Gross Vest 16 Gross Coat	49	
To the 31st of may was made 51 Gross	51	6
To the 30 of June Do. 69 & 4 Dozs.	69	4
To the 31 of July Do Do. 137 & 9 dozn.	137.	9
In the month of August 199	199.	
In the month of September 279	279.	
In the month of October 259 ½	259.	6
In the month of November 286. 9	286.	9

		Gross	Doz.
		Gross	Doz.
In the month of December	297. 8	297.	8
In January 1791	218. 6	218.	6
To the 14th February	84	84	
		1947.	

The above Buttons would average about One Dollar & 1 third per Gross. Nineteen Hundred & forty Seven Gross I made as above while I carried on the works without any Partner from the 23rd of February 1790 to the 14th of February 1791, When I then took in as Partners with me Mr. Hommoor Barney & a Brother of Mine Mr. Jonathan Mix, under the Firm of Mix Barney & Co. In which Firm we continued to do Business with about (for the most Part) Twelve workmen Constently Imployed untill the 14th of August Last in which time there was made in Said Factory Twelve Hundred & Seventy Nine Gross of Buttons which would average about One Dollar and a half Per Gross and Seventy five Gross of Skelleton Rimd Buttons which would average Three Dollars and Two thirds per Gross. We here found that the Business Could be managed by Two of the Partners without the third.

My Brother Mr. Jonathan Mix & myself made a Proposal to Mr. Barney that we would Purchase all his Right Tittle & Interest in and unto all the Stock tools & Apperatus of Said Factory. Mr. Barney then made us an Offer what he would Sell for, and we Paid him accordingly and took the works to our Selves. The Factory is now Carried on by us under the Firm of John & Jonathan Mix. We have had made since the 14th of August to the first of October 479 Gross of Buttons which would avarage about One Dollar & a half per Gross.

Sir as to the advantages or Incouragement of making Buttons I would Answer Viz. we have ever found a market for what Buttons we Could make at some prise or other; but the greatest difficulty Lies in not not geting so good Pay as we could wish: the Reason is this there is such an amazing Quantity of Buttons Importd that the Importer will dispose of them at a very low rate for Cash and the retailer in general Sells his goods for Produce; therefore he will not give us our Prise, in Cash, we are Obligded to Sell, for or Rather Barter away our Buttons for articles which we are obligded to make a very great discount to get them Into money again in order to Purchase Stock, for we Cannot Purchase One Oze. of Stock without money. The Buttons that we manufactor are universally approved of and by Tryal are daily Proved to be Preferable to the Imported Buttons.

The greatest discouragement that at preasent appears to us, is that In Europe they have been apprised of our Manufactoring buttons in America and Even Samples to my knowledge have been Carried to Europe of Buttons made in My Factory. They are now Sending over great Quantityes which are Sold of the latest Importation for one Third less than what they were Sold for one Twelvemonth Past.

We therefore Earnestly wish and hope that Congress would Early in their Approaching Session take up the Matter with Spirit and resolution and Lay such heavy Duties on the Article of Buttons that it will amount to a Prohibition of Importing Buttons into this Country. We shall then be able to Enlarge our Button Factory in a Very advantagious and Exstensive manner boath for the Publick Benefit and our Own advantage. We herewith Inclose a Sample of Such Buttons as are made in our Factory. We are now able to Turn out upwards of Two Hundred different Sort Sizes & Figures. We have about a Dozen of Workmen Constantly Imployed and are daily making Improvements. In a word with Proper Incouragments from Congress in the Prohibition of Importing Buttons &c &c &c we should Soon Inlarge our Factory so that we would be able to Turn out upwards of Four thousand Pound Sterling worth of Buttons Yearly.

John & Jonathan Mix

I am with Esteam Your most Obedient & very Humble servant

John Mix Junr.

The Honourable John Chester Esqr.

[ENCLOSURE]

John Mix, Junior, to John Chester [69]

New Haven [Connecticut] October 7th 1791

Respected Sir

Being in a very Great hurry and a Croud of business I did not give

69. ALS, Hamilton Papers, Library of Congress.

You so Perticular an account of the Skelleton Rimd. Buttons, (when I wrote you on the subject of the Button Manufactory.) as I could have wished. I therefore take this Opportunity to inform you Sir.

The Skelleton Rimd. Buttons are of those kinds which I gave you a Sample of some with Cloath with white Rims, and some with yallow, and some White Hard metal Buttons with white Rims, and some with Yallow. They are a kind of Button much Approved of, by the first Class of People, and are used on Superfine and Midling Cloaths. The Manufacturing of them is attended with a Considerable Expence and I never have hear'd of thier being made in any other Button Factory on the Continent of America but ours. The ground work of these Kind of Buttons are made much in the same manner as our Common white metal Buttons are But the makeing of the Rimms is attended with much the greatest Labour. The white Rimms. are made with Silver Plated on Copper which is thick; this goes through the Plating Mill a great number of times untill it is very thin. Then Mashienery is Constructed for Cuting out the rimms, another for Raising them and a second & third and so on that the Button and Rimm is Carried through upwards of Twenty hands or ⟨o⟩therwise handled as many times before it is fit for Market, the Stock is but trifeling the Labour and Mashienery is much the greatest on those Kind of Buttons. The Yallow Rimd is much the same Except Puting on the Silver onto the Copper. We are now Enlarging this Branch of Buttons and mean to Carry it on Exstensively with the others if we Can have Incouragement. It must of Course be a great Saving to the Country by keeping the money with us which Otherwise would be sent away in Large Quantities for the high pris'd Buttons which are not equal in Beauty goodness & Doration to those we make. There has been great Quantities of Rimd. Buttons Import from Europe which have been Sold for One Dollar & a Quarter per Dozen (Coat Buttons) which are far Inferior to ours of the Same Kind which we Sell for Six Dollars per Gross.

Sir I would Likewise Inform you that we are making Preparations for Manufactorying the Common Horn Button, and the Best Kind of Horn Buttons. Also the Paper Japand. Butt⟨on⟩. We have a Person Lately from Europe who has the Skill perfectly who is a Gentleman who is able and has Engaged to Instruct and teach us every thing Necessary in the making of them, and the Constructing the Tools and Apparatus to Carry on the same to advantage, Provided we Can have the Patronage and Support of Goverment.

I am Sir with Esteam and Respect, Your most　Obedient & very Humble servant　　　　　　　　　　　　　　　John Mix Junr.

P.S. For perticular reasons I said nothing to you Sir on the Subject of the Last mentioned Buttons, neither would I wish to have it Communicated at present to any this Side of New York.

Honle. John Chester Esqr.

[ENCLOSURE]

John Mix, Junior, to John Chester [70]

Newhaven [Connecticut] October 8th 1791.

Sir

Doubtless you may remember that I mentioned a word to you at my house with regard to my Supplying the Federal Armey with Buttons from our Factory, and that I wished for your Patronage and Influence in the matter. If Sir it is agreeable to you to mention the matter to the Secretary, I should take it as a favour. We should be able to Furnish at a very reasonable rate, and would Put USA on Each Button or any other figure or Divise that Should be required. I am Sir with Esteam &c &c Yours　　　　　　　　　　　　　　　John Mix Junr.

Honl John Chester Esq

70. ALS, Hamilton Papers, Library of Congress.

From Nathaniel Hazard

[New York, October 11, 1791]

Sir

My Friend Robert Fearon [1] Esquire, will have the Honor of delivering this to you. He is the Nephew of John Foxcroft Esquire, the late British Post Master General.[2] He has Business in Virginia to transact, respecting the Affairs of a Coll. Mercer, in which the President of the

United States had some personal Agency, so far back as 1773.[3]

He wished to know from me, in what Mode he could with most Propriety, introduce private Business, to so distinguished a public Character. I advised him to get a Line from some of his numerous respectable Acquaintances, to the Secretary of the Treasury, whose Politeness to his Countrymen of all Ranks, who wish Access to him, would doubtless be readily extended to an European Gentleman.

When we were together at Philadelphia, he learned from me, that I had paid my Respects, Sir to you, as a revered, former Fellow Citizen, & had received those Civilities, which are uniformly shewn to all such of them, as waited upon you for your Commands.

Mr. Fearon's Selection of me, as a Favor to him, is what I should wish for as an Honor, if personal Acquaintance would warrant it.

To a Desire solely, of gratifying the Wish of *a Gentleman in a strange land*, I am indebted for both the Occasion, & the Honor of, subscribing myself, at this Time,

With the highest Respect   Sir   Your most obedient, & very humble servant   Nathl. Hazard

New york 11th. Octor. 1791

ALS, Hamilton Papers, Library of Congress.
    1. See the second letter from Hazard to H, October 11, 1791.
    2. In 1761 John Foxcroft of New York became Benjamin Franklin's associate as joint Postmaster General for the colonies. Foxcroft, unlike Franklin, remained loyal to the Crown. After the American Revolution he was the New York agent for the British packets until his death on May 5, 1790.
    3. George Mercer, who rose to the rank of lieutenant colonel in the Second Virginia Regiment during the French and Indian War. In discussing Washington's varied activities in 1773, Douglas Southall Freeman has written:
    "Washington now disclosed once more his familiar weakness in being unwilling to say 'No' to a request that meant a material increase in the load of business he already carried. John Mercer, the able and contentious attorney who possessed vast appetite for land, had died on the 14th of October, 1768, at the age of 64. He left much property . . . and many debts. His son James was so interested in the law that he neglected his own affairs; George, the other son, Washington's former aide, remained in England, where he had a romantic but, for the time being, an impoverished marriage. Soon it was thought that George Mercer's bride would receive a fortune, in anticipation of which he had high-priced slaves purchased in considerable number for his Virginia plantations. At the next turn of the wheel, George and James Mercer were at cross purposes and with their interests so confused that Washington and one or two other of their friends had to try to untangle many transactions. Washington, as usual, had most of the work to do." (Freeman, *Washington,* III, 330–31.)

From Nathaniel Hazard

[New York, October 11, 1791]

Sir

I should not have so soon addressed you again but to apologize for a Freedom, I reluctantly took, & would not have done *for any American*.[1] An english Gentleman Robert Fearon Esqr. has Business respecting the Estate & Affairs of a Coll. Mercer in Virginia, in which in 1773 the President had a personal Agency. At his Request, I *barely* present him for *official Information*. He is the Gentleman who dined with me in Company lately with Dr. Johnson [2] & Mr. Wolcott.[3] He has been regularly bred to the Law at the Temple, & came out from England to Virginia, from whence his Uncle John Foxcroft Esqr. I believe originally came, I mean the late Postmaster General. He has Letters from Governor Franklyn [4] & others to distinguished Characters in America. He is here much caressed by the English. He does not admire however I find Sir John Temple.[5] I became acquainted with Mr. Fearon on my late Journey to Philadelphia, I found him a polite amiable young Gentleman, & was flattered with the Attachment he shewed me after I had apprised him, to prevent Misapprehension, that I was a plain Citizen & not a fashionable Man. He hurried from Philad to return with me. We had a gay & agreeable Tour especially on our Way to Philad, attended with some very odd & laughable Adventures. He had Letters to the British Consul,[6] & several eminent Merchants in Philad. He barely made his Bow to the Consul. His Wish is an american Introduction, & no Doubt he has Curiosity to see the American Premier. The Earl of Wycombe's [7] three Curiosities are to see New England, the President, & Premier. Mr. Fearon who returns to England in the Spring, will give a better Account of America, I suspect, than the Marquis of Lansdowne's Son. He staid a very few Days in New york. Dr. Johnson dined one Day with him at Sir John's; he said he was a well behaved young Gentleman & appeared to be fond of Information. Sir John asked Leave of Coll. Burr [8] to introduce him, he I believe never went. He travelled Post thro' New England. Dr. Dwight [9] (who was lately in Town) marvelled that he left New haven, on Commencement Day. He is to go from Boston to Virginia by Sea. If this is the british Mode of acquiring Information—God help them! I presume this young Lord will be a proper Bureau Aid du Camp to Lord Sheffield; who I pray fervently will attack Mr. Coxe.[10] I should glory in volunteering with him, as an Aid.

Mr. Fearon returns to America to settle in his Profession in Virginia. He is an *unbiassed* young Englishman, offers well as to at least decent Abilities. His Billetts discover Wit, as well as Politesse. I mean to correspond with him, when he settles, & learn truly the Interior of So. Politics. He is domestic with a Number of principle People there. An ill Impression has been attempted upon him, as to the President's Inacessibility & Distance; it was done by a *Refugee* Officer. I effaced it. Fearon is domestic with Governor Franklyn, yet appears to be a Whig. He is observant, & I dare say the British Premier will catechise him.

I go to Connecticut to attend the Assembly with my fraternal Friend, Mr. Maxwell [11] on Business, he has Edwards [12] our Advocate & Pilot. I will press Turn Pike Roads & the national Manufactures in Jersey upon my Connecticut acquaintance. Laurence will I beleive try it here in January.[13] I will write from New haven.

Vale

P.S. I am afraid you will think me intrusive in Fearon's Business. A Letter to Mr. Coxe, would not have gratified him. He told me, thus "Bond will I know, present me in Form, but I want to reconnoitre 'en famille' both President & Premier." I also feel uneasy at my last, unguarded, written Chat. As a public Man, I respect you more highly than any Man living, Ledyard's Death, *as a Friend*, ought to wound me more deeply that any private Man's in Existence.[14] I know your Time is more than filled up. I wish *barely* Three Words "All is well" & two Letters—thus, A.H.

Inclosed is Peter Pendulum.[15] It came from the East. O. W.[16] when here said Halt! on that Business. I have wrote Halt! & I mean to *say* Halt! next Week. I have sent unknown to Fenno [17] "Ventoso." [18] It is a general & liberal Squib. There is a Parson Palmer [19] at Philadelphia, an Universalist. I will borrow your Envelope. Please to read the next Letter, I write to him, & *suppress* it, if you think best.

Bogert [20] can explain, why I trouble you now with my Letter to him, if an Apology is necessary.

Octor. 11th. 1791

ALS, Hamilton Papers, Library of Congress.

1. See Hazard's first letter of October 11 to H.

2. William Samuel Johnson was president of Columbia College from 1787 to 1800. He had been a delegate from Connecticut to the Constitutional Convention and was one of the first two Senators elected from Connecticut. He resigned from the Senate in 1791 because the shift in the Government from New York City to Philadelphia would have made it impossible to continue his duties as president of Columbia.

3. Oliver Wolcott, Sr.

4. William Franklin, the son of Benjamin Franklin, had been the royal governor of New Jersey from 1763 to 1776. A Tory, he lived in England after the American Revolution.

5. Temple was British consul general at New York.

6. Phineas Bond was British consul at Philadelphia.

7. Earl Wycombe, son of the Marquis of Lansdowne, inherited his father's titles in 1805.

8. Aaron Burr.

9. Timothy Dwight, a Congregational minister who in 1795 became president of Yale College, was at this time the head of a coeducational school in Greenfield Hill, Connecticut.

10. Tench Coxe in 1791 wrote a rebuttal entitled *A Brief Examination of Lord Sheffield's Observations on the Commerce of the United States* (Philadelphia, 1791) to Lord Sheffield's *Observations on the Commerce of the American States with Europe and the West Indies; including the several articles of import and export; and on the tendency of a bill now depending in Parliament* (London; J. Debrett, 1783).

11. William Maxwell was a New York City tobacconist and merchant. An entry for October, 1791, in the records of the Connecticut Assembly reads as follows: "Upon the Memorial of William Maxwell of New York Shewing to this Assembly that at the Time the British Army took possession of New York in September 1776, he was possessed of Bills of Credit emitted by this State to the Amount of £567.5.0 Lawfull Money which he hath retained in his Possession to this Time and was unavoidably prevented from Lodging them in the Treasury of this State agreeably to the requirement of an Act of this Assembly passed in the year 1778" (*Connecticut State Records*, VII, 364).

12. Pierpont Edwards, the youngest son of Jonathan Edwards, was United States attorney for the District of Connecticut.

13. This is a reference to either Nathaniel Lawrence, an assemblyman from Queens, or John Laurance, a New York City lawyer and a close friend of H, who at this time was a member of the House of Representatives.

14. Presumably this is a reference to Isaac Ledyard's attempt to secure the Federalist nomination for Aaron Burr in the New York gubernatorial election in 1792. See Ledyard to H, February 1, 1792.

15. This is a reference to an article, dated October 1, 1791, and signed "Peter Pendulum," which was reprinted from the *New York Daily Gazette* in *The* [Hartford] *Connecticut Courant*, October 24, 1791. The article satirized the attacks on John Adams which the Republicans made in the summer and fall of 1791. Presumably the article was sent to Hazard before it was published.

16. Oliver Wolcott, Sr.

17. John Fenno, publisher of the [Philadelphia] *Gazette of the United States.*

18. This newspaper article was published in the [Philadelphia] *Gazette of the United States,* October 22, 1791.

19. Elihu Palmer, a native of Connecticut, who had preached in 1788 and 1789 in a Presbyterian church in Newton, Long Island, had been forced after six months to relinquish his pulpit because of disagreement with church policy. He then went to Philadelphia where he preached as a Universalist.

20. Cornelius J. Bogart, a New York City lawyer, was a member of the New York Assembly in 1791.

From Jeremiah Olney

Custom House
Providence 11th. October 1791

Sir.

In directing the District Attorney to file a Libel against the Brigt. Betsey, John Arnold Master, from Bordeaux, and then acquainting you with the Case and the favorable circumstances attending the breach of the Law, I acted, in my Idea, so perfectly consonant to a plain and positive Law, and your Instructions, that I thought Malice itself could not blame me;[1] but some Interested Men (particularly Welcome Arnold Esquire, who was before much offended with me for putting his Bond in Suit)[2] have clamoured loudly against me, with a view of exciting Prejudices in the Minds of some Persons unfavorable to the executive part of my Conduct: They say I had no right, when it appeared there was fraud intended, to have given the information to the Attorney, until after I had received your directions to do it; That after the information was given, it was my Duty, on application of the Owner, to have taken a Bond, and released the Vessel; That even after the Libel was filed and a special Court ordered by the Judge to be held on the 17th instant in this Town, it was in my power to withdraw the Action; and which, on the receipt of your Letter of the 24th ulto., it was my Duty immediately to do, that she might proceed on a foreign Voyage. As neither the Law nor your Instructions submit anything to my discretion in the Case of this Vessel, I conceived myself not warranted to comply with the several particulars above mentioned, the first of which was not Requested, but is now said to be what I ought to have done. I am anxious to do my Duty, and whatever I believe that to be I shall invariably execute, regarless of the Consequences; but then it is certainly reasonable to Hope for, and I flatter myself I shall have, your Approbation and Support. If Sir, it shall appear to you that I have done my Duty in this Affair, I respectfully and earnestly entreat, in order to heal my wounded Feelings, that you would generously signify your Approbation of my Conduct at an early period.

With the highest respect, I have the honor to be &c.

Jereh. Olney Collr.

Alexr. Hamilton Esqr.
Secy of the Treasury.

ADfS, Rhode Island Historical Society, Providence; copy, RG 56, Letters from the Collector at Providence, National Archives.
1. See Olney to H, September 15, 1791, and H to Olney, September 24, 1791.
2. See Olney to H, July 19, 1791; Welcome Arnold to H, July 15, 1791; H to Arnold, July 22, 1791; H to Olney, July 22, 1791.

To George Washington

[Philadelphia, October 11, 1791]

Sir,

The Post of this day has brought me your letter of the 7th. instant,[1] the commands of which shall with great care & no less pleasure be executed.

I wrote you on the sixth a letter; of which the enclosed is a copy.

With the truest & most respectful attachment, I have the honor to remain Sir, &c.

A. Hamilton

Philadelphia
11th. Octo: 1791.

LC, George Washington Papers, Library of Congress.
1. Letter not found.

To George Washington

Philadelphia
Octr. 11. 1791

Sir

Lord Wycomb [1] having mentioned to me his intention to pay you his respects at Mount Vernon, I beg your permission to present him to you.

The personal acquirements and merits of his Lordship conspire with a consideration for the friendly dispositions and liberal policy of his father, the Marquis of Lansdown, towards this country, to constitute a claim in his favour to cordial notice.

I have the honor to be With the most respectful attachment, Sir, Your obedient & humble servant   A Hamilton

The President of the United States

ALS, George Washington Papers, Library of Congress; copy, Hamilton Papers, Library of Congress.
    1. Earl Wycombe. See Nathaniel Hazard to H, October 11, 1791.

To Otho H. Williams

Treasury Department
Octr. 11th. 1791.

Sir,

Your letter of the 3rd instant has been received. There can be no doubt that horses and other live stock imported from foreign countries must be considered as an object of trade, or vendible commodity, and of course as subject to duties.

To obviate the adoption of this rule in a general sense, I think it however necessary to observe that I consider negroes to be exempted from duties on importation. A formal question has in another case been put to me on this point.[1]

I am   Sir   Your obedt Servant   A Hamilton

Otho. H. Williams Esqr
Collr. Baltimore

LS, Columbia University Libraries.
    1. This sentence is in H's handwriting.

To Edmund Randolph

[*Philadelphia, October 12, 1791.* On October 18, 1791, Randolph wrote to Hamilton: "The attorney-general of the United States does himself the honor of replying to the questions, propounded by the secretary of the Treasury of the United States, in his letter of the 12th of October 1791." *Letter not found.*]

From Nathaniel Gorham [1]

Boston Oct. 13th 1791.

Sir

In contemplating yours relative to the manufactories of this State,[2] I am apprehensive we shall not make so good a figure as in reality we ought to do and the reason is that the goods & articles made in this State are of such a nature as not to appear in a very conspicuous light, altho they are not the less usefull.

About twenty years ago the importation of European goods into this State was nearly double to what it is at present. This will be accounted for by some People by asserting that the Connecticut trade has taken a turn from hence to N York. This is in a great degree true, but it must be observed that this place never posse⟨ss⟩ed the whole of it; a considerable part allways going to N York.

But it is further to be observed that a great part of New Hampshire & allmost all Vermont has come into existence since the period above mentioned, & a great part of those People come down to Boston to trade especially in the Winter, fully equal in my opinion to those who came from Connecticut—besides which the People in this State have very much increased within twenty Years.

How then is it to be accounted for that the Importations are not now so large? I answer because the People in their own Families & for their own use manufacture double to what they did 20 years ago. It is now worth the observation of the curious traveler through N England to observe (more especially out of the great Roads) the cloathing of the Country Family, & he will find their common cloath allmost wholly made by themselves. Let him at night veiw the Bed & beding & he will find it the same from the Bed Tyck to the Pillow case. This has given a most powerful check to the importations, &

ALS, Hamilton Papers, Library of Congress.
1. Gorham was supervisor of the revenue for Massachusetts.
2. See "Treasury Department Circular to the Supervisors of the Revenue," June 22, 1791.

with other concuring causes has rendered the People of this Country at the present moment the happiest on the face of the Earth & so far as I can recollect historey, does not furnish any instance of a People equally happy. In short I believe it is not in the case of Human nature to be exceeded & the People seem sensible of it—all uneasiness and murmuring being at an end & good humour & chearfullness universally privaling. Those branches of business that are carried on to any effect & of importance are contained in the several inclosed papers. They will some or all of them probably succeed which will be a stimulous to further attempts, & I believe little or no doubt can be entertained but that we shall be manufacturing as fast as circumstances make it necessary or convenient.

I am with great esteem & regard Sir Your Most Humble Servt
Nath Gorham

Hon Alexander Hamilton Esqr

[E N C L O S U R E] [3]

The Sail Cloth Factory in Boston [4] employs about 200 Women & Girls together with about 50 Men, the whole of the latter with a major part of the former depend solely on the factory for a maintenance. At present only 30 Looms are improv'd, which produce from 45 to 50 pieces of Duck ℔ week, though the Works are Capable of turning out 90 or 100 ps ℔ week, provided a sufficient supply of Flax could be obtain, and at a price that would envisage the prosecution of it to that extent.

The Government Bounty [5] of 8/ a ps. (which ceases at the close of this year) enables the Proprietors to give the present high price of 6½d Le Mony pr. ld for Flax: but should that exorbitant price continue & the Legislature refuse any further aid, the Proprietors must be necessitated, either to advance upon the price of their Cloth or *discontinue* the Manufacture, as hitherto it has not afforded a profit of one pr Cent (independent of the Bounty) upon the Capital em-

3. D, Hamilton Papers, Library of Congress.
4. The Boston Duck or Sail Manufactory had been established in 1788. See Samuel Breck to H, September 3, 1791.
5. See Breck to H, September 3, 1791, note 5.

ploy'd. In the first case the Merchant who purchases the Cloth would be disgusted, and would again commence the Importation of Russian Canvas and would undersell them so far, as to discourage the use of the American Cloth; so that either alternative must terminate in the Abolition of the Manufacture.

The Buildings already erected have cost upwards of 4000 Dollars, and the Tools &ca employ'd have stood them in above 2200 Dollars, so that 6200 Dollars of the Capital remains totally inactive, and Should the Proprietors be reduc'd to the necessity of annihilating the Business they must be subjected to *at least* the loss of one half the cost of the Buildings & Tools. But on the other hand, Should the General Government or their own State continue to patronize it by affording a Bounty or laying an additional Duty on *foreign Duck* they may encourage the present Proprietors to continue the Business till such time as the Country may get into the practise of growing three times the quantity of flax they do at present, when, & not till then will the article be obtain'd at a rational price, as previous to the Revolution & at the Commencemt: of the Manufacture the best of flax could be bought at 4 d & 4¼ d. pr. ld which shews the necessity that the Cultivation of the Raw Material should go *hand in hand* wth ye Manufactures.

[ENCLOSURE] [6]

The State of the Nail Manufacture in this Commonwealth is rather discouraging, at present, than otherways, as there is not sufficient brought to the Market to answer the Demand, owing in some measure to ye increas'd cultivation of their farms, as most of the workmen in that Business are Farmers, and attend to the Nail making, only in the Winter season, except in the Towns of Bridgwater, Norton & Taunton, where they have regular & Steady Establishments that affords constant employment to a great number of workmen, one concern only in the latter Town turns out a hundred ton of Nails in a year. And the Deficiency of the business may in some part be owing to an Act of the Legislature, that obliges the several sizes of Nails to be made of a proper length & thickness So as to afford a thousand nails

6. D, Hamilton Papers, Library of Congress.

for the weight assignd to each Denomination,[7] which checks their obstinate propensity, *to do as they please*, and fabricate the Nails So large as to count only 800 for the weight that ought to produce a 1000. The price being advanc'd from 5/9 to 6/8 ℔ m for 10d Nails by the Cask, will induce great exertions in the Manufacture after ye harvest is in.

Previous to the Revolution there were annually Imported into this Commonwealth about 7 or 800 ton of Nails, and for several years past very *inconsiderable* quantities have been brought from Europe. So that insted of depending on a foreign supply they have not only manufactur'd Sufficient for home Consumption but have *exported* large quantities to the southern states.

[ENCLOSURE][8]

The various manufactories of the Commonwealth of Massachusetts, finish upwards of Ten Thousand dozen pair of cotton and wool cards yearly; two thirds of these are exported to the several States; they average at the price of Five Dollars and an half per dozen, and produce Fifty five thousand dollars. Four fifths of the whole are made in the Town of Boston. One house alone completes Six thousand dozen per annum: This gives employment to at least One thousand Six hundred women and children, who stick them: If to them, we add the great number of persons, who are busied in manufacturing Thirty thousand Sheep Skins; those who make eight million of Tacks; others engaged in the wood work; and the hands employed in cutting wire, and completing the cards, this manufacture may be allowed to furnish the principal means of subsistence to Two thousand five hundred people.

About one hundred and fifty casks of wire at Twenty five pounds per cask, are imported annually, which is all that depends on a foreign source. There is a hope, that even this trivial import will shortly cease, as some ingenious mechanicks have in contemplation a work of this kind.

The importation of tacks, which at the commencement of these

7. "An Act for Regulating the Manufacture of Nails Within this Commonwealth, & for Repealing All Laws Heretofore Made for that Purpose," *Acts and Laws of the Commonwealth of Massachusetts,* 1790–1791 (Boston, 1895), 72–74 [March 10, 1791].
8. D, Hamilton Papers, Library of Congress.

works, was common, is now nearly abolished. The tacksmiths, within Twenty miles of the capital, furnish sufficient for home consumption, and export a great quantity abroad.

The manufactory of Mr. Giles Richards and company,[9] is reputed the largest in the Commonwealth. Their improvements in cutting wire have excited the attention of Judicious Europeans; and models of two of their principal machines, were lately purchased by an English Gentleman for nearly one hundred pounds sterling. These Gentlemen are daily profiting by new and happy inventions, which diminish the toil of labor, expedite work, and lessen the price of cards. The present year they have completed machines, for cutting boards, which form both the concave and convex parts, to great perfection, at a very few strokes. A lath, is also invented for turning the handles either oval, flat or round, with great ease and facility. At present the works are in such perfection, that Eight men can turn out Fifty dozen per day.

9. Giles Richards and Company operated a wool and cotton card factory at No. 2 Hanover Street in Boston.

From Timothy Pickering

Philadelphia Octr. 13. 1791.

Dear Sir,

When I received your letter of the 13th of August,[1] I did not consider it with the attention which would have been necessary if at that time I had attempted to answer the questions you propose. Now it appears to me impossible to do it, with any degree of precision. It then struck me that certain communications to the Society of Agriculture of this city [2] would have furnished the principal documents required, on the subject at large: but upon a review of them (after a lapse of several years,) I find I was mistaken.

In my late absence from the city, I meant to have made enquiries, in the counties thro' which I travelled in this state; but here also I was disappointed; not meeting with any farmers sufficiently informed.

From the farms in my neighbourhood [3] (from which you naturally expected me to collect accurate information) no conclusions can be drawn. Their peculiar situation in respect to title & their quality rendering them exceptions to most of the farms in the United States.

Their title being in suspense between the claimants under Connecticut
& Pennsylvania, prevents their due cultivation & improvement; and the
parts under cultivation are almost exclusively the bottom (or inter-
vale) lands adjacent to the river susquehannah and its branches. The
residue of the country is without inclosures, where the cattle range
at large, and where, till within four years past, the people cut wood
for timber & fuel at discretion, without regarding their own lines of
property. This singular state of the Wyoming farms precludes the
idea of fixing their value. Their contents, generally are 300 acres, of
which, upon an average, not 30 acres are reclaimed from a state of
nature. The average produce of their cultivated grounds I estimate as
follows—

Wheat	15 bushels per acre	
Rye	12	
Oats	25	Without
Buckwheat	15	manure.
Indian Corn	25	
Hay	1½ ton	

Mr. Bordley of Maryland (in a pamphlet published in 1784)[4] remarks,
That Mr. Young,[5] the English Travelling farmer, has ascertained, that
289 acres are the average size of farms in England; of which 140 are
in grass; & the remaining 149 are called arable; altho' only 112 give
crops; the residue, 37 acres, contains the buildings, orchard &c. Mr.
Bordley estimates the average size of Maryland farms at 240 or 250
acres exclusive of woods; and their average produce at 6 bushels of
wheat & 12 of Indian Corn per acre. An intelligent Jersey farmer
(in a communication to the Agricultural Society here) rated the
average produce of wheat in that state to be under 6 bushels. Doctor
Tilton [6] thus states the produce of land in the Delaware state "an
acre of ground will produce of Timothy from one to two tons of
dry forage; of red clover, from 2 to 3 tons; of Indian corn, from
15 to 50 bushels; of wheat from 6 to 20 bushels; of barley and rye,
from 10 to 35 bushels; of oats and buckwheat from 15 to 30 bushels;
of Irish potatoes, from 100 to 300 bushels." If the doctor meant that
the mean quantities should be considered as the average produce, the
land in the Delaware state must be more fertile or better cultivated
than the land of any of the old states in the union.

I have made a few enquiries relative to the sizes of farms and their divisions into meadows, pastures, arable & wood land, in this state & Connecticut: but the answers were not satisfactory; and as your application to me respected only land in "my quarter" it may be useless to state them.

As it is thus in my power to give you only such very imperfect information relative to the subject of your investigation, I hope you may have taken measures to obtain from others what will answer your design. I think, however, it will be impossible to ascertain the requisite facts with precision: for I doubt whither one American farmer in a thousand has determined by actual admeasurement, the sizes of his fields and their produce.

I am & c.

A. Hamilton Esqr.
Secy of the Treasury

ADF, Massachusetts Historical Society, Boston.
1. "Treasury Department Circular," August 13, 1791.
2. The Philadelphia Society for the Promotion of Agriculture, which had been founded in 1785.
3. Pickering's farm was in Luzerne County, Pennsylvania. This was in the Wyoming Valley, which was claimed by both Pennsylvania and Connecticut.
4. John Beale Bordley, *A Summary View of the Courses of Crops, in the Husbandry of England & Maryland; with a Comparison of their Products; and a System of Improved Courses, Proposed for Farms in America* (Philadelphia, 1784).
5. Arthur Young was at this time editing the *Annals of Agriculture*, which continued publication until 1809.
6. Dr. James Tilton served as a physician with the Continental Army throughout the American Revolution. After the war he practiced medicine in Dover, Delaware, served in the Continental Congress in 1783 and 1784, and was commissioner of loans for Delaware from 1785 to 1801. He eventually gave up the practice of medicine to devote his time to farming. He wrote several essays on agriculture.

From William Seton

[New York] 13th. October 1791

Sir

I am honored with your Letters of the 8th & 10th. The Commissioner of Loans [1] not having required the anticipated Credit of Twenty Thousand Dollars, the Treasurers Check for Thirty thousand

Dollars is all that has passed to his Credit. I delivered your Letter to the Commr. of Loans upon the subject of the Transfer to the Books of the Treasury for the Debt purchased by me for Account of the United States,[2] and as soon as he receives a supply of Books (I think he termd it so) he would be able to comply with your request and to furnish me with the Certificate necessary to be transmitted to you, which between this and Monday he expects to do.

I have the honor to be &c.

LC, Bank of New York, New York City.
    1. John Cochran.
    2. Letter not found. See H to Seton, October 3, 8, 10, 1791; Seton to H, October 1, 6, 7, 1791.

From William Ellery

Collector's Office [Newport, Rhode Island]
Oct. 14th 1791

Sir

Inclosed is the form of the bond and oath given and taken by the Exporters of Distilled Spirits in this District. Please to revise, and correct them, and return them, or to furnish me with other forms as soon as may be convenient.

It is made a question whether by the addition to the provisions contained in the fortieth and forty-first Sects. of the Act intituled an Act to prove more effectually for the Collection of duties &c the privilege of giving bond with Condition for the payment of the duties on teas in two years from the date of the bond is extended to teas imported from Europe or from any other Country than China.[1] An early solution of this question will greatly oblige &c.[2]

I am Sir Yr. most obedt: servant   Wm Ellery Collr

A Hamilton Esqr.
Secry Treasy.

LC, Newport Historical Society, Newport, Rhode Island.
    1. This reference is actually to Sections 41 and 42 of "An Act to provide more effectually for the collection of the duties imposed by law on goods, wares and merchandise imported into the United States and on the tonnage of ships or vessels" (1 Stat. 168–69 [August 4, 1790]). For the mistake in numbering the sections of the Collection Law, see H to Richard Harison, April 26, 1791, note 2. These two sections read in part as follows:

"*Sec. 41. And be it further enacted*, That all duties on goods, wares and merchandise imported, shall be paid or secured to be paid, before a permit shall be granted for landing the same. And where the amount thereof on goods imported in any ship or vessel, on account of one person only, or of several persons jointly interested, shall not exceed fifty dollars, the same shall be immediately paid; but where the said amount shall exceed fifty dollars, the same may, at the option of the proprietor or proprietors, consignee or consignees, be either immediately paid or secured by bond, with condition for the payment thereof, if accruing upon articles of the produce of the West Indies, in four months; if accruing on Madeira wines, in twelve months; if accruing upon any other goods, wares or merchandise, other than teas imported from China, in six months. . . .

Sec. 42. *Provided always, and be it further enacted*, That all teas imported from China may, at the option of the proprietor or consignee thereof, be deposited in the custody of the collector with whom the same shall be entered, or the duties thereon secured by bond, with one or more sureties, to the satisfaction of the collector, with condition for the payment of such duties within twelve months; and in case of depositing such teas, they shall be kept at the charge of the person or persons depositing the same. . . ."

"An Act making farther provision for the collection of the duties by law imposed on Teas, and to prolong the term for the payment of the Duties on Wines," in Section 1, provided in part that "in addition to the provisions contained in the fortieth and forty-first sections of the act, intituled 'An act to provide more effectually for the collection of the duties imposed by law on goods, wares and merchandise imported into the United States, and on the tonnage of ships or vessels,' as they regard the payment, or securing the payment of the duties on teas, it shall be lawful for every importer of teas, if he or she shall elect so to do, to give his or her bond to the collector of the district in which any of the said teas shall be landed, in double the amount of the duties thereupon, with condition for the payment of the said duties in two years from the date of such bond . . ." (1 *Stat.* 219 [March 3, 1791]).

2. Ellery endorsed the letter book copy of this letter "Answd. Nov. 17." H's reply has not been found.

From Thomas Lowrey [1]

Alexandria in New Jersey October 14th. 1791.

Sir!

Agreeably to my promise when I last had the pleasure of seeing you, I am to inform you of the prices of the sundry articles of Provisions, Fuel, Labour &c. in the upper part of Hunterdon County & of Sussex County within this State, from twenty to forty Miles above Trenton in the Neighborhood of the Delaware and Raritan Rivers, & shall proceed in such order as appears to me regular Vizt.

ALS, Hamilton Papers, Library of Congress.

1. Lowrey, a resident of Flemington, New Jersey, was a member of the New Jersey Assembly, United States marshal in New Jersey, and a stockholder and director of the Society for Establishing Useful Manufactures. In this letter Lowrey is discussing a possible site for the society.

Wheat Flour	15/. ℔ Cwt.
Rye ditto	10/. do.
India Corn.	3/. ℔ Bushl.
Buckwheat	2/. do.
Pork	3d. @ 3½ ℔ lit
Beef	2d. @ 2½ do.
Mutton	2½ @ 3. do.
Veal	2. @ 2½ do.
Butter	7 @ 8. do.
Potatoes	1/6 @ 2/. ℔ Bushl.
Turnips	9 @ 10d. do.

Poultry of all kinds very plenty & low Priced.

The above quoted prices have been nearly the Average for these many years past, but there are instances of some of the articles rising at certain periods, and some other periods lower than the above quoted prices, particularly wheat flour.

The article of Fuel, as Wood, is at present in the above described limits, abundant, and may be purchased standing at the rate of one shilling per Cord, & if delivered at any place of Landing may be had at the rate of, from seven shillings and six pence to Ten shillings ℔ Cord, for I should suppose one hundred years to come, as there are vast quantities of Wood on the Hills adjoining the Delaware for one hundred Miles up, which with ease may be collected & rafted down on the Water. I would further observe the article of Coal as in my opinion worthy of a degree of consideration for a future resource as to fuel, and shall here take the liberty to mention that the Mountains on the Susquhannah in the Neighborhood of Wyoming and up the Lakawanick [2] (which is not far distant from the Delaware, and on the same Direction of Mountains which Cross the Delaware) contain in their Bowels, quantities of Coal, of the Kindly [3] or blazing kind almost inexhaustable. They are found so near the surface as to require very little trouble or expence in mining, & answer effectually every purpose for which coal is usually employed except tempering Scythes &c. and this can be easily remidied by a small addition of Charcoal.

2. The Lackawanna River rises in the northeastern part of Pennsylvania about fifteen miles from the Delaware and flows southwesterly through Scranton into the Susquehanna River.

3. A mining term meaning to have promising mineral qualities.

From this circumstance as the distance is not very considerable the conjecture is a natural one and far from being improbable that the mountains on the Delaware are also impregnated with this valuable and useful material. To this opinion I am not led merely by conjecture, for in the periodical Floods which we have in the Delaware it has been frequently observed that stumps of Trees which were brought down by the Torrent had small quantities of Stone Coal adhearing to their roots. This then puts it past a conjecture that the Coal exists on the Delaware, and the period I hope is not far distant when the Discovery of its local situation will be made, so as to be a principal aid in the Establishment of Manufactories in this part of the Country.

As to the hire of Labour, I shall also give you as exact an account as I am able. The Labour of an able bodied Man may be obtained for, from fifteen to eighteen Pounds per annum if found in provisions and Lodgings, if found by himself, the Labour may be obtained at, from twenty five to twenty eight Pounds per annum. The Labour of a Woman as above from seven to eight Pounds, if found, if on the contrary the same allowance for finding themselves as above. Those prices for Labour it is to be considered is to be applied to prime hands, and the proportion may be easily calculated as to inferiors & youths of both sexes, according to the weight of the Labour.

With respect to the transportation of produce down the Delaware, as far as to where the tide meets the Current, or Trenton Landing, is by Boats commonly called Durham Boats, which carry with great safety, from Ten to Twenty Tons burthen down, & will bring from four to eight Tons up. The cause of the difference of burthen in these Boats, is calculated for the purpose of keeping one or both of them employed as the Water Suits. The smaller description are altogether employed when the River is so low as not to admit the large ones to carry a load, but there is a probability of the Navigation of the River being much improved, by the obstructions being removed, which were in several of the falls in the River. This work has been carried into effectual execution in some places last Summer, & it is Thought will be generally so in the event. When this improvment is effected it will admit of Boats of much greater Burthen & will consequently reduce the price of freights. Thes Boats for the most part go down to Philadelphia with almost all the Produce raised in the Country.

The average time of these Boats in making their trips is four to five days going and coming. The freight of the large boat for one trip is from seven to eight Pounds and the small one in proportion as the former takes five hands to work it, the latter but three.

The soil of the Country is extensively luxuriant. The Hills covered with wood, the Vallies fine arable Land, & largely proportioned with Meadow Ground. The healthy situation of this part of the Country is so well known as not to need any explanation on that head.

The situation of Musconectcong River which empties into the Delaware, is not more than 45 Miles from the City of Philadelphia by land, & seventy Miles by Water. Its being so remote from the Cities of Philadelphia & New York, will ever prevent the rise of Provisions and Fuel. The most eligible Stream for heavy Works, or Works of any kind within my knowledge in this State, is the abovementioned Musconectcong, where materials for erecting Buildings of every kind are in abundance & Cheap. Vizt. Square Timber, Boards, Shingles, Slate, Stone, Stone lime &c &c. Boards of inch & quarter Thick from 50/. to 60/. ℔ M feet. Shingles from 50/ to 60/. ℔ M, first quality. Stone easily to quarry and at hand, good Stone Lime delivered at seven pence ℔ Bushl. Sand also at hand. There is a Mountain sixteen Miles up the River from this situation, which will produce any quantity of Slate.

I hope to be in Philadelphia in the course of the ensuing Week when I intend to do myself the pleasure of waiting on you in Person. In the interim I beg leave respectfully to submit the foregoing & remain,   sir   Your very obedt. & humble Servant   Thomas Lowrey

Alexander Hamilton Esqr:
Secretary of the Treasury

From Thomas Smith

Loan Office [Philadelphia] Pennsa Octr 14th 1791

Sir,

I have received Two hundred and forty nine thousand two hundred and fifty four pounds 10/ ½ equal to Six hundred and seventy five thousand one hundred and one Drs $33/100$ in the assumed debt of this

State for which I have given descriptive receipts, have registered and numbered them & Carried them to the Comptroller of this State's Office,[1] who has examined them and declares them genuine. He is now making the necessary discriminations whither they are assumable or not. The Comptroller informs me that there is about 200,000 dollars in the hands of individuals which are dated after the first of January 1790 and that there is about 300,000 drs more which have not been presented at this Office. I have endeavoured to obtain from the People who are in the possession of the Certificates dated after the 1st Jany 1790 a list of them or the amount but they knowing they could not be received have neglected it. The greater part of those Certificates have been issued for Certificates of an earlier date. The Interest on the Certificates which I have received is generally indorsed paid (to the 1st Jany 1792) the words of the Indorsement are Prepaid in full.[2]

The large Quantitys of Certificates, Old emission money &ca.[3] Received for funding with the State debt business Returns &ca will keep the whole of the Clerks of this Office *industriously* employed to the 1st of Jany at least.

Numbers of people have presented Certificates, Contl. money & State Debt Certs. since the 30th of septr.

I have the honor &c

Honble: Alexander Hamilton secy Treasy.

LC, RG, 53, Pennsylvania State Loan Office, Letter Book, 1790–1794, Vol. "615-P," National Archives.
1. John Nicholson.
2. See Smith to H, June 6, 1791.
3. For background to the loan office business to which Smith is referring, see Nathaniel Appleton to H, February 5, 1791, note 1.

From George Washington

Mount Vernon Octr. 14th. 1791

(Private)

My dear Sir,

When I addressed a private letter to you a few days ago [1] I had no more idea that Monday the 24th. instt. was the day appointed for the meeting of Congress, than I had of its being dooms-day until it was mentioned to me in a letter which I have just received from Mr. Lear (who was under the like mistake). It had taken such deep root in my mind that the *last* monday in the month was the time that I never consulted the Law [2] or made any enquiry about it and meant to move leizurely on in the course of next week for Philadelphia & for that purpose had directed Page [3] to send off his Stage Coach so as to be at George-Town on tuesday the 18th. This discovery, however, will oblige me, as soon as I am provided with the means, to accelerate my Journey, and it induces me at the same time to urge you more earnestly to be prepared against my arrival with what my last requested.

How far, in addition to the several matters mentioned in that letter, would there be propriety do you conceive, in suggesting the policy of encouraging the growth of Cotton, & Hemp in such parts of the United States as are adapted to the culture of these articles? The advantages which would result to this Country from the produce of articles which ought to be manufactured at home is apparent but how far bounties on them come within the powers of the Genl. Government or it might comport with the temper of the times to expend money for such purposes is necessary to be considered and without a bounty is given I know of no means by which the growth of them can be *effectually* encouraged.

The establishment of Arsenals in convenient & proper places is, in my opinion, a measure of high national importance meriting the serious attention of Congress; and is one of those measures which ought to be brought to their view.

Yesterday I received the resignation of John Spotswood Moore Surveyor of West Point in this state. I mention it now, that if opportunities should present, you may make the necessary enquiries into the fitness of Alexr. Moore, his Brother whom he recommends as a Successor.

With affectionate regard   I am ever Yours   Go: Washington

ALS (photostat), George Washington Papers, Library of Congress; LC, George Washington Papers, Library of Congress.

1. Letter not found.

2. "An Act fixing the time for the next annual meeting of Congress" (1 Stat. 198 [March 2, 1791]) provided "That after the third day of March next, the first annual meeting of Congress shall be on the fourth Monday of October next."

3. Stephen Page, deputy sheriff of Philadelphia, operated a stagecoach business.

From Thomas Lowrey

Alexandria New Jersey 15th: October 1791.

Sir!

I did myself the pleasure of writing you yesterday and as an immediate conveyance presented itself, I must confess that being eager to come forward with what information lay in my power, as early as possible, through hurry I had omitted one very particular observation which I fully intended to have made. I have therefore taken the Liberty to address you again and shall make my omission the subject of this Letter.

In my letter of yesterday the method of transportation down & up the Delaware and also the Price of Freights constituted a part & I should have observed that altho' this transportation will consequently be attended with expence to a Manufactoring Society, I would here place against such charge the low price at which Fuel can be obtained in this part of the Country, & in order to strengthen a calculation which has been had on that part of the business, a Number of Gentlemen would readily enter into contract, safely to insure & conduct all materials and products of the manufactory to & from the Mouth of Musconectcong to the Landing of Trenton for the consideration of the difference which may be between the price of Fuel & provisions for the supply of the Manufactory, (which may be estimated) between the situation on the Musconectcong and any other situation which may shew a colour of competition. I am induced to observe this in particular knowing that several surveys have been made of the different Streams of Water, within this State, & perhaps several yet about to be made in, *or near* it.

As I mentioned in my letter of yesterday my hopes of waiting on you in Person in the course of the ensuing Week I still hold, when I shall explain myself more fully than the bounds of a letter will reasonably admit.

I remain respectfully,   sir,   Your very obedt. & hum: servant

Thomas Lowrey

Alexander Hamilton Esquire
Secretary of the Treasury

ALS, Hamilton Papers, Library of Congress.

From James McHenry [1]

Baltimore 15 Octbr. 1791.

The electors of the Senate of Maryland have chosen me one of the Senate of our State legislature, and many of my friends are urgent that I should accept. As yet I have given no answer. If you still entertain the project you mentioned to me when in Philadelphia it may somewhat influence my determination. Perhaps the complexion of several European powers, as it respects France, and the claims for succours she may bring forward under the 11th article of the treaty of alliance,[2] in case of being attacked, may render the presence of a ministerial character necessary at the Hague, as a spot which can afford a tolerable view of the parties likely to be concerned.[3] Perhaps too it is an eligible situation to forward our commerce with the Northern nations as well as England, at least it would seem a position which might enable a qualified person to watch the course of trade, and improve favorable conjunctures. But if the chief object would be your loans or financial operations I think I could give you entire satisfaction. I have been led thus far into a change of sentiment, since we spoke together on this subject, by an alteration in my health, which I flatter myself would be benefited by the voyage and the new materials with which the employment would furnish my mind. Should things take the turn you wi⟨sh⟩, you will readily conceive that I ought to be allowed some time for preparations as I must take my family with me.

But whether here or elsewhere, in sickness or heal⟨th⟩ I shall always my dear Hamilton be your sincere friend.   James McHenry

ALS, Hamilton Papers, Library of Congress.

1. McHenry, who had served as George Washington's secretary during the American Revolution, had attended the Constitutional Convention and the Maryland Ratifying Convention. He was a member of the Maryland Assembly from 1788 to 1790.

2. Article 11 of the Treaty of Alliance of 1778 with France reads: "The two Parties guarantee mutually from the present time and forever, against all other powers, to wit, the united states to his most Christian Majesty the present Possessions of the Crown of france in America as well as those which it may acquire by the future Treaty of peace: and his most Christian Majesty guarantees on his part to the united states, their liberty, Sovereignty, and Independence absolute, and unlimited, as well in Matters of Government as commerce and also thair Possessions, and the additions or conquests that their Confederation may obtain during the war, from any of the Dominions now or heretofore possessed by Great Britain in North America, conformable to the 5th. & 6th

articles above written, the whole as their Possessions shall be fixed and assured to the said States at the moment of the cessation of their present War with England" (Miller, *Treaties*, II, 39–40).

3. At this time the United States had neither a minister nor a chargé d'affaires at The Hague. During the Confederation period American affairs at The Hague had been handled by an agent, Charles F. W. Dumas, a Swiss national.

From Jeremiah Olney

Providence, October 15, 1791. "Enclosed is my Return of Exports from July to September inclusive, amounting to 55,805 Dollars & 33 Cents. . . ."

Copy, Rhode Island Historical Society, Providence; copy, RG 56, Letters from the Collector at Providence, National Archives.

From William Skinner

United States Loan Office, [Hillsboro] North Carolina. October 15th. 1791.

Sir

The state of North Carolina, (as was expected) continued to press their Certificates on me to be received on Loan, Agreable to your orders,[1] I received them, amounting agreable to Mr. Child's[2] own calculation, aparently to 409.570. dolls. & 17 Cents, for which I have given a rect. agreable to orders. The 22.415. dolls. & 10 Cents which had been brot. in by Duncan Mc.Rae for Duncan Mcauslen,[3] for which I had given a rect. is no⟨t⟩ acknowledg'd to be part of the Pubs. Certificates.[4] The inclosd. is in Substance a copy of the rect. given for the Certificates recd. on account of the State.

I am most Respectfully Your most obedient Servant. W Skinner.

Honble, Alexander Hamilton Esqr.

[E N C L O S U R E][5]

United States Loan Office. [Hillsboro] North Carolina. 30th. Septr. 1791.

Thereby acknowledge to have received into my office, of Francis Child Esqr. on account of the State of North Carolina, Sundry Certificates of the said State's debt, amounting in the whole agreable to Mr. Child's own Calculation to four hundred & nine thousand, five hundred & Seventy dollars, and Seventeen Cents, which Certificates are to remain in my Office, subject to the Decision of the Secretary of the Treasury of the United States; before any further proceedings be had thereon, in consequence of the said Deposit. Given under my hand &c &c.

Copy, North Carolina Department of Archives and History, Raleigh. This letter was enclosed in H's "Report to the Governor of North Carolina," July 31, 1794.
  1. See H to Skinner, September 8, 1791.
  2. Francis Child was comptroller of North Carolina.
  3. See Skinner to H, August 29, 1791.
  4. In "Report to the Governor of North Carolina," July 31, 1794, this account is described as "lodged in the hands of the Commissioner of Loans by a certain Duncan McAulan and by him transferred to the State of North-Carolina" (copy, North Carolina Department of Archives and History, Raleigh).
  5. Copy, North Carolina Department of Archives and History, Raleigh. This document was enclosed in H's "Report to the Governor of North Carolina," July 31, 1794.

From George Joy [1]

London 16th. Octr: 1791

Alexander Hamilton Esqre.

Sir

I know not how far the documents I requested from you before I left America (Vizt. pr my letter 20th Octr: 1790) [2] might have enabled me to obtain such information respecting any arrangements forming here or in Amsterdam, for speculations &ca. in American Debt, as would be worth your attention. Without them, however, little information has occurred wch I was not pretty well assured you must receive advices of from other Channels (or the witholding those documents under an Idea of Impropriety in such Communications would not have prevented my writing you); and the Communication of the opinions I have met with on your financial arrangements were not alone sufficient to warrant my troubling you with a letter wch

ALS, Hamilton Papers, Library of Congress; LS, Hamilton Papers, Library of Congress.
  1. Joy had been a merchant in New York City from 1787 to 1790. At the end of 1790 he settled in London.
  2. Letter not found.

could not arrive with you until the Effect of your plans should constitute a higher panegyrick than the Encomiums of the best skilled and most experienced in subjects of this Nature; or I might have informed you that on the subject of your Bank Report[3] the Gentn: I have conversed with both here and in Amsterdam have expressed a full approbation and admiration, of that sound Judgement wch could hazard an opinion that the irredeemable quality of the 6 pr Ct stock should be consider'd an equivalent for taking a lower rate of Interest than the Contract entitled the holders to, when the Debt itself was to be bought for less than half it's nominal value, which opinion the Event has verified; and that the same person who under those Circumstances would hazard such an opinion, wch had so much the appearance of a sanguine and immature disposition, should exhibit such wariness and precaution not to commit himself on the Subject of establishing a plurality of Branches; the Utility of wch will probably be dictated by Experience, but which will grow more naturally and with less danger to the root from being gradually cherished.

The recommendation to the Maintenance of the Inviolability of property and Contracts and the truly valuable Consequences expected to be derived therefrom are register'd among the number of Instances of your opinion of the necessity and good policy of literally maintaining the public faith—hardly have the United States escaped the Censure, the most *expensive* as well as most destructive of all Governments—that of a breach of the public faith. The operation of the funding Bill[4] by new modelling the Debt and particularly by placing the Indents on a three pr Ct. Interest must have been considered compulsory, were it not for the provision in the Bill that the Contracts of those who should not subscribe should not be impaired but remain in full force and virtue; and as it is it has been attended with immense difficulty to Individuals who were so circumstanced that they could not retain their property of this kind until the *presumed* Ability of the Country should be so fully *ascertained* by Experience that they could with Confidence make a demand according to the express tenor of their Certificates. I know an Instance in wch principal to a large Amount (say 140 M Dollars) was given in Exchange for Interest

3. "Second Report on the Further Provision Necessary for Establishing Public Credit (Report on a National Bank)," December 13, 1790.

4. "An Act making provision for the (payment of the) Debt of the United States" (1 *Stat.* 138–44 [August 4, 1790]).

upon the terms of 1⅔rds Dollars Principal for one dollar Indents; so fully confident was one of the Parties, from the attempts made under the old Government to make an early provision for calling in the Indents, and the common Ideas, that pending the Ability of the Public to pay the Principal they would exert their first Efforts to discharge the Interest. I say I know this fact and 'tis to my cost I know it, as the Loss thus sustained by the Party has render'd him incapable of paying his Creditors among whom I myself stand the most formidable and to a very alarming Amount. By loaning more than fifty thousand pounds sterling in the Month of March last at an Interest of 5 pr Ct: free of all Charges I have prevented a sacrifice of near 300 M Dollars of this species of Debt, and a large amot: of the foreign Debt of So: Carolina on wch I have an hypothecation, wch have since risen very much in value; but on the Justice of the Public by making this debt equal to the specific Contract on wch it stands, either by an actual payment or by funding it at such rate of Interest as will bring it up to it's nominal value, I depend for the means of re-imbursing the sums for wch I am thus Creditor to the Public. You may remember, sir, (if your very important avocations have not intervened to prevent it) a suggestion I once took the liberty to make to you that on a presumption that the revenue granted would pay 4½ @ 5 pr Ct: on the full amount of the Debt; as much might be hired in Europe for 3 @ 5 Years as would make up the deficiency, under Condition, that, if it should be ascertained by an average of that number of years that the revenue was competent to the payment of that Interest without risque of deficiency, you should be intitled to receive such sum from the Parties on a similar Interest as would pay the whole Debt, if required, or such part thereof as the present holders would not choose to subscribe on the same Conditions. In this opinion I am fully confirmed, with this addition that if no Infringement had been made upon existing Contracts, or if the Ability of the Government being now ascertained those who have waited the Event, render an Assurance that their Contracts should not be infringed, should meet that Justice wch the Constitution and the funding Bill, as well as the specific Tenor of their demands entitle them to; the Money might in all probability be hired at a lower rate of Interest even than 4½ pr Ct:

There is now an attempt making in this City to loan Money on American security at 4½ pr Ct: I have not yet ascertained whether

'tis an accot: of our Government or private speculation and am apprehensive I cannot know until after the sailing of this ship. If it is for
Government you will know it of Course; if not such information as
I may obtain shall be at your service. The Object, I understand, is
either to purchase or pay off the french Loans. 'Tis pity that an opportunity for paying that Debt at so very favorable an Exchange as
the present should be lost. 'Tis probable that the Reflux of Money to
France in Consequence of the Completion of the Revolution which is
now pretty generally acknowledged to be beyond any material Controversy, will soon induce an alteration in the Exchange favorable to
that Country tho' the general Market Rate of Interest in Europe may
not be materially or for any length of time alter'd thereby.

It would render me very essential service to be informed by you
of any measures adopted or likely to be pursued for the early discharge of the unsubscribed Debt; or for admitting any proportion
thereof in payment of Loans of Money at the same or a less rate of
Interest than what the U.S. have lately paid; being confident that
such a plan might be pursued with advantage to the Character of the
U.S. as a people, with a certain ultimate benefit to the finances of the
Country and perhaps an immediate diminution of the annual Expenditure or, at all Events, of the just annual claims upon the public.
I pretend not to any Claim to such information but such as arises from
a sincere disposition to repay the Obligation by any personal services;
or (which I know to be more acceptable to you) by any services wch
it may be in my power to render you in your official Capacity by the
Communication of facts that may come within my knowledge. Were
the sum larger I might with Confidence urge such information being
early conveyed to me as an Object of Policy. Circumstanced as I am an
early arrangement or an early assurance under the Authority of your
opinion of the probability of such arrangement may make the *difference* between 300 M Dollrs (say three hundred thousand Dollars)
of this debt and more than £30 M stlg (say thirty thousand pounds
sterling) of the foreign Debt of So: Carolina being held by *foreigners*
or a *Citizen* of the U.S. I have so large a sum to pay in Holland on the
first day of April next (for wch I must be providing myself some
Weeks before) that in the fullest Confidence and satisfaction that no
dishonorable advantage will be suffer'd by you to be taken of my
situation to purchase for the Government at an under value I will

frankly confess to you that it will not only be impossible for me to hold them unless such arrangement be, at least in a train of formation; but I shall be obliged to abandon them to foreigners at a very low rate perhaps, under the fetters in wch they are held, not more than 10/. pr £, not only suffering thereby the loss of those benefits wch from an unshaken Confidence in the Magnanimity of the Government, even in the most trying times, and my consequent speculations in the funds, I had a reasonable right to expect; (for any part of wch my prospects of payments are very much clouded) but the loss of very heavy Sums for which I am actually in advance without the prospect of re-imburse-ment but from the above source. I say were the sum larger I should with Confidence urge this Argument; as it is you may not perhaps think it unworthy your attention. If so, knowing as I do your opinion of the difference in a political View between paying a *larger* annuity * abroad or a *smaller* at home, it would be a needless waste of your time to bring before you any Arguments on the subject. You will readily conceive from what I have written above that I should be able in Case the Funds were put on a more respectable footing to loan such sums on an hypothecation of them as would prevent the necessity of a sacrifice by Sale.

I have confined myself above to the promise of furnishing you with any information that may occur to me. A cordial aversion from the imputation of having led any of my friends to expect from me what in the Event I may find myself unable to perform prevents my making you a tender of more important services; and I do not feel warranted to assure myself of the Ability to raise large loans for the public (tho' some Connections I am now forming make it presumeable). I would, however, gladly bring forward in the line of a Co-adjutor such powers as I may possess in aid of such plan; being very desirous of establish-ing a *precedent* wch would prevent the advantage naturally taken of your having *given* a large Interest to *ask* a large Interest—a Circum-stance wch however *trifling* it must appear to a reasoning mind does actually occasion (especially when combined with the Circumstance of an *apparent,* magnified by the Money lenders into a *real,* breach of Contract) a demand for a larger Interest than is paid by States less able to pay their debts and subject to numerous evils operating a greater risque of the Capital than can be supposed to exist with us; and

* I mean a larger Interest on the sum actually received from a Foreigner.

such *Precedent* I presume may be successfully established by Loans at a lower rate of Interest tho' the unsubscribed Arrears of Interest or even the 3 pr. Ct. Stock were receivable for a large proportion of the Amount.

I mention the modification of the unsubscribed Debt in some such way, as perhaps more likely to meet the Concurrence of the Legislature; tho' for my own part I am clearly of opinion that to fund it according to the express tenor of the Contract *redeemable ad libitum* would be most profitable as well as on all other accounts the best mode that could be pursued. It would effectually preclude any just Complaint of a breach of Contract and therefore must meet the Concurrence of the Creditors; it would enhance the Credit and respectability of the U.S. and enable them to loan Money in future at as low Interest as any State in Europe; and they might in a *very short time* avail themselves of the Consequence of those pacific principles resulting from the enlightened and improving State of Society to loan at a *much* lower rate than your prudence would suffer you to hazard a Conjecture of in your report of Janry 1790.[5]

Any Apology for the length of this letter would only add to what is already extended far beyond what I intended troubling with. I therefore finish it with the Assurance that I am with perfect Esteem and Respect,

Sir,   Your obedt. & very hble servt.

Geo: Joy

Address No. 56 Hatton Garden.

5. "Report Relative to a Provision for the Support of Public Credit," January 9, 1790.

From George Joy

(Duplicate)

Alexander Hamilton Esqre.   London 16th. Octr. 1791

sir

I beg leave to submit to you the following Calculations and Observations wch led to the Conclusions in my letter of this date—and

ALS, Hamilton Papers, Library of Congress.

first in Corroboration of what I have there said respecting the french debt that " 'tis pity the opportunity of paying it at so very favorable an Exchange as the present should be lost."

The sum due to foreign Officers Vizt: 186,427 Dollars * pays an annual Interest of 6 pr Ct; of this debt therefore

100 Dollrs. now pay	6 Drs.
100 Dollrs. @ 22 Excha.† (say 22d stlg pr demi Ecu or 3 livres) would be equal to or be paid for at 73 Drs. 66⅔ cents the Interest on wch if loand at 4 pr Ct: would be only	2 – 94⅔ Cents
leaving a benefit to the U.S. of more than half the Annuity Viz.	3 Drs 5⅓ Cents Pr Ct.

* I think you contemplate this and all the debt payable in France as redeemable at the pleasure of our Government. I observe there is an express provision for it in the loan of the 16th. July 1782 for 18 millions of livres.[1] I have no Copy of that for 6 millions for 1783 but presume it must contain the same proviso.[2]

† 30d. Stg pr demi Ecu[3] (the rate here contemplated as the par of Exchange) is the precise *rate* of Excha: used at our Treasury Vizt: 108 sous pr Dollar of 4/6 Sterlg.

1. Article 2 of the "Contract between the King [of France] and the Thirteen United States of North America, signed at Versailles July 16, 1782," reads as follows: ". . . His Majesty . . . has consented that the payment of the capital in ready money at the royal treasury be in twelve equal payments of 1,500,000 livres each, and in twelve years only, to commence from the third year after a peace."

Article 4 of the contract reads as follows: "The payment of the said eighteen millions of livres tournois shall be in ready money at the royal treasury of His Majesty at Paris, in twelve equal parts and at the terms stipulated in the above second article. The interest of the said sum, at five per cent per annum, shall commence with the date of the treaty of peace, and shall be paid at every period of the partial payments of the capital, and shall diminish in proportion with the payments; the Congress of the said United States being left, however, at liberty to free themselves sooner from this obligation by anticipated payments in case the state of their finances will admit" (Miller, *Treaties*, II, 51–52).

2. Article 3 of the "Contract between the King [of France] and the Thirteen United States of North America, signed at Versailles February 25, 1783," reads as follows: "The new loan of six millions livres tournois, the subject of the present contract, shall be refunded and reimbursed in ready money at His Majesty's royal treasury in six equal portions of a million each, with interest at five per cent per annum, and in six periods, the first of which shall take place in the year 1797, and so on from year to year until 1802, when the last reimbursement shall be completed."

Article 5 reads as follows: "The interest of the capital of the six million shall diminish in proportion to the reimbursements . . . Congress and the United States reserving, however, the liberty of freeing themselves by anticipated payments, should the state of their finances admit" (Miller, *Treaties*, II, 120–21).

3. A silver coin equal to two livres ten sous.

Again . . 100 Dollrs now pay . . . . 6 –
73–66⅔ @ 4½ pr Ct: would pay . 3 – 31½
Annual benefit to the U.S. . . 2 – 68½

The above Calculations are at what the Excha: has stood at for some time past, it is now risen to 23⅛ at wch rate the following are computed

Vizt: 100 Drs. now pay . . . . . . 6.
@ Excha: 23⅛ the principal might be discharg'd
for 77–8⅓ Cts loaned at 4 pr Ct. . . . . . 3 – 8⅓
Annual benefit to the U.S. . . . . . 2 – 91⅔

Again . . 100 Dollrs. now pay . . . . 6 –
77–8⅓ loan'd at 4½ would pay . 3 – 46⅞
bonus 2 – 53⅛

We will now suppose the Excha: to rise to 24
At this Excha: 100 Drs wch now pay . . . 6 –
might be discharged for 80 wch at 4 pr Ct.
would pay . . . . 3 – 20
leaving a benefit to the U.S. of 2 – 80

Again . . 100 Dollrs. pay . . . . . 6 –
80 Drs. loaned at 4½ would pay . 3 – 60
leaving to the U.S. an annual
bonus of . . . . . . 2 – 40

That part of the French Debt wch pays 5 pr Ct: may be thus stated
100 Dollrs pay . . . . . . 5 –

Excha: 22: 73–66⅔ loan'd at 4 pr Ct: would
pay . . . . 2 – 94⅔
Annual bonus to the U.S. . . . 2 – 5⅓

Again . . 100 Dollrs. pay . . . . . 5 – –
73–66⅔ @ 4½ pr Ct: would pay 3 – 31½
Annual bonus to the U.S. . . . 1 – 68½

Again . . 100 Drs. now pay . . . . 5 –
Excha: 23⅛ 77–8⅓ @ 4 pr Ct: . . . . 3 – 8⅓
Annual bonus to the U.S. . . . 1 – 91⅔

Again . . 100 Dollrs now pay . . . . 5 –
77–8⅓ @ 4½ . . . . . . 3 – 46⅞
Annual bonus to the U.S. . . . 1 – 53⅛

Again	100 Dollrs. now pay	5 –
Excha: 24	80 Dollrs. loaned at 4 pr Ct:	
	would pay	3 – 40
	Annual Bonus to the U.S.	1 – 80
Again	100 Dollrs. pay	5 – –
	80 Drs. @ 4½ pr Ct:	3 – 60
	Bonus to the U.S.	1 – 40

I cannot but remark here how fully the application of the smallest of those Surpluses to the reduction of the principal would evince the Doctrine in your report of Janry. 1790 [4] that the great secret of Finance is to obtain an Excess of Revenue beyond the Expenditure; and if this were effected in Consequence of the present Government holding inviolable existing Contracts, how fully would it confirm the Assertion in the General's Circular Letter to the Governors of the different States on leaving the Army that Honesty in States as well as Individuals must ever be found the best and soundest policy.[5] I quote from Memory—perhaps not literally but I am confident I am not mistaking in the substance.

The following Calculations are consonant to my Suggestion of benefits to be derived to the U.S. by admitting a proportion of the unsubscribed Debt in part payment of Loans to be contracted &ca:— and I shall confine myself to that part of the unsubscribed Debt wch pending the ascertaining of the Ability of the Government to discharge all its Obligations, and while there was hazard of inability received a temporary provision very inadequate to what was made for other parts of the Debt having on no principle a higher Claim. The advantages to result to the U.S. are on a Comparison of what they now pay (not what the unsubscribing Creditor is entitled to receive) with what they would pay in the Event of loans being contracted on the following principles.

300 Dollrs. 6 pr Ct Stock now pay	18
100 Drs. Indents . . . do:	3
	21

4. "Report Relative to a Provision for the Support of Public Credit," January 9, 1790.
5. See George Washington's circular to the states, June 8, 1783 (*GW*, XXVI, 483–96).

400 Dollrs. loaned at 5 pr Ct: (¼ receivable in Indents) would pay . . . } 20

being less than is now paid . . . . 1 Dr. pr Annum
   on 400—equal to ¼ th pr Ct:

On every 100 Dollrs. you pay 2 Drs. pr ann: of the Principal, stopping thereby an Interest of 12 Cents for wch if you hire the Money at 5 pr Ct: you pay *10* Cents * leaving to the U.S. to operate a reduction of the principal 2 Cts pr 100 Dollrs. whereas by the above mode you would have *25* Cts pr Ann: to apply to this purpose. It will be needless to repeat the Increase of benefit in this View under the following Calculations.

Again . as above 21
   400 Dollrs. loan'd @ 4½ (¼ receivable
     in Indents) 18

being less than is now paid . . . 3 or ¾ pr Ct.
Again . as above 21
   400 Drs. loan'd at 4 pr Ct: (¼ receivable
     in Indents) 16

  being less than is now paid . . . 5 or 1¼ pr Ct:
Again 200 Dollrs. 6 pr Cts now pay . 12 –
   100 Drs Indents 3

   300 Drs. loan'd at 5 pr Ct: would
     pay the same Sum . . . 15.

(a) If this plan should meet the Acquiescence of the Creditors therefore the Object would be valuable but no specific gain on a Comparison with what is now paid

Again . as annex'd 15
   300 Dollrs. loaned at 4½ pr Ct
   (⅓rd payable. in Indents) } 13 – 50
   would pay . . . . .
   leaving on 300 Drs. Principal
   an Annuity of . . . . . 1 – 50 equal to ½ pr Ct:

* If you have an Excess of revenue that will do this so be it; but it does not in any degree alter the principle of Calculation while the Market rate of Interest or the benefit that the Government might derive from the Use of it is not less than 5 pr Ct:

Again . as above . . . . . .   15 –
    300 Drs. loaned at 4 pr Ct: would
        pay . . . . . .   12 –
        Annual Bonus . . . . $\overline{3}$ equal to 1 pr Ct

The following Calculations apply to that part of the Debt wch now pays 5 pr Ct: Vizt:

    400 Dollrs. 5 pr Ct: foreign Debt
        now pay . . . . .   20 –
    100 Drs. Indents . . . . $\underline{3 –}$
                        23 –

    500 Dollrs. loaned at 4½ (⅕th
        Indents) would pay . . . $\underline{22 – 50}$
        leaving a Bonus to the U.S. of   – 50 or ⅟₅₀
                             say ⅟₁₀ pr Ct.

Again . As above 23
    500 Drs. loaned at 4 pr Ct: (⅕th
        Indts) 20
        Annual Bonus . . . . . $\overline{3}$ or ⅗ pr Ct:

Again 300 Drs 5 pr Cts now pay . . $\overline{15}$
    100 Do. Indents " . . 3
    $\overline{400}$ Drs. loaned at 4½ (¼
        Indts) would pay the same . 18 – – so that

(a) The observation (a) annex'd applies here.
Again . as above . . . . .   18 – –
    400 Drs. loaned at 4 pr Ct: (4¼
        Indts) would pay . . . .   16 –
          Annual Bonus . . . $\overline{2.}$ equal to ½ pr Ct

118 Dollars Omnium or 100 Dollrs Registered Debt bearing Interest from 31st Decr 1787 have been funded and may be computed as follows Vizt:

    66⅔rds pay annually . . . . . . 4 Dollrs.
    33⅓ deferr'd for 10 years com-
        puting the value of money
        at 5 pr Ct: is worth ⅓rd
        of 61 drs 39 cts & abot: ³⁄₁₆
        of a Cent (this being very
        nearly the Value of 100

Dollrs. on the above principle) say 20 Drs 46⁶⁄₁₆
Cts wch at 5 pr Ct: (the
same rate of Interest) pay
annually .   .   .   .   .   1 Dr. 2⅓ Cts.
18 Drs back Interest at 3 pr Ct: .   54
118 Dolls: thus pay what is equal
to an annuity of .   .   .   5 – 56⅓

being 4 Drs 71⁴⁷⁄₁₀₀ Cts (say 4 Drs. 71½ Cts) pr Ct:—computing the value of Money at 6 pr Ct: and the Interest also
wch is nearer the Value at the time of subscribing and (considering the irredeemable quality of the deferred as well as the
6 pr Ct Stock) perhaps a more proper mode of ascertaining the
comparative benefit—instead of 4–71½ this would amount to 4
Drs. 78⁹⁄₁₀ Cts (say 4–79) and without considering the subscrib-
ability of a great part of it to the national Bank, the benefit resulting
from the irredeemable quality of the Debt under the actual fall that
has taken place and the fair prospects of a farther fall in the Market
rate of Interest may be fairly computed at 21 Cents pr Ann: *at
least;* making 5 pr Ct:. I will not trouble you with a long round of
Calculations on the benefits the U.S. might derive from opening
new Loans for the discharge of the unsubscrib'd Debt on a Comparison of such loans with what they have paid as above, but will
observe that if loans were opened to the full Amount at 5 pr Ct for
those purposes receivable either in specie or in any part of the Debt
and any specie received thereon appropriated *bona fide* to the redemption of such part of the Debt as may not be subscribed and the stock
created by these loans made redeemable at the pleasure of the Government; or (wch would on some Accots be better) on one, two or
three Years Notice being given to the Creditors; the benefit wch
the Government would thus derive from the fall in the Market rate
of Interest would very shortly shew this to be far the more profitable
Arrangement. Loans at 4½ would be far within either of the above,
independent of other advantages; but were it not that the sound of
a six pr Ct: Interest might alarm the Legislature and occasion delay,
singular tho' the opinion may appear, had I had as great a propensity
to, as I have had aversion from, embarking in political pursuits and

had I even acquired reputation therein I should not be afraid to risque it on the opinion, that to fund it at 6 pr Ct: at once redeemable ad libitum, or on short Notice, would have the advantage of every other plan. Among others it would have that of raising them so rapidly as to prevent foreigners getting them at an under value. It would increase and *hasten* the Ability of the Government to loan at a low Interest from the Circumstance of it's thus meeting the tenor of the Contract at the moment of their finding themselves able to do it (and I hope and trust that the Government of the U.S. is now in a Condition above asking favors of its Creditors). It would enable the Agents of the U.S. to promote and benefit by a fair Competition of the Money lenders without leaving it in the power of a few interested persons to discourage them by insinuations of broken faith. In short, beside the Convenience of having a large proportion of the debt redeemable on the fall of the Market rate of Interest, it would give that spring to the Credit of the U.S. that can only be derived from the Assurance that the Government is able and ever has been willing to meet it's Obligations with respectability, magnanimity and honor.

With much respect and Esteem   I remain,   sir,   Your very hble servt: Geo: Joy

To George Washington

[Philadelphia, October 16, 1791]

Sir,

I have the honor of your letter of the 10th. instant.

Mine to you of the 6th., which was sent by duplicates, will have informed you of the then state of the business of the Supervisorship of the District of Delaware. I have, within two days, received a letter from Mr. Vining [1] stating that an absence from home had delayed the receipt of my letter,[2] & the ascertaining of Mr. Barratt's [3] inclination in regard to the office; but at the same time expressing his conviction that it would be accepted. As a further explanation is to be expected, I conclude to defer applying for the Commission; especially as the late Supervisor [4] continues to act, & the public service will not, I presume, suffer.

Governor Clayton's application,[5] thro' me, in favor of his son, was communicated to you on the day it was received,[6] which was two days before your departure from this place. You reserved the matter for enquiry in the course of your passage thro' the State; & when you wrote to me respecting Mr Barratt, I concluded that the appointment of young Mr. Clayton [7] had appeared to you inexpedient. He was represented to me as a *very young* man who had had slender opportunities of being acquainted with business.

With the most respectful & truest attachment, I have the honor to be &c.   A: Hamilton

Philadelphia
16th Octob: 1791.

LC, George Washington Papers, Library of Congress.
  1. John Vining, Federalist member of the House of Representatives from Delaware. Letter not found.
  2. Letter not found.
  3. Andrew Barratt.
  4. Dr. Henry Latimer.
  5. Joshua Clayton. See Washington to H, October 10, 1791.
  6. Letter not found.
  7. James Clayton.

To Robert Ballard [1]

[*Philadelphia, October 17, 1791.* According to the dealer's description of this letter, it relates to the "duty on spirits distilled from domestic and foreign materials." *Letter not found.*]

Sold by Harvard Trust Company, Cambridge, Massachusetts, 1962.
  1. Ballard was surveyor of the port of Baltimore.

To Henry Knox

[Philadelphia] Oct 17th [1791]

Dear Sir

The following are the particulars in the Presidents Letter [1] which he expects you to prepare.

Expeditions against the Indians. Every pacific measure was previously tried to produce accom~ & avoid expence. More pointed laws with penalties to rest⟨r⟩ain our own people. This & good faith may produce tranquillity.

Treaties with Cherokees & six Nations *& reasons.*
I annex to the first the hints in the Presidents letter.
Yrs. Affect   A Hamilton

You will of course add any other things that occur on *any point.*

Gen Knox

ALS, Massachusetts Historical Society, Boston.
1. This letter has not been found, but it is presumably the one mentioned in George Washington to H, October 14, 1791, and it obviously contained a request for material for Washington's message to Congress.

Treasury Department Circular to the District Judges

Treasury Department
October 17. 1791

Sir,

A question has occurred whether upon a Petition being presented in order to the mitigation or remission of any forfeiture, which may have been incurred, the Judge to whom it is presented may release the Vessel or goods forfieted, upon taking some proper surety to abide the event.[1]

I deem it not proper to give an opinion respecting the construction of the law in this particular; but I think it expedient to say that if such a proceeding should appear to the Judge, before whom the matter is brought, legal, I shall have no objection to its being adopted, due care being observed as well with regard to the competency of the sum, in which the security may be taken as of the sureties themselves.

On the point of the sufficiency of the sum I should be glad that the Officers interested in the forfieture might be satisfied.

With great consideration I have the honor to be Sir Your obedt Servant   A Hamilton

LS, to James Duane, New-York Historical Society, New York City; LS, Massachusetts Historical Society, Boston.
1. See "An Act to provide for mitigating or remitting the forfeitures and penalties accruing under the revenue laws, in certain cases therein mentioned" (1 *Stat.* 122–23 [May 26, 1790]).

From George Washington

George-Town [Maryland] Octo. 17th. 1791

My dear Sir,

I am thus far on my way to Philadelphia, and if the disagreeableness of the weather (for it is now raining) does not prevent it, shall proceed to Bladensburgh at least to night; but be my dispatch what it probably may, the mail which leaves this tomorrow, will arrive in Philadelphia before me.

This being the case, and time pressing, I forward the enclosed suggestions of Mr. Jefferson and Mr. Madison,[1] who are both at this place and from whom I requested information of the several matters that had occurred to them, proper for communication.

I am always and sincerely   Yours.   G.W——n.

LC, George Washington Papers, Library of Congress.
  1. These "suggestions" were for Washington's message to Congress.

From William Ellery

Collector's Office [Newport, Rhode Island]
Oct. 18th 1791

Sir,

The bark Polly Ebenezer Shearman master, which sailed from this Port for Hamburgh May 25th 1791 arrived here from that place on the 14th. of this month with a valuable cargo, and on the 15th. the master delivered a report and manifest in writing. Among other articles specified therein are four casks containing gin; which Gin being in casks of less than fifty gallons capacity, and not in cases jugs or bottles is I conceive imported contrary to the 33d. Section of the Act repealg. after the last day of June next the duties laid on distilled Spirits imported from abroad &c.[1] This gin belongs to the mate of the bark, and the master and was imported in casks to save expences. As the vessel sailed before the Law took place, the master was ignorant of it, and there did not appear to be the least intention of fraud. I have thought it more adviseable to take those casks of gin into custody and to wait your direction, than to commence a prosecution agst the vessel and gin, in the first instance which might involve the concerned in unnecessary expence. Please to honour me with your directn. as early as may be convenient.[2]

I am Sir,   Yr. most obedt. servant   Wm Ellery Collr

A Hamilton Esqr
Secry of Treasy

LC, Newport Historical Society, Newport, Rhode Island.
    1. 1 *Stat.* 207 (March 3, 1791). Section 33 of this act provided "That after the last day of June next, no spirituous liquors except gin or cordials in cases, jugs or bottles, shall be brought from any foreign port or place, in casks of less capacity than fifty gallons at the least, on pain of forfeiting of the said spirits, and of the ship or vessel in which they shall be brought."
    2. Ellery endorsed the letter book copy of this letter "Answrd. Oct. 26." H's reply has not been found.

From Henry Lee

[Alexandria, Virginia, October 18, 1791]

My dear sir.

My assiduity has been exercised to procure for you a riding horse ever since my return.[1] My success has not been equal to my hopes, & indeed it is not easy to accomodate you with a horse as you require one very gentle, which is not commonly a quality to be found in horses of the best sort.

Mr Giles [2] will deliver you the best I could get, & I beleive among the safest & most agreable that this country possesses.

He is less addicted to starting & stumbling than riding horses generally are, & is peculiarly well gaited.

He excels in a short gallop which to me is the easiest gait.

But he is old & subject on long journeys to fail in one of his legs. This latter appurtenance will not be consequential to you as you want him only for daily airings & short rides.

Indeed he regards the injury in his leg so little as seldom to complain of it even in severe rides.

If he suits you he will continue yours. If he does not suit you write to me wherein, that I may in my next choice adapt myself exactly to your taste. This I can readily do while at Richmond &

in this case I will exchange for the horse now sent as he is to me very agreeble.

I hope Mrs. Hamilton has returned to you with restored health & that she may long live to make you happy.

with the most sincere affection I am always yours

Henry Lee

oct. 18th. 1791 Alexa.

ALS, Hamilton Papers, Library of Congress.
  1. See Lee to H, August 22, 1791.
  2. Presumably William G. Giles of Petersburg, a Virginia attorney and Congressman, who was a Republican leader in the House of Representatives.

To Benjamin Lincoln

Treasury Department
October 18 1791

Sir,

The post of this day brought me your letter of the 7th instant.

I am pained that my having desired a second return of your purchases of the public debt should have caused you uneasiness. Be assured that an idea of inattention on your part had no share in producing that request. Your first statement with the vouchers was handed over to the Auditor, and was not particularly in my mind, when I wrote. If it had been before me it would have prevented the call upon you (except for a specification of what is hereafter required); to which I was, in some sort, led by a memorandum sent me from the Auditors Office, implying, as I understood it, that those particulars were wanting. Indeed some other enquiries, imperfectly answered, had led to another mistake; which was that the transfers of the Stock itself to the books of the Treasury, had not been completed. The contrary is now discovered.

The only imperfection which I at present perceive regards the place or places where the purchases were made. I take it for granted Boston will answer the further enquiry; but as an offical report of a necessary fact by me ought to be founded on some authentic document, I must give you the trouble of noting in your statement the place or places of purchase. And accordingly I return to you, for this purpose, that which you last transmitted.

As to the interest I will have the Commissioner of Loans [1] author-ised to pay you as well as the dividents which have been struck in the name of the Trustees [2] as those which have been struck in your own name. The final settlement must wait for some future order of the Trustees.

I request that the statement with the place or places noted may be returned to me as speedily as possible.

With great consideration and esteem   I am, Sir, Your Obed Ser-vant   Alex Hamilton

Benjamin Lincoln Esqr
Boston.

LS, RG 36, Collector of Customs at Boston, Letters from the Treasury, 1789–1808, National Archives; copy, RG 56, Letters to the Collector at Boston, National Archives; copy RG 56, Letters to Collectors at Small Ports, "Set G," National Archives.

1. Nathaniel Appleton was commissioner of loans for Massachusetts.
2. The commissioners of the sinking fund.

From Edmund Randolph

[Philadelphia, October 18, 1791]

The attorney-general of the United States does himself the honor of replying to the questions, propounded by the secretary of the Treasury of the United States, in his letter of the 12th of October 1791,[1] as follows.

1st. The Commissioners, appointed in pursuance of the act, in-corporating the bank of the United States,[2] have no power, as such, to superintend the election of directors, or to interfere therein.

By the first section of that act, subscriptions towards constituting the stock were to be opened, under the superintendance of such per-sons, not less than three, as should be appointed *for that purpose* by the President of the United States; the President was to appoint them *accordingly;* and the subscriptions were to continue open, until the whole of the stock should be subscribed.

The fifth section provides, that as soon as the sum of 400,000 dollars,

DS, RG 60, Copies of Opinions, National Archives.
1. Letter not found.
2. "An Act to incorporate the subscribers to the Bank of the United States" (1 *Stat.* 191–96 [February 25, 1791]).

in gold and silver, shall have been actually received on account of the subscriptions to the said stock, notice thereof shall be given by the persons, under whose superintendance the same shall have been made, in at least two public gazettes, printed in the city of Philadelphia; that the said persons shall at the same time, in like manner, notify a time and place within the said city, at the distance of ninety days from the time of such notification, for proceeding to the election of directors; that it shall be lawful for such election to be then and there made, and that the persons, who shall then and there be chosen, shall be the first directors.

These are the only clauses, which relate to the commissioners.

By the former clause their authority would have been concluded, as soon as the whole of the stock was subscribed.

Nor was it extended by the latter farther than to enable them to notify the time and place for proceeding to the election of directors, that is, the time and place, when and where the persons, capacitated to elect, should proceed to elect.

The commissioners will, I suppose, appear with the Books, that it may be known, who were the original subscribers. But this duty naturally arises from their possession of those books, which are the best evidence of the original rights. The superintendance of the election has no analogy to such a possession.

2ndly. But does the smallest necessity exist, why the commissioners, as such, should become the judges or superintendants of the election, or in any manner intermeddle in it? Is it not familiar to the experience of every day, that persons assemble, with equal priveleges of suffrage, and without the preeminence of any one of them, in order to constitute a body for the management of business? The first step is to appoint a moderator or chairman. In the present instance, the stockholders may with ease choose one or more persons to receive, and count the votes, to report the numbers, minute the proceedings, and notify to the newly-elected directors their nomination. This seems to be a completion of the work.

3rd. Altho' in the 5th. section of the act, which requires the first election of directors, it is not said, by whom it shall be made; yet is the connection between that and the 4th. section so intimate, as to render it certain that it must be made by the stockholders, or proprietors of the capital stock.

Whether these terms be synonimous, or not it is immaterial here to examine. It is sufficient to say, that no man can be one or the other, except by virtue of an original subscription, or an assignment duly made of that subscription. Here lies the essence of the difficulty. Can an assignment be made before the first election of directors? The Script, it is true, may be contracted for; may be delivered into the hand of the purchaser; and the price may be actually paid. But it is a creature of the bank-law, and its Mode of transfer depends upon that law. Accordingly it is declared, in the 12th section, that the stock of the said corporation shall be assignable and transferable, according to such rules, as shall be instituted in that behalf, by the laws and ordinances of the same. Now the election of directors preceeds the institution of laws and ordinances concerning the assignment and transfer of stock; and therefore no assignment of transfer can, as yet, be legally made. It is true indeed, that the delivery of Script amounts to an agreement to transfer the stock, when the laws and ordinances shall be instituted; and the seller will be compelled in a court of law to perform all acts, which shall be hereafter necessary to the transfer. But an agreement to transfer is not an actual transfer. Hence I conclude, that no holder of purchased script can be now accepted, (merely in right of his purchase) as a voter for directors.

It is proper, however, to take notice of three objections, which may be urged against these positions. The first is, that the giving of a power to the corporation to ordain rules of transfer does not exclude the usual modes of transfering personal property before those rules shall be formed. The second, that the provision, that *after* the first election no share shall confer a right of suffrage, which shall not have been holden three calender months, previous to the day of election, implies, that *at* the first election shares assigned confer a right of suffrage; and the Third, that if the present assignees be shut out, either a sufficient number of stockholders may not be found to elect, or the original subscribers, who do not retain a shilling of interest, will be admitted to a vote, without any attachment to the common welfare.

To the first objection I answer, that the nature of script must be an acknowledgment of a certain subscription to the bank of the United States: that it does not resemble a corporeal chattel, to which delivery constitutes a complete right but rather a chose in action, concerning which the purchaser cannot without the aid of a statute use his own name judicially, but must use that of the original proprietor. Besides, the third section had already vested the corporation with ample power to regulate transfers; and the twelfth would have been nugatory, had it not been intended to prevent transfers from being full alienations, without an observance of the rules to be established.

The force of the second objection is destroyed, when we recollect; that, altho' it be admitted that at the first election, shares acquired at any time before, howsoever short, would give a vote, yet the clause undoubtedly had in view, what every body expected, that the subscription would be filled by degrees; and therefore that no subscriber, even on the day preceding the first election, should be deprived of a vote. The objection is also founded on too distant an implication, to counteract reasoning, otherwise weighty.

The consequence of the foregoing sentiments undoubtedly is, (as a branch of the third objection expresses) that original subscribers, who may have sold out and who no longer have a fellow-feeling for the success of the scheme, will be admitted to vote.

Is this the genuine construction of the law? If it be, it is not for any man to discuss the propriety of its consequences, I confess, that a consequence, extravagantly absurd, ought to lead us to be confident, that congress never contemplated it. But in many of the States we meet with a similar instance with the present. In certain elections none but freeholders can vote. In this none but stockholders or proprietors of capital stock can vote. Let it be supposed, that the freeholder has agreed in writing to convey to another his freehold, has received the purchase money and delivered the possession; as in the case of Script, the original subscriber may have agreed to sell, has indorsed upon it an assignment and delivered it, so indorsed, to the purchaser. This agreement as to the freehold would be considered in the States, to which I refer, as giving an equitable title only to the buyer, and reserving the legal title to the vendor. So in Script, the purchasers have the equitable while the original subscribers retain the legal title. Who would vote in the case of the freehold? The holder of the legal title. Who by a parity of reason ought to vote for directors? The person, who, being the original subscriber, is alone known, as the holder of the legal title. I have seen none of those indorsements or writings, by which Script has been attempted to be transferred: and therefore will not undertake to say, whether they amount to a substitution of the purchaser, as the proxy of the seller. He, who claims to be a proxy, ought to exhibit, if not a regular letter of attorney, at least some authentic appointment to the office. I have distinguished also between the real interest, and the right of voting at the first election. Hence the conveyance of one does not absolutely insolve the other. But I can concieve, that the words of those indorsements, may perhaps be broad enough, to justify a demand of the rights of a proxy.

4th.   The proxies, however, of no subscriber can have more votes, than himself. For example, four shares subscribed by one man, cannot by being divided into the hands of four proxies, confer four votes, as would have been the case, if each of them had subscribed a share. But what is to be done, if a subscriber has appointed several proxies? He may appoint, what number he pleases; but if they are divided, they cannot be called the proxies of an individual (if I may be permitted so to speak) integrally. To be the real proxies then, they must concur. It may perhaps be presumed, that, if the subscriber were in the division of his shares among his proxies to make them representatives respectively of so many, as would give them one or more votes, each might vote by himself. But their power being that of proxies only, they cannot claim separate suffrages; because they spring from the separate holding of stock in one person or in other words from separate subscriptions.

5th.   The fifth question being answered in the foregoing observations, I forbear to repeat the answer. But I will now recapitulate the general result.

1st.   That the commissioners cannot, as such superintend, or intermeddle in the election.

2nd   That the stockholders can easily of themselves provide judges of the election.

3rd.   That the original subscribers, whether holding interest or not, or their proxies, have the only right of voting.

4th.   That proxies may be made by any authentic act.

5th   And that all the proxies of the same subscriber must concur.

I pass by the possibility of a schism between the original subscribers or their proxies, and the assignees, as they are called, and of the election of two sets of directors. For this makes no part of your enquiry; and would be remedied by the commissioners, delivering up the books and money to that set, whom they think to be duly elected.

Edm: Randolph

To the Secretary of the Treasury

From William Seton

[New York] 18 Oct 1791

sir

I had the honor to write you on the 13th. since which, Indisposition has till this day prevented my obtaining from the Office the Certificates necessary to transfer to the Books of the Treasury the Debt purchased by me for account of the United States. They are now enclosed & I hope will be in full time. I have the honor to be with the greatest respect sir &c.

LC, Bank of New York, New York City.

From Benjamin Lincoln

Boston Oct 20 1791

Sir

When I first received your orders for supplying the Cutter [1] I attempted to bring the men to the established ration fixed by Congress. The moment our design was known a good Crew left the vessel. I was therefore obliged to supply as the Merchants supply or suffer the Cutter to remain in port. The latter I thought would be more difficult for me to justify than given the men the supply generally received on board merchant men. I therefore put a certain supply of provisions into the care of the Capt who had proper tubs made in which he could secure the provisions under lock. By the inclosed returns of the provisions expended You will be convinced that the rations for the men have Cost 12 Cents ℔ day. Upon the receipt of your letter fixing the ration at 9 Cents and specifying the several articles which should constitute a ration an attempt was again made to bring the people to it but without success. We cannot here Ship men for the Cutter unless the supplies can be augmented & be what men receive on common Merchant voyages. Matters must remain in their present State untill I shall have your farther direction.

Secretary of the Treasury

LC, Massachusetts Historical Society, Boston; two copies, RG 56, Letters from the Collector at Boston, National Archives.
1. "Treasury Department Circular to the Collectors of the Customs," September 21, 1791.

From Jeremiah Olney

Providence, October 20, 1791. "Enclosed is my weekly Return of Cash No. 63, the Balance of which is 4,322 Dolls. & 56¼ Cents. Two small Errors in my last Quarter's Accot., discovered since their transmission, make the Balance due to the United States on the 30th of Septr., stand in my Books, thus—

In Bonds uncancelled	58,922..81
In Cash on hand	5,519..78
	64,442..59

I enclose a Draft of the Treasurer in favor of Wm. Seton Esqr. No. 2362, for 1,000 Dollars, which I have paid and charged to the United States. . . . I have recd. your favor of the 7th Instant. The Explanation of your Meaning, relative to Coasting Vessels without proper Papers, is sufficiently clear and satisfactory. . . ."

ADfS, Rhode Island Historical Society, Providence; copy, RG 56, Letters from the Collector at Providence, National Archives.

From Baron von Steuben[1]

New York le 20me d'Octobre [1791]

De tout temps c'etait ma destiné de rencontrer ces Génies Extraordinaires qu'on Apelle Originaux de sorte que je ne suis pas surpris de me trouver en contact avec le Quaker Churchman.[2] Ce Philosophe magnetisé m'a communiqué ses idées et ses Chimeres; Je m'interesse à sa curiosité de vouloir reconnaitre ce point magnetique, dont nous connaissons l'effêct depuis des Siecles, et dont nous ignorons toujours la cause.

Ce point se trouve actuellement dans notre proximité; les Etats

Unis et le gouvernement Anglois en Canada peuvent atteindre ces Regions (dans une saison calculée) sans beaucoup de depense ni de difficulté.

Les lettres que Churchman m'a communiqué de plusieurs Accadémies des Sciences en Europe denoncent, généralement l'importance de ces decouvertes et Observations qu'il desire de faire; et une ambition patriotique me fait desirer que le gouvenement des Etats Unis ne soit pas tout à fait inattenif aux propositions de mon Philosophe magnetic.

Je suis bien loin de me noyer dans ses Deluges de Deucalion [3] et de Noah, dont il donne le calcul, ni de garantir l'exactitude de ses dimentions de longitudes par la Boussole; mais Je ne vous cache pas ma Curiosité sur les observations du point magnétique du Nord, et s'il est possible la cause de sa Variation.

Daignez parcourir les observations des Académies de Petersbourg, et de Berlin que M. Churchman vous communiquera et si vous les trouvez un Object digne de votre curiosité et attention, soyez le protecteur de mon Quaker et de son Hobby Horse.   steuben

ALS, Hamilton Papers, Library of Congress.
   1. H had become friendly with von Steuben during the American Revolution when the baron was inspector general of the Continental Army. At the close of the war von Steuben settled in New York and engaged in the development of a large tract of land north of Utica which the New York legislature granted to him in 1786.
   2. John Churchman, a Quaker of Calvert, Maryland, was a surveyor, land speculator, businessman, cartographer, and scientist. In 1787 he presented to the American Philosophical Society a paper giving a new theory of the variation of the magnetic needle. Other scientists in Europe and the United States rejected Churchman's theory. Although James Madison supported Churchman's petition to Congress in 1790 for funds to finance an expedition to locate the magnetic pole, Congress did not act favorably on this petition.
   3. In Greek legend Deucalion was the King of Phthia in Thessaly. When Zeus decided to destroy all mankind with a flood, Deucalion built an ark in which he and his wife Pyrrha survived the flood.

From Horatio Gates [1]

[New York, October 23, 1791]

Dear Sir.

If I am too troublesome in making the following Request, it is your own Fault, for you have encouraged me to do it. My agent, Mr. William Alexander, Mercht: in Richmond, Virginia, has by my direction, placed in the Hands of The Commissioner of Loans of that

State[2] Military Certificates, belonging to me, ammounting 14037 Dollars, & 52 Cents, to be Funded in my Name. I have lately sent Mr. Alexander a letter of Attorney, to enable him to Transferr that Stock, from the Loan Office in Virginia, to you, at the Treasury in Philadelphia, & my request is, that you will be so obliging, as to order it, to be further transferred in my Name to The Loan Office here. Amongst the Multitude of your Friends, and Admirers, believe me, there is few, if any, more Sincerely so.

Than Dr. Sir   Your Affectionate Friend & Servant   H G's

Rose Hill[3] 23d: Octr. 1791

ADfS, MS Division, New York Public Library.
  1. Following the American Revolution, Gates lived on his plantation in Virginia. In 1790 he emancipated his slaves and moved to New York City.
  2. John Hopkins.
  3. "Rose Hill" was Gates's ninety-acre farm two or three miles north of New York City.

From Nathaniel Peabody [1]

Atkinson, New Hampshire, October 24, 1791. Recommends to Hamilton's "friendly Notice the Honble Jereh. Smith[2] Esqr. one of the Representatives lately Gone on from this State to the Congress of the united States." Also recommends James MacGregore[3] for the position of Federal marshal.

ALS, Hamilton Papers, Library of Congress.
  1. Peabody was a New Hampshire physician and politician. A veteran of the American Revolution and a member of the Continental Congress in 1779 and 1780, he was a member of the New Hampshire Senate in 1791.
  2. Before his election to Congress in March, 1791, Jeremiah Smith had been a lawyer in Peterborough, New Hampshire.
  3. James MacGregore of Londonderry, New Hampshire, was state excise master in the seventeen-eighties and a member of the New Hampshire legislature in 1791.

From William Seton

[New York] 24 Oct 1791

sir

A Circumstance has occured respecting the Treasurers dfts on the Bank of Maryland which I take the liberty of mentioning to you.

We negotiated several of them the other day & when the holders presented them at the Bank for payment they deducted ⅛ ℀ Cent altho' the amount was named in their Bank & post Notes. This has occured before with the Collectors to the Southward but not that I have heard of with the Banks, for in fact the Treasurers dfts on the Cashier are the same as the Checks of an individual Depositor, and the partys expect to receive the full value without deduction. There may some reason exist for it of which I am ignorant. I hope therefore you will excuse my troubling you upon the subject, but as it may militate against our disposal of such bills after we have given credit for them to the Treasury, I wish to know whether the mode is right.

I have the honor to be &c.

LC, Bank of New York, New York City.

From William Ellery

[*Newport, Rhode Island*] *October 25, 1791.* "Yesterday the Brig: Seven Brothers [1] was condemned, no person appearing to claim her, and defend against the Libell. The person referred to in my letter of the 10th. of this month, who was a seaman on board the Sloop Betsy when the breach of the Revenue laws was made for which she was forfeited, and for whom a summons was issued, appeared before the District Judge and made his deposition, by which he appeared to be utterly ignorant of every thing that took place after the arrival of said Sloop in this District prior to her being entered. I shall summons the man who was mate of the vessel at the time mentioned, and if he should be as ignorant as the person referred to, the success of the cause against Cotrell [2] must principally depend on the testimony of a person who swore in the case of the Sloop Betsy and will swear again in this prosecution that he knew Cotrell's voice and that he heard him tell the hands who were unlading the vessel in the night not to speak so loud. . . ."

LC, Newport Historical Society, Newport, Rhode Island.
  1. See Ellery to H, July 11, August 2, 23, October 4, 10, 1791.
  2. See Ellery to H, August 2, 23, 26, 29, September 19, October 4, 1791.

From Jeremiah Olney

Providence, October 25, 1791. Acknowledges Hamilton's "Letter of the 14th instant,[1] covering part of the Margin of the Certificate of Registry . . . granted for Sloop Susannah. . . ."

ADfS, Rhode Island Historical Society, Providence; copy, RG 56, Letters from the Collector at Providence, National Archives.

1. As this letter deals with routine Treasury Department matters, it has not been printed (LS, Rhode Island Historical Society, Providence; copy, RG 56, Letters to the Collector at Providence, National Archives; copy, RG 56, Letters to Collectors at Small Ports, "Set G," National Archives).

To William Ellery

[*Philadelphia, October 26, 1791.* On November 7, 1791, Ellery wrote to Hamilton: "I have received your Letter of the 26th. of October last." *Letter not found.*]

From Joseph Whipple

Portsmo New Hamp. Octo. 26. 1791

Sir

Having collected & discharged the Several bills against the Revenue Cutter Scammel, I now transmit you herewith Inclosed my Account for the Vessel, & Vessels Stores. The Stores with Some Small disbursments amounts to 157 $\frac{88}{100}$ Dolls. and the Vessel to 1255 $\frac{95}{100}$ Dolls. which includes every article applied to her use except 12 pieces of Sail Cloth Sent from Boston by Genl Lincoln [1] of which I have no account nor directions respecting the payment. It will be observed that the Vessel exceeds your limitation by 155 Dolls. besides 12 ps. Sail Cloth not accounted.

Finding it impossible to Contract with any person on whom I could depend for a good Vessel fitted to the Sea, I proceeded in the usual way in practice here of contracting with the Carpenters for the Hull & in procuring the other articles on the lowest terms given in Cash. I determined on the dimentions for a Vessel whose bills together by calculation would amount only to the Sum limitted. But conceiving it to be conformable to your directions, as well as in my own opinion proper, that Cap Yeaton [2] Shoud give Such directions respecting the Rigging & fitting the Vessel as Should in his Opinion be most conducive to her usefulness, I submitted the directions for masting, rigging, Sails & finishing to him, injoining the Strictest œconomy in the manner of finishing the Vessel, urging the Necessity of not exceeding the apportionment to this Vessel of the Monies for the Service appropriated. But Capt. Yeaton conceiving differently from me in the outfitting of the Vessel submitted to him; the amount exceeds by nearly 300 Dollars my calculation & expectations—which arises principally from an excess in the Sails, rigging & Joyners work according to my Idea of the necessity of them. In the Stores furnished there is a Small deviation from the list transmitted, some articles being left out & not purchased & others added which were more necessary. I conceive It will be proper that colours should be added to the Stores which is yet witheld. I must acknowledge myself disappointed that the Vessel exceeds my calculations which I must impute to my confidence in Capt. Yeaton & his Zeal for the Good of the Service rather than to his extravagancy.

Cap. Yeaton has received from Boston 10 Muskets & 10 pr. of Pistols in bad order which I have caused to be repaired & fitted for Sea use.

I have paid the Officers & peoples wages and the Officers Rations to the 30th. of September, but omit for the present to transmit the Accounts till the forms intended Shall be forwarded or till final directions shall be given respecting the Seamens rations, to which my letter of the 7th. instant has reference.

The Wages & Rations paid to the 30th. Sep. & the Cost of the provisions now on board amount to Dolls. 538.15 which with the Account now transmitted Amounts to Dolls. 1951.98 & is the whole amount of payments on account of the Scammel.

I have the honor to be &c   J. W.

Hon. Alex. Hamilton Esqr Secy.

ADfS, RG 36, Collector of Customs at Portsmouth, Letters Sent, 1791–1792, Vol. 3, National Archives; copy, RG 56, Letters from the Collector at Portsmouth, National Archives.

1. Benjamin Lincoln, collector of customs at Boston.
2. Hopley Yeaton, captain of the New Hampshire revenue cutter.

From Oliver Wolcott, Junior

T.D
C. Off 26. Oct. 1791.

Sir,

I take the liberty to request that the opinion of the Attorney General of the United States may be taken on the question arising out of the following state of facts.

On the twenty first day of October 1780 congress resolved that the Officers of the Army who should *continue in service to the end of the war* should be intittled to receive half pay during life.[1]

On the 22d. of March 1783. the grant of half pay for life was commuted for a grant of five years full pay, to those Officers who were *then in service and should continue therein to the end of the war.*[2]

On the 23d. of April 1783, Congress expressed it as their opinion, *that the time of the men engaged to serve during the war, did not expire untill the ratification of the definitive Treaty of Peace.*[3]

On the 11th. of April 1783. a proclamation for declaring *a Cessation of Arms* between the United States of America & his Britannic Majesty, was published by Congress.[4]

In consequence of resolutions of Congress passed on the 23d. of April, the 26th. of May, the 11th. of June & the 9th. of August 1783. the Army was *furloughed* & the troops returned to their respective homes.[5]

On the 18th. of October 1783 a proclamation was published by Congress, for discharging that part of the Army which had been engaged to serve during the War, from & after the 3d. day of Nov. 1783. [6]

In the month of September 1783. an Officer of the rank of Major in the Army who had been previously dismissed on furlough died; and his representatives claim the amount of five years full pay, under the grant made on the 22d of March 1783.

The question resulting from the facts before stated, on which the opinion of the Attorney General is requested, is, *whether, an Officer who died in September 1783, continued in service untill the end of the war, so as to intittle his representatives to receive the grant of commutation for half pay during life?*

I am Sir with the greatest   respect your obed ser

The Honble Alexr. Hamilton Esqr
Secy of the Treas

ADf, Connecticut Historical Society, Hartford.
1. JCC, XVIII, 958–59.
2. JCC, XXIV, 207–09.
3. JCC, XXIV, 269–71.
4. JCC, XXIV, 238–41.
5. JCC, XXIV, 273, 364–65, 390, 496.
6. JCC, XXV, 703.

From John Neville [1]

Pittsburgh, October 27. 1791.

Sir,

Herewith I return your form filled in the best manner I am able at present. I beg leave to mention, that in a new Country like this where farming is not yet reduced to system, it is difficult to form an Estimate as you wish. Our farms are generally new—the eldest not exceeding twenty years.

In order to give you as good an idea as possible, I have divided them into three classes—annexing the just value of each class, and have averaged the product. I believe this rule would apply as equally here as any other. I have extended my enquiries to two or three different farms of each Class.

Should the method which I have adopted not answer your intention, or be too inexplicit; I will with the greatest pleasure make any further enquiries that you may think necessary.

I have the honor to be,   Sir,   With much respect,   Your Obedt. hble Servt.   John Nevill.

Alex Hamilton Esqr.

LC, George Washington Papers, Library of Congress; copy, George Washington Papers, Library of Congress.
1. Neville had served in the American Revolution as a colonel and after the war was a member of the Supreme Executive Council of Pennsylvania and a delegate to the Pennsylvania Ratifying Convention. In November, 1791, he was appointed inspector of Survey No. 4 in Pennsylvania.
Neville's letter was written in reply to "Treasury Department Circular," August 13, 1791.

Value of Farm.		averaged value 16/8.	Quantity consumed by Cattle and Poultry.	Prices
Kinds of Land.	Acres of arable Land.	47.		
	Acres of pasture land.	10.		
	Acres of Meadow.	7.		
	Acres of Wood-land.	250.		
Annual Product	Bushels of wheat.	150.		3/9.
	Bushels of Rye.	150.	30.	2/6.
	Bushels of Corn.	250	200	2/.
	Bushels of Oats.	160	60.	1/6.
	Bushels of Barley.	50.		3/9.
	Bushels of Buck wheat.	50.		1/6.
	Bushels of Potatoes.	200.	160.	1/10.
	Other roots and Vegetables in value.	Considerable quantities of pumkins, turnips &c. whose value I cannot ascertain.		
	Black Cattle.	4.		
	Horses.	2.		
	Sheep.	6.		
	Hogs.	15.		
	Dozens Poultry.	6.		
	lbs Tobacco.	a small quty. for own consumption.		
	Cords of wood consumed in fuel.	Without number.		
	Hay.	8. Tons.	6.	50/- ℔ Ton.

Lands divided into three classes.

1st Class—25/. ℔ acre
2d do—15/. do.
3d. do.—10/. do.

Kinds of Land & their annual products averaged.

2. LC, George Washington Papers, Library of Congress.

Account with Reinhard Kahmer

[Philadelphia, October 29, 1791]

Reinhard Kahmer bot for Cornal Hamilton at Sundred times

1791

october 19th	To . . 3 . . bushels of potatoes at 2s/9	£0 . .8 . .3	
	To a ½ . . peck of pears	0 . .1 . .10½	
	To . . a ½ . . bushel of turnips	0 . .1 . .3	
	To . . 3 . . bunches of Carrotts & Cabeges	0 . .0 . .9.	
	To . . 8 . . ld beef at 3 ½	0 . .2 . .4	
	To . . 12 ½ . . ld mutton at 4 ½ d	0 . .4 . .8	
	To . . . . buns & Som yearbs	0 . .1 . .8. ½	
20 . .	To . . 6 . . ld beef at 3 1/2	0 . .1 . .9.	
	To . . 2 . . bushels of Apels	0 . .5 . .0	
	To . . 8 . . ld butter at 1/3	0 . .10. .0	
21 . .	To . . 17 . . ld beef at 6s 1 ld suet at 8d	0 . .9 . .2	
	To . . 3 . . Dozen of Eggs	0 . .3 . .0	
	To . . 13 ½ . . ld mutton at 5d	0 . .5 . .7 ½	
	To . a ½ . . peck pears & Spinnag	0 . .2 . .3.	
	To onions . . 5 ½ endif 3d & Salrey 8d	0 . .1 . .4 ½	
	To . . a copel of fouls	0 . .2 . .0	
	To . . a basket	0 . .1 . .11. ½	
22 . .	To . . 7 ¾ . . ld veal at 7d	0 . .4 . .6	
	To . . 7 ½ . . ld beef at 5	0 . .3 . .1 ½	
	To . . time & parsly	0 . .1 . .6.	
	To . . a Set of Calfs feet	0 . .0 . .6	
	To . . 1 ½ . . bushel of turnips at 2s 6d	0 . .3 . .9.	
	To . . Eggs & Cabeges	0 . .2 . .6. ½	
	To . . Quals tripe	0 . .2 . .6	
	To . . 13 . . ld mutton at 4d	0 . .4 . .0	
24 . .	To . . 9 . . ld beef at 4d	0 . .3 . .0	
	To . . 2 . . bushels of turnips 2s/6d	0 . .5 . .0	
	To . . 4 . . fouls at 3/9	0 . .3 . .9.	
25 . .	To . . 5 . . bushels of potatoes at 2/9	0 . .13. .9.	
	To . . 10 ½ . . ld Corn beef at 3	0 . .4 . .4 ½	
	To . . 20 . . ld pork at 4 1/2	0 . .7 . .6.	
	To . . 14 . . ld mutton at 4	0 . .4 . .8	
	To . . . . Cabages	0 . .3 . .4.	
	To . . ½ . . bushel of Cramberis	0 . .3 . .6	
	To . . 12 . . Dozen of Eggs at 10d & 4 Dozen & 9 at 3/9	0 . .13. .9.	
	To . . 6 . . ld butter at 1/4	0 . .8 . .0	
29 . .	To . . a tung salt	0 . .2 . .6	
	To . . 13 . . ld mutton at 4 1/2	0 . .4 . .10 ½	
	To . . 3 . . teal at 1/3 a pice & Carrits 6d	0 . .4 . .3	
	To . . . . Swete potatoes	0 . .0 . .11.	
		£8 . .7 . .10	

AD, Hamilton Papers, Library of Congress.

Treasury Department Circular
to the Commissioners of Loans

Treasury Department
Oct. 29th. 1791

sir,

Mistakes have been frequently made by the Commissioners of Loans, in the certificates directed to me for the purpose of transferring stock from one office to another; either by erroneously indenting the marginal Check, or otherwise. And whenever inaccuracies of this kind have occurred, it has been thought adviseable to return such certificates to the holders, with some indefinite intimation, of their not being in proper order, and that of course they were to be returned to the office where they issued.

It being essential to know that the alterations required be actually made by the officer, and not by the parties; it is my desire that in every case, where an error shall be corrected by you, either by issuing a new certificate, in lieu of the one returned; or by making such alteration in the identical certificate itself, you will note the circumstance on the back of it.

Although the want of accuracy here noticed, has been partial only; yet a desire to obviate inconveniencies for the future, induces me to recommend circumspection in the execution of this business to the officers in general.

I am   Sir   Your obedt Servant   A Hamilton

LS, to Nathaniel Appleton, Pierpont Morgan Library, New York City; LS, to James Tilton, Delaware Historical Society, Wilmington.

From Joseph Whipple

Portsmouth, New Hampshire, October 29, 1791. "Inclosed herewith I transmit my quarterly Account for the Support & Maintenance of the Lighthouse in this State, & for the repairs to the 30th. of September past. The extraordinary quantity of Glass used in the repairs in this quarter was occasioned by the Oil taking fire in the Lantern & breaking the Windows, by which the building was in imminent danger of distruction. The cause of its taking fire I have not been able clearly to investigate, but am apprehensive it arose from the improper construction of the Vessel containing the Oil, which has been in use many years; It is an open pan about 20 inches diameter & 3 or 4 inches deep, the wick being Supported in it by an Iron plate (or piece of hoop) crossing, & Sunk in it, to the level of the Surface of the Oil. The Oil in use being fish oil, I find affords a very indifferent light, & as an improvement to the light I had procured Oil of a better quality & that was more free to burn—in the first tryal the accident happnd, which renders it necessary to lay this kind of Oil aside, till Such alteration is made in the Construction of the Lamps as will admit of the use of Spermaceti Oil with Safety. . . ."

ALS, RG 26, Lighthouse Letters Received, Vol. "B," New Hampshire and Massachusetts, National Archives; copy, RG 36, Collector of Customs at Portsmouth, Letters Sent, 1791–1792, Vol. 3, National Archives; copy, RG 56, Letters from the Collector at Portsmouth, National Archives.

From John Halsted [1]

Perth Amboy [New Jersey] Octor. 31st: 1791.

Sir

Having seen your plan, for the formation of a Manufacturing Company,[2] and the reasons you have assigned for establishing it in this State, with the Idea, that the plan is too extensive to be carried into full effect in one place to the best advantage to adventurers, induces me to request you to propose to the subscribers, this place, or its Vicinity, for one of the places of Manufactory, and the principal place of sale. To encourage which, I take the liberty to inclose a sketch of the Town, the waters Eastward which is the best and principal Harbour, with a Farm of four Hundred Acres, contigious to the Town for sale in whole or in part; [3] and I annex some proposals to the Company respecting the same, which I have to request, you will lay before them, or their Committee, as you shall find most proper.

The Proprietors of the Farm, propose to lay out forty acres, in four equal squares, to be divided into such Lots, as the Company shall approve, and to give to the Company on half the same, reserving the other half to themselves, and occasionally to sell to the Company or any other Persons at reasonable rates, such additional lands, as they may incline to purchase, or to sell them the whole Farm, if it shall best suit them on a view of it.

The Farm is within three fourths of a Mile of the Town. There are several situations well calculated for erecting a Town on, particular two, very convenient for Transporting by Water, to or from the Town or Elsewhere, the Navigation being little interupted in the severest Winters; There is a good situation for a Tide Mill, on a Creek sufficient to answer all the purposes, of grinding for the Manufactorers, and perhaps some other purposes; The situations are very healthy, pleasant, and conveniently situated to collect the articles at, that may be Manufactured at other places, or to supply them with materials from. On said Farm, there is Clay of the best quality for bricks, which may be made at a landing to save expence of Carting, also Clay, of tried and approved quality for Earthenware. The convenience of Transportation by Water will secure a supply of fuel, provisions, and raw materials for Manufacturing, as well as an easy access, to purchasors of Manufactures, or conveyance of them to other markets.

The Owners of the Farm, will be reasonable in their demand, and as they wish to promote every thing, that will tend to advance publick good, they would in case of a Sale, cheerfully subscribe the full amount to the factory.

There are some Lots in this Town, the most convenient, and best calculated for Wharves, Warehouses, and dwelling for Superintendants, or others, for sale.

Not having any safe method of laying the above proposals, and plan, before the subscribers, induced me to Inclose it to you for that purpose, and will I hope be deemed a sufficient excuse for my giving you this trouble.

I am very respectfully   Sir   your most Obedient Humble Servant
John Halsted.

The Honble Alexander Hamilton Esquire
Secy. of the Treasury
Philadelphia

ALS, Hamilton Papers, Library of Congress.
  1. Halstead was collector of customs at Perth Amboy.
  2. The Society for Establishing Useful Manufactures. See "Prospectus of the Society for Establishing Useful Manufactures," August, 1791.
  3. D, Hamilton Papers, Library of Congress. The heading on this map reads:

"A Sketch of Perth Amboy with a Farm of 400 Acres in it's Vicinity with the Streets & Roads discribed." A note states that Crane Creek adjacent to the farm "is navigable for Vessels of 40 Tons or upwards, as high as the place marked A, where a good tide-mill may be conveniently erected."

From Jeremiah Olney

Custom-House,
Providence 31st. Octr. 1791.

Sir.

The Schooner Alice, Jabez Andrus Master, entered here the 29th. instant, from Bonavista,[1] loaded with Salt only, a Manifest, as usual, being exhibited to the Inspector who first went onboard within this District. This Morning I recd. a Letter from Jona. Maltbie, Master of the Argus Cutter,[2] informing me, that One of his Mates went onboard the said Schooner and found no Manifest: This Information, he says, he gives in consequence of Directions from you: I wish Sir, to know whether it is your Meaning that every Master of a Vessel from a foreign Port should be prosecuted agreeable to the 12th Section of the Collection Law,[3] for the Penalty incurred by *neglecting* to have Manifests onboard on his arrival within Four leagues of the Land? I shall omit the Prosecution of Capt. Andrus until I am favored with your reply.

I have the Honor to be &c   Jereh. Olney Collr.

Alexr. Hamilton Esqr.
Secy. of the Treasy.

ADfS, Rhode Island Historical Society, Providence; copy, RG 56, Letters from the Collector at Providence, National Archives.

1. A port on the east coast of Newfoundland.
2. Jonathan Maltbie. The *Argus* was the Connecticut revenue cutter.
3. Section 12 of "An Act to provide more effectually for the collection of the duties imposed by law on goods, wares and merchandise imported into the United States, and on the tonnage of ships or vessels" reads as follows: "*And be it further enacted*, That if the master or other person having the charge or command of any ship or vessel laden as aforesaid, and bound to any port or place in the United States, shall not, upon his arrival within four leagues of the coast thereof, or within the limits of any district thereof, where the cargo of such ship or vessel or any part thereof is intended to be discharged, produce such manifest or manifests in writing, to the proper officer or officers upon demand thereof, and also deliver such copy or copies thereof as aforesaid according to the directions of this act in each case, or shall not give an account of the destination of such ship or vessel, which he is hereby required to do, upon request of such officer or

officers, or shall give a false account of the said destination, in order to evade the production of the said manifest or manifests, the said master or other person having the charge or command of such ship or vessel, shall forfeit for every such refusal, neglect or offence, a sum not exceeding five hundred dollars. And if such officer or officers first coming on board, in each case within the distance or limits aforesaid, shall neglect or refuse to certify on the back of such manifest or manifests, the production thereof, and the delivery of such copy or copies respectively, as are herein before directed to be delivered to such officer or officers; every such officer, so neglecting or refusing, shall forfeit and pay the sum of five hundred dollars" (1 *Stat.* 157 [August 4, 1790]).

To the Senate and the House of Representatives [1]

[Philadelphia, October 31, 1791]

Arrangement made by the President of the United States, with respect to the subdivisions of the several districts thereof into surveys, the appointment of officers, and the assignment of compensations, pursuant to the act of Congress, passed the third day of March, 1791, entitled "An act repealing, after the last day of June next, the duties heretofore laid upon distilled spirits, imported from abroad, and laying others in their stead; and also upon spirits distilled within the United States, and for appropriating the same." [2]

New Hampshire forms one survey of inspection. The duties of inspector are performed by the supervisor; to this office Joshua Wentworth has been appointed. His compensation is a salary of five hundred dollars, and a commission of one half per centum.

Massachusetts forms three surveys of inspection. No. 1 consists of the province of Maine; No. 2, of the counties of Essex, Middlesex,

ASP, Finance, I, 110–11.
    1. This document should be compared with George Washington to H, March 15, 1791.
    An entry in the *Journal of the House* for November 1, 1791, reads as follows:
    "A message, in writing, was received from the President of the United States, by Mr. Lear, his Secretary, as followeth:
                                    'United States, *October 31st,* 1791.
Gentlemen of the Senate and of the House of Representatives:
    I send you, herewith, the arrangement which has been made by me, pursuant to the act, entitled, "An act repealing, after the last day of June next, the duties heretofore laid upon distilled spirits imported from abroad, and laying others in their stead; and also upon spirits distilled within the United States; and for appropriating the same," in respect to the subdivisions of the several districts, created by the said act, into surveys of inspection, the appointment of officers for the same, and the assignment of compensations.   G. Washington'"
(*Journal of the House,* I, 445.)
    2. 1 *Stat.* 199–214 (March 3, 1791).

Worcester, Hampshire, and Berkshire; No. 3, of the residue of the State. Nathaniel Gorham has been appointed supervisor; his compensation is a salary of eight hundred dollars, and a commission of one half per cent. The supervisor performs the duties of inspector of survey No. 1. Jonathan Jackson has been appointed inspector of survey No. 2, and Leonard Jarvis, for survey No. 3. The compensation to each of these inspectors is a salary of five hundred dollars, and a commission of one half per cent.

Rhode Island forms one survey. The duties of inspector are performed by the supervisor. John S. Dexter has been appointed to this office, with an allowance of a salary of five hundred dollars, and a commission of one half per cent.

Connecticut forms one survey. The duties of inspector are performed by the supervisor, who is John Chester. His compensation is a salary of six hundred dollars, and a commission of one half per cent.

Vermont forms one survey, of which the supervisor performs the duties of inspector. Noah Smith has been appointed to this office. His allowance is a salary of four hundred dollars, and a commission of one half per cent.

New York forms one survey, of which the supervisor acts as inspector. William S. Smith has been appointed to this office, with a salary of eight hundred dollars, and a commission of one half per cent.

New Jersey forms one survey. The supervisor performs the duties of inspector. To this office, Aaron Dunham has been appointed. His compensation is a salary of four hundred dollars, and a commission of one half per cent.

Pennsylvania forms four surveys. No. 1 consists of the city and county of Philadelphia, and the counties of Bucks and Montgomery; No. 2, of the counties of Berks, Northampton, Luzerne, and Northumberland; No. 3, of the counties of Delaware, Chester, Lancaster, York, Dauphin, Cumberland, Franklin, Mifflin, and Huntingdon; No. 4, of the counties of Bedford, Westmoreland, Washington, and Alleghany. The supervisor for the district, George Clymer, acts as inspector of survey No. 1. His compensation is a salary of one thousand dollars, and a commission of one half per cent. James Collins has been appointed inspector of survey No. 2, Edward Hand, of survey No. 3, and John Neville, of survey No. 4. The allowance to each of these inspectors, is a salary of four hundred and fifty dollars, and a commission of one per cent.

Delaware forms one survey, of which the supervisor acts as inspector. His compensation is a salary of four hundred dollars, and a commission of one per cent. Henry Latimer, who was appointed supervisor, has resigned his office.

Maryland forms two surveys. No. 1 comprehends the counties of St. Mary's, Somerset, Calvert, Queen Anne's, Caroline, Kent, Charles, Talbot, Dorchester, Baltimore, Ann Arundel, Worcester, Hartford, Cecil, and Prince George's. No. 2 consists of the counties of Montgomery, Washington, Frederick, and Alleghany. The supervisor of the district, George Gale, officiates as inspector of survey No. 1. His compensation is a salary of seven hundred dollars, and a commission of one per cent. Philip Thomas has been appointed inspector of survey No. 2, with a salary of four hundred and fifty dollars, and a commission of one per cent.

Virginia has been divided into seven surveys of inspection. No. 1 consists of the counties of Lancaster, Northumberland, Richmond, Westmoreland, King George, Caroline, Hanover, Henrico, Charles City, James City, Warwick, Elizabeth City, York, Gloucester, Mathews, Middlesex, Essex, King and Queen, King William, and New Kent; No. 2 of the counties of Stafford, Prince William, Fairfax, Loudon, Fauquier, Culpepper, Orange, Albemarle, Louisa, and Spottsylvania; No. 3, of the counties of Goochland, Fluvanna, Amherst, Bedford, Franklin, Henry, Patrick, Pittsylvania, Halifax, Charlotte, Mecklenburg, Lunenburg, Nottoway, Amelia, Powhatan, Cumberland, Buckingham, Prince Edward, and Campbell; No. 4, of the counties of Princess Anne, Chesterfield, Norfolk, Isle of Wight, Sussex, Surry, Prince George, Dinwiddie, Brunswick, Greensville, Southampton, Nansemond, Accomac, and Northampton; No. 5, of Frederick, Berkley, Hampshire, Hardy, Monongalia, Ohio, Harrison, Randolph, Pendleton, Augusta, Rockingham, and Shenandoah; No. 6, of the counties of Rockbridge, Botetourt, Montgomery, Wythe, Washington, Russel, Greenbrier, and Kenhawa; No. 7 consists of the district of Kentucky. Edward Carrington has been appointed supervisor, with a salary of one thousand dollars, and a commission of one per centum. Drury Ragsdale has been appointed inspector of survey No. 1; Edward Stevens, of No. 2; Mayo Carrington, of No. 3; Thomas Newton, of No. 4; Edward Smith, of No. 5; James Brackenridge, of No. 6; and Thomas Marshall, on No. 7. The compensations to these officers are, to each, a salary of four hundred and fifty dollars, and a commission of one per cent.

North Carolina forms five surveys. No. 1 consists of the counties of Wilmington, Onslow, New Hanover, Brunswick, Bladen, Duplin, Anson, Richmond, Moore, Cumberland, Robertson, and Sampson; No. 2, of the counties of Carteret, Hyde, Beaufort, Pitt, Craven, Jones, Dobbs, Johnson, and Wayne; No. 3, of the counties of Currituck, Camden, Pasquotank, Perquimons, Chowan, Gates, Hartford, and Tyrrel; No. 4, of the counties of Northampton, Martin, Halifax, Nash, Edgecomb, Warren, Franklin, Caswell, Orange, Randolph, Granville, Wake, and Chatham; No. 5, of the counties of Mecklenburg, Montgomery, Roan, Iredel, Surry, Stokes, Rockingham, Guilford, Lincoln, Rutherford, Burke, and Wilkes. William Polk has been appointed supervisor, and a salary of seven hundred dollars, and a commission of one per cent., have been assigned him as a compensation. James Read has been appointed inspector of survey No. 1; John Daves, of No. 2; Thomas Benbury, of No. 3; John Whitaker, of No. 4; and Joseph McDowel, the elder, of No. 5. The compensations to the inspectors of surveys No. 1, 2, and 3, are, to each, a commission of two per centum; those inspectors being also officers of the customs. A salary of four hundred and fifty dollars, and a commission of one per cent., have been assigned as a compensation to the inspectors of surveys No. 4 and 5, respectively.

South Carolina forms three surveys. No. 1 consists of the counties of Colleton, Berkeley, Washington, Marion, Bartholomew, Charleston, Granville, Hilton, Lincoln, Shrewsbury, Winton, Orange, and Lewisburg; No. 2, of the counties of Winyaw, Williamsburgh, Liberty, Kingston, Darlington, Chesterfield, Marlborough, Clarendon, Clermont, Lancaster, Kershaw, Richland, Fairfield, Chester, and York; No. 3, of the counties of Edgefield, Abbeville, Newbury, Laurens, Union, Spartanburg, Greenville, and Pendleton. The duties of inspector of survey No. 1, are performed by the supervisor, Daniel Stevens, to whom a salary of seven hundred dollars, and a commission of one per cent., have been assigned as a compensation. Benjamin Cudworth has been appointed inspector of survey No. 2, and Sylvanus Walker, of No. 3. The compensation assigned to the inspector of survey No. 2, is a salary of three hundred dollars, and a commission of two per centum; to the inspector of survey No. 3, a salary of four hundred and fifty dollars, and a commission of one per cent.

Georgia forms one survey. The supervisor, John Matthews, officiates as inspector; the compensation assigned him, is a salary of five hundred dollars, and a commission of one per cent.

The commission, in each case, is computed upon the nett product of the duties on spirits distilled within the jurisdiction of the officer, to whom it is allowed; which nett product is determined by deducting, at each stage of the compensaton, all preceding charges.

With regard to the ports, the following arrangements have been made: At the ports at which there are both a collector and a surveyor, the latter has been appointed an inspector; where there is a collector only, he has been appointed; and where there is a surveyor only, he has been appointed. The ports at which neither collector nor surveyor resides, have been placed under the inspection of the collector or surveyor of the district to which they belong, as the one or the other is the inspector of the revenue for the port where he resides. The duties of these inspectors are confined to spirits imported from abroad; and, as they bear an analogy to those which they have been accustomed to perform, no compensation has been assigned. The officers, directed by the 18th section of the law to be appointed by the supervisors,[3] have been denominated collectors of the revenue. Their number has been, of necessity, left to the discretion of the supervisor,[4] with these general intimations, that they should be, in all cases, as few as the proper execution of the business would permit; and that, in regard to the collection of the duties on stills, one for each county would suffice; but this regulation necessarily varies as the stills are more or less dispersed. Where they are much scattered, two, three, or more counties, have been assigned to the same person. The compensation to these officers is a commission on the sums collected by each, of two per centum on the product of the duties on spirits distilled from foreign materials, and of four per centum on the product of the duties arising from spirits distilled from domestic materials, whether

3. Section 18 of this act reads as follows: "*And be it further enacted*, That the supervisor of each district shall appoint proper officers to have the charge and survey of the distilleries within the same, assigning to each, one or more distilleries as he may think proper, who shall attend such distillery at all reasonable times, for the execution of the duties by this act enjoined on him" (1 *Stat.* 203).

4. See enclosure to "Treasury Department Circular to the Collectors of the Customs," May 26, 1791.

per gallon, or by the still. This difference was dictated by the different nature of the business.

By order of the President of the United States.

Alexander Hamilton, *Secretary of the Treasury.*
Treasury Department, *October* 31, 1791.

From Thomas Smith

Loan Office [Philadelphia] Pennsa. Octr. 31st. 91

Sir

I now forward abstra[c]t of Old Emission Money Certificates & Indents received agreeable to act of Congress [1] from the 17th day of Sept. to the 30th sept Inclusive. The Old Emission Money Certificates & Indents are this day forwarded to the Auditors office. Numbers of People have presented Certificates of the United states & state Debt for the purpose of funding since the 1st of Octr.

I am &c

Honble Alexr Hamilton
Secty Treasy U States

LC, RG 53, Pennsylvania State Loan Office, Letter Book, 1790–1794, Vol. "615-P," National Archives.
1. "An Act making provision for the (payment of the) Debt of the United States" (1 *Stat.* 138–44 [August 4, 1790]).

From Thomas Williams [1]

[*Richmond, October 31, 1791.* On June 19, 1793, Williams wrote to Hamilton: "I rote you the 31 of Octobr 1791." *Letter not found.*]

1. See H to John Hopkins, April 2, 1791.

To Wilhem and Jan Willink, Nicholaas and Jacob Van Staphorst, and Nicholas Hubbard

Treasury Department,
October 31st. 1791.

Gentlemen,

I have directed the Treasurer of the United States to draw upon you for one million of Guilders, at the same sight as in the last case.[1] These Bills will be discharged out of the loan of 6.000.000[2] of Guilders, mentioned in the letters of Mr. Short and yourselves, of August last.

I am &c.   Alexander Hamilton.

Messrs. Willink, Van Staphorst,
& Hubbard. Amsterdam.

Copy, RG 233, Reports of the Treasury Department, 1792–1793, Vol. III, National Archives. This letter was enclosed in H's "Report on Foreign Loans," February 13, 1793.
  1. See H to Willink, Van Staphorst, and Hubbard, March 18, 1791.
  2. The Holland loan of September, 1791. For a description of this loan, see William Short to H, August 31, 1791.

From John Dexter [1]

[*October, 1791. Letter not found.*]

[E N C L O S U R E]

Moses Brown to John Dexter [2]

Providence 22d. 7th Mo. [– October 15] 1791

Esteemed Friend
    I duly recd, thy Lre, of the 7th Inst with a Copy of a Lr, from the

  1. Dexter was supervisor of the revenue for Rhode Island. Although Dexter's covering letter has not been found, he apparently forwarded the two letters printed below to H sometime in October, 1791.
  2. ALS, Hamilton Papers, Library of Congress. Brown was a prominent Providence merchant and philanthropist. After the American Revolution he became interested in cotton manufacturing and in 1789 was instrumental in founding the Providence firm of William Almy and Smith Brown. Later in the same year he persuaded Samuel Slater to settle in Providence and construct there his cotton manufacturing machinery.
    On July 7, 1791, Dexter had written to Brown as follows: "I take the liberty to send you the enclosed, being the copy of a letter which I received a day or two since, from the secretary of the treasury, and to request you to give me, as soon as convenient, in writing, such information as you may possess, (and which the secretary is solicitous to obtain,) on the subjects stated in his letter. You will readily conceive that a transmission of the information requested, to the secretary, may involve consequences favourable to the manufacturing interest in this state. I address myself to you on this subject with the more confidence from a full conviction, that as no one in the state has more at heart the encouragement of our infant manufactures—has been more indefatigable and liberal in the estab-

Secy of the Treasury of the 22d Ulo [3] inclosed, and as a subject of promoting Manufactures in this country has been adviseable Object in my view for years past, I shall chearfully give every information in my power which may contribute to further the views of the National Legislature or Assist the Secy. in forming a plan for promoting Manufactures in the United States.

The Spermacity Manufactory was extensive here, before the late War, it commenced in this Town about 1754. When Most of the Headmatter Caught in this Country was, with the Oil, carried to England but as Experience was gained in working and an increased quantity thereby got Out of a barrel, the price for saving it seperate from the Oil was increased and the Whalemen incouraged to save the headmatter first before they did the Oil, and the Increase of the Fishery was greatly promoted by the bounty given on the Headmatter above the price of the Body Oils so that from 80 to 130,000 lb Weight of Spermacity candles were Annualy Made here from the year 1760 to 1776 According to the success of the Fishery from this Town and Nantuckett from whence We imported the greater part. The Whale Fishery being broken up by the War; and but little gone into from hence Since, together with the great impoverishment of the people of the Island of Nantuckett by the War, who have not yet rose to One half their Vessels they had before and the Manufacturers of Candles there Working Most of the Heads Caught there, that Valuable Branch seems to be Lost to the Town and I am prety clear there is not half the Quantity of Spermaceti Candles made in America Any One year Since the War as was made in this *Town, only,* for several years before It. The Spermaceti Whale are Drove from their Usual Feeding Ground so that the Oil caught is principaly from the Right Whale or bone Whale, as is allso the case of the Fisheries from England and France from which Whale, no SpermaCety is Taken but from the Body Oil of SpermaCeti Whale a small proportion is Extracted which is Made Up with the Headmatter & principaly carryed to the Westindia Markett as well from England as America.

The Distilleries of Spirits have been Antient in this Town One

lishment, improvement and use of them than yourself, so no one can possibly possess a more competent knowledge of their commencement, progress, and present state" (White, *Samuel Slater,* 93–94).

3. See "Treasury Department Circular to the Supervisors of the Revenue," June 22, 1791.

Large One for Spirits and Two for Gin Since the peace but as the Import Laws & Revenue thereby Collected will best shew their present state I shall not add respecting them. We had One sugar house before the war, One erected about or near the Close of it and another Since, the last of these, only is at Present Supplyd or wrought in, probably owing to the Difficulty of Obtaining Stock Sufficient to Make the Business an Object to the Owners, Like Our SpermaCeti Manufacturies.

In the Spring of the year 1789 some persons in this Town had procured Made a Carding Mashine, a Jenney and a Spining Fraim to work by hand After the manner of Arkwrights Invention, Taken principaly from Models belonging to the State of Massachusets which was Made at their Expence by Two persons from scotland who took their Ideas from Observation and not from Experience in the Business,[4] These Mashines made here not Answering the purpose & Expectations of the proprietors and I being desireous of perfecting them if possible, and the Business of the Cotton Manufactury so as to be usefull to the Country I purchased them, and by great Alterations, the Carding Mashine & Jenny was made to answer The Fraim with One Other or nearly the same Construction made from the same Moddle and Tryed witout success at East Greenwich, which I allso purchased, I attempted to set to Work by Water and Made a Little yarn so as to answer for Warps, but being so Imperfect both as to the Quality and Quantity of the yarn that their progress was Suspended till I could procure a person who had Wrought or seen them wrought in Europe for as yet we had not, late in the fall I recd a Letter from a young Man then lately Arived at New york from Arkwrights works in England informing Me his scituation, that he could hear of no perpetual Spining Mills on the Continent but Mine & proposed to come and work them.[5] I wrote him & he came Accordingly, but on viewing the Mills he declined doing anything with them and proposed Making a New One Useing such parts of the Old as would Answer, We had by this time got several Gennies and some Weavers at Work on Linnen Warps, but had not been able to get Cotton Warps to a Usefull Degree of perfection on the Jennies and Altho I had found the

4. Joseph Alexander and James McKerries.
5. Samuel Slater's letter to Brown dated December 2, 1789, and Brown's reply, dated December 10, 1789, are printed in White, *Samuel Slater*, 72–73.

Undertaking much more Arduous than I Expected both as to the Attention Necessary and the Expence, being Necessitated to Employ Workmen of the most Transient kind and on whom Little Dependence could be placed and to Collect Materials to Compleat the Various Mashines from Distant parts of the Continent however We, I say, We (because I had Committed the Immediate Mannagement of the Business to my son in Law Wm. Almy and kinsman Smith Brown under the firm of Almy & Brown) contracted with the young Man from England to Direct and Make a Mill in his own way which he did and it answered a Much better purpose than the former but still imperfect for want of Other Mashines such as Cards of a Different Construction from those Already Made and remadeover, with various other Mashines preparitory to the Spining, all which with the Necessary Mechanicks Skilled in Working of Wood, Iron, Brass &c &c was more than Twelve month Compleating before we could get a single Warp of Cotton perfected, During this Time Linnen Warps were wove and the Jennie Spining was performed in Different Sellers of Dwelling Houses but finding the Illconvenience of this We have now a Factory House & Dye House Erected and Occupie Other Buildings for the Singing, Callendering & other Mashines. There being a Variety of Branches in the Perfecting of the Cotton Business, as, the Picking, Soaping Pressing, Stoveing or Drying the Cotton, ropeing it by hand or on Mashines, Spining, Bobbin winding, Weaving, Cutting for Velvets or other Cut goods, Singing or Dressing, Bleaching Dying and Finishing, renders it more Difficult and requires longer Time to perfect than many Other Branches of Business in a Country where there are very few acquainted with it, but when Each Branch is Learned it May be Extended to Any length Necessary by Means of the great Advantage of the Mashines in the saving of Labour. There has been Made in this Factory of Almy & Browns Since the 1st of the 1st Mo last Velveteens Velverets, Corduroys, Thicksets a variety of Fancy cutt goods Jeans, Denims, Velures, Stockenets, Pillows or Fustians &c &c as ⅌ Acct at Bottom, 326 ps Costg 7823 yards There are allso Several Other persons who Manufacture Cotton & Linnen goods by the Carding Mashines & Jennies but when they Make all Cotton Goods they have the Warps from Almy & Browns Mills, Samuel slater the young Man from England being allso Concernd therein. The Dying and Finishing is allso Chiefly done by their Workmen. There are allso Cotton & Linnen Goods Manufactured at East Greenwich, their Cotton Warps are Made at the Afforesaid Mills, The Quantities Manufactured by those several Persons and Others in the Common way of family Work I expect will be given an Account of by them selves or Collected by the Mechanical & Manufacturing Society in this Town; [6] I therefore refer to them. For the Degree of Maturity Our Cotton Manufactury has Obtained and their Different Qualities I refer to the Pattrons of the Mill yarn and Goods Made from Warps of it herewith sent, the prices sold at are allso Marked.

As to the Impediments underwhich this Business Labours I beg leave to Observe. No Encouragement has been given by any Laws of this state nor by any Donation of any Society or Individuals but Wholey began Carried on and thus far perfected at private Expence.

Our Commencing the Business at a period when from the great Extent of it in England and Ireland, and Other causes, Many became bankrupts, their goods were sold at Vendue and shipt to America in large Quantities, the 2 or 3 last years Lower than Ever before, add to this, which is much the Greatest, Brittish Agents have been Out in this and I presume, some Other Manufacturing Towns with Large Quantities of Cotton Goods for Sale and strongly Solisiting Corrispondence of people in the Mercantile Line to Receive their Goods at a very long Cr say 18 mo, which is 6 and 9 more than has been Usual heretofore, doubtless for the Discouragement of the Manufactory here, This bate has been too Eagerly taken by Our Merchants who from their Activity in Business Mostly Trade Equal to, or beyound their Capital and so are induced by the long Cr, to receive the Goods in expectation of Turning them to Advantage before the Time of payments but the great Quantities which some have on hand we have reason to expect will disappoint them, but Others being induced by the same Motive are supplyd and then the Quantities of Brittish goods of these kinds on hand, Exceeding the Markett Obstruct the sale of Our Own Manufacturys without the Merchant trading in them getting his Usual Proffits by them, this English Trade therefore in time would be reduced for want of Proffits, but when the Actual Sales of British goods fail, of the cotton Manufactury, they are Sent and left here on Commissions. This I am informed by good Authority was the Polacy of the English Manufacturers, formed into Societies

6. The Providence Association of Mechanics and Manufacturers.

for the purpose, about 10 or 12 years ago, when the Cotton Business began in Ireland, Agents were sent Out into the Manufacturing Towns of that Nation to Disperse such goods as was made there at a Less price than they could at first be Made, in order to break up the Business, which it is said would have had the Effect if the Irish parliament and the society for promoting Manufactures had not Taken up the Subject and granted Large Bounties, [7] Such as Effectualy Enabled the Manufacturer Soon to Vie with those of England in Supplying their Own Markett, and they now Export great Quantities. I Mention this Circumstance to Shew the Attention of the people of Ireland to Establish this Valuable Manufacture, and When it is Considered that, Cotton, The raw Material May be raised in the United States and not in Ireland, how Much More Attention Ought Our Legislature to pay to this Object? Which brings Me to the subject of Raising Cotton in Our Southern States which we find by Experience is as Imperfect and more so, than the Manufacturing when raised; This I presume is Much Owing to the promiscuous Gathering and saving of this Article from the podd,* in which it Grows, some of which like fruit on a Tree are fair and full Grown while Others are not, in the picking of which and takeing the cotton Out of the podd care should be taken that it be kept separate, and the thin membrance which lines the podd and some times comes off with the cotton in it's Seperation from them, should then be sevor'd and the clean full Grown preserved to Work on the Mashines, the Other will Answer to work by hand, but as the Cotton Must be Clean before it works well on the Mashine the present production in the Mixed Manner in which it is Brought to

---

* The frequent Shifting of the seeds of this as of Most Annual plants not Natural to the place of Raising, would most probably add to the perfection of the produce.

7. See, for example, 21 and 22 Geo. III, C. 8 (1781–1782); 25 Geo. III, C. 11 (1785). The "society for promoting Manufactures" was the Dublin Society, which was established by a group of prominent Dublin citizens in June, 1731, to improve manufacturing, farming, and other useful arts in Ireland. In January, 1737, it began publication of the *Dublin Society's Weekly Observations*, devoted to spreading information on brewing, agriculture, and flax husbandry. In 1746 the society applied for and received an annual grant of five hundred pounds from the government to enable it to continue its policy of offering premiums on manufactured products of Irish origin. In 1750 the society was incorporated as the Dublin Society for Promoting Husbandry and Other Useful Arts in Ireland. In addition to the annual grant of five hundred pounds, the society received substantial sums from the Irish House of Commons to enable it to continue its activities. See, for example, 3 Geo. III, C. 1 (1763).

Markett does not Answer a good purpose, the unripe short and durty part being so inveloped with that which would be good if Seperated propperly at first, so Spoils the Whole as to discourage the Use of it in the Mashines and Obliges the Manufacturer to have his supply from the Westindies Under the Discouragement of the Impost, [8] rather than Work our own production: a Circumstance Truly Mortifying to those who from Motives of Promoting the Produce and Manufactures of Our Own Country as well as from Interest, have been at large Expences & Trouble to Effect so Desireable an Object. I therefore beg leave to suggest the Idea of some Encouragement to the raiseing and Saving of Cotton Clean & good fit for the Manufacturers, as well as some Encouragement on the goods Manufactured, This perhaps may be Effected by Applying a Bounty on the raw Materials of the 1st Quality Suitable for the Business and on the goods Manufactured Equally to be paid Out of Additional Impost on all Cotton & Cotton & Linnen Goods & Cotton Yarn Imported into these states from abroad, May I not allso be permitted on this Ocation to suggest the propriety of Suspending the Impost on the first Quality of Cotton till Our Southern States could supply Such as would Answer to Work on Mashines. I have Mention'd Yarn, as the Importation of that Article from India has been Suggested by the late Manufacturing, Committee in Philadelphia [9] at which time no good yarn had been made fit for Warps, but as the Manufactury of the Mill Yarn is done by Children from 8 to 14 years old It is as near a Total Saving of Labour to the Country as perhaps Any Other that can be named, and there fore no Importation of the yarn Ought to be Admitted without a Large Impost if at all, as the Seccry May be assured that Mills and Mashines may be Erected in Different places in One year Sufficient to make all the Cotton yarn that may be Wanted in the United states both for Warps and for Knitting & Weaving Stockins, Was Encouragement given to protect the Manufacturer from being intercepted in the sale by foreign Importation, but from this Circumstance and that of the Abillities of the Manufacturing Interest of Great Brittain to Intercept the sale of Our Own Goods, at a price as low as theirs has been here-

8. Section 1 of "An Act making further provision for the payment of the debts of the United States" stipulated a duty of three cents per pound on cotton (1 *Stat.* 180 [August 10, 1790]).

9. Presumably the Pennsylvania Society for the Encouragement of Manufactures and the Useful Arts.

tofore sold by Our Importing Merchants, the Actual Combination of them in the case of Ireland and Most probably Our present Circumstance, forms a very great Discouragement to Men of Abilities to lay Out their propperty in Extending Manufacturies, the preparation for which even before they can be perfected Must be lost if they cannot be Continued. I have been lengthy on this subject not only because My family have Engaged in it, but because I conceive from the Advantages of the Mills & Other Mashines and the Raiseing of the Raw Materials Among Ourselves, this Country may avail itself of One of the Most Valuable Manufactures from which every part of the Union May be Supplyed. I apprehend this subject would have been laid before Congress by the United representation of the Cotton Manufacturers had not some states Liberaly Contributed to the promotion of it particularly the Massachusets, and the incorporated Company at Beaverly largely partaken of their bounty [10] in proportion to what they have done, Whether under an Idea that the Assistance they had recd would have Enabled them to go on, while Others would be under a Necessity of discontinuing the Business as some have in fact tho't best to do for want of that Assistance in the same Government Viz the Factory at Worcester,[11] or what Ever Other Reasons the Beaverly company may have, they have not come forward as Expected. The Publick Spirit of the Massachusets on this subject as well as Pennsylvania Are to be Applauded and in Justice to the Latter I Mention this Circumstance, The Publication of their grant to a Certain person for a Certain Mashine [12] in this Manufactory reaching England & Comeing to the Knoledge of the Workmen at Arkrights Mills Ocationd the workman before mentioned, privately comeing to America [13] and perfecting the first Water Spining in the United states

10. The Beverly Cotton Manufactory, which was founded in 1787. See George Cabot to H, September 6, 1791, note 4.

11. The cotton manufactory at Worcester, Massachusetts, had been established by a group of prominent Worcester businessmen in 1789.

12. This grant, which was passed by the Pennsylvania legislature on October 3, 1788, was made to John Hague for "introducing into this state a carding machine by means of which the establishment of a proposed extensive cotton manufactory may be greatly facilitated" ("An Act to Recompense John Hague for Introducing into This State a Useful Machine for Carding Cotton," *Pennsylvania Statutes,* XIII, 138–39).

13. George S. White describes Slater's motives for coming to the United States as follows: "During the last year or two of his apprenticeship, his thoughts as to his future course, and the establishment of the business on his own account, were

that I have heard of, 'tho I am informed a Company from England are now about to Erect Mills near New York for which the Mashinery is Making at Newhaven.[14] It is an Undoubted fact Authenticated to Me by Divers persons from England that the King has frequently made proclamation against any Trademen Leaving the Kingdom & Called on his officers for their most Vigilant Watch against it as well as against any Draughts of Mashinery being carried Out,[15] this allso Should excite Our Attention to those Advantages which they find of so much Consequence to that Country.

The Manufactory of Iron into Blisterd steel Equal in Quality to English has been began within about 12 Mo. in this Neighbourhood and is Carried only by Oriel Wilkinson who informs Me he can Make good Business at 10/ ℔ Ct for the steel in Blisters, Returning Weight for Weight with the Iron Manufactured. The Drawing into Barrs to any shape being an Additional Charge.

Beside the foregoing I had in Contemplation some remarks on Various Other Manufactures carried on within this District such as the Making of Woolen & Linnen Cloths, Riging, Lines & Twine, Pigg & Bar Iron, Sliting it into Rods roleing into plates & Hoops, Makeing it into Shovels & Spades, hot & Cold Nails, Anchors, paper mill & Cloathiers Screws, Wool and Cotton Cards with the Mashines for Cutting 800 Teeth in a Minute, Paper Mills, Fulling Mills Chocolate Mills & Snuff Mills by Water and Ginning of Cotton As well by Water as Improved foot Wheels &C &C. but having been more Lengthy on the subject of the Cotton Business than I Expected and the Time having nearly come when the Secry May want to Apply the Information he gets I delay no longer the Closeing a Letter I had

---

turned towards this country, by various rumours and reports which reached Derbyshire, of the anxiety of the different state governments, here, to encourage manufactures. The newspaper account of a liberal bounty (£100) granted by the legislature of Pennsylvania, to a person, who had imperfectly succeeded in constructing a carding machine, to make rolls for jennies, and the knowledge that a society had been authorised by the same legislature for the promotion of manufactures, induced him finally to push his fortune in the western hemisphere" (White, *Samuel Slater*, 37).

14. Presumably this is a reference to the firm of Dickson, Livingston, and Company which was at this time drawing up plans for a cotton factory on an island in the East River. The partnership consisted of "David Dickson, late of Moore Place, Moorfields, County of Middlesex, England, and Andrew Stockholm, late of Nantes, France, but now of New York, John Robert Livingston of New York, and John Leary, Jr., formerly of Boston but now of New York, all merchants and lately partners" (Bagnall, *Textile Industries*, I, 184).

15. See, for example, 21 Geo. III, C. 37 (1781); 22 Geo. III, C. 60 (1782).

so long ago began, and Omit saying Any thing further upon them, Apprehending the Society here will Include them & others so far as may be Necessary. My Apology for the Delay of My Answer to thy Lre, is only Absence from and Engagements when at home. If any Information worth the Reading Over this Long Letter can be derived I shall be glad and thou Art at Liberty to forward the same to the Secry. if thou thinks propper without further Apology for its incorrect state.

I am respectfully his & thy friend   Moses Brown

Providence 15th. 10th Mo. 1791.

Account of the Cotton, and Cotton & Linnen Goods Manufactured by Almy & Brown Since the Commencement of the Business say abt. 15th. of 6 Mo. 1789 to the 1st. of 1st. Mo. 1791.

45 ps. Corduroys	Contg	1090 yards	Sold from 3/6 to 4/4 ℔ yd.
25 ps. Royal Ribs Denims &c		558 yds	3/ to 4/
13 Cottonetts		324	2/6 to 3/.
79 Janes		1897	2/ to 2/6
27 Fustians		687	1/8 to 2/
189 ps		4556 yds	

From the 1st of the 1st Mo. 1791. to the Date being 10 Months

30 ps. Velverets	Contg	669	4 to £ 4/6
30 ps. Thicksets		745	3/6 to 4/.
45 ps Corduroys		1001	3/6 to 4/.
26. Fancy Goods Cords &C.		664	3/6 to 4/.
55 Royal Ribbs Denims &C.		1284	3/ to 4/.
74 Janes.		1769	2/ to 2/6
66 Fustians		1691	1/8 to 2/
326 ps	Contg	7823 yds	

John Dexter Esq Supervisor   Providence

[ENCLOSURE]

Report of a Committee Appointed to Obtain Information on Manufacturing in Providence [16]

[Providence, October 10, 1791]

The Committee appointed on the 19th. July last, to obtain a State-

16. DS, Hamilton Papers, Library of Congress.

ment of the Manufactures in this Town [17] &c. asks Leave to report.

That they have obtained from the several Manufacturers the Information contained in the following Statements.

Hat Making.

Quantity manufactured in the Year 1790.

121 Beavers, at 8 Dolls. each,

1327 Castors, at 18 to 48 Dollrs. pr. Dozen

4564 Felts, of diff. Qualities, from 5 to

12 Dolls. ℔ Dozen.

The Increase of the Business the present Year computed at One Third of the whole Amount of what was manufactured the Year past.

This Business was established in this Town in the Year 1730, of late great Improvements have been made and we flatter ourselves, that in a short Time Hats made in this Town will equal any imported in Elegance, as they always have in Durability exceeded them, owing to the Excellency of the Materials. The Quantity manufactured might be greatly encreased (except in Hats made of Beaver) was the Sale sufficiently extensive, and consequently the Prices might be diminished—altho it is allowed that Hats made in America are now sold as low in Proportion to their Quality, as those imported, the foreign Coarse Hats being very unprofitable to the Purchaser. And as the Country abounds with Materials, it is our Opinion that the Manufacture might in a short Time be extended to the full Consumption of the United States—and Hats become a great Article of Exportation if the Impediments were removed—some of which (as it appears to be the Wish of the Hon. the Secretary of the Treasury) we shall take the Liberty to mention. The Scarcity of Beaver and some other Furrs, produced in the Back Country is a great Impediment, which arises not from the Nature of the Country, but from other Nations being principally possessed of the extensive Furr Trade of the vast Continent, which enhances the Prices of Furrs so greatly, that Beaver Hats, which before the Revolution was sold at 5 Dollars, and sometimes at a Guinia, cannot now be afforded at less than 8

17. This was a committee of the Providence Association of Mechanics and Manufacturers. Dexter had sent a copy of the "Treasury Department Circular to the Supervisors of the Revenue," June 22, 1791, together with a request for information on manufacturing, to the association on July 9, 1791 (ALS, Rhode Island Historical Society, Providence).

Dolls. while the Price of Wool Hats are diminished considerably. If this Trade was commanded by the United States, it might prove a great Source of Wealth, exclusive of the manufacture of Furrs among ourselves. The Duty on imported Hats is so small [18] that it does not operate as a Check on Importations, where long practised, especially where Trade is managed by the Agents of Foreigners, who thro regard to the Interest of the Houses which employ them will do all in their Power to discourage the Manufactures of the Country where they acquire their Wealth. The Manufacturers in the Eastern States still feel the good Effects of a heavy Impost which some Years past was laid on foreign Hats,[19] but even in those States Importations are again made, which if attended with success must operate greatly to our Discouragement from which Government alone can defend us.

The necessary Trimmings, Bow Strings, &c. which are almost entirely imported, might, in our Opinion, with a small Governmental Encouragement, be manufactured among ourselves.

As to the mineral Substances necessary to coloring we pretend not to judge, as we are ignorant of the Expence attending their Preparation.

Block-making.

3496 Feet made in the Year 1790.

No return since. Workmen more than get Employ. Materials Plenty, and easily obtained.

Tanning & Currying.

In this Town and Vicinity the present Years Stock in Hides *Tanned*

Calf Skins,	3010
Goat	3226
Sheep,	451
Hides *curried, for diff Uses,*	1710
Calf Do.	1325
	4278

18. Under "An Act making further provision for the payment of the debts of the United States" (1 *Stat.* 180–82 [August 4, 1790]) the duty on fur hats was seven and one-half percent ad valorem.

19. In Rhode Island, for example, the legislature had at its June, 1785, session imposed the following duties on hats: "every beaver hat, six shillings, every castor hat, three shillings, every felt hat, one shilling and six pence" (*Records of Rhode Island*, X, 115).

Goat,   451
618 pr. of Boot Legs, from 1 to 2½ Dolls. pr.
Calf Skins, 18 Dolls. pr Doz.

The Embarassment on the Business of Tanning and Currying at present and for some Time past hath been very considerable, owing to the large Quantities of Leather imported from the West Indies, the Duty on which is small in Proportion to many other Articles.[20] We hope the Subject will be duly considered by the Hon. A. Hamilton, and such Information given to Congress, as may be proper and beneficial to those who carry on so great and necessary a Branch of the mechanic Business.

Saddle & Harness-making.
Made within one Year past.
999 Saddles, from 6 to 14 Dolls.
164 Sets Harness, for 4, 2 & 1 Horse Carriages,
  This Business might be carried on to a much greater Extent, if there were sufficient Sales for the Work, considerable Quantities of which are Yearly exported.

Fringe and Web-weaving
Made in 1790—1100 yd. Girth Webb—1350 yds. Fringe, 360 yd Lace. equall to any, and at a lower Rate than can be imported, so that the Maker (*Jonathan Hill*) wishes for nothing but to be known.

Woolen Cloth.
Manufactured in this Town & Vicinity, in the Year 1790 in the Factories & private Families, 30,000 yds. of all Qualities—a proportionable Quantity the present Year and was the raising of Sheep duly encouraged, a sufficient Quantity might be manufactured for the whole of the Inhabitants.

Boot & Shoe-making
Shoes made within one Year past, 15,356 Pair, from ⅔ds to 1½ Dolls. *Boots*, 215 pr. from 3⅓ to 8 Dolls.
  The Embarrassment this Business labours under is the Importation from Europe, which tends to undervalue the Price of our Work to the great Discouragement of our Workmen

20. The duty on leather was seven and one-half percent ad valorem.

Nails.

Manufactured in this Town, in 1790.

3,000,000,	Prices			Drs.	Cents
		20d ⅌. Hund.			
		10d ⅌. H.		1	
		8d ⅌. H.			88
		6d. ⅌. H.			75
		4d ⅌. H. (cut)			33
		3d ⅌. H.			25
		2d ⅌. H.			21

As the Materials for carrying on this Business, abounds in the Country; and as many Country Peoples, Boys, as well as Men work at it in the Winter Season, it appears, that Nails have and may still be manufactured cheaper than can be imported, especially since we have Slitting Mills sufficient to furnish the whole Country with Rods.

Edge Tools

4500 Scythes, Axes, & Drawing Knives, made in the Year 1790. As to Materials the like Observations may be made as in the foregoing Business.

Clock-making.

From January to August, 1791—has been made 6 Eight Day Clocks, from 33⅓ Dolls. to 40 Dolls. Might with the same Hands be made 3 Times that Number. There is as many if not more imported from Europe, than made in this Country.

Chocolate Manufacture.

Made in the Year 1790, 60,000 lbs @ 9d ⅌ lb.
Much the same Proportion continues to be made, but the Duty on Cocoa so much exceeds the Duty on imported Chocolate,[21] that if continued will discourage my Increase of that manufacture.

Soap and Candle-making.

In 1790—Candles made, 40,000 lb.   @ 6d ⅌ lb.
     Hand Soap,   10,000,   @ 5d ⅌ lb.

and continues in the same Proportion but labours under Embarrassment by Reason of large Quantities imported into the Southern States, with very little Profit to the federal Chest.

21. The duty on chocolate was five percent ad valorem; on cocoa a duty of one cent per pound was charged.

Coach and Chaisemaking

Made in 1790—56 Carriages of diff. Sorts.

Silver and plated Work

Made in 1790—   100 pr. Silver Buckles.
1400 pr. Plated Do.
80 Doz. Silver Spoons diff. Sizes.

This Business might be generally extended, especially in plated Work, there being more Hands than are fully employed—and large Sums, are sent to Europe, particularly for Coach & Chaise plated Harness Trimmings, which might be as well made here, and more durable, at nearly the same Prices.

Card-making.

Made 1790—2550 Pair, and by a Return for 6 Months past, it appears there has been made 100 Dozen Cotton, @ 8 Dolls ℔ Doz.
and 120 Doz. Wool, @ 5 D. ℔ Doz.

As this is a most necessary Business, so it is most profitable to the Public, as it employs Numbers of poor Children, who, while they are earning Somthing towards their Subsistence, are prevented from contracting bad Habits, and are introduced thereby to a Habit of Industry, by which we may hope to see them become useful Members of Society. It were to be wished that the Wire could be drawn in this Country.

Brass-founders Work.

Of all Kinds made in this Town Yearly to a large Amount, but by Reason of the great Variety of Articles, the Prices cannot be ascertained, but the Makers say as cheap, if not cheaper, and as good, if not better, than any imported from Europe.

Engines for extinguishing Fire!

There has been one made this season, equal to any that have been imported, and the Maker Daniel Jackson is ready to receive Orders for any Size, from 266⅔ds to 933⅓ Dolls Price.

Joiner's & Moulding Tools.

Made annually to the Amount of 1000 Dollrs, the particular Prices, by Reason of the great Variety cannot be ascertained but are at present sold something higher than those imported—the Workmen not having full Employ—but as the Materials are so easily obtained the Prices might be reduced upon Par with imported Tools if there was Vent for large Quantities.

Paper Manufacture

From the 1st. of January to 1st. October, 1791 has been made in this Town.

1584 Rh. Writing Paper, the average Price 2⅛ Dolls ℔ R.

340 Rh. Printing, @ 1⅔ ds

840 Wrapping, @ ⅚th. D.

153 Groce fine Paste Boards, 12 Dolls. ℔ Groce.

3000 lb. Sugar Loaf Paper, @ 8⅓ Dolls. ℔ Hund.

2000 lb Candle Do. @ 8½ D. ℔ H.

7300 lb Sheathing D. @ 3¼ D. ℔ H.

4800 lb Paste Boards
Do for Bookbinding } @. 4 D: ℔ H.

Paper, at present the most estensive Branch of Manufacture that is carried on in America, labours under great Disadvantages by Reason of the great Importations of the various Kinds of Coarse Paper, such as Paste Board, Sugar Loaf & Sheathing Paper.

Leather Dressing & Glove-Making.

From the 1st. of January to 1st. October, 1791.

Skins, wash Leather dressed, 125 Doz. @ 3 Dolls. ℔ Doz.

Ditto, tanned for Card Leather, 125 Doz. @ 3⅓ Dolls. ℔ D.

Women's long Gloves made, 200 Doz. @ 3⅓ ℔ Doz.

Do. Habit, 583 Doz. @ 3 Dolls.

Slit & rolled Iron Work

There is in the Vicinity of this Town, a *Slitting Mill*, which in the Year 1790, slit about 50 Tons Nail Rods—at the same Place was made 50 Doz. Iron Shovels, which now sell, the best made at 8 Dolls. ℔ Doz. but if the Business was extended so as to employ 3 Master Workmen there might be enough made to supply all the New England States, and the best Kind sold at 7 Dolls. ℔ Doz. There is also some Iron Hoops rolled at the same Mill.

Cotton Goods

Of diff Sorts manufactured from 1st. Jany to 1st. October, 1791.

    In Mess Almy & Browns Factory.　*No Return.*[22]

      In Mr. Wm. Potters,　　2164 yds.

          M Lewis Pecks　　　2500 Do.

          Mr. Andrew Dexters,　466 Do.

          Mr Jas. McKerns,　　700 Do.

The Prices by the Piece are

      Double twilled Cord,　　⅔ ds Dolls. ℔ Yd.

      Do. Fancy Cord,　　　⅔ ds Doll.

      Jeans, on an Average,　⅓ ds. Doll.

      Fustians,　　　　　　15½ Cents

As this Manufacture is growing in Consequence, and engages the Attention of Gentlemen not immediately concerned in the Mechanic Arts we doubt not it will find able Advocates—therefore think it unnecessary to enlarge in this Place.

There is large Quantities of Cabinet and Chair Work *Cordage*, Coppersmiths, Braziers and Pewterers Works made in this Town, of which we have been able to obtain no regular Statement but the Manufacturers of Pewter complain that they labour under a great Discouragement by being obliged to work large Quantities of old Pewter, which being of a base Quality, imported from Bristol and Liverpool, and sold here for London-make, they cannot, by Reason of the Scarcity of *Block-Tin*, make it equal to the London Standard, and at the same Time work up all the old Pewter in the Country.

Your Committee have only to remark upon the foregoing Statements, that if there is any Thing expressed, which should be thought forward in pointing out the Impediments attending the Prosecution

22. Almy and Brown's return apparently was not received until this report was completed. It later was inserted on a separate sheet and reads as follows:
   "Manufactured by Almy & Brown from the ⟨comm⟩encement of their buiseness to the 1st. of Day 1st Mo 1791.
        Corduroys Royal Ribs
        Denims Cottonets Janes
        and Fustians———189 peices—4556 yards
        ⟨Fr⟩om the 1st of 1st Mo 1791 to the present Date
        ⟨Ve⟩lverets thicksett Corduroys
        ⟨F⟩ancy Cords Ribs Janes & Ca 326 p 1819 yds."

of any Branch of Manufactures they are persuaded it arises from an honest Zeal for promoting the best Interest of the United States—and in full Confidence in the parental Regard of the Supreme Legislature of the Union. And it is the Boast of Americans, that instead of living under a Government which spurns at the Subject, for the Representation of any Thing that operates as a Grievance, those who fill the first Offices in Government are encouraging them to make such Representations, as may serve to give necessary Information; and we doubt not that altho there are very few in Congress whose *immediate Interest* is concerned, yet a sincere Regard for the *general Interest* will animate that truly honorable Body to give all the Encouragement which they can (consistent with a proper Regard to the Revenue) to that Class of Citizens who in Proportion to their Property pay so large a Share of the public Expence.

Signed by Order and in Behalf of The Committee,

William Richmond, Chairman

Provd. Oct: 10, 1791.

A true Copy from the Journals:

B: Wheeler,[23] Secy to the Ass.

23. Bennett Wheeler was a Providence printer and editor of the Federalist newspaper the [Providence] *United States Chronicle*. He was the first secretary of the Providence Association of Mechanics and Manufacturers after its establishment in 1789 and held the post for six years.

From John Daves

Collectors Office Port of New Bern [North Carolina]
November 1st. 1791.

Sir,

In obedience to your request to be informed what mode is customary among Merchants in this District for calculating the Tare upon Sugars, Coffee, &c.[1] I have made the following Statement, which was also my mode of calculating the Tare until the present Act of Congress entitled "An Act to provide more effectually for the collection of the duties imposed by Law on Goods, Wares and Merchandize, imported into the United States, and on the Tonage of Ships and Vessels"[2] required that I should vary my mode, since which I have strictly gone conformable to that Act.

I have also in obedience to your directions of the 5th. of August last,[3] enclosed an exact copy of the Table of Duties, Fees &c. which I have constantly set up in my Office in conformity to the 54th section of the Collection Law.[4]

With much respect I have the honour to be, Sir, Your Most Obedt. Servt.

The Honourable Alexr. Hamilton Esqr.

Copy, RG 56, Letters from the Collector at New Bern, National Archives.
1. "Treasury Department Circular to the Collectors of the Customs," May 13, 1791.
2. 1 *Stat.* 145–78 (August 4, 1790).
3. "Treasury Department Circular to the Collectors of the Customs," August 5, 1791.
4. Daves is actually referring to Section 55, rather than 54, of this act (1 *Stat.* 173). For an explanation of the confusion over the numbering of the sections of this act, see H to Richard Harison, April 26, 1791, note 2. Section 55 reads as follows: "*And be it further enacted,* That every collector, naval officer, and surveyor, shall cause to be affixed and constantly kept in some public and conspicuous place of his office, a fair table of the rates of fees and duties demandable by law, and shall give a receipt for the fees he shall receive, specifying the particulars; and in case of failure therein, shall forfeit and pay one hundred dollars, to be recovered with costs, in any court having cognizance thereof, to the use of the informer; and if any officer of the customs shall demand or receive any greater or other fee, compensation or reward, for executing any duty or service required of him by law, he shall forfeit and pay two hundred dollars for each offence, recoverable in manner aforesaid for the use of the party grieved."

To William Short

Treasury Department
November 1st. 1791

Sir,

I have barely time by this opportunity to inform you That I have directed the Treasurer to draw for One Million of florins on account of the last loan of six millions [1] and towards the close of the present month shall direct him to draw for another million. I calculate that the whole amount of the loan will have been received before the second set of draughts are presented.

I remain with great consideration & regard   Sir   Your obedt Servant.   Alexander Hamilton

Willm Short Esqr

LS, William Short Papers, Library of Congress; copy, William Short Papers, Library of Congress. A copy of this letter was enclosed in H's "Report on Foreign Loans," February 13, 1793.
1. The Holland loan of September, 1791. For a description of this loan, see Short to H, August 31, 1791.

From John Fry

London 2nd Novr. 1791.

Mr. Alexr. Hamilton

Dear Sir

The interest you must necessarily take in all information relative to the state of American Credit in Europe, having so essentially contributed to its establishment, induces me to communicate some facts, which from peculiar circumstances I am possibly better acquainted with than most others. The American Funds had inspired no Confidence in this market 'till they had acquired a high price at home & three months ago a sale of them must have been effected here with the greatest difficulty. The Case is now so materially alter'd that one friend of mine has bought & sold near a Million of Dollars, chiefly 6 ⅌ Ct. Stock, & another about half that amount, at prices gradually increasing from 98 to 120 ⅌ Ct. which latter price when exchange is at 175 ⅌ Ct in Philaa. is equal to 25/. Three per Cts. have also risen & are now at from 72 to 75 ⅌ Ct. & it appears to me that no fluctuations in America will have any essential influence on the rates in this Market whilst the sources of Revenue on which the Interest depends remain productive & secure. The Orders from France for Am Stock in London would indeed much enhance the present price had not such unfavorable accounts of Stock been lately receiv'd from Philaa.[1] Nevertheless the price does not sink because nobody here knows what to do with money. If it be an object with you, Sir, now the funds bear so fair a price, to promote the Sale of them here, *that the encumber'd Landholder* in America may eventually feel the benefit of that Capital which in this City is superabundant & unproductive, it can easily be effected by any plan for the payment in London of Interest on them, which shall be known, as I hinted to Mr. Tench Coxe, to be honor'd with your patronage. This view may also be promoted by facilitating foreign transfers. When I left Philada.

in August last I had heard much of the little value of money in this my native City, but the facts which since my arrival have come to my immediate knowledge have nevertheless surprised me; the market rate of Interest is really before 4 ⅌ Cent & for any uncertain periods money will scarcely command 2½ Cent ⅌ ann~. *All* the American Stock in Holland is effectually lock'd up from Sale, by deposits as security for Loans, notes for which are circulated, with private engagements for the Interest, that command 130 ⅌ Ct. The plans on which these loans have been obtained are various, but all immensely advantageous to those who purchased Certificates, & borrow'd in this way to continue their purchases. I have sent some considerable Orders to Philaa. for Stock & besides have offer'd whilst I remain in London to sell for those friends of mine who wish it at a half ⅌ Ct. Commn. which I hope will contribute to releive the American Market.

I shall be very sorry if this short address trespass too much on the time you so advantageously employ in the service of our Country to the real aggrandisement of your ministerial reputation at home & *abroad*. A desire to communicate serviceable information if in my power is my sole motive for writing ⟨& since⟩ I shall not return to settle in Philaa. before June ⟨if any⟩ thing very important on these Subjects should ⟨arise⟩ I m⟨ay⟩ still take the Liberty of hazarding intrusion on ⟨a⟩ moment of your leisure.

I am with the highest personal respect & esteem   Yours very sincerely   John Fry
                                Mercht. of Philadelphia
                                at No. 19 Grace Church Street
                                London.

ALS, Hamilton Papers, Library of Congress.
   1. This is a reference to a sharp decline in security prices in Philadelphia in August, 1791. See Fisher Ames to H, August 15, 1791, note 6.

To Horatio Gates

Philadelphia Nov 2. 1791

Private

My Dear Sir

The certificate mentioned in your letter of the 22d. of October [1] has not yet appeared at the Treasury.

When it does, your wish will be answered.

I will not tell you how high a value I set on the expression of your friendship; but I will tell you with great sincerity that I am very truly & affectionately

Yr. Obedient servant   A Hamilton

Horatio Gates Esqr

ALS, MS Division, New York Public Library.
1. H made a mistake, for Gates's letter is dated October 23.

From Benjamin Lincoln

Boston Novr. 2d. 1791

Sir

In May 1790 The Schooner Industry arrived in this District from Ireland with no other than an old State Register. The apology was that as she was owned in Virginia & there had not been time for her to renew her papers. This was accepted And the master Mr. Russell,[1] the Ships friend, were informed that their conduct was irregular & that the vessel could not be entitled to the rights of a Ship of the United States should she proceed with the old papers. She went however an other voyage returned here in Sept following at which time we considered her as liable to pay the foreign tonnage & which we receved. A few days since the same vessel entered here from Virginia with a New Register which she received there in April last. A demand is now made by Mr. Russel in behalf of the owner in Virginia for a return of the Foreign tonnage. As I do not feel my self authorised to comply with the demand, Mr. Russel has requested that I would state the matter to you for your decision which will end the question however you may decide.

In the exception of goods not chargable with a duty are *dying woods* amd *dying drugs*.[2] I find these very indefinite terms and that the revenue suffers in consequence thereof. Would it not be well for you sir in a circular letter, that there might be a practice uniform, thru the whole, to say what are considered as dying woods especially dying drugs for if every article is to pass as a dying drug which is in any proposition used in dying the Apothicary will pay few duties indeed. Verdigrise for instance is used by the dyers & painters. Many articles are used partly by the dyers partly by the painters, & partly by the compounders of medicine which makes it difficult to determine when we are right.

Under the 4th Ulto I suggested to you that in my opinion three out of four of our boat men might be discharged untill the spring without injury to the revenue. As you have not in any letter since mentioned the suggestion I am quite at a loss to know whether you approve or not the idea. As they were engaged by your Special direction I do not feel my self autherised, tho~ as I said before they cannot be useful to the public, to discharge them without your permission.

I am &c

Secy of the Treasury

LC, Massachusetts Historical Society, Boston; LC, incorrectly dated November 27, 1791, RG 36, Collector of Customs at Boston, Letter Book, 1790–1797, National Archives; two copies, one incorrectly dated October 27, 1791, RG 56, Letters from the Collector at Boston, National Archives.

1. Thomas Russell, a Boston merchant.
2. See Section 1 of "An Act making further provision for the payment of the debts of the United States" (1 *Stat* 180–81 [August 10, 1790]).

To James McHenry

[Philadelphia, November 2, 1791]

My Dr. Mc.

Your letter of the 15 of October came duly to hand and an answer has only be[en] delayed through extreme hurry.

My views on the point you mentioned cannot have changed and I am glad to know how you stand. All that confidence or attachment on my part could dictate will be employed. But nothing is certain. And nothing ought to be suspended on the event.

Indeed I cannot perceive how the one thing ought to interfere with the other. A change of position upon an unforseen circumstance is as common in politick as in war.

Yrs. Affect & sincerely   A Hamilton

Novembr 2d. 1791
Js. McHenry Esqr

ALS (photostat), James McHenry Papers, Library of Congress.

To Edmund Randolph

[*Philadelphia, November 2, 1791.* On November 9, 1791, Randolph wrote to Hamilton: "I do myself the honor of answering your letter of the 2d. instant." *Letter not found.*]

From Jeremiah Olney

Custom House,
Providence 3rd Novr. 1791

Sir.

Edward Peterson, Master of the Sloop Friendship, burthen Sixty-three Tons, arrived here Yesterday from New-York; from whence, he says, he brought a Certified Manifest and Permit to proceed, stopped at Newport, entered his Vessel, left the Manifest and Permit at the Custom House, landed part of his Freight, and proceeded with the remainder (consisting of the Articles contained in the enclosed copy of the Inspector's Return) to this Place, without a certified Manifest or Permit. I have taken the Goods into possession; and have acquainted the District Attorney [1] with this Transaction, that he may proceed against the Master and Goods as the Law [2] directs.

I have also been under the disagreeable necessity of taking into possession Six Chests of Bohea Tea, which, with Forty Bushels of Apples, composed the Freight of the Sloop Clementina, burthen 29 64/95 Tons, Samuel Westcott Master, this Day arrived here from Newport, with neither Manifest nor Permit to proceed; which he says he forgot to call for at the Office to obtain.[3] This information I have likewise communicated to the District Attorney.

I have the Honor to be &c. Jereh. Olney Collr.

Alexr. Hamilton Esquire
Secy. of the Treasury.

ADfS, Rhode Island Historical Society, Providence; copy, RG 56, Letters from the Collector at Providence, National Archives.

1. William Channing was district attorney for Rhode Island.
2. Section 67 of "An Act to provide more effectually for the collection of the duties imposed by law on goods, wares and merchandise imported into the United States, and on the tonnage of ships or vessels" (1 *Stat.* 176 [August 4,

1790]) provided the "mode of prosecuting and recovering penalties and forfeitures."

3. See Henry Marchant to H, October 8, 1791.

To James Taylor and Abishai Thomas [1]

Treasury Department Novr. 3rd 1791

Gentlemen,

The measures taken to ascertain the fact, whether *the State of
North Carolina has ever issued its own certificates in lieu of those
of the United States* [2] not yet having produced the desired information, as inconveniences would arise from longer delay of a determination of the question which arises on the eighteenth section of the Act
making provision for the debt of the United States.[3]

I take the liberty to request the favor of you to give me such
information as you may possess concerning the above mentioned fact
together with your opinions of the real state of the thing.

I have the honor to be, with   great consideration   Gentlemen
Your obedt Servant   Alexander Hamilton [4]

Abisha Thomas & James
Taylor Esqrs Agents for
North Carolina

LS, Duke University Library.
1. Taylor and Thomas were agents of the state of North Carolina to support
the claims of that state in the final settlement of accounts between the states.
2. See "Treasury Department Circular to the Governors of the States," June
27, 1791, and "Treasury Department Circular to the Commissioners of Loans,"
May 27, June 6, 1791.
3. 1 *Stat.* 144 (August 4, 1790). For Section 18, see "Treasury Department
Circular to the Commissioners of Loans," May 27, 1791, note 1.
4. The following endorsement appears on the back of this letter: "Secy of the
Treasury to the Agents 3rd Novr 1791 reced & Answered the 11th." This is a
mistake, for Taylor and Thomas answered H's letter on November 14, 1791. The
endorsement on the draft of their letter to H reads: "To the Secy. of the
Treasury 14 Nov. 91 in answer to his of the 3rd."

Report on the Estimate of Expenditures for 1792 [1]

[Philadelphia, November 4, 1791
Communicated on November 4, 1791][2]

[To the Speaker of the House of Representatives]

The Secretary of the Treasury respectfully reports to the House of Representatives the Estimates herewith transmitted, No. I, II, III, IV.

	Dollars.	Cents.

The first, relating to the Civil List, or the expenditure for the support of Government during the year 1792, (including incidental and contingent expenses of the several departments and offices) amount to . . 328.653.56.

The second, relating to certain liquidated claims upon the treasury; to certain deficiencies in former estimates for the current service, and to a provision in aid of the fund heretofore appropriated for the payment of certain officers of the Courts, Jurors, witnesses &c . . . . 197.119.49.

The third, relating to the department of War, shewing the stated expenditure of that department, for the year 1792 . . . . 357.731.61.

The amount of a year's pensions to invalids . . 87.463.60 ⅔

Pay and subsistence to sundry officers, for which no appropriation has yet been made, . . . 10.490.36.

Arrearages due upon Indian affairs for the year 1791, and the sum supposed to be necessary for the year 1792 . . . . 39.424.71

Expenses incurred for the defensive protection of the frontiers for the years 1790 and 1791, and for which no appropriation has yet been made . . 37.339.48.

Amounting together to, Dollars, ... 1.058.222.81 ⅔

As appears by Number 4, which contains a summary of the three preceding ones, exhibiting in one view the total sum, as above stated, for which an appropriation is requisite.

The funds, out of which the said appropriation may be made, are,

Copy, RG 233, Reports of the Secretary of the Treasury, 1790–1791, Vol. I, National Archives; copy, RG 233, Reports of the Treasury Department, 1791–1792, Vol. II, National Archives.

1. There are numerous arithmetical errors in this report which have not been noted.

2. The communicating letter may be found in RG 233, Reports of the Secretary of the Treasury, 1790–1791, Vol. I, National Archives. The report was read in the House of Representatives on November 7, 1791 (Journal of the House, I, 449).

first, the sum of six hundred thousand dollars reserved annually out of the duties on imports and tonnage, by the Act making provision for the debt of the United States, for the support of the government thereof:[3] And secondly, such surplus as shall have accrued to the end of the present year, upon the revenues heretofore established, over and above the sums necessary for the payment of interest on the public debt during the same year, and for the satisfying of other prior appropriations.

Judging from the returns heretofore received at the Treasury, there is good ground to conclude, that that surplus, together with the above-mentioned sum of six hundred thousand dollars, will be adequate to the object.

All which is humbly submitted   Alexr. Hamilton
                                                                           Secretary of the Treasury.

ESTIMATE OF THE EXPENDITURES FOR THE CIVIL LIST OF THE UNITED STATES, *together with the Incidental and Contingent Expenses of the several Departments and Offices for the Year 1792.*[4]

No. I

	Dollars.	Cents.
For compensation to the President of the United States	25.000.	
That of the Vice-president	5.000.	
Compensation to the Chief Justice	4.000.	
Ditto of five Associate Judges at 3500 dollars per annum each	17.500.	

To the Judges of the following Districts, Viz:

Maine	1.000.
New Hampshire	1.000.
Vermont	800.
Massachusetts	1.200.
Rhode Island	800.
Connecticut	1.000.
New York	1.500.
New Jersey	1.000.
Pennsylvania	1.600.
Delaware	800.
Maryland	1.500.
Virginia	1.800.
Kentucky	1.000.
North Carolina	1.500.
South Carolina	1.800.

3. See Section 1 of "An Act making provision for the (payment of the) Debt of the United States" (1 *Stat.* 138–39 [August 4, 1790]).

4. Copy, RG 233, Reports of the Secretary of the Treasury, 1790–1791, Vol. I, National Archives.

Georgia . . . . 1.500.
Attorney General . . . . 1.500.

72.800.

Compensation to the Members of Congress, estimating the attendance of the whole number for six months, Viz:

	Dolls. Cts.

Speaker of the House of Representatives,
  at twelve dollars per day . . . . . 2.190.
Ninety four members at six dollars ℔
  day . . . . 102.930.
Travelling expenses, computed at . . . 16.000.

121.120.

To the Secretary of the Senate one years
  salary . . . . 1.500.
Additional allowance estimate for six
  months, at two dollars per day . . 365.

1.865.

Principal Clerk to the Secretary of the Senate, for the
  same time at three dollars per day 547.50
Engrossing Clerk to ditto, estimated for the same time
  at two dollars per day . . . . 365.
Chaplain to the Senate estimated for six months, at five
  hundred dollars per annum . . . . 250.
Doorkeeper to the Senate, for the same time, at three
  dollars per day 547.50
Messenger to the Senate for the same time at two dollars
  per day . . . . 365.
Clerk of the House of Representatives, for
  one year's salary . . . . 1.500.
Additional allowance, calculated for six ⎱
  months at two dollars per day . . . ⎰ 365.

1.865.

Principal Clerk in the Office of the Clerk of the House
  of Representatives, estimated for six months, at three
  dollars per day 547.50
Engrossing Clerk for the same time, estimated at two
  dollars per day . . . . 365.
Chaplain to the House of Representatives, estimated for
  six months at five hundred dollars per annum . . 250.
Serjeant at Arms estimated for the same time at four
  dollars per day . . . . 730.
Doorkeeper of the House of Representatives, estimated
  for six months at three dollars per day 547.5
Assistant doorkeeper for do. at two dollars per day . 365.

129 730.

TREASURY DEPARTMENT

Secretary of the Treasury . . . . . 3.500.
Assistant of the Secretary of the Treasury 1.500.
Nine Clerks, at five hundred dollars each 4.500.

Messenger and Office-keeper . . . .   250.

                                                                9 750.

Comptroller of the Treasury . . . .   2 000.
principal Clerk . . . .   800.
Ten Clerks at five hundred dollars each .   5 000.

                                                                7 800.

Treasurer . . . .   2 000.
principal Clerk . . . .   600.
Additional ditto . . . .   500.
Messenger and Office-keeper . . . .   100.
Two Clerks appointed to count and ex- ⎫
   amine the old and new emissions of   ⎪
   Continental money and indents at 500 ⎬
   dollrs. ℔ Ann. . . . . ⎭ 1 000.

                                                            4.200.

Auditor of the Treasury . . . . .   1 500.
principal Clerk . . . .   800.
Sixteen Clerks to ditto at 500 dollars per
   annum. . . . .   8.000.

                                                        10.300.

Register of the Treasury . . . . .   1.250.
Three Clerks on the books and accounts of
   impost and tonnage and excise accounts,
   at 500 dollars each . . . . . .   1 500.
Two ditto on ditto of receipts and expenditures of public monies . . . .   1 000.
Twelve Clerks on the books of the six per
   cent, three per cent, and deferred stocks,
   of the domestic and assumed debts, including those necessarily engaged in
   filling up certificates, forming dividends
   of quarterly interest, and doing other
   parts of this branch of the Treasury
   records, 500 dollars each . . . .   6.000.
Two Clerks on the books of the Loan
   Officers and General Loan Officers business, 500 dollars each . . . . . .   1 000.
Three Clerks on the books of the registered or unfunded debt, including a
   Clerk employed on the dividends of
   interests payable thereon at 500 dollars
   each . . . .   1 500.
Three Clerks on the books and accounts of
   the late government, at 500 dollars each   1 500.
One for keeping the accounts of the register of ships &c. &c. under the Act for
   registering vessels, regulating the coasting trade and other purposes therein
   mentioned.[5] . . . .   500.

                                                        14.250.

Three Office keepers and Messengers for
   the Comptroller's, Auditor's and Reg-
   ister's Offices, at 250 dollars each . .   750.

5. 1 *Stat.* 55–65 (September 1, 1789).

LOAN OFFICERS.

For,	New Hampshire	650.
	Massachusetts	1 500.
	Rhode Island	600.
	Connecticut	1 000.
	New York	1 500.
	New Jersey	700.
	Pennsylvania	1 500.
	Delaware	600.
	Maryland	1 000.
	Virginia	1 500.
	North Carolina	1 000.
	South Carolina	1 000.
	Georgia	700.

13.250.

60.300.

DEPARTMENT OF STATE.

The Secretary of State . . . . . . 3 500.
One Chief Clerk . . . . 800.
Three Clerks at 500 dollars each . . . 1 500.
Clerk for foreign languages . . . . . 250.
Office keeper and Messenger . . . . . 250.

6.300.

DEPARTMENT OF WAR.

Secretary of the Department . . . . 3 000.
Chief Clerk, ... 600.
Six Clerks at 500 dollars each . . . . 3 000.
Paymaster to the troops and Commissioner
   of Army Accounts, ... 1 250.
Three Clerks to do. at 500 dollars each . . 1 500.
Messenger and Office keeper . . . . 250.

9.600.

BOARD OF COMMISSIONERS FOR THE SETTLEMENT OF THE
ACCOUNTS BETWEEN THE UNITED STATES AND THE
INDIVIDUAL STATES, VIZ:

Three Commissioners at 2250 dollars per
   annum . . . . 6 750.
Chief Clerk . . . . 600.
Eleven Clerks at 500 dollars each . . . 5 500.
Messenger and doorkeeper . . . . . 250.

13.100.

GOVERNMENT OF THE WESTERN TERRITORY.

District Northwest of the River Ohio.

Governor, for his salary as such, and
   for discharging the duties of Superintendant of Indian Affairs—Northern
   department . . . . 2 000.
The Secretary of said District . . . 750.
For stationery, office-rent and printing
   patents for land, &c. &c. . . . . 350.
Three Judges at 800 dollars per annum 2 400.

District Southwest of the River Ohio

Governor for his salary as such, and for discharging the duties of Superintendant of Indian Affairs–southern department	2 000.
Secretary of said District	750.
For Stationery, office rent &c. &c.	350.
Three Judges, at 800 dollars per annum	2 400.
	11.000.

GRANT TO BARON STEUBEN.

His annual allowance by Act of Congress[6] . . . . 2.500.

PENSIONS GRANTED BY THE LATE GOVERNMENT.

Issac Van Vert ⎱ A pension of 200 dollars ⎱ John Paulding ⎰ per ann. to each, pursuant ⎰ David Williams ⎰ to an Act of Congress of 3d. November 1780[7]	600.
Dominique L. Eglize, per Act of Congress 8th. August 1782[8]	120.
Joseph Traverse, per ditto[9]	120.
Youngest children of the late Major General Warren, per Act of 1st. July 1780[10]	450.
Youngest son of General Mercer, per Act of 8th April 1777,[11] estimated at	400.
James McKensie, ⎱ per Act of 10th. of Sept. Joseph Brussels, ⎰ 1783[12] entitled to a pension John Jordan, ⎰ of 40 dollars each, per annum	120.
Elizabeth Bergen, per Act of 21st. August, 1781[13],	53.33
Joseph De Beauleau, per Act of 5th. August 1782,[14]	100.
Richard Gridley, per Acts of 17th. November 1775, and 26th. February 1781[15]	444.40
Lieutenant Colonel Touzaid per Act of 27th. of October 1788[16]	360.
	2.767.73
	42.767.73

6. "An Act for finally adjusting and satisfying the claims of Frederick William de Steuben" (6 *Stat.* 2 [June 4, 1790]).

7. *JCC,* XVIII, 1009–10.

8. *JCC,* XXII, 457.

9. *JCC,* XXII, 456–57.

10. *JCC,* XVII, 581.

11. *JCC,* VII, 243.

12. This act was passed September 15, 1783 (*JCC,* XXV, 569).

13. This act was passed August 24, 1781 (*JCC,* XXI, 908).

14. *JCC,* XXII, 428–29.

15. *JCC,* III, 358–59; XIX, 197.

16. Although there is no account in *JCC* of a pension granted on this date to Lewis Tousard, "An Act allowing Lieutenant-Colonel Tousard an equivalent for his pension for life" (6 *Stat.* 15 [April 30, 1794]) reads as follows: "*Be it enacted,*

FOR INCIDENTAL AND CONTINGENT EXPENSES RELATIVE TO THE CIVIL LIST ESTABLISHMENT

Under this head are comprehended firewood, stationery together with printing work, and all other contingent expenses of the two Houses of Congress, rent and office expenses of the three several departments, viz: Treasury, State, War, and of the General Board of Commissioners.

Secretary of the Senate, his estimate	4 500.
Clerk of the House of Representatives, ditto	5.500.

TREASURY DEPARTMENT

Secretary of the Treasury, per Estimate .		800.
Comptroller . . . . . . ditto .		300.
Auditor . . . . ditto .		873.33
Register, (including new books for the assumed debt) . . ditto .		1 500.
Treasurer . . . . . . ditto .		850.
Rent of the Treasury and taxes, ... ditto .		650.
Ditto of an Office taken for the Register and taxes		200.
Wood for the department (Treasurer's excepted)		600.
Occasional and extra clerk in the several offices of the Treasury, estimated at 4 Clerks through the year, at 500 dollars each		2 000.
		7 773.33.

DEPARTMENT OF STATE.

Including the expense attending the collection of the laws of the several States, for publishing the laws of the first Session of the second Congress of the United States, for the collection of newspapers from different States, and gazettes from abroad, and for an index to the laws passed at the first, second and third sessions of the first Congress &c. . . . . 1 332.50.

DEPARTMENT OF WAR.

Secretary at War, per estimate . . .	600.
Contingencies for the officers acting as paymaster General and Commissioner of Army accounts, per his estimate .	100.
	700.
General Board of Commissioners, as per estimate . .	750.
	20.555.83.
Dollars . .	328.653.56.

Treasury Department,
Register's Office, 4th. November 1791.

Joseph Nourse, Register

&c., That there be allowed to Lieutenant-Colonel Tousard three thousand six hundred dollars, in full discharge of his pension of three hundred and sixty dollars for life."

No. II

ESTIMATE OF THE SUMS NECESSARY FOR DISCHARGING CERTAIN LIQUIDATED CLAIMS UPON THE UNITED STATES, FOR MAKING GOOD DEFICIENCIES IN FORMER ESTIMATES, FOR AIDING THE FUND APPROPRIATED FOR THE PAYMENT OF CERTAIN OFFICERS OF THE COURTS, JURORS AND WITNESSES, AND FOR THE ESTABLISHMENT OF TEN CUTTERS.

His most christian Majesty has a claim on the United States, upon an Account settled at the Treasury, 28th. of February 1791, being for sundry supplies to the ships Confederacy, Dean and Saratoga, from the king's magazines at Cape Francois, during their stay at said place, in the year 1781.

Amount of said Account	29.029.68.	
From which deduct a payment made on account from the appropriation of 50.000 dollars granted by Congress for the discharge of accounts finally settled at the Treasury	20.000.	
Leaves a balance to be provided for		9.020.68

Oliver Pollock, late Commercial Agent for the United States at New Orleans, has a claim on the United States, for sundry supplies, for cloathing, arms, and other military stores under the acts of Congress of 6th. February 1781, October 22d. 1782, and 28th. September 1785,[17] principal sum due 1st. July 1786, as per account settled at the Treasury . . . . 81.657.94.

Interest thereon to 31st. December 1791 . . . . . 26.947. 8.

108.605. 2

To make good deficiencies in the last year's estimate for the Civil List establishment

Principal Clerk of the Senate from 1st. July 1791, to 31st December, 184 days, at three dollars per day . .	552.
Principal Clerk to the House of Representatives, 184 days, at three dollars per day	552.
Engrossing Clerk to ditto, at two dollars per day . .	368.
Engrossing Clerk to the Senate from 24th. October to 31st. Decr. 1791, 69 days, at two dollars per day .	138.
Compensation to the Secretary of the Senate, 69 days at two dollars per day	138.
Ditto to the Clerk of the House of Representatives, 69 days, at two dollars per day	138.
Deficient appropriation for the third Judge, district south of the river Ohio	800.
Ditto . . . for the District of Vermont . . .	660.
Marshall of said District	175.
To the Attorney General, additional allowance to his salary, granted by an Act 3d. March 1791,[18] for one year	400.
Ditto to the Comptroller of the Treasury . . .	400.

17. JCC, XIX, 118–19; XXIII, 680–81; XXIX, 776–77.

18. See Section 4 of "An Act supplemental to the act 'establishing the Treasury Department,' and for a farther compensation to certain officers" (1 Stat. 215).

Ditto to the Auditor . . . .   400.
Ditto the the Register . . . .   250.

4 971.

For so much short estimated in the last year's appropriation for the Register's office, the number of
Clerks being encreased by the funding system, be-
yond the number then contemplated . . . .   500.
Commissioners of Loans in the several States, for the
payment of such sums as they shall necessarily expend, for the hire of clerks to assist in executing the
duties of their several offices, and also for stationery,
on the settlement of their several accounts at the
Treasury, under the Act of Congress of 3d. of March
1791,[19] estimated at . . . .   16.000.
An additional sum may likewise be computed so as to
extend the allowance for necessary clerk-hire to the
end of the year 1791, should such be deemed ex-
pedient . . . .   5.000.

21.000.

To make good deficient appropriations in the former
grants of Congress for the contingent expenses of
the several offices of the

TREASURY DEPARTMENT.

The contingent expense of said department from 13th.
September 1789, to 30th. September 1791, as per accounts settled at the Treasury, to . . . . . .   10.070.71.
For the discharge of sundry accounts against the department and for contingencies from 1st. October
to 31st. December 1791 . . . .   1.965.64.

11.036.35

Deduct the actual payment made from appropria-⎱
tions heretofore granted . . . .⎰   9.236.35.

Leaves to be appropriated to make good deficiencies
of the appropriations granted for the years 1789,
1790 and 1791 . . . .   2.800.
Additional expense which attends the enumeration of
the inhabitants of the United States
The following Marshals have had their accounts settled
at the Treasury, Viz;

For . . .		
Maine, amounts to .	. 1 796.13.	
New Hampshire	. 1 679.77.	
Massachusetts	. 2 892.18.	
Rhode Island	. 531.17.	
Connecticut .	. 1 834.	
Pennsylvania .	. 4 958.33.	
Delaware	. 708.94.	
Maryland	. 2 622.22.	
Virginia .	. 4 253.90.	
North Carolina .	. 6 029.54.	
Georgia .	. 1 416.61.	
	28.722.79.	

19. "An Act for making compensation to the Commissioners of Loans for
extraordinary expenses" (1 *Stat.* 216).

Estimate of the following States, the accounts whereof have not been settled, Viz:

Vermont	1 700.
New York	3 500.
New Jersey	3 000.
Kentucky	1 700.
South Carolina . . .	3 000.

12.900.

41.622.79.

Deduct this sum provided for by a former appropriation . . . . 21.850.

Remains to be appropriated as a fund to make good deficiencies . . . . 19.772.79.

To Clerks of Courts, Jurors, Witnesses &c. for so much deficient in the fund provided by the Act which prescribes their payment from the monies arising from fines, forfeitures and penalties.[20]

Amount of their accounts settled at the treasury . . . . 5.075.57.

Estimate for accounts not settled to 31. Decr. 1791. . . . . 2,372.57. } 7 448.14.

Deduct this amount discharged from monies arising from "fines, forfeitures and penalties" . . . . . 2.372.57 / 2 448.14.

Leaves to be appropriated . . . . 5.000.

For the purchase of Hydrometers for the use of the officers of the customs and inspectors of the revenue . . . . 1 000.

For arranging and fixing (in numerical order) into books to be prepared for that purpose, the negociable certificates of the United States, which have been, or may be hereafter, cancelled at the treasury. Three Clerks to be employed in preparing, affixing and numbering the books, at 500 dollars each . . . 1 500.

150 books, paper and binding . . . . 800.

Contingent expenses . . . . 150.

2 450.

For expenses towards the safe keeping and prosecution of persons committed for offences against the United States . . . . 4 000.

For the support and maintenance, and repairs of lighthouses, beacons, piers, stakes and buoys . . . . 16.000.

A farther deficiency in the approriations heretofore made for building and equipping ten Cutters . . . 2 000.

Total Dollars 197.119.49

Treasury Department,
Register's Office, 4th. November 1791.

Joseph Nourse, Register

---

20. "An Act providing compensations for the officers of the Judicial Courts of the United States, and for Jurors and Witnesses, and for other purposes" (1 Stat. 216–17 [March 3, 1791]).

No. III

ESTIMATE OF THE EXPENSES OF THE WAR DEPARTMENT FOR THE YEAR 1792.

PAY OF THE TROOPS.

Infantry—Two Regiments

			Dollars. Cents
1 Major General .	. . . . at 125 dollrs. per month . .		1 500.
2 Lieutenant Colonels Commandants	. . . . . 60		1 440.
6 Majors	40		2 880.
1 Quarter Master .	. . . . 60		720.
2 Inspectors	30		720.
1 Aid de Camp .	. . . . . 40		480.
1 Brigade Major .	. . . . 40		480.
1 Chaplain	50		600.
24 Captains	30		8 640.
24 Lieutenants	22		6 336.
24 Ensigns	18		5 184.
2 Paymasters	5		120.
6 Adjutants	10		720.
6 Quarter Masters	5		360.
2 Surgeons	30		720.
8 Surgeons mates	24		2 304.
96 Serjeants	5		5 760.
96 Corporals	4		4 608.
6 Senior Musicians	5		360.
42 Musicians	3		1 512.
1584 Privates	3		57.024.
		Dollrs. . . .	102.468.

Artillery—One Battalion

1 Major Commandant .	. . . at 45 dollars per month . .		540.
4 Captains	30		1 440.
8 Lieutenants	22		2 112.
1 Adjutant	10		120.
1 Quarter Master	5		60.
1 Paymaster	5		60.
1 Surgeons mate	24		288.
16 Serjeants	5		960.
16 Corporals	4		768.
1 Senior Musician	5		60.
7 Musicians	3		252.
264 privates	3		9.504.
			16.164.

pay of { Infantry . . . . 102.468.
{ Artillery . . . . 16.164.

Dollars, ... 118.632.

The troops on the old establishment, amounting to 430, for which the difference of pay to be added to the new establishment, which for the aforesaid 430 non commissioned officers and privates, amount to   10.640.

Dollars, . . . 129.272.

DEDUCTIONS.

For Clothing.

112 Serjeants,	.	at 1 dollar	40 Cents per month	.	1 881.60
112 Corporals,	. . at 1	.	15	. . .	1 545.60
7 Senior musicians	1	. .	40	. . .	117.60
49 Musicians,	. . . .		90	. . .	529.20
1848 privates	. . . .		90	. . .	19.958.40
					24.032.40

For Hospital Stores.

2128 non commissioned officers and privates at 10
cents pr. month . . . . 2 553.60.

26.586.

pay of the Troops . . . Dollars . . . 102.686.

SUBSISTENCE.

	RATIONS.
1 Major General . . . . . at 15 rations per day . . .	5 475.
1 Lieutenant Colonel, Commandant, with the emoluments of a Brigadier General 12	4 380.
1 Lieutenant Colonel Commandant . 6	2 190.
7 Majors 4	10.220.
1 Quarter master 6	2.190.
2 Inspectors 3	2 190.
Aid de Camp 4	1 460.
1 Brigade Major 4	1 460.
28 Captains 3	30.660.
32 Lieutenants 2	23.360.
24 Ensigns 2	17.520.
2 Surgeons 3	2.190.
9 Surgeons mates 2	6.570.

Or money in lieu thereof, at the option of the said Officers a
the contract price at the posts respectively, where the ration
shall become due . . . .
2128 Noncommissioned officers and privates, at one ration per day 776.720.

Rations . . . 886.585.

886.585 rations, at 13½ cents per ration . . . Dollars . . . 119.688.97.

CLOTHING.

2 128, non commissioned officers and privates,
272 Contingencies.
2 400. Suits of Clothing at 20 dollars per suit . Dollars, . . . 48.000.

FORAGE.

1 Major General . . . . . at 20 dollars per month . .	240.
1 Lieutenant Colonel with the emolument of Brig: General	} 16	192.
1 Lieutenant Colonel Commandant 12	144.

7 Majors	 10	. . . .	840.
1 Quarter Master	 12	. . . .	144.
1 Aid de Camp	 10	. . . .	120.
1 Brigade Major	 10	. . . .	120.
2 Inspectors	 10	. . . .	240.
2 Surgeons	 10	. . . .	240.
9 Surgeons mates	 6	. . . .	648.
7 Adjutants	 6	. . . .	504.
7 Quarter Masters	 6	. . . .	504.
3 Paymasters	 6	. . . .	216.
			4.152.

HOSPITAL DEPARTMENT.

For medicines, instruments, furniture and Stores for the Hospitals 6.000.

QUARTER MASTER'S DEPARTMENT.

Including the transportation of the recruits to the frontiers, the removal of the troops from one station to another, the transportation of clothing, ordnance and military stores for the troops on the frontiers; the necessary removal of ordnance and military stores; the hire of teams and pack horses; the purchase of tents, boats, axes, camp kettles, boards, firewood, company-books, stationery for the troops, and all the other expenses in the Quarter Masters department . . . .   50.000.

ORDNANCE DEPARTMENT.

For the salaries of the Storekeepers at the . . . .
several Arsenals.

Viz:

Springfield . . (Massachusetts) . . . . .   480.

Fort Renssellaer, and it's dependencies,
(New York) . . . . . . 120.
Subsistence at one dollar per week . 52.

                 172.

West point (New York) . . . .   480.
Philadelphia (Pennsylvania) . . . . . .   500.
Carlisle . . . ditto . . . .   60.
Fort Pitt . . ditto . . . .   360.
New London, (Virginia) . . . . . .   430.
Manchester . ditto . . . .   50.
Charleston (South Carolina) . . . . .   100.
Three assistants, one at Springfield, one at West-
point, and one at Philadelphia at 15 dollars per
month each . . . .   540.

Not included in former estimates . .   3.172.
The Salary of Storekeeper at Fort Pitt from 15th.
of February to 31st. Decemr. 1791, at 30 dollars
per month . . . .   315.
The Salary of the Storekeeper at Carlisle from
25th. October 1789, to 31st. December 1791, at
5 dollars per month 130.83⅔

                                  445.83⅔

RENTS

Philadelphia	666.66⅔	
New London	350.	
Manchester	66.66⅔	
Not included in former estimates . .		1 083.33⅓

Rent at Manchester from 10th. June 1787, to 31st.
December 1791, is four years six months and
twenty days, at the rate of dolls. 66. 66⅔ per
annum 303.48

Laborers at the several Arsenals, ...	400.	
Coopers, armorers and carpenters, employed occasionally at the several Arsenals	600.	
		1.000.
Ten armorers, at five dollars per month . . .		600.
Two conductors of military stores at the rate of twenty five dollars per month, including rations,		600.
Dollars, . . .		7.204.65.

INVALIDS.

The annual allowance of the Invalids of the United States, from
4th. March 1792, to 4th. March 1793.

New Hampshire	4.074.66⅔
Massachusetts	12.721. 8
Rhode Island	2.981.
Connecticut	7.227.50
New York	16.188.
New Jersey	4.474.26⅔
Pennsylvania	16.149.32
Delaware	2.016.
Maryland	6.678.
Virginia	9.443.33⅓
North Carolina	886.
South Carolina . . . conjectural	4 000.
Georgia	624.44.
Dollars . . .	87.463.60⅔

CONTINGENCIES OF THE WAR DEPARTMENT.

For Maps, hiring expresses, allowances to officers for extra expenses,
printing, loss of stores of all kinds, advertising and apprehending
deserters . . . . 20.000.

MONIES DUE FOR FORMER SERVICES, BEING PAY AND SUBSISTENCE OF SUNDRY
OFFICERS OF THE LATE ARMY OF THE UNITED STATES, AND FOR PAY OF
THE LATE MARYLAND LINE, FOR WHICH NO APPROPRIATIONS HAVE BEEN
MADE.

Pay and subsistence of Jeremiah Green, surgeon's mate, quota of Rhode
Island, raised under the Act of Congress of the 20th. October 1786[21]   228.

21. JCC, XXXI, 891–93.

Subsistence due to John Elbert, surgeon's mate to the late 5th. Mary-
land, regiment, for 1782 and 1783 . . . .   76.85
Pay due Lieut. James Simmons of Colo. Washington's Dragoons, for
January, February and March 1782 . . . .   100.
Pay of sundry officers of the late Maryland Line, for balance of pay
due them for 1782 and 1783, as per statement of 10th. July 1787 . .   406.66.
Pay for the non-commissioned officers and privates of said line, for
balance of four months pay of 1783, per said Statement . . . .   9 678.85.
                                         Dollars . . . 10.490.36.

INDIAN DEPARTMENT.

The expences in the Indian department for the various objects thereof,
in the year 1791, as per accounts 23.424.71
Balance on hand of former appropriations, 30th. March, 1791 . . .   9.000.
Balance to be provided for the year 1791 . . . .   14 424.71.

For the year 1792.

There will probably be required, for the various objects of the⎫
Indian department, for the ensuing year, the sum of . . . . .⎬ 25.000.
                                         Dollars . . . 39.424.71.

ESTIMATE OF THE EXPENSES WHICH HAVE BEEN INCURRED FOR THE DEFENSIVE PROTECTION
OF THE FRONTIERS AGAINST THE INDIANS, DURING THE YEARS 1790 AND 1791, BY VIRTUE
OF THE AUTHORITY VESTED IN THE PRESIDENT OF THE UNITED STATES, BY THE ACTS
RELATIVE TO THE MILITARY ESTABLISHMENT, PASSED THE 29TH. SEPTEMBER 1789,
AND THE 30TH. APRIL 1790,[22] AND FOR WHICH NO APPROPRIATIONS HAVE BEEN MADE.

ACCOUNTS ACTUALLY PRODUCED.

PENNSYLVANIA.

Alleghany Militia 1791.

                                                Dollars. Cts.
From 22nd. March to 22d. May, 1 Captain, 2 Lieutenants,
  1 Ensign, 5 Serjeants, 4 Corporals, 76 privates . . .   1 346.96

Westmoreland Militia 1791.
The payrolls, not being correct, were withdrawn, conjectural 2 301. 4

Washington Scouts 1790.
Four men, aggregate 325 days 297.85

Monongalia Militia 1791.
From 13th. April to 12th. July, 1 Ensign, 2 Serjeants, 19
privates 231.60
N:B: 17 men, who left their posts, not included.

VIRGINIA

Randolph Militia 1791.
From 10th. May to 22d. August, 1 Captain, 1 Lieutenant,
  1 Ensign, 3 Serjeants, 2 Corporals, 48 privates . . . .   1.295.40.

22. "An Act to recognize and adapt to the Constitution of the United States
the establishment of the Troops raised under the Resolves of the United States
in Congress assembled, and for other purposes therein mentioned" (1 *Stat.* 95–

Ohio Scouts 1790.
Eight men aggregate, 864 days . . . .   792.

Harrison Scouts 1790.
Eight men aggregate, 808 days 740.66⅔

             Kenhawa Rangers and Scouts .   1.163.66⅔

Mason Scouts 1790.
Twelve men aggregate 587 days . . . .   538. 8.
These men were not all in service at the same time

Jefferson Scouts 1790.
Fourteen men aggregate 746 days . . . . . .   682.16.
These men were not all in service at the same time

Lincoln Scouts 1790.
Four men aggregate, 376 days 344.66⅔

Monongalia Scouts 1790.
Six men aggregate, 566 days 518.82

Mercer Scouts 1790.
Four men aggregate 394 days . . . .   361.16.

Woodford Scouts 1790.
Four men aggregate, 351 days 321.74

Rangers 1790.
Fifteen men, 28 days each 90.25

Militia 1791.
From 29th April to 3d. July, 1 Major, 1 Captain, 1 Lieutenant 1 Ensign, 4 Serjeants, 3 Corporals, 56 privates—
pay . . . .   695.30.

                                                 1.107.29

Madison Scouts 1790.
Six men aggregate, 233 days . . . .   213.58.

Bourbon Scouts 1790.
Eight men aggregate, 384 days—Pay . . . .   320.
The Scouts are a species of patroles, who are the best
hunters or woodsmen of the frontiers, and are advanced
constantly to discover the traces of the Indians. From
the great danger and fatigue of their services, they have
been in the habit of receiving from the State of Virginia
5/6ths. of a dollar per day, while employed. They were
adopted for a short space of time, by the general government, on an exigency during the spring of the year
1790, as a more efficacious, satisfactory and œconomical
expedient, than calling out the militia promiscuously.

Militia 1791.
From 6th. May to 11th. July, 1 Captain, 1 Lieutenant, 1
Ensign, 3 Serjeants, 43 privates—Pay 446.49

96); "An Act for regulating the Military Establishment of the United States"
(1 *Stat.* 119–21).

Rations, including the rations for the Militia of Woodford
above mentioned . . . .   393.60.

                                                         1.160. 9.

TERRITORY OF THE UNITED STATES NORTHWEST OF THE OHIO.

Washington Militia 1791.
Stationed at Waterford
From 1st. July to 25th. July, 1 Ensign, 1 Serjeant, 1 Corpo-
ral, 15 privates—Pay . . . .   60.

Stationed at Marietta 1791.
From 1st. July to 20th. July, 1 Captain, 2 Serjeants, 2 Corporals, 38 privates—Pay . . . .   108.

Stationed at Belleprè 1791.
From 1st. July to 22d. July, 1 Lieutenant, 1 Serjeant, 1 Corporal, 20 privates—Pay . . . .   69.76.

Stationed at Marietta 1791.
From 7th. January to 31st. March, 1 Lieutenant, 2 Serjeants,
1 Corporal, 30 privates—pay and rations .   640.18.
1791—From 1st. April to 1st. July, 1 Captain, 1 Lieutenant,
1 Serjeant, 1 Corporal, 36 privates.—pay and rations .   625.41.

Stationed at Belleprè 1791.
From 9th. January to 1st. April, 1 Captain, 1 Serjeant,
1 Corporal, 22 privates—pay and rations . . . . .   461.58.
1791—From 1st. April to 1st. July, 1 Lieutenant, 1 Serjeant,
1 Corporal, 18 privates—pay and rations . . . .   362.36.

Stationed at Waterford 1791.
From 10th January to 31st. March, 1 Ensign, 1 Serjeant,
1 Corporal, 20 privates—pay and rations. . . . . .   338.76.
1791—From 1st. April to 30th. June, 1 Ensign, 1 Serjeant,
1 Corporal, 16 privates—pay and rations . . . . .   222.60.

Stationed at Fort Harmer 1790.
From 28th. September to 9th. of November, 2 Serjeants,
2 Corporals, 26 privates—pay . . . .   134.40.

                                                         3.023. 5.

TERRITORY OF THE UNITED STATES NORTH-WEST OF THE OHIO.

Lieutenant Colonel Sproat, his pay from 1st. October, to
5th. November 1790, and from 2d. January to 20th.
July 1791 . . . .   456.

Fort Knox Militia.
These companies were under the command of
Majr. Hamtramck.
       1 Major and 1 Adjutant included.
26 and 33 days service—2 Lieutenants, 1 Ensign, 2 Serjeants, 42 privates—pay . . . .   156.36.
26 and 33 days service—1 Captain, 1 Lieutenant, 1 Ensign,
2 Serjeants, 45 privates—pay . . . .   240.86.

                                                         397.22.

TERRITORY OF THE UNITED STATES, SOUTH OF THE OHIO.

Davidson and Summer. 1790.

At different periods—1 Captain, 1 Serjeant, 35 privates—

pay	239. 2.	
Rations . . .	129.16.	
		368.18.

A conjectural estimate of the expense of the Militia, called out by virtue of the orders of the President of the United States, on the 10th. of March 1791, at a time of great alarm upon the frontiers, and before any arrangements of levies could be raised and brought forward for their protection. The accounts of the actual services not being yet produced.

This estimate comprehends the several counties, from Fort Pitt to the falls of the Ohio, the counties of Russell, Wythe, and Washington in Virginia and the counties on the territories of the United States south and north-west of the Ohio, not included in the foregoing estimate,　　20.000.

Dollars, . . . 37.339.48.

RECAPITULATION

Pay of the troops	102.686.
Subsistence	119.688.97.
Clothing	48.000.
Forage	4.152.
Hospital Department	6.000.
Quarter Masters department	50.000.
Ordnance department	7.204.64.
Contingencies of the War department . . .	20.000.
Stated annual expenses . . .	357.731.61.
Extra expenses—Annual allowance to invalids, . 87.463.60⅔	
Monies due for former services for which appropriations have not been made . . . . . . 10.490.36.	
Indian department . . . . 39.424.71.	
Expenses incurred for the defensive protection of the frontiers, for which appropriations have not been made . . . . 37.339.48.	
	174.718.15⅔
Dollars, . . .	532.449.76⅔

War-Office, October 27th. 1791.

H: Knox. Secretary at War.

Treasury Department,
Register's Office, November 4th. 1791.

I certify, that the within Statement is a true copy of the original estimate filed on record in this Office.

Joseph Nourse, Register.

No. IV [23]

GENERAL ESTIMATE FOR THE SERVICES OF THE ENSUING YEAR.

CIVIL LIST.

For compensation to the President, Vice President, Chief Justice, and Associate Judges .	51.500.	
Ditto to the District Judges	21.300.	
Members of the Senate, House of Representatives and their Officers	129.730.	
Treasury department	60.300.	
Department of State	6.300.	
Department of War	9.600.	
Board of Commissioners	13.000.	
Government of the Western Territory . .	11.000.	
Grant to Baron Steuben	2.500.	
Pensions granted by the late Government . .	2.767.73.	
Incidental and contingent expenses of the Civil List Establishments	20.555.83.	
		328.653.56

EXTRAORDINARIES.

For discharging certain liquidated claims on the United States	117.625.70.	
To making good deficiencies in the civil list establishments	49.043.79.	
Clerks of Courts, Jurors, Witnesses &c. . .	5.000.	
Maintenance of lighthouses, and repairs . .	16.000.	
Keeping prisoners	4.000.	
Arranging the public securities	2.450.	
Purchase of Hydrometers	1.000.	
Building and equipping ten cutters	2.000.	
		197.119.49

WAR DEPARTMENT.

Stated annual expenses	357.731.61.	
Annual allowance to invalids	87.463.60⅔	
For former deficient appropriations . . .	47.829.84.	
Indian Department	39.424.71.	
		532.449.76⅔
Dollars, . .		1.058.222.81⅔.

Treasury Department
Registers Office, 4th. November 1791.

Joseph Nourse, Register.

23. In MS this was incorrectly written "No. III,"

From William Ellery

Newport [Rhode Island] November 7, 1791. "I have received your Letter of the 26th. of October last,[1] delivered the Gin taken into my Custody which was imported in the Bark Polly [2] in Casks under legal capacity, and shall make similar communications where I discover any deviations from the requisitions of the Laws. I would be much obliged to you for an answer to my letter of the 14th. of last month respectg. the form of bond on oath taken and given by Exporters of Distilled Spirits, and respectg. the addn. to the proviss. contd. in the 40 & 41 Sects. of the Act intituled an Act to provide more effectually for the collection of duties &c. . . ."

LC, Newport Historical Society, Newport, Rhode Island.
  1. Letter not found.
  2. See Ellery to H, October 18, 1791.

Report of the Commissioners of the Sinking Fund

[Philadelphia, November 7, 1791
Communicated on November 7, 1791] [1]

[To the President of the Senate]

The Vice President of the United States and President of the Senate, The Chief Justice, The Secretary of State, The Secretary of the Treasury and the Attorney General respectfully report to the Congress of the United States of America.

That pursuant to the Act intitled an Act making provision for the reduction of the public debt [2] and in conformity to two resolutions agreed upon by them one on the fifteenth day of January [3] another on the 15th. day of August last [4] and severally approved by the President of the United States, they have caused purchases of the said debt to be made through the Agency respectively of Samuel Meredith Treasurer of this United States, William Seton Cashier of the Bank of New York, Benjamin Lincoln Collector of the District of Boston and Charlestown and William Heth Collector of the District of Bermuda Hundred, to the amount of Eight hundred fifty two thousand, six hundred seventy seven dollars & forty six Cents, and for which there have been paid Five hundred forty eight thousand, Nine hundred twenty four Dollars and fourteen Cents in specie, as will more particularly appear by the several documents No I to VIII [5] herewith submitted as part of this Report and which specify the places where, the times when, the prices at which, and the persons of whom the said purchases have been made. That though the statements of Willm Seton and Benjamin Lincoln have not yet passed through the forms of a settlement it appears by the document No. VIII being a certified transcript from the books of the Treasury that the amount of the stock by them respectively reported to have been purchased has been duly transferred to the said Books.

That the purchases now and heretofore reported amount in the whole to One million, one hundred thirty one thousand, three hundred sixty four Dollars and seventy six Cents, for which there have been paid six hundred ninety nine thousand, one hundred sixty three dollars and thirty Eight Cents in specie.

Signed in Behalf of the Board John Adams

D, RG 46, Reports of the Commissioners of the Sinking Fund, National Archives.
1. *Annals of Congress*, III, 27–28.
2. 1 *Stat.* 186–87 (August 12, 1790).
3. This is a mistake, for this resolution was adopted on January 18, 1791. For the resolution and its date, see "Meeting of the Commissioners of the Sinking Fund," January 18, 1791.
4. For this resolution, see "Meeting of the Commissioners of the Sinking Fund," August 15, 1791.
5. D, RG 46, Reports of the Commissioners of the Sinking Fund, National Archives. These eight enclosures are printed in *ASP, Finance*, I, 112–20.

From Henry Marchant

Rhode Island District
Newport Nov. 8th 1791

In pursuance of an Act of the Congress of the United States "to provide for mitigating or remitting forfeitures and penalties, accruing under the Revennue Laws in certain Cases therein mentioned" [1] I have received the Petition of James Maxwell and Dunken Thelley both of said District Traders in Company hereto annexed And thereupon caused William Ellery, Collector, and Robert Crooke Naval Officer of Newport District and Nathl. Phillips Surveyor for the Port of Warren within sd Newport District the Persons claiming a moiety of Three Hogsheads of West India Rum upon forfeiture thereof, if such forfeiture should take Place; and also William Channing Esqr. Atty of the United States for Rhode Island District to be noticed to appear before me and shew Cause if any they have, against the mitigation or Remission of the forfeiture thereof and who have signified to me that they have no Cause to offer against the Remission prayed for by the Petitioners Nor had they any Reason to disbelieve the Facts and Circumstance as stated and set forth in said Petition. Whereupon I proceeded to examine further into the circumstances of the Case in a summary Manner And it appears by the manifest of the Cargo of the Sloop Dolphin Sheffield Weaver Master, delivered to Enoch Sawyer Dy Collr. for the Port of Plank Bridge State of North Carolina, Sepr. 2d. 1791 that said three Hogsheads of Rum were included therein And that the sd. Captain was permitted with said Sloop Dolphin to proceed from that Port for the Port of New York, with the Cargo contained in said manifest the said three Hhd of Rum being part. And which same Manifest and permit He the sd. Capt. did upon his Arrival at the sd. Port of New york deliver to Chs. Tillinghast Depy. Collr. of that Port, or by Copy and certificate thereof from the sd. Chs. Tillinghast Depy Colr. It also appears by the Certificate of Nathl. Phillips Surveyor for the sd. Port of Warren, that the Origl. Certificates (which were also produced to me) given to James Maxwell (one of sd. Owners of the said Rum who went the Voyage with the sd. Capt.) by Isaac Gregory Inspector of the Port of Plank Bridge agrees with the Marks, Numbers &c on each of the said three Hhds. of Rum taken and seized at the sd. Port of Warren. That by Letter to me from the said Nathl. Phillips Surveyor, it appears the Capt. & the sd. Maxwell one of the sd. owners came in very sick, & unable to take any Care of the Vessel or Cargo. That the other Owner immediately of his own accord, mentioned to him the said three Hhds of Rum. That Maxwell Chace Mate of said Sloop on solemn Oath to him by me administered, declared that he well knew all the Matters and Things set forth in said Petition to be true, and that he was not any Ways interested in the Subject Matter thereof. Whereupon it appears to me that the Statement of Circumstances set forth in said Petition are true. All which I do hereby certify to the Secretary of the Treasury of the United States of America.

Hy. Marchant
Judge of the Dst. Court for
Rhod: District

Copy, Rhode Island Historical Society, Providence.
1. 1 *Stat.* 122–23 (May 26, 1790).

From William Short

Paris Nov. 8. 1791.

Sir

Of the six million loan lately made, three millions of florins have been remitted & have yielded 8,170,000₶.[1] I had intended that the rest should be kept in the hands of the bankers to answer your draughts for 2½ millions of florins & such other demands as might arise. But some days ago the commissaries of the treasury [2] requested I would direct our bankers to pay theirs f 560,000, in order to face a demand against them at the Hague for that sum in the course of this month. As our bankers wrote to me [3] at the same time that they had informed those of France they were ready to do it on recieving my orders I supposed it proper to give them. The commissaries of the treasury proposed to fix the exchange at 44. which being somewhat more advantageous than the then rate I accepted without hesitation. There still remains of this loan to answer your demands f 2,440,000. Should your bills for the whole amount of 2½ millions arrive before any new loan is made the bankers will undoubtedly find no difficulty in making the temporary advance of f 60,000. They suspect probably that you will draw on them for a part of this loan, but they cannot form an idea of the amount unless they have been informed from America.

In their last letter to me of the 24th. of Octobr. they informed me that they had received the greater part of the loan. I suppose it probable it is completed at present. They add that the present high rate of British stocks & favorable exchange had induced great numbers of the Dutch capitalists to sell out & that cash had become so abundant in consequence thereof that they had great hopes the U.S. would be able to make a loan at Amsterdam before the expiration of the year a 4½ p. cent interest. It is much to be desired that this should be effected before the 1st. of January next as I learn from them a tax is to [be] levied on all loans made after that time.

I mentioned to you in my last of the 10th. ulto that I had authorized the opening a loan at Antwerp if it could be done at 4½ p. cent interest & 5. p. cent commission. Since then there has been an increase of cash & the Emperor has opened a loan at Amsterdam at 4. p. cent (which as I am told has not failed though it has not fully succeeded). These circumstances facilitating the American loans, Mr. Morris recieved for answer from his correspondent at Antwerp [4] that he had taken measures for carrying the loan into effect, I suppose by consulting with the brokers, & should come immediately to Paris to conclude the affair with me. He did not know my intention of going to Antwerp & was to leave that place as soon after his letter that it would have been impossible to have stopped him. He is expected here daily. As soon as any thing is done you shall be immediately informed of it. I shall notwithstanding go to Amsterdam as mentioned formerly & for the reason there given.[5]

My last letters from London [6] confirm what had been formerly mentioned & add that it would be improper to attempt a loan there at present, but that one may be counted on in the course of the winter or spring. They add that nothing further can be said before I go there which will be indispensable if the idea is to be prosecuted, & the sooner the better in order to prepare the way. I shall be able whilst in Holland & after knowing the success of new loans there & in Antwerp, better to judge of what should be done with respect to London, bearing in mind that, ceteris paribus, loans in this latter place would be preferred by you. On the whole if the administration of the U.S. continues to have the same success at home their prospects abroad for the next year will become still more bright, as they will be exonerated of their arrears, & enable them to dictate the mode of liquidating their foreign debt. Allow me to congratulate you most cordially on so propitious an event & to assure you at the same time of the sentiments of sincere attachment & profound respect with which I have the honor to be   Sir   Your most obedient   & most humble servant   W Short

The Honble
Alexander Hamilton Secretary of the Treasury Philadelphia

ALS, letterpress copy, William Short Papers, Library of Congress.

1. The Holland loan of September, 1791. For a description of this loan, see Short to H, August 31, 1791. On October 24, 1791, Willink, Van Staphorst, and Hubbard wrote to Short: "We have remitted to the National Treasury . . . Eight Millions One Hundred seventy Thousand Livres cury for account of the United States, Which is about the Three Millions of Guilders You desired us to remit provisionally to the Commissaries" (LS, Short Family Papers, Library of Congress).

2. The commissioners of the French Treasury.

3. Willink, Van Staphorst, and Hubbard to Short, October 24, 1791 (LS, Short Family Papers, Library of Congress).

4. Charles John Michael de Wolf, an Antwerp banker. On October 19, 1791, Gouverneur Morris wrote to Short that Wolf had opened the Antwerp loan (ALS, William Short Papers, Library of Congress). The English translation of the contract for this loan reads as follows:

"On this thirtieth day of November one thousand seven hundred and ninety one, before me John Gerard Deelen, Notary of Antwerp, admitted by the sovereign council of Barbant, in the presence of the witnesses hereafter named, appeared Mr William Short, chargé d'affair of the United States of America at the court of France, at present in this City, and to the witnesses known; exhibiting a power from Mr Alexander Hamilton Secretary of the Treasury of the said united states, dated the first of September 1790, authorising him the said William Short, by virtue of a power of substitution from the President of the United States to the said Alexander Hamilton, dated August the 28th 1790, to borrow under the acts of Congress of the 4th and 12th of August 1790, in any part of Europe, a certain limited sum of money, and to pass and execute such contracts, as he the said William Short shall judge necessary for that purpose: all agreeably to the documents deposited in the Office of C. J. M. De Wolf, Banker of this City, where the said Documents remain for the inspection and satisfaction of the Lenders.

"And the said William Short by virtue of the said power and authority, did acknowledge to have received from sundry Persons, for the use of the united States, the sum of Three millions of florins, money of exchange of Brabant, agreeably to the receipts subjoined to each Obligation of one thousand florins, money aforesaid, as hereafter mentioned; and did declare to be indebted on behalf and on account of the united States, to the said Persons, to the amount of the sum aforesaid, renouncing expressly the exception of monies untold. And the said William Short by virtue of the power aforesaid did promise to re-imbourse the said sum of three millions of florins, money of exchange of Brabant to the said Persons, through the office of C. J. M. De Wolf free of all charges whatsover, within fifteen Years after the date of the first of December 1791, under the clauses and conditions hereafter stipulated, to wit:

"That the said sum of three millions of florins money of exchange of Brabant shall not be demandable, during the term of eleven Years, from and after the first of December 1791: That at that period the sum of 600,000 florins money as aforesaid shall be reimbursed, and the like payments shall be continued from year to year in such manner, that the whole of the said Capital of three millions of florins shall be repaid and extinguished at the end of fifteen years. The united states shall however be at liberty to discharge part, or the whole of the said Capital sum sooner; but always in payments of intire obligations of one thousand florins each.

"In the mean time there shall be paid by the united States aforesaid, on the capital sum, an annual interest of 4½ per cent., to commence from the first of December 1791, and to continue until the principal shall be redeemed, which interest shall be paid upon checks, signed by Mr Gouy, employed in the office of C. J. M. De Wolf, or by such of the proprietors of the obligations as shall have preferred to hold them in their own names.

"That after the expiration of eleven years, the redemption of the obligations shall be determined by Lottery, six hundred numbers to be drawn at the time of each installment, in the presence of a Notary and Witnesses, at the office of C. J. M. De Wolf in the City of Antwerp, where the aforesaid principal, and the interest due, shall be paid, as shall be announced in the public papers.

"And the said William Short by virtue of his power aforesaid did declare, that C. J. M. De Wolf, Banker of this City, shall be the Director of this negociation; promising in the name of his constituents, that the Amount of the yearly interest, as well as the reimbursements, hereinbefore stipulated, shall be remitted annually to the said Director, free of all charges to the lenders. And that the present obligation of three millions of florins, or any part thereof, shall never be subject to any Tax or imposition, already laid, or hereafter to be laid by the united States, or by any of the individual states; and that in case of dissension among the said united States, or in the event of actual war, between them and the sovereign of the Belgic provinces, no impediment shall arise from either of these causes in the regular discharge of the interest, nor in the reimbursement of the principal, under any pretext whatsoever.

"And in order to give full effect to this instrument, the said William Short by virtue of the power aforesaid, doth further promisse and declare, that neither the united States, nor any of the said individual states shall enter into any convention, treaty of peace, or other engagement public or private, which might be prejudicial, or contrary to any of the clauses of this contract; and that the same shall be ratified by the President of the united States as soon as possible, and authentic copy of the ratification as well as a translation of the original, deposited at the office of the said Director, there to remain with the authentic Copies, Commissions, and powers of the said William Short, until the said principal and interest shall be discharged.

"And it is agreed, that three thousand Copies of this obligation shall be printed, each for one thousand florins, money of exchange of Brabant, with the name, or in blank, at the choice of the lenders, signed by the said William Short and numbered from 1 to 3000, and countersigned by C. J. M. De Wolf, certifying that the number of the said obligations does not exceed three thousand; which obligations with the receipts annexed shall be delivered up by the proprietors at the respective periods of reimbursement.

"And for the due performance of the aforesaid Contract the said William Short pledges the good faith of the United States, by virtue and authority of the acts of Congress of the 4th and 12th of August 1790, expressly renouncing in the name of the said united States of America the benefit of duobus vel pluribus reis debendi, as well as far as may be necessary, the benefit of ordinis divisionis et excussionis, the effects of which being known to him; promising never to avail himself thereof. . . ." (Copy, RG 59, Records Relating to Foreign Accounts, 1782–1797, Letters, Accounts, and Contracts, National Archives.)

5. See Short to H, October 10, 1791.

6. Robert Burton and Alexander Donald to Short, October 4, 1791 (LS, William Short Papers, Library of Congress); Burton and Donald to Short, October 11, 1791 (LS, William Short Papers, Library of Congress).

From Richard Harison

New York 9th: Novr. 1791

Sir,

In Consequence of your Directions to the Collector of this Place [1] a Suit was commenced against Anthony Libbey upon the registring Act,[2] for not bringing a duplicate Manifest of his Cargo from the Port he belonged to in the District of Maine. His Cargo had been previously landed and disposed of by Permission from the proper Officers who did not suspect any Misconduct. Upon an Examination into the Circumstances of his Case at Judge Duane's [3] Chambers in the Presence of the Collector it appeared that the whole Value of the Cargo was not equal to two hundred Dollars, and at the Place of Purchase did not amount to much more than half of that Sum. It appeared also from the Testimony of the Mate that the Error of the Captain (if any) had proceeded from Accident, and the Collector declared that he had long known and always found him a most punctual and honest Man. In this Situation of Things I did not suppose it prudent to proceed any farther against the Captain without your Directions, especially as the 29th. Section of the registring Act confines the Penalty to Cases where the Value of the Cargo is equal to two hundred Dollars.[4]

I beg Leave also to remind you of the Account which I exhibited some Time ago against the United States.[5] You must recollect Sir that we have no Table of Fees for criminal Cases, the State Government allowing an Annual Salary to it's Attorney Genl. The National Govt. has not indulged the District Attornies in that Way.[6] Therefore it was thôught most proper to adopt similar Allowances to those given in the State Supreme Court for equal Services in civil Causes,[7] tho' these Allowances in many Instances have been supposed inadequate, and it is usual to recieve additional Compensation from the Clients whose Business we transact. It would be very agreable to know what Government will determine with Respect to their Officers, whose Time and Attention must frequently be employed for the public Service in Cases for which at present there is no Provision.

I have now completed the Business entrusted to me with Respect to West Point.[8] A Fine with Proclamations has been duly levied, and the Deeds to lead the Uses are with the Secretary of the State to be recorded in his Office. This Precaution I thought proper, tho' I had no particular Orders for that Purpose. As you have been consulted at different Periods with Regard to this Business I beg to know (if you do not consider it as improper to interfere) what Disposition I am to make of the Title Deeds for this Property. It has been my own Idea that they should be lodged in the Secretary of State's Office, but as I recollect that Genl. Knox appeared to entertain a different Opinion, I wish to recieve explicit Directions upon the Subject. You can inform me whether it will be necessary to apply to the President, or to whom I should address myself.

With the highest Respect &ca. I remain Sir, Your most obedt Servt.

Hon. Alexr. Hamilton Esqr.
Secry Treasury. U.S.

LC, New-York Historical Society, New York City.

1. John Lamb. Letter not found.

2. "An Act for Registering and Clearing Vessels, Regulating the Coasting Trade, and for other purposes" (1 *Stat.* 55–65 [September 1, 1789]).

3. James Duane, Federal judge for the District of New York.

4. Section 29 of this act reads as follows: "*And it be further enacted,* That if the master of any ship or vessel, of the burthen of twenty tons or upwards, licensed to trade as aforesaid, and having on board goods, wares or merchandise, of the value of two hundred dollars or upwards, shall depart with the said ship or vessel from any port, with intent to go to another district, without such manifest and permit, except as is herein after provided, the master or owner of such ship or vessel shall forfeit and pay the sum of four hundred dollars for every such offence; and all goods, wares and merchandise, of the value of two hundred dollars or upwards, which shall be found on board any such ship or vessel after her departure from the port where the same were taken on board, without being contained in, and accompanied with such manifest as is herein before directed, except as is herein after excepted, shall be subject to seizure and forfeiture" (1 *Stat.* 63).

5. Harison to H, June 28, 1791.

6. Section 35 of "An Act to establish the Judicial Courts of the United States" stipulated that the United States attorney in each district "shall receive as a compensation for his services such fees as shall be taxed therefor in the respective courts before which the suits of prosecutions shall be" (1 *Stat.* 92–93 [September 24, 1789]).

7. For the fees allowed attorneys in the New York Supreme Court, see *Laws of the State of New York*, II, 129–30.

8. This is a reference to the purchase by the United States of additional land at West Point. See "Report on the Petition of Stephen Moore," June 3, 1790, and "An Act to authorize the purchase of a tract of land for the use of the United States" (1 *Stat.* 129 [July 5, 1790]).

From Thomas Mifflin [1]

[Philadelphia, November 9, 1791]

Sir,

It gave me great pleasure to receive the report of the Comptroller General of this State, upon the Business of the Lake Erie purchase; from which it appears, that the Comptroller General of the United States has concurred with him, in fixing the Consideration money of that purchase at 151, 640^{25}/$_{100}$ Dollars, and in the mode of payment. I have, therefore, referred the papers to the Attorney General of Pennsylvania, with instructions to confer with you, on the proper conveyances to be made; [2] and, as soon as they are compleated, you will receive a warrant, in favor of the Treasurer of the United States, for the above sum. Let me request, that you will be so good as to expedite this last Act of negociation; and believe me to be, with great Respect,

Sir,   Your most Obedient Servant   Thomas Mifflin.

Philadelphia, 9th. November 1791.
To Alexander Hamilton, Esquire, Secretary of the Treasury, of the United States.

LC, Division of Public Records, Pennsylvania Historical and Museum Commission, Harrisburg.

1. For background to this letter, see Mifflin to H, September 26, 1791, and H to Mifflin, September 28, 1791.

2. An entry in the executive minutes of Pennsylvania for November 9, 1791, reads as follows: "A Warrant was signed by the Governor authorizing and directing the Treasurer of this State to pay to the Treasurer of the United States, or to his order for the use of the United States the sum of one hundred and fifty one thousand six hundred and forty dollars and twenty five cents either in Loan Office Certificates of the United States, their specie value reduced by the Scale of depreciation—in Certificates of final settlement issued by the Commissioners of the States or departments—or in Certificates commonly called registered debt with the interest which may be due thereon untill the tenth day of June 1791 the same being a payment in full of the consideration money for the purchase of a certain Tract of Land on Lake Erie by this State from the United States agreeably to the Terms of the Contract and the Law authorising the Governor to Conclude the same" (*Pennsylvania Archives*, 9th ser., I, 276).

From Edmund Randolph

Philadelphia Nov: 9. 1791.

Sir

I do myself the honor of answering your letter of the 2d. instant [1] upon the subject of the North Carolina certificates.

The 13th. section of the funding act [2] admits, that subscriptions may be made to the loan payable in the principal and interest of the certificates or notes which, prior to a certain day, were issued by the respective states as acknowledgments or evidences of debts, by them respectively owing, except certificates, issued by the commissioners of army accounts in the state of North Carolina, in the year 1786. These last certificates are, I presume, now out of the question.

But how can redeemed certificates be a subscription of *debt?* Is a debt once due, but now paid off, still a debt? I cannot comment upon this question, with any hope of making it clearer, than it is at its first appearance.

For its redeemed debt of the foregoing description, each state will, I suppose, be a ⟨creditor⟩ [3] of congress. But the great settlement of accounts bet⟨ween the⟩ United States and the individual States must em⟨brace that⟩ debt. The subscription excluded it; as may be ⟨more fully seen⟩ by a reference to the 17th. section. [4]

I have ⟨the honor⟩ to be   ⟨with respect⟩ & esteem   ⟨your obedt.⟩ serv.   Edmd. Randolph

To the Secretary of the Treasury

ALS, RG 60, Copies of Opinions, National Archives; copy, North Carolina Department of Archives and History, Raleigh. The copy was enclosed in H's "Report to the Governor of North Carolina," July 31, 1794.

1. Letter not found.
2. For Section 13 of "An Act making provision for the ⟨payment of the⟩ Debt of the United States" (1 *Stat.* 138–44 [August 4, 1790]), see Thomas Smith to H, June 6, 1791, note 1.
3. Words within broken brackets have been taken from the copy.
4. For Section 17 of the Funding Act, see Smith to H, June 6, 1791, note 1.

To William Ellery

[*Philadelphia, November 10, 1791.* On November 21, 1791, Ellery wrote to Hamilton: "On the 19th. instant I recd. your letter of the 10th." [1] *Letter not found.*]

1. This was presumably the same as H to Jeremiah Olney, November 10, 1791.

To William Heth

[*Philadelphia, November 10, 1791.* On November 20, 1791, Heth wrote to Hamilton: "Your private favor of the 10th. Inst found me at home." *Letter not found.*]

To Charles Lee

Treasury Department
November 10 1791

Sir

Mr Gray's letter of the 9th Ultimo,[1] relative to the seizure made by you of the Ship Washington, and of five Casks of Brandy, has been received.

To obviate inconveniencies which the Owners might suffer by a delay, I have no objection to an immediate restoration of the Vessel and Brandy, provided the parties enter into Bond, with sufficient security, conditioned, that they will abide the event of my decision, when the subject shall come before me, in due course, from the Judge of the District of Virginia.[2]

I am, Sir, Your Most Obedt Servant, A Hamilton

Charles Lee Esqr.
Alexandria.

LS, RG 56, Letters to and from the Collector at Alexandria, National Archives; copy, RG 56, Letters to Collectors at Small Ports, "Set G," National Archives.
1. Letter not found. Vincent Gray was the deputy collector of customs at Alexandria, Virginia.
2. H is referring to the procedure for the remission of fines and forfeitures under the provisions of Section 43 of "An Act repealing, after the last day of

June next, the duties heretofore laid upon Distilled Spirits imported from abroad, and laying others in their stead; and also upon Spirits distilled within the United States, and for appropriating the same" (1 *Stat.* 209 [March 3, 1791]).

From Benjamin Lincoln

Boston 10th Novr. 1791

Sir

Inclosed is our tonnage Abstract commencing with July and ending with September. By a late instruction from the Treasury department we are called upon to make return to what port the several vessels entered here are destined, in what Kingdom State or Islands such ports are situated. All are in our return which are not in port have left it for places unknown to us. From the peculiar situation of this District, nearly in the center of the State and from it being the great mart thereof, are the Causes of this uncertainty. Vessels from other districts enter and unload here & proceed afterwards in ballast to their own districts. Departing in ballast precludes the necessity of Clearing out and leaves us much at a loss for the destination of so large a proportion of Vessels which enter here. We can only say that all such vessels Saving those mentioned in the return departed since the close of it, are gone coastwise or are in port.

By the inclosed abstract of duties you will have, I think, a pleasing view of the productiveness of the revenue in this district. I cannot omit mentioning circumstances as pleasing as interesting that the duties are paid with great cheerfulness & punctuality and that no suit has been brought on any bond for more than a year past.

Secy Treasury

LC, Massachusetts Historical Society, Boston; LC, RG 36, Collector of Customs at Boston, Letter Book, 1790–1797, National Archives; two copies, RG 56, Letters from the Collector at Boston, National Archives.

From Jeremiah Olney

Providence, November 10, 1791. "On the arrival of the Sloop Clementina from Newport, the Third instant, the Master informed me that there were *Six* Chests of Tea onboard; but there proved to be only *Five:* my Letter [1] was written before the Inspector, who had orders to Store it, made his Return; which will account for the mistake. The Apples, being of a perishable nature, were delivered to the Consignee, who, in case of condemnation, is to account for them. . . ."

ADfS, Rhode Island Historical Society, Providence.
1. Olney to H, November 3, 1791.

To Jeremiah Olney

Treasury Department
November 10 1791

Sir

I have, on consideration, deemed it expedient to authorize you to receive, in payment of duties, the notes of the Bank of Providence, payable in specie on demand.[1] For the greater safety in so doing I have requested the President of that institution [2] to furnish you with his signature, that of the Cashier and such Checks as may be sufficient to enable you to detect Counterfeits. It is my wish also that you will transmit, once in every week, to the Bank of Providence such monies as appear as the balance of your weekly returns, after defraying the expences of your Office, paying the other Officers &ca. For each of these payments you will obtain duplicate receipts, one of which you will transmit to me, retaining the other in your hands. Any monies that may be necessary to pay such of the undermentioned Bills as are not taken up, you will be careful to retain.

I am, Sir, Your Obedt Servant.   A Hamilton

Draughts remaining unpaid
No 2282 in favor of Tench Francis [3] for Dolls   500
   2345   Ditto   1000
   2415   Ditto   500
   2433   Wm Seton [4]   500

Jere. Olney Esqr.
Collr. Providence.

LS, Rhode Island Historical Society, Providence; copy RG 56, Letters to the Collector at Providence, National Archives; copy, RG 56, Letters to Collectors at Small Ports, "Set G," National Archives.

1. See the second letter from Olney to H, October 8, 1791.
2. John Brown was president of the Providence Bank.
3. Francis was cashier of the Bank of North America.
4. Seton was cashier of the Bank of New York.

Receipt from William Pearce [1]

[Philadelphia, November 10, 1791]

Received Philadelphia November 10. 1791 of Alexander Hamilton One hundred and fifty Dollars on account of Machines.

Wm. Pearce

D, in writing of H and signed by Pearce, Hamilton Papers, Library of Congress.
1. For "A List of Mr Willm Pearce's Machines," see "Receipt from William Pearce," August 20, 1791, note 2.

George Washington to John Kean [1]

Philadelphia, November 10, 1791. Approves of Kean's decision to remain in the service of the Federal Government in spite of his appointment as cashier of the Bank of the United States. Thinks it will be advisable for him to remain a commissioner until the commission expires in July, 1792.

Df, in writing of H, RG 59, Miscellaneous Letters, 1790–1799, National Archives.
1. Kean had been appointed in August, 1789, as one of the commissioners for settling the United States accounts with the individual states. He was reappointed in August, 1790. On October 25, 1791, he was appointed cashier of the Bank of the United States.

From John Beale Bordley [1]

Wye (on the Eastern shore of Maryland)
11 Novr. 1791.

Dear Sir,

The method in which I proceeded on the enquiry, was this: In conversation with farmers, I expressed a wish to be informed of

LC, George Washington Papers, Library of Congress; copy, George Washington Papers, Library of Congress.
1. Bordley, a lawyer and landowner on the Eastern Shore of Maryland, moved to Philadelphia in 1791. He had been instrumental in the formation in 1785 of the Philadelphia Society for the Promotion of Agriculture and was vice president of the society until his death in 1804.
H sent a copy of this letter to the President, who in turn sent a selection of

several particulars in rural concerns, that seem to me to have been too little thought of by Husbandmen. On explaining my meaning they approved of the design & promised to recollect what they could of those matters, and that they would communicate the result to me. Having thus prepared them, I sometime after delivered to them printed papers containing the particulars of my enquiries, and requested they would fill up the blanks in those papers. The last step was to wait on them at their houses.

The information contained in the paper which I have now the honor to deliver to you, is all that could be obtained. The farmers received the papers with hearty intentions to fill up the blanks, without conceiving there was any difficulty in the execution; yet the only reason of there not being other answers to the questions, is solely from the difficulty—to *them* the impossibility of fulfilling their design & promise; for they kept no minutes, & their attention to the bulk of the articles, as they acknowledged with concern, had been trifling. On this occasion I had the pleasure to hear several of the farmers declare, that being, by the enquiry, led to think on the numerous particulars in the paper, they had determined in future to make some account of them, as they conceive it will be considerably advantageous to them.

The little introduction to the piece was meant to soften it from an appearance it might have of an inventory of their Effects; and I think that if the *value* of things, especially of the Land, can be omitted, the quantities would be more readily, if not also in more numerous instances, obtained: and there would be less danger of a jealousy that the enquiry is meant for political purposes. In one instance only there appeared a suspicion that such a use was intended. It was the last conversation I had on the subject with some farming gentlemen. "It may be said by some people that Mr: B. is a politician, and that he wants to know the value of Country Estates that they may be taxed."

The value of Lands as reported by the proprietors, probably is less to be depended on, than if it was collected from conversations with the people from the several States. Ask any man what his Land would sell for, or is worth, he cannot find a moderate rate. The land in the

---

such letters on American agriculture to Arthur Young, the English agricultural authority. See *GW*, XXXII, 71.

Bordley's letter was written in reply to "Treasury Department Circular," August 13, 1791.

present case is fully worth the sum it is rated at; but yet in my opinion, it could not be now sold, on time, for that price. No article is so slow of sale, as Land at this time.

I have the honor to be &c.   Beale Bordley.

Alex. Hamilton Esquire

[ENCLOSURE] [2]

The following account is of a farm in Talbot County (State of Maryland) of *middling* goodness; with the *medium* produce of it's last four years Crops. It contains about 450 acres, of which 180 are woodland, 270 arable, & of this 110 are pasture. The value of the whole, as it might be expected to sell on time, according to present opinion is £2,500.

It's Produce, in common, the medium of 4 years, follows.

	qt'y.	value
Wheat	700–	£263. 0.0.
Rye		
Corn	450	£67. 0.0.
Oats		
Barley		
Buckwheat		
Potatoes, with fruit, other roots & vegetables in value. —		50. 0.0
Tobacco	5000 ld.	50. 0.0
Wood for fuel, cord	160	20 0.0
Hay, tons	5	25. 0.0
Pulse (Peas &c)		
Hemp	20 ld	10.0
Flax	100	2.10.0
Wool	200	10. 0.0
Butter	400	20. 0.0
Cotton, Cheese, fruit		

	value
Cattle 35; calves annually raised 5;	£120. 0.0

2. LC, George Washington Papers, Library of Congress.

Horses 20; Colt,   do.   do.   1; 250. 0.0
Sheep 80; Lambs do.   do.   30; 75. 0.0
Hogs, anny. killd. or sold   30; . . . .   60. – –
Poultry pr year—dunghill 400—Turkies 100. Ducks 90.

The quantities & values are generally in round numbers, which has a suspicious appearance. But the worthy farmer after considering well each article, stated them partly from memory, partly from notes or scraps of paper, & thought it best to omit fractional quantities & sums as he had not perfect minutes. It is the accot. of an honest, candid man, who wou'd not have given it, if he had not believed it to be generally just.

To Jabez Bowen

[*Philadelphia, November 11, 1791*. Letter listed in dealer's catalogue. *Letter not found.*]

LS, sold by Stan V. Henkels, Jr., April 13, 1917, Lot 160.

From William Ellery

Collector's Office
Port of Newport [Rhode Island] Novr. 11 1791

Sir,

At the Session of the Genl. Assembly, which ended the last week, I desired a leading member of the Lower House to move for a Cession of the Light House &c to the United States,[1] if he should think the motion would succeed. He conversed with some members of the Upper House upon the subject who had formerly opposed it, they said there was time enough to cede hereafter, and thought it best to hold their right as long as they could. Under these circumstances he deemed it unseasonable to make the motion. In my letter of the 18th. of July last, I gave you an account of the condition in which the Light House was, what repairs were necessary, the estimated expence, and asked your directions whether repairs should be made or not. As this is the season for falling weather, and the Winter is advancing I

wish to receive your directions in this regard as soom as may be convenient.

I am considered as Superintendant of the Light-House, but I have
no appointment, and no compensation is allowed for my trouble. The
United States are debited in my books for monies advanced for the
Use of the Light-House, but no Warrant has issued, by which I could
give them Credit. I wish that these matters might be adjusted.

Permit me, in addition to what I have heretofore written, in my
letters of the 31st. of January [2] and the 18th. of July last, respecting
an allowance and an adequate compensation for my services as Collector, to observe, that the Collector of this District, on account of
the number of ports of delivery in it, is involved in greater difficulty
and trouble than they experience who have a smaller number of
Officers to superintend. He is obliged to maintain a constant intercourse with the Supervisors by letters, to examin the accounts of a
variety of Inspectors, and to rectify errors as they arise, and this you
are sensible, Sir, requires much time, care, and attention. While I
continue in office, I shall discharge my duty, as far as I know it, with
fidelity; and I will not believe that my services will go unrewarded.

I am, Sir,   Yr. most obedt. servt.   Wm Ellery Collr

A. Hamilton Esqr
Secry Treasy.

LC, Newport Historical Society, Newport, Rhode Island.
    1. See Ellery to H, March 7, May 9, July 4, 1791.
    2. This letter had not been located when Volume VII of *The Papers of
Alexander Hamilton* was published. It has since been located in the Newport
Historical Society and will be printed in a supplementary volume.

To Samuel Jones [1]

[*Philadelphia, November 11, 1791.* "I do not consider myself as at
liberty to authorise anything; and so much are the circumstances
effaced from my memory that I do not even feel myself competent
to advise." [2] *Letter not found.*]

ALS, sold at American Art Association, November 24, 1924, Lot 333.
    1. Jones, a prominent lawyer of Queens County, New York, had served in the
New York Assembly from 1786 to 1790 and had been a member of the New York
Ratifying Convention in 1788.
    2. Text taken from extract of letter in the dealer's catalogue.

From John Lamb [1]

[*New York, November 11, 1791.* On November 20, 1791, Hamilton wrote to Lamb: "Your private letter of the 11th. instant duly came to hand." *Letter not found.*]

1. Lamb was collector of customs in New York City.

To Jeremiah Olney

Treasury Department
November 11 1791

Sir

Your letter of the 31st Ultimo relative to the Schooner Alice, Jabez Andrus Master, has been received.

The question, therein stated, turns upon the following points; whether the vessel belongs in the whole or in part to a Citizen or inhabitant of the United States; and if she was within four leagues of the coast, or within the limits of any district of the United States when the manifest was demanded by the Officer: then, and in every such case, the master must be prosecuted for the penalty incurred by the 12th Section of the Collection law.[1]

I am, Sir, Your Most Obed Servant.   A Hamilton

Jere. Olney Esqr.
Providence.

LS, Rhode Island Historical Society, Providence; copy, RG 56, Letters to the Collector at Providence, National Archives; copy, RG 56, Letters to the Collectors at Small Ports, "Set G," National Archives.
1. See Olney to H, October 31, note 3.

To William Seton

[*Philadelphia, November 11, 1791.* On November 17, 1791, Seton wrote to Hamilton: "I am honoured with your Letters of the 11th & 14th." *Letter of November 11 not found.*]

Treasury Department Circular
to the Collectors of the Customs

Treasury Department,
November 11, 1791.

Sir,

An order having been transmitted to me from the honorable House of Representatives, to make certain returns, relative to the exports, imports and tonnage of the United States, I find it necessary to press your immediate transmission of all such documents as are to come from your Office, to the 30th of September last.[1]

A case, which has been represented to me, renders it necessary to intimate to the Collectors of the Customs that I do not conceive the allowance for damage, provided in the collection law, can be made to importers, unless such damage shall be certified by the appraisers, appointed as the act directs, "to have taken place during the voyage." [2]

I am, Sir, Your obedient Servant, A Hamilton

LS, to Sharp Delany, Bureau of Customs, Philadelphia; L[S], to Benjamin Lincoln, RG 36, Letters from the Treasury, Vol. 5, National Archives; LS, to Otho H. Williams, Office of the Secretary, United States Treasury Department; copy, to Otho H. Williams, RG 56, Circulars of the Office of the Secretary, "Set T," National Archives; L[S], Circulars of the Treasury Department, Library of Congress; copy, United States Finance Miscellany, Treasury Circulars, Library of Congress.

1. An entry in the *Journal of the House* for November 10, 1791, reads as follows: "*Ordered,* That the Secretary of the Treasury do report to this House the amount of the exports from the several districts within the United States respectively; also, of duties arising on imports and tonnage, from the twenty-ninth of September, one thousand seven hundred and ninety, to the thirtieth of September, one thousand seven hundred and ninety-one" (*Journal of the House,* I, 452).

2. See Section 37 of "An Act to provide more effectually for the collection of the duties imposed by law on goods, wares and merchandise imported into the United States, and on the tonnage of ships or vessels" (1 *Stat.* 166–67 [August 4, 1790]).

To Otho H. Williams

Treasury Department
November 11 1791

Sir

I have, on consideration, concluded to authorise you to allow the Officers and crew of the revenue cutter twelve cents per ration, instead of nine cents, mentioned in my circular letter of the 21st September. But the allowance claimed for expences of board is inadmissible; their pay and rations must be considered as a full compensation.

I am, Sir, Your Obed Servant. Alexander Hamilton

Otho H Williams Esqr.
Baltimore.

LS, Columbia University Libraries.

From John Daves

New Bern [*North Carolina*] *November 12, 1791.* "In looking out to procure the sundry stores necessary for the Revenue Cutter now building for the North Carolina Station, I find it impossible to procure the whole of the articles in this place or neighbourhood, and not supposing myself justafiable in sending public money abroad to purchase them, I have to request you will be pleased to direct them to be purchased agreeable to the memorandum inclosed, and forward them to this place or Washington[1] as soon as may be convenient. . . ."

Copy, RG 56, Letters from the Collector at New Bern, National Archives.
1. Washington, North Carolina.

To Benjamin Lincoln

Treasury Department
November 12 1791

Sir

I have received your letter of the 4th Ultimo, inclosing a duplicate receipt, No 345, of the Bank of Massachusetts for a payment of twenty five thousand Dollars, made by you into that Bank.

With regard to the boatmen, I fully approve of your idea, upon the strength of what you suggest, that the service will not suffer by dismissing three of them during the winter season.

I am, Sir, with great consideration,   Your Most Obed Servt

Benjamin Lincoln, Esqr.
Collector, Boston.

L[S], RG 36, Collector of Customs at Boston, Letters from the Treasury, 1789–1807, Vol. 4, National Archives; copy, RG 56, Letters to the Collector at Boston, National Archives; copy, RG 56, Letters to Collectors at Small Ports, "Set G," National Archives.

From William Short

Paris Nov: 12. 1791

Sir

Since my last of the 8th. inst. sent by the French packet, the person expected from Antwerp [1] of whom I then spoke to you has arrived. This letter written in haste & despatched by the post of to-day in the possibility of its arriving at L'Orient in time for the packet, is merely to inform you of the result of my interview with Mr. Wolf of Antwerp the name of the person in question.

I informed you some time ago that I had authorized his opening a loan at 4½ p. cent interest & 5. p. cent commission.[2] At that time no attempt had been made by the Emperor to reduce the rate of interest & circumstances in general were not so favorable to such an object as at present. Of course as Mr. Wolf had not opened the loan but had desired as a condition that I should stipulate not to open any more in Holland at an higher rate of interest, I thought myself founded to consider my former authorization given him as so far void that I might propose to him new terms of commission determining however to grant the 5. p. cent if the rate of interest could not be lowered without it. He insisted for some time on the necessity of being allowed at least 5. p. cent on account of the loan for the U.S. being a new thing, the greater commission he is consequently obliged to allow the undertakers &c. &c. I found so many arguments however to oppose to all these that he at length consented & seems well satisfied to take 4. p. cent for commission, all charges &c. as at Amsterdam, with which I am well persuaded you will be highly satisfied as being applied to a loan at a reduced rate of interest. I have always considered it proper to have the charges on the loans reduced with the utmost rigour, more for the credit of the borrowing power than on account of a small economy. The rate of interest being for the most part the same, the real criterion by which the well informed judge of the credit of the several borrowing powers is the commission they pay on their loans.

This loan will be opened so as to date from the 1st of next month & Mr Wolf assures me that it will be carried through with eclat. He had taken all the preliminary measures in such a manner before leaving Antwerp as to put this matter beyond all question in his own mind. The duration of this loan & mode of re-imbursement will be the same as those made at Amsterdam. Mr. Wolf desired that the U. S. should stipulate not to re-imburse any part before a certain number of years, but as he did not seem to think this essential I have determined to preserve that privilege, although there is little probability of its being made use of within the term of five or six years which he desired. The amount of the loan is to be three millions of florins. Mr. Wolf wished much that I should authorize him to extend it on the same conditions to six millions if, as he was well persuaded, he should find it practicable in the course of a few months. I have not consented to this however because I have thought it best to reserve to the U. S. the right of reducing the rate of interest or commission on the next loan if found practicable, & also because if the bankers at Amsterdam should also make the loan which I have authorized them to open for three millions if it can be done previous to the 1st. of January so as to avoid the tax they mentioned to me,[3] I shall not consider myself at liberty under your letter of the 1st. of Aug. last, to have any additional sum borrowed at 4½. p. cent interest, exclusive of charges. As you have never said any thing to me expressly about the re-imbursement of the Spanish debt [4] & that to the Farmers-general,[5] I shall wait until I hear further from you unless it should become essential to attend to them sooner in which case I shall suppose myself implicitly authorized to apply thereto the money which may be on hand.

I know not what effect the opening this loan at Antwerp will have at Amsterdam. It will certainly produce ill humour among those who are employed in our loans there & who have been accustomed to think that their city was entitled to a monopoly of them. As the present situation of the U. S. however with respect to their arrears to the French government & other exigencies puts them above the effects of such ill humour it is probable it will not be shewn.

I have mentioned to you [6] that the bankers informed me a tax was to be laid by the Dutch government on all loans made after the 1st. of Jany next & that they were of opinion they could have one undertaken at 4½. p. cent interest previous to that period. I have authorized them in that case to do it provided the commission be fixed at 4. p. cent [7] I have as yet no answer, but you may count on being immediately informed of what shall be done in this as well as the loan at Antwerp.

My late letters to you have been of Aug. 8. 23. 30. 31. Sep 3. 23. Oct 10. Nov 8. I have the honor to be most respectfully   Sir   Your most obedient humble servant   W. Short

The Honble
Alexander Hamilton Secretary of the Treasury, Philadelphia.

ALS, letterpress copy, William Short Papers, Library of Congress.
    1. Charles John Michael de Wolf.
    2. See Short to H, October 10, 1791.
    3. See Willink, Van Staphorst, and Hubbard to Short, August 25, 1791, printed as an enclosure to Short to H, August 31, 1791. This matter is also discussed in Short to Willink, Van Staphorst, and Hubbard, November 11, 1791 (ALS, letterpress copy, William Short Papers, Library of Congress).
    4. The Spanish loan of 1781. For a description of this debt, see H to Short, September 1, 1790, note 19.
    5. For a description of this debt, see H to Short, September 1, 1790, note 26.
    6. See Short to H, November 8, 1791.
    7. Short to Willink, Van Staphorst, and Hubbard, November 11, 1791 (ALS, letterpress copy, William Short Papers, Library of Congress).

To William Constable [1]

Philadelphia, November 14, 1791. ". . . the whole money for interest on the Stock of your friends in Antwerp has been paid as well that on the separate as on the joint stock; in confidence that you will find me a further bond of indemnification respective the separate stock. The truth is that the Gentlemen in Question have not acted like men of business; for, I believe by the law of their country as well as ours a power from A B & C to receive interest upon stock standing *in their names* is no more a power to receive interest on stock standing in the name of A & B than a power from *William Constable* to receive interest on Stock standing in his name would be a power to receive interest on Stock standing in the name of *Alexander Hamilton*. Certain political considerations neverless conspiring with a wish to accomodate you determined me to pass over the obstacle resulting from so radical a defect. But you must tell that Gentlemen that they must transact their business with more accuracy in future. . . ."

ALS, from a typescript supplied by Mr. Elisha K. Kane, Kane, Pennsylvania.
  1. Constable was a prominent New York merchant and speculator.

From John Jay

[*New York, November 14, 1791*. On December 5, 1791, Hamilton wrote to Jay: "Your letter of the 14th of November duly came to hand." *Letter not found.*]

To William Seton

[*Philadelphia, November 14, 1791*. On November 17, 1791, Seton wrote to Hamilton: "I am honoured with your Letters of the 11th & 14th." *Letter of November 14 not found.*]

From James Taylor and Abishai Thomas

Office of the Agents of No. Carolina [Philadelphia]
November 14th 1791

Sir

This Afternoon we were honor'd with yours of the 3rd instant, in which you request to be informed, *"Whether the State of North Carolina has ever issued its own Certificates in lieu of those of the United States,"* together with our *"opinion of the real state of the thing."* In answer to the first after giving the most ample investigation to the subject which the means in our power would admit, we inform you that there is no public act, record, or document in our possession or within the knowledge of either of us which can induce us to believe that that State hath ever issued any Certificates of that description, and we may add that if such a transaction had ever taken place in that State, we conceive that we could not be unacquainted with it. Our "opinion of the real state of the thing" being founded on the result of our enquiries on the subject of the information solicited, we consider the foregoing as fully to include that opinion as any thing we could add on the occasion.

We have the honor to be with the utmost consideration   Sir Your very obt Servts.

Df, in the writing of Abishai Thomas, North Carolina Department of Archives and History, Raleigh; copy, incorrectly dated November 12, 1791, North Carolina Department of Archives and History.

From William Ellery

Newport [Rhode Island] November 15, 1791. ". . . At a District Court held at Providence the last week came on the trial United States vs Thomas Cotrell [1] for aiding and assisting in unlading the Sloop Betsy James Bissel Master without a permit when the Jury found a Verdict for the Plaint. for four hundred Dollars, and Cost of Suit. . . ."

LC, Newport Historical Society, Newport, Rhode Island.
   1. See Ellery to H, August 2, 23, 26, 29, September 19, October 4, 1791.

From Tobias Lear

United States 15th. Novr. 1791.

By the Presidents command T. Lear has the honor to transmit to the Secretary of the Treasury a letter from Messrs. Triol, Roux & Co. enclosing a copy of a memorial presented by them to the National Assembly of France.[1]

The President wishes when the Secretary may have leisure, that he would take the subject of said memorial into consideration & report thereon to the president.   Tobias Lear
                                                    S. P. U. S.

LC, George Washington Papers, Library of Congress.
   1. This letter and petition concerned the redemption of loan office certificates

acquired by Triol, Roux, and Company, Marseilles merchants, in return for a ship and supplies sold in the United States during the American Revolution. A translation of the letter, dated June 15, 1791, and a copy of the memorial to the French Assembly, dated June 1, 1791, may be found in RG 59, Miscellaneous Letters, 1790–1799, National Archives.

To William Ellery

[*Philadelphia, November 16, 1791.* On December 5, 1791, Ellery wrote to Hamilton: "I have recd. your letters of the 16th & 17th of the last month." *Letter of November 16 not found.*]

From William R. Davie [1]

Halifax, No Carolina, Nov. 17th. 1791.

Sir,

I mentioned to my friend Judge Iredell [2] when I saw him last at Newbern my intentio⟨n⟩ of moving our next Assembly to address Congress on the subject of receiving our *pap⟨er⟩* money in the revenue of the United States collected in this State; and requested him to have a conversation with you on the business, that I might avail myself of your opinion of its propriety and success.

This measure has been suggested to me, by the objections that are made here to the colle⟨ct⟩ion of the excise in *specie;* the real difficu⟨l⟩ty with which I foresee it will be attended, and its certain operation on the value or exchange of our paper currency: but independent of the policy and convenience of such a measure, I think the State may very wel⟨l⟩ require it of Congress as a matter of Justi⟨ce.⟩ The first emission of this money was ⟨made⟩ for the express purpose of paying the Continental line; [3] the second to purchase Tobacco to pay the interest of the Federal debt,[4] and to answer these purposes more effectually both emissions were made a tender in discharge of private contracts, and have been so received. It is also to be observed, that both these emissions amounting to two hundred thousand pounds were made several years before the constitution was formed, and that this incumbrance made a part of our political situation at its adoption, and had grown out of the old confederation: so that leaving this State to struggle with the task of supporting the credit of this money, even against the measures of Congress, surely has the appearance of great injustice, especially after a general Assumption of the State debts.

The effects of such a measure would I am certain be highly beneficial to the people of this Country, and I think not injurious to the General Government; the paper money which is now generally at ten shillings to the dollar would rise instantly to *par*, a benefit the people would attribute to its proper cause; the commercial part of the State would be relieved from great and very distressing difficulties, and the demand for *specie* created by the duties would no longer operate injuriously on the value of our paper money; it would effectually remove the only rational ground of complaint made against the excise, in the interior and western parts of the State, that is the difficulty or as they say impossibility, of procuring specie sufficient to pay that Tax: And would also prevent a very delicate and perhaps dangerous question, that must otherwise soon arise on executions issuing from the Federal Court. These appear to me as objects of some moment, and I take it, form only a part of the good consequences of this measure. There are not more than £140,000, now in circulation, the balance having been taken up by the sinking fund and destroyed, and as the money would certainly rise to par I think the Federal Treasury would run little risk in receiving it; and I cannot prevail upon myself to entertain the idea, that the General Government is so unwieldy a machine as to be incapable of being accommodated to the interests and situations of the different States.

Our Assembly meet at Newbern the first monday of December, and should you think proper to write to me on this subject you will please to direct to me at that place. I would undertake that the State shall give the most satisfactory assurances that the sinking fund Tax [5] shall be continued; and that the Assembly will pass any other law that might be necessary to secure the Treasury of the United States.

I know very well that Gentlemen in official situations are in the habit of respecting no communication, but such as wears the garb of confidence or office. I have no claim to either footing and was I not well persuaded, even from the slight acquaintance I have with you, that you possess a mind of a very different ⟨cast,⟩ I should not have troubled you with this letter.

I have the Honor to be with great respect your mo obd
William R. Davie

ALS, Hamilton Papers, Library of Congress.

1. Davie, a lawyer and Federalist politician, was a representative from the borough of Halifax in the North Carolina state legislature.

2. James Iredell of North Carolina was an Associate Justice of the United States Supreme Court.

3. In 1783 the North Carolina legislature passed "An Act for emitting One Hundred Thousand Pounds in Paper Currency, for the purposes of government for seventeen hundred and eighty three, for the redemption of paper currency now in circulation, and advancing to the Continental officers and soldiers part of their pay and subsistance. . ." (Clark, *State Records of North Carolina,* XXIV, 475–78).

4. On December 29, 1785, the North Carolina legislature passed "An Act for emitting One hundred thousand Pounds paper Currency, for the Purposes therein expressed." This law was enacted because of the "pressing circumstances of our domestic and foreign debts" (*The Laws of the State of North-Carolina, Passed at Newbern, December, 1785* [New Bern: Printed by Arnett & Hodge, Printers to the State, 1786], 8–9).

5. This tax had been provided by "An Act for emitting One hundred thousand Pounds paper Currency, for the Purposes therein expressed" passed by the North Carolina legislature on December 29, 1785. Section XII provided that "the tax of six-pence on every hundred acres of land, one shilling and six-pence on every poll, and one shilling and six-pence on every hundred pounds value of town property, shall be levied in each and every year, to commence and be first paid for the year one thousand seven hundred and eighty-six; which shall be a sinking fund to sink the paper money in circulation, no part of which shall again go into circulation except the commission given for the collection of said tax" (*Laws of the State of North-Carolina . . . December, 1785,* 9).

To William Ellery

[*Philadelphia, November 17, 1791.* On December 5, 1791, Ellery wrote to Hamilton: "I have recd. your letters of the 16th & 17th of the last month." *Letter of November 17 not found.*][1]

1. This letter was written in reply to Ellery to H, October 14, 1791.

To Benjamin Lincoln

Treasury Department
November 17 1791

Sir

Your letter of the 2nd instant has been duly received.

You were perfectly right in charging the Schooner Industry with the rate of foreign Tonnage. As the fact stands, it does not appear that the law authorises a restitution; and the parties, in pursuing a second voyage without a Register, after having been once indulged, and admonished, and after sufficient time and opportunity were given them, to procure the necessary papers, can have no claim to further forbearance, even if there was a discretion to grant it.

The 4th Section of the Tonnage ⟨act allows a⟩ [1] restitution of the foreign Tonnage, ⟨which has⟩ been paid on Ships or Vessels of the United States under certain circumstances, *prior to the passing of that act*, which was in July, and can therefore not apply to any case subsequent to it.[2]

To obviate the difficulty in respect to the terms "dying wood and dying drugs" I shall consider whether an enumeration cannot be formed of those articles. In the mean time I incline to a liberal interpretation of the terms in favor of manufactures.

In mine of the 12th instant I consented that you might discharge so many of the boatmen during the winter season as in your opinion should be deemed proper.

I am, Sir,   with great consideration   Your Most Obed Servant.

Benjamin Lincoln Esqr.
Boston.

L[S], RG 36, Collector of Customs at Boston, Letters from the Treasury, 1789–1807, Vol. 4, National Archives; copy, RG 56, Letters to the Collector at Boston, National Archives; copy, RG 56, Letters to Collectors at Small Ports, "Set G," National Archives.

1. The words within broken brackets have been taken from the copy in RG 56, Letters to the Collector at Boston, National Archives.

2. Section 4 of "An Act imposing duties on the tonnage of ships or vessels" reads as follows: *"Be it therefore further enacted,* That in all cases in which the said foreign duty shall have been heretofore paid on ships or vessels of the United States, whether registered at the time of payment or afterwards, restitution thereof shall be made, and that no such foreign duty shall hereafter be demanded on the said ships or vessels" (1 *Stat.* 136 [July 20, 1790]).

From William Seton

Bank of New York 17 Novr 1791

Sir

I am honoured with your Letters of the 11th & 14th.[1] The sale of the Bills on Amsterdam shall be arranged at the rate of 6 ⅌ Ct Interest for the term of Credit agreeable to your desire, and furnished in a few days.

Mr Hill [2] was this day paid the Seven thousand Dollars, and Inclosed in his receipt for the same which is Charged to the United States. I have the Honor to be &c

Alexr. Hamilton Esqr
Sy. of Ty. of the US.

LC, Bank of New York, New York City.
1. Letters not found.
2. William Hill was a New York City merchant who had formerly been associated with William Duer in the West Indian trade.

Treasury Department Circular
to the Collectors of the Customs

Treasury Deparmt.
Nov. 17. 1791.

Sir

On considering several representations which have been made to me relative to the rations for the cutters,[1] I have determined on the following mode of conducting the business.

A price not exceeding twelve cents for each man per diem may be agreed for by you with the Captain or any other person, who will contract to supply the necessary articles. It is hoped that this will enable you to conduct the business in a manner which will be satisfactory to the seamen and consistent with a proper execution of the public service. Should you find it practicable to obtain this supply for less than twelve cents per man per day, your concern for the public interests will, I assure myself, prompt you to do it. The officers may receive the same articles with the seamen [2] or the sum stipulated for them as they may prefer the one or the other.

I have already observed that rations from the date of each commission is all that it is in the power of the officers of the Treasury to admit as compensation for board prior to the officers living on board the cutters.[3] Accounts for the time prior to the date of the commissions may be rendered to the Auditor of the Treasury (in those instances wherein it has not been already done) with such testimonials of their having been engaged and actually in service as in each case they may be able to adduce. It will lie with the examining and accountant officers of this department to determine how far they can be legally admitted.

The number of men and boys being limited by law it is not in my power to add to them.[4]

It will be proper that quarterly accounts terminating as in the customs should ⟨be⟩ regularly transmitted in your own mode ⟨un⟩til forms shall be sent to you.

I am, Sir, Your obedt. servant

L[S], to Benjamin Lincoln, RG 36, Collector of Customs at Boston, Letters from the Treasury and Others, 1790–1817, Vol. 10, National Archives; L[S], to Otho H. Williams, Office of the Secretary, United States Treasury Department; LS, to Jedediah Huntington, New London Custom House Records, Federal Records Center, Boston; copy, United States Finance Miscellany, Treasury Circulars, Library of Congress; copy, RG 56, Circulars of the Office of the Secretary, "Set T," National Archives.

1. See Benjamin Lincoln to H, October 4, 20, 1791; Joseph Whipple to H, October 7, 1791.

2. "Treasury Department Circular to the Collectors of the Customs," September 21, 1791. See also H to Otho H. Williams, November 11, 1791.

3. "Treasury Department Circular to the Collectors of the Customs," July 8, 1791.

4. Section 63 of "An Act to provide more effectually for the collection of the duties imposed by law on goods, wares and merchandise imported into the United States, and on the tonnage of ships or vessels" states that "there shall be to each of the said boats or cutters, one master, and not more than three mates, first, second, and third, four mariners and two boys" (1 *Stat.* 175 [August 4, 1790]).

To Otho H. Williams

Treasury Department
Nov. 17. 1791.

Sir

There will not be found any provision for the payment of Mr. Edward Swift, whom Captain Gross[1] has shipt to do the duty of Mr. James Forbes now absent,[2] unless Mr. Forbes from a sense of justice and propriety allows it to be done out of his money. It would be well for you to intimate this to Captain Gross, and the more so as he in a former instance made an appointment of his officers, which can only be done by the President of the United States.

I am, Sir, Your most obedt. servt.　　　　Alex Hamilton

Otho H. Williams Esq.
Collector Baltimore.

LS, Columbia University Libraries.
  1. Simon Gross was captain of the revenue cutter for Maryland.
  2. Forbes, third officer of the Maryland revenue cutter, was serving aboard another ship until the completion of the Maryland cutter.

To Tobias Lear

[*Philadelphia*] *November 18, 1791.* "The President has directed that a commission be made out for Mr Morris,[1] now second mate— as *first* Mate of the N Y Cutter. . . ."

LC, George Washington Papers, Library of Congress.
  1. Richard Valentine Morris of New York.

To Benjamin Lincoln

Treasury Department
November 18 1791

Sir

Inclosed is an application which has been made to the President.

I request your opinion, as to the competency of the present allowance, or as to what would be a competent one, if you think the present deficient.[1] When you communicate it, you will please to send back the representation now transmitted.

I am, with great consideration, Sir,   Your Obed Servant.

Alex Hamilton

Benjamin Lincoln Esqr
Boston.

LS, RG 36, Collector of Customs at Boston, Letters and Papers re Lighthouses, Buoys, and Piers, 1789–1819, Vol. I, National Archives.
  1. The "allowance" under consideration was that of the Portland lighthouse keeper. See Lincoln to H, December 1, 1791.

Receipt from William Pearce

[*Philadelphia*] *November 18, 1791.* "Received November 18. 1791 of Alexander Hamilton Fifty Dollars on account of Machines for a Cotton Manufactory." [1]

D, in the handwriting of H and signed by Pearce, Hamilton Papers, Library of Congress.

1. For "A list of Mr Willm Pearce's Machines," see "Receipt from William Pearce," August 20, 1791, note 2.

Report on Imports for the Year Ending September 30, 1790

Treasury Department
Nov. 18. 1791.
[Communicated on November 18, 1791] [1]

[To the President of the Senate]

Sir

In pursuance of the order of the Senate,[2] I have the honor to transmit a return of the Imports of the United States so modified as to convey a considerable portion of the information which I conceive they require.[3] I beg leave to observe that this document is a part of a set of papers relative to imports, exports and tonnage, which have been some time in preparation at the Treasury. Some others which are completed will be transmitted to the Senate as soon as they shall have been transcribed.

I have the honor to be, Sir   with the greatest respect,   Your most obedient   & most humble servant   Alexander Hamilton
Secy of the Treasury

The Vice President of the United States
and President of the Senate.

LS, RG 46, First Congress, 1789–1791, Reports of the Secretary of the Treasury, National Archives.

1. *Annals of Congress,* III, 31.
2. Although it is stated in the *Annals of Congress* that the Senate requested a report on imports on February 16, 1791, the only Senate order for that date is a request for a report on exports. See *Annals of Congress,* II, 1801; III, 31.
3. This enclosure, which is entitled "A General Statement of Goods, Wares, and Merchandise, imported into the United States, from the 1st of October, 1789, to the 1st of September, 1790," is printed in *ASP, Commerce and Navigation,* I, 35–43.

From James McHenry

Annapolis 19th Novr. 1791.

My dear Sir.

Since taking my seat in the Senate, which I have done more in conformity with your opinion than my own,[1] I have used the opportunity it affords of conversing with Mr. Wm. Perry the gentleman I mentioned to you when in Philada. as a person well qualified for Auditor, and have discovered that had he been appointed he would not have refused. I have two reasons for telling you this now. That you may keep him in mind should such a vacancy occur as one that may be fully relied on. That you may also know that beside his being independent or wealthy, he exerted his whole influence to establish our government, continues to exert it for its daily preservation, and possesses a large share of public confidence, especially on the eastern shore where he resides & for which he is a Senator, circumstances which might render him ⟨pe⟩culiarly proper for an officer in the excise ⟨in⟩ case of a new arrangement of the system.

An opinion prevails in our house of ⟨del⟩gates that our constitution wants mending and ⟨now⟩ Mercer Pinkney & Craik [2] are to lead in the business. They do not venture I mean the two first for the last is rather federal,[3] to expose their true reason tho' they have not been able to conceal it. I cannot tell how the project may terminate but I like our constitution as it stands and trust the people having heretofore found it a good one will not easily be brought to any radical alterations.

Adieu.

James McHenry

ALS, Hamilton Papers, Library of Congress.
1. See McHenry to H, October 15, 1791; H to McHenry, November 2, 1791.
2. These three men were all lawyers and all members of the Maryland House of Delegates. John F. Mercer was a resident of Anne Arundel County, William Pinckney was a resident of Harford County, and William Craik was a resident of Port Tobacco.
3. Mercer refused to remain at the Federal Convention in 1787 and opposed ratification of the Constitution at the Maryland Ratifying Convention. At the Maryland Convention Pinckney opposed the ratification of the Constitution.

From William Heth

Shillelah [1] [Virginia] 20th. Novr. 1791

Dear Sir

Your private favor of the 10th. Inst found me at home.[2] The death of a most tenderly beloved, & only daughter and the Peculiarly distressing situation of my dear companion in affliction, has chiefly confined me here for three weeks past.[3] There has been but little to do at the Office.

In conceiving that, I *had reasons* for apologising in the manner I did, for the frequency of my observations; you were right. But you were very wide of the true cause. I never looked for replys to many of my letters. To questions only, I expected answers. But my dear Sir, I dont know, whether I can venture, even in this private way, to tell you *why* my latter communications have been made with so much reluctance, and that, since June last, I have discontinued making notes on the operations of the Revenue laws, and of such articles, as appeard to be proper objects for higher duties, and of transmitting my observations thereon, as formerly: Because, I have some reason to suspect that the contents of certain letters written by me in May last, as well as I recollect—if not of one of my private letters also, hath been communicated by a certain Clerk in your Office, to a Collector in this State. However, as it is my present intention to see you in January or Feby next I will then, inform you fully of those circumstances, which will enable you to Judge of the propriety of my Suspicions. At present allow me only to say, that, two of my brother Collectors in June last, insinuated to me that my voluminous letters to you, were very troublesome & disagreeable. One of them observed that "by my writing so much, I should be little attended to." The other declaring, with some degree of self approbation that, "*he* had written but one letter since he had been in Office"—meaning I suppose a letter of observations remarks &c &c. At another conversation, on my Saying that I had perhaps consumed as much paper in pointing out the defects & imperfections of the coasting act,[4] as all my fees under it would purchase—& that I had got quite tired of abusing it—he replyd with a laugh that "he understood" or "that the fear was, that I had long since *tired you* with my correspondence." These observations were made to me in a manner which clearly indicated an opinion that I had considered myself as a man of more information & consequence, in the line of my duty, than any body else, and that, I should be *full as well esteemed by you, if was less communicative.* However sensibly this Idea, affected my feelings—Yet, having ever entertained the most humble opinion of my abilities & consequence, I was readily enough, disposed to think that, *their* opinions were very Just: especially when I recollected that, I had not received any answers from you on subjects & to questions which appear to me of importance sufficient to require an immediate reply. Such for Instance, as my earnestly beging last spring to be favord with your construction of the short law respecting Lead "printed & stained or colourd goods—or manufactures of cotton or of linen or both." (This may not be a correct quotation as it is from Memory. The law is Still differently construed by the Collectors.) [5] I therefore determind never to trouble you as I had done—but barely do my duty—answer such questions as you might ask, &, like my neighbours, trudge thru the business of my office, with as little trouble to myself as possible. But I found, after a long struggle that my *pride—ambition —Zeal* for the public service,—or, call it what you will—would not suffer me to remain *altogether* in so negative a character. Hence it was, that I made apologies for some of the many observations which had occur'd to me & which my duty told me was indispensible. You may easily guess the relief which yo⟨ur⟩ present polite, & condescending favor has given to my feelings.

Mr. Campbell, our present Attorney for this District, has confirmd the opinion of Mr. Nelson [6] respecting certain fees under the coasting act. To *this* gentlemans great talents & abilities you are doubtless no stranger. His reasonings thereon I will transmit to you, with my first Official letter.

I am Dear sir,   With the highest respect   & most sincere affection
Yr very hbe st   W Heth

The Hnble
Colo Alex Hamilton

ALS, Hamilton Papers, Library of Congress.
1. Shillelah was one of three Virginia estates owned by Heth.
2. Letter not found.
3. Heth's two-year-old daughter had died on October 31.
4. "An Act for Registering and Clearing Vessels, Regulating the Coasting Trade, and for other purposes" (1 *Stat.* 55–65 [September 1, 1789]).
5. Heth is referring to "An Act to explain and amend an act intituled 'An act making further provision for the payment of the debt of the United States'" (1 *Stat.* 198 [March 2, 1791]). His letter to H has not been found.
6. On October 31, 1791, the President nominated Alexander Campbell as "Attorney for the United States in the Virginia District, vice William Nelson, Jr. resigned." The appointment was confirmed by the Senate on November 7 (*Executive Journal,* I, 86, 88).

To John Lamb

[Philadelphia, November 20, 1791]

Dear Sir

Your private letter of the 11th. instant duly came to hand.[1] The inquiry concerning Mr. Rhinelander's case has been officially answered.[2]

The apples you mention are not yet received, but all the other articles you have been so obliging as to forward have been received; and Mrs. Hamilton joins me in acknowlegements for them. She also desires her compliments to Mrs. Lamb. These marks of friendly attention are particularly acceptable. I only fear they may occasion you some trouble.

Yrs. with great rest   A Hamilton

Phil Nov 20. 1791

ALS, Mr. Ben Weisinger, New York City.
   1. Letter not found.
   2. Letter not found.

From William Ellery

[*Newport, Rhode Island*] *November 21, 1791.* "On the 19th. instant I recd. your letter of the 10th.[1] authorizing me to receive, in payment of Duties, the Notes of the Bank of Providence, payable in Specie on Demand, advising me that you have requested the President of that Institution to furnish me with checks, expressing your wish that I should 'Transmit once in every week to the Bank of Providence such monies as appear as the balance of my weekly returns, after defraying the expences of my Office, paying the other Officers &ca., and directing me to retain any monies necessary to pay such of the Bills undermentioned in that letter, as are not taken up.' All the Bills or draughts undermentioned in said Letter have been paid. The manner in which I am to transmit the monies referred to I presume have been, or will be pointed out. The communication by water between this Town and the Town of Providence is interrupted by ice a great part of the Winter, and the balance of weekly returns remaining in my hands after defraying the expenses mentioned, may some times be too heavy to be carried by the Post on horse-back; and I suppose that the United States are not to pay the expence of transportation. In your Circular Letter of the 14 Oct. 1789 a copy of which was transmitted to me, the Collectors are to exchange, under a restriction, any Specie which may, at any time, be in their hands for the Notes of the Banks of North America and New york. Is such exchange to be continued? and am I to exchange Specie for the Notes of the bank of Providence? . . ."

LC, Newport Historical Society, Newport, Rhode Island.
   1. Letter not found. This was presumably the same as H to Jeremiah Olney, November 10, 1791.

From John Fitzgerald [1]

Alexandria [Virginia] Novr. 21st. 1791

My dear Sir

It is with great reluctance I write you particularly as Congress is sitting & I am satisfied you have full employment for every moment of your time, yet I cannot forbear soliciting your kind assistance in favor of establishing a Branch of the National Bank in this town, to effect which a memorial is forwarded to the Directors stating some of the Advantages which would result to the public from it.

I flatter myself that from the Collector's [2] returns made to you, the Importance of our trade will justify us in this request; add to this that within these last twelve Months we have had a very great accession of Inhabitants; the Improvements made & making for the accomodation & safety of shipping are very considerable, & no town in the United states has a more extensive & fertile back Country for its support. These reasons join'd with what is set forth in the memorial will I hope induce you to think with me that a Branch of the Bank establish'd here will afford benefit to the public as well as to that part of the Community more immediately connected with the place, & be assur'd that were not these my real Sentiments I would not (interested as I am in the event) request you to support the measure. If time permits I shall be happy in a line from you on this subject. [3]

Believe me to be with unfeign'd regard & Esteem   Dear Sir   Yr.
Mo Obed Servt.   John Fitzgerald

ALS, Hamilton Papers, Library of Congress.
   1. Fitzgerald, a resident of Alexandria, had served as aide-de-camp to George
Washington during the American Revolution.
   2. The collector at Alexandria was Charles Lee.
   3. H wrote on the envelope of Fitzgerald's letter: "Ansd June 28." H's letter
to Fitzgerald has not been found.

To Jedediah Huntington

Treasury Department
Nov. 21. 1791.

Sir

From some inadvertence your letter, relative to vessels which put
into the district of Newport,[1] was placed among the answered letters,
and has therefore lain without due attention.

It is the duty of the Collectors of the several districts to pay attention to all vessels arriving within the same by whatever cause they may
be led thither. If forty eight hours are likely to elapse after the
arrival it becomes a matter of obligation on the master to enter, and
of duty in the Collector to see that he does so. In making this entry
certain duties fall upon the officers of the customs, for which a compensation is equitably and legally due. By the form of the law the
tonnage must be secured to be paid in such district, though the master
of the vessel shall have declared his intention to proceed to another
port, and the impost must be secured to be paid, either at the port
in which the vessel is, or in that to which she shall be destined. This
service and certifying the manifest is attended with some care and
trouble to the officer, and they are deemed by the legislature necessary
to the protection of the revenue. Under these views of the subject
I do not perceive that the vessels belonging to any other district, which
shall stop at Newport, can, after the expiration of the time prescribed
by law, be exempted from entry.[2]

I am, Sir   with great consideration,   Your most obedt ⟨servt.⟩
                                              Alexander Hami⟨lton⟩
Jedediah Huntington, Esquire,
Collector,
New London.

LS, MS Division, New York Public Library.
1. Letter not found.
2. See Sections 16–20 of "An Act to provide more effectually for the collection of the duties imposed by law on goods, wares and merchandise imported into the United States, and on the tonnage of ships or vessels" (1 *Stat.* 158–60 [August 4, 1790]).

From Charles Marshall and Christopher Marshall, Junior [1]

Philada. Novemr. 21st. 1791.

Respected Frd.

Since we have had the Pleasure of Conversing with thee on the Subject of our Manufactures of Sal Glauber, Sal Ammoniac, & Volatile Spirits, We have thought proper to withdraw our Proposal of a Duty on Sal Ammoniac, & Volatile Spirits, the former being an Article, as we mentioned to thee before, that we are enabled to supply, not only the United States, but to Ship Considerable Quantities to Europe, & as its admitted in England in British Vessels free of Duty, it may be impolitic in us, lest it may be the Means of our being restrained from that Market. Yet we desire in thy Report,[2] particular mention may be made of such a Manufactory being established here.

The only Object we are now anxious to obtain a Duty on, is, the Sal Glauber. In our Letter,[3] we mentioned 4d. pr. lb. but on our Consultation with thee, 2d. pr. lb. was suggested. We therefore now desire thou wilt please reconsider the Matter, & if thou thinks proper, propose Three Cents pr. pound.

As thou desired us to furnish thee with the Prices, Sal Glauber has been imported from London Several Years past, we here annex them, by which thou may see how the prices have been reduced from Time, to Time.

1783 Septemr. 1st	. . . . .	35/ ℔ Cr. Sterg.
1786 Augt	4	. . . . .	32/
1787 Feby	21	. . . . .	28/
1789 March	3	. . . . .	26/
1790 Feby	17	. . . . .	21/
1791 March		. . . . .	15/

We are, with due Respects, Thy Frds.

Chrisr Junr & Charles Marshall

Alexander Hamilton Esqr.

LS, Hamilton Papers, Library of Congress.

1. Charles Marshall and his brother, Christopher Marshall, Jr., were Philadelphia druggists.

2. On January 15, 1790, the House of Representatives ordered H "to prepare and report to this House, a proper plan or plans . . . for the encouragement and promotion of such manufactories as will tend to render the United States independent of other nations for essential, particularly for military supplies" (*Journal of the House*, I, 141–42). H's "Report on the Subject of Manufactures" was presented in the House on December 5, 1791.

3. Letter not found.

From Jeremiah Olney

Custom-House,
Providence 21st. Novr. 1791.

Sir.

Agreeable to the directions in your Letter of the 10th Instant, I shall on Thursday next, pay into the Bank of Providence, the Balance of my weekly Return of Cash, and continue to do the same, on that Day in every Week, deducting only my Commissions, the Drafts you mention being all paid, and Office Expences are always included in the Return. I wish to be informed Sir, whether the Money thus deposited will be considered at the Treasury as accounted for by me; If so, it will be proper to charge it to the United States, and the retained duplicate Receipt will serve as a Voucher.

I enclose a Draft No. 2282, for 500 Dolls. which I have paid and charged.

I have the honor to be &c. Jereh. Olney Collr.

Alexr. Hamilton Esqr.
Secy. of the Treasury

ADfS, Rhode Island Historical Society, Providence.

From William Seton

[New York] 21 Novr 1791

Dear sir,

It is with reluctance I intrude upon your time, but I feel so interested in what has lately passed at Phia.[1] that I cannot refrain indulging myself with some conversation with you on the subject. No doubt you was informd that our Directors immediately after the Directors at Pa. of the Bank of the U. S. were known, wrote a Letter stating their reasons for reserving the 300 Shares of Stock & making a tender of them to that Institution.[2] It appears to me that some how or other, this Letter was prevented from having its proper effect—for we find Committees were appointed who reported in favour of Branches, but took no notice of the offer or of the State Banks. Last Thursday only our President[3] recd an answer to the Letter, saying that the Directors there had resolved that it was inexpedient for the Bank of the US. to commit any part of its Capital in the State Banks, & politely declined our offer. This with the report of the Committee seems to establish the point, that there will be a branch here independent of this Institution—from which every one inferrs its consequent annihilation & our Stock after having rose to upwards of 50 is fallen to less than 18 ℈ Cent. I cannot bring myself to think it would be either for the general Interest of the public or for the particular interest of the B of the US. that this Institution should clash with their operations, when it is evident that by a juncture we could so essentially aid the Public, to the benefit of both Institutions—⟨however⟩ it is to be feared that a ⟨imputation⟩ or a wish on their part to destroy us, would revive State Politicks to the prejudice of the General Government & give a handle to party, surely some mode may yet be found out to avert the evil. From the great support the Institution has recd from you I trust you will think the subject worthy your attention & if the mode already pointed out is insufficient, that in your wisdom you will be able to point out some other that will bring about so desirable an object as a union with the ⟨two⟩. The Situation of the Bank is at present highly flourishing, but much will depend upon your fatherly care to keep it so. Too sudden an extinction of the public money would oblige us to check our discounts as too large a proportion for the dealers to be able with ease to pay up, especially if the reception of the Impost was taken out of our hands at the same time tho both [of] them we must expect, yet I hope the mode of doing it will be pointd out by you. I hope you will excuse my intruding upon your time.

There are 3 Dividends & the Surplus due to you in Bank, in all amtg to 291 Dolls. Will [you] be so good as to authorize me to sign the Books for you that they may be carried to the credit of your private Account.

I have the honor to be with the highest respect Dear sir Your Obliged Obed Hue Ser

ADf, Bank of New York, New York City.

1. This is a reference to the fact that the directors of the Bank of the United States had recently voted to establish branch banks in New York City, Boston, Baltimore, and Charleston, South Carolina. See James O. Wettereau, "The Branches of the First Bank of the United States," *The Journal of Economic History*, II (December, 1942), Supplement, 74.

2. In August, 1791, the Bank of New York increased its capital stock to nine hundred thousand dollars and reserved one sixth of this amount (or three hundred shares) for ownership by the Bank of the United States. But, as Seton indicates, the directors of the Bank of the United States refused this offer. See Davis, *Essays*, II, 54–57.

3. Gulian Verplanck.

To George Washington

Treasury Departmt. 21st. Novr. 1791.

The Secretary of the Treasury has the honor respectfully to submit to the President of the United States a Contract between the Collector of New-London [1] and Nathaniel Richards for the supply of the Light house in that District for one year to end on the first day of October 1792. This agreement is on terms somewhat more favorable than those of the preceding year. A Contract between the Collector of New London & the keeper of the Lighthouse is likewise respectfully submitted, which being as low as that for the preceding year & being among the most moderate of those compensations, the Secretary does not perceive any ground of exception against it. [2]

Alexander Hamilton

LC, George Washington Papers, Library of Congress.

1. Jedediah Huntington.

2. At the bottom of this letter is written: "Note. The above mentioned Contracts were approved by the President U S on the 23d. Novr. 1791."

From Wilhem and Jan Willink, Nicholaas and Jacob Van Staphorst, and Nicholas Hubbard

[*Amsterdam, November 21, 1791.* On February 14, 1792, Hamilton wrote to Willink, Van Staphorst, and Hubbard: "I am just honored with your several favours of Nov 21st & 24th & December 2d." *Letter of November 21 not found.*]

To Samuel Gerry [1]

[*Philadelphia, November 22, 1791*. Asks Gerry to secure the papers which belonged to the office of the Marblehead collector of customs and which were in the possession of the estate of the late collector, Richard Harris.[2] *Letter not found.*]

LS, sold at American Art Association, February 28, 1927, Lot 138.
  1. Gerry was collector of customs at Marblehead, Massachusetts.
  2. Summary of letter taken from catalogue of the American Art Association.

To Jedediah Huntington

Treasury Department
Nov. 22. 1791.

Sir

I do not think, it will be necessary to require a refund from the officers of the revenue cutter in consequence of the payments to them at eleven cents per ration,[1] as mentioned in your letter of the 10th. October.[2]

It is very much my wish that the article of rum may be as sparingly supplied as possible. Country rum at half a jill per man per day is, as I understand, as large an allowance as is usual in many of the ports, and it appears in every view desirable to confine it to that quantity.

The contracts for the light house are received, and submitted to the President.[3]

I am, Sir   Your obedt. servant   Alex Hamilton

Jedediah Huntington Esq.
Collector
New London.

LS, MS Division, New York Public Library.
  1. For the arrangements concerning rations on the revenue cutters, see "Treasury Department Circular to the Collectors of the Customs," September 21, November 17, 1791.
  2. Letter not found.
  3. See H to George Washington, November 21, 1791.

From William Short

Paris Nov. 22. 1791.

Sir

In my two last letters of the 8th: & 12th: inst. I informed you of the then position of affairs at Antwerp & Amsterdam. Nothing new can have taken place with respect to Antwerp as I then mentioned to you that a loan was to be opened there for three millions of florins at 4½. p. cent interest & 4. p. cent commission. I shall leave this place in two days so as to sign the contract there at the end of the month.

I mentioned to you also that I had authorized the opening a loan for the same sum & on the same terms at Amsterdam.[1] I have just recieved a letter from the commissioners there in which they inform me that they have postponed it in hopes of being able to raise a loan the beginning of the next month at 4. p. cent interest, & ask my authorisation to do it with an augmentation of charges.[2] This has surprised me very agreeably & I shall of course in answering their letter approve what they have done & give them the authorization they desire. I shall be extremely happy to find their hopes realized & shall take care to inform you of the progress of this business immediately on my arrival there. They state the charges as being somewhat above 5. p. cent.

It is too late now to stop the loan ordered at Antwerp as the prospectus will have been published two days ago, or I should do it; having some apprehensions it may prevent the bankers opening the one they speak of at 4. p. cent. In that case however I shall really suspect they have held out these hopes merely to have a pretext for saying that the translation of our loans to Antwerp prevented the reduction of the rate of interest to 4. p. cent at Amsterdam. It is unfortunately too true that such stratagems are considered as legitimate among the most delicate of those who deal in money in the markets

ALS, letterpress copy, William Short Papers, Library of Congress.

    1. Short to Willink, Van Staphorst, and Hubbard, November 11, 1791 (ALS, letterpress copy, William Short Papers, Library of Congress).

    2. Willink, Van Staphorst, and Hubbard to Short, November 14, 1791 (LS, Short Family Papers, Library of Congress); Willink, Van Staphorst, and Hubbard to Short, November 17, 1791 (LS, Short Family Papers, Library of Congress).

of these countries. A very short time will shew however what opinion is to be formed of the prospect which they thus hold out, & which they say is produced by extraordinary & unexpected circumstances, particularly the immense & unforeseen sales of British stock. Such a reduction in the rate of interest is an event pregnant with such a variety of good consequences that it should be aimed at by every possible means. There was every reason to believe it would be effected in the course of the next year, but I own I did not flatter myself with it sooner.

Since my last I have recieved your two letters of Sep. 2. & Oct. 3. As it is the intention of the U.S. to make up the depreciation I am glad to have been informed of it thus early. I communicated it to the commissaries of the treasury who intended as they told me making objections to such payments in future. This astonished me the more as it would be objecting to recieve from a debtor what they pay to a considerably greater amount annually to their creditors. It is well to have anticipated their reclamations since the intention of the U.S. is such. I am persuaded the Ministry would have been too prudent to have rendered public such reclamations & should suppose it highly probable Ternant [3] had acted of himself. The commissaries of the treasury were highly pleased with my communication. I desired they would fix some basis which should be equally just for both parties; it was agreed between us that it would be to ascertain what would have been the rate of exchange between Paris & Amsterdam if gold & silver had continued to circulate in France. They said they would consider of this subject, but nothing has been as yet proposed. I did not mention the mode of selling them my bills for specie,[4] because their laws, & the accidental circumstances of the revolution having rendered gold & silver as articles of merchandize considerably dearer in France than they would have been in the ordinary course of things it is not just that the U. S. should support this real & intrinsic increase. In my letter to which you allude [5] the depreciation was stated as about half the value of exchange. Since then depreciation, I mean the comparison difference between assignats & specie, has gone on much more rapidly

3. Jean Baptiste de Ternant, French Minister Plenipotentiary to the United States.
4. Treasury bills drawn at Amsterdam.
5. Short to H, June 3, 1791.

than the difference of exchange. There are various & obvious reasons for this.

I have communicated this intention of the U. S. to M. de Lessart who has the interim of the department of foreign affairs.[6] I have not as yet however an answer from him owing probably to the unsettled state of the department.

I had from a former letter concieved that you would have preferred London to Amsterdam in order to establish a credit there.[7] I shall attend however in the manner you desire to what you say on this subject in your letter of Sep. 2.

It gave me much pleasure to find by your last letter that you had noticed to the bankers at Amsterdam the momentary fall in our stock there.[8] The reduction of the rate of interest will of course, as it has hitherto been, be in future the object of our efforts agreeably to your desire, & I am exceedingly happy to have been able to offer you such favorable hopes respecting it, being ever desirous to convince you of my zeal, & give you assurances of the sentiments with which I have the honor to be Sir, you most obedient servant.

W: Short

The Honble.
Alexander Hamilton Secretary of the Treasury, Philadelphia.

6. In 1791 Claude Antoine de Valdec de Lessart was successively Minister of the Interior, Minister of Marine, and Minister of Foreign Affairs.
7. See H to Short, August 1–2, 1791.
8. H to Willink, Van Staphorst, and Hubbard, October 3, 1791.

To George Washington

Treasury Departmt. 22d. Novr. 1791.

The Secretary of the Treasury has the honor respectfully to submit to the President of the United States, a Contract made by the Collector of Portsmouth [1] for keeping & supplying the Light house at the mouth of that harbour for six months. It is supposed that this agreement has been confined to the term of six months in order to a future commencement in the beginning of the year. The conditions of it are the same as those of the preceding Contract, provided the supply be made in Hake Oil, & the extra expence of Spermaceti Oil, if it should be found necessary, does not appear liable to exception.[2]

Alexander Hamilton

LC, George Washington Papers, Library of Congress.
1. Joseph Whipple.
2. At the bottom of this letter is written: "Note. The above-mentioned Contract was approved by the President of the United States on the 23d. of Novr. 1791."

To Joseph Whipple

[*Philadelphia, November 22, 1791.* On December 10, 1791, Whipple wrote to Hamilton: "I have recd. your letter of the 22 Ulto." *Letter not found.*]

From Richard Wylly [1]

Loan Office, Georgia, November 22, 1791. "I have the honor of enclosing you my account against the United States for Stationary, Printers bill and hire of a Clerk. . . . As I did most of the business myself until the 25 of June I only employed a Person occasionally to assist me; after which time I found I could not dispatch the business without a Clerk constantly to attend in the Office, to whom I allowed at the rate of 400 dollars ℔ annum, which I hope You will not think too much, as there are Merchants Clerks here who received larger Salaries. I did not keep an exact account of the Stationary, but I suppose it amounted to what I have charged. . . ."

ALS, RG 217, Miscellaneous Treasury Accounts, 1790–1894, Account No. 1911, National Archives.
1. Wylly was commissioner of loans for Georgia.

To Jeremiah Olney

Treasury Department Novr. 23rd 1791

Sir,

Your letter of the 11th October has been duly received.

Although, if it had occurred to you to forbear the institution of a suit, until application could have been made in due course for a remission of the forfeiture incurred, I should under the circumstances, of the case have approved of your conduct, yet it is certain, that you were strictly in order in every step you took and have furnished no cause for disapprobation or censure. You would not have been justifiable, in withdrawing the Action, which had been commenced, upon the receipt of my letter of the 24th of September, as has been supposed.

I feel a persuasion too, from the manner in which you stated the case to me, [as well as my general impression of your sentiments and views,] [1] that you not having proceeded in the mode above intimated, rather than in that, in which you did proceed, was occasioned by an impression on your mind, that the latter was most consonant with your duty.

With great consideration   I remain Sir   Your obedt Servant

Alexander Hamilton

Jereh. Olney Esqr
Collector of Providence

LS, Rhode Island Historical Society, Providence; copy, RG 56, Letters to the Collector at Providence, National Archives; copy, RG 56, Letters to Collectors at Small Ports, "Set G," National Archives.
1. The material within brackets is in H's handwriting.

Report on Imports for the Year Ending September 30, 1790

Treasury Department
Nov. 23. 1791.
[Communicated on November 24, 1791] [1]

[To the President of the Senate]
Sir

I have the honor to transmit to the Senate, in further obedience to their order,[2] an estimate exhibiting the value, *at the several places of shipment,* of all foreign goods, wares and merchandize imported into the United States, during the year ending on the 30th. day of September 1790.[3] The principal objects of this document are to exhibit the portion of our consumption which is supplied by each foreign nation, and the aggregate value of the whole of our importations.

I have the honor to be with the greatest respect, Sir,   Your most obedt. & most humble servt.   Alexander Hamilton

The Vice President of the United States
and President of the Senate.

LS, RG 46, Reports of the Secretary of the Treasury, National Archives.
1. *Annals of Congress*, III, 31.
2. Although the entry in the *Annals of Congress* states that the Senate order was dated February 16, 1791, the only order recorded for that date is a request for a report on exports rather than imports. See *Annals of Congress*, II, 1801.
3. This "estimate," which is not printed in *ASP, Commerce and Navigation*, has not been found.

To William Constable [1]

[Philadephia, November 24, 1791]

Dr Sir

I have examined the draft herewith returned & perceive no objection to it. It can have no effect in severing the joint responsibility of the persons for what remains.

I infer from the draft & take for granted the fact is that this release to part of the Obligers is pursuant to an arrangement between the whole. This is necessary to the propriety of the measure towards them. They agreeing, the present form of the thing is indifferent to you.

Yrs. truly   A H

Nov 24. 1791

Wm. Constable Esq

ALS, New-York Historical Society, New York City.
1. For background to this letter, see H to Constable, November 14, 1791.

To Benjamin Lincoln

Treasury Department
Nov. 24, 1791.

Sir

The President has received a petition from the keeper of the light house at Portland (Joseph Greenleaf) setting forth that his compensation is fixed below the rate at which he can afford to perform the service. It is understood that it was not a matter of contract, but that it was fixed at that rate after his appointment to the duty. Your opinion on the sufficiency of the allowance and on the degree to which it may be expedient, if at all, to increase it, are desired.[1]

I am, Sir,   Your most obedt. servant

Benj. Lincoln Esq.
Collector
Boston.

L[S], RG 36, Collector of Customs at Boston, Letters and Papers re Lighthouses, Buoys, and Piers, 1789–1819, Vol. 4, National Archives; copy, RG 56, Letters to Collectors at Small Ports, "Set G," National Archives; copy, RG 56, Letters to the Collector at Boston, National Archives.
   1. This sentence is in H's handwriting.

To James Madison

[Philadelphia, November 24, 1791]

Dear Sir

You will oblige me by taking the trouble to peruse the Report [1] which accompanies this; and if the weather permit, I will call upon you sometime tomorrow or next day to converse on the subject of it. I remain with great esteem and regard   D Sir Yr Obed ser

A Hamilton

It will not be disagreeable to me if after perusal you hand it over to Mr. Jefferson.

Philadelphia Nov 24th
Mr. Madison

ALS, University of Virginia.
   1. Presumably this is a reference to H's "Report on the Subject of Manufactures," December 5, 1791.

From Jeremiah Olney [1]

Providence, November 24, 1791. "Though I have no doubt but that the Schooner Alice was within Four leagues of Land when the Officer from on board the Argus Cutter demanded a Manifest of Captain Andrus; yet I have thought it prudent, before I commence a Prosecution, to put the question to Capt. Maltbie, in a letter which I have

written to go by this Post. The Vessel is the property of Messrs.
Brown & Francis of this Town. . . ." [2]

ADfs, Rhode Island Historical Society, Providence.
1. For background to this letter, see Olney to H, October 31, 1791, and H
to Olney, November 11, 1791.
2. John Brown and John Francis, Providence merchants.

From Wilhem and Jan Willink, Nicholaas and Jacob Van Staphorst, and Nicholas Hubbard

[*Amsterdam, November 24, 1791.* On February 14, 1792, Hamilton
wrote to Willink, Van Staphorst, and Hubbard: "I am just honored
with your several favours of Nov. 21st & 24th & December 2d." *Letter
of November 24 not found.*]

To Alexander Dallas [1]

Treasury Department, November 25, 1791. "I request you to make
my acknowlegements to the Governor [2] for the Copy of the Laws
transmitted to me by his direction. . . ." [3]

ALS, Mr. Alexander Hamilton, New York City.
1. In January, 1791, Dallas was appointed secretary of the state of Pennsylvania.
2. Thomas Mifflin.
3. An entry in the executive minutes of Pennsylvania for November 22, 1791,
reads as follows: "Copies of the Laws passed in the last Session of the General
Assembly were this day transmitted to Thomas Jefferson Esquire Secretary of
State; to Alexander Hamilton Esquire Secretary of the Treasury of the United
States; and to Henry Knox Esquire Secretary at War" (*Pennsylvania Archives,*
9th ser. I, 285).

From Nathaniel Hazard

[New York, November 25, 1791]

Sir

In one of my hasty Memorandums,[1] I mentioned an Intention of
writing from New-haven, I had however but little Time, as I was
engaged in Leveeing the great; (on Mr Maxwell's [2] Petition, whom

AL, Hamilton Papers, Library of Congress.
1. See Hazard to H, October 11, 1791.
2. William Maxwell. See Hazard to H, October 11, 1791.

I went purposely to serve) in eating & drinking with them; & paying some Attention to Mrs. H——d, who accompanied me. Upon the whole, I concluded to postpone my Remarks untill I got back to New york. Why I have delayed so long is of little Consequence to yourself, it is however of some to me. I began a Sheet of detached Minutes 3d. Novemr. (as I see they are dated) & completed it at detached Interludes, in the Course of some Days. I then disliked them & recollected with Vexation, my Scribble of a Sheet by young Remsen,[3] its superfluous Matter, as well as slovenly Manner, & above all the Absurdity of my taking on myself upon the Strength of a *personal* Acquaintance of Twenty four Hours only, in *Fact,* to give a Letter of Introduction to you.[4] I had however some pardonable Views, for they were not *personal,* but national. I have lately received a Letter from Mr. Fearon of some Length. He writes me he had a Letter to you from his Aunt, an old Acquaintance of yours he understands, which nullified my intrusive one of Course. He dwells on his Reception with Animation. He begs me to correspond with him, gives me his Virginia Address, at Richard Harrison's[5] Esqr, Petersburg, calls me a Politician; himself a humble Enquirer after all that a *young Republican* ought to know. I shall give him just as much *real* politicial Information, as his Patron Governor Franklin may chuse to ⟨amuse⟩ himself with.

As it scarcely ever was my Good Fortune, to write a long Letter that did not require a subsequent Commentary, I must go back, & in Justice to a certain Person now in Philadelphia,[6] (who professes, & indeed evidences a real personal Friendship for me) observe that my Jealosy has been perhaps unfoundedly awakened on the Score of his "*Redrawing Confidence from me*" as I believe I termed it to you in my long Script by young Remsen.[7] I took it for granted that in Consequence of my Friend & NameSake's[8] having served him so ably in the Senator Business, he would of Course promote his desired State Appointment of Attorney General. My friend was lamenting to me

3. This is a reference to one of the sons of Henry Remsen, Jr., a New York City merchant who had nine children.
4. See Hazard to H, October 11, 1791, which introduced Robert Fearon.
5. This is presumably the Richard Harrison, a Virginia merchant, who was appointed auditor in the Treasury Department on November 29, 1791.
6. Aaron Burr.
7. Letter not found.
8. Nathaniel Lawrence. See Hazard to H, September 30, 1791.

that Harrison [9] wished it, he believed, who would certainly meet your Countenances. I replied, "I did not know that, if you was not committed, I thought it not unlikely, that his Patron (C B) [10] would be readily gratified, it could do no Harm for me to hint it to you." This Conversation, I mentioned substantially to my Friend's Patron, (who is his (L——e's) Deity, I tell him). He (C.B) recoiled at the Idea of such Communication to you, as being a Patron, or that such was his Wish & disavowed to me, his patronizing any one, for that Place. I felt hurt & disappointed for my Friend, tho I dared not tell him the Cause. I talked warmly & I presume groundlessly, in general Terms about redrawing Confidence. I had taken for granted what was not allowed, & had to all reasonable *Apperance*, been asking for a Stranger to me (as C.B then was) a Favor, of at least a political Stranger to him, I mean yourself. He had good ostensible Cause for being startled, on this Occasion. The last Conversation I had with him was just before he went Westward & I to N. England. It was of some Length. I recapitulated the Origin, & Cause of our political Communion, its Progress & my Wishes as to Future Operations. I also recapitulated the first interesting Conversation, I had with him at his own House, by which I meant to renew in his Memory, decently, Sentiments then avowed by me in Language, which should make this Impression. "Sir you profess yourself my Friend, I accept it thankfully, but conditionally; remember, you will find me at least, your political Enemy, if you oppose the System adopted for this Country, which I think all ought to support." At the Close of our Conversation, I took occasion to "anticipate, the Pleasure it would give me, to see the World disappointed, at an unexpected Combination of Talents & Measures." Assent was given to this with apparent Cordiality, & if my wretched Memory does not deceive me; *casual* Difference of Opinion, was barely hinted at, as *possible*, but in the Main I understood, all would be well. Two Persons, whom all the World knows to be opposed to a proper System, were introduced by him, in Words very much like these "I shall not renounce my Acquaintance, with M——n & J——n [11] as Men of Science."

We met several Times accidentally, & had gay Conversations,

9. Richard Harison, United States attorney for the District of New York.
10. Colonel Burr.
11. Madison and Jefferson.

previous to this last one, which was at my House. I had sent him a long Letter of Mr. Bogert's [12] about his Lodgings & he called to see me. I have wrote two Letters to him since my Return, on Edwards [13] & my own Affairs, with *some* Connecticut Politics. With you I have *none* to with-hold. I am not a political Trinitarian. I cannot believe in "Three Beings equal in Substance, Power & Glory" nor even Two. Under that Impression, I speak & write. I have received promptly by Return of Post, Answers to the Letters I have wrote him, which evidence his Penetration & Address. He has a Right to shew some Attention to me. His Brother in Law, who is a great & popular Law-Character,[14] as well as his Uncle the District Attorney;[15] he acknowledged to me, in our first explanatory Conversation had both declared to him, my early & useful Patronage. It was at a time, when I could *act* the Patron. They have great Influence in their State. Of the Purity & Sincerity of my Friendship for them, they have no Doubt, & not an ill Opinion of the Soundness of my political Creed. We shall (C.B. & myself) correspond gaily, indeed we have commenced in that Style. Politics from that Quarter, (I mean confidential) I neither expect or wish, untill I can write one Letter which will equally serve there & with yourself.

I inclose for your Amusement, Trumbull's [16] last Letter to me. He communes with very few intensly. He is a Man of a very independent Spirit. He is avowedly the Friend of C H——n.[17] Doctor Johnson [18] is so likewise, as you shall presently judge. The Doctor spoke humbly of J——n at Edwards Table. At his Lodgings, I asked him what he tho't of M——n, as compared with H——n, "He (M——n) ought not to be mentioned in the same Day with H——n." I know his Opinion of most public Characters. He is rather too reserved in giving his Opinions, considering his Independence of Station. In a Tete a Tete with him at the College, before I last went to

12. Cornelius J. Bogart. See Hazard to H, October 11, 1791.
13. Pierpont Edwards. See Hazard to H, October 11, 1791.
14. Burr's brother-in-law was Tapping Reeve, who in 1784 founded at Litchfield, Connecticut, one of the country's first law schools.
15. This is a reference to Pierpont Edwards, the son of Jonathan Edwards. Burr's mother was Pierpont Edwards's sister.
16. John Trumbull, poet and member of the Hartford Wits, who is best known as the author of *M'Fingal*. In 1789 he became state's attorney for the county of Hartford.
17. Colonel Hamilton.
18. William S. Johnson, president of Columbia College.

N. England, in a gay Conversation I said to him "Doctor, Strangers accuse you, of too acquiescent a Manner in Conversation. The World ought to know, what your Friends know, that you don't refuse giving your Opinion, when necessary or useful." My Acquaintance has been of long Standing with this great & good Man, he knows that I have a filial Regard & Veneration for him, & that his Fame is dear to me.

I mentioned, (in my preceding Letter to Mr. Trumbull) Mr. Coxe's Numbers on Sheffield [19] highly, & wished his Opinion; I also told him confidentially, I had corresponded with him on Subjects of Commerce & Manufactures; I satirized him for an imaginary Disappointment at an Election, & consoled him with the Philosophy I had shewn on the *only Occasion* I had ever been willing to serve which was the Winter you wished me (as John Murray [20] told me) to go to Albany. You will please to return me Trumbull's Letter, as soon as convenient. Let me remark here, that Wolcott, [21] when last in this Place, thought it prudent *at this Time*, to postpone attacking J——n. He thought it would injure the V.P.[22] When I gave Wolcott's Reasons to Trumbull, at Hartford, Trumbull spoke peevishly about it, & said he would not postpone, for his Part. Says I, "You will scare Wolcott to Death." Trumbull replies "let him be scared then, it is Time Somebody should be." I then said Wolcott had intimated to me, that the Publication of the Letter "on political Heresies" was done sorely against the Will of J——n, & that he believed it had been explained so, as to remove *personal* Animosity, "No such Thing" said Trumbull. Now Trumbull was several Hours with the V.P. at Hartford, when he was coming on in October to Congress. Of what passed, I know not a Tittle, nor wished to know. I never ask Questions of my Friends, of so delicate a Nature, I neither make, or wish useless Confidences, by which I mean such as are not necessary for my Guidance, in my Efforts to serve them. It appears to me however, that Oliver,[23] must either have misjudged, or been misinformed. I shall leave it to Mr. Trumbull *alone*, to rectify this Mistake with Mr. Wolcott. I thought

19. See Hazard to H, October 11, 1791, note 10.
20. Murray was a New York City merchant.
21. Oliver Wolcott, Jr.
22. The Vice President, John Adams. This is a reference to the controversy over Jefferson's letter in the American edition of Thomas Paine's *Rights of Man.* See "Thomas Jefferson's Notes on a Conversation with Alexander Hamilton," August 13, 1791, note 1.
23. Oliver Wolcott, Jr.

this, a necessary explanatory Appendage, to what I had mentioned on this Business, to you in my Letter by young Remsen or a subsequent one. Mr. Trumbull taught me to think highly of the V.P. I had once, much disliked him; & very causelessly. I even supposed, he was bred a Tradesman. I once thought, from a Report, that circulated here; that Mr. Coxe, was not in easy Circumstances; Accident led you, (talking to me of his future Views) to undo this Error. At Mr. Edwards' Table I dined often. We had all the distinguished & influential Characters of both Houses, by Squads. The last Day, I dined there, were present, the Governor,[24] Lieut. Governor, [25] Doctor Johnson, Mr. Trumbull (the Pair),[26] Genl. Chandler,[27] & others of the Council &c &c to the Number of 15 or 16. Some Gentleman at Table, I forget who, introduced Mr. Coxe's Remarks on Sheffield; I listened silently to the Approbation, given them; at last some other Gentleman, I know not who, said he had understood, Mr. Coxe's Circumstances were not easy; I waited to hear it contradicted, it was not; untill, I mentioned, that I had lately been in Philadelphia, on Business; that I learned there, by mere Accident, in the Course of Conversation, directly the Reverse. My Authority was disinterested, & unquestionable; I could take upon myself peremptorily, to assert it was a gross Mistake. At this Table, Mr. Edwards, ridiculed, J——n & M——n's Tour; in which they scouted silently thro' the Country, shunning the Gentry, communing with & pitying the Shayites, & quarrelling with the Eatables; nothing good enough for them.[28] Trumbull will give this Tour, a Canto, if Southern Smoke, provokes a North-East Gale, of stinging Satire. They are supremely contemned by the Gentlemen of Connecticut, which State I found on a Review right as to national Matters. Partizans will differ, but I found Co. H——n has no Enemies on either Side. Mr. J——y [29] is popular, as a learned & just Judge, & his Manners assimilate well with the Gravity of their stable, grave Men. The originating, as well as executing those Measures, wch

24. Samuel Huntington.
25. Oliver Wolcott, Sr.
26. This is a reference to John Trumbull, the poet, and John Trumbull, the painter of the American Revolution.
27. John Chandler, a member of the Connecticut Board of Assistants.
28. Jefferson and Madison made a trip through the Northeast in the spring of 1791. See Robert Troup to H, June 15, 1791.
29. John Jay.

have operated so essentially in producing the national Character & Prosperity are ascribed to *their proper Source*.

The Dignity of Human Nature, has not been raised in my Opinion by my late leisureable Tour, in Connecticut. As to Politics, I acted the Statesman there, said little (on that Score) heard much, & asking no Questions I excited no Suspicions, & fairly passed behind the Curtain. I suppose *State* Politics, are a Miniature of *National*. How limited are those in their Views, as to an honest *national Frame*, who oppose a large Representation in Congress, merely because it hurts the relative Influence of their respective States. Are not the many, full as governable as the few, by Talents & Virtue? Three, or four young Men, sway the Connecticut lower House. Two I well knew, the other Two Edwards made me acquainted with. This House consists of 150 Members. Very few really very great Men, appear in [an] Age. I once thought this mere Cant. But how many very great Men have we in America? Men who know human Nature & how honorably, to influence & operate upon Temper & Character? When Walpole said every Man had his Price,[30] he only meant, every Man had his Tendo Achilles. I am convinced more & more that a mental Aristocracy, bordering upon Monarchy is the Design of Heaven, in every Age of every Nation. I dont accuse the Pravity of the human Heart because there are so few wise, or even well informed Hearts. Relatively considered, I suspect I am now a better informed Statesman, than many first Rate *State* Characters, & blush for human Wisdom when I reflect on my own Littleness; & look back. Last July, I was as uninformed on political Subjects, as any bookish Trader, well could be. From May to July I corresponded not only lengthily for me, with Mr. Coxe, & Governor Paterson [31] But my Friend Trumbull brightened the ancient Chain of friendly Correspondence with several two Sheet Letters. Personal Affairs on both Sides, & the Politics of the State of Connecticut, as they respected my Friend Edwards, induced a Correspondence of unusual *Length*, between him & me, for he loves neither Bills—nor Epistolary Letters, as he ought to do. "He loves not Plays, as thou dost Anthony" I said to Trumbull at

---

30. The saying "every man has his price" was attributed to Sir Robert Walpole, head of the British cabinet from 1721 to 1742.
31. William Paterson was governor of New Jersey.

Hartford, pointing out their different Tastes & probable Pursuits. With Ledyard [32] my unreserved Correspondence, increased in Consequence of the others. I pass a Sunday once a Month, & pick up, by Stipulation, all Letters of Treason, against the State or Decency. These correspondences super added, to my commercial ones, & counting House Business, made me unusually sedentary, & gave me two or three strange Dizzinesses in my Head. The last alarmed me; I was writing to Edwards. I flung down my Pen. "d——n it, it will kill me. I will go & see him; (taking another Turn across the Room) & Trumbull too." These two with Ledyard are all the *Intimates* I have. N. L——e is but an Apprentice of 4 Years Service; of Yesterday comparatively; I have *worn* the others many ages & they have *worn* well. Edwards & Trumbull each 20 years, Ledyard—13. I was off (for N.E) in eight Hours, made my Tour to Newhaven & Hartford & back in 6 days; the ninth I arrived at Greenbush,[33] at Midnight, after paddling one Mile & walking another in a Thunder Gust, & reimbarked, with Mrs. H——d (who was there & expected me) the same Day for New york.

I supposed that Edwards was intimate with Co. H——n; thro him, I wished to sound what might be hoped, for Ledyard, at whose House, I had engaged myself to dine the Sunday following. The first News he had, I was gone to N. England. Little did he then, or ever since suspect that he was the impulsive Motive. I passed the Day with Edwards, he gave me his Views, told me his Relation here,[34] wished much to ⟨–⟩ him. I cautioned him, about him as a probable Rival. On my Return, I went to the House of (C.B) to sound him as to Possibility of Clash with my Friend Edwards, & to know his political System; the rest you will remember, I presume. One of the most influential Characters in Connecticut, a Mr. Mitchell,[35] observed in a large Company, at Edwards's, composed of the Speaker [36] & leading Members of the lower House that Mr. J——y would contest the Vice-President-ship. I told him the contrary Idea obtained amongst our best informed

32. Isaac Ledyard. See Hazard to H, October 11, 1791.
33. Greenbush is on the west bank of the Hudson River opposite Albany.
34. Aaron Burr.
35. Stephen Mix Mitchell of Hartford, a distant relative of Pierpont Edwards.
36. Thomas Seymour, representative in the Connecticut Assembly from Hartford.

Politicians. Another Remark was C. B——r. coming in thro' a certain Party Influence. I left this Matter to explain itself.

From minor Statesmen, let me return to one just coming forward, whose Talents, are equal I beleive, to the Attainment of a very great Character. I hope confidently & beleive wait not indifferently, to see it established. In my last (I think it was) to T. C——e,[37] I mentioned this Person, *unqualifiedly*, as one who would possess, as great & as *merited Influence*, upon both Houses, as any Man in either House. After "*Influence*" the Words, *I trust*, were strongly in my Mind, but Delicacy forbad that in a Letter to Mr. C——e; which I can properly do to yourself. This Person (C.B.) has an Address not resistable by common Clay; he has Penetration, Fire, incessant Perseverance, animatedly active Execution, & could if so unwise, as to pursue so wrong a Course, mar Councils & Systems, more I suspect than any Individual I know in either House. I repeat my firm & confident Hope & Belief, that a Man of so eminent & universal Talents, cannot but employ them, in such a Manner as to evidence himself, a truly great Man.

By a very great Man, I mean one, who effects the greatest Quantity of public Good, by Means well adapted; pure & honorable, in the Sight of God; of Men of real Sense & Honor; & an intuitively self exploring Conscience.

To such a Man, & under such serious Impressions, I once more declare, that I am disinterestedly & truly

His sincere Friend & faithful humble Servant

Novemr. 25th 1791

P. S. I have inclosed Trumbull's Letter, & mentioned his Conversation, I feel a well-founded Confidence, that he has no greater Reserves to yourself, than to me, or I should not have committed an ostensible Act of Indiscretion.

37. Tench Coxe.

Report on Tonnage for the Year Ending September 30, 1790

Treasury Department, *November* 25, 1791.
[Communicated on November 28, 1791] [1]

[To the President of the Senate]
Sir:

In further obedience to the order of the Senate,[2] I have the honor to transmit a return of the Tonnage of all the vessels employed in the import, coasting, and fishing trades of the United States, for one year, ending on the 30th September, 1790.[3] This document will be found to exhibit the degree in which American and foreign vessels participate in every branch of the commerce of the United States, except the export trade, for which a similar return is now in preparation.

I have the honor to be, with the highest respect, sir, your most obedient and most humble servant,

Alexander Hamilton, *Secretary of the Treasury.*
The Vice President *of the United States and* President *of the Senate.*

ASP, *Commerce and Navigation,* I, 44.
  1. *Annals of Congress,* III, 32–33.
  2. Although it is stated in the *Annals of Congress* that the Senate requested a report on imports on February 16, 1791, the only Senate order for that date is a request for a report on exports (*Annals of Congress,* III, 31; II, 1801). See "Report on Imports for the Year Ending September 30, 1790," November 18, 1791; "Report on Imports for the Year Ending September 30, 1790," November 23, 1791.
  3. This return is printed in *ASP, Commerce and Navigation,* I, 45–47.

To William Seton

[Philadelphia] November 25. 1791

My Dear Sir

I seize the first moment of leisure to answer your letter of the 21st.

Strange as it may appear to you, it is not more strange than true, that the whole affair of branches was *begun, continued* and *ended;* not only without my participation but *against my judgment.* When I say against my judgment, you will not understand that my opinion was given and overruled, for I never was consulted, but that the steps taken were contrary to my private opinion of the course which ought to have been pursued.

I am sensible of the inconveniences to be apprehended and I regret them; but I do not know that it will be in my power to avert them.

Ultimately it will be incumbent upon me to place the public funds in the keeping of the branch; but *it may be depended upon* that I shall *precipitate nothing,* but shall so conduct the transfer as not to embarrass or distress your institution. I have not time to say more at present except that if there *are finally* to be two institutions, my regard for you makes me wish you may feel yourself at liberty to take your fortune with the Branch which must preponderate.

With great regard   I remain   Yrs   A Hamilton

Wm. Seton Esquire

ALS, The Andre deCoppet Collection, Princeton University Library.

From Oliver Wolcott, Junior

T.D
C. Off Nov. 25. 1791

Sir,

Applications are frequently made respecting accounts which remain dependg in this Office, on which I have already delivered my opinion and made reports while I served in the Office of Auditer of the Treasury.

In some cases special appeals were made to my predecessor in Office,[1] & in other cases when no appeals were made; the principles on which the accounts were stated, appear to be interesting to the public & to the claims of individuals.

As it was clearly intended by the Legislature in their Act for establishing the Treasury Department that all accounts, should be examined by the Comptroller of the Treasury, for reasons affecting the public, & for the purpose of securing to claimants an appeal from settlements made by the Auditer;[2] I have supposed that considerations of duty to the public & to individuals, as well as motives of delicacy which respect myself, required that accounts of this description should be made subject to some special regulation.

I therefore have taken the liberty to make this representation & to request that you would cause such arragements to be made as shall in your judgement be suitable & expedient.

I have the honour to be with the greatest respect Your obed servt   O.W.

To the Honle A H.

ADfS, Connecticut Historical Society, Hartford.

1. Wolcott had succeeded Nicholas Eveleigh as comptroller of the Treasury.

2. Section 3 of "An Act to establish the Treasury Department" reads as follows: "*And be it further enacted*, That it shall be the duty of the Comptroller to superintend the adjustment and preservation of the public accounts; to examine all accounts settled by the Auditor, and certify the balances arising thereon to the Register; to countersign all warrants drawn by the Secretary of the Treasury, which shall be warranted by law; to report to the Secretary the official forms of all papers to be issued in the different offices for collecting the public revenue, and the manner and form of keeping and stating the accounts of the several persons employed therein. He shall moreover provide for the regular and punctual payment of all monies which may be collected, and shall direct prosecutions for all delinquencies of officers of the revenue, and for debts that are, or shall be due to the United States" (1 *Stat. 66* [September 2, 1789]).

From Benjamin Hawkins [1]

Senate Chamber [Philadelphia] 26 novr. 1791

Dear Sir,

The legislature of North Carolina will soon be in Session,[2] and I think it of considerable importance, that they should be informed of the *Reasons* Why you have refused to that State, the *right*, claimed by their executive, to subscribe their certificates or notes, issued prior to the first of January 1790, and received into the treasury.[3] I therefore request the favour of you to give me such information on this subject as you may judge proper.

I request the favour also of your opinion on the 17 sec. of the act making provision for the debt of the United States.[4] That you may clearly comprehend my object in this request, I will state the following Quere; Is the State of North Carolina entitled to receive from the United States, an interest ℔ centum per annum, upon so much of the sum, as shall not have been subscribed, equal to that which would have accrued on the deficiency, had the same been subscribed, in trust for the non subscribing creditors; to continue until there shall be a settlement of accounts between the United States & the individual States &ca.?

I have the honor to be, very Sincerely Dear Sir   your most obt. servt.   Benjamin Hawkins

Honbe. Alexander Hamilton
Secretary of the Treasury.

Copy, North Carolina Department of Archives and History, Raleigh.
  1. Hawkins had been commercial agent of North Carolina and a member of the North Carolina House of Commons during the American Revolution. He served in the Continental Congress during the Confederation and was a member of the North Carolina Ratifying Convention in 1789. In the November, 1789, session of the North Carolina legislature he was elected to the United States Senate.
  2. The North Carolina legislature convened on December 5, 1791.
  3. See H to William Skinner, September 8, 1791.
  4. For the relevant provisions of Section 17 of "An Act making provision for the (payment of the) Debt of the United States" (1 *Stat.* 138–44 [August 4, 1790]), see Thomas Smith to H, June 6, 1791, note 1.

To Jedediah Huntington

[*Philadelphia, November 26, 1791.* Orders Huntington to "pay annually to the Surveyor of Stonington the Sum allowed by the Collection law. . . ." [1] *Letter not found.*] [2]

LS, sold at Swann Galleries, May 19, 1949, Lot 12.
  1. "An Act to provide more effectually for the collection of the duties imposed by law on goods, wares and merchandise imported into the United States, and on the tonnage of ships or vessels" (1 *Stat.* 145–78 [August 4, 1790]).
  2. Quotation taken from an extract in dealer's catalogue.

From William Ellery

[Newport, Rhode Island]
Collrs Off: Novr. 28 1791

Sir,

This will be attended with my weekly return of monies recd. and paid.

I have recd. your circular letter of the 11th. of this month respectg.

the allowance for damaged goods, and shall pay due regard to your sentiments on that subject.

The Brig Seven Brothers, by my direction,[1] was at the public auction put up at five hundred Dollars. Colo. Topham, the former owner, with a number of others attended the sale; but no body bid more, she remains on my hands. She is an old brig & her sails and rigging bad; but in the opinion of the Custom House Officers and others is worth much more than the sum at which she was put up. I shall do the best with her I can; but the season of the year, the circumstances of Hispaniola,[2] and the aversion of merchants to purchase vessels in her situation, will I am advised prevent a speedy disposal of her.

Thomas Cotrell in order to avoid an execution, and apprehensive of further prosecution and a gaol has left this State. Since his Departure, I have recd. a letter from him, wrote I suppose before he quitted Newport; in which, after a melancholy description of his situation, he wrote me "if I could be assured from you that there would be no more prosecutions I would return and make myself as easy as possible, but to stay here, and be cast into prison, which must be the case if any more prosecutions was to take place, it is more than I can bear; therefore I am obliged to quit the State, but where I shall go I cannot tell." I cannot give him any assurances; nor shall I answer his letter.

In my letter of the 21st. of this month I mentioned that the balance of weekly returns remaining in my hands might sometimes be too heavy to be carried by the Post. My apprehension in that respect has ceased; for I believe that the payments of duties will hereafter be principally if not altogether made in Providence Bank Notes. I also in that letter asked whether I was to exchange Specie for those Notes. The President of that Bank [3] has been at this Office, and furnished me with Checks. In the Denominations of the Notes are half dollar, one dollar and two dollar notes, and I am otherwise informed that there are a number as low as for one Shilling Lawful Money. These low denominations were, I presume, intended to give an extensive circulation through the State; but I suspect that in the provision Markets, among the huxters, seamen, and some others of the lower class of inhabitants in the Southern part of the State, those Notes will be not readily received, unless they should be exchangeable for Specie at this or some other Office; and if they should be exchangeable at my Office, and any Specie should be paid for duties, the business of it will be very much embarrassed by frequent applications for such exchanges. The President of the bank, to facilitate the circulation of its Notes in this part of the State has proposed to some Merchants of this town to receive such Specie as may be in my Office in his behalf and to exchange it for bank Notes; but as this would occasion much trouble, and he would not allow a commission for the Service, no one, as yet, is disposed to undertake it. However desirous the Proprietors of the Providence Bank may be that its notes should be exchanged at this Office, the circumstance last mentioned shows that it is not strongly expected; and for the reason given I hope it will not be admitted. I wish to have your direction with regard to the mode of transmitting my weekly balances to Providence as early as may be convenient.

I am Sir   Yr. most obedt. servant   Wm Ellery

A Hamilton Esqr
Secry of Treasy:

LC, Newport Historical Society, Newport, Rhode Island.
    1. See Ellery to H, July 11, August 2, 23, October 4, 10, 25, 1791.
    2. This is a reference to the insurrection which took place in Santo Domingo in August, 1791.
    3. John Brown, a leading Providence merchant and businessman and brother of Moses Brown, had been appointed president of the newly founded Providence Bank on October 4, 1791.

From Jeremiah Olney

Providence, November 28, 1791. "Your circular Letter of the 11th Instant, to which I shall pay due attention, induces me to ask whether any allowance (which has been demanded here) is to be made in ascertaining the Duties on broken and unshelled Coffee and Cocoa of an inferior quality generally purchased in the West Indies at about half the price of Merchantable? You will oblige me Sir, by giving me your Opinion upon this Matter. . . ."

ADfS, Rhode Island Historical Society, Providence.

From John Ross [1]

[Philadelphia, November 29, 1791]

Dear Sir

The inclosed [2] is Sent for your peruseal, and the letter Sketched for Mr Flint [3] for your consideration, and to be altered by you if necessary. If however approved to be Sent in its present form, be pleased to Sign it, and I shall, convey it to be signed by the Other Commissioners,[4] at N York & delivered. Excuse my troubling you.

With much Respect I am   Yours &ca   J: Ross

Nov. 29th. 1791.

Alexander Hamilton Esqr.

[ENCLOSURE]

Royal Flint to John Ross [5]

New York Nov. 15. 1791.

Sir

I have before me your favor of the 11th instant and am sorry I can make no reply that will give you satisfaction. The partners of the late firm of Daniel Parker & Co have not yet exhibited their accounts in such a manner as to render a close of them practicable. Nor have I now, any more than I always have had, the least expectation that this object will ever be accomplished. If the Commissioners of the trust think proper I will put the bonds into the hands of an Attorney to be put in suit. The Books of the company are all as forward for settlement, as they can be, with the documents I have already received. Mr Grant who knows more of this business than any other person will be here in ten days; after I have seen him I will write you more fully. In the mean time I have the honer to be   sir   with great respect   your obed srvt   Royal Flint

Jno Ross Esq

[ENCLOSURE]

Trustees for Daniel Parker and Company to Royal Flint [6]

Philadelphia 30th November 1791

Sir

Our last to you was dated 23d. of April and having now before us your letter to Mr. Ross of the 15th. Instant informing him that your application to the respective Partners of the late Firm of Daniel Parker & Co. have had no Effect in forwarding the Settlement of their Accots. with each other and that moreover, you have no expectation now of this objects being accomplished. That being the case Sir! we conceive it incumbent on us, as Commissioners appointed in the Act which invest the power and trust in you, to discharge our duty as much as possible, accordingly, we give it as our opinion that the Bonds of the Partners be immediately put in Suit for the Penalty.

The Creditors are suffering, and have much cause to complain of Neglect and delays on the part of Daniel Parker & Co. In Justice therefore to them, We do by this further authorize you to pursue every possible Legal measure, under the Powers you are possessed of, to facilitate the Recovery of the Penaltys for their Security. We are

Sir Your most humble Servants

Royal Flint Esqr.
Joint Agent & Trustee for
Daniel Parker & Co. & for their Creditors.
New York.

LS, Hamilton Papers, Library of Congress.
   1. Ross was a Philadelphia merchant.
   This letter deals with the complicated negotiations that attended the liquidation of Daniel Parker and Company. In 1788 Andrew Craigie, who was Parker's agent, concluded an agreement with Parker's Philadelphia creditors. Under this agreement a board of trustees or arbitrators, on which the creditors were to be represented, was to be established to settle the various claims. As trustees Craigie wished to have H, William Seton, John Murray, Jonathan Burrall, John Ross, and John Holker. It is not possible to ascertain whether all these men agreed to serve as commissioners, but Ross's letter to H indicates that both were trustees. The trustees' efforts to satisfy Parker's Philadelphia creditors are described briefly in Davis, *Essays*, I, 254–59.

2. See enclosure, Royal Flint to Ross, November 15, 1791.

Originally a resident of Connecticut, Flint became a prominent New York businessman. In the seventeen-eighties he had been closely associated in several business ventures with William Duer and Jeremiah Wadsworth.

3. See enclosure, Trustees for Daniel Parker and Company to Flint, November 30, 1791.

4. I.e., the trustees. See note 1.

5. ALS, Hamilton Papers, Library of Congress.

6. Copy, Hamilton Papers, Library of Congress.

From Oliver Wolcott, Junior

T. D
C Off Nov 29th. 1791

Sir

I have the honour to submit to your consideration and decision a form for regulating the manner of rendering the accounts of expences of the revenue Cutters and take the liberty to request your instructions respecting the rate of Commissions to be allowed.

I have &

The Honble A H

[ENCLOSURE] [1]

T.D
C. Office

Sir

Enclosed you will receive a form for stating the accounts of the Revenue Cutters and your direction.

It will be expedient that an account should be opened in your books for the expences incurred under this agency, which will be closed quarterly and for the amount of which you will debit the United States in your quarterly account Current as Collector of the Revenue for the district of   .[2]

The rations of the Officers & Mariners you will please to allow according to such prices as shall from time to time be authorized by the Secretary of the Treasy.

A Commission of   [3] ₱ Cent is allowed for your extra trouble in this business which you will please to charge in the abstract of expences to be rendered according to the inclosed form, independent of and in addition to, the Commission to which you are otherwise by Law intittled.

I am &c

ADf, Connecticut Historical Society, Hartford.
  1. ADf, Connecticut Historical Society.
  2. Space left blank in MS.
  3. Space left blank in MS.

To William Short

Duplicate

Treasury Department
November 30 1791

Sir

Your letters of the 23rd. and 31st. of August and 3d of September remain unacknowledged. Mine to you of the 1st. of August 2nd. September and 3rd. of October will much abrige what is necessary to be said at this time.

The prices of the public debt here rendering it questionable whether it be any longer the interest of the United States to prosecute the idea of purchases with monies borrowed at 5 ℔ Cent, and there being reasons of the moment against beginning the redemption of the six per Cents, I have concluded to forbear drawing for the second Million of Guilders mentioned in my letter of the 1st. instant. Except therefore one million of the last six which has been drawn for, the intire loan is to be applied to European purposes.

In directing this application you will bear in mind that there will be payments to be made on account of the Dutch Loans for which the proper reservations are to be made.

In your letter of the 23d. of August you mention that "in June next the first reimbursement is to take place on the loans made at Amsterdam," and the Commissioners in some of their letters speak of the time of that reimbursement as approaching.

Hence I conclude that some mistake has arisen, as by the Contracts in the Treasury it appears that the first payment of principal of the first Dutch Loan namely that for 5,000.000 of florins contracted the 17th of June 1782 is not to take place till the 1st. of June 1793.[1]

It will be proper to have an explanation with the Commissioners on this point; lest an error should have crept into the copies of the Contract sent to the Treasury; which however from the whole circumstances appears scarcely possible.

All payments for interest or otherwise which shall be necessary to be made upon the Dutch Loans during the year 1792 are intended to be made out of the monies borrowed abroad which will leave in the Treasury here the sums that ought to be remitted for interest as a part of the two millions of Dollars authorised to be borrowed by the act making provision for the reduction of the public debt.[2]

After the year 1792 remittances for interest will go from hence. But it is probable that for some time to come, we shall have to depend on loans abroad for the reimbursement of the installments of principal, which may be falling due.

I observe the idea that a *Guarantee* would be necessary, in the case of a Loan made in England. This circumstance I was not apprised of. It appears to me inadmissible.

I also observe what has passed concerning the charges on the last loan. You will perceive from my letters above referred to the light in which this subject of charges has presented itself to my view.

With the truest consideration and esteem   I have the honor to be, Sir,   Your most Obedt servant   Alexander Hamilton

William Short Esqr.

LS, William Short Papers, Library of Congress. A copy of this letter was enclosed in H's "Report on Foreign Loans," February 13, 1793.
   1. For a description of this loan, see Willink, Van Staphorst, and Hubbard to H, January 25, 1790, note 15. The contract was dated June 11, 1782.
   2. 1 *Stat.* 186–87 (August 12, 1790).

To Angelica Church

Philadelphia
November   [1] 1791

My Dear friend

What is the reason that we have been so long without a line from you? Does your affection for us abate? If it does you are very ungrateful: for *I* think as kindly as ever of My Dear *Sister in Law* and *Betsey* has lately given me stronger proof than she ever did before of her attachment to you. Guess if you can what this is. If you can't guess, you must wait for an explanation until we meet once more.

You may think this as remote as a *certain day*, that pious folks talk so much about. But you will be disappointed—*I hope too agreeably*. Things are tending fast to a point, which will enable me honorably to retreat from a situation in which I make the greatest possible sacrifices to a little *empty praise*, or if you like the turn better, to a disposition to make others happy. But this disposition must have its limits.

Will you be glad to see us in Europe? For you will never come to America.

This will be delivered to you by Mr. Morris, son of Robert Morris.[2] He is not a *dilatanti fellow;* but he is a deserving young man. And you must be civil to him.

Betsey joins me in embracing you and in assuring you that we are ever most Affectionately Yrs.

Adieu

A Hamilton

Mrs. Church

ALS, Judge Peter B. Olney, Deep River, Connecticut.
  1. Space left blank in MS.
  2. Robert Morris, Jr., who at this time was on his way to London on business.

Memorandum from Oliver Wolcott, Junior [1]

[*Philadelphia November, 1791*]. Encloses extract of a letter, dated August 22, 1785, from Nathanael Greene to the President of Congress. Observes that "Baron Glaubeck was allowed pay as a Captain from March 9, 81. to August. 24 1782 [2] & pd. . . . A sum far less than Genl. Green had advanced."

ALS, Hamilton Papers, Library of Congress.
  1. Wolcott prepared this memorandum for use in connection with H's "Report on the Petition of Catharine Greene," December 23, 1791.
  2. See "An Act to allow the Baron de Glaubeck the pay of a Captain in the Army of the United States" (6 *Stat.* 1 [September 29, 1789]). Baron Glaubeck had served as aide-de-camp to Brigadier General Daniel Morgan during the American Revolution.

To Nathaniel Appleton

Treasury Department
December 1. 1791.

Sir

I have directed the Treasurer to transmit you draughts for fifty five thousand dollars towards payment of the quarter's interest ending the 31st. of December. These draughts are with blanks for the direction as heretofore, and may be filled with the name either of the Collector of Boston or of the Cashier of the Bank of North America, New York or Massachusetts. One half of these bills may at once be disposed of, if a demand occurs, upon either of the Banks of North America or New York. For the residue it is presumed you will find sufficient sums in the Bank of Massachusetts and in the hands of the Collector of Boston. There appeared to be on the 13th. of November a balance of twenty two thousand two hundred and fifteen dollars in the hands of the latter. You will however do well to consult with him, in order to ascertain what sum you may rely upon in time.

You will without delay inform me how far there is a probability that the sum transmitted, together with the former draughts remaining in your hands, will be adequate to the object, and you will report to me weekly the amount of the sales you shall make.

I am, Sir,   Your obedt. servant   A Hamilton

PS   You will of course understand that you are to make use of the drafts which have remained in your hands, equally with those now announced, as far as may be necessary.[1]

Nathl. Appleton Esq.
Commissioner of Loans
Massachusetts.

LS, The Bostonian Society, Boston.
   1. The postscript is in H's handwriting.

From Benjamin Lincoln

Boston Decr. 1 1791

Sir

Your favours of the 17th & 18th were received last evening by post. The one referred to in your letter to Capt williams [1] did not come to hand.

I wish my opinion had not been asked relative to the present allowance made the keeper of the Light House at Portland as the sum given was named by me and thought to be as much as the public ought to give for keeping it in the best manner. I did not consider whether the sum was sufficient to support Mr. Greenleaf [2] & family or not. I considered only the service to be performed and what sum would compensate a man for doing it. I considered that the Light-House was situated on the main Land in the vicinity of a good neighbourhood and not more than half a mile from an open road on which is much traveling. That whoever keept the light house might carry on the business of a Smith, a Shoemaker, a weaver, a taylor &c &c or that he might do the business of a common day labourer among the farmers—besides a mans time might be well spent part of the season in fishing. I also considered that in addition to the eighty dollars there was a convenient House owned by the public for which the light House keeper would not pay any rent nor for the garden & for a small barn which is building. I also considered that as Labour & provisions are in this State the Eighty dollars, the house rent &c would nearly pay a man for his whole time.

When I mentioned the Eighty dollars I knew a person of character who could produce very ample recommendations, that would gladly keep the lights for a less Sum. I did not think I should be justified in putting it at so low a price as he fixed it for. It did not appear to me that it would be a full compensation for the services which must be render.

It may be said that the sum of Eighty dollars bears no proportion to what is given for keeping other light Houses in the State. Though I did not think this ought to have any weight in the decision of the simple question what was a reasonable compensation for keeping the

Light House at Portland Yet the difference will not appear very great when it is considered that the others are on Islands, which cannot be approached at some seasons of the year for a long time together, far removed from any other inhabitants or on long Isthmuses one I think is thirteen miles & the other not much less. This makes it necessary to keep two men at the least and in some places more constantly at the light Houses and their detached situation excludes them in a degree from those employments which did they exercise would much aid their support.

I have been thus particular in the statement of this matter because I had before given my opinion because I find a Host of Petitioners applying for a much larger sum and because hereby that you may be poss[ess]ed of a state of facts necessary to making up a final judgment on the Question.

On the whole if the Question is whether Eighty dollars are a sum sufficient to support Capt Greenleaf & family I should answer No. If it is, whether Eighty dollars will compensate for the labours in keeping the Light House and whether it can be attended for that sum I should answer yea.

I hope soon being in Philadelphia and give a general state of all the light-Houses & their supplies in this State.

Secy of the Treasury

LC, Massachusetts Historical Society, Boston; LC, RG 36, Collector of Customs at Boston, Letter Book, 1790–1797, National Archives; two copies, RG 56, Letters from the Collector at Boston, National Archives.
   1. John Foster Williams was master of the Massachusetts revenue cutter. Letter not found.
   2. Joseph Greenleaf was the keeper of the lighthouse at Portland.

From William Short

Antwerp Dec. 1. 1791

Sir

I arrived here the day before yesterday & learned from M de Wolf that the loan mentioned to you in my letters of the 12th. & 22d of November was already contracted for, except a small portion which

ALS, letterpress copy, William Short Papers, Library of Congress.

he reserved for the public according to the usage of this place & which he should continue open ten or fifteen days. The loan is to be dated from to-day & the undertakers are to have five months to furnish the money in equal portions monthly with the privilege of furnishing it sooner if they please as at Amsterdam. He has no doubt it will be furnished much sooner.

I passed the act before the Notary yesterday, a copy of which will be forwarded to you with this letter if it can be prepared in time, to obtain on it the ratification promised. The terms of interest & commission have been already mentioned to you.[1]

The amount of this loan will be remitted to France in proportion as it is recieved here, as well to avoid double interest as to leave it the smallest time possible at the risk of the U.S. Nothing was settled before I left Paris as to the manner of indemnifying France for depreciation. I mentioned to you why the sale of my bills for specie at Paris would be disadvantageous.[2] The government do not remit this money to Holland, as you had been informed. On the contrary they have specie brought from thence to satisfy such demands in France as exact specie. I imagine that the indemnity must be made them at the close of the payments by estimation formed on principles which it will not be difficult to agree about. The price of exchange is regularly & daily settled. The price of gold & silver is published also daily, but the manner in which this commerce is carried on & its accidental fluctuations render it by no means a true standard or one which would suit the U.S.

I had the honor of informing you in my late letters of the payments made out of the loan of six millions [3] conformably to my orders.[4] They amounted to three millions of florins which I had desired the bankers of the U.S. to remit to France & f 560,000. paid to the French bankers at Amsterdam. I had supposed of course there would remain in their hands of the 6,000,000, f 2,440,000 which was the part you had directed to be kept at your disposition except the f 60,000 paid above the f 500,000 to the French bankers as formerly mentioned. I

1. The contract for the Antwerp loan was sent to H on December 15, 1791. See Short to H, December 15, 1791. For an English translation of this contract, see Short to H, November 8, 1791, note 4.
2. See Short to H, November 22, 1791.
3. The Holland loan of September, 1791. For a description of this loan, see Short to H, August 31, 1791.
4. See Short to H, September 23, October 10, November 8, 1791.

have lately recieved however a letter from our bankers in which they state f 2,200,000 as the whole of the balance that will remain in their hands.[5] How this happens I cannot say, but suppose they must have received other orders for disposing of this money as mine extend only to f 3,560,000. Should your draughts be recieved for the f 2,500,000, directed to be reserved, still I do not apprehend any inconvenience, as if no loan should be previously made at Amsterdam, the deficiency may at the worst be supplied from hence.

You will have learned from my several letters the progress of affairs here & at Amsterdam. Before having any reason to believe that the U.S. would be able to reduce the rate of interest this year at Amsterdam, & assured by our bankers that all loans made there after that period would be subjected to a tax of 1. p. cent, I authorized a loan here at 4½. p. cent interest & 5. p. cent commission. Circumstances becoming more favorable before that authorisation was acted under I determined to endeavour to make use of them to ameliorate the terms of commission & succeeded in the manner mentioned to you. During this time the bankers represented to me that the increasing abundance of money at Amsterdam gave them hopes that they might succeed in effecting a loan at 4½ p. cent. early enough to avoid the tax & therefore requested my authorisation for them to sieze the first favorable moment to conclude an engagement with the undertakers at 4½. p. cent. Nothing was said about charges, but their former letters left me no doubt that they counted on an augmentation, & they wrote me soon afterwards in answer to my letters on the subject that the reduction of interest would of course augment the charges, they could not say how much precisely until authorized to make propositions to the undertakers. As soon as I had fixed the business of the loan at Antwerp I limited them to the same charges of 4. p. cent & authorised their opening a loan at 4½. p. cent interest for f 3,000,000 if it could be done before the operation of the tax.[6] In answer they say they postpone it in hopes of soon effecting a loan at 4. p. cent interest with an augmentation of charges somewhat above five p. cent, & desire my authorisation as mentioned to you in my last.[7] I mentioned to you also that it was then too late to stop that agreed for here, under

5. Willink, Van Staphorst, and Hubbard to Short, November 14, 1791 (LS, Short Family Papers, Library of Congress).

6. Short to Willink, November 11, 1791 (ALS, letterpress copy, William Short Papers, Library of Congress).

7. Willink, Van Staphorst, and Hubbard to Short, November 14, 1791 (LS,

circumstances quite different from those then stated at Amsterdam; & the effect I apprehended it might produce on our bankers there to whom it had been notified since their writing above, although it is probable they had either information or suspicions respecting it sooner. I was not mistaken in my apprehensions. On my arrival here I found a letter from them waiting for me in which they express fully their mortification at a loan being opened here.[8] They gave various reasons to shew the impropriety & danger it may be of to the credit of the U.S. & finally desire that if any opportunity should present itself for stopping it that it may be done as being "absolutely necessary to insure the success of a loan at Amsterdam at 4. p. cent."

Their letter may be reduced to the following substance which I give you in its own order. Their surprize that it did not occur to me from the relation they stand in to the U.S. to ask their opinion upon the measure, that they would then have told me that Antwerp is not a new source of credit to the U.S. as the monied men here place their money in the loans in Holland, that the Undertakers will be piqued at this & avail themselves of any circumstance to shew their resentment, that those who operate a solitary piece of business will not be as well disposed if as able as they are, to advance any monies for regular payment of interests, that borrowing money out of Amsterdam would denote the credit of the U.S. being exhausted there & be a mortifying reflection, though an untrue one, on the respectability of the U.S., that a debtor's borrowing money here, there & wherever he can find lenders supposes great wants or small means of satisfying them & be a basis of discredit, that borrowing at different places under the same power limited as to its amount, may prevent giving the moral certainty required in such cases where personal respectability & credit are out of the question, of the power's not being exceeded. They had misconstrued an expression in my letter which I used in notifying to them this loan, so as to infer that the wants of the U.S. were considerable, & that therefore the offers from Antwerp had been accepted; & they say in consequence that if I had deigned to inform them confidentially of the extent of these wants they would have informed me candidly how far they could be supplied there. Whereas I meant that the wants of the U.S. were such that they were suffi-

---

Short Family Papers, Library of Congress); Willink, Van Staphorst, and Hubbard to Short, November 17, 1791 (LS, Short Family Papers, Library of Congress).

8. Willink, Van Staphorst, and Hubbard to Short, November 24, 1791 (LS, Short Family Papers, Library of Congress).

ciently master of them to execute the design of reducing the rate of interest even at the risk of diminishing the sums loaned.

I answered their letter yesterday [9] & found no difficulty in obviating the several objections they made. On the whole I continued the authorization of making the loan at 4. p. cent interest informing them that no more would be made at an higher rate, that this was authorised here, as they knew, before any hopes were held out of reducing the interest below 5. p. cent this year at Amsterdam & that it had been too late to have revoked it or I should have done it not from any apprehension that it could prevent a loan at 4. p. cent at Amsterdam, but because it was better raising money at 4. p. cent than 4½. & that if the loan was not effected at 4. p. cent I should remain fully persuaded that the hopes they had held out had been too sanguine & never believe they had been frustrated by this loan which was already engaged. I observed also that I supposed the dispositions of the undertakers would depend very much on those by whom they were employed, but that if not & they were sufficiently unjust to desire any other monopoly of the loans of a country than that which arises from negotiating them on better terms, I should imagine they (the bankers) would agree with me that it was an additional reason for desiring not to depend solely on their will. I know not what effect my letter will produce though I cannot doubt that if any opportunity presented itself in this moment for exercising their resentment with some degree of efficacity that it would be made use of. As that cannot be done however, interest will probably resume its proper weight & induce them to exert themselves as hitherto. Should they not effect the loan at 4. p. cent it will be an indisputable proof to me, that the suspicions they had entertained of the loan here, had more influence in exciting the hopes they held out than its accomplishment can have had in frustrating them.

I own however that I wait with some degree of anxiety for the event, for although what I have mentioned, is my firm persuasion yet it is possible you may think otherwise; & even the possibility of the measure which I have taken, procrastinating so desirable an event as the reduction of the interest on the loans to 4. p. cent, would augment much the distrust I have always entertained as to myself in

9. Short to Willink, Van Staphorst, and Hubbard, December 1, 1791 (ALS, letterpress copy, William Short Papers, Library of Congress).

this business & which I took the liberty of communicating to you.[10]

In any event however I cannot doubt Sir that you will consider the authorisation given for the loan here, as indisputably proper at the time & under the circumstances it was given, with which you were regularly made acquainted. I must add also in justice to myself that if any doubts could possibly have been entertained respecting the measure at that time, they would have been removed by the confidence of the advantages resulting from it, entertained & expressed by Mr. Morris with so much constancy & uniformity,[11] & whose opinions could not but have weight with me proportioned to the proofs of the confidence reposed in him by the President of the United States.

This letter will be sent by the way of London & will be followed soon by another informing you of what shall have been done at Amsterdam, & adding assurances of the respect & attachment with which I have the honor to be Sir, you most obedient humble servant

W: Short

The Honble.
Alexander Hamilton Secretary of the Treasury Philadelphia

10. See Short to H, October 10, 1791.
11. See Short to H, July 24–25, 1791.

To Nathaniel Appleton

Treasury Department
December 2 1791

Sir

I have upon reflexion concluded to authorise You to dispose of the whole of the draughts mentioned in my letter of yesterday upon either of the Banks of North America or New York in preference to the other mode then proposed. But in case you should find no demand for the whole or part of the draughts upon the two banks; it is to be understood that you are at liberty to avail yourself of the alternative first mentioned, as to the residue.

I am, Sir   Your Obed Servant.   Alexander Hamilton

Nathaniel Appleton Esqr.
Commr of Loans
Massachusetts

LS, The Bostonian Society, Boston.

To Joseph Whipple

[*Philadelphia, December 2, 1791.* On December 17, 1791, Whipple wrote to Hamilton: "I received by the last post your letter of the 2nd Instant." *Letter not found.*]

From Wilhem and Jan Willink, Nicholaas and Jacob Van Staphorst, and Nicholas Hubbard

[*Amsterdam, December 2, 1791.* On February 14, 1792, Hamilton wrote to Willink, Van Staphorst, and Hubbard: "I am just honored with your several favours of Nov 21st & 24th & December 2d." *Letter of December 2 not found.*]

To John Adams

Treasury Department
Dec. 3. 1791.

Sir

I have the honor to inform you that I have issued a warrant for the sum of five thousand two hundred and fifty six dollars in favor of the Secretary of the Senate (Samuel A. Otis Esq.) for the purpose of discharging the compensations due to the members of that body, grounded upon a pay roll certified by you to the 30th. ultimo inclusive. I take the liberty of communicating to the Senate that this mode will be pursued till they shall signify their pleasure in regard to some other mode of proceeding.

I have the honor to be,   with the greatest respect,   Sir,   your most obedt.   & most humble servt.   Alexander Hamilton

The Vice President of the United State
& President of the Senate.

LS, RG 46, Second Congress, 1791–1793, Records of the Office of the Secretary of the Senate, National Archives.

To Nathaniel Appleton

Treasury Department December 3d 1791

sir

On the receipt of this letter I request You to deposit in the Bank of Massachusetts for sale, the Bills of the Treasurer of the united States for 55,000 Dollars, (or such of them as remain unsold) which have been transmitted to you agreably to my letter of the 1st instant.[1]

I am, sir, Your Obedt Servt   Alexander Hamilton

Nathl: Appleton Esqr
Commissr of loans
Massachusetts

LS, The Bostonian Society, Boston.
1. See also H to Appleton, December 2, 1791.

To John Chaloner [1]

[Philadelphia, December 3, 1791]

Sir

I request you will not take any step respecting the land mortgaged by Mr. Holker [2] for Mr. Church's debt without first consulting me.[3]

I am Sir   Your obedient servt   Alex Hamilton

December 3d. 1791
John Chaloner Esqr.

ALS, Historical Society of Pennsylvania, Philadelphia.
1. During the seventeen-eighties Chaloner, a Philadelphia merchant, had served as the Philadelphia agent for John B. Church and Jeremiah Wadsworth.
2. John Holker, who had served as inspector general of manufactures in France, came to the United States in 1778, where he served as marine agent of France. In September, 1781, he was appointed French consul general for New York, New Jersey, Pennsylvania, and Delaware. During the seventeen-eighties and seventeen-nineties he was a shareholder in the Scioto Company and a principal figure in the bankruptcy proceedings of Daniel Parker and Company. See John Ross to H, November 29, 1791, note 1. In 1784, together with other Philadelphia businessmen, he participated in founding the Bank of North America.
3. H handled Church's affairs in the United States.

From William Ellery

[*Newport, Rhode Island*] *December 5, 1791.* "I have recd. your letters of the 16th [1] & 17th [2] of the last month, and the contents of them will be duely regarded. The construction you give to the Provision in the Act of the 3d. of March 1791 I am happy to find corresponds with the opinion I had entertained. . . ." [3]

LC, Newport Historical Society, Newport, Rhode Island.
   1. Letter not found.
   2. Letter not found. This letter was written in reply to Ellery to H, October 14, 1791.
   3. See Ellery to H, October 14, 1791.

To Philip A. Hamilton [1]

Philadelphia December 5
1791

I received with great pleasure My Dear Philip the letter which you wrote me last week.[2] Your Mama and myself were very happy to learn that you are pleased with your situation and content to stay as long as shall be thought for your good. We hope and believe that nothing will happen to alter this disposition.

Your Master also informs me that you recited a lesson the first day you began, very much to his satisfaction. I expect every letter from him will give me a fresh proof of your progress. For I know that you can do a great deal, if you please, and I am sure you have too much spirit not to exert yourself, that you may make us every day more and more proud of you.

Your Mama has got an Ovid for you and is looking up your Mairs introduction.[3] If it cannot be found tomorrow another will be procured and the books with the other articles she promised to send you will be forwarded in two or three days.

You remember that I engaged to send for you next Saturday and I will do it, unless you request me to put it off. For a promise must never be broken; and I never will make you one, which I will not fulfil as far as I am able. But it has occurred to me that the Christmas holidays are near at hand, and I suppose your school will then break up for some days and give you an opportunity of coming to stay with us for a longer time than if you should come on Saturday. Will it not be best for you, therefore, to put off your journey till the holidays? But determine as you like best and let me know what will be most pleasing to you.

A good night to my darling son.   Adieu   A Hamilton

Master Philip A Hamilton

ALS, facsimile in George Shea, *The Life and Epoch of Alexander Hamilton: A Historical Study* (Boston, 1880), 7.

1. Philip Hamilton, H's eldest son, was born in 1782. On November 26, 1791, Moore Furman, a resident of Trenton, New Jersey, wrote: "Mr. and Mrs. Hamilton came to town last night they have brought their son to put to boarding school to our Episcopal Church Parson" (*The Letters of Moore Furman* [New York, 1912], 90). William Frazer was the Episcopal rector of St. Michael's Church in Trenton under whom Philip Hamilton studied.

2. Letter not found.

3. John Mair, *An Introduction to Latin Syntax; or, an exemplification of the rules of construction, as delivered in Mr. Ruddiman's Rudiments. To which is subjoined, an Epitome of ancient history. . .* (Edinburgh, 1775).

To John Eager Howard

Treasury Department
Dec. 5th. 1791.

Sir.

It appearing to me, that the attention of the Legislature of Maryland may be necessary to the removal of an inconvenience under which the subscribers of the debt of that state now lie, I do myself the honor to make the requisite communication to your Excellency.

The 18th. section of the act making provision for the debt of the United States suspends the payment of interest in respect to the debt of any State which shall have issued its own certificates in exchange for those of the United States, until it shall be satisfactorily made to appear, that the certificates issued for that purpose by such state have been *re-exchanged* or *redeemed*, or until those, which shall not have been re-exchanged or redeemed shall be *surrendered* to the United States.[1] It is understood that the measure contemplated in this section was adopted by the State of Maryland, that is, that a sum of state certificates was issued in exchange for an equal sum of certificates of the federal debt, and that although a part of those state certificates has been redeemed, others to a considerable amount have not been re-exchanged or redeemed, but that many of them have been subscribed to the loan of the assumed debt.[2] It will conduce as well to the order of the finances as to the convenience of the public creditors, [the payment of Interest to whom must otherwise be suspended,] [3] if measures can be taken by the government of Maryland to make the balance unredeemed and unexchanged to appear, and if they should direct the surrender of the amount of such balance in certificates of federal debt in their old form. Should the surrender of them in that form be impracticable from the circumstance of the subscription of federal debt, which was directed by the legislature, an equal sum of six per cent, deferred and three per cent stock, in such proportions as the balance or deficiency would produce on subscription, may be paid in lieu of the certificates in their old form. This will be at the election of the state, and can be affected by no circumstance but their own convenience, as there can be no pecuniary advantage or disadvantage in either mode.

Should this subject require further explanation, the Commissioner of Loans,[4] on your signifying your desire to him, can probably possess you of the necessary information, or should any thing occur which he cannot elucidate, it will give me great satisfaction to make the necessary communication.

I have the honor to be with the greatest respect, Sir.   Your most obedt. & most humble servant   Alexander Hamilton
                                                     Secretary of the Treasury

His Excellency
The Governor of Maryland.

LS, from the original in the New York State Library, Albany; copy, RG 56, Letters 2nd Comptroller, 2nd Auditor, Executive of Maryland and Georgia, 1789–1833, National Archives; copy, RG 56, Miscellaneous Letters Sent, "Set K," National Archives.

    1. 1 *Stat.* 144 (August 4, 1790). See also "Treasury Department Circular to the Commissioners of Loans," May 27, 1791; "Treasury Department Circular to the Governors of the States," June 27, 1791.

    2. Maryland had provided for the exchange of loan office certificates for state certificates in "An Act proposing to the citizens of this state, creditors of congress on loan-office certificates, to accept this state for payment, on the terms therein mentioned" which was passed by the Maryland legislature in 1783 (*Laws of Maryland, Made and Passed at a Session of Assembly, begun and held at the city of Annapolis, on Monday the Fourth of November, in the year of our Lord*

one thousand seven hundred and eighty-two [Annapolis: Printed by Frederick Green, Printer to the State, n.d.], Ch. XXV [January 15, 1783]). An authority on this subject has written:

"When Congress ceased paying interest on loan office certificates in 1782, Maryland at once invited her federal creditors to exchange their securities for state notes. Not all the loan office creditors availed themselves of this offer, but the state assumed $214,712 specie value. In later years the government of Maryland invested in other types of public securities and by 1790 owned $661,000 specie value of the federal public debt." (E. James Ferguson, "State Assumption of the Federal Debt During the Confederation," *Mississippi Valley Historical Review*, XXXVIII [December, 1951], 417.)

3. The bracketed words are in H's handwriting.
4. Thomas Harwood, commissioner of loans for Maryland.

To John Jay

Philadelphia December 5
1791

My Dear Sir

Your letter of the 14th of November [1] duly came to hand.

A temporary absence from this place, some ill health, and much occupation have delayed an acknowlegement 'till this time.

Aware of the inconveniences, to which you refer, from the want of a proper provision for defraying the expences of the Courts— I inserted in the estimate presented at the beginning of the session [2] a sum for an appropriation in aid of the fund heretofore designated,[3] which has not been found sufficiently productive. I was not consulted when that provision was made or I could have foretold that it would prove inadequate.

Accounts from all quarters bespeak the same content which you mention as prevailing in the Country which has fallen under your observation.

There is I hope no danger of the error you mention, though the passions of some folks would in particular respects lead to it, if they could have their way.

Mrs. H joins in Compliments to Mrs. Jay.

With respectful & affectionate attachment   I remain Dr Sir   Your Obed serv   A Hamilton

The Honble Chief Justice Jay

ALS, Columbia University Libraries.

1. Letter not found.

2. See "Report on the Estimate of Expenditures for 1792," November 4, 1791.

3. See "An Act providing compensations for the officers of the Judicial Courts of the United States, and for Jurors and Witnesses, and for other purposes" (1 *Stat.* 216–17 [March 3, 1791]).

INDEX

COMPILED BY JEAN G. COOKE

Abbeville County, S.C., 429
Accomack County, Va., 279, 428
Adams, —— (Mr.), 301
Adams, John, 104, 533, 534; attacks on, 367; commissioner of sinking fund, 68, 93, 176, 476-77; *Discourses on Davila*, 33-34; *letter to*, 558
Adams, John (N.H.), 297
Adams, John Quincy: "Publicola," 33-34
Adams, William: promissory note from, 35
Agriculture: in Bucks County, Pa., 124-27; in Connecticut, 332, 333, 334, 344; in Delaware, 376-77; in Great Britain, 376-77; Hamilton's request for information on, 35-37; in Luzerne County, Pa., 375-77; in Maryland, 376-77, 490-93; in New Jersey, 376; in Pennsylvania, 114-18; in Pittsburgh, Pa., 419-20; in Virginia, 303
Albany, N.Y., 7, 87, 196, 533, 536
Albemarle County, Va., 428
Alburg, Vt., 91
Alchorne, Stanesby, 4-5
Alexander, Joseph, 434
Alexander, William, 413-14
Alexandria, Va.: and branch of Bank of the U.S., 515-16; collector of customs at, *see* Lee, Charles; deputy collector of customs at, *see* Gray, Vincent; surveyor of port of, *see* Hanson, Samuel
Alice, 425, 495, 528-29
Allegany (Alleghany) County, Md., 130, 428
Allegheny County, Pa., 427
Allibone, William: *letter from*, 244
Allon (Allou), —— (M.), 267-69
Almy, William, 432, 435, 441, 448

Almy and Brown, 432, 435, 441, 448
Amelia County, Va., 428
American Academy of Arts and Sciences: Hamilton's election to, 104-5, 196-97, 237
American Philosophical Society, 413
American Revolution, 5, 10, 32, 38, 114, 143, 210, 211, 212, 246, 265, 277, 299, 324, 341, 342, 346, 349, 352, 358, 364, 367, 373, 374, 377, 386, 413, 414, 419, 432, 433, 442, 503, 541, 549
Ames, Fisher: *letters from*, 55-59, 187-88
Amherst County, Va., 428
Amsterdam, 22, 64, 132, 165, 229, 233, 432, 520, 529, 553, 554, 558; loans at, 97, 133, 136, 313, by Holy Roman Empire, 480, tax on foreign loans, 480, by U.S., 100, 315 (*see also* Loans); and payment of U.S. foreign debt, 161; rate of exchange at, 159-60, 523-24; speculations in U.S. debt at, 388-93; U.S. bankers at, *see* Willink, Van Staphorst, and Hubbard; and U.S. stocks and bonds, 20-21, 272, 274; U.S. treasury bills at, 70, 506-7, 523. *See also* Short, William; United Netherlands
Andrews, Elezur, 346; *letter to* John Treadwell, 348-49
Andrus, Jabez, 425, 495, 528-29
Annapolis, Md., 260
Anne Arundel County, Md., 428, 511
Anson County, N.C., 429
Antifederalists, 247
Antwerp, 22, 500; loans at, 101, Russian loan at, 20, 228. *See also* Loans; Morris, Gouverneur
Appleton, Nathaniel: *letters from*, 10-11, 153; *letters to*, 10, 241, 550, 557,

Appleton, Nathaniel (*Continued*) 559; and Benjamin Lincoln, 284, 294-95; and payment of interest on public debt, 406; Treasury Department circulars to, 14-15, 78, 422
Apprentices: in hat industry, 337
Argus, 425, 528-29
Arkwright, Sir Richard, 434, 439
Arnold, John, 206-7, 368, 525-26
Arnold, Jonathan, 29
Arnold, Thomas: *letter to*, 29
Arnold, Welcome, 29, 295-96; and Jeremiah Olney, 368-69
Arsenals, 384
Ascension, 309
Aspenwell, Prince, 355
Assignats, *see* France
Assistant Secretary of the Treasury, *see* Coxe, Tench; Duer, William
Assumption of state debts, 80; and Holland loans, 141; and Maryland, 561-63; and North Carolina, 27-28, 32-33, 122-23, 154-55, 191-92, 387-88, 456, 503-5; and Pennsylvania, 382-83, 431; and Rhode Island, 153-57; and South Carolina, 9-10, 154-55
Atkinson, N.H., 414
Attorney General: compensation of, 459, 464. *See also* Bradford, William; Randolph, Edmund
Auditor of the Treasury Department, 405, 430; candidates for the office of, 511; and revenue cutters, 507-8. *See also* Harrison, Richard; Wolcott, Oliver, Jr.
Augusta County, Va., 428
Avera, Thomas, 281

Bagwell, Hickerson, 281
Bailey, Anselm, 275; *letter to* Thomas Newton, Jr., 280
Ballard, Robert, 37, 181-82; *letter to*, 401
Baltimore, Md.: Bank of the U.S., branch at, 518-20; collector of customs at, *see* Williams, Otho H.; deputy collector of customs at, *see* Delozier, Daniel; surveyor of the port of, *see* Ballard, Robert; warden for the port of, 18
Baltimore County, Md., 428
Bankers of U.S. in Amsterdam, *see* Willink, Van Staphorst, and Hubbard

Bank of Boston, *see* Massachusetts Bank
Bank of Maryland, 414-15
Bank of New York, 86, 506, 550-57; and Bank of the U.S., 55, 187, 538-39, branch of, 519-20, oversubscription of, 60-61; cashier of, *see* Seton, William; charter of, 55; and John Cochran, 264; director of, 184 (*see also* King, Rufus); incorporation of, 55; and Samuel Meredith, 69-70, 265; notes of, 120, 515; president of, *see* Verplanck, Guilian; president and directors of, 77, 265, *letters to*, 71, 182, 219, 236; and purchase of public debt, 68-69, 71-73, 77, 122, 176, 202
Bank of North America, 550, 557, 559; cashier of, *see* Francis, Tench; director of, *see* Bingham, William; notes of, 5, 515
Bank of Providence, *see* Providence Bank
Bank of the U.S., 151; and Bank of New York, 55, 187, 519-20, 538-39; branches of, 55, 58, 187, 255-60, 389, 518-20, 538-39, cashiers, 258-59, directors, 258-59, notes of, 259-60, plan for establishing, 258-60, presidents of, 258, request for, 515-16; cashier of, *see* Kean, John; constitution of, 255; and contracts, 389; debts of, 256; deposits of, 256; directors of, 406, 407-8, election of, 157, 201-2, 406-7; and Holland loans, 141, 160-61; laws of, 408; limitations of, 255-56; and Massachusetts Bank, 56-59, 187; and New York State, 123; and Philadelphia, 201-2; "Plan for establishing departments of the Bank of the United States," by Oliver Wolcott, Jr., 258-60; and President of U.S., 406; profits of, 256, 258; and property, 389; and proxies, 406-11; and public faith, 389; and state banks, 55-59, 519-20; stock of, 61, 113-14, 259, oversubscription of, 58, 59-61, 114, speculation in, 59-61, 71, 74-75, 75-76, 185; subscribers of, meeting of, 157-58, and voting rights, 406-11; subscription of, 113-14, 406-7; and trade, 57; and U.S. Government, 57; Oliver Wolcott, Jr., on, 255-60
Banks: capital stock of, 256-57; and deposits, 257; and interest rates, 257;

and manufactures, 146; operations of, 256-57; profits of, 256-57
Baring, Sir Francis, 204-5
Barney, Hommoor, 360
Barns, Asa, 349
Barratt, Andrew, 211-12, 288-89, 317, 400-1
Barrell, Joseph, 45
Bartholomew County, S.C., 429
Barton, William, 26-27, 213, 304-5
Batavia, 42, 43
Bath, District of Maine, 29
Bayard, William, 31-32, 112, 158
Beale, Daniel, 49
Beaufort County, N.C., 429
Beaulieu, Louis Joseph de (Joseph De Beauleau): pension, 462
Beckley, John, 34
Beckwith, George, 270; conversations with Hamilton, 29-30, 104; *letter from*, 265-66
Bedford, Gunning, Jr., 211-12
Bedford County, Pa., 427
Bedford County, Va., 428
Belfast, 86
Bellepré, 473
Belmont, Pa., 114
Benbury, Thomas, 429
Benezet, Daniel, 28
Bengal, 45, 54
Bergen, Elizabeth: pension, 462
Berkeley County, S.C., 429
Berkeley County, Va., 428
Berks County, Pa., 427
Berkshire, England, 5
Berkshire County, Mass., 427
Berlin, 413
Berlin, Conn.: manufacturing at, 346-47
Bermuda Hundred, Va., 476-77
Betsey, 206-7, 236-37, 285, 368-69, 525-26
Betsy, 6, 29, 95-96, 110-11, 118-19, 215, 283, 308-9, 415, 502
Beverly, Mass., 106; cotton manufactory at, 177, 439
Bingham, William: *letters from*, 285-86, 287; *letter to*, 285; and Society for Establishing Useful Manufactures, 285-86
Binghamton, N.Y., 285
Biscoe, George, 69-70; *letter to*, 106
Bissell, James, 6, 502
Bladen County, N.C., 429
Bladensburg, Md., 403

Blankets: manufacture of, 147
Blocks: manufacture of, 443
Board of Treasury, 239-40
Board of War, 114
Boehm, Edmund, 204-5
Bogart, Cornelius J., 367, 368, 532
Bolton, *see* Boulton
Bombay, 43, 45
Bonavista, Newfoundland, 425
Bond, Phineas, 365-67
Boon, Gerrit, 8
Bordeaux, France, 206, 236, 368
Bordley, John Beale, 376-77; *letter from*, 490-93; Treasury Department circular to, 35-37
Boston, Mass., 34, 45, 119, 182, 187, 213, 321, 332, 366, 371, 374, 375, 416, 417, 440; assessors of, 188; Bank of the U.S., branch of, in, 518-20, directors of, 201-2; collector of customs at, *see* Lincoln, Benjamin; manufacturing in, 162-63, of duck in, 372-73, of sailcloth in, 372; naval officer of port of, 225; surveyor of port of, *see* Melville, Thomas
Boston Duck or Sail Cloth Manufactory, 163, 372
Boston Glass House, 163
Botetourt County, Va., 428
Boudinot, Elias (N.J.), 152, 173
Boudinot, Elias (N.Y.), 130
Boulton (Bolton), Matthew, 103
Bounties: on cotton, 438; on duck, 162-63; on glass, 162-63; on head matter, 433; on manufactures, 384; in Massachusetts, 372-73; on mulberry trees, 355-56; for potash, 345; on sailcloth, 163; George Washington on, 384; for wool manfactures, 322, 327, 343
Bowen, Jabez, 78; *letters to*, 80, 493
Brackenridge, James, 429
Bradburn, Butler, 303
Bradford, William, 88-90
Bradley, ——— (Mr.), 359
Bragg, John, 121
Brandy, *see* Distilled spirits
Brantsen, Gerard, 228-29
Brasher, Ephraim, 70
Brass: manufacture of, 147, in Connecticut, 324, in Providence, R.I., 446
Breck, Samuel: *letter from*, 162-63
Breck, ——— (Mrs. Samuel), 163
Bridgewater, Mass., 373

Bristol, Conn.: manufacturing at, 346-47
Bristol, England, 448
Bristol, R.I., 308-9
British East India Co., 43, 45
Brown, James: *letter to*, 113-14
Brown, John, 183-84, 209-11, 213-14, 305-6, 529, 542-43; *letter to* William Irvine, 210-11
Brown, Moses, 305-6, 543; *letter to* John Dexter, 432-41
Brown, Smith, *see* Almy and Brown
Brown and Francis, 213-14. *See also* Brown, John; Francis, John
Browning, —— (Capt.), 5-6, 95
Brownson, Stephen, 347
Brunswick County, N.C., 429
Brunswick County, Va., 428
Brussels, Joseph: pension, 462
Buchanan, Robert, 88-90
Buckingham County, Va., 428
Bucks County, Pa., 123, 427
Bull, Martin, 347
Burdick, Oliver, 205
Burke County, N.C., 429
Burlington, Vt., 91
Burr, Aaron, 247, 365, 367, 530-32, 536, 537
Burr, Josiah, 319
Burr, Oliver, 334
Burr, O., and Co.: *letter to* John Chester, 336-38; manufacturing of hats, 334-35
Burral and Gruman, 341
Burrall, Jonathan, 545
Burton, Robert: and U.S. loan in London, 99, 100, 227-28, 312-13, 482
Bush, George, 307
Butler, Richard (Gen.), 209-11
Buttons: imports from Europe, 361, 362; manufacture of, in Connecticut, 324, 347, 358-61, 362-63

Cabinets: manufacture of, in Connecticut, 339-40, in Providence, R.I., 448
Cabot, Andrew, 177
Cabot, George, 439; *letter from*, 177-80; *letter to*, 106
Cabot, John, 177
Calin, 51
Callahan, John, 225
Calvert, Md., 413
Calvert County, Md., 428
Cambridge, Mass., 104, 196
Camden, N.C., 69-70

Camden, S.C., 212
Camden County, N.C., 429
Campbell, Alexander, 513
Campbell, William: *letter from*, 173-75
Campbell County, Va., 428
Canada: fur trade, 337-38
Candal, William, 321, 354, 355
Candles: manufacture of, in Providence, R.I., 445; manufacture of spermaceti candles, in Providence, R.I., 433, 434
Canton, China, 13; trade with, 38-55; U.S. consul at, *see* Shaw, Samuel; vice-consul at, *see* Randall, Thomas; viceroy of, 46
Cape Fear, N.C.: lighthouse on, 173-75
Cape Fear River, 175, 249-50; stakage of, 317
Cape Francois, *see* Cap-Français
Cape Henry, Va.: lighthouse at, 19, 310
Cape of Good Hope, 45, 49
Cap-Français (Cape Francois), 6, 26, 464
Capital: lack of, and manufactures, 145; raising of, for manufactures, 146-47
Carding machines, 434, 435, 439. *See also* Cotton, manufacture of
Cards: manufacture of, in Providence, R.I., 446
Cargell, Benjamin, 354, 355
Carlisle, Pa., 469
Caroline County, Md., 428
Caroline County, Va., 428
Carpets: manufacture of, 147
Carriages: manufacture of, in Connecticut, 323, 346, 351
Carrington, Edward, 130, 428; *letters from*, 275-82, 299-304; *letter from* Thomas Newton, Jr., 278-79; *letter from* Drury Ragsdale, 280-82; *letter from* Edward Stevens, 300-4
Carrington, Mayo, 428-29
Carteret County, N.C., 429
Cartwright, Edmund, 86
Casks: manufacture of, in Connecticut, 346
Caswell County, N.C., 429
Cayenne, French Guiana: cotton from, 180
Cazenove, Théophile, 8, 31-32
Cecil County, Md., 428

Chace, Maxwell, 478
Chaloner, John: *letter to*, 559
Chamberlayne, Edward P., 281
Chandler, John, 534
Channing, William, 5-6, 95-96, 205, 206-7, 283-84, 304-5, 368, 455, 478
Charles City County, Va., 428
Charles County, Md., 428
Charleston, S.C., 10, 164, 170, 469; and Bank of the U.S., 201-2, branch of, 518-20; collector of customs at, *see* Holmes, Isaac; duties paid at, 3-4; and "Excise Law," 9; naval officer for the port of, 143
Charleston County, S.C., 429
Charlestown, Mass., 119
Charlotte County, Va., 428
Chatham, Conn.: manufacturing at, 349-50
Chatham County, N.C., 429
Cherokees: treaty with, 402
Chester, John, 214-15, 357, 427; *letter from*, 318-63; *letter from* O. Burr and Co., 336-38; *letter from* Elisha Colt, 324-27; *letter from* Peter Colt, 319-24; *letter from* Joseph P. Cooke, 334-35; *letter from* James Davenport, 340-41; *letter from* William Hillhouse, 332-34; *letter from* Benjamin Huntington, 329-30; *letter from* Amasa Learned, 338-39; *letters from* Christopher Leffingwell, 330-31, 332; *letters from* John Mix, Jr., 357-58, 358-61, 361-63, 363; *letter from* Roger Newberry, 341-46; *letter from* Jonathan Palmer, Jr., 339-40; *letter from* Heman Swift, 328-29; *letter from* John Treadwell, 346-49; *letter from* Chauncey Whittelsey, 349-53; *letter from* William Williams, 353-57
Chester, Pa., 213
Chester County, Pa., 427
Chester County, S.C., 429
Chesterfield County, S.C., 429
Chesterfield County, Va., 428
Chew, Benjamin, 212, 288-89
Child, Francis, 122-23, 191-92, 387-88
Child labor, *see* Labor
China: admeasurement of ships in, 39, 40; and debts, 54; Emperor of, 51; and export duties, 44; and frauds, 49, 143; government of, 38, 39; and Hong merchants, 39, 40, 43, 45, 46, 47, 48, 50-51, 52, 53, 54; and import

duties, 44; mandarins, influence of, 39, 40, 42, 44, 46, 47, 48, 49, 50, 51; monopoly in, 40; tea, 13, 378-79; trade with, 38-55, 143-44, frauds in, 53; viceroy of, 47, 48. *See also* Canton; Ginseng
Chocolate: manufacturing of, in Providence, R.I., 440
Chowan County, N.C., 429
Church, Angelica Schuyler (Mrs. John B.), 4-5; *letters to*, 266-67, 548-49
Church, John B., 112, 289, 559; *letter from*, 4-5
Churchman, John, 412-13
Cincinnati, 211
Civil list: "Estimate of the Expenditures for the Civil List . . . for the year 1792," 458-63; and Holland loans, 141
Clarendon County, S.C., 429
Clark, Peleg, 94
Clarke, John, 105
Clayton, James, 318, 400-1
Clayton, Joshua, 317-18, 400-1
Clementina, 305, 455, 488
Clermont County, S.C., 429
Clinton, George, 246-47; *letter from* George Washington, 206
Clocks: manufacture of, in Providence, R.I., 445
Cloth: manufacture of, in Virginia, 280-82
Clymer, George, 427
Coaches: manufacture of, in Providence, R.I., 446
Coal: produced in Connecticut, 344
"Coasting Act," 512; and smuggling, 198-99. *See also* Congress of U.S., acts of, "An Act for Registering and Clearing Vessels, Regulating the Coasting Trade, and for other purposes"
Coasting trade: and distilled spirits, 198-99; ships in, 243, 412, 538, duties on, 28, fees of, 107, 198, 295
Cobb, Nathan, 332
Cochran, John, 264, 288; *letter to*, 307; and purchase of public debt, 296, 306, 310-11, 377-78
Cocoa: duty on, 445, 543
Coffee: duty on, 543; tare on, 449
Cogdell, John, 218
Coins and coinage, 101-3; of France, 103; information on, 228; Spanish dollars, 4-5, 52-53

Coit, Daniel L., 319, 339
Coit and Lathrop, 339
Colchester, Conn.: manufacturing at, 319, 321, 329
Collectors of customs: at Alburg, Vt., see Keyes, Stephen; at Alexandria, Va., see Lee, Charles; at Annapolis, Md., see Davidson, John; at Baltimore, Md., see Williams, Otho H.; at Bermuda Hundred, Va., see Heth, William; at Boston, Mass., see Lincoln, Benjamin; at Charleston, S.C., see Holmes, Isaac; at Frenchman's Bay, District of Maine, see Jordan, Meletiah; at Georgetown, S.C., see Cogdell, John; at Great Egg Harbor, N.J., see Benezet, Daniel; at Marblehead, Mass., see Gerry, Samuel, and Harris, Richard; at New Bedford, Mass., see Pope, Edward; at New Bern, N.C., see Daves, John; at New London, Conn., see Huntington, Jedediah; at Newport, R.I., see Ellery, William; at New York City, see Lamb, John; at Nottingham, Md., see Biscoe, George; at Perth Amboy, N.J., see Halsted, John; at Philadelphia, see Delany, Sharp; at Plankbridge, N.C., see Gregory, Isaac; at Portsmouth, N.H., see Whipple, Joseph; at Providence, R.I., see Olney, Jeremiah; at Wilmington, Del., see Bush, George; at Wilmington, N.C., see Read, James; and abstract of duties, 488; and Bank of New York, 69-70; and certificates of registry, 15, 16, 107, 108, 119-20, 180, 181, 197-98, 215, 222, 225, 284, 308, 309, 416; and coasting vessels, 107, 109, 295, 412; compensation of, 260-61, 494; and customhouse fees, 81, 107, 109, 119, 120, 197-98, 199, 217-18, 450; and drawbacks, 189-90; and hydrometers, 262, 272; and impost, 516-17; and moieties, 111; monthly schedule of bonds, 5, 309; and Providence Bank, 518; and public debt, interest on, 190; returns of, 197, 488, of bonds, 222, of exports, 132, of quarterly accounts, 132, 223, of tonnage, 295; and revenue laws, infractions of, 26-27; and ships, admeasurement of, 11-12, 16-17, 18, 82-83, 95, 107, 109, 119-20, 197-98, 208, 222-23, condemned, 283, entry of, 516-17, licenses, 120, 308, manifests, 199, 295, 455, registers, 18, 82-83, 213, 284, 295, 453, 505, seizures of, 6, 78-79; and smuggling, 83-84, 132; and state of public monies, 222-23; and supervisors of the revenue, 85, 430; and thermometers, 83, 262, 272; and tonage duties, 516-17; and treasurer of U.S., 69-70, 222, 260; and weekly return of monies, 5, 93, 120, 132, 215, 284, 309, 412, 541. See also Treasury Department circulars to the collectors of the customs
Collectors of revenue: appointment of, 430; and "Excise Law," 304; for New Hampshire, see Wentworth, George; in North Carolina, 84-85
Colleton County, S.C., 429
Collins, James, 427-28
Colon, ——— (Mrs.), 274
Colt, Elisha: letter to John Chester, 324-27
Colt, Peter: letter to John Chester, 319-24
Columbia, 45, 48
Columbia College, 367, 532; president of, see Johnson, William Samuel
Commerce: with northern Europe, 386. See also Trade
Commercial treaty: conversation about, with Jean Baptiste de Ternant, 290-92; wih Great Britain, 291-92
Commissioner for settling accounts between U.S. and the individual states, 490
Commissioners of loans: for Delaware, see Tilton, James; for Georgia, see Wylly, Richard; for Maryland, see Harwood, Thomas; for Massachusetts, see Appleton, Nathaniel; for New York, see Cochran, John; for North Carolina, see Skinner, William; for Pennsylvania, see Smith, Thomas; for Rhode Island, see Bowen, Jabez; for Virginia, see Hopkins, John; clerks for, 525; compensation of, 461; expenses of, 465; mistakes of, 422; and public debt, 14-15, interest on, 242; and Rhode Island, 156; and Secretary of Treasury, 14-15; stationery for, 525; and U.S. Government stock, 244-45. See also Treasury Department cir-

culars to the commissioners of loans

Committee Appointed to Obtain Information on Manufacturing in Providence: *letter to* John Dexter, 441-49

Comptroller of the Treasury, *see* Eveleigh, Nicholas; Wolcott, Oliver, Jr.

Condict, Silas: *letter to* Aaron Dunham, 193-94

Confederacy, 464

Confederation, 387

Congress of U.S., 413; and admeasurement of ships, 16; and commerce of U.S., 16; compensation of members of, 459; and distilled spirits, 13; and foreign loans, 233; and French loans, 394; and "Funding Act," 154-55; and import duties, 3-4; and indents of interest, 88-90; meeting of, 383-84; and North Carolina paper money, 503-5; and public debt, purchase of, 244-45, report on, 271; and return of duties, 223; and shipbuilding, 16; and tonnage duties, 37; George Washington's message to, 402, 403. *See also* House of Representatives; Senate

Congress of U.S., acts of: "An Act to allow the Baron de Glaubeck the pay of a Captain in the Army of the United States" (September 29, 1789), 549; "An Act allowing Lieutenant-Colonel Tousard an equivalent for his pension for life" (April 30, 1794), 462-63; "An Act to authorize the purchase of a tract of land for the use of the United States" (July 5, 1790), 484; "An Act declaring the assent of Congress to certain acts of the states of Maryland, Georgia, Rhode Island and Providence Plantations" (August 11, 1790), 18, 38; "An Act to establish the Judicial Courts of the United States" (September 24, 1789), 483-84; "An Act to establish the Treasury Department" (September 2, 1789), 539-40; "An Act for the establishment and support of Lighthouses, Beacons, Buoys, and Public Piers" (August 7, 1789), 208-9; "An Act to explain and amend an act intituled 'An act making

further provision for the payment of the debt of the United States' " (March 2, 1791), 513; "An Act for finally adjusting and satisfying the claims of Frederick William de Steuben" (June 4, 1790), 462; "An Act fixing the time for the next annual meeting of Congress" (March 2, 1791), 384; "An Act for giving effect to the several Acts therein mentioned, in respect to the State of Rhode Island and Providence Plantations" (June 14, 1790), 29; "An Act imposing duties on the tonnage of ships or vessels" (July 20, 1790), 506; "An Act to incorporate the subscribers to the Bank of the United States" (February 25, 1791), 114, 255-60, 406-11; "An Act for making compensation to the Commissioners of Loans for extraordinary expenses" (March 3, 1791), 465; "An Act making further provision for the collection of the duties by law imposed on Teas, and to prolong the term for the payment of the Duties on Wines" (March 3, 1791), 262-63, 378-79, 560; "An Act making further provision for the payment of the debts of the United States" (August 10, 1790), 13-14, 438, 443, 453-54; "An Act making provision for the (payment of the) Debt of the United States" (August 4, 1790), 1, 72-73, 80, 88-90, 154, 156, 263-64, 389, 390, 431, 456, 458, 486, 540-41, 561-63; "An Act making Provision for the Reduction of the Public Debt" (August 12, 1790), 1, 67-68, 72-73, 244-45, 271, 293-95, 476-77, 548; "An Act to provide for mitigating or remitting the forfeitures and penalties accruing under the revenue laws, in certain cases therein mentioned" (May 26, 1790), 11-12, 205-6, 207, 304-5, 402, 477-78; "An Act to provide more effectually for the collection of the duties imposed by law on goods, wares and merchandise imported into the United States, and on the tonnage of ships or vessels" (August 4, 1790), 17, 18, 78-79, 83-84, 111, 189-90, 198-99, 378-79, 425-26, 449-50, 455-56, 476, 495,

Congress of U.S. acts of (*Continued*) 496, 506-8, 516-17, 541; "An Act providing compensations for the officers of the Judicial Courts of the United States, and for Jurors and Witnesses and for other purposes" (March 3, 1791), 466, 563-64; "An Act to recognize and adapt to the Constitution of the United States the establishment of the Troops raised under the Resolves of the United States in Congress assembled, and for other purposes therein mentioned" (September 29, 1789), 471; "An Act for Registering and Clearing Vessels, Regulating the Coasting Trade, and for other purposes" (September 1, 1789), 11-12, 15-17, 81-83, 94-95, 109, 119, 120, 197-99, 215, 224, 225, 460, 483-84, 512-13; "An Act to regulate the Collection of the Duties imposed by law on the tonnage of ships or vessels, and on goods, wares and merchandises imported into the United States" (July 31, 1789), 111, 118-19, 189-90; "An Act for regulating the Military Establishment of the United States" (April 30, 1790), 471-72; "An Act repealing, after the last day of June next, the duties heretofore laid upon Distilled Spirits imported from abroad, and laying others in their stead; and also upon Spirits distilled within the United States, and for appropriating the same" (March 3, 1791), 9-10, 84-85, 186, 188, 206-7, 217-18, 236-37, 248-49, 303-4, 403-4, 426-31, 487-88; "An Act supplemental to the act 'establishing the Treasury Department,' and for a farther compensation to certain officers" (March 3, 1791), 464

Connecticut, 35, 367, 368, 377, 458, 461, 465, 532, 546; "An Act in alteration of the Act entituled an Act to promote the making of Raw Silk within this State" (May, 1784), 356; "An Act for the Encouragement of Certain Manufactures within this State" (May, 1788), 322, 343; "An Act for the encouragement of the Woolen Manufacture within this State" (January, 1789), 322; agriculture in, 332, 333, 334, 344; apprentices, tax on, 330; Board of Assistants, 334, 534; bounty for woolen manufactures, 343; coal production, 344; codfishing, 329; comptroller of public accounts of, 91; Council, members of, 328, 329, 334, 346, 353; duties paid in, 3; flax production, 333; governor of, *see* Huntington, Samuel; Nathaniel Hazard on, 529-37; hemp production, 344; inspector of revenue, *see* Chester, John; invalid pensions in, 470; legislature of, 321, 322, 329, 332, 334, 339, 341, 349, 350, 366, 367, 535, 536; lieutenant governor of, *see* Wolcott, Oliver, Sr.; lighthouse in, 520; lottery in, 321, 322-23, for wool manufactures, 325, 354; manufactures in, 318-63, of brass, 324, of buttons, 324, 347-48, 358-61, 362-63, of cabinets, 339-40, of carriages, 323, 346, 351, of casks, 346, of cotton, 320, 331, 332, 335, 340-41, 343, 347, 351, 354, of cotton cards, 344, of crockery, 331, domestic, 320-21, 326, 328, 332-33, 342, 347, 353, 355, of duck, 319-20, of earthenware, 346, of furniture, 323, of geneva, 350, of hats, 324, 334, 336-38, 339, 341, 345, 348, 349, of iron, 323, 328-29, 331, 335, 344, 350, 351, of leather, 323, 338-39, 344-45, 351, of linen, 319, 320, 328, 329, 340, 341, 342, 343-44, 348, 350, 353, 355, of lumber, 345, of nails, 334, 341, 342, 344, 351, of pewter, 324, of potash and pearlash, 335, 345, 350, 351, of rope, 338, of rum, 350, of saddlecloth, 336, 338, of saddles, 345, of sailcloth, 338, 340, of saltpeter, 346, of shoes and boots, 349, of silk, 349, 354, 355-57, of silver, 324, of snuff, 350, of steel, 349, 352-53, of stockings, 320, 357, of tin, 324, of tools, 342, 351, 354, of tow cloth, 342, value of, 323, of wood, 323, of wool, 324-27, 328, 329, 332, 333, 340, 342, 343, 347, 348, 351, 353-54, 355, of wool cards, 344; mulberry tree cultivation in, 355-56, 357; poll tax in, 330, 337; quarries in, 350; revenue cutter for, 96, 309, 425; scarcity, of wool in, 326, 333, of machines, 327; shipbuilding in, 329,

338; slitting mills in, 335; supervisor of revenue for, see Chester, John; survey of inspection in, 427; tax laws of, 329-30; and trade with Massachusetts, 371; U.S. attorney for the District of, 367 (see also Edwards, Pierpont); U.S. Senator from, see Johnson, William Samuel; and Wyoming Valley, 376-77

Connecticut River, 214, 345

Connecticut Society of Silk Manufacturers, 356-57

Constable, William, 25, 152, 157-58; letters to, 500-1, 527; and speculation in U.S. securities, 74-75

Constitution (U.S.), 503; adoption by Rhode Island, 29; ratification of, 247, 511; signer of, see Bedford, Gunning, Jr., and Williams, William

Constitutional Convention, 367, 386, 511; delegates to, see Johnson, William Samuel, and Pinckney, Charles Cotesworth

Continental Army, 377; Artillery, 38; Corps of Engineers, 246; deputy quartermaster general of southern department, 142-43; and half-pay, 418-19; inspector general, 412-13, 462, 475

Continental Congress, 114, 123, 334, 541; acts of, 462, 464, 470; bills of credit, 27-28; members of, 353 (see also Brown, John; Grayson, William; Irvine, William; Latimer, Henry; Peabody, Nathaniel; Peters, Richard; Smith, Melancton; Tilton, James; Wynkoop, Henry); and Pennsylvania land purchase, 239-40; president of, 549; resolutions of, 27-28, 418-19

Continental line, 503-5

Continental loan officers: for North Carolina, 27-28

Contracts: and Bank of the U.S., 389; for clothing, 110; lighthouses, 19, 520, 524-25; and Pennsylvania land purchase, 239-40; for stakage of Cape Fear River, 249-50, 317, of Neuse River, 121-22; for supply of western posts, 244, 289-90

Cooke, Joseph, 213-14

Cooke, Joseph P., 336, 341; letter to John Chester, 334-35

Cooper, William: letter to, 8

Cooperstown, N.Y., 8

Cordage: manufacture of, in Providence, R.I., 448; sale of, in China, 39-42

Corn: in Virginia, 275

Cornwall, Conn.: manufacturing at, 328-29

Corporations: and manufacturing, 252

Cory, William, 108

Cotterell, Thomas, 6, 118-19, 215, 283, 308, 415, 502, 542

Cotton: bounties on, 438; and China trade, 43, 44-45, 143; duties on, 438; growth of, in Virginia, 276; manufacture of, 86, 147, 177-80, 184, in Connecticut, 320, 321, 331, 332, 335, 340-41, 343, 344, 347, 351, 354, in Great Britain, 437, in Ireland, 436, machines for, 86, in Massachusetts, 439, mechanics for, 216-17, in Providence, R.I., 432, 434-40, 448, and Samuel Slater, 432, and Society for Establishing Useful Manufactures, 24-25, 74, 184, 214, in South Carolina, 170, in Virginia, 279, 280, 281, 301-3; in South, defects of, 437-38; from West Indies, 438

Cotton cards: manufacture of, 374

Counterfeiting: of Continental loan office certificates, 27-28

Courts: Federal, compensation of judges of, 458, 475

Cox, John Henry, 49

Cox, Peter, 92

Coxe, Tench, 214, 366-67, 451, 533, 534, 535, 537; and authorship of prospectus of Society for Establishing Useful Manufactures, 144; A Brief Examination of Lord Sheffield's Observations on the Commerce of the United States, 376; letter from, 143-44; and Society for Establishing Useful Manufactures, 269; and supervisors of revenue, 85

Craig, Andrew, 8

Craigie, Andrew, 56, 545

Craik, William, 511

Crane Creek, 425

Craven County, N.C., 429

Creditors: and domestic loan of 1790, 154-55; and "Funding Law," 263-64

Crockery: manufacture of, in Connecticut, 331

Croghan, George, 8

Crooke, Robert, 205, 478

Cudworth, Benjamin, 207, 429-30
Culp, Daniel, 304
Culpeper County, Va., 428
Cumberland County, N.C., 429
Cumberland County, Pa., 427
Cumberland County, Va., 428
Cundall, William, see Candal
Currituck County, N.C., 429
Customs: boat, 200; houses, 17, 180, 222-23; officers, and forfeitures, 6, and informers, 309, and moieties, 215, 304-5, 478, and sale of condemned ship, 111. See also Collectors of customs; Duties; Revenue; Revenue cutters; Ships
Cuyler, Jacob, 196
Cuyler, Richard, 196

Dabney, James, 302
Dallas, Alexander: letter to, 529
Danbury, Conn.: manufacturing at, 334-35, 336-38, 341
Dangerfield, Bathurst, 35
Danville, Va., 210
Darlington County, S.C., 429
Dauphin County, Pa., 427
Davenport, James, 319, 334; letter to John Chester, 340-41
Daves, John, 225; compensation of, 429; letters from, 449-50, 497
Davidson, John: letter to, 260
Davidson: troops at, 474
Davie, William R.: letter from, 503-5
Davis, Samuel, 194-95, 293
Deane, 464
De Beauleau, Joseph, see Beaulieu, Louis Joseph de
Debt, see Assumption of state debts; Public debt
Declaration of Independence, 353
Deelen, John Gerard, 481
Delany, Sharp: letter from, 286; letters to, 189, 189-90, 307; Treasury Department circular to, 496
Delaware, 121, 458, 461, 465; agriculture in, 376-77; auditor of, 289; commissioner of loans for, see Tilton, James; duties paid in, 3; invalid pensions in, 470; president of, see Clayton, Joshua; regiment, 212; supervisor of revenue for, 317, 400-1 (see also Barratt, Andrew; Latimer, Henry); survey of inspection, 428; U.S. judge for the District of, see

Bedford, Gunning, Jr.; U.S. Representative from, see Vining, John
Delaware County, Pa., 427
Delaware River, 171, 244, 379, 380, 381, 382, 385
Delozier, Daniel: letter from, 163-64
Demerara, British Guiana, 180
Denmark: and China trade, 39, 53
Department of State, see State Department
Department of Treasury, see Treasury Department
Department of War, see War Department
D'Eprémesnil, Duval, see Eprémesnil, Duval d'
Derby, John, 45
Derbyshire, England, 440
Detroit, 266
Dewey, John, 346
Dexter, Andrew, 448
Dexter, John S., 214-15, 442; compensation of, 427; letter from, 432-49; letter from Moses Brown, 432-41; letter from Committee Appointed to Obtain Information on Manufacturing in Providence, 441-49
Dexter, Stephen, 206-7
Dickinson, John, 86
Dickson, David, 440
Dickson, Livingston, and Co., 440
Digges, Thomas, 81, 86
Dighton, Mass., 284
Dinwiddie County, Va., 428
Distilled spirits, 18-19; and coasting trade, 198-99; and domestic materials, 248; duties on, 2, 401, 426-31; export of, 309; exporters of, 378, 476; and foreign materials, 248; gin, forfeiture of, 403-4; import of, 13; imported class, 249; "old stock," 217-18, 248; seizures of, 206-7, 236, 248-49, 285; and South Carolina, 9-10; in Virginia, 302-4. See also "Excise Law"; Supervisors of the revenue
Distilleries: in Connecticut, 350; in Massachusetts, 187-88; in New Hampshire, 186; in North Carolina, 84-85; in Providence, R.I., 433-34; in Virginia, 279, 302-4
District of Maine, see Maine
Dobbs County, N.C., 429
Dolphin, 478
Domestic manufactures: in Connecti-

cut, 320-21, 326, 328, 332-33, 334, 342, 347, 353, 355; in Rhode Island, 436; in Virginia, 299-304

Donald, Alexander, 99-100, 482; and London loan, 227-28, 312-13

Donald and Burton, 312-13

Donnaldson, John, 310

Dorcaster, England, 86

Dorchester, Lord: address to western Indians, 265-66, 270

Dorchester County, Md., 428

Dordrecht, Holland, 101

Dove, 18-19

Dover, Del., 211, 377

Drawbacks, 189-90

Drayton, Stephen, 142-43

Droz (Drost), Jean Pierre, 101-3, 228

Drugs: duty on, 517-18; manufacture of, 517-18

Duane, James, 483-84; *letter from*, 25; *letter to*, 11-12; Treasury Department circular to, 402

Dublin Society for Promoting Husbandry and Other Useful Arts in Ireland, 437

Dublin Society's Weekly Observations, 437

Duck: bounty on, in Massachusetts, 163; manufacture of, 162-63, in Boston, 372-73, in Connecticut, 319-20

Duer, William, 24-25, 90, 152, 507, 546; and Bank of the U.S. stock, 61, 74-75; Hamilton on, 74-75; *letters from*, 30, 71; *letter to*, 74-75; and Scioto Co., 253-55; and Society for Establishing Useful Manufactures, 267-69

Dumas, Charles F. W., 387

Dunham, Aaron: compensation of, 427; *letter from*, 193-94; *letter from Silas Condict*, 193-94

Duplin County, N.C., 429

Dutch, *see* United Netherlands

Dutch East India Co.: Holland loan for, 134, 139

Duties, 37; abstracts of, 488; on buttons, 361; in China, 44; on coasting ships, 28; on cocoa, 445, 543; on coffee, 543; collection of, 503-4; on cordage, 278; on cotton, 438; on distilled spirits, 2, 9-10, 401; drawback of, 189-90; on drugs and dyeing wood, 453-54, 506, 517-18; on grindstones, 223-24; on hats, 443; import, 327, 330, 458; on leather, 339, 444; on livestock, 273, 370; on molasses, 19; on Negroes, 370; payment of, and Providence Bank, 489-90, 514-15; on pumpings, 19; refund of, 29; report to Congress on, 3-4; return of, 223; on rum, 187-88; statement of, 2-4; on teas, 378-79. *See also* Tonnage, duties

Dwight, Timothy, 365, 367

Dycas's hydrometer, 212-13

Dyeing woods and drugs: duties on, 453-54, 506, 517-18

Earthenware: manufacture of, in Connecticut, 346

Eastern Shore, Md., 490, 511

East Greenwich, R.I.: manufacturing at, 434, 436

East Hartford, Conn., 350

East River, 440

Eastwood, James, 15

Eastwood, Thomas, 15

Eddy (Eddie), Thomas, 202-3

Edenton, N.C., 121

Edgecombe County, N.C., 429

Edgefield County, S.C., 429

Edinburgh, University of, 287

Edwards, Jonathan, 367, 532

Edwards, Pierpont, 366-67, 532, 534, 535, 536

Eells, Cushing, 332

Elbert, John, 471

Eliot, Jared: treatise on field husbandry, 356

Elizabeth (Elizabethtown), N.J., 87, 172, 189

Elizabeth City County, Va., 428

Ellery, William, 181, 205, 305, 478; *letters from*, 5-6, 18-19, 93-96, 110-11, 118-20, 180-81, 214-15, 223-24, 283-84, 307-9, 378-79, 403-4, 415, 476, 493-94, 502, 514-15, 541-43, 560; *letters to*, 25, 105, 207, 226, 416, 487, 503, 505; and supervisor of revenue, 494

Elliot, Robert, 244, 288

Elliot and Williams, 243-44, 289-90; *letter to*, 287-88

Elliott, Aaron (father), 349, 352

Elliott, Aaron (son): *letter to Hezekiah Lane*, 352-53

Emigrants: and labor force, 145

Empress of China, 38, 39, 41, 42

England, *see* Great Britain

English, Andrew, 163

Eprémesnil, Duval d', 254-55

Essex County, Mass., 426

Essex County, Va., 428

"Estimate of the Expenses . . . for the Defensive Protection of the Frontiers Against the Indians . . . ," 471-74

"Estimate of the Sums Necessary for Discharging certain Liquidated Claims upon the United States . . . ," 464-66

Europe, 374, 434; abundance of money in, 451-52; imports from, 279, 282, 324, 331, 338, 348, 446, of buttons, 359, 361, 362, of shoes and boots, 444, of tea, 378-79; manufactures in, 251, 252; procurement of machines in, 147; recruitment of labor in, 147; U.S. credit and stock in, 451-52, information about, needed, 315-16

Eveleigh, Nicholas, 539-40

"Excise Law": and assumption of state debts, 9-10; and collectors of revenue, 304; and North Carolina, 504; and South Carolina, 9-10; in Virginia, 303-4. *See also* Congress of U.S., acts of, "An Act Repealing, after the last day of June next, the duties heretofore laid upon Distilled Spirits imported from abroad, and laying others in their stead; and also upon Spirits distilled within the United States, and for appropriating the same"

Executive departments: heads of, 30

Exports: return of, 16, 81, 387, 496, 510

Fabrics: manufacture of, 145-46

Fairfax County, Va., 428

Fairfield County, Conn.: manufacturing in, 334-35

Fairfield County, S.C., 429

Farmers-General, 315, 499, 500

Farming, *see* Agriculture

Farmington, Conn.: manufacturing at, 319, 321, 322, 346-48

Fauquier County, Va., 428

Fayetteville, N.C., 85, 122

Fearon, Robert, 363-64, 366, 530

Federal District, 246

Federalists, 32, 173, 177

Fenner, Arthur, 157

Fenno, John, 366, 368

Ferret, 105, 195

Finch, Joseph, 5, 95, 180

Fire engines: manufacture of, in Providence, R.I., 446

Fishing: for cod, 329; ships, 538

Fitzgerald, John: *letter from*, 515-16

Flagg, John, 297, 299

Flax, 162: production of, in Connecticut, 333; in Virginia, 275, 276. *See also* Linen

Flemington, N.J., 379

Flint, Royal: *letter from* Trustees for Daniel Parker and Co., 545-46; *letter to* John Ross, 544-46

Fluvanna County, Va., 428

Forbes, James, 508-9

Foreign debt, *see* Public debt

Foreign loans, *see* Loans

Foreign officers: debt due, 22, 97, 315, 394-96

Forfeitures, 111; of gin, 403-4; mitigation and remission of, 402, 525-26

Forrest, Thomas, 264

Fort Harmar, 473

Fortitude, 16, 108

Fort Knox, 473

Fort Pitt, 210, 211, 469, 474

Fort Rensselaer, 469

Fort Washington, 211

Fort William and Mary, 242-43

Foster, Theodore: *letter from*, 12; *letter to*, 153-57

Fox, George: *letter from*, 204-5

Fox, Nathaniel, Jr., 281

Foxcroft, John, 363-65

France, 15, 165, 451; agent at Canton, 52; *arrêt* of August 30, 1784, 290, 292; assignats, depreciation of, 2, 23, 66, 129, 141, 159-60, 315, 523-24, 553; bankers at Amsterdam, 142, 479, 553-54; chargé d'affaires in U.S., *see* Otto, Louis; and Chinese silk, 53; coins of, 103; Commissaries of the National Treasury, and payment of U.S. debt to France, 227, 229, 479, 481, 523-24; Committee of Finance, 64; Comptroller General of Finance, *see* Lambert, Charles; conditions in, 30, 254, 391; constitution, 229; consul general for Delaware, New Jersey, New York, and Pennsylvania, *see* Holker, John; Director General of Finances, *see* Necker, Jacques; émigrés, 254; Estates General, 255; Farmers-General, 315, 499, 500; fisheries,

433; Genoese Minister at, *see* Spinola, Christoforo Vincenzo de; Inspector General of Manufactures, *see* Holker, John; King of, 228, 229, 290, 394, 464; loans, 394 (July 16, 1782), 394 (February 25, 1783); manufactures in, 252; marine agent, *see* Holker, John; Minister for Foreign Affairs, *see* Lessart, Claude Antoine de Valdec de, *and* Montmorin Saint-Herem, Armand Marc, comte de; Minister of Interior, *see* Lessart; Claude Antoine de Valdec de; Minister of Marine, *see*, Lessart; Claude Antoine de Valdec de; Minister Plenipotentiary to U.S., *see* Ternant, Jean Baptiste de; money, commission on, 228, rate of exchange, 22, 553; National Assembly, 502-3, decrees of, 290, 292, and U.S. debt to France, 65, 66; Parlement of Paris, 254-55; and Scioto Co., 253; trade with China, 39; Treaty of 1778, 290, 386-87, of commerce, 104, 290-92; United Netherlands, Minister to, *see* Brantsen, Gerard; and U.S., 29-30; U.S. debt to, 22, 63-67, 97, 132-33, 315, and Antwerp loan, 553-54, payment of, 98, 129, 135-36, 140, 141-42, 159-60, 161, 165, 227, 229, 394-96, proposal to purchase, 62-63, and revolt in Haiti, 219-20, 225-26, 238, 265, and Schweizer, Jeanneret, and Co., 161, speculation in, 390-91; and U.S. debt to foreign officers, 315; U.S. legation, secretary to, *see* Short, William; U.S. loan in, possibility of, 1-2, 3; U.S. tonnage duties, claims against, 290-92; vice consul to U.S., *see* La Forest, Antoine René Charles Mathurin de

Francis, John, 183-84, 213-14, 529
Francis, Tench: drafts of, 489-90; payment of interest on public debt, 78, 550
Franking: and treasurer of U.S., 270
Franklin, Benjamin, 204-5, 364, 367
Franklin, William, 365-67, 530
Franklin, William Temple, 204-5
Franklin, Conn.: manufacturing at, 329
Franklin County, N.C., 429
Franklin County, Pa., 427
Franklin County, Va., 428
Fraser, Thomas, 79, 163-64

Frauds: and China trade, 143; and revenue, 206-7
Frazer, William, 561
Frederick County, Md., 130, 428
Frederick County, Va., 428
French and Indian War, 364
Frenchman's Bay, District of Maine, 260-61, 261-62
French West Indies: U.S. trade with, 290, 292
Friendship, 455
Frontier: protection of, 471-74
Fry, John: *letter from*, 451-52
Funded debt, *see* Public debt
Funding, 431
Furman, Moore, 561
Furniture: manufacture of, in Connecticut, 323
Furs: and hat manufactures, 337-38; imported from Europe, 338; sale of, in China, 39, 42; scarcity, 442

Gale, George, 428; *letter to*, 164
Gallipolis, 255
Gardner, William: Treasury Department circular to, 14-15
Gates, Horatio: *letter from*, 413-14; *letter to*, 452-53
Gates County, N.C., 429
Geerman, Christian, 16
Geneva: distillation of, in Connecticut, 350
Genoa, 23: possibility of U.S. loan at, 1, 22, 98-101, 136, 314-15
Georgetown, Md., 289, 384, 403
Georgetown, S.C., 218
Georgia, 288, 459, 461, 465; commissioner of loans for, *see* Wylly, Richard; duties paid in, 3; invalid pensions in, 470; Superior Court of, 289; supervisor of revenue for, *see* Matthews, John; survey of inspection in, 430; U.S. Senator from, *see* Gunn, James
Germany: imports from, 338
Gerry, Samuel: *letter to*, 521
Gervais, John, 253-55
Giddens, Francis, 303, 304
Giles, William G., 404-5
Gin, *see* Distilled spirits
Ginseng: sale to China, 38-44
Glasgow, Scotland, 345
Glass: manufacture of, 162-63
Glastonbury, Conn.: manufacture of cotton at, 321

Glaubeck, Baron de, 549
Gloucester County, Va., 428
Gloves: manufacture of, in Providence, R.I., 447
Goochland County, Va., 428
Goodintent, 261-62
Gordon, William, 94
Gore, Christopher, 55; and Bank of the U.S., 187
Gorham, Nathaniel, 162-63, 427; *letter from*, 371-75
Gouy, ——— (Mr.), 481
Grace, 52
Graham, John: *letter to*, 113-14
Grand, ——— (Mr.), 544
Grand and Co., *see* Le Grand, Ferdinand, and Co.
Grangers and Elys mill, 345
Granville County, N.C., 429
Granville County, S.C., 429
Gray, Vincent, 487; *letter from*, 307
Grayson, William, 32
Great Britain, 34, 165, 322, 337, 364, 433, 439, 440; apprenticeship laws, 337; army of, 367; Board of Trade, president of, 4-5, 289; Cabinet, 4; and China trade, 39, 41, 45, 49-50, 51-52, 53, 143-44; consul at Philadelphia, 365-67; consul-general at New York City, 365, 367; cotton manufacturing in, 80, 436, 437, machinery, 434; customs revenue, 12; excise, 12; and export of machinery, 440; farms in, 376-77; fisheries, 433; imports from, 301, 339; King of, 440; labor in, 4, 179, emigration of, to U.S., 324, 440; loans in, 101; manufactures in, 4, and manufactures in U.S., 325, 436-37, 438-39; Minister Plenipotentiary to U.S., 4-5, 30, 289, 291; mint, assay master of, 4-5; and Gouverneur Morris's mission to, 63-64; Navigation Act, 4, 289; and occupation of New York City, 367; Parliament, 5; post on Lake Champlain, 206; postmaster general for the colonies, 363-65; representative to U.S., *see* Beckwith, George; salt duty, 12; statutes, 11-12, 352, 437, 440; Superintendent of Indian Affairs, 266; tonnage laws, 11-12; trade in Northwest, 266; and U.S., 29-30, attitude toward, 289, proposed treaties with, 291-92; U.S. loan in, 548; wool manufactures in, 326, 327

Great Egg Harbor, N.J., 28
Great Kanawha River, 277
Green, James, Jr., 27-28
Green, Jeremiah, 470
Green, John, 38
Greenbrier County, Va., 428
Greenbush, N.Y., 536
Greene, Catharine (Mrs. Nathanael), 549
Greene, Nathanael, 549
Greenfield Hill, Conn., 367
Greenleaf, Joseph, 527, 551-52
Greenman, Jeremiah, 35
Greenville County, S.C., 429
Greenville County, Va., 428
Gregory, Isaac, 69-70, 478
Grenville, Lord, 30, 104, 266
Grey, Robert, 45, 46
Gridley, Richard: pension, 462
Griffin, Cyrus, 487-88
Grindstones: duties on, 223-24
Gross, Simon, 508-9
Grosvenor, Lemuel, 355
Groton, Conn.: manufacturing at, 329
Guest, Henry: *letter from*, 144
Guilford County, N.C., 429
Gunn, James, 289

Hague, John, 439
The Hague, 386-87, 479
Haiti: revolt in, 219-20, 238, 542-43; and U.S. debt to France, 219-20, 225-26, 265
Halifax, N.C., 85, 503, 505
Halifax County, N.C., 429
Halifax County, Va., 428
Hall, William: contract with, 80-81; *letters from*, 121, 171-72
Halsted, John: *letter from*, 423-25
Ham, William, 35
Hamburg, 403
Hamilton, Alexander: on Bank of the U.S. branches, 538-39; and John B. Church, 5, 559; conversations with George Beckwith, 29-30, 104; on William Duer, 74-75; election to American Academy of Arts and Sciences, 104-5, 196-97, 237; horse for, 31, 92, 404-5; Henry Lee on, 31-32; as Daniel Parker and Co. trustee, 545; Rhode Island Senators on, 155, 157; on William Short, 2-3; sinking fund commissioner, 67-68; on speculation in Bank of the U.S. stock,

76; in wax museum, 59. *See also* Society for Establishing Useful Manufactures

Hamilton, Elizabeth, 4, 163, 266-67, 405, 514, 549, 563; *letter from*, 8; *letters to*, 6-7, 24, 25-26, 87-88, 172-73

Hamilton, James, 7, 24, 26, 246

Hamilton, Philip A.: *letter to*, 560-61

Hammond, George, 4-5, 30, 289, 291

Hampshire County, Mass., 427

Hampshire County, Va., 428

Hamtramck, John F. (Maj.), 473

Hand, Edward, 427-28

Hanks, Benjamin, 355

Hanks, Uriah, 355

Hanover County, Va., 428

Hanson, Samuel, 200, 262-63

Hardy County, Va., 428

Harford County, Md., 428, 511

Harison, Richard, 16-17, 82-83, 107, 197-98, 247, 530-31; *letter from*, 483-84

Harison, Samuel, 200, 262-63

Harris, Richard, 521

Harrison, Richard, 530

Harrison County, Va., 428

Hartford, Conn., 319, 532, 533, 536; manufacturing at, 345, of wool, 320, 322-23, 324-27

The [Hartford] *Connecticut Courant*, 367

Hartford County, Md., *see* Harford County, Md.

"Hartford Wits," 532

Hartford Woolen Manufactory, 322-23, 324, 347; history of, 324-25

Harvard College, 197

Harwood, Thomas, 562-63

Hathaway, Robert, 18, 37

Hats: duty on, 443; manufacture of, 147, in Connecticut, 324, 334, 336-38, 339, 341, 345, 348, 349, in Providence, R.I., 442-43; prices of, 336-37

Havre de Grace, Md., 37

Hawk (*Hawke*), 18, 37

Hawkesbury, Baron, 4-5, 289

Hawkins, Benjamin: *letter from*, 540-41

Hawse, —— (Mrs.), 281

Hazard, Nathaniel: *letters from*, 246-47, 363-64, 365-68, 529-37

Hazard, —— (Mrs. Nathaniel), 530, 536

Head of Elk, Md., 211, 317

Hemp: Massachusetts bounty on, 162-63; production of, in Connecticut, 344, in Virginia, 275, 276

Hempstead, N.Y., 247

Henchman, Thomas, 204-5

Henrico County, Va., 428

Henry County, Va., 428

Hertford, N.C., 35

Hertford County, N.C., 429

Heth, William: *letter from*, 511-13; *letter to*, 487; and sinking fund, 476-77

Hill, Jonathan, 444

Hill, William, 110, 507

Hillhouse, William: *letter to* John Chester, 332-34

Hillsboro, N.C., 27, 84, 122, 387

Hilton County, S.C., 429

Hispaniola, 15, 542; imports of hides from, 339. *See also* Haiti

Hobart, Samuel, 99, 105, 297

Hogguer, Grand, and Co., 142, 479; and payment of U.S. debt to France, 553-54

Holker, John, 545, 559

Holland, *see* United Netherlands

Holland Land Co., 8

Holland loans, *see* Loans

Hollins, John, 281

Holly, John, 108

Holly, Jonathan William, 340

Holmes, Isaac, 181

Holy Roman Empire: consul of, 53; loans of, 480, 498; trade with China, 39

Hook, Conrad, 70

Hooper, George: *letter from*, 173-75

Hope, 42, 54-60, 163-64

Hopkins, John, 413

House of Representatives: clerk of, *see* Beckley, John; compensation of officials of, 459, 464, 475; *letter to*, 426-31; and manufactures, 517-18; order of, 496; report to, 456-75

Houston (Houstoun), John, 288-89

Howard, James, 281

Howard, John Eager: *letter to*, 561-63

Howard, Samuel, 281

Hubbard, William, 319

Hudson River, 536

Hughes, James Miles, 246-47

Hunt, —— (Dr.), 55

Hunterdon County, N.J., 269, 379

Huntingdon County, Pa., 427

Huntington, Benjamin, 330, 332; *letter to* John Chester, 329-30

Huntington, Jedediah: *letter from,* 309; *letters to,* 106, 516-17, 521, 541; and lighthouse contract, 520; Treasury Department circulars to, 15-17, 221, 507-8

Huntington, Samuel, 534; *letter from,* 91

Hyde County, N.C., 429

Hydrometers: expense, 4, 475; purchase of, 466. *See also* Collectors of customs; Dycas's hydrometer

Imperial East India Co., 39

Import duties, *see* Duties

Imports: and manufacturing, 371; report on, 510, 526-27; return of, 16, 81, 496; statement of duties on, 2-4

Impost, *see* Duties

India, 43; and China trade, 45; import of yarn from, 438; trade, 143

Indian department: expenses, 471, 474, 475

Indians: Lord Dorchester's address to, 265-66, 270; expedition against, 210-11, 401-2, 457; expenses of protection against, 471-74. *See also* Cherokees; Kickapoo Indians; Six Nations

Indian Superintendent of the Northern District, 209-11

Industry, 453, 505

Ingersoll, Jared, 88-90, 485; *letter to* Thomas Mifflin, 239-40; and Pennsylvania land purchase, 239-40, 245-46

Innes, Harry, 211

Inspectors of the ports, 198; of Bristol, R.I., *see* Munro, William; of New London, Conn., 205; of Plankbridge, N.C., *see* Gregory, Isaac; and collectors of customs, 199-200

Inspectors of the revenue (of surveys): for Connecticut, *see* Chester, John; for Kentucky, *see* Marshall, Thomas; for Maryland, *see* Thomas, Philip; for Massachusetts, *see* Jackson, Jonathan, *and* Jarvis, Leonard; for North Carolina, *see* Benbury, Thomas, *and* Daves, John, *and* McDowell, Joseph, Sr., *and* Read, James, *and* Whitaker, John; for Pennsylvania, *see* Collins, James, *and* Hand, Edward, *and* Neville, John; for Rhode Island, *see* Dexter, John S.; for South Carolina, 9, 175-76 (*see also* Cudworth, Benjamin;

Walker, Silvanus); for Virginia, *see* Brackenridge, James, *and* Carrington, Mayo, *and* Marshall, Thomas, *and* Newton, Thomas, Jr., *and* Ragsdale, Drury, *and* Smith, Edward, *and* Stevens, Edward; appointment of, 84-85; certificates for, 84-85; duties of, 430

Interest, *see* Public debt

Invalid pensions, 470, 474; for 1792, 457; payment of, 10

Iredell, James, 503, 505

Iredell County, N.C., 429

Ireland, 453; cotton manufacturing in, 216-17, 436; Dublin Society for Promoting Husbandry and Other Useful Arts in Ireland, 437, 439; House of Commons, 437

Iron: manufacture of, in Connecticut, 323, 328-29, 331, 335, 344, 350, 351, in New Jersey, 193, in Providence, R.I., 440, 447, in Virginia, 277, 281; sale of, in China, 39, 42

Iron ore: in Virginia, 277

Irvine, William, 209-11; *letter from* John Brown, 210-11

Isle of Wight County, Va., 428

Jackson, Daniel, 446

Jackson, Jonathan, 427

Jacquett, Peter, 211-12

James City County, Va., 428

James River, 277

Jarvis, Leonard, 427

Jarvis, Samuel, 341

Jay, John, 534, 536; *letters from,* 196, 501; *letter to,* 563-64; sinking fund commissioner, 68, 93, 476-77

Jay, Sarah Livingston (Mrs. John), 563

Jay, 43

Jeanneret, François, 22-23

Jefferson, Thomas, 1, 30, 228, 531, 532, 533; conversation with Hamilton, 33-34; and Alexander Donald, 99; and Jean Pierre Droz, 101; and Hamilton's "Report on Manufactures," 528; *letter from,* 129; *letter to* Ferdinand Le Grand, 103; *letters to,* 111-12, 129; and William Pearce, 86; Pennsylvania laws, 529; and Schweizer and Jeanneret, 62; sinking fund, commissioner of, 67-68, 93, 476-77; and John Cleves Symmes, 269; tour of New England, 534;

trip to Virginia, 185; and George Washington's message to Congress, 403; and West Point, 484

Jenny, 43

Jersey: manufacture of, in Virginia, 301

Johnson, James, 206-7

Johnson, Sir John, 266

Johnson, Seth, 56

Johnson, William Samuel, 365, 367, 532, 534

Johnson County, N.C., 429

Jones, Samuel, 16-17, 82-83, 107, 197, 198; *letter to*, 494

Jones County, N.C., 429

Jordan, John: pension, 462

Jordan, Meletiah: *letters from*, 260-61, 261-62

Joy, George: *letters from*, 388-93, 393-400

Kahmer, Reinhard: account with, 421

Kanawha (Kenhawa) County, Va., 428

Keais, Nathan: *letter from*, 121-22

Kean, John: *letter from* George Washington, 490

Kent County, Del., 212

Kent County, Md., 428

Kentucky, 209, 428, 458, 466; inspector of revenue for, *see* Marshall, Thomas; militia of, 210-11; and James Wilkinson, 211

Kershaw County, S.C., 429

Keyes, Stephen: *letter to*, 91

Kickapoo Indians, 210-11

Killingly (Killingsly), Conn.: manufacturing at, 320, 321, 322, 354

Killingworth, Conn.: manufacturing at, 349, 351, 352

King, Alexander, 342: *letter to* Roger Newberry, 343-46

King, John, 281

King, Rufus, 55; *letter from*, 59-61; *letter to*, 75-76

King and Queen County, Va., 428

King George County, Va., 428

King's College, 287

Kingston County, S.C., 429

King William County, Va., 280, 281, 428

Knox, Henry, 211, 226, 474; *letters to*, 270, 401-2; and Pennsylvania laws, 529; and West Point, 484

Krakatoa Island, 43

Labor: child, 145, 374, 438, 446; European, 147; Great Britain, from, 324, in, 4; high price of, 145, 345; scarcity of, in Connecticut, 323, 327, 356; women, 145, 342

Lackawanna River, 380

Lafayette, Marie Joseph du Motier, marquis de, 30, 104

La Forest, Antoine René Charles Mathurin de, 265, 306-7

Lake Champlain, 206

Lake Erie: and Pennsylvania land purchase, 239-40, 245-46, 485

Lamb, Jandine (Mrs. John), 514

Lamb, John, 262, 483-85; *letter from*, 495; *letter to*, 514

Lambert, Charles Guillaume, 64

Lancaster, Duchy of, 5

Lancaster County, Pa., 427

Lancaster County, S.C., 429

Lancaster County, Va., 428

Lane, Hezekiah, 349; *letter from* Aaron Elliott, 352-53; *letter to* Chauncey Whittelsey, 352

Lanneau, Bazile, 171

Lansdowne, Marquis of, 367, 370

La Roche, Jean Baptiste de, 74-75

Latesta, Roderick, 16

Lathrop, Joshua (Dr.), 332, 339

Latimer, Henry, 211-12, 400-1, 428

Laurance, John, 366, 367

Laurens County, S.C., 429

Lawrence, —— (Mr.), 94

Lawrence, Nathaniel, 246-47, 366, 367, 530-31, 536

Lead: in Virginia, 277; sale of, in China, 39, 42

Lear, Tobias, 212, 250, 384, 426; *letters from*, 34-35, 61-67, 67, 164, 181-82, 207, 502-3; *letters to*, 130, 175-76, 509

Learned, Amasa, 329, 330, 332, 339; *letter to* John Chester, 338-39

Leary, John, Jr., 440

Leather: duties on, 444; imports of, 444; manufacture of, in Connecticut, 323, 338-39, 344-45, 351, in Providence, R.I., 443-44, 447, in Virginia, 278, 282

Lebanon, Conn.: manufacturing at, 319, 321, 353-55

Ledyard, Isaac, 366-67, 536

Lee, Charles, 307, 515-16; *letters from*, 81-83, 218; *letters to*, 200, 202, 203, 235-36, 262-63, 487, 487-88

Lee, Henry: *letters from,* 31-32, 92, 404-5

Leffingwell, Christopher, 329, 339; *letters to* John Chester, 330-31, 332

L'Eglize, Dominique: pension, 462

Le Grand, Ferdinand, 100-1; *letter from* Thomas Jefferson, 103

Le Grand, Ferdinand, and Co., 100, 142

Le Havre, 128, 228

L'Enfant, Pierre Charles, 246

LeRoy, Herman, 31-32, 112, 152, 158; and Society for Establishing Useful Manufactures, 24-25

LeRoy and Bayard: *letters from,* 157-58, 201-2; *letters to,* 112, 181

LeRoy, Bayard, and McEvers, 158

Lessart, Claude Antoine de Valdec de, 524

Lewisburg County, S.C., 429

Libbey, Anthony, 483

Liberty County, S.C., 429

Lighthouses: on Cape Fear, N.C., 173-75; on Cape Henry, Va., 19, 310; in Connecticut, 520; contracts, 19; maintenance and repairs, 466, 475; in New Hampshire, 241-43, 422-23; at New London, Conn., 520, 521; at Newport, R.I., 180; at Portland, District of Maine, 131-32, 208-9, 509, keeper of, 527-28, 551-52; at Portsmouth, N.H., 524-25; in Rhode Island, 493-94; in South Carolina, 67, 70

Lincklaen, Jan, 8

Lincoln, Benjamin, 182, 416-17; *letters from,* 107-8, 130-32, 194-95, 284-85, 293-95, 411-12, 453-54, 488, 551-52; *letters to,* 13-14, 83-84, 208-9, 218-19, 225, 244-45, 293, 405-6, 497-98, 505-6, 509, 527-28; and payment of interest on public debt, 78, 550; and sinking fund, 476-77; Treasury Department circulars to, 496, 507-8

Lincoln County, N.C., 429

Lincoln County, S.C., 429

Linen: manufacture of, 147, in Connecticut, 319, 320, 321, 328, 329, 340-41, 342, 343-44, 348, 350, 355, in Providence, R.I., 435, 436, 440, in South Carolina, 170, in Virginia, 301-3

Lipscomb, Bernard, 281

Lipscomb, Charles, 281

Lisbon, Conn.: manufacturing at, 329

Liverpool, 164, 448

Livestock: duty on, 273, 370

Livingston, Edward, 246-47

Livingston, John Robert, 440

Livingston, Philip, 152

Livingston, Robert R., 246-47

Loan office: certificates of, 263-64, 485, 561-63. *See also* Commissioners of loans

Loans: at Antwerp, possibility of U.S. loan at, 1, 20, 22, 98-99, 228, 272, 313-14, opened, 480-82, 498-500, 522-23, 552-57, Russian loan at, 20, and U.S. credit, 555; domestic loan of 1790, 10-11, and Maryland, 561-63, and New York, 123, and North Carolina, 27-28, 122-23, 154, 191-92, 387-88, 486, 540-41, and Pennsylvania, 310, and Rhode Island, 153-57, and South Carolina, 154, speculation in, 204-5, stock of, 60-61, subscribers to, 88-90; foreign, 1-4, extension of, 161, interest and charges on, 1, and public debt, 547-48, and William Short's instructions, 1-4; French, of July 16, 1782, 65-66, 394, of February 25, 1783, 394, possibility of U.S. loan from the, 1-2, 3, 22, 315; Genoa, possibility of U.S. loan in, 1-2, 3, 22, 315; Genoa, possibility of U.S. loan in, 1-2, 136, 314-15; Holland, 1-2, 3, 20-23, 522, and Antwerp loan, 498-500, and assumption of state debts, 141, of August, 1790, 111-12, 137, 160, 162, 230, and Bank of the U.S., 141, 160-67, charges on, 21, 97, 140, 160-61, 165-70, 226-27, 272, 524, 554, 556, and civil list, 141, and French loan of July 16, 1782, 140, of March, 1791, 21-22, 66, 111-12, 135, 136, 140, 162, 230, 231, 234-35, 314, new loan proposed, 556, and payment of U.S. debt to France, 65, reimbursement of, 97, 547-48, of September 14, 1782, 547-48, of September, 1791, 21-22, 98, 128, 132-36, 164-67, 226-27, 229-32, 232-35, 311-12, 314, 316-17, 431-32, 450-51, 479, 481, 547-48, 553, tax on, 134, 136, 139-40, 480, 500, 554, and U.S. domestic debt, 141; London, possibility of U.S. loans at, 1, 98-100, 135, 136, 166, 227-28, 312-13, 480, 548; payment of, and unsubscribed public debt, 396-400; William Short's power for making, 20; Spanish loan of 1781, 499-500

London, 4, 5, 23, 45, 99, 112, 161, 201, 204, 213, 388, 393, 448, 451, 517, 524, 557; possibility of U.S. loan in, 1, 98-100, 135, 136, 166, 227-28, 312-13, 480; speculations in U.S. debt, 388-93

Londonderry, N.H., 414

Lorient (L'Orient), France, 498

Lotteries: in Connecticut, 321, to encourage manufacturing, 322-23, 325, 354; in Massachusetts, to encourage manufacturing, 178; and Society for Establishing Useful Manufactures, 148

Loudoun County, Va., 301, 428

Louisa County, Va., 301, 428

Lovell, James, 225

Low, Nicholas, 24-25, 152

Lowrey, Thomas, 91, 385; *letter from*, 379-82

Lucretia, 225

Lumber: manufacture of, in Connecticut, 345, in Virginia, 275

Lunenburg County, Va., 428

Lurana, 15, 108

Luzerne County, Pa., 427; agriculture in, 375-77

Lydia, 214-15

Lyman, Daniel, 94, 111, 205

Lyme, Conn.: manufacturing at, 329

Lyon, —— (Mr.), 94

MacAuslan, Duncan, 122-23, 387-88

McClenachan, Blair, 152, 264

McComb, Eleazer, 289

McComb, John, Jr.: lighthouse at Cape Henry, Va., 19, 310

McConnell, Matthew, 24-25, 152

McDowell (McDowel), Joseph, Sr., 85, 429

McEvers, Charles, Jr., 157-58, 201

M'Fingal (John Trumbull), 532

MacGregore, James, 414

McHenry, James: *letters from*, 386-87, 510-11; *letter to*, 454-55

Machines: for cotton manufacturing, 434-35; and dearness of labor, 145; and labor, 435; procurement of, in Europe, 147; scarcity of, in Connecticut, 327

McKensie, James: pension, 462

McKern, James, 448

McKerries, James, 434

McMahin, Robert, 70

Macnaughten, Auly: *letter from*, 173-75

McRae, Duncan, 122-23, 191, 387-88

McRae, John, 79, 164

McStephens, James, 249-50, 317

Madeira, 43

Madison, James, 413, 531, 532; and Hamilton's "Report on Manufactures," 528; *letter to*, 528; New England tour, 534; and George Washington's message to Congress, 403

Madras, 43, 44

Magee, James, 42

Maine, 107, 243, 426, 458, 465, 483; and Beverly Cotton Manufactory, 178

Mair, John: *An Introduction to Latin Syntax* . . . , 560-61

Malay settlements, 51

Maltbie, Jonathan, 425, 528-29

Manchester, England, 177

Manchester, Va., 469, 470

Mansfield, Conn.: manufacturing at, 354, 355-57

Manufactures: and active wealth, 144-45; and banks, 146; of blankets, 147; of blocks, 443; in Boston, Mass., 162-63; and bounties, 162-63, 322, 327, 343, 345, 355-56, 372-73, 384, 433, 438; of brass, 147, 324, 446; and brewery, 148; and British rivalry with U.S., 436-37, 438-39; of buttons, 347-48, 358-61, 362-63; of cabinets, 339-40, 448; of candles, 433, 434, 445; capital for, 146, 147; of cards, 344, 446; of carpets, 147; of carriages, 323, 346, 351; of casks, 346; of chocolate, 446; of clocks, 445; of cloth, 280-82; in Connecticut, 318-63; of copper, 448; of cordage, 448; and corporations, 252; of cotton, 147, 170, 177-80, 279, 280, 281-82, 301-3, 320, 321, 331, 332, 335, 340-41, 343, 347, 351, 354, 432, 434-40, 448; of crockery, 331; domestic, 320-21, 326, 328, 332-33, 334, 342, 347, 353, 355, 436; of drugs, 517-18; of duck, 319-20; and dyeing woods and drugs, 506; of earthenware, 346; in Europe, 251, 252; and

Manufactures (*Continued*)
exemptions, 327; of fabrics, 145-46; Federal encouragement of, 327, 330, 438, 449; of fire engines, 446; of foreign material, duty on, 223-24; in France, 252; of fringe and web, 444; of furniture, 323; of geneva, 350; of gloves, 447; in Great Britain, 4, 436, 437; of grindstones, 223-24; of hats, 147, 324, 334, 336-38, 339, 341, 345, 348, 349, 442-43; and House of Representatives, 517-18; impediments to, in U.S., 145; and imports, 371-72; in Ireland, 436; of iron, 147, 193, 277, 282, 323, 328-29, 331, 335, 344, 350, 351, 440, 447; and labor supply, 145, 354; of lead, 277; of leather, 278, 282, 323, 338-39, 344-45, 351, 443-44, 447; of linen, 147, 170, 301-3, 319, 320, 321, 328, 329, 340, 341, 342, 343-44, 348, 350, 353, 355, 435, 436, 440; and lotteries, 148, 178, 321, 322-23, 325, 354; of lumber, 345; in Massachusetts, 178, 371-75; of nails, 334, 341, 342, 344, 351, 445; national, 366; in New Jersey, 193-94; of paper, 147, 440-47; of pasteboard, 147; of pewter, 324, 448; of potash and pearlash, 335, 345, 350, 351; of pottery, 147; in Providence, R.I., 432-49, Report of a Committee Appointed to Obtain Information on Manufacturing in, 441-49; and public debt, 145; of ribbons and tapes, 147; of rope, 278, 338; of rum, 350; of saddlecloth, 336, 338; of saddles, 345; of sailcloth, 147, 213, 338, 340; of saltpeter, 346; of shoes and boots, 147, 279, 280, 301-3, 349, 444; of silk, 194, 349, 354, 355-57; of silver, 324, 446; of snuff, 350, 440; of soap, 445; in South Carolina, 170-71; and speculation, 327; of steel, 349, 352-53, 440; and stock of U.S., 146; of stockings, 147, 279, 280, 281, 282, 301-3, 320, 357; of sugar, 434; tax on, 300; of thread, 147; of tin, 324; of tools, 342, 351, 354, 445, 446-47; of tow cloth, 342; value of, 323; in Virginia, 275-82, 299-304; George Washington on, 384; of wood, 323; of wool, 279, 281-82, 301-3, 320, 322-23, 324-27, 328, 329, 332, 333, 340, 342, 343, 347, 348, 351, 353-54, 355, 440, 444. *See*

also Society for Establishing Useful Manufactures
Maple sugar: manufacture of, 8
Marblehead, Mass., 521
Marchant, Henry, 215, 283-84, 308, 415; *letters from,* 205-6, 304-5, 477-78
Marenty Bay, Vt., 279
Marietta, 473
Marion County, S.C., 429
Marlboro (Marlborough) County, S.C., 429
Marseilles, 503
Marshall, Charles: *letter from,* 517-18
Marshall, Christopher, Jr., 517-18
Marshall, Thomas, 121, 250; contract with, 73-74; *letter from,* 267-69
Marshall, Thomas (Ky.), 35, 130, 429
Martin, Alexander, 27-28, 123, 191-92
Martin, Thomas, 105, 208-9, 213
Martin County, N.C., 429
Maryland, 81, 177, 289, 458, 461, 465; acts of, 18, "An Act proposing to the citizens of this state, creditors of congress on loan-office certificates, to accept this state for payment, on the terms therein mentioned" (January 15, 1783), 562-63; agriculture in, 376-77, 490-93; and assumption of state debts, 561-63; commissioner of loans for, *see* Harwood, Thomas; constitution of, 511; and domestic loan of 1790, 561-63; duties paid in, 3; inspector of revenue, *see* Thomas, Philip; invalid pensions in, 470; legislature of, 18, 386, 510-11, 561; line, pay for, 470, 471; and loan office certificates, 561-63; Ratifying Convention, 386, 511; revenue cutter for, captain of, *see* Gross, Simon, officers for, 238, 508-9, rations for, 497; state certificates, 561-63; subscribers to the public debt, 561-63; supervisor of the revenue for, *see* Gale, George; surveys of inspection in, 428; tonnage duties in, 38
Massachusetts, 38, 243, 458, 461, 465; "An Act for Regulating the Manufacture of Nails Within this Commonwealth, & for Repealing All Laws Heretofore Made for that Purpose," 373-74; bounties in, 372-73, on duck, 163, on hemp, 162-63; Circuit Court, 195; commissioner of

loans for, *see* Appleton, Nathaniel; distillers, 187-88; duties paid in, 3, 4; inspectors of the revenue for, *see* Jackson, Jonathan, *and* Jarvis, Leonard; invalid pensions in, 10, 470; labor prices in, 179; lotteries in, 178; manufacturing in, 371-75, of cotton, 177-80, 439, of cotton and wool cards, 374, encouragement of, 178, machinery for, 434, of nails, 373-74, of tacks, 374-75; revenue cutter for, 130-31, 411-12, captain of, *see* Williams, John Foster, construction of, 208, crew of, 284, 454, 497-98, 506, expenses of, 293, rations for, 285, 297-98; supervisor of the revenue for, *see* Gorham, Nathaniel; surveys of inspection in, 426-27; trade with Connecticut, 371, with New York, 371; U.S. attorney for the District of, *see* Gore, Christopher; U.S. Representative from, *see* Ames, Fisher; U.S. Senator from, *see* Cabot, George

Massachusetts Bank, 187, 550; and Nathaniel Appleton, 559; and Bank of New York, 187; and Bank of the U.S., 56-59, as branch of, 56, subscription to, 56; cashier of, 78, 550; and Benjamin Lincoln, 218-19, 284, 497-98; paper of, 57

Mathews County, Va., 428

Matthews, John, 430

Maxwell, James, 477-78

Maxwell, William, 366-67, 529-30

Mecklenburg County, N.C., 429

Mecklenburg County, Va., 428

Melville (Melvill), Thomas, 107, 182, 208

Menema, Daniel, 247

Mercer, George, 363-64, 365

Mercer, Hugh (Brig. Gen.): pension to son of, 462

Mercer, James, 364

Mercer, John, 364

Mercer, John F., 511

Meredith, Samuel, 120; and Bank of Maryland, 414-15; and Bank of New York, 265; bills of, 69, 176, 559; and collectors of the customs, 69-70, 222, 260; drafts of, 260, 412, 550; franking privilege, 270; Holland loan of September, 1791, 450-51; invalid pensions, 10; Pennsylvania land purchase, 485; public debt, payment

of interest on, 78, purchase of, 185, 190; and sinking fund, 476-77; and Willink, Van Staphorst, and Hubbard, 431-32

Meyer, John, 172-73

Middlesex, England, 440

Middlesex County, Mass., 426, 428

Middletown, Conn., 352; manufacturing at, 319, 321, 349-51

Mifflin, Thomas, 529; *letters from*, 239-40, 310, 485; *letter from* Jared Ingersoll, 239-40; *letters to*, 92-93, 245-46

Mifflin County, Pa., 427

Militia: and defense against Indians, 471-74

Minima, *see* Menema

Mints: Great Britain, 4-5; information on, 228, in Holland, 101, 228-29

Mitchell, Stephen Mix, 536

Mix, John, Jr.: *letters to* John Chester, 357-58, 358-61, 361-63, 363

Mix, Jonathan, 360

Mix, Barney, & Co.: and manufacture of buttons, 360

Moïse, 52

Molasses: duty on, 19

Money: abundance of, in Europe, 451; and China trade, 143-44

Monongalia County, Va., 428

Monopoly: in China, 40; in Massachusetts, 163

Monqua, 46, 47, 48

Montgomery County, Md., 130, 428

Montgomery County, N.C., 429

Montgomery County, Pa., 427

Montgomery County, Va., 428

Montmorin Saint-Herem, Armand Marc, comte de, 64

Montville, Conn.: manufacturing at, 329, 332-34

Moore, Alexander, 384

Moore, John Spotswood, 385

Moore County, N.C., 429

Morgan, David, 549

Morris, Gouverneur, 204-5; and Antwerp loan, 313-14, 480-81, 557; and British ministry, 63-64; *letter from* George Washington, 61-62; *letter to* George Washington, 63-67; and U.S. debt to France, 61-67

Morris, Richard Valentine, 130, 509

Morris, Robert, 99, 189-90, 204-5, 549

Morris, Robert, Jr., 549

Morrison, John, 79, 164

Morristown, N.J., 193
Mort, Joseph, 121, 171; contract with, 90-91
Mount Vernon, 203, 212, 220, 370
Mulberry trees: in Connecticut, bounty on, 355-56, cultivation of, 357
Munro, William, 308-9
Murdaugh, Josiah, 35
Murray, John, 533, 545
Musconetcong River, 382, 385
Musk: and China trade, 143

Nails: manufacture of, in Connecticut, 334, 341, 342, 344, 351, in Massachusetts, 373-74, in Providence, R.I., 445
Nankeen: China trade, 53
Nansemond County, Va., 428; manufacturing in, 278
Nantes, France, 440
Nantucket: and whaling, 433
Nash County, N.C., 429
Naval officers: for the port of Boston, Mass., see Lovell, James, of Charleston, S.C., 143, of Newport, R.I., see Crooke, Robert, of Providence, R.I., see Thompson, Ebenezer; and moieties, 111
Naverson, John, 70
Necker, Jacques, 63
Negroes, 278, 282, 327; duties on, 370
Nelson, William, Jr., 513
Neuse River, 121-22
Neville, John, 427-28; letter from, 419-20; Treasury Department circular to, 35-37
Newark, N.J., 267
New Bedford, Mass., 18; collector of customs at, 94
New Bern, N.C., 121, 225, 497, 503, 504; collector of customs at, see Daves, John
Newberry, Roger: letter from Alexander King, 343-46; letter to John Chester, 341-42
Newberry (Newbury) County, S.C., 429
New Brunswick, N.J., 24, 25, 74, 144
New Castle Island, N.H., 242-43
New England, 365, 371, 531, 533; and Bank of the U.S., 202
Newfoundland, 195
New Gate Prison, Conn.: manufacturing at, 342
New Hampshire, 371, 458, 461, 465;

distilleries in, 186; duties paid in, 3; invalid pensions in, 470; legislature of, 414; lighthouse in, maintenance of, 241-43, 422-23; manufacture of sailcloth in, 213; revenue cutter for, 105, 107-8, 208, account of, 416-17, captain of, see Yeaton, Hopley, officers for, 297-99; supervisor of revenue for, see Wentworth, Joshua; survey of inspection in, 426; U.S. Representative from, see Smith, Jeremiah
New Hanover County, N.C., 429
New Haven, Conn., 365, 366, 440, 529, 536; manufacturing at, 318, 319, 321, 322, 357-58, 361-63
New Jersey, 341, 458, 461, 466; agriculture in, 376; duties paid in, 3; governor of, see Franklin, William, and Paterson, William; invalid pensions in, 470; legislature of, 194, 379, and incorporation of Society for Establishing Useful Manufactures, 80-81; manufacturing in, 193-94; and Society for Establishing Useful Manufactures, 24, 80-81, 85-86, 146, 148, 152, 366; supervisor of revenue for, see Dunham, Aaron; survey of inspection in, 427; U.S. marshal for the District of, see Lowrey, Thomas; U.S. Representative from, see Boudinot, Elias
New Kent County, Va., 428
New London, Conn., 214, 355; collector of customs at, see Huntington, Jedediah; inspector of the port of, 205; lighthouse, 520, 521; manufacturing at, 319, 321, 338-39
New London, Va., 469, 470
New London County, Conn.: manufacturing in, 329, 330-31, 332-34, 338-39
Newman, William, 281
Newport, Del., 211
Newport, R.I., 108, 181, 214, 305, 308, 403, 455, 488, 514, 516, 542; collector of customs at, see Ellery, William; lighthouse at, 180; naval officer for the port of, 205, 478; surveyor of the port of, 94, 111, 205
Newton, Thomas, Jr., 275, 429; letters from, 19, 310; letter from Anselm Bailey, 280; letter from Robert Twiford, 279; letter to Edward Carrington, 278-79
Newton, N.Y., 368

New York City, 16, 25, 32, 38, 42, 45, 55, 56, 69, 87, 121, 142, 149, 150, 190, 201, 202, 220, 246-47, 274, 338, 364, 365, 367, 368, 382, 388, 440, 455, 478, 483, 530, 536, 544, 546; Bank of the U.S., branch of, 518-20, election of directors of, 201-2, speculation in stock of, 74; British consul general at, 365-67; British occupation of, 367; collector of customs at, *see* Lamb, John; Committee of 100, 38; deputy collector of customs at, 478; Marine Society of, 38; and purchase of public debt, 67-68; speculation in, 185; stock market decline in, 58

New York County, N.Y., 247

New York Daily Gazette, 367

New York State, 8, 152, 337, 345, 458, 461, 466; attorney general of, 483 (*see also* Burr, Aaron); and Bank of the U.S., 123; commissioner of loans for, *see* Cochran, John; constitution of 1777, 247; Council of Appointment, 246-47; and domestic loan of 1790, 123; duties paid in, 3; governor of, *see* Clinton, George; invalid pensions in, 470; iron exports to, 335; legislature of, 247, 368, 413, 494; Ratifying Convention of, 247, 494; revenue cutter for, 130, 509; speculation in lands of, 204-5; state regents, 247; supervisor of revenue for, *see* Smith, William S.; Supreme Court, 483-84; survey of inspection in, 427; trade with Massachusetts, 371; U.S. attorney for the District of, *see* Harison, Richard; U.S. judge for the District of, *see* Duane, James; U.S. Representative from, *see* Laurance, John; U.S. Senators from, *see* Burr, Aaron, *and* Schuyler, Philip

Nicholas, 108, 181

Nicholson, John, 92, 239-40, 264, 485; and assumption of state debts, 382-83; and Pennsylvania land purchase, 245-46

Norfolk, Va., 278

Norfolk County, Va., 428; manufacturing in, 278

Northampton County, N.C., 429

Northampton County, Pa., 427

Northampton County, Va., 279, 428

North Carolina, 458, 461, 465; accounts with U.S., 456, 501-2, 540-41; "An Act for emitting One Hundred Thousand Pounds in Paper Currency, for the purposes of government for seventeen hundred and eighty three, for the redemption of paper currency now in circulation, and advancing to the Continental officers and soldiers part of their pay and subsistance . . ." (1783) 503, 505, "An Act for emitting One hundred thousand Pounds paper currency, for the Purposes therein expressed" (December 29, 1785), 503, 505; and assumption of state debts, 27-28, 32-33, 122-23, 154-55, 191-92, 356, 387-88, 503-5; certificates of, 32-33, 486; collector of revenue for, 84-85; commercial agent for, 540-41; commissioner of loans for, *see* Skinner, William; comptroller of state of, 33, 122-23, 191-92, 387-88; Continental loan officer for, 27-28; distilleries in, 84-85; and domestic loan of 1790, 27-28, 122-23, 154, 191-92, 387-88, 486, 540-41; duties paid in, 3; and Federal debts, 503-5; governor of, *see* Martin, Alexander; inspectors of revenue for, *see* Benbury, Thomas, *and* Daves, John, *and* McDowell, Joseph, Sr., *and* Read, James, *and* Whitaker, John; invalid pensions in, 470; legislature of, 27-28, 33, 503, 504, 540, 541; paper money of, 503-5; and public debt, 27-28; Ratifying Convention, 541; revenue cutter for, 497; sinking fund tax, 504-5; supervisor of revenue for, *see* Polk, William; surveys of inspection in, 429; treasurer of, 33; treasury of, 122; U.S. Representative from, *see* Williamson, Hugh; U.S. Senator from, *see* Hawkins, Benjamin

North Kensington, R.I., 6, 111, 223-24

Northumberland County, Pa., 427

Northumberland County, Va., 428

Northwest Territory: militia, expenses of, 473

Norton, Mass., 373

Norwich, Conn., 91; manufacturing at, 319, 321, 329-30, 330-31, 332, 339, 341

Nottingham, Md., 69-70, 106

Nottoway County, Va., 428

Nourse, Joseph: register of the Treasury, 88, 89, 474, 475; report on duties on imports, 2-4

Nova Scotia, 195

Observations on the Commerce of the American States with Europe and the West Indies . . . (Lord Sheffield), 367
Ohio County, Va., 428
Ohio River, 210, 211, 255
Olney, Jeremiah, 304-5; *letters from,* 26-27, 35, 108-9, 181, 206-7, 213-14, 285, 305-6, 368-69, 387, 412, 416, 425-26, 455-56, 488-89, 518, 528-29, 543; *letters to,* 78-79, 96, 183-84, 236-37, 270, 295-96, 489-90, 495, 525-26; Treasury Department circulars to, 15-17, 222-23
O'Neill, Terence, 216-17
Onslow County, N.C., 429
Orange County, N.C., 429
Orange County, S.C., 429
Orange County, Va., 428
Oriolle, ———— (Capt.), 52
Osborn, John: petition of, 11-12
Ostend, 39
Otis, Samuel A., 558
Otsego County, N.Y., 8
Otsego Patent, 8
Otto, Louis G., 62, 291-92
Ovid, 560

Page, Charles, 218, 235
Page, Stephen, 384
Paine, Thomas: *The Rights of Man,* 34, 533
Palmer, Elihu, 366, 368
Palmer, Jonathan, Jr., 541; *letter to* John Chester, 339-40
Pankikoa, 39, 40
Pankikoa (son), 47, 48
Panton, John (Jonathan) A., 51
Paper: manufacture of, 147, in Providence, R.I., 440, 447
Paper hangings: manufacture of, 147
Paper money, 188; in North Carolina, 503-5; old emissions, 383; in Pennsylvania, 431; and state banks, 57-58
Paris, 1, 64, 100, 553; and payment of foreign debt at, 161; and payment of U.S. debt to France, 62-63, 227; possibility of U.S. loans at, 22, 315; rate of exchange at, 142, 159-60, 229, 523-24; U.S. chargé d'affaires at, *see* Short, William
Parker, Daniel, 38
Parker, Daniel, and Co., 544, 559;

trustees for, *letter to* Royal Flint, 595
Parnell, David, 281
Parrot, John, 297
Parsons, Jasper, 286-87
Pasquotank County, N.C., 429
Passaic River, 121, 268, 269; Falls, 171-72, as site for Society for Establishing Useful Manufactures, 267-69
Pasteboard, 147
Paterson, William, 535
Paterson, N.J., 172, 319; and Society for Establishing Useful Manufactures, 24
Patrick County, Va., 428
Patten, John, 211-12
Paulding, John: pension, 462
Payne, John, 121
Peabody, Nathaniel: *letter from,* 414
Peace, 29
Pearce, William: receipts from, 85-86, 184, 214, 490, 509-10
Pearson, Eliphalet, 105; *letter from,* 196-97; *letter to,* 237
Peck, Lewis, 448
Peck, William, 95, 283-84, 308-9
Pendleton County, S.C., 429
Pendleton County, Va., 428
"Pendulum, Peter," 366, 367
Pennsylvania, 86, 152, 212, 380, 458, 461, 465, 485; acts of, 529, "An Act to Recompense John Hague for Introducing into This State a Useful Machine for Carding Cotton" (October 3, 1788), 439; agriculture in, 114-18, 124-27; and assumption of state debts, 382-83, 431; attorney general of, *see* Bradford, William, *and* Ingersoll, Jared; commissioner of loans for, *see* Smith, Thomas; comptroller general of, *see* Nicholson, John; Court of Errors and Appeals, 212; and domestic loan of 1790, 310; duties paid in, 3; governor of, *see* Mifflin, Thomas; inspectors of revenue for, *see* Collins, James, *and* Hand, Edward, *and* Neville, John; invalid pensions in, 470; Lake Erie land purchase, 92-93, 239-40, 245-46, 485; legislature of, 114, 239; manufactures, encouragement of, 439, 440; militia, expenses, 471; Ratifying Convention, 419; register general of, 310; secretary of state, 529; Society for the Encourage-

ment of Manufactures and the Useful Arts, 438; supervisor of revenue for, *see* Clymer, George; Supreme Court of, 88; Supreme Executive Council, 419; surveys of inspection, 427-28; treasurer of, 485; U.S. Representative from, *see* Wynkoop, Henry; and Wyoming Valley, 376-77

Pensions: expense of, 475. *See also* Invalid pensions

Pequest River, 121

Perquimans County, N.C., 429

Perry, William, 511

Perth Amboy, N.J., 423-25

Peterborough, N.H., 414

Peters, Richard: *letter from*, 114-18; Treasury Department circular to, 35-37

Petersburg, Va., 164, 405

Peterson, Edward, 455

Petitions: of Massachusetts distillers, 187, 188; of John Osborne, 11-12; of Peleg Saunders, 205-6, 214

Pewter: manufacture of, in Connecticut, 324

Phelps, ——— (Mr.), 344

Philadelphia, 5, 24, 32, 38, 57, 61, 82, 86, 114, 121, 149, 150, 187, 211, 212, 213, 244, 253, 269, 291, 332, 368, 381, 384, 386, 403, 407, 414, 427, 438, 451, 469, 470, 511, 518-20, 530, 534, 552; and Bank of the U.S., 201-2; British consul at, 365-67; collector of customs at, *see* Delany, Sharp; deputy sheriff of, 384; duties paid at, 2; and purchase of public debt, 68; speculation in Bank of the U.S. stock at, 452; and stock market decline, 58

[Philadelphia] *Gazette of the United States*, 368

Philadelphia Society for the Promotion of Agriculture, 114, 375, 377, 490

Phillips, Nathaniel, 478

Pickering, Timothy: *letters from*, 113, 375-77; *letter to*, 96; Treasury Department circular to, 35-37

Pickett, George: *letter to*, 113-14

Pierce, Benjamin, 261-62

Pinckney, Charles Cotesworth: *letter to*, 9-10

Pinckney, William, 511

Pinqua, 46, 47, 48, 49

Pintard, John M., 45

Pitkin, William, 350

Pitt, William, 228

Pitt County, N.C., 429

Pittsburgh, Pa., 210; agriculture in, 419-20

Pittstown, N.J., 269

Pittsylvania County, Va., 428

Plankbridge, N.C., 69-70, 478

Platt, Richard, 24-25

Playfair, William: *letter from*, 253-55

Pleasants, John P., 288-89

Polk, William, 429; *letter from*, 84-85

Pollock, Oliver, 464

Poll tax: in Connecticut, 322, 330, 337

Polly, 164, 403, 476-77

Pomfret, Conn.: manufacturing at, 354-55

Pope, Edward, 94

Porcelain: and China trade, 53

Porter, David, 238

Portland, District of Maine: lighthouse at, 131-32, 208-9, 509, 527-28, 551-52

Portsmouth, N.H., 186, 197; collector of customs at, *see* Whipple, Joseph; lighthouse at, 524-25; surveyor of the port of, 105, 208-9, 213

Portsmouth, Va., 279

Port Tobacco, Md., 511

Portugal: and trade with China, 41

Postmaster General, *see* Pickering, Timothy

Postmasters: deputy, 113

Potash and pearlash: bounties for, 345; manufacture of, in Connecticut, 335, 345, 350, 351

Potomac River, 200

Potter, Thomas, 108, 181

Potter, William, 448

Pottery: manufacture of, 147

Powhatan County, Va., 428

Premiums, *see* Bounties

President of U.S.: compensation of, 458, 475. *See also* Washington, George

Prices: of manufactured goods, in Connecticut, 323

Prince Edward County, Va., 428

Prince George County, Va., 428

Prince Georges County, Md., 428

Princess Anne County, Va., 428; manufacturing in, 278

Prince William County, Va., 428

Property: and Bank of the U.S., 389

Providence, R.I., 5, 12, 108, 283, 308, 455, 502, 529; Association of Mechanics and Manufacturers, 442, 449; collector of customs at, *see* Olney, Jeremiah; distilling in, 433-34; manufactures in, 432-49, of blocks, 443, of brass, 446, of cabinets, 448, of candles, 433, 434, 445, of cards, 446, of chocolate, 440, of clocks, 445, of coaches, 446, of copper, 448, of cordage, 448, of cotton, 434-40, 448, of fire engines, 446, of fringe and web, 444, of gloves, 447, of hats, 442-43, of iron, 440, 447, of leather, 443-44, 447, of linen, 435, 436, 440, of nails, 445, of paper, 440, 447, of pewter, 448, of shoes and boots, 444, of silver, 446, of snuff, 440, of soap, 445, of steel, 440, of sugar, 434, of tools, 445, 446-47, of wool, 440, 444; naval officer for the port of, 304-5; The Providence Association of Mechanics and Manufacturers, 436; "Report of a Committee Appointed to Obtain Information on Manufacturing in," 441-49; surveyor of port of, 26-27, 213, 304-5

Providence, 26

Providence Bank, 305-6; and collectors of customs, 489-90, 518, 542; notes of, 489-90, 514-15, 542-43; president of, *see* Brown, John

[Providence, R.I.] *United States Chronicle,* 449

Public creditors: definition of, 89; and unsubscribed debt, 393

Public debt, 66, 72-73; and Bank of New York, 68-69; certificates of, 32-33, 88-90; and commissioners of loans, 14-15; deferred, 11, 60, 68, 72, purchase of, 77, 110, 122, 176; to Farmers-General, 499, 500; foreign, 1, 67, payment of, 161; and foreign loans, 547-48; to foreign officers, 22, 97, 394-96; to France, 22, 63-67, 97, 132-33, 315, and Antwerp loan, 553-54, and Haitian revolt, 219-20, 225-26, 238, 265, payment of, 98, 129, 135-36, 140, 159-60, 161, 165, 227, 229, 394-96, 523-24, proposal to purchase, 62-63, 161, speculation in, 390-91; funded, 10-11, 68; and Holland loans, 141; indents of interest, 88-90; interest on, payment of, 14-15, 190, 241, 406, 458, 550; and man-

ufactures, 145; nonsubscribers, 88-90, 389; and public creditors, 89; purchase of, 67-68, 68-69, 71-73, 93, and Bank of New York, 77, and foreign loans, 161, Hamilton on, 71-73, and Benjamin Lincoln, 293-95, 405, purpose of, 71-73, and William Seton, 68-69, 77, 110, 122, 176, 182, 184, 185, 190, 202-3, 271, 288, 296, 306, 310-11, 377-78, 411, and sinking fund, 67-68, 77, 476-77; registered debt, 89, 485; speculation in, 65, 185, at Amsterdam and London, 388-93; and state certificates, 32-33, 91; subscribers to, 72-73, 88-90; unsubscribed, 391, 393, 396-400. *See also* Assumption of state debts; Loans; North Carolina

"Publicola," 33-34

Pumpings: duty on, 19, 180-81

Putnam, Daniel, 320

Queen Annes County, Md., 428

Queens County, N.Y., 247, 367, 494

Ragsdale, Drury, 275, 428-29; *letter to* Edward Carrington, 280-82; manufactures by, 281; on manufactures in Virginia, 299; report of, 278

Randall, Thomas (Mass.): *letter from,* 38-55

Randall, Thomas (N.Y.), 38

Randolph, Beverley, 210-11

Randolph, Edmund: Attorney General, 33, 192, opinion requested, 418-19; commissioner of sinking fund, 67-68, 93, 476-77; *letters from,* 88-90, 263-64, 406-11, 486; *letters to,* 370-71, 455

Randolph County, N.C., 429

Randolph County, Va., 428

Raritan River, 121, 269, 379

Read, James, 84-85, 250, 317-18, 429

Reeve, Tapping, 532

Register of the Treasury Department, *see* Nourse, Joseph

Reid, Joseph, 53

Remsen, Henry, Jr., 530, 534

"Report on Imports for the Year Ending September 30, 1790" (November 18, 1791), 510

"Report on Imports for the Year Ending September 30, 1790" (November 23-24, 1791), 526-27

"Report on the Establishment of a Mint" (January 28, 1791), 101
"Report on the Estimate of Expenditures for 1792" (November 4, 1791), 456-75, 563-64
"Report on the Subject of Manufactures" (December 5, 1791), 37, 163, 177, 518, 528
"Report on Tonnage for the Year Ending September 30, 1790" (November 25-28, 1791), 538
"Report Relative to a Provision for the Support of Public Credit" (January 9, 1790), 393, 396
"Report to the Governor of North Carolina" (July 31, 1794), 191-92
Republicans, 367
Revenue: and duties, 488; and frauds, 198; laws, evasions of, 6, 26-27, 96, 217-18, 309, 415; and smuggling, 109
Revenue cutters: appropriation for, 466; for Connecticut, 96, 309, 425; expenses of, 475, 546-47; for Maryland, 236, 497, 508-9; for Massachusetts, 130-31, 208, 411-12, crew of, 284, 454, 497-98, 506, expenses of, 293, rations for, 285, 297-98; for New Hampshire, 105, 107-8, 195, 208, account of, 416-17, officers of, 297-99, 509, rations for, 297-98; for New York, 130; for North Carolina, 497; officers of, 34-35; rations for, 221, 507-8, 521; for Rhode Island, 35, 96, 528-29
Rhinelander, —— (Mr.), 514
Rhode Island, 458, 461, 465, 470; "An Act relative to certain securities heretofore granted by this state, and for repealing certain acts of the legislature of this state hereinafter mentioned" (June, 1791), 154, 155; and assumption of state debts, 153-57; bounties, 433; and commissioners of loans, 156 (see also Bowen, Jabez); and Constitution (U.S.), 29; Court of Admiralty of, 12; deputy U.S. marshal for the District of, 283; and domestic loan of 1790, 153-57; duties paid in, 3; finances, 155-56; governor of, see Fenner, Arthur; inspector of revenue, see Dexter, John S.; invalid pensions in, 470; legislature of, 12, 156, 443, 493; lighthouse in, 493-94; paper money of, 155-56; and Providence Bank, 306;
Ratifying Convention, 29; revenue cutter for, 35, 96, 528-29; supervisor of revenue for, see Dexter, John S.; survey of inspection in, 427; U.S. attorney for the District of, see Channing, William; U.S. District Court of, 5, 95, 502; U.S. judge for the District of, see Marchant, Henry; U.S. marshal for the District of, see Peck, William; U.S. Senator from, see Foster, Theodore, and Stanton, Joseph, Jr. See also Providence, R.I.
Ribbons and tapes: manufacture of, 147
Richards, Giles, 375
Richards, Nathaniel, 520
Richards, Samuel, 319
Richards, Giles, and Co., 375
Richeson, Peter, 281
Richland County, S.C., 429
Richmond, William, 449
Richmond, Va., 114, 277, 404, 413
Richmond County, N.C., 429
Richmond County, Va., 428
Roan County, N.C., see Rowan County, N.C.
Robertson County, N.C., see Robeson County, N.C.
Robeson County, N.C., 429
Rochon, Alexis Marie de, 228
Rockbridge County, Va., 428
Rockingham County, N.C., 429
Rockingham County, Va., 428
Roosevelt, Isaac, 246-47
Rope: manufacture of, in Connecticut, 338, in Virginia, 278
"Rose Hill," 414
Ross, John: letter from, 544-46; letter from Royal Flint, 544
Rotterdam, 8
Rouse, William, 171
Rowan County, N.C., 429
Ruffin, James, 281
Ruffin, Sterling, 281
Rum: distillation in Connecticut, 350; duty on, 187-88; and evasion of revenue laws, 217-18; seizure of, 215; smuggling of, 189
Russell, Thomas, 453-54
Russell County, Va., 428, 474
Russia, 137, 162-63; loan at Antwerp, 20, 228
Rutherford County, N.C., 429
Rutledge, Edward, 9

Saddlecloth: manufacture of, in Connecticut, 336, 338

Saddles: manufacture of, in Connecticut, 345

Sag Harbor, N.Y., 309

Sailcloth: bounty on, 163; manufacture of, 147, 162-63, in Boston, 372, in Connecticut, 338, 340, in New Hampshire, 213

St. Clair, Arthur (Maj. Gen.): Indian expedition, 210-11; and John Cleves Symmes, 237-38, 269

St. Croix, 286-87

St. Johns, New Brunswick, 262

St. Marys County, Md., 428

St. Michael's Church (Trenton, N.J.), 561

St. Petersburg, Russia, 413

Salem, Mass., 45, 194

Sally, 25, 94

Salter, Manasseh: account with, 274

Saltpeter: manufacture of, in Connecticut, 346

Sampson County, N.C., 429

Santo Domingo, *see* Haiti

Saratoga, 464

Saunders, Peleg, 205-6, 214

Savannah, Ga.: French vice consul at, 269, 306-7

Sawyer, Enoch, 478

Scammell, 195, 297, 416, 417

Schuyler, Angelica, *see* Church, Angelica Schuyler

Schuyler, Peter, 246-47

Schuyler, Philip, 247

Schuylkill River, 114

Schweizer, Jean Gaspar, 22-23

Schweizer, Jeanneret, and Co.: proposal to purchase U.S. debt to France, 22-23, 61-63, 161

Scioto Co., 74-75, 559; William Playfair on, 253-55

Scioto River, 211

Scotland, 282, 434

Scott, Charles (Brig. Gen.), 210, 211

Scouts: and Indian defense, 472

Scranton, Pa., 380

Scriba, George, 16

Sea Horse, 51

Sea otter skins, 45-49

Searl, ——— (Mr.), 285

Sears, Isaac, 42

"Second Report on the Further Provision Necessary for Establishing Public Credit (Report on a National Bank)" (December 13, 1790), 389

Second River, 268

Secretary of Navy, *see* Stoddert, Benjamin

Secretary of State, *see* Jefferson, Thomas

Secretary of Treasury, *see* Hamilton, Alexander

Secretary of War, *see* Knox, Henry

Securities, public, *see* United States, stocks and bonds

Seizures: of distilled spirits, 248-49; of rum, 215

Senate: and appointments, 84-85, 93, 171, 513; compensation of, 558; expenses of, 459, 464, 475; *letter to,* 426-31; orders of, 510, 526-27, 538; president of, *see* Adams, John; reports to, 510, 526-27, 538; secretary of, *see* Otis, Samuel A.

Seton, William, 56, 172-73, 219, 236, 307, 412; draft of, 489-91; *letters from,* 69-70, 77, 110, 122, 176, 176-77, 202, 202-3, 264, 265, 288, 296, 377-78, 411, 414-15, 506-7, 518-20; *letters to,* 14, 68-69, 71-73, 86, 93, 184, 185, 190, 248, 271, 306-7, 310-11, 495, 501, 538-39; and payment of interest on public debt, 78, 550; and William Pearce, 86; and purchase of public debt, 68-69, 71-73, 182; and sinking fund, 476-77; trustee for Daniel Parker and Co., 545

Seven Brothers, 5-6, 95, 283, 308, 309, 415, 542

Seymour, Thomas, 536

Shaw, Samuel, 38, 39, 42-43, 54

"Shayites," 534

Shearman, Ebenezer, 403

Sheffield, Lord, 366, 367, 533, 534

Shenandoah County, Va., 428

Sherman and Procter, 17-18

Ships: admeasurement of, 11-12, 16-17, 18, 37, 82-83, 95, 107, 109, 119-20, 197-98, 208, 222-23, in China, 39, 40, foreign, 16-17, 83, 198, 200, 208, 222-23; certificates of registry of, 81; fishing, 223-24; licenses, 119-20; manifest, 199; registers of, 15, 16, 18, 82-83, 94, 106, 107, 108, 183, 213, 453, and collectors of customs, 295; report on, 81; sale of condemned,

283; seizures of, 6; shipbuilding, in Connecticut, 329, 338, in customs districts, 16; tonnage of, 11-12

Shoes and boots: imports of, 444; manufacture of, 147, in Connecticut, 349, in Providence, R.I., 444, in Virginia, 279, 280, 301-3

Short, William, 62, 110, 274, 432; Hamilton on, 2-3; instructions to, 1-4; *letters from*, 20-23, 97-103, 128, 132-42, 164-70, 226-35, 311-17, 479-82, 498-500, 522-24, 552-57; *letters from* Willink, Van Staphorst, and Hubbard, 136-42, 229-32; *letters to*, 1-4, 158-62, 272, 450-51, 547-48; *letters to* Willink, Van Staphorst, and Hubbard, 167-70, 232-35, 316-17; loans, authority to make, 132, charges and commissions on, 132-42, 166-70; and Gouverneur Morris, 63-64; powers of, 20, 112, 161; and Schweizer and Jeanneret proposals, 63-65

Shrewsbury County, S.C., 429

Shykinkoa, 41, 42

Silk: Chinese, 53, 143; manufacture of, in Connecticut, 349, 354, 355-56, 356-57, in New Jersey, 194

Silver: manufacture of, in Connecticut, 324, in Providence, R.I., 446

Simmons, James, 471

Simpson, William, 218

Sinking fund, 93; commissioners of, 185, and Benjamin Lincoln, 293-95, meeting of, 67-68, and purchases of public debt, 68-69, 71-73, 77, 185, 190, 244-45, 271, 288, 296, 406, report of, 244-45, 271, 476-77, resolution of, 68-69. *See also* Adams, John; Hamilton, Alexander; Jay, John; Jefferson, Thomas; Randolph, Edmund

Six Nations: treaty with, 402

Skinner, William: *letters from*, 27-28, 122-23, 387-88; *letters to*, 7, 32-33, 191-92

Slater, Samuel, 439-40; and cotton manufactures, 432, 434, 435

Slaves: in Virginia, 276, 281

Slitting mills: in Connecticut, 328, 335; in Rhode Island, 445, 447; in Virginia, 282

Slocum, Pardon T., 18-19

Smith, Benjamin: *letter from*, 173-75

Smith, Edward, 429

Smith, George, 49-50

Smith, Jeremiah, 414

Smith, Jonathan B., 34

Smith, Melancton, 246-47

Smith, Noah, 427

Smith, Samuel Harrison, 34

Smith, Thomas: *letters from*, 73, 382-83, 431

Smith, William Loughton, 201-2

Smith, William Stephens, 427

Smuggling, 194-95; and "Coasting Act," 198-99; and coasting fees, 109; of cotton, 83-84; prevention of, 132, 208; of rum, 189

Snuff: manufacture of, in Connecticut, 350, in Providence, R.I., 440

Soap: manufacture of, in Providence, R.I., 445

Société de Vingt-Quatres, 75

Society for Establishing Useful Manufactures, 319, 341; attorneys for, 152; capital for, 145-46, 147; capital stock of, 150-51; directors of, 73, 90-91; discussion of, 250-52; exemption from taxation, 151; formation of, 24; governor of, *see* Duer, William; incorporation of, 80-81, 148-53; labor for, 145; machines for, 84-85, 121, 184, 214, 490, 509-10; management of, 149; meeting of, 74-75; organization of, 148-53; power of attorney to Hamilton, 24-25; prospectus of, 144-53, discussion of, 250-52; site for, 121, 144, 146, 171-72, 379-82, 385, 423-25; subscribers to, 24-25; subscription book of, 74, 285-86; weaknesses of, 250-52. *See also* Hall, William; Marshall, Thomas; Mort, Joseph

Somerset County, Md., 428

South Carolina, 458, 461, 466; "An Act for loaning to the United States, a sum of the Indents of this State under certain Limitations therein mentioned" (February 19, 1791), 154, 155; and assumption of state debts, 9-10, 154-55; debt of, 390-91; and domestic loan of 1790, 154; duties paid in, 3; and excise tax, 9-10; inspectors of the revenue for, 9, 175-76 (*see also* Cudworth, Benjamin; Walker, Silvanus); invalid pensions in, 470; legislature of, 10; lighthouse in, 67, 70; manufactures

South Carolina (*Continued*)
in, 170-71; Ratifying Convention, 10; supervisor of revenue for, *see* Stevens, Daniel; surveys of inspection in, 9, 429-30; U.S. attorney for the District of, *see* Rutledge, Edward; U.S. Representative from, *see* Smith, William Loughton

Southern states, 445; cotton, raising of, 437-38; exports to, from Connecticut, 323, 339, 340, 341, 342

Southampton County, Va., 428

Southington, Conn.: manufacturing at, 346-47, 348-49

South Sea Bubble, 74

Southwest Territory: militia, expenses of, 474

Southworth, Constant, 354; *letter to* William Williams, 355-57

Spain: dollars, 52-53; loan of 1781, 499-500

Spartanburg County, S.C., 429

Specie: and foreign loans, 2; and stock of U.S., 146

Speculation: and Bank of the U.S., 69-70, 74-75, 75-76; and banks, 58; in land, *see* Symmes, John Cleves; and manufactures, 323-24, 327; in New York City, 185; in Philadelphia, 452; in securities, 157-58; in U.S. debt to France, 22-23; in U.S. securities, 112

Spinning frame, 434. *See also* Cotton, manufacture of

Spinning jenny, 86, 434, 435. *See also* Cotton, manufacture of

Spinning mule, 86

Spinola, Christoforo Vincenzo de, 101

Spotsylvania County, Va., 428

Springfield, Mass., 469

Stafford County, Va., 428

Stamford, Conn., 334; manufacturing at, 319, 321, 340-41

Stanton, Joseph, Jr., 157

Starke, William, 281

State Department: expenses of, 461, 475, incidental, for 1792, 463

States: accounts of, 456, 461, 486; banks, 55-59, 519-20; debt, 11, 91; and "Excise Law," 9-10; and Society for Establishing Useful Manufactures, 149

Statutes of U.S., *see* Congress of U.S., acts of

Steel: manufacture of, in Connecticut,

349, 352-53, in Providence, R.I., 440

Steuben, Frederick William Augustus Henry Ferdinand, baron von: grant to, 462, 475; *letter from*, 412-13

Stevens, Daniel, 9-10, 429; *letter from*, 170-71; *letter from* Silvanus Walker, 170-71

Stevens, Edward, 428-29; *letter from*, 286-87; *letter from* Charles Yancey, 302-4; *letter to* Edward Carrington, 300-3; and manufactures in Virginia, 299-304

Stills, *see* Distilled spirits

Stock: of Bank of the U.S., 259; as capital for manufactures, 146

Stockholm, Andrew, 440

Stockings: manufacture of, 147, in Connecticut, 320, 357, in Virginia, 279, 280, 281, 282, 301-3

Stoddert, Benjamin, 289

Stokes County, N.C., 429

Stonington, Conn., 214, 215; manufacturing at, 329, 339-40

Stratford, Conn.: manufacturing at, 319, 321

Stringer, Samuel (Dr.), 7

Suffield, Conn., 342; manufacturing at, 343-46

Suffolk County, Mass., 293

Sugar: manufacture of, 434; seizure of, 78-79; tare on, 449; and trade with China, 43

A Summary View of the Courses of Crops in the Husbandry of England and Maryland . . . (John Beale Bordley), 377

Summer: troops at, 474

Supervisors of the revenue: and collectors of customs, 430; and collectors of revenue, 430; compensation of, 85; for Connecticut, *see* Chester, John; for Delaware, 317, 400-1 (*see also* Barratt, Andrew; Latimer, Henry); for Georgia, *see* Matthews, John; for Maryland, *see* Gale, George; for Massachusetts, *see* Gorham, Nathaniel; for New Hampshire, *see* Wentworth, Joshua; for New Jersey, *see* Dunham, Aaron; for New York, *see* Smith, William S.; for North Carolina, *see* Polk, William; for Pennsylvania, *see* Clymer, George; postage for, 113; for Rhode Island, *see* Dexter, John S.; for South Carolina, *see* Stevens,

Daniel; and surveyors of the port, 430; for Vermont, *see* Smith, Noah; for Virginia, *see* Carrington, Edward. *See also* Treasury Department circulars to the supervisors of the revenue

Supreme Court: associate judges of, compensation of, 475; Chief Justice of, compensation of, 458, 475. *See also* Jay, John

Surinam, 19; cotton from, 180

Surry County, N.C., 429

Surry County, Va., 280, 428

Surveyors of the port, 200; and admeasurement of ships, 12, 18, 83, 107, 119-20, 208; of Alexandria, Va., *see* Hanson, Samuel; of Baltimore, Md., *see* Ballard, Robert; of Boston, Mass., *see* Melville, Thomas; and distilled spirits, 199; and moieties, 111; of New Bedford, Mass., 94; of Newport, R.I., *see* Lyman, Daniel; of North Kingston, R.I., *see* Updike, Daniel Eldridge; of Portsmouth, N.H., 105 (*see also* Martin, Thomas); of Providence, R.I., *see* Barton, William; and seizures, 26-27; and ships' manifests, 199; and ships' registers, 180, 183; of Stonington, Conn., *see* Palmer, Jonathan, Jr.; and supervisors of revenue, 430; of Warren, R.I., *see* Phillips, Nathaniel

Susannah, 416

Susquehanna River, 376, 380

Sussex County, N.J., 379

Sussex County, Va., 428

Swan, James: proposal to purchase U.S. debt to France, 22-23

Swan, Timothy, 345

Swanwick, John, 189-90, 204-5

Sweden: trade with China, 39, 53

Swift, Edward, 508

Swift, Heman: *letter to* John Chester, 328-29

Symmes, John Cleves: and land speculation, 237-38, 269

Tabor, Job, 319

Tacks, manufacture of, 374-75

Talbot County, Md., 428, 492

Tarboro, N.C., 85

Tare: on coffee, 449; on sugar, 449

Taunton, Mass., 373

Taxes: in Connecticut, 328-29, 337; on property, 188. *See also* Duties; "Excise Law"; Tonnage, duties

Taylor, —— (Mr.), 344

Taylor, James: *letter from*, 501-2; *letter to*, 456

Tea: and China trade, 52, 53; Chinese, 38, 46, 48, 49, 51, 55, purchase of, 42-43, 45; consumption of, 143; duty on, 13-14, 378-79; moiety upon forfeiture of, 304-5; regulations on importation of, 262-63; varieties of, 13-14

Telles, John, 190

Temple, Sir John, 365, 367

Ternant, Jean Baptiste de, 22, 29, 104, 129, 161; conversation with Hamilton, 290-92; *letter from*, 219-20; *letter to*, 220; and revolution in Haiti, 225-26, 238; and U.S. debt to France, 159-60, 523-24

Thelley, Dunken, 477-78

Thomas, Abishai: *letter from*, 501-2; *letter to*, 456

Thomas, Philip, 130, 428

Thompson, —— (Capt.), 43

Thompson, —— (Mr.), 344

Thompson, Ebenezer, 304-5

Thomson, Erasmus, 225

Thread: manufacture of, 147

Tilden, Daniel, 354

Tillinghast, Charles, 478

Tillotson, Thomas, 246-47

Tilton, James, 376-77; Treasury Department circular to, 422

Tin: in China trade, 51; manufacture of, 324

Tinker, Stephen, 121

Tobacco: production of, in Virginia, 275, 276

Tonnage: and China trade, 143; duties, 16, 29, 37, 81, 109, and admeasurement of ships, 223, and coasting vessels, 295; foreign, 453, 505-6, French claims against, 290-92, and restitution of, 506; laws, 11-12; report on, 510, 538; return of, 295, 496

"Tonnage Act," 506; French objections to, 290-92

Tools: manufacture of, in Connecticut, 342, 354, in Providence, R.I., 445, 446-47

Toomer, Henry, 249-50, 317; *letter from*, 173-75

Topham, John, 95, 542

Tousard, Lewis (Lt. Col.): pension to, 462-63
Tow cloth: manufacture of, in Connecticut, 342
Towler, William, 281
Trade: and Bank of the U.S., 57; with China, 38-55, 143-44; with France, 290-92; with French colonies, 290; with India, 143
Traverse, Joseph: pension, 462
Treadwell, John: *letter from* Elezur Andrews, 348-49; *letter to* John Chester, 346-48
Treasurer of U.S., *see* Meredith, Samuel
Treasury Department, 196; Assistant Secretary of, *see* Coxe, Tench, *and* Duer, William; auditor of, 539-40 (*see also* Harison, Richard; Wolcott, Oliver, Jr.); bills at Amsterdam, 523; clerk of, *see* Meyer, John; comptroller of, *see* Eveleigh, Nicholas, *and* Wolcott, Oliver, Jr.; expenses, 459-60, 463, 464-65, 475; register of, *see* Nourse, Joseph; Secretary of, *see* Hamilton, Alexander; treasurer of, *see* Meredith, Samuel
Treasury Department circular to ——, August 13, 1791, 35-37
Treasury Department circular to the district judges, October 17, 1791, 402
Treasury Department circulars to the collectors of the customs, August 5, 1791, 15-17; September 20, 1791, 217-18; September 21, 1791, 221; September 21, 1791, 222-23; November 11, 1791, 496; November 17, 1791, 507-8
Treasury Department circulars to the commissioners of loans, August 4, 1791, 14-15; August 18, 1791, 78; October 29, 1791, 422
Treasury Department circulars to the supervisors of the revenue, June 22, 1791, 275, 318, 433, 442; September 30, 1791, 248-49
Treaties: with Cherokees, 402; with France (1778), 290-92, 386-87, of commerce, proposed, 104; with Great Britain, 292; with Six Nations, 402
Trenton, N.J., 269, 379, 381, 385, 561
Trinidad, 213
Trinidada, 183, 213-14

Triol, Roux, and Co., 502-3
Trumbull, John (painter), 534
Trumbull, John (poet), 532, 533, 534, 535, 536, 537
Trumbull, Jonathan, 319
Trustees of the sinking fund, *see* Sinking fund, commissioners of
Turnpikes, 366
Twiford, Robert, 275; *letter to* Thomas Newton, Jr., 279
Tyrrell County, N.C., 429

Union County, S.C., 429
United Netherlands, 8, 553; banking houses of, 32; bills on, 77; China trade, 39; and Chinese silk, 53; French bankers at, *see* Hogguer, Grand, and Co.; Minister to France, 228-29; mint in, 101; and Paris exchange, 65; rate of exchange at, 62; U.S. commissioners at, *see* Willink, Van Staphorst, and Hubbard. *See also* Loans
United States: accounts, with Richard Harison, 483-84, of marshals, 465, with North Carolina, 501-2, with states, 456, 461, 486, 540-41; Army, 363, hospital department, 469, 474, ordnance department, 469, 474, quartermaster's department, 469, 474; attorneys for the District of Connecticut, *see* Edwards, Pierpont, of Massachusetts, *see* Gore, Christopher, of New York, *see* Harison, Richard, of Rhode Island, *see* Channing, William, of South Carolina, *see* Rutledge, Edward, of Virginia, *see* Campbell, Alexander, *and* Nelson, William, Jr.; and Bank of the U.S., 57; compensation of attorneys, 483-84; consuls, 17; courts, expenses of, 563-64; credit in Europe, 128, 451-52, 555; judge for the District of Delaware, *see* Bedford, Gunning, Jr., of New York, *see* Duane, James, of Rhode Island, *see* Marchant, Henry; liquidated claims on, 464-66; manufactures in, 144-45, aid to, 146; marshals for New Jersey, *see* Lowrey, Thomas, for Rhode Island, *see* Peck, William; publicity in Europe, 315-16; and Society for Establishing Useful Manufactures; 149; stocks and bonds, 20, 21, 60,

71-72, 110, 272, 274, 451-52, 524; vice consuls, 17. *See also* Sinking fund
United States bankers in Amsterdam, *see* Willink, Van Staphorst, and Hubbard
United States commissioners, *see* Willink, Van Staphorst, and Hubbard
United States v *Brigantine Seven Brothers*, 95
United States v *Joseph Finch*, 95
Updike, Daniel Eldridge, 6, 111, 223-24
Usher, George, 118, 283
Usher, Hezekiah, 119, 283
Utica, N.Y., 413

Van Beeftingh and Boon, 8
Van Rensselaer, Margaret Schuyler (Mrs. Stephen), 172-73
Van Rensselaer, Stephen, 173
Van Vert, Isaac: pension, 462
"Ventoso," 366, 368
Vermont, 328, 344, 371, 458, 464, 466; map of, 91; supervisor of revenue for, *see* Smith, Noah; survey of inspection in, 427
Vernier, Theodore, comte de Montorient, 64
Verplanck, Guilian, 71, 519-20
Versailles, 394
Vice President of U.S.: compensation of, 458, 475. *See also* Adams, John
Vining, John, 211-12, 288-89, 400-1
Virginia, 32, 82, 99, 177, 185, 363, 365, 366, 367, 453, 458, 461, 465, 530; agriculture in, 303-4; census returns of, 278; commissioner of loans for, *see* Hopkins, John; crops of, 275-76; distilleries in, 279, 302-4; duties paid in, 3; and "Excise Law," 303-4; fulling mills in, 277; governor of, *see* Lee, Henry, *and* Randolph, Beverley; inspectors of revenue for, *see* Brackenridge, James, *and* Carrington, Mayo, *and* Marshall, Thomas, *and* Newton, Thomas, Jr., *and* Ragsdale, Drury, *and* Smith, Edward, *and* Stevens, Edward; invalid pensions in, 470; labor in, 275-76; legislature of, 32, 210, 299; manufacturing in, 275-82, 299-303, of cloth, 280-82, of cotton, 279, 280, 281-82, of iron, 277, 282, of lead, 277, of leather, 278, 282, of rope, 278, of shoes, 279, 280, of stockings, 279, 280, 281, 282,

of wool, 279, 281-82; militia expenses, 471-73; raw materials in, 276-77; Second Regiment, 364; slave labor in, 276; slitting mills in, 282; staple crops of, 275; supervisor of revenue for, *see* Carrington, Edward; surveys of inspection in, 428-29; trades in, 278; U.S. attorney for the District of, *see* Campbell, Alexander, *and* Nelson, William, Jr.; U.S. District Court, 235, judge of, *see* Griffin, Cyrus; U.S. Representatives from, *see* Brown, John, *and* Giles, William G.; U.S. Senator from, *see* Grayson, William
Von Steuben, *see* Steuben
Vreeland's Point, N.J., 269

Wabash River, 210
Wadsworth, Jeremiah, 319, 357, 546, 559
Wake County, N.C., 429
Walker, Robert, 319
Walker, Silvanus (Sylvanus), 35, 429-30; *letter to* Daniel Stevens, 170-71
Wallingford, Conn.: manufacture of silk at, 318
Walpole, Sir Robert, 535
War Department: expeditions of, 457; expenses of, 467-74, 475, incidental, for 1792, 463; and invalid pensions, 10; Secretary of, *see* Knox, Henry
Warren, James, 59
Warren, Joseph (Maj. Gen.): pension to children of, 462
Warren, Mercy (Mrs. James), 59
Warren, R.I., 478
Warren, 295
Warren County, N.C., 429
Warwick County, Va., 428
Wash, William, 303
Washington, George, 32, 363-64, 365, 366, 367; on agriculture, 490; aide-de-camp to, 515-16; and Alburg, Vt., 91; and Antwerp loan, 481-82; appointments of, 84-85, 130, 164, 175-76, 297, 508, 509; and arsenals, 384; and Robert Ballard, 181-82; and Bank of the U.S., 406; and Beverly Cotton Manufactory, 177; bounties, 384; and call for militia, 474; and contracts, 242, 249-50, 520, 521, 524-25; and "Excise Law," 9, 426-31; and Indians, 401-2; *letters from*, 211-12, 238, 269-70, 296, 317-18, 383-84, 403;

Washington, George (*Continued*)
   letter from Gouverneur Morris, 63-
   67; *letters to,* 70, 142-43, 209-11,
   225-26, 237-38, 249-50, 288-89, 369,
   369-70, 400-1, 520, 524-25; *letter to*
   George Clinton, 206; *letter to* John
   Kean, 490; *letter to* Gouverneur
   Morris, 61-62; and lighthouse in
   South Carolina, 67; on manufactures, 384; and George Mercer, 365;
   message to Congress, 402, 403;
   money for, 203; and Gouverneur
   Morris, 557; and William Pearce,
   86; ratification of Holland loans,
   111-12; revolt in Haiti, 219-20; and
   Schweizer and Jeanneret's propos-
   als, 61-63; secretary of, *see* Lear,
   Tobias; and William Short, 1-4; and
   sinking fund, 476-77; and state gov-
   ernors, 396; and Jean Baptiste de
   Ternant, 129, 292; tour of South,
   61; and U.S. debt to France, 61-67
Washington, William (Col.), 471
Washington, N.C., 15, 121, 497
Washington, 43, 52, 487
Washington County, Md., 428
Washington County, N.Y., 247
Washington County, Pa., 427
Washington County, S.C., 429
Washington County, Va., 428, 474
Waterford: troops at, 473
Watt, James, 103
Wayne County, N.C., 429
Weaver, Sheffield, 478
Webster, Alexander, 246-47
Wentworth, George, 186
Wentworth, Joshua, 272-73, 426; *let-
   ter from*, 186; *letter to*, 105
Westcott, Samuel, 455
Westerly, R.I., 205-6
Western posts: supply of, 244
Western territory, 209-11; expenses of,
   461-62, 475
Westgate, Samuel, 304-5
West Indies, 321, 433, 543; cotton ex-
   ports, 438; exports to, 323, 339; im-
   ports from, 379, of leather, 444;
   trade of, 507
Westmoreland County, Pa., 427
Westmoreland County, Va., 92, 428
West Point, 384, 469; land for, 483-84
Whales, 433
Whampoa, China, 44, 50
Wheat: production of, in Virginia,
   275, 276

Wheeler, Bennett, 449
Whipple, Joseph, 524-25; *letters from*,
   105, 195, 197-200, 212-13, 241-43, 297-
   99, 416-17, 422-23; *letters to*, 216,
   272-73, 525, 558
Whitaker, John, 85, 429
White, Judson, 336, 338
White, Russell, 334-35
Whiteside (Whitesides), William, 55
Whittelsey, Chauncey, 319; *letter from*
   Hezekiah Lane, 352; *letter to* John
   Chester, 349-51
Wilkes County, N.C., 429
Wilkinson, James, 210-11
Wilkinson, Oriel, 440
Willard, Joseph, 104
Willett, Marinus, 246-47
Williams, David: pension, 462
Williams, Elie, 244, 288
Williams, John Foster, 107-8, 130-31,
   293, 298, 299, 551
Williams, Otho H., 243-44, 287-88;
   letters from, 37-38, 273; *letters to,*
   17-18, 79, 238, 289-90, 370, 497, 508-
   9; Treasury Department circulars
   to, 496, 507-8
Williams, Thomas: *letter from,* 431
Williams, William: *letter from* Con-
   stant Southworth, 355-57; *letter to*
   John Chester, 353-55
Williamsburg County, S.C., 429
Williamson, Hugh, 32-33
Willing, Thomas, 189-90, 204-5
Willing, Morris, and Swanwick, 189-90
Willink, Wilhem and Jan, Nicholaas
   and Jacob Van Staphorst, and Nicholas Hubbard, *see* Willink, Van
   Staphorst, and Hubbard
Willink, Van Staphorst, and Hubbard,
   20-23, 63, 164-65, 272, 500; *letters
   from,* 110, 520-21, 529, 558; *letters
   from* William Short, 167-70, 232-35,
   316-17; *letters to,* 274, 431-32; *letters
   to* William Short, 136-42, 229-32;
   and U.S. debt to France, 63, 160,
   553-54; and U.S. loans, at Antwerp,
   554-56, in Holland, 314, 522, 554-56,
   charges on, 98, 132-42, 160-61, 166,
   226-27, 554-55, ratification of, 111-
   12, reimbursement of, 547-48, of
   September, 1791, 128, 311-12, 479,
   481; and U.S. stock, 524
Willkings, M. R.: *letter from,* 173-75
Wilmington, Del., 183, 211, 213, 289,
   307

Wilmington, N.C., 84, 173, 249-50; collector of customs at, *see* Read, James
Wilmington County, N.C., 429
Windham, Conn., 354
Windham County, Conn.: manufacturing in, 353
Windsor, Conn.: manufacturing at, 341-42
Windsor, England, 5
Wine: and China trade, 39, 42, 43; duty on, 379
Winton County, S.C., 429
Winyaw County, S.C., 429
Wiscasset, District of Maine, 29
Withers, Thomas: *letter from,* 173-75
Wolcott, Oliver, Sr., 365, 366-68, 534
Wolcott, Oliver, Jr., 143, 246-47, 533; auditor of the Treasury, 539-40; on Bank of the U.S., 255-60; comptroller of the Treasury, 14-15, 186, 239-40, and Pennsylvania land purchase, 239-40, 245-46, 485, and subscription to loans, 241; *letters from,* 28, 158, 255-60, 418-19, 539-40, 546-47; memorandum from, 549; "Plan for establishing departments of the Bank of the United States," 258-60
Wolf, Charles John Michael de: loan at Antwerp, 20, 480-82, 498-500, 552-57
Women: and manufactures, 145, in Boston, 374
Wood: manufactures of, in Connecticut, 323
Wool: manufacture of, in Connecticut, 320, 322-23, 324-27, 328, 329, 332, 333, 340, 342, 343, 347, 348, 351, 355, in Providence, R.I., 440, 444, in Virginia, 279, 281, 301-3; production of, in Virginia, 276
Wool cards: manufacture of, in Connecticut, 344, in Massachusetts, 374
Worcester, Mass., 345; cotton manufactory at, 439
Worcester County, Md., 428
Worcester County, Mass., 427
Wycombe, Earl, 365, 367, 369-70
Wye, Md., 490
Wylly, Richard: *letter from,* 525
Wynkoop, Henry: *letter from,* 123-27; Treasury Department circular to, 35-37
Wyoming Valley: claimed by Pennsylvania and Connecticut, 376-77
Wythe County, Va., 428, 474

Yale College, 358, 367; president of, 365, 367
Yancey, Charles, 301-4; *letter to* Edward Stevens, 302-4
Yarn: manufacture of, in Virginia, 279
Yeaton, Hopley, 195, 297-99, 416-17
York County, Pa., 427
York County, S.C., 429
York County, Va., 428
Yorkshire, England, 86
Young, Arthur, 37, 376, 377, 490-91; *Annuals of Agriculture,* 377

Zuell, —— (Mr.), 345

35623